Formula 5.3

$$\text{DEPRECIATION PER UNIT OF PRODUCT} = \frac{\text{ORIGINAL COST} - \text{RESIDUAL VALUE}}{n}$$

Formula for finding the depreciation per unit of product when using the units-of-product method

where n = the number of product units in the life of the asset

Formula 5.4

$$k = \frac{\text{WEARING VALUE}}{\dfrac{n(n+1)}{2}}$$

Formula for finding the value of one part (constant of proportion) when using the sum-of-the-years-digits method

where Wearing Value = $\dfrac{\text{Original}}{\text{Cost}} - \dfrac{\text{Residual}}{\text{Value}}$

Formula 5.5

$$d = 2 \times \frac{1}{n}$$

Formula for finding the rate of depreciation when using the simple declining-balance method

where n = the number of years in the life of the asset

Formula 5.6

$$d = 1 - \sqrt[n]{\frac{\text{RESIDUAL VALUE}}{\text{ORIGINAL COST}}}$$

Formula for finding the rate of depreciation when using the complex declining-balance method

Formula 6.1

$$\text{AMOUNT OF DISCOUNT} = \text{RATE OF DISCOUNT} \times \text{LIST PRICE}$$

Finding the amount of discount when the list price is known

Formula 6.2

$$\text{NET PRICE} = \text{LIST PRICE} - \text{AMOUNT OF TRADE DISCOUNT}$$

Finding the net amount when the amount of discount is known

Formula 6.3A

$$\text{NET PRICE FACTOR (NPF)} = 100\% - \% \text{ DISCOUNT}$$

Finding the net price factor (NPF)

Formula 6.4A

$$\text{NET PRICE} = \text{NET PRICE FACTOR (NPF)} \times \text{LIST PRICE}$$

Finding the net amount directly without computing the amount of discount

Formula 6.5A

$$\text{NET PRICE FACTOR (NPF) FOR THE DISCOUNT SERIES} = \text{NPF FOR THE FIRST DISCOUNT} \times \text{NPF FOR THE SECOND DISCOUNT} \times \ldots \times \text{NPF FOR THE LAST DISCOUNT}$$

Formula 6.6A

$$\text{NET PRICE} = \text{NET PRICE FACTOR FOR THE DISCOUNT SERIES} \times \text{LIST PRICE}$$

Finding the net amount directly when a list price is subject to a series of discounts

Formula 6.7

$$\text{RATE OF TRADE DISCOUNT} = \frac{\text{AMOUNT OF DISCOUNT}}{\text{LIST PRICE}}$$

Finding the rate of discount

Formula 6.8

SINGLE EQUIVALENT RATE OF DISCOUNT FOR A DISCOUNT SERIES

Finding the single rate of discount that has the same effect as a given series of discounts

$$= 1 - \text{NPF FOR THE DISCOUNT SERIES}$$
$$= 1 - [(1 - d_1)(1 - d_2)(1 - d_3) \ldots (1 - d_n)]$$

Formula 6.9A

$$\text{SELLING PRICE} = \text{COST} + \text{EXPENSES} + \text{PROFIT}$$

Basic relationship between selling price, cost, expenses such as overhead, and profit

or

$$\text{S} = \text{C} + \text{E} + \text{P}$$

fifth edition

contemporary
business
mathematics

with Canadian applications

S. A. Hummelbrunner

Prentice Hall Canada Inc., Scarborough, Ontario

Canadian Cataloguing in Publication Data

Hummelbrunner, S. A. (Siegfried August)
   Contemporary business mathematics with
Canadian applications

5th ed.
ISBN 0-13-769019-3

1. Business mathematics.   I. Title.

HF5691.H85 1998   650'.01'513   C97-930781-3

Prentice-Hall, Inc., Upper Saddle River, New Jersey
Prentice-Hall International (UK) Limited, London
Prentice-Hall of Australia, Pty. Limited, Sydney
Prentice-Hall Hispanoamericana, S.A., Mexico City
Prentice-Hall of India Private Limited, New Delhi
Prentice-Hall of Japan, Inc., Tokyo
Simon & Schuster Southeast Asia Private Limited, Singapore
Editora Prentice-Hall do Brasil, Ltda., Rio de Janeiro

ISBN 0-13-769019-3

Acquisitions Editor: Sarah Kimball
Senior Marketing Manager: Ann Byford
Developmental Editor: Maurice Esses
Production Editor: Kelly Dickson
Substantive/Copy Editor: Anita Smale
Production Coordinator: Deborah Starks
Permissions Research: Karen Becker
Art Direction: Mary Opper
Cover Design: Alex Alter
Cover Image: Tom Collicott/Direct Stock
Interior Design: David Murphy/ArtPlus Limited Design Consultants
Page Layout: Compeer Typographic Services Limited

1 2 3 4 5   CC   02 01 00 99 98

Printed and bound in the USA.

Visit the Prentice Hall Canada Web site! Send us your comments, browse our catalogues, and more at **www.phcanada.com**. Or reach us through e-mail at **phcinfo_phcanada@prenhall.com**.

Credits:
Page 301, Reprinted with permission from Fidelity Investments Canada Limited; Page 346, Canada Trust; Page 387, Investor's Group; Page 429, Reprinted with permission from the Canadian Imperial Bank of Commerce; Page 504, Investor's Group; Page 620, Reprinted with permission from The Globe and Mail; Page 661, Canada Investment & Savings; Page 717, Used with permission from Yamaha Motor Canada.

Brief Table of Contents

Table of Contents

PART THREE   **Mathematics of Finance and Investment   360**

Preface

INTRODUCTION

Contemporary Business Mathematics is intended for use in introductory mathematics of finance courses in business administration programs. In more general application it also provides a comprehensive basis for those who wish to review and extend their understanding of business mathematics.

The primary objective of the text is to increase the student's knowledge and skill in the solution of practical financial and mathematical problems encountered in the business community. It also provides a supportive base for mathematical topics in finance, accounting and marketing.

ORGANIZATION

Contemporary Business Mathematics is a teaching text using the objectives approach. The systematic and sequential development of the material is supported by carefully selected and worked examples. These detailed step-by-step solutions presented in a clear and uncluttered layout are particularly helpful in allowing students, in either independent studies or in the traditional classroom setting, to carefully monitor their own progress.

Each topic in each chapter is followed by an exercise containing numerous drill questions and application problems. The review exercise and self-test at the end of each chapter and the case studies are designed to assist in the integration of the material studied.

The first four chapters and Appendix I (Review of Basic Algebra) are intended for students with little or no background in algebra and provide an opportunity to review arithmetic and algebraic processes.

The text is based on Canadian practice, and reflects current trends utilizing available technology—specifically the availability of reasonably priced electronic pocket calculators.

Students using this book should have access to calculating equipment having a power function and a natural logarithm function. The use of such calculators eliminates the arithmetic constraints often associated with financial problems and frees the student from reliance on financial tables.

The power function and the natural logarithm function are often needed to determine values which will be used for further computation. Such values should not be rounded and all available digits should be retained. The student is encouraged to use the memory to retain such values.

When using the memory the student needs to be aware that the number of digits retained in the registers of the calculator is greater than the number of digits displayed. Depending on whether the memory or the displayed digits are used, slight differences may occur. Such differences will undoubtedly be encountered when working the examples presented in the text. However, they are insignificant and should not be of concern. In most cases the final answers will agree, whichever method is used.

Students are encouraged to use preprogrammed financial calculators though this is not essential. The use of preprogrammed calculators facilitates the solving of most financial problems and is demonstrated extensively in chapters 9 to 16.

NEW TO THIS EDITION

This fifth edition represents a major revision of the text. To reflect current practices in Canada and to better suit the needs of users of this book, many important changes have been made in content and organization.

In Chapter 1 (Review of Arithmetic), a new applications section on Taxes has been added, which deals with GST, PST, and Property Tax. Futhermore, to make the review of arithmetic more complete, sections on Fractions and Percent have been inserted in this chapter.

In Chapter 2 (Review of Basic Algebra), a new section has been added to stress the importance of understanding Formula Manipulation.

In Chapter 3 (Ratio, Proportion, and Percent), three new applications sections have been added: one on Currency Conversions, one on Personal Income Taxes, and one on Index Numbers (including the Consumer Price Index).

In Chapter 4 (Linear Systems), a discussion of the Slope-Intercept Form of linear equations has been added.

The pricing terminology has been revised throughout Chapter 6 (Trade Discount, Cash, Discount, Markup, and Markdown). New diagrams have been added to illustrate clearly the various relationships along the merchandizing chain.

In Chapter 8 (Simple Interest Applications), new sections on Treasury Bills and on Personal Lines of Credit have been added.

Chapters 11-13 on Annuities have been reorganized in order to avoid the sort of repetition found in the earlier editions.

In Chapter 14 (Amortization of Loans), a new section on Residential Mortgages in Canada has been added.

A slightly shorter treatment of Bond Valuation has been combined with a discussion of Sinking Funds to form the new Chapter 15.

The old chapter on Depreciation, Depletion, and Capitalization has been omitted to make room for the new topics and new features added for this edition. Coverage of this material is now introduced earlier in the book.

The pedagogical elements of the previous edition have been retained. But in response to requests and suggestions by users of the book, we have added numerous new features for this edition (as described below).

FEATURES

- A careful effort has been made with this edition to add features that will enhance applications and facilitate learning.

- A new friendlier design has been created for the book making it more accessible to today's student.

- A new box opens each chapter to emphasize the practical applications of the material to follow:

> Depreciation calculations and break-even analysis can be used in everyday situations. If you run a small business out of your home, such as an income tax or bookkeeping service, you are eligible to depreciate your computer and office furniture. This will reduce the income tax you pay on your business income. If you are in the market for a new car or other appliance, you can use break-even analysis to compare current costs to future savings. The concept of spending money to save money needs to be tempered with the time factor. A large box of cereal is not a bargain if it goes stale before you eat it. A new car that uses little gas doesn't save you money if you go broke paying for the new car.

- A set of learning objectives is listed near the beginning of each chapter.

- A new Business Math News Box is presented in each chapter. This element consists of short excerpts based on material appearing in newspapers or magazines, followed by a set of questions. These boxes demonstrate how widespread business math applications are in the real world:

BUSINESS MATH NEWS BOX

Yamaha recently ran the following advertisement:

Lease a New

Virago 1100	Big Bear 4×4
for $175*	for $148*
per month for 36 months with $1500.00 down.	per month for 36 months with $1200.00 down.

*Plus applicable taxes, freight, and PDI. Does not include insurance, licence, or registration fees. Limited time offer. Consumer may be required to purchase leased goods at the end of the lease term for $3919.83 for Virago™ and $2417.01 for Big Bear™ plus applicable taxes. See your dealer for return of refinancing options.

QUESTIONS

To answer these questions, assume the combined PST and GST tax rate is 15%. Assume freight, PDI, insurance, licence, and registration costs are the same whether you lease or buy a vehicle.

1. Suppose the Virago 1100 has a Manufacturer's Suggested Retail Price (MSRP) of $7995.00 plus taxes.
   a) If you can earn 10% on your money, is it cheaper to lease or buy this motorcycle?

- A new Did You Know? Box in each chapter offers interesting mathematical facts:

DID YOU KNOW?

When the bank's loan officer is determining how expensive a house you can afford to buy, one rule of thumb used is the calculation of two and a half times your gross family income. The chart below will give you an idea of what you can afford and the size of your 5% down payment. In order to qualify for a 5% down payment, your mortgage must be insured by Canada Mortgage and Housing Corporation (CMHC), and you must be a first-time purchaser of a principal residence.

On a Family Income Of:	You Could Afford a House Up To:	And Your 5% Down Payment Would Be:
$50 000	$125 000	$6 250
55 000	137 500	6 875
60 000	150 000	7 500
100 000	250 000	12 500

- Numerous Examples with worked out Solutions are provided throughout the book. Many of these examples offer easy to follow step by step instructions:

EXAMPLE 2.6G

Given $S = P(1 + i)^n$, solve for i.

$S = P(1 + i)^n$

$\dfrac{S}{P} = (1 + i)^n$ ———————————— right side was multiplied by P, so divide both sides by P

$\sqrt[n]{\dfrac{S}{P}} = 1 + i$ ———————————— taking a root is the undoing of a power

$\sqrt[n]{\dfrac{S}{P}} - 1 = i$ ———————————— 1 was added, so subtract 1 from both sides

- The Programmed Solutions using calculators have, where appropriate, been maintained from earlier editions; however, they have been completely redesigned to be clearer to the user. New Spreadsheet applications have been incorporated in Chapter 5 (for depreciation schedules), Chapter 8 (for loan repayment schedules), Chapter 9 (for the accumulation of principal), Chapter 14 (for amortization schedules), and Chapter 15 (for sinking fund schedules).

- Key Terms are introduced in the text in boldface type. A Glossary at the end of each chapter lists the terms with their definitions.

- Main Equations are highlighted in the chapters and repeated in a Summary of Formulae at the ends of the chapters. Equations have been labelled and presented throughout in such a way as to distinguish between main formulae and equivalent formulae. Each main formula is presented in colour and labelled numerically (with the letter A suffix if equivalent forms are presented later). By contrast, equivalent formulae are presented in black and labelled with the number of the related main formula followed by the letter B or C. Thus, for example, the first three boxed equations in Chapter 9 are all forms of the same formula. The first formula, $S = P(1 + i)n$, is presented in colour and labelled Formula 9.1A. The second formula, $P = S/(1 + i)n$, is merely a rearrangement of this equation. Therefore it is presented in black and labelled Formula 9.1B. Similarly, the third formula, $P = S(1 + I) - n$ is presented in black and labelled Formula 9.1C.

- A new list of the Main Formulae is given on the inside of the front cover for easy reference.

- An Exercise set is provided at the end of each section in every chapter. In addition, each chapter contains a Review Exercise set and a Self-Test. Answers to all the odd-numbered Exercises, Review Exercises, and Self-Tests are given at the back of the book.

- A new set of Challenge Problems is provided in each chapter. As their name suggests, these problems give users the opportunity to apply the skills learned in the chapter to questions that are pitched at a higher level than the exercises:

CHALLENGE PROBLEMS

1. Two consecutive price reductions of the same percent reduced the price of an item from $25 to $16. By what percent was the price reduced each time?

2. Following a 10% decrease in her annual salary, what percent increase would an employee need to receive in future to get back to her original salary level?

- Thirty-two new Case Studies are included in the book, two near the end of each chapter. They present comprehensive realistic scenarios followed by a set of Questions. The Case Studies illustrate some of the important types of practical applications of the chapter material. One half of the Case Studies represent personal-finance applications (indicated by a credit-card logo) while the other half are business applications:

CASE STUDY 9.1 WHAT'S IN YOUR BEST INTEREST?

Marika was standing in line at the bank one day and noticed the list of interest rates paid by the bank on each type of savings account. She discovered that the bank offered four different savings accounts. The Daily Interest Savings Account had an interest rate of 3.50%. The Monthly Interest Savings Account had an interest rate of 3.60%. The Investment Savings Account had an interest rate of 4.05%. The Basic Savings Account had an interest rate of 4.00%.

When Marika reached the teller, she asked him to describe the features of each account and to explain how interest was calculated on each account. In response, the teller explained that all accounts involve compound interest, but the calculation for each is different. Compound interest on the Daily Interest Savings Account is calculated on the minimum balance in the account each day and is paid monthly. Compound interest on the Monthly Interest Savings Account is calculated on the minimum balance in the account during the month and is paid monthly. Compound interest on the Investment Savings Account is calculated on the minimum balance in the account during the month, but only when the balance remains above $5000.00 for the whole month. If the balance in the account drops below $5000.00 at any time during the month, no interest is paid that month.

Compound interest on the Basic Savings Account is calculated on the minimum balance in the account during the six-month periods ending April 30 and October 31, and is paid on April 30 and October 31.

The teller told Marika that many customers were switching their accounts from the Basic Savings Account (which used to be the only savings account banks offered) to savings accounts that paid interest more often. He advised that each account had its benefits depending on the number of transactions made through the account each month or each year. Marika finished her banking and took a brochure that summarized these accounts so that she could consider the options.one year's time if she left the money in the account for one year? Assume that the bank's interest rates will stay the same during the year.

QUESTIONS

1. Suppose Marika had a $3000.00 income tax refund that she wanted to put into a savings account. She planned to leave the money in the account for one year. Assume that the bank's interest rates will stay the same during the year.
(a) For each of the bank's four savings accounts, how much interest would Marika earn in one year's time?
(b) Which savings account would pay the most interest?

2. Suppose Marika had $6000.000 to put into a savings account.
(a) For each of the bank's four savings accounts, how much interest would Marika earn in one year's time if she left the money in the account for one year? Assume that the bank's interest rates will stay the same during the year.
(b) Which savings account would pay the most interest?
(c) Suppose Marika knew she would have to withdraw $2000.00 after ten months. Which savings account would pay the most interest?

SUPPLEMENTS

The following supplements have been carefully prepared, by the author, to accompany this new edition:

- An Instructor's Solutions Manual, providing complete solutions to all the Exercises, Review Exercises, Self-Tests, Business Math News Box questions, Challenge Problems, and Case Studies in the textbook.
- A new Instructor's Resource Manual, providing additional material on selected topics that instructors might choose to introduce in class.
- Transparency Masters of many of the Figures and Tables in the textbook.
- A Test Item File of questions organized by chapter, with the level of difficulty (i.e., easy, moderate, or difficult) indicated for each question.
- P.H. Custom Test (For Windows), a special computerized version of the Test Item File, which enables instructors to edit existing questions, add new questions, and generate tests.
- A Student's Solutions Manual, providing complete solutions to all the odd-numbered Exercises, Review Exercises, and Self-Tests in the textbook.

ACKNOWLEDGEMENTS

I am grateful to the many people who offered such helpful suggestions and recommendations for improving the book. I would particularly like to thank the following instructors for providing formal reviews for the fifth edition:

Michael Balsdon (St. Clair College)
Ross Bryant (Conestoga College)
Helen Catania (Centennial College)
Ed Fox (Niagara College)
Sharyn Jefferies (Centennial College)
Amoel Lisecki (Southern Alberta Institute of Technology)
Deborah Rosin (Keewatin Community College)
Patrick Sherlock (Nova Scotia Community College)
Janet Storey (Georgian College)
Carol Ann Waite (Seneca College)

I would like to say a particular thanks to Julia Morton of Canadore College who invested an incredible amount of work in preparing many of the new elements in this edition. Her energy and ideas were invaluable to the development of the book and her participation on this project is much appreciated.

SIEG HUMMELBRUNNER
Mississauga
October 1997

Review of Arithmetic

PART ONE

Mathematics Fundamentals and Business Applications

1

Review of Arithmetic

Suppose you owned a small business. Under Canadian tax law, you must collect the Goods and Services Tax (GST) on almost everything you sell, then remit the GST to the federal government. You are eligible for a GST refund on purchases of goods and services. To account for the GST, you have the choice of using the regular method or the quick method. By using arithmetic and the problem-solving approaches in this chapter, you should be able to determine whether you can make money using the quick method of accounting for GST.

Introduction

The basics of fraction, decimal, and percent conversions are vital skills for dealing with situations you face, not only as a small business owner, but as a consumer and investor. Although calculators and laptop computers have become common tools for solving business problems, it is still important to understand clearly the process behind the conversions between number forms, the rounding of answers, and the correct order of operations.

OBJECTIVES

Upon completing this chapter, you will be able to do the following:

1. Simplify arithmetic expressions using the order of operations.
2. Change percents to common fractions and to decimals, and change decimals and fractions to percents.
3. Solve basic problems, including arithmetic averages, and sales and property taxes, involving the fundamental operations.
4. Determine gross earnings for employees remunerated by the payment of salaries, hourly wages, or commissions.

1.1 BASICS OF ARITHMETIC

A. The basic order of operations

To ensure that arithmetic calculations are performed consistently, we must follow the **order of operations**.

If an arithmetic expression contains brackets as well as any or all of powers, multiplication, division, addition, and subtraction, we use the following procedure:

1. Perform all operations *inside* a bracket first (the operations inside the bracket must be performed in proper order);
2. Perform powers;
3. Perform multiplications and divisions in order;
4. Perform addition and subtraction.

The following "BEDMAS" rule might help you to more easily remember the order of operations:

B	E	D	M	A	S
Brackets	Exponents	Division	Multiplication	Addition	Subtraction

Most calculators now have the order of operations built in. This will allow you more freedom in doing a series of calculations. Check your calculator to see whether or not it has the order of operations built in.

EXAMPLE 1.1A

(i) $9 - 4 \times 2 = 9 - 8 = 1$ —————— do multiplication before subtraction

(ii) $(9 - 4) \times 2 = 5 \times 2 = 10$ —————— work inside the bracket first

(iii) $(13 + 5) \div 6 - 3 = 18 \div 6 - 3$ —————— work inside the bracket first, then do
$$= 3 - 3$$ division before subtraction
$$= 0$$

(iv) $18 \div 6 + 3 \times 2 = 3 + 6 = 9$ —————— do multiplication and division before adding

(v) $18 \div (6 + 3) \times 2 = 18 \div 9 \times 2$ —————— work inside the bracket first, then do
$$= 2 \times 2$$ division and multiplication in order
$$= 4$$

(vi) $18 \div (3 \times 2) + 3 = 18 \div 6 + 3$ —————— work inside bracket first, then
$$= 3 + 3$$ divide before adding
$$= 6$$

(vii) $8(9 - 4) - 4(12 - 5) = 8(5) - 4(7)$ —— work inside brackets first, then
$$= 40 - 28$$ multiply before subtracting
$$= 12$$

(viii) $\dfrac{12 - 4}{6 - 2} = (12 - 4) \div (6 - 2)$ —————— the fraction line indicates brackets as well as division
$$= 8 \div 4$$
$$= 2$$

Exercise 1.1

A. Simplify each of the following.

1. $12 + 6 \div 3$

2. $(12 + 6) \div 3$

3. $(7 + 4) \times 5 - 2$

4. $7 + 4 \times 5 - 2$

5. $5 \times 3 + 2 \times 4$

6. $5(3 + 2) - 12 \div 3$

7. $6(7 - 2) - 3(5 - 3)$

8. $8(9 - 6) + 4(6 + 5)$

9. $\dfrac{16 - 8}{8 - 2}$

10. $\dfrac{20 - 16}{15 + 9}$

1.2 FRACTIONS

A. Common fractions

A **common fraction** is used to show a part of the whole. The fraction ⅔ means two parts out of a whole of three. The number written *below* the dividing line is the *whole* and is called the **denominator**. The number written *above* the dividing line is the *part* and is called the **numerator**. The numbers 2 and 3 are called the **terms of the fraction**.

A **proper fraction** has a numerator that is *less* than the denominator. An **improper fraction** has a numerator that is *greater* than the denominator.

EXAMPLE 1.2A

$\dfrac{3}{8}$ ← numerator ← denominator ——— a proper fraction, since the numerator is less than the denominator

$\dfrac{8}{3}$ ← numerator ← denominator ——— an improper fraction, since the numerator is greater than the denominator

B. Equivalent fractions

Equivalent fractions are obtained by changing the *terms* of a fraction without changing the value of the fraction.

Equivalent fractions in higher terms can be obtained by multiplying both the numerator and the denominator of a fraction by the same number. For any fraction, we can obtain an unlimited number of equivalent fractions in higher terms.

Equivalent fractions in lower terms can be obtained if both the numerator and denominator of a fraction are divisible by the same number or numbers. The process of obtaining such equivalent fractions is called *reducing to lower terms*.

DID YOU KNOW?

Delectable Numbers

A *delectable number* is defined as a number in which all the digits from 1 to 9 appear only once. As well, the first digit is exactly divisible by 1, the first two digits are exactly divisible by 2, the first three digits exactly by 3, and so on, until the whole number is exactly divisible by 9. One delectable number is 381654729. Check that this number is delectable, and see if you can find any others.

EXAMPLE 1.2B

(i) Convert ¾ into higher terms by multiplying successively by 2, 2, 3, 5, 5, and 11.

Solution

$$\frac{3}{4} = \frac{3 \times 2}{4 \times 2} = \frac{6}{8} = \frac{6 \times 2}{8 \times 2} = \frac{12}{16} = \frac{12 \times 3}{16 \times 3} = \frac{36}{48} = \frac{36 \times 5}{48 \times 5} = \frac{180}{240}$$

$$= \frac{180 \times 5}{240 \times 5} = \frac{900}{1200} = \frac{900 \times 11}{1200 \times 11} = \frac{9900}{13\,200}$$

$$\text{Thus } \frac{3}{4} = \frac{6}{8} = \frac{12}{16} = \frac{36}{48} = \frac{180}{240} = \frac{900}{1200} = \frac{9900}{13\,200}$$

(ii) Reduce ²¹⁰/₂₅₂ to lower terms.

Solution

$$\frac{210}{252} = \frac{210 \div 2}{252 \div 2} = \frac{105}{126}$$

$$= \frac{105 \div 3}{126 \div 3} = \frac{35}{42}$$

$$= \frac{35 \div 7}{42 \div 7} = \frac{5}{6}$$

The fractions ¹⁰⁵/₁₂₆, ³⁵/₄₂, and ⁵/₆ are lower term equivalents of ²¹⁰/₂₅₂.

The terms of the fraction ⁵/₆ cannot be reduced any further. It represents the simplest form of the fraction ²¹⁰/₂₅₂. It is the *fraction in lowest terms.*

C. Converting common fractions into decimal form

Common fractions are converted into decimal form by performing the indicated division to the desired number of decimal places or until the decimal terminates or repeats. We place a dot above a decimal number to show that it repeats. For example, $0.\dot{5}$ stands for 0.555….

EXAMPLE 1.2C

(i) $\dfrac{9}{8} = 9 \div 8 = 1.125$

(ii) $\dfrac{1}{3} = 1 \div 3 = 0.3333\ldots = 0.\dot{3}$

(iii) $\dfrac{7}{6} = 7 \div 6 = 1.16666\ldots = 1.1\dot{6}$

D. Converting mixed numbers to decimal form

Mixed numbers are numbers consisting of a whole number and a fraction, such as 5¾. Such numbers represent the *sum* of a whole number and a common fraction and can be converted into decimal form by changing the common fraction into decimal form.

EXAMPLE 1.2D

(i) $5\frac{3}{4} = 5 + \frac{3}{4} = 5 + 0.75 = 5.75$

(ii) $6\frac{2}{3} = 6 + \frac{2}{3} = 6 + 0.6666... = 6.66666... = 6.\dot{6}$

(iii) $7\frac{1}{12} = 7 + \frac{1}{12} = 7 + 0.083333... = 7.083333... = 7.08\dot{3}$

E. Rounding

Answers to problems, particularly when obtained with the help of a calculator, often need to be rounded to a desired number of decimal places. In most business problems involving money values, the rounding needs to be done to the nearest cent, that is, to two decimal places.

While different methods of rounding are used, for most business purposes the following procedure is suitable.

1. If the first digit in the group of decimal digits that is to be dropped is the digit 5 or 6 or 7 or 8 or 9, the last digit retained is *increased* by 1.
2. If the first digit in the group of decimal digits that is to be dropped is the digit 0 or 1 or 2 or 3 or 4, the last digit is left *unchanged*.

EXAMPLE 1.2E

Round each of the following to two decimal places.

(i) 7.384 —————→ 7.38 ————— drop the digit 4

(ii) 7.385 —————→ 7.39 ————— round the digit 8 up to 9

(iii) 12.9448 ————→ 12.94 ————— discard 48

(iv) 9.32838 ————→ 9.33 ————— round the digit 2 up to 3

(v) 24.8975 ————→ 24.90 ————— round the digit 9 up to 0; this requires rounding 89 to 90

(vi) 1.996 —————→ 2.00 ————— round the second digit 9 up to 0; this requires rounding 1.99 to 2.00

(vii) 3199.99833 ——→ 3200.00 ————— round the second digit 9 up to 0; this requires rounding 3199.99 to 3200.00

F. Complex fractions

Complex fractions are mathematical expressions containing one or more fractions in the numerator or denominator or both. Certain formulae used in simple interest and simple discount calculations result in complex fractions. When you encounter such fractions, take care to use the order of operations properly, whether computing manually or with the help of a calculator.

EXAMPLE 1.2F

(i) $\dfrac{420}{1600 \times \frac{315}{360}} = \dfrac{420}{1600 \times 0.875} = \dfrac{420}{1400} = 0.3$

(ii) $500\left(1 + 0.16 \times \dfrac{225}{360}\right)$

$= 500(1 + 0.10)$ ———— multiply 0.16 by 225 and divide by 360

$= 500(1.10)$ ———— add inside bracket

$= 550$

(iii) $1000\left(1 - 0.18 \times \dfrac{288}{360}\right) = 1000(1 - 0.144)$

$= 1000(0.856)$

$= 856$

(iv) $\dfrac{824}{1 + 0.15 \times \frac{73}{365}} = \dfrac{824}{1 + 0.03} = \dfrac{824}{1.03} = 800$

(vi) $\dfrac{1755}{1 - 0.21 \times \frac{210}{360}} = \dfrac{1755}{1 - 0.1225} = \dfrac{1755}{0.8775} = 2000$

Exercise 1.2

A. Reduce each of the following fractions to lowest terms.

1. $\dfrac{24}{36}$

2. $\dfrac{28}{56}$

3. $\dfrac{210}{360}$

4. $\dfrac{330}{360}$

5. $\dfrac{360}{225}$

6. $\dfrac{360}{315}$

7. $\dfrac{144}{360}$

8. $\dfrac{360}{288}$

9. $\dfrac{25}{365}$

10. $\dfrac{115}{365}$

11. $\dfrac{365}{73}$

12. $\dfrac{365}{219}$

B. Convert each of the following fractions into decimal form. If appropriate, place a dot above a decimal number to show that it repeats.

1. $\dfrac{11}{8}$

2. $\dfrac{7}{4}$

3. $\dfrac{5}{3}$

4. $\dfrac{5}{6}$

5. $\dfrac{11}{6}$

6. $\dfrac{7}{9}$

7. $\dfrac{13}{12}$

8. $\dfrac{19}{15}$

C. Convert each of the following mixed numbers into decimal form.

1. $3\dfrac{3}{8}$

2. $3\dfrac{2}{5}$

3. $8\dfrac{1}{3}$

4. $16\dfrac{2}{3}$

5. $33\dfrac{1}{3}$

6. $83\dfrac{1}{3}$

7. $7\dfrac{7}{9}$

8. $7\dfrac{1}{12}$

D. Round each of the following to two decimal places.

1. 5.633   2. 17.449   3. 18.0046   4. 253.4856

5. 57.69875   6. 3.09475   7. 12.995   8. 39.999

E. Simplify each of the following.

1. $\dfrac{54}{0.12 \times \frac{225}{360}}$

2. $\dfrac{264}{4400 \times \frac{146}{365}}$

3. $620\left(1 + 0.14 \times \dfrac{45}{360}\right)$

4. $375\left(1 + 0.16 \times \dfrac{292}{365}\right)$

5. $2100\left(1 - 0.135 \times \dfrac{240}{360}\right)$

6. $8500\left(1 - 0.17 \times \dfrac{216}{360}\right)$

7. $\dfrac{250\,250}{1 + 0.15 \times \frac{330}{360}}$

8. $\dfrac{2358}{1 + 0.12 \times \frac{146}{365}}$

9. $\dfrac{3460}{1 - 0.18 \times \frac{270}{360}}$

10. $\dfrac{2901}{1 - 0.165 \times \frac{73}{365}}$

1.3 PERCENT

A. The meaning of percent

Fractions are used to compare the quantity represented by the numerator with the quantity represented by the denominator. The easiest method of comparing the two quantities is to use fractions with denominator 100. The preferred form of writing such fractions is the *percent* form. **Percent** means "per hundred," and the symbol % is used to show "parts of one hundred."

PERCENT means HUNDREDTHS ⟶ % means $\dfrac{}{100}$

Accordingly, any fraction involving "hundredths" may be written as follows:

(i) as a common fraction $\dfrac{13}{100}$

(ii) as a decimal   0.13

(iii) in percent form   13%

B. Changing percents to common fractions

When speaking or writing, we often use percents in the percent form. However, when computing with percents, we use the corresponding common fraction or decimal fraction. To convert a percent into a common fraction, replace the symbol % by the symbol $\dfrac{}{100}$. Then reduce the resulting fraction to lowest terms.

EXAMPLE 1.3A

(i) $24\% = \dfrac{24}{100}$ ————————————— replace % by $\frac{}{100}$

$= \dfrac{6}{25}$ ————————————— reduce to lowest terms

(ii) $175\% = \dfrac{175}{100} = \dfrac{7 \times 25}{4 \times 25} = \dfrac{7}{4}$

(iii) $6.25\% = \dfrac{6.25}{100}$

$= \dfrac{625}{10\ 000}$ ————————— multiply by 100 to change the numerator to a whole number

$= \dfrac{125}{2000} = \dfrac{25}{400} = \dfrac{5}{80}$ ————— reduce gradually or in one step

$= \dfrac{1}{16}$

(iv) $0.8\% = \dfrac{0.8}{100} = \dfrac{8}{1000} = \dfrac{1}{125}$

(v) $0.025\% = \dfrac{0.025}{100} = \dfrac{25}{100\ 000} = \dfrac{1}{4000}$

(vi) $\dfrac{1}{4}\% = \dfrac{\frac{1}{4}}{\frac{100}{1}}$ ————————— replace % by $\frac{}{\frac{100}{1}}$

$= \dfrac{1}{4} \times \dfrac{1}{100}$ ————————— invert and multiply

$= \dfrac{1}{400}$

(vii) $\dfrac{3}{8}\% = \dfrac{\frac{3}{8}}{\frac{100}{1}} = \dfrac{3}{8} \times \dfrac{1}{100} = \dfrac{3}{800}$

(viii) $33\frac{1}{3}\% = \dfrac{33\frac{1}{3}}{100}$ ————————— replace % by $\frac{}{100}$

$= \dfrac{\frac{100}{3}}{\frac{100}{1}}$ ————————— convert the mixed number $33\frac{1}{3}$ into a common fraction

$= \dfrac{100}{3} \times \dfrac{1}{100}$

$= \dfrac{1}{3}$

$$\text{(ix)} \quad 216\tfrac{2}{3}\% = \frac{216\tfrac{2}{3}}{100} = \frac{\frac{650}{3}}{\frac{100}{1}} = \frac{\overset{13}{\cancel{650}}}{3} \times \frac{1}{\underset{2}{\cancel{100}}} = \frac{13}{6}$$

Alternatively

$$216\tfrac{2}{3}\% = 200\% + 16\tfrac{2}{3}\% \quad\underline{\hspace{3cm}}\quad \text{separate the multiple of 100\%}$$
$$\text{(that is, 200\%) from the remainder}$$

$$= 2 + \frac{\frac{50}{3}}{\frac{100}{1}}$$

$$= 2 + \frac{50}{3} \times \frac{1}{100}$$

$$= 2 + \frac{1}{6}$$

$$= \frac{13}{6}$$

C. Changing percents to decimals

Replacing the symbol % by $\frac{1}{100}$ indicates a division by 100. Since division by 100 is performed by moving the decimal point *two places to the left*, changing a percent to a decimal is easy to do. Simply drop the symbol % and move the decimal point two places to the left.

EXAMPLE 1.3B

(i) $52\% = 0.52$ $\underline{\hspace{2.5cm}}$ drop the percent symbol and move the decimal point two places to the left

(ii) $175\% = 1.75$

(iii) $6\% = 0.06$

(iv) $0.75\% = 0.0075$

(v) $\dfrac{1}{4}\% = 0.25\%$ $\underline{\hspace{2cm}}$ first change the fraction to a decimal

$\qquad = 0.0025$ $\underline{\hspace{2cm}}$ drop the % symbol and move the decimal point two places to the left

(vi) $\dfrac{3}{8}\% = 0.375\%$

$\qquad = 0.00375$

(vii) $\dfrac{1}{3}\% = 0.\dot{3}\%$ $\underline{\hspace{2cm}}$ change the fraction to a repeating decimal

$\qquad = 0.00\dot{3}$ $\underline{\hspace{2cm}}$ drop the % symbol and move the decimal point two places to the left

(viii) $\dfrac{5}{8}\% = 0.625\%$

$\qquad = 0.00625$

D. Changing decimals to percents

Changing decimals to percents is the inverse operation of changing percents into decimals. It is accomplished by multiplying the decimal by 100%. Since multiplication by 100 is performed by moving the decimal point *two places to the right*, a decimal is easily changed to a percent. Move the decimal point two places to the right and add the % symbol.

EXAMPLE 1.3C

(i) $0.36 = 0.36(100\%)$ ——————— move the decimal point two places to the
$= 36\%$ right and add the % symbol

(ii) $1.65 = 165\%$

(iii) $0.075 = 7.5\%$

(iv) $0.4 = 40\%$

(v) $0.001 = 0.1\%$

(vi) $2 = 200\%$

(vii) $0.0005 = 0.05\%$

(viii) $0.\dot{3} = 33.\dot{3}\%$

(ix) $1.1\dot{6} = 116.\dot{6}\%$

(x) $1\frac{5}{6} = 1.8\dot{3} = 183.\dot{3}\%$

E. Changing fractions to percents

When changing a fraction to a percent, it is best to convert the fraction to a decimal and then to change the decimal to a percent.

EXAMPLE 1.3D

(i) $\frac{1}{4} = 0.25$ ————————— convert the fraction to a decimal

$= 25\%$ ————————— convert the decimal to a percent

(ii) $\frac{7}{8} = 0.875 = 87.5\%$

(iii) $\frac{9}{5} = 1.8 = 180\%$

(iv) $\frac{5}{6} = 0.8\dot{3} = 83.\dot{3}\%$

(v) $\frac{5}{9} = 0.\dot{5} = 55.\dot{5}\%$

(vi) $1\frac{2}{3} = 1.\dot{6} = 166.\dot{6}\%$

Exercise 1.3

A. Change each of the following percents into a decimal.

1. 64%
2. 300%
3. 2.5%
4. 0.1%

5. 0.5%
6. 85%
7. 250%
8. 4.8%

9. 450%
10. 7.5%
11. 0.9%
12. 95%

13. 6.25%
14. 0.4%
15. 99%
16. 225%

17. 0.05%
18. $8\frac{1}{4}$%
19. $\frac{1}{2}$%
20. $112\frac{1}{2}$%

21. $9\frac{3}{8}$%
22. $\frac{3}{4}$%
23. $162\frac{1}{2}$%
24. $\frac{2}{5}$%

25. $\frac{1}{4}$%
26. $187\frac{1}{2}$%
27. $1\frac{3}{4}$%
28. $\frac{1}{40}$%

29. $137\frac{1}{2}$%
30. $\frac{5}{8}$%
31. 0.875%
32. $2\frac{1}{4}$%

33. $33\frac{1}{3}$%
34. $166\frac{2}{3}$%
35. $16\frac{2}{3}$%
36. $116\frac{2}{3}$%

37. $183\frac{1}{3}$%
38. $83\frac{1}{3}$%
39. $133\frac{1}{3}$%
40. $66\frac{2}{3}$%

B. Change each of the following percents into a common fraction in lowest terms.

1. 25%
2. $62\frac{1}{2}$%
3. 175%
4. 5%

5. $37\frac{1}{2}$%
6. 75%
7. 4%
8. 225%

9. 8%
10. 125%
11. 40%
12. $87\frac{1}{2}$%

13. 250%
14. 2%
15. $12\frac{1}{2}$%
16. 60%

17. 2.25%
18. 0.5%
19. $\frac{1}{8}$%
20. $33\frac{1}{3}$%

21. $\frac{3}{4}$%
22. $66\frac{2}{3}$%
23. 6.25%
24. 0.25%

25. $16\frac{2}{3}$%
26. 7.5%
27. 0.75%
28. $\frac{7}{8}$%

29. 0.1%
30. $\frac{3}{5}$%
31. $83\frac{1}{3}$%
32. 2.5%

33. $133\frac{1}{3}$%
34. $183\frac{1}{3}$%
35. $166\frac{2}{3}$%
36. $116\frac{2}{3}$%

C. Express each of the following as a percent.

1. 3.5
2. 0.075
3. 0.005
4. 0.375

5. 0.025
6. 2
7. 0.125
8. 0.001

9. 0.225
10. 0.008
11. 1.45
12. 0.0225

13. 0.0025   14. 0.995   15. 0.09   16. 3

17. $\frac{3}{4}$ 18. $\frac{3}{25}$ 19. $\frac{5}{3}$ 20. $\frac{7}{200}$

21. $\frac{9}{200}$ 22. $\frac{5}{8}$ 23. $\frac{3}{400}$ 24. $\frac{5}{6}$

25. $\frac{9}{800}$ 26. $\frac{7}{6}$ 27. $\frac{3}{8}$ 28. $\frac{11}{40}$

29. $\frac{4}{3}$ 30. $\frac{9}{400}$ 31. $\frac{13}{20}$ 32. $\frac{4}{5}$

1.4 APPLICATIONS – AVERAGES

A. Basic problems

When electronic calculators are used to solve problems, the accuracy of the final answer is often influenced by the number of decimal positions used for intermediate values. To avoid introducing rounding errors, keep intermediate values unrounded.

EXAMPLE 1.4A

The local cooperative received $36\frac{3}{4}$ tonnes of feed at $240 per tonne. Sales for the following five days were

$3\frac{5}{8}$ tonnes, $4\frac{3}{4}$ tonnes, $7\frac{2}{3}$ tonnes, $5\frac{1}{2}$ tonnes, and $6\frac{3}{8}$ tonnes.

What was the value of inventory at the end of Day 5?

Solution

$$\text{Total sales (in tonnes)} = 3\frac{5}{8} + 4\frac{3}{4} + 7\frac{2}{3} + 5\frac{1}{2} + 6\frac{3}{8}$$

$$= 3.625 + 4.75 + 7.6666667 + 5.5 + 6.375$$

$$= 27.9166667$$

$$\text{Inventory (in tonnes)} = 36.75 - 27.9166667 = 8.8333333$$

$$\text{Value of inventory} = 8.8333333 \times 240 = 2119.999992 \cong \$2120.00$$

EXAMPLE 1.4B

Complete the following excerpt from an invoice.

Quantity	Unit Price	Amount
72	$0.875	$ _____
45	$66\frac{2}{3}¢$	_____
54	$83\frac{1}{3}¢$	_____
42	$1.3\dot{3}	_____
32	$1.375	_____
Total		$ _____

Solution

$$72 \times \$0.875 = \qquad\qquad\qquad \$\ 63.00$$

$$45 \times 66\tfrac{2}{3}\cancel{c} = 45 \times \$0.66\dot{6}$$

$$= 45 \times \$0.6666667 = \$\ 30.00$$

$$54 \times 83\tfrac{1}{3}\cancel{c} = 54 \times \$0.83\dot{3}$$

$$= 54 \times \$0.8333333 = \$\ 45.00$$

$$42 \times \$1.3\dot{3} = 42 \times \$1.3333333 = \$\ 56.00$$

$$32 \times \$1.375 = \qquad\qquad\qquad \$\ 44.00$$

$$\underline{}$$
$$\$238.00$$

B. Problems involving simple arithmetic average

The *arithmetic mean* of a set of values is a widely used average found by adding the values in the set and dividing by the number of those values.

EXAMPLE 1.4C

The marks obtained by Jim Pearson for the seven tests comprising Section 1 of his Mathematics of Finance course were 82, 68, 88, 72, 78, 96, and 83.

(i) If all tests count equally, what was his average mark for Section 1?

(ii) If his marks for Section 2 and Section 3 of the course were 72.4 and 68.9 respectively and all section marks have equal value, what was his course average?

Solution

(i) Section Average $= \dfrac{\text{Sum of the Test Marks for the Section}}{\text{Number of Tests}}$

$$= \dfrac{82 + 68 + 88 + 72 + 78 + 96 + 83}{7}$$

$$= \dfrac{567}{7}$$

$$= 81.0$$

(ii) Course Average $= \dfrac{\text{Sum of the Section Marks}}{\text{Number of Sections}}$

$$= \dfrac{81.0 + 72.4 + 68.9}{3}$$

$$= \dfrac{222.3}{3}$$

$$= 74.1$$

EXAMPLE 1.4D

Monthly sales of Sheridan Service for last year were:

January	$13 200	July	$13 700
February	11 400	August	12 800
March	14 600	September	13 800
April	13 100	October	15 300
May	13 600	November	14 400
June	14 300	December	13 900

What were Sheridan's average monthly sales for the year?

Solution   Total sales $=$ 164 100

$$\text{Average Monthly Sales} = \frac{\text{Total Sales}}{\text{Number of Months}} = \frac{164\ 100}{12} = \$13\ 675$$

C. Weighted average

If the items to be included in computing an arithmetic mean are arranged in groups or if the items are not equally important, a *weighted arithmetic average* should be obtained. Multiply each item by the numbers involved or by a weighting factor representing its importance.

EXAMPLE 1.4E   During last season, Fairfield Farms sold strawberries as follows: 800 boxes at $1.25 per box in the early part of the season; 1600 boxes at $0.90 per box and 2000 boxes at $0.75 per box at the height of the season; and 600 boxes at $1.10 per box during the late season.

(i) What was the average price charged?
(ii) What was the average price per box?

Solution   (i) The average price charged is a simple average of the four different prices charged during the season.

$$\text{Average Price} = \frac{1.25 + 0.90 + 0.75 + 1.10}{4} = \frac{4.00}{4} = \$1.00$$

(ii) To obtain the average price per box, the number of boxes sold at each price must be taken into account; that is, a weighted average must be computed.

$$
\begin{array}{lll}
800 \text{ boxes @ } \$1.25 \text{ per box} & \longrightarrow & \$1000.00 \\
1600 \text{ boxes @ } \$0.90 \text{ per box} & \longrightarrow & 1440.00 \\
2000 \text{ boxes @ } \$0.75 \text{ per box} & \longrightarrow & 1500.00 \\
\underline{600} \text{ boxes @ } \$1.10 \text{ per box} & \longrightarrow & \underline{660.00} \\
\underline{5000} \text{ boxes} \longleftarrow \text{ TOTALS} & \longrightarrow & \underline{\$4600.00}
\end{array}
$$

$$\text{Average Price per Box} = \frac{\text{Total Value}}{\text{Number of Boxes}} = \frac{4600.00}{5000} = \$0.92$$

EXAMPLE 1.4F   The Dutch Coffee Shop creates its house brand by mixing 13 kg of coffee priced at $7.50 per kg, 16 kg of coffee priced at $6.25 per kg, and 11 kg of coffee priced at $5.50 per kg. At what price should the store sell its house blend to realize the same revenue as it could make by selling the three types of coffee separately?

Solution

$$
\begin{array}{lll}
13 \text{ kg @ } \$7.50 \text{ per kg} & \longrightarrow & \$\ 97.50 \\
16 \text{ kg @ } \$6.25 \text{ per kg} & \longrightarrow & 100.00 \\
\underline{11} \text{ kg @ } \$5.50 \text{ per kg} & \longrightarrow & \underline{60.50} \\
\underline{40} \text{ kg} \longleftarrow \text{ TOTALS} & \longrightarrow & \underline{\$258.00}
\end{array}
$$

$$\text{Average Value} = \frac{\text{Total Value}}{\text{Number of Units}} = \frac{258.00}{40} = \$6.45$$

The house blend should sell for $6.45 per kg.

EXAMPLE 1.4G   The credit hours and grades for Dana's first term courses are listed here.

Course	Credit Hours	Grade
Accounting	5	A
Economics	3	B
English	4	C
Law	2	D
Marketing	4	A
Mathematics	3	A
Elective	2	D

According to the grading system A's, B's, C's, and D's are worth 4, 3, 2, and 1 quality points respectively. Based on this information, determine

(i) Dana's average course grade;

(ii) Dana's grade-point average (average per credit hour).

Solution   (i) The average course grade is the average quality points obtained:

$$\frac{4 + 3 + 2 + 1 + 4 + 4 + 1}{7} = \frac{19}{7} \cong 2.71$$

(ii) The average obtained in part (i) is misleading since the credit hours of the courses are not equal. The grade-point average is a more appropriate average because it is a weighted average allowing for the number of credit hours per course.

Course	Credit Hours	×	Quality Points	=	Weighted Points
Accounting	5	×	4	=	20
Economics	3	×	3	=	9
English	4	×	2	=	8
Law	2	×	1	=	2
Marketing	4	×	4	=	16
Mathematics	3	×	4	=	12
Elective	2	×	1	=	2
	23	←	Totals	→	69

$$\text{Grade-Point Average} = \frac{\text{Total Weighted Points}}{\text{Total Credit Hours}} = \frac{69}{23} = 3.00$$

EXAMPLE 1.4H

A partnership agreement provides for the distribution of the yearly profit or loss on the basis of the partners' average monthly investment balance. The investment account of one of the partners shows the following entries.

Balance, January 1	$25 750
April 1, withdrawal	3 250
June 1, investment	4 000
November 1, investment	2 000

Determine the partner's average monthly balance in his investment account.

Solution

To determine the average monthly investment, determine the balance in the investment account after each change and weigh this balance by the number of months invested.

Date	Change	Balance	×	Invested	=	Value
January 1		25 750	×	3	=	77 250
April 1	−3250	22 500	×	2	=	45 000
June 1	+4000	26 500	×	5	=	132 500
November 1	+2000	28 500	×	2	=	57 000
		Totals		12		311 750

$$\text{Average Monthly Investment} = \frac{\text{Weighted Value}}{\text{Number of Months}} = \frac{311\ 750}{12} \cong \$25\ 979.17$$

EXAMPLE 1.4I

Several shoe stores in the city carry the same make of shoes. The number of pairs of shoes sold and the price charged by each store are shown below.

Store	Number of Pairs Sold	Price per Pair
A	60	$43.10
B	84	38.00
C	108	32.00
D	72	40.50

(i)   What was the average number of pairs of shoes sold per store?

(ii) What was the average price per store?

(iii) What was the average sales revenue per store?

(iv) What was the average price per pair of shoes?

Solution

(i) The average number of pairs of shoes sold per store

$$= \frac{60 + 84 + 108 + 72}{4} = \frac{324}{4} = 81$$

(ii) The average price per store

$$= \frac{43.10 + 38.00 + 32.00 + 40.50}{4} = \frac{153.60}{4} = \$38.40$$

(iii) The average sales revenue per store

$$
\begin{array}{rl}
60 \times 43.10 = & \$\ 2\ 586.00 \\
84 \times 38.00 = & 3\ 192.00 \\
108 \times 32.00 = & 3\ 456.00 \\
72 \times 40.50 = & \underline{2\ 916.00} \\
& \$12\ 150.00
\end{array}
$$

$$\text{Average} = \frac{12\ 150.00}{4} = \$3\ 037.50$$

(iv) The average price per pair of shoes

$$= \frac{\text{Total Sales Revenue}}{\text{Total Pairs Sold}} = \frac{12\ 150.00}{324} = \$37.50$$

Exercise 1.4

A. Answer each of the following questions.

1. Heart Lake Developments sold four lakefront lots for $27 500 per hectare. If the size of the lots in hectares was 3¾, 2⅔, 3⅝, and 4⅚ respectively, what was the total sales revenue of the four lots?

2. Five carpenters worked 15½, 13¾, 18½, 21¼, and 22¾ hours respectively. What was the total cost of labour if the carpenters were each paid $12.75 per hour?

3. A piece of property valued at $56 100 is assessed for property tax purposes at ⁶⁄₁₁ of its value. If the property tax rate is $3.75 on each $100 of assessed value, what is the amount of tax levied on the property?

4. A retailer returned 2700 defective items to the manufacturer and received a credit for the retail price of $0.8̇3̇ or 83⅓¢ per item less a discount of ⅜ of the retail price. What was the amount of the credit received by the retailer?

5. Extend the following invoice.

Quantity	Description	Unit Price	$
64	A	$0.75	_____
54	B	$83\frac{1}{3}$¢	_____
72	C	$0.375	_____
42	D	$1.3̇3̇	_____
		Total	_____

6. Complete the following inventory sheet.

Item	Quantity	Cost per Unit	Total
1	96	$0.875	_____
2	330	$16\frac{2}{3}¢$	_____
3	144	$1.75	_____
4	240	$1.6\dot{6}$	_____
		Total	_____

B. Solve each of the following problems involving an arithmetic average.

1. Records of Sheridan Service's fuel oil consumption for the last six-month period show that Sheridan paid 38.5 cents per litre for the first 1100 litres, 41.5 cents per litre for the next 1600 litres, and 42.5 cents per litre for the last delivery of 1400 litres. Determine the average cost of fuel oil per litre for the six-month period.

2. On a trip, a motorist purchased gasoline as follows: 56 litres at 49.0 cents per litre; 64 litres at 60.5 cents per litres; 70 litres at 51.5 cents per litre; and 54 litres at 54.5 cents per litre.

   (i) What was the average number of litres per purchase?

   (ii) What was the average cost per litre?

   (iii) If the motorist averaged 8.75 km per litre, what was her average cost of gasoline per kilometre?

3. The course credit hours and grades for Bill's fall semester are given below. At his college, an A is worth six quality points, a B four points, a C two points, and a D one point.

   Credit hours: 3 5 2 4 4 2
      Grade: B C A C D A

   What is Bill's grade-point average?

4. Kim Blair invested $7500 in a business on January 1. She withdrew $900 on March 1, reinvested $1500 on August 1, and withdrew $300 on September 1. What is Kim's average monthly investment balance for the year?

1.5 APPLICATIONS – PAYROLL

Employees can be remunerated for their services in a variety of ways. The main methods of remuneration are salaries, hourly wage rates, and commission. While the computations involved in preparing a payroll are fairly simple, utmost care is needed to ensure that all calculations are accurate.

A. Salaries

Compensation of employees by **salary** is usually on a monthly or a yearly basis. Monthly salaried personnel get paid either monthly or semi-monthly. Personnel on a yearly salary basis may get paid monthly, semi-monthly, every two weeks, or weekly, or according to special schedules such as those used by some Boards of Education to pay their teachers. If salary is paid weekly or every two weeks, the year is assumed to consist of exactly 52 weeks.

Calculations of **gross earnings** per pay period is fairly simple. Computing overtime for salaried personnel can be problematic since overtime is usually paid based on an hourly rate.

EXAMPLE 1.5A

An employee with an annual salary of $23 296.00 is paid every two weeks. The regular workweek is 40 hours.

(i) What is the gross pay per pay period?

(ii) What is the hourly rate of pay?

(iii) What are the gross earnings for a pay period in which the employee worked six hours of overtime and is paid one-and-a-half times the regular hourly rate of pay?

Solution

(i) An employee paid every two weeks receives the annual salary over 26 pay periods.

$$\text{Gross pay per two-week period} = \frac{23\ 296.00}{26} = \$896.00$$

(ii) Given a 40-hour week, the employee's compensation for two weeks covers 80 hours.

$$\text{Hourly rate of pay} = \frac{896.00}{80} = \$11.20$$

(iii) Regular gross earnings for two-week period $896.00

Overtime pay
6 hours @ $11.20 × 1.5 = 6 × 11.20 × 1.5   100.80

Total gross earnings for pay period $996.80

EXAMPLE 1.5B

Mike Paciuc receives a monthly salary of $2080.00 paid semi-monthly. Mike's regular workweek is 37.5 hours. Any hours worked over 37.5 hours in a week are overtime and are paid at time-and-a-half regular pay. During the first half of October, Mike worked 7.5 hours overtime.

(i) What is Mike's hourly rate of pay?

(ii) What are his gross earnings for the pay period ending October 15?

Solution

(i) When computing the hourly rate of pay for personnel employed on a monthly salary basis, the correct approach requires that the yearly salary be determined first. The hourly rate of pay may then be computed on the basis of 52 weeks per year.

$$\text{Yearly gross earnings} = 2080.00 \times 12 = \$24\ 960.00$$

$$\text{Weekly gross earnings} = \frac{24\ 960.00}{52} = \$480.00$$

$$\text{Hourly rate of pay} = \frac{480.00}{37.5} = \$12.80$$

(ii) Regular semi-monthly gross earnings $= \dfrac{2080.00}{2} = \$1040.00$

Overtime pay $= 7.5 \times 12.80 \times 1.5 \qquad = \underline{144.00}$

Total gross earnings for pay period $\qquad \underline{\$1184.00}$

EXAMPLE 1.5C

Teachers with the Northern Mississagi Board of Education are under contract for 200 teaching days per year. They are paid according to the following schedule:

8% of annual salary on the first day of school;
4% of annual salary for each of 20 two-week pay periods;
12% of annual salary at the end of the last pay period in June.

Fern Brooks, a teacher employed by the board, is paid an annual salary of $51 240.00.

(i) What is Fern's daily rate of pay?

(ii) What is Fern's gross pay?
  (a) for the first pay period?
  (b) for the last pay period?
  (c) for all other pay periods?

(iii) If Fern takes an unpaid leave of absence for three days during a pay period ending in April, what is her gross pay for that pay period?

Solution

(i) Daily rate of pay $= \dfrac{51\ 240.00}{200} = \$256.20$

(ii) (a) First gross pay $= 0.08 \times 51\ 240.00 = \$4099.20$
   (b) Last gross pay $= 0.12 \times 51\ 240.00 = \$6148.80$
   (c) All other gross pay $= 0.04 \times 51\ 240.00 = \$2049.60$

(iii) Gross pay for pay period ending in April $= \$2049.60$
   Less 3 days of pay $= {}^{3}/_{200}$ of $\$51\ 240.00 \quad = \underline{768.60}$
   Gross pay $\qquad \underline{\$1281.00}$

B. Commission

Persons engaged in the buying and selling functions of a business are often compensated by a **commission**. Of the various types of commission designed to meet the specific circumstances of a particular business, the most commonly encountered are straight commission, graduated (or sliding-scale) commission, and base salary plus commission.

Straight commission is usually calculated as a percent of net sales for a given time period. Net sales are the difference between the gross sales for the time period and any sales returns and allowances.

Graduated commission usually involves paying an increasing percent for increasing sales levels during a given time period.

Salary plus commission is a method that guarantees a minimum income per pay period to the salesperson. However, the rate of commission in such cases is either at a lower rate or is not paid until a minimum sales level (called a **quota**) for a time period has been reached.

Sales personnel on commission often have a drawing account with their employer. The salesperson may withdraw funds from such an account in advance to meet business and personal expenses. However, any money advanced is deducted from the commission earned when the salesperson is paid.

EXAMPLE 1.5D

Robin Thomas receives a commission of 11.5% on his net sales and is entitled to drawings of up to $1000.00 per month. During August, Robin's gross sales amounted to $15 540.00 and sales returns and allowances were $360.00.

(i) What are Robin's net sales for August?

(ii) How much is his commission for August?

(iii) If Robin drew $875.00 in August, what is the amount due to him?

Solution

(i) Gross sales $15 540.00
     Less sales returns and allowances   360.00
     Net sales $15 180.00

(ii) Commission = 11.5% of net sales
                 = 0.115 × 15 180.00
                 = $1745.70

(iii) Gross commission earned $1745.70
       Less drawings   875.00
       Amount due $ 870.70

EXAMPLE 1.5E

Valerie works as a salesperson for the local Minutemen Press. She receives a commission of 7.5% on monthly sales up to $8000.00, 9.25% on the next $7000.00, and 11% on any additional sales during the month. If Valerie's September sales amounted to $18 750.00, what is her gross commission for the month?

Solution

Commission on the first $8000.00 = 0.075 × 8000.00   = $ 600.00
Commission on the next $7000.00 = 0.0925 × 7000.00 =   647.50
Commission on sales over $15 000 = 0.11 × 3750.00   =   412.50
Total commission for September $1660.00

EXAMPLE 1.5F

Rita is employed as a salesclerk in a fabric store. She receives a weekly salary of $575.00 plus a commission of 6¼% on all weekly sales subject to a weekly sales quota of $5000.00. Derek works in the shoe store located next door. He receives a minimum of $500.00 per week or a commission of 12.5% on all sales for the week, whichever is the greater. If both Rita and Derek had sales of $5960.00 last week, how much compensation does each receive for the week?

Solution

Rita's compensation

Base salary	$575.00
Plus commission = 6¼% on sales over $5000.00	
= 0.0625 × 960.00	60.00
Total compensation	$635.00

Derek's compensation

Minimum weekly pay $500.00
Commission = 12.5% of $5960.00 = 0.125 × 5960.00 = $745.00

Since the commission is greater than the guaranteed minimum pay of $500.00, Derek's compensation is $745.00.

C. Wages

The term **wages** usually applies to compensation paid to *hourly* rated employees. Their gross earnings are calculated by multiplying the number of hours worked by the hourly rate of pay plus any overtime pay. Overtime is most often paid at time and one-half the regular hourly rate for any hours exceeding an established number of regular hours per week or per day. The number of regular hours is often established by agreement between the employer and employees. The most common regular workweek is 40 hours. If no agreement exists, federal or provincial employment standards legislation provides for a maximum number of hours per week, such as 44 hours for most employers in Ontario. Any hours over the set maximum must be paid at least at time and one-half of the regular hourly rate.

When overtime is involved, gross earnings can be calculated by either one of two methods.

Method A
The most common method, and the easiest method for the wage earner to understand, determines total gross earnings by adding overtime pay to the gross pay for a regular workweek.

Method B
In the second method, the overtime excess (or **overtime premium**) is computed separately and added to gross earnings for all hours (including the overtime hours) at the regular rate of pay. Computation of the excess labour cost due to overtime emphasizes the additional expense due to overtime and provides management with information that is useful to cost control.

EXAMPLE 1.5G

Mario is a machinist with Scott Tool and Die and is paid $14.40 per hour. The regular workweek is 40 hours and overtime is paid at time and one-half the regular hourly rate. If Mario worked $46\frac{1}{2}$ hours last week, what were his gross earnings?

Solution

Method A

Gross earnings for a regular workweek $= 40 \times 14.40$ $= \$576.00$
Overtime pay $= 6.5 \times 14.40 \times 1.5$ $= \underline{\hspace{0.3cm}140.40}$
Gross pay $\underline{\underline{\$716.40}}$

Method B

Earnings at the regular hourly rate $= 46.5 \times 14.40$ $= \$669.60$
Overtime premium $= 6.5 \times \left(\frac{1}{2} \text{ of } 14.40\right) = 6.5 \times 7.20 = \underline{\hspace{0.3cm}46.80}$
Gross pay $\underline{\underline{\$716.40}}$

EXAMPLE 1.5H

Gloria works for $8.44 an hour under a union contract that provides for daily overtime for all hours worked over eight hours. Overtime includes hours worked on Saturdays and is paid at time and one-half the regular rate of pay. Hours worked on Sundays or holidays are paid at double the regular rate of pay. Use both methods to determine Gloria's gross earnings for a week in which she worked the following hours:

Monday	9 hours	Tuesday	$10\frac{1}{2}$ hours
Wednesday	7 hours	Thursday	$9\frac{1}{2}$ hours
Friday	8 hours	Saturday	6 hours
Sunday	6 hours		

Day	Mo	Tu	We	Thu	Fr	Sat	Su	Total
Regular hours	8	8	7	8	8			39
Overtime at time and one-half	1	2.5		1.5		6		11
Overtime at double time							6	6
Total hours worked	9	10.5	7	9.5	8	6	6	56

Solution

Method A

Gross earnings for regular hours $= 39 \times 8.44$ $=$ $\$329.16$
Overtime pay
  at time and one-half $= 11 \times 8.44 \times 1.5 = \$139.26$
  at double time $= 6 \times 8.44 \times 2$ $= \underline{\hspace{0.3cm}101.28}$ $\underline{\hspace{0.3cm}240.54}$
Total gross pay $\underline{\underline{\$569.70}}$

Method B

Earnings at regular hourly rate	$= 56 \times 8.44$	$=$	$472.64
Overtime pay			
at time and one-half	$= 11\left(\frac{1}{2} \text{ of } \$8.44\right)$		
	$= 11 \times 4.22$	$= \$46.42$	
at double time	$= 6 \times 8.44$	$= \$50.64$	97.06
	Total gross pay		$569.70

Exercise 1.5

A. Answer each of the following questions.

1. R. Burton is employed at an annual salary of $22 932.00 paid semi-monthly. The regular workweek is 36 hours.

   (a) What is the regular salary per pay period?
   (b) What is the hourly rate of pay?
   (c) What is the gross pay for a pay period in which the employee worked 11 hours overtime at time and one-half regular pay?

2. C. Hall receives a yearly salary of $23 868.00. She is paid bi-weekly and her regular workweek is 37.5 hours.

   (a) What is the gross pay per pay period?
   (b) What is the hourly rate of pay?
   (c) What is the gross pay for a pay period in which she works $8\frac{1}{2}$ hours overtime at time and one-half regular pay?

3. Carole is paid a monthly salary of $1101.10. Her regular workweek is 35 hours.

   (a) What is Carole's hourly rate of pay?
   (b) What is Carole's gross pay for May if she worked $7\frac{3}{4}$ hours overtime during the month at time and one-half regular pay?

4. Herb receives a semi-monthly salary of $863.20 and works a regular workweek of 40 hours.

   (a) What is Herb's hourly rate of pay?
   (b) If Herb's gross earnings in one pay period were $990.19, for how many hours of overtime was he paid at time and one-half regular pay?

5. An employee of a Board of Education is paid an annual salary in twenty-two bi-weekly payments of $1123.00 each. If the employee is under contract for 200 workdays of $7\frac{1}{2}$ hours each,

   (a) what is the hourly rate of pay?
   (b) what is the gross pay for a pay period in which the employee was away for two days at no pay?

6. Geraldine Moog is paid a commission of 9¾% on her net sales and is authorized to draw up to $800.00 a month. What is the amount due to Geraldine at the end of a month in which she drew $720.00, had sales of $12 660.00, and sales returns of $131.20?

7. What is a salesperson's commission on net sales of $16 244.00 if the commission is paid on a sliding scale of 8¼% on the first $6000.00, 9¾% on the next $6000.00, and 11.5% on any additional sales?

8. A sales representative selling auto parts receives a commission of 4.5% on net sales up to $10 000.00, 6% on the next $5000.00, and 8% on any further sales. If his sales for a month were $24 250.00 and sales returns were $855.00, what was his commission for the month?

9. A salesclerk at a local boutique receives a weekly base salary of $225.00 on a quota of $4500.00 per week plus a commission of 6½% on sales exceeding the quota.

   (a) What are the gross earnings for a week if sales are $4125.00?
   (b) What are the gross earnings for a week if sales amount to $6150.00?

10. A clothing store salesperson is paid a weekly salary of $250.00 or a commission of 12.5% of his sales, whichever is the greater. What is his salary for a week in which his sales were

   (a) $1780.00?
   (b) $2780.00?

11. For October, Monique Lemay earned a commission of $1884.04 on gross sales of $21 440.00. If returns and allowances were 5% of gross sales, what is her rate of commission based on net sales?

12. Jim Scott had gross earnings of $354.30 for last week. Jim earns a base salary of $270.00 on a weekly quota of $4000.00. If his sales for the week were $5124.00, what is his commission rate?

13. Doug Wilson earned a commission of $2036.88 for March. If his rate of commission is 11.25% of net sales, and returns and allowances were 8% of gross sales, what were Doug's gross sales for the month?

14. Corrie Daley had gross earnings of $337.50 for the week. If she receives a base salary of $264.00 on a quota of $4800.00 and a commission of 8.75% on sales exceeding the quota, what were Corrie's sales for the week?

15. Carlos Shastri is employed at an hourly rate of $8.42. The regular workweek is 40 hours and overtime is paid at time and one-half regular pay. Using the two methods illustrated earlier, compute Carlos's gross earnings for a week in which he worked 47 hours.

16. Kim Ferrill earns $10.60 per hour. Overtime from Monday to Friday is paid at time and one-half regular pay for any hours over 7½ per day. Overtime on weekends is paid at double the regular rate of pay. Last week Kim worked regular hours on Monday, Wednesday, and Friday, 9 hours on Tuesday, 10½ hours on Thursday, and 6 hours on Saturday. Determine Kim's gross wages by each of the two methods.

17. An employee of a repair shop receives a gross pay of $319.44 for a regular workweek of 44 hours. What is the hourly rate of pay?

18. A wage statement shows gross earnings of $361.00 for 45 hours of work. What is the hourly rate of pay if the regular workweek is 40 hours and overtime is paid at time and one-half the regular rate of pay?

1.6   APPLICATIONS – TAXES

A **tax** is defined as a "contribution levied on persons, properties, or businesses, to pay for services provided by the government." The taxes we encounter most are the **Provincial Sales Tax (PST)** and the **Goods and Services Tax (GST)**. We also pay *property taxes*, directly (the homeowner pays the municipality) or indirectly (the landlord pays the municipality). PST and GST are expressed as a percent of the value of the items or services purchased, i.e., Tax payable = Tax percent (as a decimal) × Value of purchase. Property tax rates are expressed in *mills* (to be explained below).

A. Goods and services tax (GST)

The **Goods and Services Tax (GST)** is a federal tax charged on the cost of almost all goods and services. The GST replaced the Federal Manufacturers Sales Tax on January 1, 1991. Businesses and organizations carrying out commercial activities in Canada must register with Revenue Canada for the purpose of collecting the GST if their annual revenue from GST taxable goods and services exceeds $30 000. Below that level of revenue, registration is optional.

Currently GST taxable goods and services are taxed at 7%. Registered businesses and organizations will charge the 7% GST on taxable sales and services to their customers, and they pay the 7% GST on their business purchases. Depending on the volume of taxable sales, and GST return must be submitted by each registrant to Revenue Canada at selected intervals (monthly, quarterly, annually), showing the amount of tax collected and the amount of tax paid. If the amount of GST collected is more than the amount of GST paid, the difference must be remitted to Revenue Canada. If the amount of GST collected is less than the amount of GST paid, a refund can be claimed. (While most consumers do not have this option, the government has provided GST rebate cheques to Canadians with earnings below a particular annual income level.)

EXAMPLE 1.6A   Suppose you had your car repaired at your local Canadian Tire repair shop. Parts amounted to $165.00 and labour to $246.00. Since both parts and labour are GST taxable, what is the amount of GST that Canadian Tire must collect from you?

Solution   The GST taxable amount = 165.00 + 246.00 = $411.00

GST = 7% of $411.00 = 0.07(411.00) = $28.77

Canadian Tire must collect GST of $28.77.

EXAMPLE 1.6B

Canadian Colour Company (CCC) purchased GST-taxable supplies from Kodak Canada worth $35 000 during 1997. CCC used these supplies to provide prints for its customers. CCC's total GST taxable sales for the year were $50 000. How much tax must CCC remit to Revenue Canada?

Solution

GST collected = 0.07($50 000) = $3500

GST paid = 0.07($35 000) = $2450

GST payable = 3500 − 2450 = $1050

B. Provincial sales tax (PST)

The **Provincial Sales Tax (PST)** is a provincial tax imposed by all provinces, except Alberta, on the price of most goods. In Ontario, Manitoba, Saskatchewan, British Columbia, and Prince Edward Island the PST is applied the same way as the GST, that is, as a percent of the retail price. In Quebec, the sales tax is applied after adding the GST to the retail price. Newfoundland, Nova Scotia, and New Brunswick reached an agreement with the federal government to merge their PST with the GST on April 1, 1997. For these three provinces, the blended sales tax is now 15%. All other provinces have so far rejected federal proposals to merge the two taxes.

British Columbia	7%	
Saskatchewan	7%	
Manitoba	7%	
Ontario	8%	
Quebec	8%	
Prince Edward Island	10%	
New Brunswick	15%	(blended with GST)
Nova Scotia	15%	(blended with GST)
Newfoundland	15%	(blended with GST)

EXAMPLE 1.6C

Determine the amount of provincial sales tax on an invoice of taxable items totalling $740.00 before taxes

(a) in Saskatchewan.
(b) in Quebec.

Solution

(a) In Saskatchewan, the PST = 7% of $740.00 = 0.07(740.00) = $51.80
(b) In Quebec, the PST = 8% of $740.00 + 8% of the GST on $740.00
   Since the GST = 7% of $740.00 = 0.07(740.00) = $51.80,
   the PST = 0.08(740.00) + 0.08(51.80) = 59.20 + 4.14 = $63.34

EXAMPLE 1.6D

In Ontario, restaurant meals are subject to the 7% GST as well as 8% PST on food items and 10% on alcoholic beverages. You take your friend out for dinner and spend $45.00 on food items and $27.00 on a bottle of wine. You also tip the waiter 15% of the combined cost of food items and wine. How much do you spend?

Solution

Cost of food items	$45.00
Cost of wine	27.00
Total cost of meal	$72.00

GST = 7% of $72.00   = 0.07(72.00)   = $5.04

PST = 8% of $45.00   = 0.08(45.00)   = $3.60
       = 10% of $27.00   = 0.10(27.00)   = $2.70

Total cost including taxes = $72.00 + $5.04 + $3.60 + $2.70 = $83.34
Tip = 15% of $72.00   = 0.15(72.00)   =   10.80
Total amount spent   = $83.34 + $10.80   = $94.14

C. Property tax

Municipalities raise money by a **property tax** which is a municipal tax charged on the **assessed value** of real estate, both commercial and residential. Some education taxes are also raised through this method. Property taxes are stated as a *mill rate*, as opposed to as a percent (like the PST and GST). A **mill rate** is the amount of tax per $1000 of assessed value of property. Therefore, a mill rate is equivalent to 0.1% of the assessed value of property. The assessed value of a property may be close to its market value, but does not have to be.

$$\text{Property tax} = \text{Mill rate} \times 0.001 \times \text{Assessed value of property}$$

EXAMPLE 1.6E

The municipality of Yellik lists the following mill rates for various local services:

Tax levy	Mill rate
General city	3.20
Garbage collection	0.99
Schools	10.51
Capital development	1.20

If a homeowner's property has been assessed at $120 000, find the property taxes payable.

Solution

Total mill rate = 3.20 + 0.99 + 10.51 + 1.20 = 15.9

Tax payable = total mill rate × 0.001 × assessed value

Tax payable = (15.9)(0.001)(120 000) = $1908.00

EXAMPLE 1.6F

The municipality of Verner requires a budget of $450 million to operate next year. Provincial and federal grants, fees and commercial taxes will cover $250 million, leaving $200 million to be raised by a tax on residential assessments

(i) Calculate the mill rate required to raise the $200 million if the total assessed residential value for taxation purposes is $5 billion.
(ii) Find the taxes on a building lot in Verner if it is assessed at $52 800.

Solution

(i) Rate $= \dfrac{\text{Tax Revenue Required from Residential Assessments}}{\text{Current Assessed Value}}$

$= \dfrac{\$200\ 000\ 000}{\$5\ 000\ 000\ 000} = 0.04$

For each dollar of assessed value on a residential property, each owner must pay 4 cents. Therefore, for each $1000 of assessed value, the mill rate is $0.04 \times 1000 = 40$.

(ii) Property taxes on the building lot $= 40(0.001)(52\ 800) = \$2112.00$

Exercise 1.6

A. Answer each of the following questions.

1. Cook's Department Store files GST returns monthly. If the following figures represent the store's GST taxable sales and GST it paid on its purchases for the last five months, calculate Cook's monthly GST bills. Determine if Cook's owes the government money or is entitled to a refund.

Month	Purchases	Sales
January	$147 832	$546 900
February	69 500	244 000
March	866 000	588 000
April	450 000	650 300
May	98 098	156 800

2. May's Home Income Tax business operates only during tax season. Last season May grossed $28 890 including GST. During that season she spent $8000 before GST on her paper and supply purchases. How much does May owe Revenue Canada for GST?

3. "Save the GST" is a popular advertising gimmick. How much would you save on the purchase of a T-shirt with a list price of $15.00 in an Ontario store during a "Save the GST" promotion?

4. How much would a consumer pay for the T-shirt in question 3 if the store was located in Regina, Saskatchewan?

5. During an early season promotion, a weekend ski pass was priced at $84.00 plus GST and PST at both Blackcomb Mountain, B.C., and Mont Tremblant, Quebec. What is the difference in the total price paid by skiers at the two ski resorts?

6. A retail chain sells snowboards for $625.00 plus GST and PST. What is the price difference for consumers in Toronto, Ontario, and Calgary, Alberta?

7. Calculate the property taxes on a property assessed at $125 000 if the mill rate is 22.751.

8. The town of Eudora assesses property at market value. How much will the owner of a house valued at $225 000 owe in taxes if this year's mill rate has been set at 19.368?

9. If the mill rate increases by 0.25 mill, by how much will the taxes on a property assessed at $155 500 increase?

10. A town has an assessed residential property value of $250 000 000. The town council must meet the following expenditures:

Education:	$10 050 000
General purposes:	$2 000 000
Recreation:	$250 000
Public works:	$700 000
Police and fire protection:	$850 000

(a) Suppose 80% of the expenditures are charged against residential real estate. Calculate the total property taxes that must be raised.

(b) What is the mill rate?

(c) What is the property tax on a property assessed at $175 000?

BUSINESS MATH NEWS BOX

URBAN ROULETTE

Most people know that Vancouver and Toronto are Canada's most costly cities, but by how much? Runzheimer Canada, a Toronto-based management consulting firm, recently calculated the annual cost of living in nine major cities for a middle-class family of four, living in a 1600-square-foot suburban home and owning two cars. The totals include goods and services typical for the family's size and location, as well as federal and provincial taxes.

Vancouver	$61 588
Toronto	$61 560
Ottawa	$54 506
Montreal	$54 456
Calgary	$52 183
Regina	$52 139
Winnipeg	$51 253
Saskatoon	$51 249
Edmonton	$50 720

QUESTIONS

1. Suppose you moved from Winnipeg to Vancouver. By what amount will your cost of living change?

2. Calculate the average annual cost of living in the nine cities listed.

3. By what percentage is living in Toronto more expensive than living in Saskatoon?

SOURCE: Adapted from *Maclean's Magazine*, May 6, 1996, p. 41.

REVIEW EXERCISE

1. Simplify each of the following.

   (a) $32 - 24 \div 8$

   (b) $(48 - 18) \div 15 - 10$

   (c) $(8 \times 6 - 4) \div (16 - 4 \times 3)$

   (d) $9(6 - 2) - 4(3 + 4)$

   (e) $\dfrac{108}{0.18 \times \frac{216}{360}}$

   (f) $\dfrac{288}{2400 \times \frac{292}{365}}$

   (g) $320\left(1 + 0.10 \times \frac{225}{360}\right)$

   (h) $1000\left(1 - 0.12 \times \frac{150}{360}\right)$

   (i) $\dfrac{660}{1 + 0.14 \times \frac{144}{360}}$

   (j) $\dfrac{1120.00}{1 - 0.13 \times \frac{292}{365}}$

2. Change each of the following percents into a decimal.

   (a) 185%

   (b) 7.5%

   (c) 0.4%

   (d) 0.025%

   (e) $1\frac{1}{4}\%$

   (f) $\frac{3}{4}\%$

   (g) $162\frac{1}{2}\%$

   (h) $11\frac{3}{4}\%$

   (i) $8\frac{1}{3}\%$

   (j) $83\frac{1}{3}\%$

   (k) $266\frac{2}{3}\%$

   (l) $10\frac{3}{8}\%$

3. Change each of the following percents into a common fraction in lowest terms.

   (a) 50%

   (b) $37\frac{1}{2}\%$

   (c) $16\frac{2}{3}\%$

   (d) $166\frac{2}{3}\%$

   (e) $\frac{1}{2}\%$

   (f) 7.5%

   (g) 0.75%

   (h) $\frac{5}{8}\%$

4. Express each of the following as a percent.

   (a) 2.25

   (b) 0.02

   (c) 0.009

   (d) 0.1275

   (e) $\frac{5}{4}$

   (f) $\frac{11}{8}$

   (g) $\frac{5}{200}$

   (h) $\frac{7}{25}$

5. Sales of a particular make and size of nails during a day were $4\frac{1}{3}$ kg, $3\frac{3}{4}$ kg, $5\frac{1}{2}$ kg, and $6\frac{5}{8}$ kg.

   (a) How many kilograms of nails were sold?

   (b) What is the total sales value at $1.20 per kilogram?

   (c) What was the average weight per sale?

   (d) What was the average sales value per sale?

6. Extend and total the following invoice.

Quantity	Description	Unit Price	Amount
56	Item A	$0.625	_____
180	Item B	$83\frac{1}{3}$¢	_____
126	Item C	$1.16	_____
144	Item D	$1.75	_____
		Total	_____

7. The basic pay categories, hourly rates of pay, and the number of employees in each category for the machining department of a company are shown below.

Category	Hourly Pay	Number of Employees
Supervisors	$15.45	2
Machinists	12.20	6
Assistants	9.60	9
Helpers	7.50	13

(a) What is the average rate of pay per category?
(b) What is the average rate of pay per employee?

8. Hélène Gauthier invested $15 000 on January 1 in a partnership. She withdrew $2000 on June 1, withdrew a further $1500 on August 1, and reinvested $4000 on November 1. What was her average monthly investment balance for the year?

9. Brent DeCosta invested $12 000 in a business on January 1 and an additional $2400 on April 1. He withdrew $1440 on June 1 and invested $2880 on October 1. What was Brent's average monthly investment balance for the year?

10. Maria is paid a semi-monthly salary of $800.80. Her regular workweek is 40 hours. Overtime is paid at time and one-half regular pay.

(a) What is Maria's hourly rate of pay?
(b) What is Maria's gross pay if she worked 8 ½ hours overtime in one pay period?

11. Casey receives an annual salary of $17 472.00, is paid monthly, and works 35 regular hours per week.

(a) What is Casey's gross remuneration per pay period?
(b) What is his hourly rate of pay?
(c) How many hours overtime did Casey work during a month for which his gross pay was $1693.60?

12. Tim is employed at an annual salary of $20 292.48. His regular workweek is 36 hours and he is paid semi-monthly.

(a) What is Tim's gross pay per period?
(b) What is his hourly rate of pay?
(c) What is his gross pay for a period in which he worked 12 ½ hours overtime at time and one-half regular pay?

13. Artemis is paid a weekly commission of 4% on net sales of $3000.00, 8% on the next $1500.00, and 12.5% on all further sales. Her sales for a week were $5580.00 and sales returns and allowances were $60.00.

(a) What were her gross earnings for the week?
(b) What was her average hourly rate of pay for the week if she worked 43 hours?

14. Last week June worked 44 hours. She is paid $8.20 per hour for a regular work-week of 37.5 hours and overtime at time and one-half regular pay.

    (a) What were June's gross wages for last week?
    (b) What is the amount of the overtime premium?

15. Vacek is paid a monthly commission on a graduated basis of $7\frac{1}{2}\%$ on net sales of $7000.00, 9% on the next $8000.00, and 11% on any additional sales. If sales for April were $21 500.00 and sales returns were $325.00, what were his gross earnings for the month?

16. Margit is paid on a weekly commission basis. She is paid a base salary of $240.00 on a weekly quota of $8000.00 and a commission of 4.75% on any sales in excess of the quota.

    (a) If Margit's sales for last week were $11 340.00, what were her gross earnings?
    (b) What are Margit's average hourly earnings if she worked 35 hours?

17. Last week Lisa had gross earnings of $321.30. Lisa receives a base salary of $255.00 and a commission on sales exceeding her quota of $5000.00. What is her rate of commission if her sales were $6560.00?

18. John earned a gross commission of $2101.05 during July. What were his sales if his rate of commission is 10.5% of net sales and sales returns and allowances for the month were 8% of his sales?

19. Edith worked 47 hours during a week for which her gross remuneration was $426.22. Based on a regular workweek of 40 hours and overtime payment at time and one-half regular pay, what is Edith's hourly rate of pay?

20. Norm is paid a semi-monthly salary of $682.50. Regular hours are $37\frac{1}{2}$ per week and overtime is paid at time and one-half regular pay.

    (a) What is Norm's hourly rate of pay?
    (b) How many hours overtime did Norm work in a pay period for which his gross pay was $846.30?

21. Silvio's gross earnings for last week were $328.54. His remuneration consists of a base salary of $280.00 plus a commission of 6% on net sales exceeding his weekly quota of $5000.00. What were Silvio's sales for the week if sales returns and allowances were $136.00?

22. Sean's gross wages for a week were $541.20. His regular workweek is 40 hours and overtime is paid at time and one-half regular pay. What is Sean's regular hourly wage if he worked $47\frac{1}{2}$ hours?

23. Aviva's pay stub shows gross earnings of $349.05 for a week. Her regular rate of pay is $7.80 per hour for a 35-hour week and overtime is paid at time and one-half regular pay. How many hours did she work?

24. Ramona's Dry Cleaning shows sales revenue of $76 000 for the year. Ramona's GST taxable expenses were $14 960. How much should she remit to the government at the end of the year?

25. When Fred of Fred's Auto Repair tallied up his accounts at the end of the year, he found he had paid GST on: parking fees of $4000, supplies of $55 000, utilities of $2000, and miscellaneous eligible costs of $3300. During this same time, he found he had charged his customers GST on billings that totaled $75 000 for parts and $65 650 for labour. How much GST must Fred send to the government?

26. A store located in Kelowna, B.C., sells a computer for $2625.00 plus GST and PST. If the same model is sold at the same price in a store in Kenora, Ontario, what is the difference in the prices paid by consumers in the two stores?

27. Some stores in Ontario advertise that the GST is included in the ticket price. If you pay PST on this ticket price, you are paying tax on the tax. Calculate the total tax rate if you purchase a $100 item under these conditions.

28. Two people living in different communities build houses of the same design on lots of equal size. If the person in Ripley has his house and lot assessed at $150 000 with a mill rate of 20.051 mills, will his taxes be more or less than the person in Amberly with an assessment of $135 000 and a mill rate of 22.124 mills?

29. A town has a total residential property assessment of $975 500 000. It is originally estimated that $45 567 000 must be raised through residential taxation to meet expenditures.

   (a) What mill rate must be set to raise $45 567 000 in property taxes?
   (b) What is the property tax on a property assessed at $35 000?
   (c) The town later finds that it underestimated building costs. An additional $2 000 000 must be raised. Find the increase in the mill rate required to meet these additional costs.
   (d) How much more will the property taxes be on the property assessed at $35 000?

SELF-TEST

1. Evaluate each of the following.

   (a) $4320\left(1 + 0.18 \times \dfrac{45}{360}\right)$

   (b) $2160\left(0.15 \times \dfrac{105}{360}\right)$

   (c) $2880\left(1 - 0.12 \times \dfrac{285}{360}\right)$

   (d) $\dfrac{410.40}{0.24 \times \dfrac{135}{360}}$

   (e) $\dfrac{5124}{1 + 0.09 \times \dfrac{270}{360}}$

2. Change each of the following percents into a decimal.

   (a) 175% (b) $\frac{3}{8}\%$

3. Change each of the following percents into a common fraction in lowest terms.

   (a) $2\frac{1}{2}\%$ (b) $116\frac{2}{3}\%$

4. Express each of the following as a percent.

   (a) 1.125 (b) $\frac{9}{400}$

5. The following information is shown in your investment account for last year: balance on January 1 was $7200; a withdrawal of $480 on March 1; deposits of $600 on August 1 and $120 on October 1. What was the account's average monthly balance for the year?

6. Extend each of the following and determine the total.

Quantity	Unit Price
72	$1.25
84	$16\frac{2}{3}$¢
40	$0.875
48	$1.3\dot{3}

7. Purchases of an inventory item during the last accounting period were as follows:

No. of Items	Unit Price
5	9
6	7
3	8
6	6

   What was the average price per item?

8. Ace Realty sold lots for $15 120 per hectare. What is the total sales value if the lot sizes, in hectares, were $5\frac{1}{4}$, $6\frac{1}{3}$, $4\frac{3}{8}$, and $3\frac{5}{6}$?

9. Property valued at $130 000 is assessed at $\frac{2}{13}$ of its value. What is the amount of tax due for this year if the tax rate is $3.25 per $100 of assessed value?

10. A salesperson earned a commission of $806.59 for last week on gross sales of $5880. If returns and allowances were 11.5% of gross sales, what is his rate of commission based on net sales?

11. A.Y. receives an annual salary of $26 478.40. She is paid monthly on a 38-hour workweek. What is the gross pay for a pay period in which she works 8.75 hours overtime at time and one-half regular pay?

12. J.B. earns $16.60 an hour with time and one-half for hours worked over 8 a day. His hours for a week are 8.25, 8.25, 9.5, 11.5, and 7.25. Determine his gross earnings for a week.

13. A wage earner receives a gross pay of $513.98 for 52.5 hours of work. What is his hourly rate of pay if a regular workweek is 42 hours and overtime is paid at time and one-half the regular rate of pay?

14. A salesperson receives a weekly base salary of $200.00 on a quota of $2500. On the next $2000, she receives a commission of 11%. On any additional sales, the commission rate is 15%. Find her gross earnings for a week in which her sales total $6280.

15. C.D. is paid a semi-monthly salary of $780.00. If her regular workweek is 40 hours, what is her hourly rate of pay?

16. Fred Helm of Winnipeg, Manitoba, bought a ring for $6400. Since the jeweller is shipping the ring, Fred must pay a shipping charge of $20.00. He must also pay PST and GST on the ring. Find the total purchase price of Fred's ring.

17. Bill Blake pays a property tax of $2502.50. In his community the tax rate is 55 mills. What is the assessed value of Bill's property, to the nearest dollar?

18. Suppose you went shopping and bought bulk laundry detergent worth $17.95. You then received a $2.50 trade discount, and had to pay a $1.45 shipping charge. Find the final purchase price of the detergent in your province.

CHALLENGE PROBLEMS

1. A customer in a sporting goods shop gives you a $50 bill for goods totalling $37.00. He asks that the change he receives include no coins worth $1.00 or less. Can you give this customer the correct change while meeting his request?

2. Suppose you own a small business with 4 employees, namely Roberto, Sandra, Petra, and Lee. At the end of the year you have set aside $1800 to divide among them as a bonus. You have 2 categories in place for your bonus system. An exceptional employee receives one amount and an average employee receives half that amount. You have rated Roberto and Sanda exceptional, and Petra and Lee average employees. How much bonus should each employee receive?

3. Suppose your math grade is based on the results of two tests and one final exam. Each test is worth 30% of your grade and the final exam is worth 40%. If you scored 60% and 50% on your two tests, what mark must you score on the final exam to achieve a grade of 70%?

CASE STUDY 1.1   BUSINESS AND THE GST

When the federal government introduced the Goods and Services Tax (GST), it created several accounting problems for businesses. In order to make it simpler for small businesses with annual revenues of under $30 000, the government gave these businesses the option of registering to collect and remit. If businesses choose not to register, then they do not have to charge GST on their services. The disadvantage is that they are then not eligible for a credit for the GST that they pay on their supplies. A self-employed person who does income tax or bookkeeping at home would likely be in the position of one of these businesses.

All other businesses must register. Depending on the size of the enterprise and the amount of GST collected per annum, a company will remit its GST collections on a regular basis. This could be monthly, quarterly, or annually depending on receipts. At the end of each fiscal year, each registrant must file a return summarizing the collection of GST, input tax credits (GST paid by the registrant) and periodic payments made to Revenue Canada. (Revenue Canada uses this information to calculate a business's maximum periodic installment payment for the next year.)

Medium-sized businesses are eligible for a potentially money-making option in the form of the Quick Method of Accounting. Intended to simplify GST record keeping for certain types of small businesses, the Quick Method can be used to calculate a company's GST remittance if its annual taxable revenue, including GST, is $200 000 or less. When using the Quick Method, the registrant charges customers 7% GST on sales of goods and services, but does not claim input tax credits on operating expenses and inventory purchases. The GST remittance due is calculated as a percent of the business's combined taxable revenue plus GST collected. Since the percent used in the Quick Method calculation is less than the regular 7%, the business can remit less GST even though the base is larger. Depending on the type of business, the registrant uses either a Quick Method remittance rate of 2.5% or 5%.

The 2.5% rate is for qualifying retailers and wholesalers, including grocery and convenience stores. To qualify, purchases of GST taxable goods for resale must be at least 40% of the registrant's total annual taxable sales. In addition, the remittance rate for the first $30 000 of taxable revenue in a fiscal year is reduced by 1%. This means that the registrant remits 1.5% on the first $30 000 of taxable revenue and 2.5% on the remainder.

The 5% rate is the general rate for service businesses, such as dry cleaners, repair shops, as well as retailers and wholesalers who do not qualify for the 2.5% remittance rate. The first $30 000 is charged at a rate of 4% and the remainder at 5%.

QUESTIONS

1. Bill Ford operates a GST-registered hydraulic lift repair service. His service revenue for the year is $26 000. His GST-taxable purchases amounted to $2400. Bill does not use the Quick Method of Accounting for the GST. By calculating the GST he collected and the GST he paid, determine Bill's GST remittance to Revenue Canada.

2. Bill's sister Ashley operates a fashion boutique. Her business is registered for the Quick Method of Accounting for the GST. Her GST-taxable sales were $160 000 for the year. GST-taxable purchases of goods for resale were 44% of sales. In addition, Ashley paid $485 GST on taxable services. Ashley told Bill that she is eligible for the 2.5% method and that he should register for the 5% method.

   (a) Calculate how much less GST Ashley remitted to Revenue Canada because she used the Quick Method.
   (b) Determine if Bill should take his sister's advice.

3. Steve Ford, Bill and Ashley's cousin, has been running Polar Bay Wines for the last couple of years. Based on the information that Steve's accountant filed with Revenue Canada during the prior year, Polar Wines must make monthly GST payments of $950 this year. Steve received a copy of the Goods and Services Tax Return for Registrants. He has asked his cousins for an interpretation, and they gave him the following explanation:

   Line 101   reports amount of GST-taxable revenues
   Line 103   reports amount of GST collected
   Line 106   reports amount of GST paid
   Line 109   reports amount of GST payable to Revenue Canada
   Line 110   reports amount of GST payments already made to Revenue Canada
                   this year
   Line 113   reports amount of balance to be paid or to be received

   When Steve checked his accounting records, he found the following information for the current fiscal year: GST-taxable revenue of $286 420, and purchases of $127 860. Referring to Exhibits, help Steve determine the balance of GST to be paid or to be received by calculating each line of the Goods and Services Tax Return.

REPORTING PERIOD SUMMARY

Sales & Other Revenue	101		**00**

TAX CALCULATIONS

GST Collected and GST Collectible	103		
Adjustments	104		
Total GST and Adjustments for Period (Add Lines 103 and 104)		→	105

Input Tax Credits **(ITCs)**	106		
Adjustments	107		
Total ITCs and Adjustments (Add Lines 106 and 107)		→	108

NET TAX (Subtract Line 108 from Line 105)		109

OTHER CREDITS IF APPLICABLE

Paid by Instalments	110		
Rebates	111		
Total Other Credits (Add Lines 110 and 111)		→	112

BALANCE (Subtract Line 112 from Line 109)		113

REFUND CLAIMED	114	
PAYMENT ENCLOSED	115	

CASE STUDY 1.2   # HOW MUCH ARE YOU WORTH?

Eventually, all of us look forward to buying a home or making some other large purchase, such as a boat, car, or cottage. This usually brings us to a bank manager's office and face to face with the question of whether or not we can afford our dream purchase. The bank manager will ask several questions to get a picture of your net worth. **Net worth** is calculated as the difference between a person's assets and liabilities. In layman's terms, this is the difference between what you own and what you owe. Also measured into net worth is a consideration of your potential earnings.

Suppose you have decided to purchase a home, be it a house or condo, and you must borrow some money for the purchase. The next step is to determine whether you have the financial ability to carry the costs of a mortgage and of running the home. The two most widely accepted guidelines used to estimate how much of a home buyer's income can be allocated to housing costs are the *Gross Debt Service Ratio* and the *Total Debt Service Ratio*.

The formula for calculating the Gross Debt Service (GDS) Ratio is:

$$\left(\frac{\text{monthly mortgage payment} + \text{monthly property taxes} + \text{monthly heating}}{\text{gross monthly income}}\right) \times 100\%$$

The GDS ratio should not exceed 32%.

The formula for calculating the Total Debt Service (TDS) Ratio is:

$$\left(\frac{\text{monthly mortgage payment} + \text{monthly property taxes} + \text{all other monthly debts}}{\text{gross monthly income}}\right) \times 100\%$$

The TDS ratio should not exceed 40%.

The Irwins are considering the purchase of a condo. Mrs. Irwin is a teacher with a salary of $40 000 per year. Mr. Irwin is a nurse earning $35 000. They have tallied up the potential costs of the condo and find that the mortgage will be $1100 per month, property taxes will be $1950 per year, and heating will be about $150 per month on equal billing. The Irwins also have a car loan of $275 per month, which has two more years to run. They find that they pay an average of $2400 per year on their credit cards.

QUESTIONS

1. Calculate the GDS and the TDS for the Irwins. If you were a bank manager, would you recommend the loan for their condo purchase?

2. Calculate your net worth. Calculate the GDS and TDS for you or your family.

GLOSSARY

Assessed value   a dollar figure applied to real estate by municipalities to be used in property tax calculations (can be a market value or a value relative to other properties in the same municipality)

Complex fractions   mathematical expressions containing one or more fractions in the numerator or the denominator or both

Commission   the term applied to remuneration of sales personnel based on their sales performance

Common fractions   the division of one whole number by another whole number, expressed by means of a fraction line

Denominator   the divisor of a fraction (i.e., the number written below the fraction line)

Equivalent fractions   fractions that have the same value although they consist of different terms

Fractions in lowest terms   a fraction whose terms cannot be reduced any further (i.e., whose numerator and denominator cannot be evenly divided by the same number except 1)

Goods and Service Tax (GST)   a federal tax charged on the price of almost all goods and services

Graduated commission   remuneration paid as an increasing percent for increasing sales levels for a fixed period of time

Gross earnings   the amount of an employee's remuneration before deductions

Improper fraction   a fraction whose numerator is greater than its denominator

Mill rate   the factor used with the assessed value of real estate to raise property tax revenue, expressed as the amount of tax per $1000 of assessed property value

Mixed numbers   numbers consisting of a whole number and a fraction, such as $5\frac{1}{2}$

Net worth   the difference between a person's assets and liabilities

Numerator   the dividend of a fraction (i.e., the number written above the fraction line)

Order of operations   the order in which arithmetic calculations are performed

Overtime premium   extra labour cost due to overtime

Percent (%)   a fraction with a denominator of 100

Proper fraction   a fraction whose numerator is less than its denominator

Property tax   a municipal tax charged on the assessed value of real estate, both commercial and residential

Provincial Sales Tax (PST)   a provincial tax charged on the price of most goods (usually a fixed percent of the cost of a good)

Quota   a sales level required before the commission percent is paid; usually associated with remuneration by base salary and commission

Salary   the term usually applied to monthly or annual remuneration of personnel

Salary plus commission   a method of remunerating sale personnel that guarantees a minimum income per pay period.

Straight commission   remuneration paid as a percent of net sales for a given period

Tax   a contribution levied on persons, properties, or businesses to pay for services provided by the government

Terms of a fraction   the numerator and the denominator of a fraction

Wages   the term usually applied to the remuneration of hourly rated employees

2 Review of Basic Algebra

Suppose, on the last day before the deadline, you invested this year's entire RRSP contribution in mutual funds. After the deadline, you heard that you might have been able to buy more units of the mutual fund if you had used dollar cost averaging. Now you are curious. Could you really have gotten more for your RRSP dollar by using dollar cost averaging? The skills in this chapter should help you to answer this question.

Introduction

Shifting from retirement planning to estate planning, an eccentric businessman wants to divide his n gold bars among his four children, so that the first child gets one-half of the bars, the second child gets one-fourth, the third child gets one-fifth, and the fourth child gets 7 gold bars. How many gold bars does the eccentric businessman have?

This type of "brain teaser" is an example of the use of basic algebra. We can find the answer by letting the unknown value be represented by a letter (a variable) and applying the laws of algebraic formula manipulation. Many problems in business and finance can be solved by using predetermined formulae. When these formulae are used, we need the skills of algebraic substitution and simplification to solve them.

Many problems do not fit a predetermined formula. We must then use the basics of algebra to create our own equation, and solve it to answer the problem. An equation is a statement of equality between two algebraic expressions. Any equation that has only variables (letter symbols) to the first power is called a linear equation. Linear equations can often be created to represent business problems. When you solve the equation you solve the business problem. When you finish this chapter you should feel comfortable solving linear equations. (And if you have not already solved the brain teaser above, you should be able to figure out that the eccentric businessman has 140 gold bars.)

OBJECTIVES

Upon completing this chapter, you will be able to do the following:

1. **Simplify algebraic expressions using the fundamental operations and evaluate algebraic expressions by substitution.**
2. **Simplify and evaluate powers with positive exponents, negative exponents, and exponent zero.**

3. Use an electronic calculator equipped with a power function to compute the numerical value of arithmetic expressions involving fractional exponents.
4. Write exponential equations in logarithmic form and use an electronic calculator equipped with a natural logarithm function to determine the value of natural logarithms.
5. Solve basic equations using addition, subtraction, multiplication, and division.
6. Solve equations involving formula rearrangement and algebraic simplification.
7. Solve word problems by creating equations.

2.1 SIMPLIFICATION OF ALGEBRAIC EXPRESSIONS

A. Addition and subtraction

1. Simplification Involving Addition and Subtraction

In algebra, only **like terms** may be added or subtracted. This is done by *adding* or *subtracting* the **numerical coefficients** of the like terms according to the rules used for adding and subtracting signed numbers, and *retaining* the common **literal coefficient**. The process of adding and subtracting like terms is called **combining like terms** or **collecting like terms**.

EXAMPLE 2.1A

(i) $6x + 3x + 7x$ ————————— all three terms are like terms
$= (6 + 3 + 7)x$ ————————— add the numerical coefficients
$= 16x$ ————————————— retain the common literal coefficient

(ii) $9a - 5a - 7a + 4a$
$= (9 - 5 - 7 + 4)a$
$= a$

(iii) $-5m - (-3m) - (+6m)$
$= -5m + (+3m) + (-6m)$ ——————— change the subtraction to addition
$= -5m + 3m - 6m$
$= (-5 + 3 - 6)m$
$= -8m$

(iv) $7x - 4y - 3x - 6y$ ————————— the two sets of like terms are $7x$,
$= (7 - 3)x + (-4 - 6)y$ $-3x$, and $-4y$, $-6y$, and are collected
$= 4x - 10y$ separately

(v) $5x^2 - 3x - 4 + 2x - 5 + x^2$
$= (5 + 1)x^2 + (-3 + 2)x + (-4 - 5)$
$= 6x^2 - x - 9$

2. Simplification Involving Brackets

When simplifying **algebraic expressions** involving brackets, remove the brackets according to the following rules and collect like terms.

(a) If the brackets are preceded by a $(+)$ sign or no sign, drop the brackets and retain the terms inside the brackets with their signs unchanged:
$(-7a + 5b - c)$ becomes $-7a + 5b - c$.

(b) If the brackets are preceded by a $(-)$ sign, drop the brackets and change the sign of every term inside the brackets:
$-(-7a + 5b - c)$ becomes $7a - 5b + c$.

EXAMPLE 2.1B

(i) $(7a - 3b) - (4a + 3b)$
   $= 7a - 3b - 4a - 3b$ ——————— $(7a - 3b)$ becomes $7a - 3b$
   $= 3a - 6b$ $\qquad\qquad\qquad\qquad\quad -(4a + 3b)$ becomes $-4a - 3b$

(ii) $-(3x^2 - 8x - 5) + (2x^2 - 5x + 4)$
   $= -3x^2 + 8x + 5 + 2x^2 - 5x + 4$
   $= -x^2 + 3x + 9$

(iii) $4b - (3a - 4b - c) - (5c + 2b)$
   $= 4b - 3a + 4b + c - 5c - 2b$
   $= -3a + 6b - 4c$

B. Multiplication

1. Multiplication of Monomials

The product of two or more **monomials** is the product of their numerical coefficients multiplied by the product of their literal coefficients.

EXAMPLE 2.1C

(i) $5(3a)$
   $= (5 \times 3)a$ ——————— obtain the product of the numerical
   $= 15a$ $\qquad\qquad\qquad\qquad$ coefficients

(ii) $(-7a)(4b)$
   $= (-7 \times 4)(a \times b)$ ——————— obtain the product of the numerical
   $= -28ab$ $\qquad\qquad\qquad\qquad\quad$ coefficients, -7 and 4, and the
   $\qquad\qquad\qquad\qquad\qquad\qquad\qquad$ product of the literal coefficients,

(iii) $(-3)(4x)(-5x)$ $\qquad\qquad\qquad\qquad\quad a$ and b
   $= [(-3)(4)(-5)][(x)(x)]$
   $= 60x^2$

2. Multiplication of Monomials with Polynomials

The product of a **polynomial** and a monomial is obtained by multiplying each term of the polynomial by the monomial.

EXAMPLE 2.1D

(i) $\quad 5(a - 3)$
$= 5(a) + 5(-3)$ ———————————— multiply 5 by a and 5 by (-3)
$= 5a - 15$

(ii) $\quad -4(3x^2 - 2x - 1)$
$= -4(3x^2) + (-4)(-2x) + (-4)(-1)$ — multiply each term of the trinomial
$= (-12x^2) + (+8x) + (+4)$ $\qquad$ by (-4)
$= -12x^2 + 8x + 4$

(iii) $\quad 3a(4a - 5b - 2c)$
$= (3a)(4a) + (3a)(-5b) + (3a)(-2c)$
$= (12a^2) + (-15ab) + (-6ac)$
$= 12a^2 - 15ab - 6ac$

3. Simplification Involving Brackets and Multiplication

EXAMPLE 2.1E

(i) $\quad 3(x - 5) - 2(x - 7)$
$= 3x - 15 - 2x + 14$ ——————— carry out the multiplication
$= x - 1$ ————————————— collect like terms

(ii) $\quad a(3a - 1) - 4(2a + 3)$
$= 3a^2 - a - 8a - 12$
$= 3a^2 - 9a - 12$

(iii) $\quad 5(m - 7) - 8(3m - 2) - 3(7 - 3m)$
$= 5m - 35 - 24m + 16 - 21 + 9m$
$= -10m - 40$

(iv) $\quad -4(5a - 3b - 2c) + 5(-2a - 4b + c)$
$= -20a + 12b + 8c - 10a - 20b + 5c$
$= -30a - 8b + 13c$

4. Multiplication of a Polynomial by a Polynomial

The product of two polynomials is obtained by multiplying each term of one polynomial by each term of the other polynomial and collecting like terms.

EXAMPLE 2.1F

(i) $\quad (3a + 2b)(4c - 3d)$ $\qquad$ each term of the first polynomial
$= 3a(4c - 3d) + 2b(4c - 3d)$ ——— is multiplied by the second
$\qquad$ polynomial
$= 12ac - 9ad + 8bc - 6bd$ ——— carry out the multiplication

(ii) $\quad (5x - 2)(3x + 4)$
$= 5x(3x + 4) - 2(3x + 4)$
$= 15x^2 + 20x - 6x - 8$
$= 15x^2 + 14x - 8$

C. Division

1. Division of Monomials

The quotient of two monomials is the quotient of their numerical coefficients multiplied by the quotient of their literal coefficients.

EXAMPLE 2.1G

(i) $32ab \div 8b = \dfrac{32ab}{8b} = \left(\dfrac{32}{8}\right)\left(\dfrac{ab}{b}\right) = 4a$

(ii) $24x^2 \div (-6x) = \left(\dfrac{24}{-6}\right)\left(\dfrac{x^2}{x}\right) = -4x$

2. Division of a Polynomial by a Monomial

To determine the quotient of a polynomial divided by a monomial, divide each term of the polynomial by the monomial.

EXAMPLE 2.1H

(i) $(12a + 8) \div 4 = \dfrac{12a + 8}{4} = \dfrac{12a}{4} + \dfrac{8}{4} = 3a + 2$

(ii) $(18x - 12) \div 6 = \dfrac{18x - 12}{6} = \dfrac{18x}{6} - \dfrac{12}{6} = 3x - 2$

(iii) $(12a^3 - 15a^2 - 9a) \div (-3a)$

$= \dfrac{12a^3 - 15a^2 - 9a}{-3a}$

$= \dfrac{12a^3}{-3a} + \dfrac{-15a^2}{-3a} + \dfrac{-9a}{-3a}$

$= -4a^2 + 5a + 3$

D. Substitution

Evaluating algebraic expressions for given values of the variables requires replacing the variables with the given values. The replacement or substitution of the variables by the given values takes place each time the variables appear in the expression.

EXAMPLE 2.1I

(i) Evaluate $7x - 3y - 5$ for $x = -2, y = 3$

Solution

$7x - 3y - 5$

$= 7(-2) - 3(3) - 5$ ——————— replace x by (-2) and y by 3

$= -14 - 9 - 5$

$= -28$

(ii) Evaluate $\dfrac{2NC}{P(n+1)}$ for N = 12, C = 220, P = 1500, n = 15

Solution

$$\frac{2NC}{P(n+1)} = \frac{2(12)(220)}{1500(15+1)} = 0.22$$

(iii) Evaluate $\dfrac{I}{RT}$ for I = 126, R = 0.125, T = $\dfrac{324}{360}$

Solution

$$\frac{I}{RT} = \frac{126}{0.125 \times \frac{324}{360}} = 1120$$

(iv) Evaluate P(1 + RT)   for P = 900, R = 0.15, T = $\dfrac{240}{360}$

Solution

$$\begin{aligned} P(1+RT) &= 900\left(1 + 0.15 \times \frac{240}{360}\right) \\ &= 900(1 + 0.10) \\ &= 900(1.10) \\ &= 990 \end{aligned}$$

(v) Evaluate A(1 − dt)   for A = 800, d = 0.135, t = $\dfrac{288}{360}$

Solution

$$\begin{aligned} A(1-dt) &= 800\left(1 - 0.135 \times \frac{288}{360}\right) \\ &= 800(1 - 0.108) \\ &= 800(0.892) \\ &= 713.60 \end{aligned}$$

(vi) Evaluate $\dfrac{A}{1+RT}$ for A = 1644, R = 0.16, T = $\dfrac{219}{365}$

Solution

$$\frac{A}{1+RT} = \frac{1644}{1 + 0.16 \times \frac{219}{365}} = \frac{1644}{1 + 0.096} = \frac{1644}{1.096} = 1500$$

(vii) Evaluate $\dfrac{P}{1-dt}$ for P = 1002, d = 0.18, t = $\dfrac{330}{360}$

Solution

$$\frac{P}{1-dt} = \frac{1002}{1 - 0.18 \times \frac{330}{360}} = \frac{1002}{1 - 0.165} = \frac{1002}{0.835} = 1200$$

Exercise 2.1

A. Simplify.

   1. $9a + 3a + 7a$ **2.** $6m - 2m - m$

   3. $-4a - 8 + 3a - 2$ **4.** $2x - 3y - 4x - y$

   5. $x - 0.2x$ **6.** $x + 0.06x$

   7. $x + 0.4x$ **8.** $x - 0.02x$

   9. $x^2 - 2x - 5 + x - 3 - 2x^2$ **10.** $3ax - 2x + 1 - 3 + 3x - 4ax$

   11. $(2x - 3y) - (x + 4y)$ **12.** $-(4 - 5a) - (-2 + 3a)$

   13. $(a^2 - ab + b^2) - (3a^2 + 5ab - 4b^2)$

   14. $-(3m^2 - 4m - 5) - (4 - 2m - 2m^2)$

   15. $6 - (4x - 3y + 1) - (5x + 2y - 9)$

   16. $(7a - 5b) - (-3a + 4b) - 5b$

B. Simplify.

   1. $3(-4x)$ **2.** $-7(8a)$

   3. $-5x(2a)$ **4.** $-9a(-3b)$

   5. $-x(2x)$ **6.** $-6m(-4m)$

   7. $-4(5x)(-3y)$ **8.** $2a(-3b)(-4c)(-1)$

   9. $-2(x - 2y)$ **10.** $5(2x - 4)$

   11. $a(2x^2 - 3x - 1)$ **12.** $-6x(4 - 2b - b^2)$

   13. $4(5x - 6) - 3(2 - 5x)$ **14.** $-3(8a - b) - 2(-7a + 9b)$

   15. $-3a(5x - 1) + a(5 - 2x) - 3a(x + 1)$

   16. $8(3y - 4) - 2(2y - 1) - (1 - y)$

   17. $(3x - 1)(x + 2)$

   18. $(5m - 2n)(m - 3n)$

   19. $(x + y)(x^2 - xy + y^2)$

   20. $(a - 1)(a^2 - 2a + 1)$

   21. $(5x - 4)(2x - 1) - (x - 7)(3x + 5)$

   22. $2(a - 1)(2a - 3) - 3(3a - 2)(a + 1)$

C. Simplify.

1. $20ab \div 5$

2. $30xy \div (-6x)$

3. $(-12x^2) \div (-3x)$

4. $(-42ab) \div (7ab)$

5. $(20m - 8) \div 2$

6. $(14x - 21) \div (-7)$

7. $(10x^2 - 15x - 30) \div (-5)$

8. $(-a^3 - 4a^2 - 3a) \div (-a)$

D. Evaluate each of the following for the values given.

1. $3x - 2y - 3$ for $x = -4, y = -5$

2. $\dfrac{1}{2}(3x^2 - x - 1) - \dfrac{1}{4}(5 - 2x - x^2)$ for $x = -3$

3. $\dfrac{RP(n + 1)}{2N}$ for $R = 0.21, P = 1200, n = 77, N = 26$

4. $\dfrac{I}{PT}$ for $I = 63, P = 840, T = \dfrac{216}{360}$

5. $\dfrac{I}{RT}$ for $I = 198, R = 0.165, T = \dfrac{146}{365}$

6. $\dfrac{2NC}{P(n + 1)}$ for $N = 52, C = 60, P = 1800, n = 25$

7. $P(1 + RT)$ for $P = 880, R = 0.12, T = \dfrac{75}{360}$

8. $A(1 - RT)$ for $A = 1200, R = 0.175, T = \dfrac{252}{360}$

9. $\dfrac{P}{1 - dt}$ for $P = 1253, d = 0.135, t = \dfrac{280}{360}$

10. $\dfrac{A}{1 + RT}$ for $A = 1752, R = 0.152, T = \dfrac{225}{360}$

2.2 INTEGRAL EXPONENTS

A. Basic concept and definition

If a number is to be used as a **factor** several times, the mathematical expression can be written more efficiently by using exponents:

$$5 \times 5 \times 5 \times 5 \text{ may be written as } 5^4.$$

Note: In the expression 5^4 ⟶ 5 is called the **base**

⟶ 4 is called the **exponent**

⟶ 5^4 is called the **power**

EXAMPLE 2.2A

(i) $7 \times 7 \times 7 \times 7 \times 7 = 7^5$

(ii) $(-4)(-4)(-4) = (-4)^3$

(iii) $(1.01)(1.01)(1.01)(1.01) = (1.01)^4$

(iv) $(a)(a)(a)(a)(a)(a)(a) = a^7$

(v) $(1 + i)(1 + i)(1 + i)(1 + i)(1 + i)(1 + i) = (1 + i)^6$

Definition: When 'n' is a positive integer, 'a^n' represents the product of 'n' equal factors whose value is 'a'.

$$\boxed{a^n = (a)(a)(a)(a) \ldots (a) \text{ to } n \text{ factors}}$$

a is called the **base**
n is called the **exponent**
a^n is called the **power**

$$\boxed{\text{POWER} = \text{BASE}^{\text{to the EXPONENT}}}$$

Note: If a number is raised to the exponent '1', the power equals the base.

$$5^1 = 5 \text{ and } a^1 = a;$$
$$\text{conversely, } 6 = 6^1 \text{ and } x = x^1.$$

B. Numerical evaluation of powers with positive integral exponents

1. Evaluation When the Base Is a Positive Integer

To evaluate a power, we may rewrite the power in factored form and obtain the product by multiplication.

EXAMPLE 2.2B

(i) 2^5 ———————————————————— means that 2 is a factor 5 times
$= (2)(2)(2)(2)(2)$ ———————————— power rewritten in factored form
$= 32$ ——————————————————— product

(ii) $(5)^3$ ———————————————————— 5 is a factor 3 times
$= (5)(5)(5)$
$= 125$

(iii) 1^7 ———————————————————— 1 is a factor 7 times
$= (1)(1)(1)(1)(1)(1)(1)$
$= 1$

(iv) a^n if $a = 4, n = 6$
$a^n = 4^6$
$ = (4)(4)(4)(4)(4)(4)$
$ = 4096$

2. **Evaluation When the Base Is a Negative Integer**

If a power has a negative base, the number of equal factors shown by the exponent determines the sign of the product.

(a) If the exponent is an even positive integer, the product is positive.
(b) If the exponent is an odd positive integer, the product is negative.

EXAMPLE 2.2C

(i) $(-4)^3$ ——————————————— (-4) is a factor 3 times
$= (-4)(-4)(-4)$
$= -64$ ——————————————— the answer is negative (n is odd)

(ii) $(-2)^8$ ——————————————— (-2) is a factor 8 times
$= (-2)(-2)(-2)(-2)(-2)(-2)(-2)(-2)$
$= 256$ ——————————————— the answer is positive (n is even)

   Note: -2^8 means $-(2)^8 = -(2)(2)(2)(2)(2)(2)(2)(2) = -256$

(iii) $(-1)^{55}$
$= (-1)(-1)(-1)(-1) \ldots$ to 55 factors
$= -1$

(iv) $3a^n$ for $a = -5, n = 4$
$3a^n = 3(-5)^4$
$= 3(-5)(-5)(-5)(-5)$
$= 3(625)$
$= 1875$

3. **Evaluation When the Base Is a Common Fraction or Decimal**

EXAMPLE 2.2D

(i) $\left(\dfrac{3}{2}\right)^5$ ——————————————— $\dfrac{3}{2}$ is a factor 5 times

$= \left(\dfrac{3}{2}\right)\left(\dfrac{3}{2}\right)\left(\dfrac{3}{2}\right)\left(\dfrac{3}{2}\right)\left(\dfrac{3}{2}\right)$

$= \dfrac{(3)(3)(3)(3)(3)}{(2)(2)(2)(2)(2)}$

$= \dfrac{243}{32}$

(ii) $(0.1)^4$ ——————————————— 0.1 is a factor 4 times
$= (0.1)(0.1)(0.1)(0.1)$
$= 0.0001$

(iii) $\left(-\dfrac{1}{3}\right)^3$ ——————————————— $\left(-\dfrac{1}{3}\right)$ is a factor 3 times

$= \left(-\dfrac{1}{3}\right)\left(-\dfrac{1}{3}\right)\left(-\dfrac{1}{3}\right)$

$$= \frac{(-1)(-1)(-1)}{(3)(3)(3)}$$

$$= \frac{-1}{27}$$

(iv) $(1.02)^2$

$= (1.02)(1.02)$

$= 1.0404$

(v) $(1 + i)^n$ for $i = 0.03$, $n = 4$

$(1 + i)^n = (1 + 0.03)^4$

$\qquad = (1.03)(1.03)(1.03)(1.03)$

$\qquad = 1.12550881$

C. Operations with powers

1. Multiplication of Powers

To multiply powers that have the same base, retain the common base and add the exponents.

$$\boxed{a^m \times a^n = a^{m+n}} \quad\text{———————— Formula 2.1A}$$

$$\boxed{a^m \times a^n \times a^p = a^{m+n+p}} \quad\text{———— Formula 2.1B}$$

Notice that Formula 2.1B is an extension of Formula 2.1A.

EXAMPLE 2.2E

(i) $3^5 \times 3^2$

$= 3^{5+2}$ ——————————— retain the common base 3

$= 3^7$ and add the exponents 5 and 2

(ii) $(-4)^3(-4)^7(-4)^5$

$= (-4)^{3+7+5}$ ———————— retain the common base (-4) and

$= (-4)^{15}$ add the exponents $3, 7$, and 5

(iii) $\left(\frac{1}{8}\right)^5\left(\frac{1}{8}\right) = \left(\frac{1}{8}\right)^{5+1} = \left(\frac{1}{8}\right)^6$

(iv) $(x^3)(x^5)(x) = x^{3+5+1} = x^9$

(v) $(1.06)^{16}(1.06)^{14} = (1.06)^{16+14} = 1.06^{30}$

(vi) $(1 + i)(1 + i)^5(1 + i)^{20} = (1 + i)^{1+5+20} = (1 + i)^{26}$

2. Division of Powers

To divide powers that have the same base, retain the common base and subtract the exponent of the divisor from the exponent of the dividend.

$$\boxed{a^m \div a^n = a^{m-n}} \quad\text{———————— Formula 2.2}$$

EXAMPLE 2.2F

(i) $2^8 \div 2^5$
$= 2^{8-5}$ ———————————————— retain the common base 2 and
$= 2^3$ subtract the exponent of the
                                           divisor, 5, from the exponent of
                                           the dividend, 8

(ii) $(-10)^8 \div (-10)^7$
$= (-10)^{8-7}$ ———————————————— retain the common base (-10) and
$= (-10)^1$ or -10 subtract the exponents

(iii) $\left(-\dfrac{2}{5}\right)^6 \div \left(-\dfrac{2}{5}\right)^2 = \left(-\dfrac{2}{5}\right)^{6-2} = \left(-\dfrac{2}{5}\right)^4$

(iv) $a^{15} \div a^{10} = a^{15-10} = a^5$

(v) $(1.10)^{24} \div 1.10 = (1.10)^{24-1} = 1.10^{23}$

(vi) $(1+i)^{80} \div (1+i)^{60} = (1+i)^{80-60} = (1+i)^{20}$

3. Raising a Power to a Power

To raise a power to a power, retain the base and multiply the exponents.

$$(a^m)^n = a^{mn}$$ ——————————————— **Formula 2.3**

EXAMPLE 2.2G

(i) $(3^2)^5$
$= 3^{2 \times 5}$ ———————————————— retain the base 3 and multiply the
$= 3^{10}$ exponents 2 and 5

(ii) $[(-4)^5]^3$
$= (-4)^{5 \times 3}$ ———————————————— retain the base and multiply the
$= (-4)^{15}$ exponents

(iii) $= \left[\left(\dfrac{4}{3}\right)^6\right]^{10} = \left(\dfrac{4}{3}\right)^{6 \times 10} = \left(\dfrac{4}{3}\right)^{60}$

(iv) $(a^7)^3 = a^{7 \times 3} = a^{21}$

(v) $[(1.005)^{50}]^4 = (1.005)^{50 \times 4} = 1.005^{200}$

(vi) $[(1+i)^{75}]^2 = (1+i)^{75 \times 2} = (1+i)^{150}$

4. Power of a Product and Power of a Quotient

The power of a product, written in factored form, is the product of the individual factors raised to the exponent.

$$(ab)^m = a^m b^m$$ ——————————————— **Formula 2.4**

Note: ab^2 is not the same as $(ab)^2$ since ab^2 means $(a)(b)(b)$ while
$(ab)^2 = (ab)(ab) = (a)(a)(b)(b) = a^2 b^2$.

The power of a quotient is the quotient of the dividend and the divisor raised to the exponent.

$$\left(\frac{a}{b}\right)^m = \frac{a^m}{b^m}$$ ———————————————— **Formula 2.5**

EXAMPLE 2.2H

(i) $(2 \times 3)^5 = 2^5 \times 3^5$

(ii) $(6 \times 2^7)^4 = 6^4 \times (2^7)^4 = 6^4 \times 2^{28}$

(iii) $\left(-\dfrac{5}{7}\right)^3 = \dfrac{(-5)^3}{7^3}$

(iv) $(a^3b)^4 = (a^3)^4 \times b^4 = a^{12}b^4$

(v) $\left[\dfrac{(1+i)}{i}\right]^3 = \dfrac{(1+i)^3}{i^3}$

D. Zero exponent

A zero exponent results when using the law of division of powers on powers with equal exponents.

$$3^5 \div 3^5$$
$$= 3^{5-5}$$
$$= 3^0$$

The result may be interpreted as follows.

$$3^5 \div 3^5 = \frac{3^5}{3^5} = \frac{3 \times 3 \times 3 \times 3 \times 3}{3 \times 3 \times 3 \times 3 \times 3} = 1$$

$$\boxed{3^0 = 1}$$

Similarly, $a^6 \div a^6 = a^{6-6} = a^0$

and since $a^6 \div a^6 = \dfrac{a^6}{a^6} = \dfrac{(a)(a)(a)(a)(a)(a)}{(a)(a)(a)(a)(a)(a)} = 1,$

$$\boxed{a^0 = 1}$$

In general, *any number raised to the exponent zero is 1*, except zero itself. The expression 0^0 has no meaning and is said to be *undefined*.

E. Negative exponents

A negative exponent results when the exponent of the divisor is greater than the exponent of the dividend.

$$4^3 \div 4^5$$
$$= 4^{3-5}$$
$$= 4^{-2}$$

The result may be interpreted as follows.

$$4^3 \div 4^5 = \frac{4^3}{4^5} = \frac{4 \times 4 \times 4}{4 \times 4 \times 4 \times 4 \times 4} = \frac{1}{4 \times 4} = \frac{1}{4^2}$$

$$4^{-2} = \frac{1}{4^2}$$

Similarly, $\qquad a^5 \div a^8 = a^{5-8} = a^{-3}$

and since $\qquad a^5 \div a^8 = \dfrac{a^5}{a^8} = \dfrac{(a)(a)(a)(a)(a)}{(a)(a)(a)(a)(a)(a)(a)(a)}$

$$= \frac{1}{(a)(a)(a)} = \frac{1}{a^3}$$

$$a^{-3} = \frac{1}{a^3}$$

$$a^{-m} = \frac{1}{a^m}$$ ———————————————— **Formula 2.6**

In general, a base raised to a negative exponent is equivalent to '1' divided by the same base raised to the corresponding positive exponent.

EXAMPLE 2.2I

(i) $\quad 2^{-3} = \dfrac{1}{2^3} = \dfrac{1}{8}$

(ii) $\quad (-3)^{-2} = \dfrac{1}{(-3)^2} = \dfrac{1}{9}$

(iii) $\quad \left(\dfrac{1}{4}\right)^{-4} = \dfrac{1}{\left(\dfrac{1}{4}\right)^4} = \dfrac{1}{\dfrac{1}{256}} = \dfrac{1}{1} \times \dfrac{256}{1} = 256$

(iv) $\quad \left(-\dfrac{3}{5}\right)^{-3} = \dfrac{1}{\left(-\dfrac{3}{5}\right)^3} = \dfrac{1}{\dfrac{-27}{125}} = \dfrac{-125}{27}$

Note: Since $\dfrac{-125}{27} = \dfrac{(-5)^3}{3^3} = \left(-\dfrac{5}{3}\right)^3 = \left(-\dfrac{3}{5}\right)^{-3} = \left(-\dfrac{5}{3}\right)^3$

$$\left(\frac{y}{x}\right)^{-m} = \left(\frac{x}{y}\right)^m$$ ———————————————— **Formula 2.7**

(v) $\quad (-4)^0 = 1$

(vi) $\quad (1.05)^{-2} = \dfrac{1}{1.05^2} = \dfrac{1}{1.1025} = 0.9070295$

(vii) $\quad (1 + i)^{-10} = \dfrac{1}{(1 + i)^{10}}$

(viii) $\quad (1 + i)^{-1} = \dfrac{1}{1 + i}$

(ix) $\quad (1 + i)^0 = 1$

Exercise 2.2

A. Evaluate each of the following.

1. 3^4
2. 1^5
3. $(-2)^4$
4. $(-1)^{12}$

5. $\left(\dfrac{2}{3}\right)^4$
6. $\left(-\dfrac{1}{4}\right)^3$
7. $(0.5)^2$
8. $(-0.1)^3$

9. $(-4)^0$
10. m^0
11. 3^{-2}
12. $(-5)^{-3}$

13. $\left(\dfrac{1}{5}\right)^{-3}$
14. $\left(\dfrac{2}{3}\right)^{-4}$
15. 1.01^{-1}
16. $(1.05)^0$

B. Simplify.

1. $2^5 \times 2^3$
2. $(-4)^3 \times (-4)$

3. $4^7 \div 4^4$
4. $(-3)^9 \div (-3)^7$

5. $(2^3)^5$
6. $[(-4)^3]^6$

7. $a^4 \times a^{10}$
8. $m^{12} \div m^7$

9. $3^4 \times 3^6 \times 3$
10. $(-1)^3(-1)^7(-1)^5$

11. $\dfrac{6^7 \times 6^3}{6^9}$
12. $\dfrac{(x^4)(x^5)}{x^7}$

13. $\left(\dfrac{3}{5}\right)^4\left(\dfrac{3}{5}\right)^7$
14. $\left(\dfrac{1}{6}\right)^5 \div \left(\dfrac{1}{6}\right)^3$

15. $\left(-\dfrac{3}{2}\right)\left(-\dfrac{3}{2}\right)^6\left(-\dfrac{3}{2}\right)^4$
16. $\left(-\dfrac{3}{4}\right)^8 \div \left(-\dfrac{3}{4}\right)^7$

17. $(1.025^{80})(1.025^{70})$
18. $1.005^{240} \div 1.005^{150}$

19. $[1.04^{20}]^4$
20. $\left[\left(-\dfrac{3}{7}\right)^5\right]^3$

21. $(1 + i)^{100}(1 + i)^{100}$
22. $(1 - r)^2(1 - r)^2(1 - r)^2$

23. $[(1 + i)^{80}]^2$
24. $[(1 - r)^{40}]^3$

25. $(ab)^5$
26. $(2xy)^4$

27. $(m^3n)^8$
28. $\left(\dfrac{a^3b^2}{x}\right)^4$

29. $2^3 \times 2^5 \times 2^{-4}$
30. $5^2 \div 5^{-3}$

31. $\left(\dfrac{a}{b}\right)^{-8}$
32. $\left(\dfrac{1 + i}{i}\right)^{-n}$

2.3 FRACTIONAL EXPONENTS

A. Radicals

When the product of two or more equal factors is expressed in exponential form, one of the equal factors is called the **root of the product**. The exponent indicates the number of equal factors, that is, the **power of the root**.

For example,

$25 = 5^2$ ⟶ 5 is the second power root (square root) of 25
$8 = 2^3$ ⟶ 2 is the third power root (cube root) of 8
$81 = 3^4$ ⟶ 3 is the fourth (power) root of 81
a^5 ⟶ a is the fifth root of a^5
7^n ⟶ 7 is the nth root of 7^n
x^n ⟶ x is the nth root of x^n

The operational symbol for finding the root of an expression is $\sqrt{}$. This symbol represents the *positive* root only. If the negative root is desired, a minus sign is placed in front of the symbol; that is, the negative root is represented by $-\sqrt{}$.

The power of a root is written at the upper left of the symbol as in $\sqrt[3]{}$ or $\sqrt[n]{}$.

The indicated root is called a **radical**, the power indicated is called the **index**, and the number under the symbol is called the **radicand**.

In $\sqrt[5]{32}$, the index is 5,
the radicand is 32, and
the radical is $\sqrt[5]{32}$.

When the square root is to be found, it is customary to omit the index 2. The symbol $\sqrt{}$ is understood to mean the positive square root of the radicand.

$\sqrt{49}$ means $\sqrt[2]{49}$ or 7.

In special cases, the radicand is an integral power of the root. The root can readily be found by expressing the radicand in exponential form; the index of the root and the exponent are the same.

EXAMPLE 2.3A

(i) $\sqrt{64} = \sqrt{8^2}$ ——————— the radicand 64 is expressed in exponential form as a square

$= 8$ ——————— one of the two equal factors 8 is the root

(ii) $\sqrt[5]{32} = \sqrt[5]{2^5}$ ————————— express the radicand 32 as the
fifth power of 2

   $= 2$ ————————————— one of the five equal factors 2
is the root

(iii) $\sqrt[3]{0.125} = \sqrt[3]{0.5^3} = 0.5$

In most cases, however, the radicand cannot be easily rewritten in exponential form. The arithmetic determination of the numerical value of these roots is a laborious process. But computing the root is easily accomplished using electronic calculators equipped with a power function. The problems in Example 2.3b are intended to ensure that students are able to use the power function. They should be done using an electronic calculator.

EXAMPLE 2.3B

(i) $\sqrt{1425} = 37.7492$ **Check** $37.7492^2 = 1425$

(ii) $\sqrt[5]{12\ 960} = 6.6454$ **Check** $6.6454^5 = 12\ 960$

(iii) $\sqrt[15]{40\ 000} = 2.0268$ **Check** $2.0268^{15} = 40\ 009$ (due to rounding)

(iv) $\sqrt[20]{1\ 048\ 576} = 2$ **Check** $2^{20} = 1\ 048\ 576$

(v) $\sqrt{0.005184} = 0.072$ **Check** $0.072^2 = 0.005184$

(vi) $\sqrt[7]{0.038468} = 0.6279$ **Check** $0.6279^7 = 0.03848$ (due to rounding)

(vii) $\sqrt[45]{1.954213} = 1.015$ **Check** $1.015^{45} = 1.954213$

(viii) $\sqrt[36]{0.0225284} = 0.9$ **Check** $0.9^{36} = 0.0225284$

(ix) $\sqrt{2^6} = \sqrt{64} = 8$

(x) $\sqrt[3]{5^6} = \sqrt[3]{15\ 625} = 25$

B. Fractional exponents

Radicals may be written in exponential form and fractional exponents may be represented in radical form according to the following definitions.

(a) The exponent is a positive fraction with numerator 1.

$$\boxed{a^{\frac{1}{n}} = \sqrt[n]{a}}$$ ————————— **Formula 2.8**

$$4^{\frac{1}{2}} = \sqrt{4} = 2$$
$$27^{\frac{1}{3}} = \sqrt[3]{27} = \sqrt[3]{3^3} = 3$$
$$625^{\frac{1}{4}} = \sqrt[4]{625} = \sqrt[4]{5^4} = 5$$

(b) The exponent is a negative fraction with numerator 1.

$$a^{-\frac{1}{n}} = \frac{1}{a^{\frac{1}{n}}} = \frac{1}{\sqrt[n]{a}}$$ ——————————— **Formula 2.9**

$$8^{-\frac{1}{3}} = \frac{1}{8^{\frac{1}{3}}} = \frac{1}{\sqrt[3]{8}} = \frac{1}{\sqrt[3]{2^3}} = \frac{1}{2}$$

$$243^{-\frac{1}{5}} = \frac{1}{243^{\frac{1}{5}}} = \frac{1}{\sqrt[5]{243}} = \frac{1}{\sqrt[5]{3^5}} = \frac{1}{3}$$

(c) The exponent is a positive or negative fraction with numerator other than 1.

$$a^{\frac{m}{n}} = \sqrt[n]{a^m} = \left(\sqrt[n]{a}\right)^m$$ ——————— **Formula 2.10**

$$a^{-\frac{m}{n}} = \frac{1}{a^{\frac{m}{n}}} = \frac{1}{\sqrt[n]{a^m}}$$ ——————— **Formula 2.11**

$$16^{\frac{3}{4}} = \sqrt[4]{16^3} = \left(\sqrt[4]{16}\right)^3 = \left(\sqrt[4]{2^4}\right)^3 = (2)^3 = 8$$

$$27^{\frac{4}{3}} = \sqrt[3]{27^4} = \left(\sqrt[3]{27}\right)^4 = \left(\sqrt[3]{3^3}\right)^4 = (3)^4 = 81$$

$$36^{-\frac{3}{2}} = \frac{1}{\left(\sqrt[2]{36}\right)^3} = \frac{1}{\left(\sqrt[2]{6^2}\right)^3} = \frac{1}{6^3} = \frac{1}{216}$$

For calculators, convert fractional exponents into decimals and compute the answer using the power function.

EXAMPLE 2.3C

(i) $36^{\frac{3}{2}} = 36^{1.5} = 216$

(ii) $3^{\frac{5}{4}} = 3^{1.25} = 3.948222$

(iii) $\sqrt[5]{12} = 12^{\frac{1}{5}} = 12^{0.2} = 1.6437518$

(iv) $\sqrt[8]{325^5} = 325^{\frac{5}{8}} = 325^{0.625} = 37.147287$

(v) $\sqrt[6]{1.075} = 1.075^{\frac{1}{6}} = 1.075^{0.1666667} = 1.0121264$

Exercise 2.3

A. Use an electronic calculator equipped with a power function to compute each of the following, correct to four decimals.

1. $\sqrt{5184}$

2. $\sqrt{205.9225}$

3. $\sqrt[7]{2187}$

4. $\sqrt[10]{1.1046221}$

5. $\sqrt[20]{4.3184}$

6. $\sqrt[16]{0.00001526}$

7. $\sqrt[6]{1.0825}$

8. $\sqrt[12]{1.15}$

B. Compute each of the following.

1. $3025^{\frac{1}{2}}$

2. $2401^{\frac{1}{4}}$

3. $525.21875^{\frac{2}{5}}$

4. $21.6^{\frac{4}{3}}$

5. $\sqrt[12]{1.125^7}$

6. $\sqrt[6]{1.095}$

7. $4^{-\frac{1}{3}}$

8. $1.06^{-\frac{1}{12}}$

9. $\dfrac{1.03^{60} - 1}{0.03}$

10. $\dfrac{1 - 1.05^{-36}}{0.05}$

2.4 LOGARITHMS – BASIC ASPECTS

A. The concept of logarithm

In Chapter 2, Section 2.2 and Section 2.3, the exponential form of writing numbers was discussed.

$64 = 2^6$ ⟶ the number 64 is represented as a power of 2

$243 = 3^5$ ⟶ the number 243 is represented as a power of 3

$10\,000 = 10^4$ ⟶ the number 10 000 is represented as a power of 10

$5 = 125^{\frac{1}{3}}$ ⟶ the number 5 is represented as a power of 125

$0.001 = 10^{-3}$ ⟶ the number 0.001 is represented as a power of 10

In general, when a number is represented as a base raised to an exponent, the exponent is called a logarithm. A **logarithm** is defined as the *exponent* to which a base must be raised to produce a given number.

Accordingly,

in $64 = 2^6$,   6 is the logarithm of 64 to the base 2, written $6 = \log_2 64$;

in $243 = 3^5$,   5 is the logarithm of 243 to the base 3, written $5 = \log_3 243$;

in $10\,000 = 10^4$,   4 is the logarithm of 10 000 to the base 10, written $4 = \log_{10} 10\,000$;

in $5 = 125^{\frac{1}{3}}$,   ⅓ is the logarithm of 5 to the base 125, written $\frac{1}{3} = \log_{125} 5$;

in $0.001 = 10^{-3}$, -3 is the logarithm of 0.001 to the base 10, written $-3 = \log_{10} 0.001$.

In general, if $N = b^y$ (*exponential* form)

then $y = \log_b N$ (*logarithmic* form).

EXAMPLE 2.4A

Write each of the following numbers in exponential form and in logarithmic form using the base indicated.

(i) 32 base 2

(ii) 81 base 3

(iii) 256 base 4

(iv) 100 000 base 10

(v) 6 base 36

(vi) 3 base 27

(vii) 0.0001 base 10

(viii) $\dfrac{1}{8}$ base 2

Solution	Exponential Form	Logarithmic Form

(i) Since $32 = 2 \times 2 \times 2 \times 2 \times 2$
$$32 = 2^5$$
$5 = \log_2 32$

(ii) Since $81 = 3 \times 3 \times 3 \times 3$
$$81 = 3^4$$
$4 = \log_3 81$

(iii) Since $256 = 4 \times 4 \times 4 \times 4$
$$256 = 4^4$$
$4 = \log_4 256$

(iv) Since $100\,000 = 10 \times 10 \times 10 \times 10 \times 10$
$$100\,000 = 10^5$$
$5 = \log_{10} 100\,000$

(v) Since $6 = \sqrt{36}$
$$6 = 36^{\frac{1}{2}}$$
$\frac{1}{2} = \log_{36} 6$

(vi) Since $3 = \sqrt[3]{27}$
$$3 = 27^{\frac{1}{3}}$$
$\frac{1}{3} = \log_{27} 3$

(vii) Since $0.0001 = \dfrac{1}{10\,000} = \dfrac{1}{10^4}$
$$0.0001 = 10^{-4}$$
$-4 = \log_{10} 0.0001$

(viii) Since $\dfrac{1}{8} = \dfrac{1}{2^3}$
$$\frac{1}{8} = 2^{-3}$$
$-3 = \log_2 \dfrac{1}{8}$

B. Common logarithms

While the base b may be any positive number other than 1, only the numbers 10 and e are used in practice.

Logarithms with base 10 are called **common logarithms**. Obtained from the exponential function $x = 10^y$, the notation used to represent common logarithms is $y = \log x$. (The base 10 is understood and so is not written.)

By definition then, the common logarithm of a number is the exponent to which the base 10 must be raised to give that number.

$\log 1000 = 3$ since $1000 = 10^3$
$\log 1\,000\,000 = 6$ since $1\,000\,000 = 10^6$
$\log 0.01 = -2$ since $0.01 = 10^{-2}$
$\log 0.0001 = -4$ since $0.0001 = 10^{-4}$
$\log 1 = 0$ since $1 = 10^0$

Historically, common logarithms were used for numerical calculations that were required in problems involving compound interest. However, with the availability of electronic calculators equipped with a power function, the need for common logarithms as a computational tool has disappeared. Accordingly, this text gives no further consideration to common logarithms.

C. Natural logarithms

The most common exponential function is $y = e^x$

$$\text{where } e = \lim_{n \to \infty} \left(1 + \frac{1}{n}\right)^n = 2.7182818285 \text{ approximately.}$$

The logarithmic form of this function is $x = \log_e y$ but is always written as $x = \ln y$ and called the **natural logarithm**.

Electronic calculators equipped with the universal power function are generally equipped as well with the e^x function and the $ln\ x$ function (natural logarithm function). This latter function eliminates any need for common logarithms and should be used to solve certain problems involving compound interest.

In some calculator models, the natural logarithm function ($\boxed{\ln x}$ key) is a primary function; in others, such as the Texas Instrument BA-35, the $\boxed{\ln x}$ key is a secondary function. In all cases, you must first input the number and then activate the $\boxed{\ln x}$ key by using the $\boxed{\text{CPT}}$ or $\boxed{\text{2nd}}$ key.

EXAMPLE 2.4B

Use an electronic calculator equipped with the natural logarithm key $\boxed{\ln x}$ o determine the value of each of the following.

(i) ln 2   (ii) ln 3000   (iii) ln 0.5

(iv) ln 1   (v) ln 0.0125   (vi) ln 2.71828182

Solution

(i) To evaluate ln 2,

1. Key in 2.
2. Press $\boxed{\text{CPT}}$ or $\boxed{\text{2nd}}$.
3. Press $\boxed{\ln x}$.
4. Read the answer in the display.

$$\ln 2 = 0.6931472$$

(ii) Key in 3000, press $\boxed{\text{CPT}}$ or $\boxed{\text{2nd}}$, press $\boxed{\ln x}$, read the answer in the display.

$$\ln 3000 = 8.0063676$$

(iii) ln 0.5 = -0.6931472

(iv) ln 1 = 0

(v) ln 0.0125 = -4.3820266

(vi) ln 2.718278182 = 1

REVIEW OF BASIC ALGEBRA   65

Note: 1. The natural logarithm of 1 is zero.
2. The natural logarithm of a number greater than 1 is positive, e.g. ln 2 = 0.6931472.
3. The natural logarithm of a number less than 1 is negative, e.g. ln 0.5 = −0.6931472.

D. Useful relationships

The following relationships are helpful when using natural logarithms:

1. The logarithm of a product of two or more positive numbers is the sum of the logarithms of the factors.

$$\ln (ab) = \ln a + \ln b \qquad \text{——— Formula 2.12A}$$

$$\ln (abc) = \ln a + \ln b + \ln c \qquad \text{——— Formula 2.12B}$$

Notice that Formula 2.12B is an extension of Formula 2.12A.

2. The logarithm of the quotient of two positive numbers is equal to the logarithm of the dividend (numerator) minus the logarithm of the divisor (denominator).

$$\ln \left(\frac{a}{b}\right) = \ln a - \ln b \qquad \text{——— Formula 2.13}$$

3. The logarithm of a power of a positive number is the exponent of the power multiplied by the logarithm of the number.

$$\ln (a^k) = k(\ln a) \qquad \text{——— Formula 2.14}$$

4. (i) $\ln e = 1$ since $e = e^1$
   (ii) $\ln 1 = 0$ since $1 = e^0$

EXAMPLE 2.4C

Use an electronic calculator equipped with the natural logarithm ($\ln x$) function to evaluate each of the following.

(i) $\ln[3(15)(36)]$

(ii) $\ln\left[\left(\frac{5000}{1.045}\right)\right]$

(iii) $\ln[1500(1.05^6)]$

(iv) $\ln[5000(1.045^{-1})]$

(v) $\ln\left[\left(\dfrac{4000}{1.07^{12}}\right)\right]$

(vi) $\ln[10\ 000(1.0125^{-17})]$

(vii) $\ln[1.00\ e^7]$

(viii) $\ln[2.00\ e^{-0.6}]$

(ix) $\ln\left[600\left(\dfrac{1.04^6 - 1}{0.04}\right)\right]$

(x) $\ln\left[\left(\dfrac{1 - 1.0625^{-12}}{0.0625}\right)\right]$

Solution

(i) $\ln[3(15)(36)] = \ln 3 + \ln 15 + \ln 36$
$= 1.0986123 + 2.7080502 + 3.5835189$
$= 7.3901814$

Note: You can verify the answer by first simplifying.
$\ln 3(15)(36) = \ln 1620 = 7.3901814$

(ii) $\ln\left[\left(\dfrac{5000}{1.045}\right)\right] = \ln 5000 - \ln 1.045$
$= 8.5171932 - 0.0440169$
$= 8.4731763$

(iii) $\ln[1500(1.05^6)] = \ln 1500 + \ln 1.05^6$
$= \ln 1500 + 6(\ln 1.05)$
$= 7.3132204 + 6(0.0487902)$
$= 7.3132204 + 0.2927412$
$= 7.6059616$

(iv) $\ln[5000(1.045^{-1})] = \ln 5000 + \ln 1.045^{-1}$
$= \ln 5000 - 1(\ln 1.045)$
$= 8.5171932 - 1(0.0440169)$
$= 8.4731763$

(v) $\ln\left[\left(\dfrac{4000}{1.07^{12}}\right)\right] = \ln 4000 - \ln 1.07^{12}$
$= 8.2940496 - 12(0.0676586)$
$= 8.2940496 - 0.8119032$
$= 7.4821464$

(vi) $\ln[10\ 000(1.0125^{-17})] = \ln 10\ 000 - 17(\ln 1.0125)$
$= 9.2103404 - 17(0.0124225)$
$= 9.2103404 - 0.2111825$
$= 8.9991579$

(vii) $\ln[1.00e^7] = \ln 1.00 + \ln e^7$
$= \ln 1.00 + 7(\ln e)$
$= 0 + 7(1)$
$= 7$

(viii) $\ln[2.00e^{-0.6}] = \ln 2.00 + \ln e^{-0.6}$
$$= \ln 2.00 - 0.6(\ln e)$$
$$= 0.6931472 - 0.6$$
$$= 0.0931472$$

(ix) $\ln\left[600\left(\dfrac{1.04^6 - 1}{0.04}\right)\right] = \ln 600 + \ln\left(\dfrac{1.04^6 - 1}{0.04}\right)$
$$= \ln 600 + \ln(1.04^6 - 1) - \ln 0.04$$
$$= \ln 600 + \ln (1.2653190 - 1) - \ln 0.04$$
$$= \ln 600 + \ln 0.2653190 - \ln 0.04$$
$$= 6.3969297 - 1.3268224 - (-3.2188758)$$
$$= 6.3969297 - 1.3268224 + 3.2188758$$
$$= 8.2889831$$

(x) $\ln\left[\left(\dfrac{1 - 1.0625^{-12}}{0.0625}\right)\right] = \ln (1 - 1.0625^{-12}) - \ln 0.0625$
$$= \ln (1 - 0.4831175) - \ln 0.0625$$
$$= \ln 0.5168825 - \ln 0.0625$$
$$= -0.6599397 - (-2.7725887)$$
$$= -0.6599397 + 2.7725887$$
$$= 2.1126491$$

Exercise 2.4

A. Express each of the following in logarithmic form.

   1. $2^9 = 512$ 2. $3^7 = 2187$

   3. $5^{-3} = \dfrac{1}{125}$ 4. $10^{-5} = 0.00001$

   5. $e^{2j} = 18$ 6. $e^{-3x} = 12$

B. Write each of the following in exponential form.

   1. $\log_2 32 = 5$ 2. $\log_3 \dfrac{1}{81} = -4$

   3. $\log_{10} 10 = 1$ 4. $\ln e^2 = 2$

C. Use an electronic calculator equipped with a natural logarithm function to evaluate each of the following.

   1. $\ln 2$ 2. $\ln 200$

   3. $\ln 0.105$ 4. $\ln[300(1.10^{15})]$

   5. $\ln\left(\dfrac{2000}{1.09^9}\right)$ 6. $\ln\left[850\left(\dfrac{1.01^{-120}}{0.01}\right)\right]$

THE HUNT FOR LONG-LOST FUNDS

A tip from a friend and 30 seconds on the Internet was all it took for John Alderson to track down $15 000 in a long-forgotten bank account.

If Alderson's story is unusual, it is only because of the size of his forgotten bank balance. Each year in Canada, thousands of inactive accounts are turned over to the Bank of Canada after going unclaimed for nine years. Once in federal hands, the money earns 1.5-percent interest annually for 10 years, and nothing thereafter. There are now 950 000 such dormant accounts, holding a total of $142 million. Eight accounts hold more than $100 000.

The Bank of Canada will do searches at no cost. Last year, the bank received more than 17 000 such inquiries and helped to reunite 3200 Canadians with a total of $4.4 million. "We get 200 inquiries a day," says Rachel Robinson, the bank's supervisor for unclaimed balances.

HIDDEN RICHES

Of the 950 000 dormant bank accounts that have been turned over to the federal government, most contain less than $100. A relative few, however, hold many times that figure.

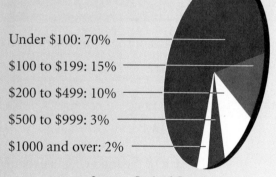

Under $100: 70%
$100 to $199: 15%
$200 to $499: 10%
$500 to $999: 3%
$1000 and over: 2%

SOURCE: Bank of Canada

QUESTIONS

1. What is the average balance in a dormant account now held by the Bank of Canada?

2. What was the average balance received by a dormant account holder last year as a result of a successful Bank of Canada search?

3. Calculate the number of dormant bank accounts in each category represented in the graph.

SOURCE: Adapted from Julie Cazzin, "The Hunt for Long-Lost Funds," *Maclean's Magazine*, September 9, 1996, p. 36.

2.5 SOLVING BASIC EQUATIONS

A. Basic terms and concepts

1. An **equation** is a statement of equality between two algebraic expressions.

$$7x = 35$$
$$3a - 4 = 11 - 2a$$
$$5(2k - 4) = -3(k + 2)$$

2. If an equation contains only one *variable* and the variable occurs with power 1 only, the equation is said to be a **linear** or **first-degree equation** in one unknown. The three equations listed above are linear equations in one unknown.

3. The two expressions that are equated are called the sides or **members of the equation**. Every equation has a left side (left member) and a right side (right member).

   In the equation $3a - 4 = 11 - 2a$,
   $3a - 4$ is the left side (left member) and
   $11 - 2a$ is the right side (right member).

4. The process of finding a replacement value (number) for the variable, which when substituted into the equation makes the two members of the equation equal, is called *solving the equation*. The replacement value that makes the two members equal is called a *solution* or root of the equation. A linear or first-degree equation has only one root and the root, when substituted into the equation, is said to *satisfy* the equation.
   The root (solution) of the equation

   $3a - 4 = 11 - 2a$ is 3 because when
   3 is substituted for a
   the left side $3a - 4 = 3(3) - 4 = 9 - 4 = 5$ and
   the right side $11 - 2a = 11 - 2(3) = 11 - 6 = 5$.

   Thus, for $a = 3$, Left Side = Right Side and 3 satisfies the equation.

5. Equations that have the same root are called **equivalent equations**.

   $$6x + 5 = 4x + 17$$
   $$6x = 4x + 12$$
   $$2x = 12$$
   $$x = 6$$

   are equivalent equations because the root of all four equations is 6; that is, when 6 is substituted for x, each of the equations is satisfied.
   Equivalent equations are useful in solving equations. They may be obtained

   (a) by multiplying or dividing both sides of the equation by a number other than zero; and
   (b) by adding or subtracting the same number on both sides of the equation.

6. When solving an equation, the basic aim in choosing the operations that will generate useful equivalent equations is to

(a) isolate the terms containing the variable on one side of the equation (this is achieved by addition or subtraction);
(b) make the numerical coefficient of the single term containing the variable equal to $+1$ (this is achieved by multiplication or division).

B. Solving equations using division

If each side of an equation is divided by the same non-zero number, the resulting equation is equivalent to the original equation.

$$15x = 45 \text{ ———————— original equation}$$

divide by 3 ⟶ $5x = 15$
or divide by 5 ⟶ $3x = 9$ } ———————— equivalent equations
or divide by 15 ⟶ $x = 3$

Division is used in solving equations when the numerical coefficient of the single term containing the variable is an integer or a decimal fraction.

EXAMPLE 2.5A

(i) $12x = 36$ ———————————— original equation

$$\frac{12x}{12} = \frac{36}{12}$$ divide each side by the numerical coefficient 12

$x = 3$ ———————————— solution

(ii) $-7x = 42$

$$\frac{-7x}{-7} = \frac{42}{-7}$$ divide each side by the numerical coefficient -7

$x = -6$

(iii) $0.2x = 3$

$$\frac{0.2x}{0.2} = \frac{3}{0.2}$$

$x = 15$

(iv) $x - 0.3x = 14$
$0.7x = 14$

$$\frac{0.7x}{0.7} = \frac{14}{0.7}$$

$x = 20$

C. Solving equations using multiplication

If each side of an equation is multiplied by the same non-zero number, the resulting equation is equivalent to the original equation.

$$-3x = 6 \quad\text{——————— original equation}$$

multiply by 2 $\longrightarrow$ $-6x = 12$ $\Big\}$ ——————— equivalent equations
or multiply by -1 $\longrightarrow$ $3x = -6$

Multiplication is used in solving equations containing common fractions to eliminate the denominator or denominators.

EXAMPLE 2.5B

(i) $\frac{1}{2}x = 3$ ——————— original equation

$2\left(\frac{1}{2}x\right) = 2(3)$ ——————— multiply each side by 2 to eliminate the denominator

$x = 6$ ——————— solution

(ii) $-\frac{1}{4}x = 2$ ——————— original equation

$4\left(-\frac{1}{4}x\right) = 4(2)$ ——————— multiply each side by 4 to eliminate the denominator

$-1x = 8$

$(-1)(-x) = (-1)(8)$ ——————— multiply by (-1) to make the coefficient of the term in x positive

$x = -8$

(iii) $-\frac{1}{7}x = -2$

$(-7)\left(-\frac{1}{7}x\right) = (-7)(-2)$ ——————— multiply by (-7) to eliminate the denominator and to make the coefficient of x equal to $+1$

$x = 14$

D. Solving equations using addition

If the same number is added to each side of an equation, the resulting equation is equivalent to the original equation.

$$x - 5 = 4 \quad\text{——————— original equation}$$

add 3 $x - 5 + 3 = 4 + 3$ $\Big\}$ ——————— equivalent equations
or add 5 $x - 5 + 5 = 4 + 5$

Addition is used to isolate the term or terms containing the variable when terms that have a negative coefficient appear in the equation.

EXAMPLE 2.5C

(i) $x - 6 = 4$ add 6 to each side of the equation to
      $x - 6 + 6 = 4 + 6$ ——————— eliminate the term -6 on the left
             $x = 10$ side of the equation

(ii) $-2x = -3 - 3x$
      $-2x + 3x = -3 - 3x + 3x$ ——————— add $3x$ to each side to eliminate the
             $x = -3$ term in x on the right side

(iii) $-x - 5 = 8 - 2x$

$-x - 5 + 5 = 8 - 2x + 5$ ——————— add 5 to eliminate the constant -5 on the left side

$-x = 13 - 2x$ ——————— combine like terms

$-x + 2x = 13 - 2x + 2x$ ——————— add $2x$ to eliminate the term in x on the right side

$x = 13$

E. Solving equations using subtraction

If the same number is subtracted from each side of an equation, the resulting equation is equivalent to the original equation.

$x + 8 = 9$ ——————— original equation

subtract 4 $x + 8 - 4 = 9 - 4$ ⎫

or subtract 8 $x + 8 - 8 = 9 - 8$ ⎭ ——————— equivalent equations

Subtraction is used to isolate the term or terms containing the variable when terms having a positive numerical coefficient appear in the equation.

EXAMPLE 2.5D

(i) $x + 10 = 6$

$x + 10 - 10 = 6 - 10$ ——————— subtract 10 from each side of the equation

$x = -4$

(ii) $7x = 9 + 6x$

$7x - 6x = 9 + 6x - 6x$ ——————— subtract $6x$ from each side to eliminate the term $6x$ on the right side

$x = 9$

(iii) $6x + 4 = 5x - 3$

$6x + 4 - 4 = 5x - 3 - 4$ ——————— subtract 4 from each side to eliminate the term 4 on the left side

$6x = 5x - 7$ ——————— combine like terms

$6x - 5x = 5x - 7 - 5x$ ——————— subtract $5x$ from each side of the equation to eliminate the term $5x$ on the right side

$x = -7$

F. Using two or more operations to solve equations

When more than one operation is needed to solve an equation, the operations are usually applied as follows.

(a) First, use addition and subtraction to isolate the terms containing the variable on one side of the equation (usually the left side).

(b) Second, after combining like terms, use multiplication and division to make the coefficient of the term containing the variable equal to $+1$.

EXAMPLE 2.5E

(i)
$$\left(-\frac{3}{5}\right)x = 12$$

$$5\left(-\frac{3}{5}\right)x = 5(12) \quad\text{—————— multiply by 5 to eliminate the denominator}$$

$$-3x = 60$$

$$\frac{-3x}{-3} = \frac{60}{-3} \quad\text{—————— divide by } -3$$

$$x = -20$$

(ii)
$$7x - 5 = 15 + 3x$$
$$7x - 5 + 5 = 15 + 3x + 5 \quad\text{———— add 5}$$
$$7x = 20 + 3x \quad\text{———— combine like terms}$$
$$7x - 3x = 20 + 3x - 3x \quad\text{———— subtract } 3x$$
$$4x = 20$$
$$x = 5 \quad\text{———— divide by 4}$$

(iii)
$$3x + 9 - 7x = 24 - x - 3$$
$$9 - 4x = 21 - x \quad\text{———— combine like terms}$$
$$9 - 4x - 9 = 21 - x - 9$$
$$-4x = 12 - x$$
$$-4x + x = 12 - x + x$$
$$-3x = 12$$
$$x = -4$$

G. Checking equations

To check the solution to an equation, substitute the solution into each side of the equation and determine the value of each side.

EXAMPLE 2.5F

(i) For $-\frac{3}{5}x = 12$, the solution shown is $x = -20$.

Check

Left Side $= -\frac{3}{5}x = \left(-\frac{3}{5}\right)(-20) = -3(-4) = 12$

Right Side $= 12$

Since the Left Side $=$ Right Side, -20 is the solution to the equation.

(ii) For $7x - 5 = 15 + 3x$, the solution shown is $x = 5$.

Check

LS $= 7x - 5 = 7(5) - 5 = 35 - 5 = 30$
RS $= 15 + 3x = 15 + 3(5) = 15 + 15 = 30$
Since the LS $=$ RS, 5 is the solution.

(iii) For $3x + 9 - 7x = 24 - x - 3$, the solution shown is $x = -4$.

Check

$$LS = 3(-4) + 9 - 7(-4) = -12 + 9 + 28 = 25$$
$$RS = 24 - (-4) - 3 = 24 + 4 - 3 = 25$$
Since LS = RS, -4 is the solution.

Exercise 2.5

A. Solve each of the following equations.

1. $15x = 45$ 2. $-7x = 35$ 3. $0.9x = 72$

4. $0.02x = 13$ 5. $\dfrac{1}{6}x = 3$ 6. $-\dfrac{1}{8}x = 7$

7. $\dfrac{3}{5}x = -21$ 8. $-\dfrac{4}{3}x = -32$ 9. $x - 3 = -7$

10. $-2x = 7 - 3x$ 11. $x + 6 = -2$ 12. $3x = 9 + 2x$

13. $4 - x = 9 - 2x$ 14. $2x + 7 = x - 5$ 15. $x + 0.6x = 32$

16. $x - 0.3x = 210$ 17. $x - 0.04x = 192$ 18. $x + 0.07x = 64.20$

B. Solve each of the following equations and check your solution.

1. $3x + 5 = 7x - 11$ 2. $5 - 4x = -4 - x$

3. $2 - 3x - 9 = 2x - 7 + 3x$ 4. $4x - 8 - 9x = 10 + 2x - 4$

2.6 EQUATION SOLVING INVOLVING ALGEBRAIC SIMPLIFICATION

A. Solving linear equations involving the product of integral constants and binomials

To solve this type of equation, multiply first, then simplify.

EXAMPLE 2.6A

(i) $3(2x - 5) = -5(7 - 2x)$
$6x - 15 = -35 + 10x$ ——————— expand
$6x - 10x = -35 + 15$ ——————— isolate the terms in x
$-4x = -20$
$x = 5$

Check

$$LS = 3[2(5) - 5] = 3(10 - 5) = 3(5) = 15$$
$$RS = -5[7 - 2(5)] = -5(7 - 10) = -5(-3) = 15$$

Since LS = RS, 5 is the solution.

(ii) $x - 4(3x - 7) = 3(9 - 5x) - (x - 11)$

$\qquad x - 12x + 28 = 27 - 15x - x + 11$ ——— expand

$\qquad -11x + 28 = 38 - 16x$ ——————— combine like terms

$\qquad -11x + 16x = 38 - 28$ ——————— isolate the terms in x

$\qquad\qquad\qquad 5x = 10$

$\qquad\qquad\qquad\ x = 2$

Check

$$
\begin{aligned}
\text{LS} &= 2 - 4[3(2) - 7] \\
&= 2 - 4(6 - 7) \\
&= 2 - 4(-1) \\
&= 2 + 4 \\
&= 6
\end{aligned}
\qquad
\begin{aligned}
\text{RS} &= 3[9 - 5(2)] - (2 - 11) \\
&= 3(9 - 10) - (-9) \\
&= 3(-1) + 9 \\
&= -3 + 9 \\
&= 6
\end{aligned}
$$

Since LS = RS, 2 is the solution.

B. Solving linear equations containing common fractions

The best approach when solving equations containing common fractions is to first create an equivalent equation without common fractions. Multiply each term of the equation by the **lowest common denominator (LCD)** of the fractions.

EXAMPLE 2.6B

(i) $\qquad \dfrac{4}{5}x - \dfrac{3}{4} = \dfrac{7}{12} + \dfrac{11}{15}x$ ——————— LCD = 60

$60\left(\dfrac{4}{5}x\right) - 60\left(\dfrac{3}{4}\right) = 60\left(\dfrac{7}{12}\right) + 60\left(\dfrac{11}{15}x\right)$ ——— multiply each term by 60

$\qquad 12(4x) - 15(3) = 5(7) + 4(11x)$ ——————— reduce to eliminate the

$\qquad\qquad 48x - 45 = 35 + 44x$ $\qquad\qquad\qquad\qquad$ fractions

$\qquad\qquad 48x - 44x = 35 + 45$

$\qquad\qquad\qquad\quad 4x = 80$

$\qquad\qquad\qquad\quad\ x = 20$

Check

$$\text{LS} = \frac{4}{5}(20) - \frac{3}{4} = 16 - 0.75 = 15.25$$

$$\text{RS} = \frac{7}{12} + \frac{11}{15}(20) = 0.5833333 + 14.6666667 = 15.25$$

Since LS = RS, 20 is the solution.

(ii) $\qquad \dfrac{5}{8}x - 3 = \dfrac{3}{4} + \dfrac{5x}{6}$ ——————— LCD = 24

$24\left(\dfrac{5x}{8}\right) - 24(3) = 24\left(\dfrac{3}{4}\right) + 24\left(\dfrac{5x}{6}\right)$

$\qquad 3(5x) - 72 = 6(3) + 4(5x)$

$\qquad 15x - 72 = 18 + 20x$

$\qquad\qquad -5x = 90$

$\qquad\qquad\quad x = -18$

Check

$$\text{LS} = \frac{5}{8}(-18) - 3 = -11.25 - 3 = -14.25$$

$$\text{RS} = \frac{3}{4} + \frac{5}{6}(-18) = 0.75 - 15.00 = -14.25$$

Since LS = RS, the solution is -18.

C. Solving linear equations involving fractional constants and multiplication

When solving this type of equation, the best approach is first to eliminate the fractions and then to expand.

EXAMPLE 2.6C

(i)
$$\frac{3}{2}(x - 2) - \frac{2}{3}(2x - 1) = 5 \quad\text{——— LCD} = 6$$

$$6\left(\frac{3}{2}\right)(x - 2) - 6\left(\frac{2}{3}\right)(2x - 1) = 6(5) \quad\text{——— multiply each side by 6}$$

$$3(3)(x - 2) - 2(2)(2x - 1) = 30 \quad\text{——— reduce to}$$
$$9(x - 2) - 4(2x - 1) = 30 \qquad\text{eliminate fractions}$$
$$9x - 18 - 8x + 4 = 30$$
$$x - 14 = 30$$
$$x = 44$$

Check

$$\text{LS} = \frac{3}{2}(44 - 2) - \frac{2}{3}(2 \times 44 - 1) = \frac{3}{2}(42) - \frac{2}{3}(87) = 63 - 58 = 5$$

$$\text{RS} = 5$$

Since LS = RS, 44 is the solution.

(ii)
$$-\frac{3}{5}(4x - 1) + \frac{5}{8}(4x - 3) = \frac{-11}{10} \quad\text{——— LCD} = 40$$

$$40\left(\frac{-3}{5}\right)(4x - 1) + 40\left(\frac{5}{8}\right)(4x - 3) = 40\left(\frac{-11}{10}\right)$$

$$8(-3)(4x - 1) + 5(5)(4x - 3) = 4(-11)$$
$$-24(4x - 1) + 25(4x - 3) = -44$$
$$-96x + 24 + 100x - 75 = -44$$
$$4x - 51 = -44$$
$$4x = 7$$
$$x = \frac{7}{4}$$

Check

$$\text{LS} = -\frac{3}{5}\left[4\left(\frac{7}{4}\right) - 1\right] + \frac{5}{8}\left[4\left(\frac{7}{4}\right) - 3\right]$$

$$= -\frac{3}{5}(7 - 1) + \frac{5}{8}(7 - 3)$$

$$= -\frac{18}{5} + \frac{5}{2} = -\frac{36}{10} + \frac{25}{10} = -\frac{11}{10}$$

$$\text{RS} = -\frac{11}{10}$$

Since LS = RS, the solution is $\frac{7}{4}$.

D. Formula rearrangement

Formula rearrangement, also known as **formula manipulation**, is the process of rearranging the terms of an equation. To solve for a particular variable, we want the variable to stand alone on the left side of the equation. If it does not already do so, then we have to rearrange the terms. Developing your skill in rearranging formulas is very important as it saves a lot of time in memorization. You need only memorize one form of any particular formula. For example, consider the formula I = Prt. Once we have memorized this formula, there is no need to memorize equivalent forms as long as we are skilled in formula rearrangement. Thus, for example, we need not "memorize" the form P = $^I/_{rt}$.

The key to formula manipulation is the concept of *undoing operations*. Addition and subtraction are *inverse operations* (that is, they *undo* each other).

Multiplication and division are inverse operations. Powers and roots are also inverses.

Before you begin formula rearrangement, study the formula to see where the variable you wish to isolate is located and what relationship it has with other variables in the formula.

EXAMPLE 2.6D

The formula for the perimeter of a rectangle is P = $2(l + w)$, where l represents length and w represents width. The perimeter of a rectangle is 82 units and the length is 30 units. Solve to find the width.

Solution

$P = 2(l + w)$ ——————————— multiply to remove brackets

$P = 2l + 2w$ ——————————— since $2l$ was added, subtract $2l$ from both sides

$\dfrac{P - 2l}{2} = w$ ——————————— since w was multiplied by 2, undo by dividing both sides by 2

$w = \dfrac{P - 2l}{2}$ ——————————— reverse members of the equation

If we know P = 82 and l = 30, then $w = \dfrac{82 - 2(30)}{2} = \dfrac{82 - 60}{2} = \dfrac{22}{2} = 11$

The width of the rectangle is 11 units.

You could have also answered this question by substituting the known values, then solving. It is more logical to rearrange the formula first, then substitute and solve.

EXAMPLE 2.6E

Given S = P(1 + i)^n, solve for P.

$$\frac{S}{(1 + i)^n} = P$$ ———————————— right side was multiplied by (1 + i)^n, so divide both sides by (1 + i)^n

EXAMPLE 2.6F

Given the formula S = $\frac{n}{2}$(2a + d), solve for d.

$$S = \frac{n}{2}(2a + d)$$

$$2S = n(2a + d)$$ ———————————— n was divided by 2, so multiply both sides by 2

$$\frac{2S}{n} = 2a + d$$ ———————————— right side was multiplied by n, so divide both sides by n

$$\frac{2S}{n} - 2a = d$$ ———————————— 2a was added, so subtract 2a from both sides

$$d = \frac{2S}{n} - 2a$$

EXAMPLE 2.6G

Given S = P(1 + i)^n, solve for i.

$$S = P(1 + i)^n$$

$$\frac{S}{P} = (1 + i)^n$$ ———————————— right side was multiplied by P, so divide both sides by P

$$\sqrt[n]{\frac{S}{P}} = 1 + i$$ ———————————— taking a root is the undoing of a power

$$\sqrt[n]{\frac{S}{P}} - 1 = i$$ ———————————— 1 was added, so subtract 1 from both sides

$$i = \sqrt[n]{\frac{S}{P}} - 1$$

Exercise 2.6

A. Solve each of the following equations and check your solutions.

1. $12x - 4(9x - 20) = 320$

2. $5(x - 4) - 3(2 - 3x) = -54$

3. $3(2x - 5) - 2(2x - 3) = -15$

4. $17 - 3(2x - 7) = 7x - 3(2x - 1)$

B. Solve each of the following equations.

1. $x - \dfrac{1}{4}x = 15$

2. $x + \dfrac{5}{8}x = 26$

3. $\dfrac{2}{3}x - \dfrac{1}{4} = -\dfrac{7}{4} - \dfrac{5}{6}x$

4. $\dfrac{5}{3} - \dfrac{2}{5}x = \dfrac{1}{6}x - \dfrac{1}{30}$

5. $\dfrac{3}{4}x + 4 = \dfrac{113}{24} - \dfrac{2}{3}x$

6. $2 - \dfrac{3}{2}x = \dfrac{2}{3}x + \dfrac{31}{9}$

C. Solve each of the following equations.

1. $\dfrac{3}{4}(2x - 1) - \dfrac{1}{3}(5 - 2x) = -\dfrac{55}{12}$

2. $\dfrac{4}{5}(4 - 3x) + \dfrac{53}{40} = \dfrac{3}{10}x - \dfrac{7}{8}(2x - 3)$

3. $\dfrac{2}{3}(2x - 1) - \dfrac{3}{4}(3 - 2x) = 2x - \dfrac{20}{9}$

4. $\dfrac{4}{3}(3x - 2) - \dfrac{3}{5}(4x - 3) = \dfrac{11}{60} + 3x$

D. Solve each of the following equations for the indicated variable.

1. $A = \dfrac{1}{2}bh$ for h

2. $Q = \dfrac{p - q}{2}$ for p

3. $F = \dfrac{9}{5}C + 32$ for C

4. $I = Prt$ for t

5. $A = P(1 + rt)$ for r

6. $P = s(1 + i)^{-n}$ for i

2.7 SOLVING PROBLEMS

One of students' biggest fears is being asked to solve a "word problem." Ironically word problems are the answer to the "what will I ever need this algebra for?" question. So think of those dreaded word problems as "practical applications." There are many different types of word problems, from money, to numbers, to mixtures, to when will the train get to the station, to who did the most work. Each type of problem has a specific method of solution, but there is a series of steps that will get you through any word problem. Before you begin the series of steps, read the problem. Then read the problem again. This is not as strange as it seems. The first reading tells you what type of question you are dealing with. It may involve money, or people, or like the brain teaser at the beginning of this chapter, gold bars. The second reading is done to find out what the question is asking you and what specific information the question is giving you. You can draw a diagram or make a chart if this will help sort out the information in the question. To solve problems by means of an algebraic equation, follow the systematic procedure outlined below.

STEP 1   *Introduce the variable* to be used by means of a complete sentence. This ensures a clear understanding and a record of what the variable is intended to represent.

STEP 2   *Translate* the information in the problem statement in terms of the variable.

STEP 3   *Set up* an algebraic equation. This usually means matching the algebraic expressions developed in Step 2 to a specific number.

STEP 4   *Solve* the equation, state a conclusion, and check the conclusion against the problem statement.

EXAMPLE 2.7A   A TV set was sold during a sale for $575. What is the regular selling price of the set if the price of the set was reduced by ⅙ of the regular price?

Solution

STEP 1   *Introduce the variable.* Let the regular selling price be represented by $x.

STEP 2   *Translate.* The reduction in price is $\frac{1}{6}x$, and the reduced price is $(x - \frac{1}{6}x)$.

STEP 3   *Set up an equation.* Since the reduced price is given as $575,

$$x - \frac{1}{6}x = 575$$

STEP 4   *Solve* the equation, state a conclusion, and check.

$$\frac{5}{6}x = 575$$

$$x = \frac{6(575)}{5}$$

$$x = 690$$

The regular selling price is $690.

Check	Regular selling price	$690
	Reduction: $\frac{1}{6}$ of 690	115
	Reduced price	$575

EXAMPLE 2.7B   The material cost of a product is $4 less than twice the cost of the direct labour, and the overhead is ⅚ of the direct labour cost. If the total cost of the product is $157, what is the amount of each of the three elements of cost?

Solution   Three values are needed, and the variable could represent any of the three. However, problems of this type can be solved most easily by representing the proper item by the variable rather than by selecting any of the other items. The *proper* item is the one to which the other item or items are *directly related*. In this problem, direct labour is that item.

Let the cost of direct labour be represented by x; then the cost of material is $(2x - 4)$ and the cost of overhead is $\frac{5}{6}x$.

The total cost is $\left(x + 2x - 4 + \frac{5}{6}x\right)$.

Since the total cost is given as $157,

$$x + 2x - 4 + \frac{5}{6}x = 157$$

$$3x + \frac{5}{6}x = 161$$

$$18x + 5x = 966$$

$$23x = 966$$

$$x = 42$$

Material cost is $80, direct labour cost is $42, and overhead is $35.

Check Material cost: $2x - 4 = 2(42) - 4 = \$80$
Direct labour cost: x $= \$42$
Overhead cost: $\frac{5}{6}x = \frac{5}{6}(42)$ $= \underline{\$35}$
Total cost $\underline{\$157}$

EXAMPLE 2.7C

Sheridan Service paid $240 for heat and power during January. If heat was $40 less than three times the cost of power, how much was the cost of heat for January?

Solution

Although the cost of heat is required, it is more convenient to represent the cost of power by the variable since heat cost is expressed in terms of power cost.
  Let the cost of power be represented by x; then the cost of heat is $(3x - 40)$ and the total cost is $(x + 3x - 40)$. Since the total cost is given as $240,

$$x + 3x - 40 = 240$$

$$4x = 280$$

$$x = 70$$

The cost of heat is $170.

Check Power: $\$ \ 70$
Heat: $3x - 40 = 3(70) - 40 = \underline{\$170}$
Total cost $\underline{\$240}$

EXAMPLE 2.7D

The Clarkson Soccer League has set a budget of $3840 for soccer balls. High quality game balls cost $36 each, while lower quality practice balls cost $20 each. If 160 balls are to be purchased, how many balls of each type can be bought to use up exactly the budgeted amount?

Solution

When, as in this case, the items referred to in the problem are not directly related, the variable may represent either one.
  Let the number of game balls be represented by x; then the number of practice balls is $(160 - x)$.

Since the prices of the two types of balls differ, the total value of each type of ball must now be represented in terms of x.

The value of x game balls is \$36x;
the value of $(160 - x)$ practice balls is \$20$(160 - x)$;
the total value is \$$[36x + 20(160 - x)]$.
Since the total budgeted value is given as \$3840,

$$36x + 20(160 - x) = 3840$$
$$36x + 3200 - 20x = 3840$$
$$16x = 640$$
$$x = 40$$

The number of game balls is 40 and the number of practice balls is 120.

Check   Number—40 + 120 = 160
Value—game balls: 36(40) = \$1440
practice balls: 20(120)   = \$2400
Total value   \$3840

EXAMPLE 2.7E

Last year, a repair shop used 1200 small bushings. The shop paid $33\frac{1}{3}$ cents per bushing for the first shipment and $37\frac{1}{2}$ cents per bushing for the second shipment. If the total cost was \$430, how many bushings did the second shipment contain?

Solution

Let the number of bushings in the second shipment be x; then the number of bushings in the first shipment was $1200 - x$. The cost of the second shipment was \$$0.37\frac{1}{2}x$ or \$$\frac{3}{8}x$, and the cost of the first shipment was \$$0.33\frac{1}{3}(1200 - x)$ or \$$\frac{1}{3}(1200 - x)$. The total cost is \$$[\frac{3}{8}x + \frac{1}{3}(1200 - x)]$. Since the total cost is \$430,

$$\frac{3}{8}x + \frac{1}{3}(1200 - x) = 430$$
$$24\left(\frac{3}{8}x\right) + 24\left(\frac{1}{3}\right)(1200 - x) = 24(430)$$
$$3(3x) + 8(1200 - x) = 10\ 320$$
$$9x + 9600 - 8x = 10\ 320$$
$$x = 720$$

The second shipment consisted of 720 bushings.

Check   Total number of bushings: 720 + 480 = 1200

Total value: $720\left(\frac{3}{8}\right) + 480\left(\frac{1}{3}\right)$

$$= 90(3) + 160(1)$$
$$= 270 + 160$$
$$= \$430$$

Exercise 2.7

A. For each of the following problems, set up an equation in one unknown and solve.

1. Eaton's sold a sweater for $49.49. The selling price included a markup of $\frac{3}{4}$ of the cost to the department store. What was the cost?

2. S&A Electronics sold a stereo set during a sale for $576. Determine the regular selling price of the set if the price of the set had been reduced by $\frac{1}{3}$ of the original regular selling price.

3. This month's commodity index decreased by $\frac{1}{12}$ of last month's index to 176. What was last month's index?

4. After an increase of $\frac{1}{8}$ of his current hourly wage, Jean-Luc will receive a new hourly wage of $10.35. How much is his hourly wage before the increase?

5. Nancy's sales last week were $140 less than three times Vera's sales. What were Nancy's sales if together their sales amounted to $940?

6. A metal pipe 90 cm long is cut into two pieces so that the longer piece is 15 cm longer than twice the length of the shorter piece. What is the length of the longer piece?

7. Ken and Martina agreed to form a partnership. The partnership agreement requires that Martina invest $2500 more than two-thirds of what Ken is to invest. If the partnership's capital is to be $55 000, how much should Martina invest?

8. A furniture company has been producing 2320 chairs a day working two shifts. The second shift has produced 60 chairs fewer than four-thirds of the number of chairs produced by the first shift. Determine the number of chairs produced by the second shift.

9. An inventory of two types of floodlights showed a total of sixty lights valued at $2580. If Type A cost $40 each while Type B cost $50 each, how many Type B floodlights were in inventory?

10. A machine requires four hours to make a unit of Product A and three hours to make a unit of Product B. Last month the machine operated for 200 hours producing a total of 60 units. How many units of Product A were produced?

11. Bruce has saved $8.80 in nickels, dimes, and quarters. If he has four nickels fewer than three times the number of dimes and one quarter more than $\frac{3}{4}$ the number of dimes, how many coins of each type does Bruce have?

12. The local amateur football club spent $1475 on tickets to a professional football game. If the club bought ten more eight-dollar tickets than three times the number of twelve-dollar tickets and three fewer fifteen-dollar tickets than $\frac{4}{5}$ the number of twelve dollar tickets, how many of each type of ticket did the club buy?

REVIEW EXERCISE

1. Simplify.

   (a) $3x - 4y - 3y - 5x$

   (b) $2x - 0.03x$

   (c) $(5a - 4) - (3 - a)$

   (d) $-(2x - 3y) - (-4x + y) + (y - x)$

   (e) $(5a^2 - 2b - c) - (3c + 2b - 4a^2)$

   (f) $-(2x - 3) - (x^2 - 5x + 2)$

2. Simplify.

   (a) $3(-5a)$ (b) $-7m(-4x)$

   (c) $14m \div (-2m)$ (d) $(-15a^2b) \div (5a)$

   (e) $-6(-3x)(2y)$ (f) $4(-3a)(b)(-2c)$

   (g) $-4(3x - 5y - 1)$ (h) $x(1 - 2x - x^2)$

   (i) $(24x - 16) \div (-4)$ (j) $(21a^2 - 12a) \div 3a$

   (k) $4(2a - 5) - 3(3 - 6a)$ (l) $2a(x - a) - a(3x + 2) - 3a(-5x - 4)$

   (m) $(m - 1)(2m - 5)$ (n) $(3a - 2)(a^2 - 2a - 3)$

   (o) $3(2x - 4)(x - 1) - 4(x - 3)(5x + 2)$

   (p) $-2a(3m - 1)(m - 4) - 5a(2m + 3)(2m - 3)$

3. Evaluate each of the following for the values given.

   (a) $3xy - 4x - 5y$ for $x = -2, y = 5$

   (b) $-5(2a - 3b) - 2(a + 5b)$ for $a = -\dfrac{1}{4}, b = \dfrac{2}{3}$

   (c) $\dfrac{2NC}{P(n + 1)}$ for $N = 12, C = 432, P = 1800, n = 35$

   (d) $\dfrac{365I}{RP}$ for $I = 600, R = 0.15, P = 7300$

   (e) $A(1 - dt)$ for $A = 720, d = 0.135, t = \dfrac{280}{360}$

   (f) $\dfrac{S}{1 + RT}$ for $S = 2755, R = 0.17, T = \dfrac{219}{365}$

4. Simplify.

   (a) $(-3)^5$ (b) $\left(\dfrac{2}{3}\right)^4$

   (c) $(-5)^0$ (d) $(-3)^{-1}$

(e) $\left(\dfrac{2}{5}\right)^{-4}$

(f) $(1.01)^0$

(g) $(-3)^5(-3)^4$

(h) $4^7 \div 4^2$

(i) $[(-3)^2]^5$

(j) $(m^3)^4$

(k) $\left(\dfrac{2}{3}\right)^3\left(\dfrac{2}{3}\right)^7\left(\dfrac{2}{3}\right)^{-6}$

(l) $\left(-\dfrac{5}{4}\right)^5 \div \left(-\dfrac{5}{4}\right)^3$

(m) $(1.03^{50})(1.03^{100})$

(n) $(1 + i)^{180} \div (1 + i)^{100}$

(o) $[(1.05)^{30}]^5$

(p) $(-2xy)^4$

(q) $\left(\dfrac{a^2b}{3}\right)^{-4}$

(r) $(1 + i)^{-n}$

5. Use an electronic calculator to compute each of the following.

(a) $\sqrt{0.9216}$

(b) $\sqrt[6]{1.075}$

(c) $14.974458^{\frac{1}{40}}$

(d) $1.08^{-\frac{5}{12}}$

(e) $\ln 3$

(f) $\ln 0.05$

(g) $\ln\left(\dfrac{5500}{1.10^{16}}\right)$

(h) $\ln\left[375(1.01)\left(\dfrac{1 - 1.01^{-72}}{0.01}\right)\right]$

6. Solve each of the following equations.

(a) $9x = -63$

(b) $0.05x = 44$

(c) $-\dfrac{1}{7}x = 3$

(d) $\dfrac{5}{6}x = -15$

(e) $x - 8 = -5$

(f) $x + 9 = -2$

(g) $x + 0.02x = 255$

(h) $x - 0.1x = 36$

(i) $4x - 3 = 9x + 22$

(j) $9x - 6 - 3x = 15 + 4x - 7$

(k) $x - \dfrac{1}{3}x = 26$

(l) $x + \dfrac{3}{8}x = 77$

7. Solve each of the following equations and check your answers.

(a) $-9(3x - 8) - 8(9 - 7x) = 5 + 4(9x + 11)$

(b) $21x - 4 - 7(5x - 6) = 8x - 4(5x - 7)$

(c) $\dfrac{5}{7}x + \dfrac{1}{2} = \dfrac{5}{14} + \dfrac{2}{3}x$

(d) $\dfrac{4x}{3} + 2 = \dfrac{9}{8} - \dfrac{x}{6}$

(e) $\dfrac{7}{5}(6x - 7) - \dfrac{3}{8}(7x + 15) = 25$

(f) $\dfrac{5}{9}(7 - 6x) - \dfrac{3}{4}(3 - 15x) = \dfrac{1}{12}(3x - 5) - \dfrac{1}{2}$

(g) $\dfrac{5}{6}(4x - 3) - \dfrac{2}{5}(3x + 4) = 5x - \dfrac{16}{15}(1 - 3x)$

8. Solve each of the following equations for the indicated variable.

(a) $I = Prt$ for r

(b) $S = P(1 + rt)$ for t

(c) $D = \dfrac{1}{E + F}$ for F

(d) $\dfrac{W_1}{S_1 T_1} = \dfrac{W_2}{S_2 T_2}$ for T_2

(e) $v = \sqrt{2gh}$ for h

9. For each of the following problems, set up an equation and solve.

(a) A company laid off one-sixth of its workforce because of falling sales. If the number of employees after the layoff is 690, how many employees were laid off?

(b) The current average property value is two-sevenths more than last year's average value. What was last year's average property value if the current average is $81 450?

(c) The total amount paid for a banquet, including gratuities of one-twentieth of the price quoted for the banquet, was $2457.00. How much of the amount paid was gratuities?

(d) A piece of property with a commercial building is acquired by H & A Investments for $184 000. If the land is valued at $2000 less than one-third the value of the building, how much of the amount paid should be assigned to land?

(e) The total average monthly cost of heat, power, and water for Sheridan Service for last year was $2010. If this year's average is expected to increase by one-tenth over last year's average, and heat is $22 more than three-quarters the cost of power while water is $11 less than one-third the cost of power, how much should be budgeted on the average for each month for each item?

(f) Monarch Swimming Pools has a promotional budget of $87 500. The budget is to be allocated to direct selling, TV advertising, and newspaper advertising according to a formula. The formula requires that the amount spent on TV advertising be $1000 more than three times the amount spent on newspaper advertising, and that the amount spent on direct selling be three-fourths of the total spent on TV advertising and newspaper advertising combined. How much of the budget should be allocated to direct selling?

(g) A product requires processing on three machines. Processing time on Machine A is three minutes less than four-fifths of the number of minutes on Machine B and processing time on Machine C is five-sixths of the time needed on Machines A and B together. How many minutes processing time is required on Machine C if the total processing time on all three machines is 77 minutes?

(h) Sport Alive sold 72 pairs of ski poles. Superlight poles sell at $30 per pair while ordinary poles sell at $16 per pair. If total sales value was $1530, how many pairs of each type were sold?

(i) A cash box contains $74.00 made up of quarters, half-dollars, and one-dollar coins. How many quarters are in the box if the number of half-dollar coins is one more than three-fifths of the number of one-dollar coins, and the number of quarters is four times the number of one-dollar coins and half-dollar coins together?

(j) Demers Manufacturing plans to allocate direct distribution costs to three product lines based on sales value for an accounting period. Product A sells for $20 per unit, Product B for $15 per unit, and Product C for $10 per unit. For last month, the number of units of Product A was five-eighths the number of units of Product B and the number of units of Product C was 16 less than three times the number of units of Product B. How much of the total direct distribution cost of $6280 is to be allocated to each product line?

SELF-TEST

1. Simplify.

   (a) $4 - 3x - 6 - 5x$

   (b) $(5x - 4) - (7x + 5)$

   (c) $-2(3a - 4) - 5(2a + 3)$

   (d) $-6(x - 2)(x + 1)$

2. Evaluate each of the following for the values given.

   (a) $2x^2 - 5xy - 4y^2$ for $x = -3, y = +5$

   (b) $3(7a - 4b) - 4(5a + 3b)$ for $a = \dfrac{2}{3}, b = -\dfrac{3}{4}$

   (c) $\dfrac{2NC}{P(n + 1)}$ for $N = 12, C = 400, P = 2000, n = 24$

   (d) $\dfrac{I}{Pr}$ for $I = 324, P = 5400, r = 0.15$

   (e) $S(1 - dt)$ for $S = 1606, d = 0.125, t = \dfrac{240}{365}$

   (f) $\dfrac{S}{1 + rt}$ for $S = 1566, r = 0.10, t = \dfrac{292}{365}$

3. Simplify.

   (a) $(-2)^3$

   (b) $\left(\dfrac{-2}{3}\right)^2$

   (c) $(4)^0$

   (d) $(3)^2(3)^5$

   (e) $\left(\dfrac{4}{3}\right)^{-2}$

   (f) $(-x^3)^5$

4. Use an electronic calculator to compute each of the following.

   (a) $\sqrt[10]{1.35}$

   (b) $\dfrac{1 - 1.03^{-40}}{0.03}$

   (c) $\ln 1.025$

   (d) $\ln[3.00e^{-0.2}]$

   (e) $\ln\left(\dfrac{600}{1.06^{11}}\right)$

   (f) $\ln\left[250\left(\dfrac{1.07^5 - 1}{0.07}\right)\right]$

5. Solve each of the following equations.

   (a) $\dfrac{1}{81} = \left(\dfrac{1}{3}\right)^{n-2}$

   (b) $\dfrac{5}{2} = 40\left(\dfrac{1}{2}\right)^{n-1}$

6. Solve each of the following equations.

   (a) $-\dfrac{2}{3}x = 24$

   (b) $x - 0.06x = 8.46$

   (c) $0.2x - 4 = 6 - 0.3x$

   (d) $(3 - 5x) - (8x - 1) = 43$

   (e) $4(8x - 2) - 5(3x + 5) = 18$

   (f) $x + \dfrac{3}{10}x + \dfrac{1}{2} + x + \dfrac{3}{5}x + 1 = 103$

   (g) $x + \dfrac{4}{5}x - 3 + \dfrac{5}{6}\left(x + \dfrac{4}{5}x - 3\right) = 77$

   (h) $\dfrac{2}{3}\left(3x - 1\right) - \dfrac{3}{4}\left(5x - 3\right) = \dfrac{9}{8}x - \dfrac{5}{6}\left(7x - 9\right)$

7. Solve each of the following equations for the indicated variable.

   (a) $I = Prt$ for P

   (b) $S = \dfrac{P}{1 - dt}$ for d

8. For each of the following problems, set up an equation and solve.

   (a) After reducing the regular selling price by ⅕, Star Electronics sold a TV set for $192. What was the regular selling price?

   (b) The weaving department of a factory occupies 400 square metres more than 2 times the floor space occupied by the shipping department. The total floor space is 6700 square metres. Determine the floor space occupied by the weaving department.

   (c) A machine requires 3 hours to make a unit of Product A and 5 hours to make a unit of Product B. The machine operated for 395 hours producing a total of 95 units. How many units of Product B were produced?

   (d) You invested a sum of money in a bank certificate yielding an annual return of ¹⁄₁₂ of the sum invested. A second sum of money invested in a credit union certificate yields an annual return of ⅑ of the sum invested. The credit union investment is $500 more than ⅔ of the bank investment and the total annual return is $1000. What is the sum of money you invested in the credit union certificate?

CHALLENGE PROBLEMS

1. In checking the petty cash a clerk counts 'q' quarters, 'd' dimes, 'n' nickels, and 'p' pennies. Later he discovers that x of the nickels were counted as quarters and x of the dimes were counted as pennies. (Assume that x represents the same number of nickels and dimes.) What must the clerk do to correct the original total?

2. Tom and Jerri are planning a 4000-kilometre trip in an automobile with five tires, of which four will be in use at any time. They plan to interchange the tires so that each tire will be used the same number of kilometres. For how many kilometres will each tire be used?

3. A cheque is written for x dollars and y cents. Both x and y are two digit numbers. In error, the cheque is cashed for y dollars and x cents, with the incorrect amount exceeding the correct amount by $17.82. Which of the following statements is correct?

   (a) x cannot exceed 70
   (b) y can equal $2x$
   (c) the amount of the cheque cannot be a multiple of 5
   (d) the incorrect amount can equal twice the correct amount
   (e) the sum of the digits of the correct amount is divisible by 9

CASE STUDY 2.1

INVESTING FOR AN EDUCATION

With our present concerns about the future of government pension plans and the relatively low current interest rates, more and more Canadians are investing in Mutual Funds. Mutual funds offer the potential for greater returns than savings accounts, and they offer investment flexibility. You can purchase units of a mutual fund as often as you like. Many investment professionals recommend purchasing units of mutual funds using the *dollar cost averaging* approach.

Dollar cost averaging is a simple, disciplined approach to buying mutual funds. You invest a fixed dollar amount in a mutual fund each month (or other regular time period), regardless of the unit price of the mutual fund. This means that in some months you can buy more units than in other months, since the unit price fluctuates. Over an extended period of time, the average cost per unit is often lower than if all units had been purchased at one time. Investors who take advantage of dollar cost averaging likely sleep better at night, never having to worry whether they made their investments at the right time. It takes the guess work out of trying to determine when units are cheapest to buy. Most mutual funds require a minimum intial investment of $500 with minimum monthly investments of $50 for dollar cost averaging.

Lindsay Pierce's grandparents wanted to help ensure she would be able to attend college. They started an education fund for her by making payments of $100 on the first day of each month into the Ethical Growth Fund. They made the first payment on June 1, 1995. Lindsay asked her grandparents to show her the history of her fund and explain to her how the calculations are made. They had kept a chart of the investments and cost per share over the time period (see below).

They explained to Lindsay that the column headed Number of Units Bought was calculated by dividing the Amount Invested by the Unit Price. For example, on July 1, 1995, the number of units bought = $100.00/$7.90 = 12.658 (rounding to 3 decimal places). Lindsay thought it rather strange that the number of units was calculated to three decimal places when money is expressed to only two places. However, she decided that rounding, in the long term, would be to her advantage.

Her grandparents continued to explain that the column headed Total Number of Units was a cumulative total of the column headed Number of Units Bought. For example, on August 1, 1995, the total number of units bought = 12.771 + 12.658 + 12.563 = 37.992.

Statement of Accounts for Lindsay Pierce
Ethical Growth Fund

Date	Amount Invested	Unit Price	Number of Units Bought	Total Number of Units	Market Value	Total Amount Invested	Excess	Average Cost Per Unit
1995								
June 1	$100.00	$ 7.83	12.771	12.771	$ 100.00	$ 100.00	$ 0	$7.83
July 1	100.00	7.90	12.658	25.429	200.89	200.00	0.89	7.87
Aug 1	100.00	7.96	12.563	37.992	302.42	300.00	2.42	7.90
Sept 1	100.00	7.93	12.610	50.602	401.27	400.00	1.27	7.90
Oct 1	100.00	7.99	12.516	63.118	504.32	500.00	4.32	7.92
Nov 1	100.00	7.95	12.579	75.697	601.79	600.00	1.79	7.93
Dec 1	100.00	8.41	11.891	87.588	736.61	700.00	36.61	7.99
1996								
Jan 1	100.00	8.43	11.862	99.450	838.36	800.00	38.36	8.04
Feb 1	100.00	8.87	11.274	110.724	982.12	900.00	82.12	8.13
Mar 1	100.00	8.79	11.377	122.101	1073.26	1000.00	73.26	8.19
April 1	100.00	9.03	11.074	133.175	1202.57	1100.00	102.57	8.26
May 1	100.00	9.19	10.881	144.056	1323.88	1200.00	123.88	8.33
June 1	100.00	9.37	10.672	154.728	1449.80	1300.00	149.80	8.40
July 1	100.00	9.13	10.953	165.681	1512.67	1400.00	112.67	8.45
Aug 1	100.00	8.88	11.261	176.942	1571.24	1500.00	71.24	8.48
Sept 1	100.00	9.22	10.846	187.788	1731.41	1600.00	131.41	8.52
Oct 1	100.00	9.46	10.571	198.359	1876.48	1700.00	176.48	8.57
Nov 1	100.00	10.04	9.960	208.319	2091.52	1800.00	291.53	8.64
Dec 1	100.00	10.84	9.225	217.544	2358.18	1900.00	458.18	8.73
1997								
Jan 1	100.00	10.76	9.294	226.838	2440.78	2000.00	440.78	8.82

The Market Value was calculated for each row by multiplying the Unit Price at that time by the total Number of Units owned. For example, on September 1, 1995, the market value = $7.93 × 50.602 = $401.27.

The Total Amount Invested was simply a total of their contributions. For example, on October 1, 1995, the total amount invested = $100.00 + $100.00 + $100.00 + $100.00 + $100.00 = $500.00. Lindsay was able to figure out that the column headed Excess was the Market Value minus the Total Amount Invested, on each date. She was pleased to see the Excess was always positive, even though it did go sharply up and down a couple of times. The Average Cost per Unit was calculated by dividing the total invested to date by the total number of units owned. For example, on December 1, 1995, the average cost per unit = $700.00/87.588 = $7.99 (rounding to 2 decimal places.) Lindsay noticed that the Average Cost per Unit stayed below the current price and she felt that she was easily going to have enough money for college.

Price per Unit on the First Business Day of Each Month for the Period June 1, 1995, to January 31, 1997

	Ethical Growth Fund	Ethical Pacific Fund
1995		
June	$ 7.83	$5.47
July	7.90	5.30
August	7.96	5.40
September	7.93	5.14
October	7.99	5.14
November	7.95	5.12
December	8.41	5.36
1996		
January	8.43	5.51
February	8.87	5.97
March	8.79	5.90
April	9.03	5.78
May	9.19	6.00
June	9.37	5.85
July	9.13	5.82
August	8.88	5.58
September	9.22	5.51
October	9.46	5.68
November	10.04	5.63
December	10.84	6.11
1997		
January	10.76	5.90

QUESTIONS

1. The Pierces have been investing for another grandchild, Tyler, as well. They invested the following amounts for him in the Ethical Growth Fund: $500 each on October 1, 1995, February 1, 1996, June 1, 1996 and October 1, 1996. Calculate Tyler's account position on January 1, 1997.

2. Lindsay is wondering if she would have been better off if her grandparents had invested the $100 per month from January 1, 1995, to January 1, 1997, in the Ethical Pacific Rim Fund instead of the Ethical Growth Fund. She obtained a listing of the price per unit of the Ethical Pacific Rim Fund from June 1, 1995, to January 1, 1997. (See the table on page 91.) Create a Statement of Accounts assuming that the investment had been made in the Ethical Pacific Rim Fund. (If you have access to a software spreadsheet program such as *EXCEL* or *Lotus 1,2,3*, use the program to generate the Statement of Accounts.) Would Lindsay have been better off on January 1, 1997, if the investment had been made in the Ethical Pacific Rim Fund?

3. Choose a mutual fund from the newspaper and for the rest of this course imagine that you are investing $50 per week. Keep a running Statement of Accounts. At the end of this course you may want to contact a mutual fund salesperson (or maybe not!).

CASE STUDY 2.2 EXPENSES ON THE ROAD

Jennifer Jamal is a consultant for the Home Insurance Company. Part of her job involves travelling to interview people in their homes or places of employment. She keeps a record of her mileage and her telephone calls. Home Insurance Company reimburses her for these expenses at the end of each month. Jennifer is allowed 30¢ per kilometer and $8.00 per day for telephone calls. In April, her mileage and telephone expenses totalled $256.00.

QUESTIONS

1. Jennifer's mileage charge was $66 less than that allowed for telephone calls. How far did Jennifer drive in April?

2. The local telephone company has decided to change its billing procedure from a $19.50 flat rate per month to $10.00 per month plus a service charge of 25¢ per local call. How many local calls could Jennifer make so that her new monthly telephone bill would not exceed the original April telephone bill?

3. In May, the Home Insurance Company indicated that it wanted to increase the mileage allowance to 35¢ per kilometer and lower the daily payment for telephone calls to $5.00 What effect would this have had on Jennifer's telephone and mileage reimbursement for April?

SUMMARY OF FORMULAE

Formula 2.1A

$$a^m \times a^n = a^{m+n}$$

The rule for multiplying two powers having the same base

Formula 2.1B

$$a^m \times a^n \times a^p = a^{m+n+p}$$

The rule for multiplying three or more powers having the same base

Formula 2.2

$$a^m \div a^n = a^{m-n}$$

The rule for dividing two powers having the same base

Formula 2.3

$$(a^m)^n = a^{mn}$$

The rule for raising a power to a power

Formula 2.4

$$(ab)^m = a^m b^m$$

The rule for taking the power of a product

Formula 2.5

$$\left(\frac{a}{b}\right)^m = \frac{a^m}{b^m}$$

The rule for taking the power of a quotient

Formula 2.6

$$a^{-m} = \frac{1}{a^m}$$

The definition of a negative exponent

Formula 2.7

$$\left(\frac{y}{x}\right)^{-m} = \left(\frac{x}{y}\right)^m$$

The rule for a fraction with a negative exponent

Formula 2.8

$$a^{\frac{1}{n}} = \sqrt[n]{a}$$

The definition of a fractional exponent with numerator 1

Formula 2.9

$$a^{-\frac{1}{n}} = \frac{1}{\sqrt[n]{a}}$$

The definition of a fractional exponent with numerator −1

Formula 2.10

$$a^{\frac{m}{n}} = \sqrt[n]{a^m}$$

The definition of a positive fractional exponent

Formula 2.11

$$a^{-\frac{m}{n}} = \frac{1}{\sqrt[n]{a^m}}$$

The definition of a negative fractional exponent

Formula 2.12A

$$\ln(ab) = \ln a + \ln b$$

The relationship used to find the logarithm of a product

Formula 2.12B

$$\ln(abc) = \ln a + \ln b + \ln c$$

The relationship used to find the logarithm of a product

Formula 2.13

$$\ln\left(\frac{a}{b}\right) = \ln a - \ln b$$

The relationship used to find the logarithm of a quotient

Formula 2.14

$$\ln\left(a^k\right) = k(\ln a)$$

The relationship used to find the logarithm of a power

GLOSSARY

Algebraic expression   a combination of numbers, variables representing numbers, and symbols indicating an algebraic operation

Base   one of the equal factors in a power

Collecting like terms   adding like terms

Combining like terms   see *Collecting like terms*

Common logarithms   logarithms with base 10; represented by the notation $\log x$

Dollar cost averaging   the method of investment in which one contributes the same amount of money at periodic intervals rather than all at once

Equation   a statement of equality between two algebraic expressions

Equivalent equations   equations that have the same root

Exponent   the number of equal factors in a power

Factor   one of the numbers that, when multiplied with the other number or numbers, yields a given product

First degree equation   an equation in which the variable (or variables) appear with power '1' only

Formula rearrangement (or **formula manipulation**)   the process of rearranging the terms of an equation

Index   the power of the root indicated with the radical symbol

Least or **lowest common denominator (LCD)**   the smallest number into which a set of denominators divides without remainders

Like terms   terms having the same literal coefficient

Linear equation   see *First degree equation*

Literal coefficient   the part of a term formed with letter symbols

Logarithm   the exponent to which a base must be raised to produce a given number

Members of an equation   the two sides of an equation; the left member is the left side; the right member is the right side

Monomial   an algebraic expression consisting of one term

Natural logarithms   logarithms with base e; represented by the notation $\ln x$

Numerical coefficient   the part of a term formed with numerals

Polynomial   an algebraic expression consisting of more than one term

Power   a mathematical operation indicating the multiplication of a number of equal factors

Power of a root   the exponent indicating the number of equal factors

Radical   the indicated root when using the radical symbol for finding a root

Radicand   the number under the radical symbol

Root of an equation   the solution (replacement value) that, when substituted for the variable, makes the two sides equal

Root of a product   one of the equal factors in the product

3 Ratio, Proportion, and Percent

Every day, in newspapers and magazines, we find articles that spew figures at us. These articles include percent increases, percent decreases, sales figures, ratios, and seemingly unrelated facts. When you finish this chapter, you will be able to decipher articles like the following, which appeared in *The Globe and Mail* on January 4, 1997:

"Seattle-based Starbucks Corp., a coffee retailer and roaster, said December, 1996, same-store sales rose 2% from a year ago. Total corporate revenue was $109.9 million (U.S.) for the five weeks ended December 29, 1996, up 39% from $79.1 million a year ago. For the same 13 weeks ended December 29, 1996, Starbucks said same-store sales increased 3%. Total corporate revenue for the 13-week period was $239.3 million, up 41% from $169.5 million a year ago. Starbucks opened 93 stores during the 13 weeks and licencees opened five stores. The company expects to open 227 new stores during the remainder of fiscal 1997, which ends October 1." (Reprinted with permission from *The Globe and Mail*.)

Introduction

Business information is often based on a comparison of related quantities stated in the form of a ratio. When two or more ratios are equivalent, a proportion equating the ratios can be set up. Allocation problems generally involve ratios, and many of the physical, economic, and financial relationships affecting businesses may be stated in the form of ratios or proportions.

The fractional form of a ratio is frequently replaced by the percent form because relative magnitudes are more easily understood as percents. This was done in the Starbucks article above. Skill in manipulating percents, finding percentages, computing rates percent, and dealing with problems of increase and decrease is fundamental to solving many business problems.

OBJECTIVES

Upon completing this chapter, you will be able to do the following:

1. Set up ratios, manipulate ratios, and use ratios to solve allocation problems.
2. Set up proportions, solve proportions, and use proportions to solve problems involving the equivalence of two ratios.
3. Find percentages, compute rates percent, and find the base for a rate percent, and then apply these skills to solve business problems.
4. Solve problems of increase and decrease including finding the rate of increase or decrease and finding the original quantity on which the increase or decrease is based.

5. Convert one country's currency to that of another using proportions and currency cross rates tables.
6. Calculate federal income taxes using federal income tax brackets and tax rates.
7. Explain how to construct an index number and use the Consumer Price Index to determine the purchasing power of the dollar and to compute real income.
8. Solve a variety of business problems involving percents.

3.1   RATIOS

A. Setting up ratios

1. A **ratio** is a comparison of the *relative* values of numbers or quantities and may be written in any of the following ways:
   (a) by using the word "to," such as in '5 to 2';
   (b) by using a colon, such as in '5 : 2';
   (c) as a common fraction, such as '5⁄2'.
   (d) as a decimal, such as '2.50';
   (e) as a percent, such as '250%.'

2. When comparing more than two numbers or quantities, using the colon is preferred.
   To compare the quantities 5 kg, 3 kg, and 2 kg, the ratio comparing the quantities is written

   $$5 \text{ kg} : 3 \text{ kg} : 2 \text{ kg}$$

3. When using a ratio to compare quantities, the unit of measurement is usually dropped.
   If three items weigh 5 kg, 3 kg, and 2 kg respectively, their weights are compared by the ratio

   $$5 : 3 : 2$$

4. The numbers appearing in a ratio are called the **terms of the ratio.** If the terms are in different units, the terms need to be expressed in the same unit of measurement before the units can be dropped.
   The ratio of 1 quarter to 1 dollar becomes 25 cents to 100 cents or 25 : 100; or the ratio of 3 hours to 40 minutes becomes 180 min : 40 min or 180 : 40.

5. When, as is frequently done, rates are expressed as ratios, ratios drop the units of measurement, even though the terms of the ratio represent different things.
   100 km/h becomes 100 : 1;
   50 m in 5 seconds becomes 50 : 5;
   $1.49 for 2 items becomes 1.49 : 2.

6. Any statement containing a comparison of two or more numbers or quantities can be used to set up a ratio.

EXAMPLE 3.1A

   (i) In a company, the work of 40 employees is supervised by five managers.
           The ratio of employees to managers is 40 : 5.

  (ii) Variable cost is $4000 for a sales volume of $24 000.
           The ratio of variable cost to sales volume is 4000 : 24 000.

 (iii) The cost of a product is made up of $30 of material, $12 of direct labour, and
           $27 of overhead.
           The elements of cost are in the ratio 30 : 12 : 27.

B. Reducing ratios to lowest terms

When ratios are used to express a comparison, they are usually reduced to *lowest* terms. Since ratios may be expressed as fractions, ratios may be manipulated according to the rules for working with fractions. Thus, the procedure used to reduce ratios to lowest terms is the same as to reduce fractions to lowest terms. However, when a ratio is expressed by an improper fraction that reduces to a whole number, the denominator '1' must be written to indicate that two quantities are being compared.

EXAMPLE 3.1B

Reduce each of the following ratios to lowest terms.

   (i) 80 : 35   (ii) 48 : 30 : 18

 (iii) 225 : 45   (iv) 81 : 54 : 27

Solution

   (i) Since each term of the ratio 80 : 35 contains a common factor 5, each term can
        be reduced.

$$80 : 35 = (16 \times 5) : (7 \times 5) = 16 : 7$$

$$\text{or} \quad \frac{80}{35} = \frac{16 \times 5}{7 \times 5} = \frac{16}{7}$$

  (ii) The terms of the ratio 48 : 30 : 18 contain a common factor 6.

$$48 : 30 : 18 = (8 \times 6) : (5 \times 6) : (3 \times 6) = 8 : 5 : 3$$

 (iii) $$225 : 45 = (45 \times 5) : (45 \times 1) = 5 : 1$$

$$\text{or} \quad \frac{225}{45} = \frac{5}{1}$$

 (iv) $$81 : 54 : 27 = (3 \times 27) : (2 \times 27) : (1 \times 27) = 3 : 2 : 1$$

C. Equivalent ratios in higher terms

Equivalent ratios in higher terms may be obtained by *multiplying* each term of a ratio by the same number. Higher-term ratios are used to eliminate decimals from the terms of a ratio.

EXAMPLE 3.1C State each of the following ratios in higher terms so as to eliminate the decimals from the terms of the ratios.

(i) $2.5 : 3$ (ii) $1.25 : 3.75 : 7.5$

(iii) $\dfrac{1.8}{2.7}$ (iv) $\dfrac{19.25}{2.75}$

Solution (i) $2.5 : 3 = 25 : 30$ ——————— multiply each term by 10 to eliminate the decimal

$= 5 : 6$ ——————— reduce to lowest terms

(ii) $1.25 : 3.75 : 7.5$
$= 125 : 375 : 750$ ——————— multiply each term by 100 to eliminate the decimals
$= (1 \times 125) : (3 \times 125) : (6 \times 125)$
$= 1 : 3 : 6$

(iii) $\dfrac{1.8}{2.7} = \dfrac{18}{27} = \dfrac{2}{3}$

(iv) $\dfrac{19.25}{2.75} = \dfrac{1925}{275} = \dfrac{7 \times 275}{1 \times 275} = \dfrac{7}{1}$

D. Allocation according to a ratio

Allocation problems require dividing a whole into a number of parts according to a ratio. The number of parts into which the whole is to be divided is the sum of the terms of the ratio.

EXAMPLE 3.1D Allocate $480 in the ratio $5 : 3$.

Solution The division of $480 in the ratio $5 : 3$ may be achieved by dividing the amount of $480 into $(5 + 3)$ or 8 parts.

The value of each part $= 480 \div 8 = 60$.
The first term of the ratio consists of 5 of the 8 parts; that is,
the first term $= 5 \times 60 = 300$ and the second term $= 3 \times 60 = 180$.

$480 is to be divided into $300 and $180.

Alternatively
$480 in the ratio $5 : 3$ may be divided by using fractions.

5 of 8 $\longrightarrow$ $\dfrac{5}{8} \times 480 = 300$

3 of 8 $\longrightarrow$ $\dfrac{3}{8} \times 480 = 180$

EXAMPLE 3.1E

If net income of $72 000 is to be divided among three business partners in the ratio $4 : 3 : 2$, how much should each partner receive?

Solution

Divide the net income into $4 + 3 + 2 = 9$ parts;
each part has a value of $72\,000 \div 9 = \$8000$.

Partner 1 receives 4 of the 9 parts ⟶ $4 \times 8000 = \$32\,000$
Partner 2 receives 3 of the 9 parts ⟶ $3 \times 8000 = \$24\,000$
Partner 3 receives 2 of the 9 parts ⟶ $2 \times 8000 = \underline{\$16\,000}$

$\qquad\qquad\qquad\qquad\qquad\qquad$ TOTAL $\quad\underline{\$72\,000}$

Alternatively

Partner 1 receives $\frac{4}{9}$ of $72\,000 = \frac{4}{9} \times 72\,000 = 4 \times 8000 = \$32\,000$

Partner 2 receives $\frac{3}{9}$ of $72\,000 = \frac{3}{9} \times 72\,000 = 3 \times 8000 = \$24\,000$

Partner 3 receives $\frac{2}{9}$ of $72\,000 = \frac{2}{9} \times 72\,000 = 2 \times 8000 = \underline{\$16\,000}$

$\qquad\qquad\qquad\qquad\qquad\qquad$ TOTAL $\quad\underline{\$72\,000}$

EXAMPLE 3.1F

A business suffered a fire loss of $224 640. It was covered by an insurance policy that stated that any claim was to be paid by three insurance companies in the ratio $\frac{1}{3} : \frac{3}{8} : \frac{5}{12}$. What is the amount that each of the three companies will pay?

Solution

When an amount is to be allocated in a ratio whose terms are fractions, the terms need to be converted into equivalent fractions with the same denominators. The numerators of these fractions may then be used as the ratio by which the amount will be allocated.

STEP 1

Convert the fractions into equivalent fractions with the same denominators.

$\dfrac{1}{3} : \dfrac{3}{8} : \dfrac{5}{12}$ ———————— lowest common denominator $= 24$

$= \dfrac{8}{24} : \dfrac{9}{24} : \dfrac{10}{24}$ ———————— equivalent fractions with the same denominators

STEP 2

Allocate according to the ratio formed by the numerators.

The numerators form the ratio $8 : 9 : 10$;
the number of parts is $8 + 9 + 10 = 27$;
the value of each part is $224\,640 \div 27 = 8320$

First company's share of claim $= 8320 \times 8 = \$\ 66\,560$
Second company's share of claim $= 8320 \times 9 = \$\ 74\,880$
Third company's share of claim $= 8320 \times 10 = \underline{\$\ 83\,200}$

$\qquad\qquad\qquad\qquad\qquad\qquad$ TOTAL $\quad\underline{\$224\,640}$

Exercise 3.1

A. Simplify each of the following ratios.

1. Reduce to lowest terms.

   (a) 12 to 32
   (b) 84 to 56
   (c) 15 to 24 to 39
   (d) 21 to 42 to 91

2. Set up a ratio for each of the following and reduce to lowest terms.

   (a) 12 dimes to 5 quarters
   (b) 15 hours to 3 days
   (c) 6 seconds for 50 metres
   (d) $72 per dozen
   (e) $40 per day for 12 employees for 14 days
   (f) 2 percent per month for 24 months for $5000

3. Use equivalent ratios in higher terms to eliminate decimals and fractions from the following ratios.

   (a) 1.25 to 4
   (b) 2.4 to 8.4
   (c) 0.6 to 2.1 to 3.3
   (d) 5.75 to 3.50 to 1.25
   (e) $\dfrac{1}{2}$ to $\dfrac{2}{5}$
   (f) $\dfrac{5}{3}$ to $\dfrac{7}{5}$
   (g) $\dfrac{3}{8}$ to $\dfrac{2}{3}$ to $\dfrac{3}{4}$
   (h) $\dfrac{2}{5}$ to $\dfrac{4}{7}$ to $\dfrac{5}{14}$
   (i) $2\dfrac{1}{5}$ to $4\dfrac{1}{8}$
   (j) $5\dfrac{1}{4}$ to $5\dfrac{5}{6}$

B. Set up a ratio for each of the following and reduce the ratio to lowest terms.

1. Deli Delight budgets food costs to account for 40 percent and beverage costs to account for 35 percent of total costs. What is the ratio of food costs to beverage costs?

2. At Bargain Upholstery, direct selling expense amounted to $2500 while sales volume was $87 500 for last month. What is the ratio of direct selling expense to sales volume?

3. A company employs 6 supervisors for 9 office employees and 36 production workers. What is the ratio of supervisors to office employees to production workers?

4. The cost of a unit is made up of $4.25 direct material cost, $2.75 direct labour cost, and $3.25 overhead. What is the ratio that exists between the three elements of cost?

C. Solve each of the following allocation problems.

1. A dividend of $3060 is to be distributed among three shareholders in the ratio of shares held. If the three shareholders have nine shares, two shares, and one share respectively, how much does each receive?

2. The cost of operating the Maintenance Department is to be allocated to four production departments based on the floor space each occupies. Department A occupies 1000 m²; Department B, 600 m²; Department C, 800 m²; and Department D, 400 m². If the July cost was $21 000, how much of the cost of operating the Maintenance Department should each production department absorb?

3. Insurance cost is to be distributed among manufacturing, selling, and administration in the ratio $\frac{5}{8}$ to $\frac{1}{3}$ to $\frac{1}{6}$. If the total insurance cost was $9450, how should it be distributed?

4. Executive salaries are charged to three operating divisions on the basis of capital investment in the three divisions. If the investment is $10.8 million in the Northern Division, $8.4 million in the Eastern Division, and $14.4 million in the Western Division, how should executive salaries of $588 000 be allocated to the three divisions?

3.2 PROPORTIONS

A. Solving proportions

When two ratios are equal, they form a **proportion**.

$$2:3 = 4:6$$
$$x:5 = 7:35$$
$$\frac{2}{3} = \frac{8}{x}$$
$$\frac{a}{b} = \frac{c}{d}$$

are proportions

Note that each proportion consists of *four terms*. These terms form an equation whose sides are common fractions.

If one of the four terms is unknown, the proportions form a linear equation in one variable. The equation can be solved by using the operations discussed in Chapter 2.

EXAMPLE 3.2A Solve the proportion $2:5 = 8:x$.

Solution

$2:5 = 8:x$ ——————— original form of proportion

$\frac{2}{5} = \frac{8}{x}$ ——————— change the proportion into fractional form

$5x\left(\frac{2}{5}\right) = 5x\left(\frac{8}{x}\right)$ ——————— multiply by the lowest common denominator = 5x

$2x = 40$

$x = 20$

Check $LS = \frac{2}{5}$, $RS = \frac{8}{20} = \frac{2}{5}$

Note: The two operations usually applied to solve proportions are multiplication and division. These operations permit the use of a simplified technique called **cross-multiplication** which involves

(a) the multiplication of the numerator of the ratio on the left side with the denominator of the ratio on the right side of the proportion, and
(b) the multiplication of the numerator of the ratio on the right side with the denominator of the ratio on the left side.

When cross-multiplication is used to solve Example 3.2, the value of x is obtained as follows:

$$\frac{2}{5} \times \frac{8}{x}$$

$$x(2) = 5(8) \quad \text{———— cross-multiply}$$
$$2x = 40$$
$$x = 20$$

EXAMPLE 3.2B

Solve each of the following proportions.

(i)
$$x : 5 = 7 : 35 \quad \text{—————— original proportion}$$
$$\frac{x}{5} = \frac{7}{35} \quad \text{—————— in fractional form}$$
$$35(x) = 5(7) \quad \text{————— cross-multiply}$$
$$35x = 35$$
$$x = 1$$

(ii)
$$2\tfrac{1}{2} : x = 5\tfrac{1}{2} : 38\tfrac{1}{2}$$
$$2.5 : x = 5.5 : 38.5$$
$$\frac{2.5}{x} = \frac{5.5}{38.5}$$
$$38.5(2.5) = x(5.5) \quad \text{————— cross-multiply}$$
$$96.25 = 5.5x$$
$$x = \frac{96.25}{5.5}$$
$$x = 17.5$$
$$x = 17\tfrac{1}{2}$$

(iii)
$$\frac{5}{6} : \frac{14}{3} = x : \frac{21}{10}$$
$$\left. \frac{\frac{5}{6}}{\frac{14}{3}} = \frac{\frac{x}{1}}{\frac{21}{10}} \right\} \quad \text{————— set up in fractional form}$$
$$\left(\frac{5}{6}\right)\left(\frac{21}{10}\right) = \left(\frac{x}{1}\right)\left(\frac{14}{3}\right) \quad \text{————— cross-multiply}$$
$$\frac{105}{60} = \frac{14x}{3}$$
$$(14x)(60) = (105)(3)$$
$$840x = 315$$
$$x = 0.375$$

B. Problems involving proportions

Many problems contain information that permits two ratios to be set up. These ratios are in proportion, but one term of one ratio is unknown. In such cases, a letter symbol for the unknown term is used to complete the proportion statement.

To assure that the proportion is set up correctly, use the following procedure.

STEP 1   Use a complete sentence to *introduce* the *letter* symbol that you will use to represent the missing term.

STEP 2   Set up the *known ratio* on the *left* side of the proportion. Be sure to retain the units or a description of the quantities in the ratio.

STEP 3   Set up the ratio using the *letter symbol* on the *right* side of the proportion. Make certain that the unit or description of the numerator in the ratio on the right side corresponds to the unit or description of the numerator in the ratio on the left side.

EXAMPLE 3.2C   Solve each of the following problems involving a proportion.

(i) If five kilograms of sugar cost \$9.20, what is the cost of two kilograms of sugar?

Solution

STEP 1   Introduce the variable.
Let the cost of two kilograms of sugar be \$$x$.

STEP 2   Set up the known ratio retaining the units.
5 kg : \$9.20

STEP 3   Set up the ratio involving the variable.
2 kg : \$$x$

Hence, $\dfrac{5 \text{ kg}}{\$9.20} = \dfrac{2 \text{ kg}}{\$x}$ —————— make certain the units in the numerators correspond

$$\frac{5}{9.20} = \frac{2}{x}$$

$$x(5) = 9.20(2)$$

$$x = \frac{18.40}{5}$$

$$x = 3.68$$

Two kilograms of sugar cost \$3.68.

(ii) If your car can travel 385 km on 35 L of gasoline, how far can it travel on 24 L?

Solution

Let the distance travelled on 24 L be n km;
then the known ratio is 385 km : 35 L;
the second ratio is n km : 24 L.

$$\frac{385 \text{ km}}{35 \text{ L}} = \frac{n \text{ km}}{24 \text{ L}}$$

$$\frac{385}{35} = \frac{n}{24}$$

$$n = \frac{385 \times 24}{35}$$

$$n = 264$$

The car can travel 264 km on 24 L.

(iii) Past experience shows that a process requires $17.50 worth of material for every $12.00 spent on labour. How much should be budgeted for material if the budget for labour is $17 760?

Solution

Let the material budget be k.

The known ratio is $\dfrac{\$17.50 \text{ material}}{\$12.00 \text{ labour}}$;

the second ratio is $\dfrac{\$k \text{ material}}{\$17\,760 \text{ labour}}$.

$$\frac{\$17.50 \text{ material}}{\$12.00 \text{ labour}} = \frac{\$k \text{ material}}{\$17\,760 \text{ labour}}$$

$$\frac{17.50}{12.00} = \frac{k}{17\,760}$$

$$k = \frac{17.50 \times 17\,760}{12.00}$$

$$k = 25\,900$$

The material budget should be $25 900.

EXAMPLE 3.2D Two contractors agreed to share revenue from a job in the ratio 2 : 3. Contractor A, who received the smaller amount, made a profit of $480 on the job. If contractor A's profit compared to revenue is in the ratio 3 : 8, determine

 (i) contractor A's revenue;

(ii) the total revenue of the job.

Solution

(i) Let x represent contractor A's revenue.

Then $\dfrac{\text{A's profit}}{\text{A's revenue}} = \dfrac{3}{8}$ ——————— known ratio

and $\dfrac{\text{A's profit}}{\text{A's revenue}} = \dfrac{\$480}{\$x}$ ——————— second ratio

$$\frac{3}{8} = \frac{480}{x}$$

$$3x = 480 \times 8$$

$$x = \frac{480 \times 8}{3}$$

$$x = 1280$$

Contractor A's revenue from the job is $1280.

(ii) Let $y represent contractor B's revenue.

Then $\dfrac{\text{A's revenue}}{\text{B's revenue}} = \dfrac{2}{3}$ ──────── known ratio

and $\dfrac{\text{A's revenue}}{\text{B's revenue}} = \dfrac{\$1280}{\$y}$ ──────── second ratio

$$\frac{2}{3} = \frac{1280}{y}$$

$$2y = 1280 \times 3$$

$$y = \frac{1280 \times 3}{2}$$

$$y = 1920$$

Total revenue $= x + y = 1280 + 1920 = 3200$

Total revenue on the job is $3200.

Alternatively

Let total revenue be $z.

Then $\dfrac{\text{A's revenue}}{\text{Total revenue}} = \dfrac{2}{5} = \dfrac{\$1280}{\$z}$

$$\frac{2}{5} = \frac{1280}{z}$$

$$2z = 1280 \times 5$$

$$z = 3200$$

Exercise 3.2

A. Find the unknown term in the following proportions.

1. $3 : n = 15 : 20$

2. $n : 7 = 24 : 42$

3. $3 : 8 = 21 : x$

4. $7 : 5 = x : 45$

5. $1.32 : 1.11 = 8.8 : k$

6. $2.17 : 1.61 = k : 4.6$

7. $m : 3.4 = 2.04 : 2.89$

8. $3.15 : m = 1.4 : 1.8$

9. $t : \dfrac{3}{4} = \dfrac{7}{8} : \dfrac{15}{16}$

10. $\dfrac{3}{4} : t = \dfrac{5}{8} : \dfrac{4}{9}$

11. $\dfrac{9}{8} : \dfrac{3}{5} = t : \dfrac{8}{15}$

12. $\dfrac{16}{7} : \dfrac{4}{9} = \dfrac{15}{14} : t$

B. Use proportions to solve each of the following problems.

1. Le Point Bookbindery pays a dividend of $1.25 per share every three months. How many months would it take to earn dividends amounting to $8.75 per share?

2. The community of Oakcrest sets a property tax rate of $28 per $1000 assessed valuation. What is the assessment if a tax of $854 is paid on a property?

3. A car requires nine litres of gasoline for 72 km. At the same rate of gasoline consumption, how far can the car travel if the gas tank holds 75 litres?

4. A manufacturing process requires $85 supervision cost for every 64 labour hours. At the same rate, how much supervision cost should be budgeted for 16 000 labour hours?

5. Suhami Chadhuri has a two-fifths interest in a partnership. She sold five-sixths of her interest for $3000.

   (a) What was the total amount of Ms. Chadhuri's interest before selling?
   (b) What is the value of the partnership?

6. Five-eighths of Jesse Black's inventory was destroyed by fire. He sold the remaining part, which was slightly damaged, for one-third of its value and received $1300.

   (a) What was the value of the destroyed part of the inventory?
   (b) What was the value of the inventory before the fire?

7. Last year, net profits of Herd Inc. were two-sevenths of revenue. If the company declared a dividend of $12 800 and five-ninths of the net profit was retained in the company, what was last year's revenue?

8. Material cost of a fan belt is five-eighths of total cost and labour cost is one-third of material cost. If labour cost is $15, what is the total cost of the fan belt?

DID YOU KNOW?

Averages and percentages can be used to describe various types of information. Statistics Canada often uses averages and percentages in its reports. For example, did you know that, in 1991, the average Canadian family had 1.2 children? And in 1991, there were 14.9 births per 1000 people? Did you know that, on average, Canadian men earn 67.4% more than Canadian women?

Sometimes you must stop and think about what statistics like these mean and how they were calculated.

3.3   THE BASIC PERCENTAGE PROBLEM

A. Computing percentages

To find percentages, multiply a number by a percent.

$$50\% \text{ of } 60 = 0.50 \times 60 = 30$$

Note: 50% is called the *rate*;
60 is called the *base* or *original number*;
30 is called the *percentage* or *new number*.

$$\boxed{\text{PERCENTAGE} = \text{RATE} \times \text{BASE}} \text{————— } \textbf{Formula 3.1A}$$

or

$$\boxed{\text{NEW NUMBER} = \text{RATE} \times \text{ORIGINAL NUMBER}}$$

To determine a percentage of a given number, change the percent to a decimal fraction or a common fraction and then multiply by the given number.

EXAMPLE 3.3A

(i) 80% of $400 = 0.80 \times 400$ ————— convert the percent into
$= 320$ a decimal and multiply

(ii) 5% of $1200 = 0.05 \times 1200 = 60$

(iii) 240% of $15 = 2.40 \times 15 = 36$

(iv) 1.8% of $\$600 = 0.018 \times 600 = \$10.80$

(v) $33\frac{1}{3}\%$ of $\$45.60 = \frac{1}{3} \times 45.60 = \$15.20$

(vi) 0.25% of $\$8000 = 0.0025 \times 8000 = \$20$

(vii) $\frac{3}{8}\%$ of $\$1800 = 0.375\%$ of $\$1800 = 0.00375 \times 1800 = \$6.75$

B. Computation with commonly used percents

Many of the more commonly used percents can be converted into fractions. These are easy to use when computing manually. The most important such percents and their fractional equivalents are listed in Table 3.1.

TABLE 3.1   Commonly used percents and their fractional equivalents

(i)	(ii)	(iii)	(iv)	(v)
$25\% = \frac{1}{4}$	$16\frac{2}{3}\% = \frac{1}{6}$	$12\frac{1}{2}\% = \frac{1}{8}$	$20\% = \frac{1}{5}$	$8\frac{1}{3}\% = \frac{1}{12}$
$50\% = \frac{1}{2}$	$33\frac{1}{3}\% = \frac{1}{3}$	$37\frac{1}{2}\% = \frac{3}{8}$	$40\% = \frac{2}{5}$	$6\frac{2}{3}\% = \frac{1}{15}$
$75\% = \frac{3}{4}$	$66\frac{2}{3}\% = \frac{2}{3}$	$62\frac{1}{2}\% = \frac{5}{8}$	$60\% = \frac{3}{5}$	$6\frac{1}{4}\% = \frac{1}{16}$
	$83\frac{1}{3}\% = \frac{5}{6}$	$87\frac{1}{2}\% = \frac{7}{8}$	$80\% = \frac{4}{5}$	

EXAMPLE 3.3B

(i) 25% of $32 = \frac{1}{4} \times 32 = 8$

(ii) $33\frac{1}{3}\%$ of $150 = \frac{1}{3} \times 150 = 50$

(iii) $87\frac{1}{2}\%$ of $96 = \dfrac{7}{8} \times 96 = 7 \times 12 = 84$

(iv) $83\frac{1}{3}\%$ of $48 = \dfrac{5}{6} \times 48 = 5 \times 8 = 40$

(v) $116\frac{2}{3}\%$ of $240 = \left(100\% + 16\frac{2}{3}\%\right)$ of 240

$$= \left(1 + \frac{1}{6}\right)(240)$$

$$= \frac{7}{6} \times 240$$

$$= 7 \times 40$$

$$= 280$$

(vi) 275% of $64 = \left(2 + \dfrac{3}{4}\right)(64)$

$$= \frac{11}{4} \times 64$$

$$= 11 \times 16$$

$$= 176$$

C. Using the 1% method

Percentages can be computed by determining 1% of the given number and then figuring the value of the given percent. While this method can be used to compute any percentage, it is particularly useful when dealing with *small* percents.

EXAMPLE 3.3C   Use the 1% method to determine each of the following percentages.

(i) 3% of $1800

Solution

1% of $1800 = $18
3% of $1800 = 3 \times 18 = $54

(ii) $\dfrac{1}{2}\%$ of $960

Solution

1% of $960 = $9.60

$\dfrac{1}{2}\%$ of $960 = \dfrac{1}{2} \times 9.60 = \$4.80$

(iii) $\frac{5}{8}$% of $4440

Solution

1% of $4440 = $44.40

$\frac{1}{8}$% of $4440 = $\frac{1}{8}$ × 44.40 = $5.55

$\frac{5}{8}$% of $4440 = 5 × 5.55 = $27.75

(iv) $2\frac{1}{4}$% of $36 500

Solution

1% of $36 500 = $365.00
2% of $36 500 = 2 × 365.00 = $730.00

$\frac{1}{4}$% of $36 500 = $\frac{1}{4}$ × 365.00 = $\underline{\quad 91.25}$

$2\frac{1}{4}$% of 36 500 $\longrightarrow$ $821.25

D. Finding a rate percent

Finding a rate means *comparing* two numbers. This comparison involves a **ratio** that is usually written in the form of a common fraction. When the common fraction is converted to a percent, a rate percent results.

When setting up the ratio, the base (or original number) is always the denominator of the fraction, and the percentage (or new number) is always the numerator.

$$\text{RATE} = \frac{\text{PERCENTAGE}}{\text{BASE}}, \text{ or } \frac{\text{NEW NUMBER}}{\text{ORIGINAL NUMBER}} \quad\text{—— Formula 3.1B}$$

The problem statement indicating that a rate percent is to be found is usually of the form

"What percent of x is y?" or
"y is what percent of x?"

This means that y is to be compared to x and requires the setting up of the ratio $y : x$ or the fraction $\frac{y}{x}$. x is the base (or original number) while y is the percentage (or new number).

EXAMPLE 3.3D   Answer each of the following questions.

(i) What percent of 15 is 6?

Solution

$$\text{Rate} = \frac{6}{15} \quad \begin{array}{l}\text{—— percentage (or new number)}\\ \text{—— base (or original number)}\end{array}$$

$= 0.40$
$= 40\%$

(ii) 90 is what percent of 72?

Solution

$$\text{Rate} = \frac{90}{72} \text{————————————— original number}$$
$$= 1.25$$
$$= 125\%$$

(iii) $9.90 is what percent of $550?

Solution

$$\text{Rate} = \frac{9.90}{550} = 0.018 = 1.8\%$$

(iv) What percent of $112.50 is $292.50?

Solution

$$\text{Rate} = \frac{292.50}{112.50} = 2.60 = 260\%$$

E. Finding the base

A great number of business problems involve the relationship from Formula 3.1A,

$$\boxed{\begin{array}{c} \text{PERCENTAGE} = \text{BASE} \times \text{RATE} \\ (\text{or NEW NUMBER} = \text{RATE} \times \text{ORIGINAL NUMBER}) \end{array}}$$

Since three variables are involved, three different problems may be solved using this relationship:

(a) finding the percentage (see Sections A, B, and C)
(b) finding the rate percent (see Section D)
(c) finding the base

Of the three, the problem of finding the rate percent is the most easily recognized. However, confusion often arises in deciding whether the percentage or the base needs to be found. In such cases it is useful to represent the unknown value by a variable and set up an equation.

EXAMPLE 3.3E

Solve each of the following problems by setting up an equation.

(i) What number is 25% of 84?

Solution

Introduce a variable for the unknown value and write the statement in equation form.

What number is 25% of 84

$$x = 25\% \text{ of } 84$$

$$x = \frac{1}{4} \times 84 \quad\rule{2cm}{0.4pt}\quad \text{change the percent to a fraction or a decimal}$$

$$x = 21$$

The number is 21.

(ii) 60% of what number is 42?

Solution

60% of what number is 42

$$60\% \text{ of} \qquad x = 42$$

$$0.6x = 42$$

$$x = \frac{42}{0.6}$$

$$x = 70$$

The number is 70.

(iii) How much is 16⅔% of $144?

Solution

$$x = 16\frac{2}{3}\% \text{ of } 144$$

$$x = \frac{1}{6} \times 144$$

$$x = 24$$

The amount is $24.

(iv) $160 is 250% of what amount?

Solution

$$160 = 250\% \text{ of } x$$

$$160 = 2.5x$$

$$x = \frac{160}{2.5}$$

$$x = 64$$

The amount is $64.

F. Applications

EXAMPLE 3.3F   Solve each of the following problems.

(i) Variable cost on monthly sales of $48 600 amounted to $30 375. What is the variable cost rate based on sales volume?

Solution

$$\text{Rate} = \frac{\text{Variable Cost}}{\text{Sales Volume}} \quad \text{——————— base for the comparison}$$

$$= \frac{30\ 375}{48\ 600}$$

$$= 0.625$$

$$= 62.5\%$$

The variable cost is 62.5% of sales volume.

(ii) What is the annual dividend on a preferred share paying 11.5% on a par value of $20?

Solution

Let the annual dividend be $x.
Since the annual dividend is 11.5% of $20,

$x = 11.5\%$ of 20
$x = 0.115 \times 20$
$x = 2.30$

The annual dividend is $2.30.

(iii) What was the amount of October sales if November sales of $14 352 were 115% of October sales?

Solution

Let October sales be represented by $x.
Since November sales equal 115% of October sales,

$14\ 352 = 115\%$ of x
$14\ 352 = 1.15x$
$$x = \frac{14\ 352}{1.15}$$
$x = 12\ 480$

October sales amounted to $12 480.

(iv) The 15% blended sales tax charged on the regular selling price of a computer sold in Halifax, Nova Scotia, amounted to $201.00. What was the total cost of the computer?

Solution

Let the regular selling price be $x.
Since the sales tax is 15% of the regular selling price,

$201.00 = 15\%$ of x
$201.00 = 0.15x$
$$x = \frac{201.00}{0.15}$$
$x = 1340$

The regular selling price is $1340.00
Add 15% of $1340   201.00
                    TOTAL COST $1541.00

Exercise 3.3

A. Compute each of the following.

1. 40% of 90

2. 0.1% of 950

3. 250% of 120

4. 7% of 800

5. 3% of 600

6. 15% of 240

7. 0.5% of 1200

8. 300% of 80

9. 0.02% of 2500

10. $\frac{1}{2}$% of 500

11. $\frac{1}{4}$% of 800

12. 0.05% of 9000

13. 0.075% of 10 000

14. $\frac{7}{8}$% of 3600

15. 2.5% of 700

16. 0.025% of 40 000

B. Use fractional equivalents to compute each of the following.

1. $33\frac{1}{3}$% of $48

2. $137\frac{1}{2}$% of $400

3. $162\frac{1}{2}$% of $1200

4. $66\frac{2}{3}$% of $72

5. $37\frac{1}{2}$% of $24

6. 175% of $1600

7. 125% of $160

8. $12\frac{1}{2}$% of $168

9. $83\frac{1}{3}$% of $720

10. $166\frac{2}{3}$% of $90

11. $116\frac{2}{3}$% of $42

12. $16\frac{2}{3}$% of $54

13. 75% of $180

14. $183\frac{1}{3}$% of $24

15. $133\frac{1}{3}$% of $45

16. 25% of $440

C. Use the 1% method to compute each of the following.

1. $\frac{1}{2}$% of $3120

2. $\frac{3}{4}$% of $2140

3. $\frac{3}{8}$% of $432

4. $\frac{4}{5}$% of $1120

5. $1\frac{1}{3}$% of $3630

6. $1\frac{1}{2}$% of $782

7. $2\frac{3}{8}$% of $944

8. $2\frac{3}{4}$% of $1632

D. Solve each of the following equations.

1. $x + 40\%$ of $x = 28$

2. $x - 20\%$ of $x = 240$

3. $x - 5\%$ of $x = 418$

4. $x + 7\%$ of $x = 214$

5. $x + 16\frac{2}{3}\%$ of $x = 42$

6. $x - 33\frac{1}{3}\%$ of $x = 54$

7. $x + 150\%$ of $x = 75$

8. $x + 200\%$ of $x = 36$

E. Find the rate percent for each of the following.

1. original amount 60; new amount 36

2. original amount 72; new amount 54

3. base $800; percentage $920

4. base $140; percentage $490

5. new amount $6; original amount $120

6. new amount $11; original amount $440

7. percentage $132; base $22

8. percentage $30; base $45

9. new amount $150; base $90

10. percentage $39; original amount $18

F. Answer each of the following questions.

1. $60 is 30% of what amount?

2. $36 is what percent of $15?

3. What is 0.1% of $3600?

4. 150% of what amount is $270?

5. $\frac{1}{2}\%$ of $612 is what amount?

6. 250% of what amount is $300?

7. 80 is 40% of what amount?

8. $120 is what percent of $60?

9. What is $\frac{1}{8}\%$ of $880?

10. $180 is what percent of $450?

11. $600 is 250% of what amount?

12. 25% of what amount is $28?

13. What percent of $70 is $350?

14. $90 is 30% of what amount?

15. 350% of what amount is $1050?

16. What is $\frac{1}{5}$% of $1200?

G. Answer each of the following questions.

1. The price of a carpet was reduced by 40%. If the original price was $70, what was the amount by which the price was reduced?

2. Labour content in an article is $37\frac{1}{2}$% of total cost. How much is the labour cost if the total cost is $72?

3. If waste is normally 6% of the material used in a production process, how much of $25 000 worth of material will be wasted?

4. If total deductions on a yearly salary of $18 600 amounted to $16\frac{2}{3}$%, how much was deducted?

5. If the actual sales of $40 500 for last month were 90% of the budgeted sales, how much was the sales budget for the month?

6. The Canada Pension Plan premium deducted from an employee's wages was $31.59. If the premium rate is 2.925% of gross wages, how much were the employee's gross wages?

7. A town's current population is 54 000. If this is 120% of the population five years ago, what was the town's population then?

8. A property was sold for 300% of what the vendors originally paid. If the vendors sold the property for $180 000, how much did they originally pay for the property?

3.4   PROBLEMS INVOLVING INCREASE OR DECREASE

A. Percent change

Problems involving a *change* (an increase or a decrease) are identifiable by such phrases as

"is 20% *more than*," "is 40% *less than*,"
"is *increased by* 150%," "is *decreased by* 30%."

The amount of change is to be added for an increase to or subtracted for a decrease from the *original number* (*base*) and is usually stated as a percent of the original number.

The existing relationship may be stated as

$$\boxed{\text{ORIGINAL NUMBER} \begin{array}{c} + \text{ INCREASE} \\ - \text{ DECREASE} \end{array} = \text{NEW NUMBER}} \quad \text{——— Formula 3.2}$$

where the change (the increase or decrease) is understood to be a *percent of the original number*.

EXAMPLE 3.4A   Answer each of the following questions.

  (i) 36 increased by 25% is what number?

   Solution

   The original number is 36;
   the change (increase) is 25% of 36. ——— in such problems the change is a
   Since the original number is known,   percent of the original number
   let x represent the new number.

   $$36 + 25\% \text{ of } 36 = x$$
   $$36 + \frac{1}{4} \times 36 = x$$
   $$36 + 9 = x$$
   $$x = 45$$

   The number is 45.

 (ii) What number is 40% less than 75?

   Solution

   The change (decrease) is 40% of 75.
   The original number is 75.
   Let x represent the new number.

   $$75 - 40\% \text{ of } 75 = x$$
   $$75 - 0.40 \times 75 = x$$
   $$75 - 30 = x$$
   $$x = 45$$

   The number is 45.

(iii) How much is $160 increased by 250%?

   Solution

   The increase is 250% of $160 and the original number is $160.
   Let the new amount be x.

   $$160 + 250\% \text{ of } 160 = x$$
   $$160 + 2.50 \times 160 = x$$
   $$160 + 400 = x$$
   $$x = 560$$

   The amount is $560.

B. Finding the rate of increase or decrease

This type of problem is indicated by such phrases as

(a) "20 is what percent *more than* 15?" or
(b) "What percent *less than* 96 is 72?"

In (a), the increase, which is the difference between 15, the original number, and 20, the number after the increase, is to be compared to the original number, 15.

$$\text{The rate of increase} = \frac{5}{15} = \frac{1}{3} = 33\frac{1}{3}\%$$

In (b), the decrease, which is the difference between 96, the number before the decrease (the original number), and 72, the number after the decrease, is to be expressed as a percent of the original number.

$$\text{The rate of decrease} = \frac{24}{96} = \frac{1}{4} = 25\%$$

In more generalized form, the problem statement is:

$$\text{``}y \text{ is what percent} \begin{Bmatrix} \text{more} \\ \text{less} \end{Bmatrix} \text{than } x?\text{''}$$

This means the difference between x, the number before the change (the original number), and y, the number after the change, is to be expressed as a percent of the original number.

$$\boxed{\text{RATE OF CHANGE} = \frac{\text{AMOUNT OF CHANGE}}{\text{ORIGINAL NUMBER}}} \quad \text{— Formula 3.3}$$

EXAMPLE 3.4B

Answer each of the following questions.

(i) $425 is what percent more than $125?

Solution

The amount before the change (the original number) is $125.
The change (increase) = 425 − 125 = $300.

$$\text{The rate of increase} = \frac{\text{AMOUNT OF INCREASE}}{\text{ORIGINAL AMOUNT}}$$

$$= \frac{300}{125} = 2.40 = 240\%$$

(ii) What percent less than $210 is $175?

Solution

The amount before the decrease is $210.
The decrease is 210 − 175 = $35.

$$\text{The rate of decrease} = \frac{35}{210} = \frac{1}{6} = 16\frac{2}{3}\%$$

C. Finding the original amount

If the quantity *after* the change has taken place is known, the quantity *before* the change (the original quantity) may be found by using the relationship stated in Formula 3.2.

EXAMPLE 3.4C Answer each of the following questions.

(i) 88 is 60% more than what number?

Solution

88 is the number after the increase;
the number before the increase is unknown.
Let the original number be x;
then the increase is 60% of x.

$$x + 60\% \text{ of } x = 88 \qquad\text{——— using Formula 3.2}$$
$$x + 0.6x = 88$$
$$1.6x = 88$$
$$x = \frac{88}{1.6}$$
$$x = 55$$

The original number is 55.

(ii) 75 is 40% less than what number?

Solution

75 is the number after the decrease.
Let the original number be x;
then the decrease is 40% of x.

$$x - 40\% \text{ of } x = 75$$
$$x - 0.4x = 75$$
$$0.6x = 75$$
$$x = \frac{75}{0.6}$$
$$x = 125$$

The original number is 125.

(iii) What sum of money increased by 175% amounts to $143?

Solution

$143 is the amount after the increase.
Let the original sum of money be x;
then the increase is 175% of x.

$$x + 175\% \text{ of } x = 143$$
$$x + 1.75x = 143$$
$$2.75x = 143$$
$$x = \frac{143}{2.75}$$
$$x = 52$$

The original amount is $52.

(iv) What sum of money when diminished by 33⅓% is $48?

Solution

$48 is the amount after the decrease.
Let the original sum of money be $x;
then the decrease is 33⅓% of x.

$$x - 33\tfrac{1}{3}\% \text{ of } x = 48$$
$$x - \frac{1}{3}x = 48, \text{ or } x - 0.3333333x = 48$$
$$\frac{2}{3}x = 48, \text{ or } 0.6666667x = 48$$
$$x = \frac{48 \times 3}{2}, \text{ or } x = \frac{48}{0.6666667}$$
$$x = 72$$

The original sum of money is $72.

Exercise 3.4

A. Answer each of the following questions.

1. What is 120 increased by 40%?

2. What is 900 decreased by 20%?

3. How much is $1200 decreased by 5%?

4. How much is $24 increased by 200%?

5. What number is 83⅓% more than 48?

6. What amount is 16⅔% less than $66?

B. Find the rate of change for each of the following.

1. What percent more than 30 is 45?

2. What percent less than $90 is $72?

3. The amount of $240 is what percent more than $80?

4. The amount of $110 is what percent less than $165?

5. What percent less than $300 is $294?

6. The amount of $2025 is what percent more than $2000?

C.   Answer each of the following questions.

1. The number 24 is 25% less than what number?

2. The number 605 is 37½% more than what number?

3. What amount increased by 150% will equal $325?

4. What sum of money decreased by 16⅔% will equal $800?

5. After deducting 5% from a sum of money, the remainder is $4.18. What was the original sum of money?

6. After an increase of 7%, the new amount was $749. What was the original amount?

3.5   PROBLEMS INVOLVING PERCENT

A. Summary of useful relationships

Problems involving percents abound in the field of business. The terminology used varies depending on the situation. However, most problems can be solved by means of the two basic relationships.

$$\boxed{\text{RATE} \times \text{ORIGINAL AMOUNT} = \text{NEW AMOUNT}} \quad \text{——— Formula 3.1A}$$

and

$$\boxed{\text{ORIGINAL AMOUNT} \genfrac{}{}{0pt}{}{+\ \text{INCREASE}}{-\ \text{DECREASE}} = \text{NEW AMOUNT}} \quad \text{——— Formula 3.2}$$

or, in the case of finding a rate percent, by means of the formulae

$$\boxed{\text{RATE} = \frac{\text{NEW AMOUNT}}{\text{ORIGINAL AMOUNT}}} \quad \text{——————— Formula 3.1B}$$

and

$$\boxed{\text{RATE OF CHANGE} = \frac{\text{AMOUNT OF CHANGE}}{\text{ORIGINAL AMOUNT}}} \quad \text{——— Formula 3.3}$$

B. Problems involving the computation of a rate percent

EXAMPLE 3.5A

Solve each of the following problems.

(i) Material content in a lighting fixture is $40. If the total cost of the fixture is $48, what percent of cost is the material cost?

Solution

$$\frac{\text{MATERIAL COST}}{\text{TOTAL COST}} = \frac{40}{48} = \frac{5}{6} = 83\frac{1}{3}\%$$

(ii) A cash discount of $3.60 was allowed on an invoice of $120.00. What was the rate of discount?

Solution

The rate of discount $= \dfrac{\text{AMOUNT OF DISCOUNT}}{\text{INVOICE AMOUNT}}$

$$= \frac{3.60}{120.00} = \frac{360}{12\,000} = \frac{3}{100} = 3\%$$

(iii) What percent increase did Nirel Walker receive if her bi-weekly salary rose from $800 to $920?

Solution

Salary before the increase (original salary) is $800;
the raise is $920 - 800 = \$120$.

The rate of increase $= \dfrac{\text{AMOUNT OF INCREASE}}{\text{ORIGINAL SALARY}}$

$$= \frac{120}{800} = 0.15 = 15\%$$

(iv) Expenditures for a government program were reduced from $75 000 to $60 000. What percent change does this represent?

Solution

Expenditure before the change is $75 000;
the change (decrease) $= 75\,000 - 60\,000 = \$15\,000$.

The rate of change $= \dfrac{\text{AMOUNT OF CHANGE}}{\text{ORIGINAL AMOUNT}}$

$$= \frac{15\,000}{75\,000} = 0.20 = 20\%$$

Expenditures were reduced by 20%.

C. Problems involving the basic percentage relationship

EXAMPLE 3.5B   Solve each of the following problems.

(i) An electronic calculator marked $39.95 in a bookstore is subject to 7% GST (goods and services tax) and 8% PST (provincial sales tax). What will it cost you to buy the calculator?

Solution

Cash price = marked price + GST + PST
$$= 39.95 + 7\% \text{ of } 39.95 + 8\% \text{ of } 39.95$$
$$= 39.95 + 0.07(39.95) + 0.08(39.95)$$
$$= 39.95 + 2.80 + 3.20$$
$$= 45.95$$

The calculator will cost you $45.95.

(ii) Sales for this year are budgeted at 112½% of last year's sales of $360 000. What is the sales budget for this year?

Solution

This year's sales $= 112\frac{1}{2}\%$ of 360 000
$$= 1.125 \times 360\ 000$$
$$= 405\ 000$$

Budgeted sales for the year are $405 000.

(iii) A commission of $300 was paid to a broker's agent for the sale of a bond. If the commission was ¾% of the sales value of the bond, how much was the bond sold for?

Solution

The commission paid $= \frac{3}{4}\%$ of the bond sale

$$300 = \frac{3}{4}\% \text{ of } x$$
$$300 = 0.75\% \text{ of } x$$
$$300 = 0.0075x$$
$$x = 40\ 000$$

The bond was sold for $40 000.

(iv) Based on past experience, Simcoe District Credit Union estimates uncollectible loans at 1¼% of the total loan balances outstanding. If, at the end of March, the loans account shows a balance of $3 248 000, how much should the credit union have in reserve for uncollectible loans at the end of March?

Solution

The provision for uncollectible loans = $1\frac{1}{4}$% of 3 248 000

1% of 3 248 000	$\longrightarrow$	$32 480
$\frac{1}{4}$ of 1% of 3 248 000	$\longrightarrow$	8 120
$1\frac{1}{4}$% of 3 248 000	$\longrightarrow$	$40 600

The credit union should have a reserve of $40 600 for uncollectible loans by the end of March.

(v) The consumer price index in July of this year was 225 or 180% of the index ten years ago. What was the index ten years ago?

Solution

This year's index = 180% of the index ten years ago

$$225 = 180\% \text{ of } x$$
$$225 = 1.80x$$
$$x = \frac{225}{1.8}$$
$$x = 125$$

The index ten years ago was 125.

D. Problems of increase or decrease

EXAMPLE 3.5C   Solve each of the following problems.

(i) Daily car loadings for August were 5% more than for July. If August car loadings were 76 020, what were the July car loadings?

Solution

Because July is earlier than August, its car loadings are the original number and are not known. Let them be represented by x.

$$x + 5\% \text{ of } x = 76 020$$
$$x + 0.05x = 76 020$$
$$1.05x = 76 020$$
$$x = \frac{76 020}{1.05}$$
$$x = 72 400$$

Car loadings in July numbered 72 400.

(ii) The trading price of shares of Northern Gold Mines dropped 40% to $7.20. Determine the trading price before the drop.

Solution

The trading price before the drop is the original value and is not known. Let it be $x.

$$x - 40\% \text{ of } x = 7.20$$
$$x - 0.4x = 7.20$$
$$0.6x = 7.20$$
$$x = \frac{7.20}{0.6}$$
$$x = 12.00$$

The trading price before the drop was $12.00.

(iii) Dorian Guy sold his house for $149 500. If he sold the house for $187\frac{1}{2}\%$ more than what he paid for it, how much did he gain?

Solution

The base for the percent gain is the original amount paid for the house. Since this amount is not known, let it be $x.

ORIGINAL AMOUNT PAID + GAIN = SELLING PRICE
$$x + 187\tfrac{1}{2}\% \text{ of } x = 149\ 500$$
$$x + 1.875x = 149\ 500$$
$$2.875x = 149\ 500$$
$$x = \frac{149\ 500}{2.875}$$
$$x = 52\ 000$$

The amount originally paid was $52 000.
Gain = 149 500 − 52 000 = $97 500.

(iv) The amount paid for an article, including 7% goods and services tax, was $100.58. How much was the marked price of the article?

Solution

The unknown marked price, represented by $x, is the base for the sales tax.

MARKED PRICE + GST = AMOUNT PAID
$$x + 7\% \text{ of } x = 100.58$$
$$x + 0.07x = 100.58$$
$$1.07x = 100.58$$
$$x = \frac{100.58}{1.07}$$
$$x = 94.00$$

The marked price of the article was $94.00.

(v) After taking off a discount of 5%, a retailer settled an invoice by paying $532.00. How much was the amount of the discount?

Solution

The unknown amount of the invoice, represented by $x, is the base for the discount.

AMOUNT OF INVOICE − DISCOUNT = AMOUNT PAID

$$x - 5\% \text{ of } x = 532$$
$$x - 0.05x = 532$$
$$0.95x = 532$$
$$x = 560$$

Discount = 5% of 560 = 0.05 × 560 = $28.00.

BUSINESS MATH NEWS BOX

SPECTRUM—STATISTICAL LORE FOR EVERYDAY LIVING

Number of bank branches and automated tellers at the end of a recent year for every 10 000 Germans, according to the Canadian Bankers Association: 3.36
For every 10 000 Americans: 5.26
For every 10 000 Canadians: 8.13

QUESTIONS

1. Find the ratio of the number of bank branches and automated tellers per German to the number per Canadian.

2. By what percent is the number of banking outlets per Canadian greater than the number of outlets per American?

3. According to these statistics, about how many bank branches and automated tellers would you expect to find in your community?

SOURCE: Adapted from Warren Clemens, "Spectrum—Statistical Lore for Everyday Living," *The Globe and Mail*, Report on Business Magazine, January 1995. Reprinted with permission from *The Globe and Mail*.

Exercise 3.5

A. Solve each of the following problems.

1. Of Purolator's 1200 employees, 2¼% did not report to work last Friday. How many employees were absent?

2. A storekeeper bought merchandise for $1575. If she sells the merchandise at 33⅓% above cost, how much gross profit does she make?

3. A clerk whose salary was $280 per week was given a raise of $35 per week. What percent increase did the clerk receive?

4. Your hydro bill for March is $174.40. If you pay after the due date, a late payment penalty of $8.72 is added. What is the percent penalty?

5. A sales representative receives a commission of 16⅔% on all sales. How much must his weekly sales be so that he will make a commission of $720 per week?

6. HRH Collection Agency retains a collection fee of 25% of any amounts collected. How much did the agency collect on a bad debt if the agency forwarded $2490 to a client?

7. A commercial building is insured under a fire policy that has a face value of 80% of the building's appraised value. The annual insurance premium is ⅜% of the face value of the policy and the premium for one year amounts to $675.

(a) What is the face value of the policy?
(b) What is the appraised value of the building?

8. A residential property is assessed for tax purposes at 40% of its market value. The residential property tax rate is 3⅓% of the assessed value and the tax is $1200.

(a) What is the assessed value of the property?
(b) What is the market value of the property?

B. Solve each of the following problems.

1. A merchant bought an article for $7.92. How much did the article sell for if he sold it at an increase of 83⅓%?

2. A retail outlet is offered a discount of 2½% for payment in cash of an invoice of $840. If it accepted the offer, how much was the cash payment?

3. A ski shop reduced its selling price on a pair of skis by 33⅓%. If the regular selling price was $225, what was the reduced price?

4. From March 1987 to March 1997, the price of gasoline increased 110%. If the price in 1987 was 33.0 cents per litre, what was the price per litre in 1997?

5. The 15% blended sales tax on a pair of shoes amounted to $11.10. What was the total cost of the shoes?

6. Ms. Daisy pays 37½% of her monthly gross salary as rent on a townhouse. If the monthly rent is $600, what is her monthly salary?

7. The annual interest on a bond is 12½% of its face value and amounts to $625. What is the face value of the bond?

8. A brokerage house charges a fee of 2¼%. If its fee on a stock purchase was $432, what was the amount of the purchase?

9. Profit last quarter decreased from $6540 in the previous quarter to $1090. What was the percent decrease in profit?

10. A wage earner's hourly rate of pay was increased from $9.60 to $10.32. What was the percent raise?

11. A property bought for $42 000 is now appraised at $178 500. What is the percent gain in the value of the property?

12. The Bank of Montreal reduced its annual lending rate from 10% to 9.75%. What is the percent reduction in the lending rate?

13. After a reduction of 33⅓% of the marked price, a fan was sold for $64.46. What was the marked price?

14. A special purpose index has increased 125% during the last ten years. If the index is now 279, what was the index ten years ago?

15. After a cash discount of 5%, an invoice was settled by a payment of $646. What was the invoice amount?

16. Sales in May increased 16⅔% over April sales. If May sales amounted to $24 535, what were April sales?

17. The working capital at the end of the third quarter was 75% higher than at the end of the second quarter. What was the amount of working capital at the end of the second quarter if the working capital at the end of the third quarter was $78 400?

18. After real estate fees of 8% had been deducted from the proceeds of a property sale, the vendor of the property received $88 090. What was the amount of the realtor's fee?

19. Employee compensation expense for August, consisting of the gross pay plus 4% vacation pay based on gross pay, was $23 400. How much was the amount of vacation pay expense?

20. In Vancouver, a car was sold for $9621.60 including 7% GST and 7% PST. How much was the provincial sales tax on the car?

3.6 APPLICATIONS—CURRENCY CONVERSIONS

One practical application of proportions is currency conversion. To perform currency conversions, we use exchange rates. An **exchange rate** is the value of one nation's currency expressed in terms of another nation's currency. In other words, the exchange rate tells us how much of one currency we need in order to buy one unit of another currency. By using proportions and exchange rate tables (sometimes called *currency cross rate* tables), we can convert easily from one currency to another.

A. Using Proportions

Suppose we were told that the U.S. dollar is worth $1.39 Canadian today. How would we calculate the exchange rates between the Canadian dollar and the U.S. dollar? Since there are two currencies involved, we can express the exchange rate in two different ways.

First, we can set up the exchange rate converting U.S. dollars to Canadian dollars. To do so, set up the ratio:

$$\frac{\text{CANADIAN DOLLARS}}{\text{U.S. DOLLARS}} = \frac{\$1.39}{\$1.00} = 1.39 \quad\underline{\hspace{1cm}}\quad$$ 1.39 is the exchange rate for converting U.S. dollars to Canadian dollars

To convert U.S. dollars to Canadian dollars, multiply the number of U.S. dollars by 1.39. Thus, to convert $10 U.S. to Canadian dollars, calculate: $10.00 × 1.39 = $13.90.

Second, we can set up the exchange rate converting Canadian dollars to U.S. dollars. To do so set up the ratio:

$$\frac{\text{U.S. DOLLARS}}{\text{CANADIAN DOLLARS}} = \frac{\$1.00}{\$1.39} \doteq 0.72 \quad\underline{\hspace{1cm}}\quad$$ 0.72 is the exchange rate for converting Canadian dollars to U.S. dollars

To convert Canadian dollars to U.S. dollars, multiply the number of Canadian dollars by 0.72. Thus, to convert $10 Canadian to U.S. dollars, calculate: $10.00 × 0.72 = $7.20.

In general, if we know the exchange rate from currency A to currency B (ratio $^B/_A$), then we can find the exchange rate from currency B to currency A by taking the reciprocal of the original ratio (i.e., $^A/_B$).

If both rates are known, choosing which exchange rate to use can be confusing. The best way to choose the exchange rate is to express the exchange rate as a proportion of two currencies so that the wanted currency is in the numerator of the known ratio.

EXAMPLE 3.6A

Suppose you wanted to convert $150 Canadian into U.S. dollars. You read in the newspaper that one U.S. dollar is worth 1.39 Canadian dollars, and that one Canadian dollar is worth 0.72 U.S. dollars. Which exchange rate should you use?

Solution

Let the number of U.S. dollars be x. The wanted currency is U.S. dollars.

Known ratio $\dfrac{\$0.72 \text{ U.S.}}{\$1 \text{ Canadian}}$

Second ratio $\dfrac{\$x \text{ U.S.}}{\$150 \text{ Canadian}}$

Proportion $\dfrac{\$0.72 \text{ U.S.}}{\$1 \text{ Canadian}} = \dfrac{\$x \text{ U.S.}}{\$150 \text{ Canadian}}$

$$\frac{0.72}{1} = \frac{x}{150}$$

Then cross-multiply:
$x = 0.72(150)$
$x = 108.00$

Therefore $150 Canadian is $108 U.S.

EXAMPLE 3.6B

While travelling in the United States, you filled your gas tank with 13.3 U.S. gallons of gas at a cost of $17.56 U.S.

(i) How much did the fillup cost you in Canadian funds if one Canadian dollar cost 0.74 U.S. dollars?

Solution

Let the amount in Canadian dollars be x.

$$\frac{1 \text{ C\$}}{0.74 \text{ US\$}} = \frac{x \text{ C\$}}{17.56 \text{ US\$}}$$

$$\frac{1}{0.74} = \frac{x}{17.56}$$

$$1(17.56) = x(0.74)$$

$$x = \frac{17.56}{0.74}$$

$$x = 23.73$$

The fillup cost $23.73 in Canadian funds.

(ii) What was the cost of gas per litre in Canadian funds, if one U.S. gallon is equivalent to 3.6 litres?

Solution

Since 1 U.S. gallon = 3.6 litres,
13.3 U.S. gallons = 3.6(13.3) = 47.88 litres
From (i), $17.56 US = $23.73 Canadian.

$$\text{Cost per litre} = \frac{23.73}{47.88} = \$0.4956 \text{ Canadian}$$

The cost per litre in Canadian funds was $0.4956.

B. Using cross rate tables

Cross rate tables are commonly found in newspapers and business and travel magazines. They show the exchange rates between a number of currencies. One example is shown in Table 3.2. Notice that exchange rates are often given to more decimal places than the usual two places for dollars and cents. To convert currency A into currency B, first find currency A in the column headings (along the top of the table). Then find currency B in the row headings (along the left side of the table). The exchange rate is the number where the column and row intersect. For instance, from Table 3.2, the exchange rate to convert Canadian dollars to U.S. dollars is 0.73043.

EXAMPLE 3.6C

Convert $55.00 Canadian into German deutschmarks.

Solution

First, to find the exchange rate from Canadian dollars to German deutschmarks (DM), locate the Canadian dollars (C$) column in Table 3.2. Move down the C$ column until you come to the Deutschmark row. The exchange rate is 1.25236.

TABLE 3.2 Currency cross rates

	C$	US$	DM	Yen	£	Fr. fr.	Sw. fr.	A$
Canadian $	...	1.36905	0.79849	0.01124	2.19281	0.23682	0.92522	1.07792
U.S. $	0.73043	...	0.58324	0.00821	1.60170	0.17298	0.67581	0.78735
Deutschmark	1.25236	1.71455	...	0.01407	2.74619	0.29658	1.15871	1.34995
Japanese yen	88.99	121.82	71.05	...	195.13	21.07	82.33	95.92
British pnd.	0.45604	0.62434	0.36414	0.00512	...	0.10800	0.42193	0.49157
French franc	4.22264	5.78100	3.37173	0.04745	9.25943	...	3.90687	4.55167
Swiss franc	1.08082	1.47970	0.86303	0.01215	2.37004	0.25596	...	1.16504
Australian $	0.92771	1.27008	0.74077	0.01043	2.03429	0.21970	0.85834	...

$$\text{Conversion} = 55.00 \times 1.25236$$
$$= 68.8798 \text{ DM, or } 68.88 \text{ DM}$$

EXAMPLE 3.6D Suppose you are taking a trip from Canada to France, and then to Japan. Convert $100 Canadian to French francs, then convert the French francs to Japanese yen. Use the exchange rates in Table 3.2.

Solution

(i) From Table 3.2, the exchange rate for Canadian dollars (C$) to French francs is 4.22264.

$$\text{Conversion} = 100 \times 4.22264$$
$$= 422.264 \text{ French francs}$$

(ii) From Table 3.2, the exchange rate for French francs (Fr. fr.) to Japanese yen is 21.07.

$$\text{Conversion} = 422.264 \times 21.07$$
$$= 8897.1025 \text{ Japanese yen}$$

You can check this answer by converting $100 Canadian to Japanese yen. However, the answers may differ slightly due to rounding.

Exercise 3.6

A. Answer each of the following questions.

1. How many U.S. dollars can you buy for $750.00 Canadian if one Canadian dollar is worth $0.7452 U.S. dollars?

2. How many Canadian dollars can you buy for $750.00 U.S. if one Canadian dollar is worth $0.7452 U.S. dollars?

3. Suppose the exchange rate was $0.73 U.S. for each Canadian dollar. What is the price, in Canadian dollars, of a flight to Florida costing $149.00 in U.S. dollars?

4. What is the price of gasoline per litre in Canadian dollars if a U.S. gallon of gasoline costs $1.24 U.S.? One U.S. dollar is worth $1.36 Canadian, and one U.S. gallon is equivalent to 3.6 litres.

B. Use the Currency Cross Rates in Table 3.2 on page 131 to make each of the following conversions.

1. Convert $350 U.S. to Canadian dollars.

2. Convert $200 Canadian to Australian dollars.

3. Convert $175 U.S. to Swiss francs.

4. Convert 250 British pounds to Japanese yen.

5. Convert $550 Australian to German deutschmarks.

3.7 APPLICATIONS—PERSONAL INCOME TAXES

Personal income taxes are taxes imposed by the federal and provincial governments on the earned income of residents of Canada. The federal government collects and refunds income taxes based on the income you calculate on your income tax return each year.

Federal tax rates vary currently from 17% to 29% of taxable income. The tax rates increase as your income increases. The 1997 federal income tax brackets and tax rates are shown in Table 3.3.

TABLE 3.3   1997 Federal income tax brackets and tax rates

Taxable Income (income tax brackets)	Tax Rates
$29 590 or less	17%
$29 590 to $59 180	$5 030 plus 26% of income over $29 590
Over $59 180	$12 724 plus 29% of income over $59 180

The income tax brackets are adjusted annually for changes in the Consumer Price Index (CPI) in excess of 3%. The CPI is discussed further in Section 3.8. If the CPI increases by less than 3% during a year, there is no increase in the tax brackets. Due to low inflation in Canada, the tax brackets and tax rates shown for 1997 have remained the same since 1992.

The **marginal tax rate** is the rate at which your next dollar of earned income is taxed. Your marginal tax rate increases when your earnings increase and you move from a lower tax bracket to a higher tax bracket. It decreases if your earnings decline and you move into a lower tax bracket. Due to the variety of provincial tax rates and surtaxes, the combined federal-provincial marginal tax rates vary from province to province.

For taxpayers in the highest tax bracket, the 1997 combined federal-provincial marginal tax rates, including surtaxes, for the provinces and territories were:

British Columbia	54.2%	New Brunswick	51.1%
Alberta	46.1%	Prince Edward Island	50.3%
Saskatchewan	52.0%	Nova Scotia	50.0%
Manitoba	50.4%	Newfoundland	53.3%
Ontario	51.8%	Northwest Territories	44.4%
Quebec	52.9%	Yukon Territory	46.6%

EXAMPLE 3.7A

Use the tax brackets and rates in Table 3.3 to compute the federal tax for Jim, Juan, and Jane, who are declaring taxable income, respectively, of

(i) $29 000

(ii) $58 000

(iii) $87 000

Solution

(i) Federal tax for Jim = 17% of $29 000
$$= 0.17(29\ 000)$$
$$= \$4930.00$$

(ii) Federal tax for Juan = $5030 + 26% of ($58 000 − $29 590)
$$= 5030 + 0.26(28\ 410)$$
$$= 5030 + 7386.60$$
$$= \$12\ 416.60$$

(iii) Federal tax for Jane − $12 724 + 29% of ($87 000 − $59 180)
$$= 12\ 724 + 0.29(27\ 820)$$
$$= 12\ 724 + 8067.80$$
$$= \$20\ 791.80$$

Therefore, Jim, Juan, and Jane must report federal tax of $4930.00, $12 416.60, and $20 791.80 respectively.

Taxpayer	Taxable Income	Increase in Income		Federal Tax	Increase in Federal Tax	
Jim	$29 000			$ 4 930		
Juan	58 000	$29 000	(100%)	12 417	$ 7 487	(152%)
Jane	87 000	58 000	(200%)	20 792	15 862	(322%)

For an increase in income of 100%, the federal tax increases more than 150%. For an increase in income of 200%, the federal tax increases more than 320%.

Exercise 3.7

A. Use the 1997 federal income tax brackets and rates listed below to answer each of the following questions.

Taxable Income (income tax brackets)	Tax Rates
$29 590 or less	17%
$29 590 to $59 180	$5 030 plus 26% of income over $29 590
Over $59 180	$12 724 plus 29% of income over $59 180

1. Victor calculated his 1997 taxable income to be $49 450. How much federal income tax should he report?

2. Sonja reported a taxable income of $86 300 on her 1997 income tax return. How much federal income tax should she report?

3. How much federal income tax should Marilyn report if she earned taxable income of $32 920 and $7700 from her two jobs?

4. In early 1997, Julian's gross pay increased from $28 000 per year to $32 000 per year.

   (a) What was the annual percent increase in Julian's pay before federal income taxes?
   (b) What was the annual percent increase in Julian's pay after federal income taxes were deducted?

3.8 APPLICATIONS—INDEX NUMBERS

A. The nature of index numbers

An **index number** results when you compare two values of the same thing measured at different points in time. The comparison of the two values is stated as a ratio, then expressed as a percent. When the percent symbol is dropped, the result is called an index number.

EXAMPLE 3.8A

The price of a textbook was $40.00 in 1993 and $50.00 in 1999. Compare the two prices to create an index number.

Solution

The change in price over the time period 1993 to 1999 can be measured in relative terms by writing the ratio

$$\frac{\text{Price in 1999}}{\text{Price in 1993}} = \frac{50.00}{40.00} = 1.25 = 125\%$$

An index number can now be created by dropping the percent symbol. The price index is 125.

To construct an index number, you must select one of the two values as the denominator of the ratio. The point in time at which the denominator was measured is called the **base period**. In Example 3.8A, 1993 was chosen as the base period. The chronologically earlier time period is usually used as the base period.

The index for the base period is always 100. The difference between an index number and 100 indicates the relative change that has taken place. For Example 3.8A, the index number 125 indicates that the price of the book in 1999 was 25% higher than in 1993.

Indexes provide an easy way of expressing changes that occur in daily business. Converting data to indexes makes working with very large or small numbers easier and provides a basis for many types of analysis. Indexes are used in comparing and analyzing economic data and have become a widely accepted tool for measuring changes in business activity. Two of the more common indexes frequently mentioned in the media are the Consumer Price Index (CPI) and the Toronto Stock Exchange 300 Composite Price Index (TSE 300).

B. The Consumer Price Index and its uses

The **Consumer Price Index** (CPI) is the most widely accepted indicator of changes in the overall price level of goods and services. In Canada, a fixed "basket" or collection of goods and services is used to represent all Canadian goods and services. The prices of the items in this collection are monitored and are used to represent the price change of all goods and services. The Canadian Consumer Price Index is currently based on 1986 price levels and is published monthly by Statistics Canada. For example, the December 1996 consumer price index of 136.80 indicated that the price level increased 36.80% from 1986 (the base year) to December 1996.

You can use the Consumer Price Index to determine the *purchasing power of the Canadian dollar* and to compute *real income*.

The **purchasing power of the dollar** is the reciprocal of the consumer price index; that is,

$$\text{Purchasing Power of the Dollar} = \frac{\$1}{\text{Consumer Price Index}} (100)$$

EXAMPLE 3.8B

The CPI was 133.90 for December 1995 and 136.80 for December 1996. Determine the purchasing power of the Canadian dollar for the two months, and interpret the meaning of the results.

Solution

The purchasing power of the dollar for December 1995

$$= \frac{\$1}{133.90} (100) = \$0.7468$$

The purchasing power of the dollar for December 1996

$$= \frac{\$1}{136.80} (100) = \$0.7310$$

This means the dollar in December 1995 could only purchase about 75% of what it could purchase in 1986 (the base year). In December 1996, the dollar could purchase even less (about 73% of what it could purchase in 1986).

The CPI can be used to eliminate the effect of inflation on income by adjusting **nominal income** (income stated in current dollars) to **real income** (income stated in base-period dollars).

$$\text{REAL INCOME} = \frac{\text{INCOME IN CURRENT DOLLARS}}{\text{CONSUMER PRICE INDEX}}(100)$$ ———— **Formula 3.4**

EXAMPLE 3.8C   Heather's income was $35 000 in 1986, $43 000 in 1991, and $51 000 in 1996. The Canadian CPI was 126.2 in 1991 and 136.8 in 1996. The CPI base year is 1986.

(i) Determine Heather's real income in 1991 and 1996.

(ii) Comment on the changes in nominal income compared to changes in real income.

Solution   (i) Real income in 1991 = $\dfrac{\text{Nominal Income}}{\text{CPI in 1991}}(100) = \dfrac{43\,000}{126.2}(100) = \$34\,073$

Real income in 1996 = $\dfrac{\text{Nominal Income}}{\text{CPI in 1996}}(100) = \dfrac{51\,000}{136.8}(100) = \$37\,281$

(ii) To compare nominal income with real income, it is useful to determine income changes in absolute and relative terms.

Year	1986	1991	1996
Nominal Income	$35 000	$43 000	$51 000
Simple price index	$\frac{35\,000}{35\,000}(100)$	$\frac{43\,000}{35\,000}(100)$	$\frac{51\,000}{35\,000}(100)$
	= 100.00	= 122.9	= 145.7
Absolute ($) increase		$8 000	$16 000
Relative (%) increase		22.9%	45.7%
Real Income	$35 000	$34 073	$37 281
Simple price index	$\frac{35\,000}{35\,000}(100)$	$\frac{34\,073}{35\,000}(100)$	$\frac{37\,281}{35\,000}(100)$
	= 100.00	= 97.4	= 106.5
Absolute ($) increase		($927)	$2281
Relative (%) increase		(2.6%)	6.5%

While Heather's income in 1991 increased 22.9% over her 1986 income, her purchasing power, reflected by her 1991 real income, actually decreased by 2.6% over the five-year period. From 1986 to 1996, her nominal income increased by 45.7% over her 1986 income. Her real income increased 6.5%, indicating that real income increased during the period 1991 to 1996.

Exercise 3.8

A. Solve each of the following problems.

1. Using 1989 as the base period, compute a simple price index for each of the following commodities. Interpret your results.

Commodity	Price in 1989	Price in 1999
Bread (loaf)	$0.92	$1.44
Tires	$85.00	$94.00
Computer	$2100.00	$1450.00

2. Using 1993 as the base period, compute a series of simple price indexes for the price of gold for the period 1993 to 1997. Interpret your results.

Year	1993	1994	1995	1996	1997
Price per gram	$12.46	$11.85	$11.02	$13.84	$10.04

B. Solve each of the following problems.

1. The Consumer Price Index for 1992 was 128.1 and 136.8 for 1996.

   (a) Determine the purchasing power of the dollar in 1992 and 1996 relative to the base year 1986.
   (b) Compute the purchasing power of the dollar in 1996 relative to 1992.

2. Kim's annual incomes for 1986, 1992, and 1996 were $24 000, $36 000, and $31 800 respectively. Given that the Consumer Price Index for the three years was 100.0, 128.1, and 136.8 respectively, compute Kim's real income for 1992 and 1996.

REVIEW EXERCISE

1. Set up ratios to compare each of the following sets of quantities. Reduce each ratio to its lowest terms.

   (a) twenty-five dimes and three dollars

   (b) five hours to 50 min

   (c) $6.75 for thirty litres of gasoline

   (d) $21 for three-and-a-half hours

   (e) 1440 words for 120 lines for 6 pages

   (f) 90 kg for 24 ha (hectares) for 18 weeks

2. Solve each of the following proportions.

   (a) $5 : n = 35 : 21$

   (b) $10 : 6 = 30 : x$

   (c) $1.15 : 0.85 = k : 1.19$

   (d) $3.60 : m = 10.8 : 8.10$

   (e) $\dfrac{5}{7} : \dfrac{15}{14} = \dfrac{6}{5} : t$

   (f) $y : \dfrac{9}{8} = \dfrac{5}{4} : \dfrac{45}{64}$

3. Compute each of the following.

   (a) 150% of 140

   (b) 3% of 240

   (c) $9\frac{3}{4}$% of 2000

   (d) 0.9% of 400

4. Use fractional equivalents to compute each of the following.

   (a) $66\frac{2}{3}$% of \$168

   (b) $37\frac{1}{2}$% of \$2480

   (c) 125% of \$924

   (d) $183\frac{1}{3}$% of \$720

5. Use the 1% method to determine each of the following.

   (a) $\dfrac{1}{4}$% of \$2664

   (b) $\dfrac{5}{8}$% of \$1328

   (c) $1\frac{2}{3}$% of \$5400

   (d) $2\frac{1}{5}$% of \$1260

6. Answer each of the following questions.

   (a) What is the rate percent if the base is 88 and the percentage is 55?

   (b) 63 is what percent of 36?

   (c) What is ¾% of \$64.00?

   (d) 450% of \$5.00 is what amount?

   (e) \$245 is 87½% of what amount?

   (f) 2¼% of what amount is \$9.90?

   (g) What percent of \$62.50 is \$1.25?

   (h) \$30 is what percent of \$6?

   (i) 166⅔% of what amount is \$220?

   (j) \$1.35 is ⅓% of what amount?

7. Answer each of the following questions.

   (a) How much is \$8 increased by 125%?

   (b) What amount is 2¼% less than \$2000?

   (c) What percent less than \$120 is \$100?

(**d**) $975 is what percent more than $150?

(**e**) $98 is 75% more than what amount?

(**f**) After a reduction of 15%, the amount paid for a CD player was $289. What was the price before the reduction?

(**g**) What sum of money increased by 250% will amount to $490?

8. D, E, and F own a business jointly and share profits and losses in the same proportion as their investments. How much of a profit of $4500 will each receive if their investments are $4000, $6000, and $5000 respectively?

9. Departments A, B, and C occupy floor space of 80 m², 140 m², and 160 m² respectively. If the total rental cost for the floor space is $11 400 per month, how much of the rental cost should each department pay?

10. Four beneficiaries are to divide an estate of $189 000 in the ratio $\frac{1}{3} : \frac{1}{4} : \frac{3}{8} : \frac{1}{24}$. How much should each receive?

11. Three insurance companies have insured a building in the ratio $\frac{1}{2}$ to $\frac{1}{3}$ to $\frac{2}{5}$. How much of a fire loss of $185 000 should each company pay?

12. A hot water tank with a capacity of 220 L can be heated in twenty minutes. At the same rate, how many minutes will it take to heat a tank containing 176 L?

13. If the variable cost amounts to $130 000 when sales are $250 000, what will variable cost be when sales are $350 000?

14. Gross profit for April was two-fifths of net sales, and net income was two-sevenths of gross profit. Net income was $4200.

(**a**) What was the gross profit for April?

(**b**) What were net sales for April?

15. In a college, ⁴/₉ of all employees are faculty and the ratio of the faculty to support staff is 5 : 4. How many people does the college employ if the support staff numbers 192?

16. In the last municipal election, 62¹/₂% of the population of 94 800 was eligible to vote. Of those eligible, 33¹/₃% voted.

(**a**) What was the number of eligible voters?

(**b**) How many voted?

17. An investment portfolio of $150 000 consists of the following: 37¹/₂% in bonds, 56¹/₄% in common stock, and the remainder in preferred shares. How much money is invested in each type of investment security?

18. A sales representative's orders for May were 16⅔% less than her April orders, which amounted to $51 120.

    (a) How much were the sales rep's orders in May?

    (b) By what amount did her orders decrease?

19. The appraised value of a property has increased 233⅓% since it was purchased by the present owner. The purchase price of the property was $120 000, its appraised value at that time.

    (a) How much is the current appraised value?

    (b) How much would the owner gain by selling at the appraised value?

20. The direct material cost of manufacturing a product is $103.95, direct labour cost is $46.20, and overhead is $57.75.

    (a) What is the percent content of each element of cost in the product?

    (b) What is the overhead percent rate based on direct labour?

21. Inspection of a production run of 2400 items showed that 180 items did not meet specifications. Of the 180 that did not pass inspection, 150 could be reworked. The remainder had to be scrapped.

    (a) What percent of the production run did not pass inspection?

    (b) What percent of the items that did not meet specifications had to be scrapped?

22. The price of a stock a week ago was $56.25 per share. Today the price per share is $51.75.

    (a) What is the percent change in price?

    (b) What is the new price as a percent of the old price?

23. A wage earner's hourly rate of pay increased from $6.30 to $16.80 during the last decade.

    (a) What has been the percent change in the hourly rate of pay?

    (b) What is the current rate of pay as a percent of the rate a decade ago?

24. A firm's bad debts of $7875 were 2¼% of sales. What were the firm's sales?

25. A ski shop lists ski boots at 240% of cost. If the ski shop prices the DX2 Model at $396.00, what was the cost of the ski boots to the dealer?

26. A property owner listed his property for 160% more than he paid for it. The owner eventually accepted an offer 12½% below his asking price and sold the property for $191 100. How much did the owner pay for the property?

27. A marina listed a yacht at 33⅓% above cost. At the end of the season, the list price was reduced by 22.5% and the yacht was sold for $15 500. What was the cost of the yacht to the marina?

28. A & E Holdings' profit and loss statement showed a net income of 9¾% or $29 250. Twenty percent of net income was paid in corporation tax and 75% of the net income after tax was paid out as dividends to Alice and Emile, who hold shares in the ratio 5 to 3.

   (a) What was the revenue of A & E Holdings?

   (b) How much was the after-tax income?

   (c) How much was paid out in dividends?

   (d) What percent of net income did Alice receive as a dividend?

29. A farm was offered for sale at 350% above cost. The farm was finally sold for $330 000 at 8⅓% below the asking price.

   (a) What was the original cost of the farm to the owner?

   (b) How much gain did the owner realize?

   (c) What percent of the original cost does this gain represent?

30. Suppose it costs $325.50 Canadian to purchase $237.62 U.S.

   (a) What is the exchange rate?

   (b) How many U.S. dollars will you receive if you convert $725 Canadian into U.S. dollars?

31. Media Marketing of Atlanta, Georgia, offers a three-day accommodation coupon for a Hilton Head resort in South Carolina at a promotion price of $216.00 Canadian. If the exchange rate is $1.36 Canadian per U.S. dollar, what is the value of the coupon in U.S. dollars?

32. Veronica calculated her 1997 taxable income to be $83 450.00. How much federal income tax should she report if she is in the top tax bracket, which is taxed at $12 724 plus 29% of income over $59 180?

33. Suppose the Consumer Price Index in the year 2000 is 148.0, with 1986 as the base year.

   (a) What is the purchasing power of the dollar in the year 2000 compared to 1986?

   (b) What is the real income, relative to 1986, of a wage earner whose income amounted to $62 900 in 2000?

SELF-TEST

1. Compute each of the following.

   (a) 125% of $280

   (b) $\frac{3}{8}$% of $20 280

   (c) $83\frac{1}{3}$% of $174

   (d) $1\frac{1}{4}$% of $1056

2. Solve each of the following proportions.

   (a) $65 : 39 = x : 12$

   (b) $\frac{7}{6} : \frac{35}{12} = \frac{6}{5} : x$

3. The results of a market survey indicate that 24 respondents preferred Brand X, 36 preferred Brand Y, and 20 had no preference. What percent of the sample preferred Brand Y?

4. Departments, A, B, and C occupy floor space of 40 m², 80 m², and 300 m² respectively. If the total rental for the space is $25 200 per month, how much rent should Department B pay?

5. Past experience shows that the clientele of a restaurant spends $9.60 on beverages for every $12.00 spent on food. If it is expected that food sales will amount to $12 500 for a month, how much should be budgeted for beverage sales?

6. After a reduction of 16⅔% of the marked price, a pair of boots sold for $60.00. What was the marked price?

7. A bonus is to be divided among four employees in the ratio $\frac{1}{2} : \frac{1}{3} : \frac{1}{5} : \frac{1}{6}$. What is each employee's share of a bonus of $40 500?

8. Alanna Fawcett's hourly rate of pay was increased from $11.00 to $12.54. What was the percent raise?

9. A bicycle was sold for $287.50. The selling price included 15% blended sales tax. Find the amount of sales tax on the bike.

10. A microwave oven originally advertised at $220.00 is reduced to $209.00 during a sale. By what percent was the price reduced?

11. A special consumer index has increased 100% during the last 10 years. If the index is now 360, what was it 10 years ago?

12. Mr. Braid owned ³⁄₈ of a store. He sold ²⁄₃ of his interest in the store for $18 000. What was the value of the store?

13. Suppose it cost $0.802 Canadian to purchase one German deutschmark.

    (a) How much would it cost in German deutschmarks to purchase one Canadian dollar?

    (b) How many German deutschmarks would you need to buy 500 Canadian dollars?

14. If one Canadian dollar is equivalent to $0.7625 U.S., how much do you need in Canadian funds to buy $800.00 U.S.?

15. Suppose a taxpayer is in the tax bracket where federal income tax is calculated as $5030 plus 26% of income over $29 590. How much federal income tax must he report if he earns $48 750?

16. What is the purchasing power of the dollar relative to the base year of 1986 if the Consumer Price Index is 144.9?

CHALLENGE PROBLEMS

1. Two consecutive price reductions of the same percent reduced the price of an item from $25 to $16. By what percent was the price reduced each time?

2. Suppose you own a fastfood outlet and buy 100 kg of potatoes that are 99% water. After leaving them outside for a few days, you are told that they are now only 98% water. Assuming that they have simply lost some water only, how much do the potatoes now weigh?

3. Luis ordered 4 pairs of black socks and some additional pairs of blue socks from a clothing catalogue. The price of the black socks per pair was twice that of the blue. When the order was filled, it was found that the number of pairs of the two colours had been interchanged. This increased the bill by 50% (before taxes and delivery charges). Find the ratio of the number of pairs of black socks to the number of pairs of blue socks in Luis's original order.

4. Following a 10% decrease in her annual salary, what percent increase would an employee need to receive in future to get back to her original salary level?

CASE STUDY 3.1 FRANCHISE FINANCES

Market research in the gourmet coffee business is fairly simple: Count the customers at the rival café, and if there's a long line every morning, open another one nearby.

That's one of the ways Starbucks Corp. became the leading retailer of specialty coffee in the United States. But now that the Seattle chain has more than 1100 outlets, the rival café is likely to be another Starbucks.

In the Dupont Circle area of Washington, D.C., two Starbucks vie for business a block apart. In San José, California, two shopping malls at a major intersection both have Starbucks stores. In Vancouver, B.C., the company opened a new coffee house across the street from an existing Starbucks. More are on their way: Starbucks plans to open 325 stores in fiscal 1997 and aims to have a total of 2000 by the year 2000.

But the steady proliferation of stores has its price. Though, overall, Starbucks sales are still growing quickly, the rate of growth is slowing at existing stores. Annual sales growth at stores open at least 13 months slid to 7% last year from 19% in 1993 and have continued to shrink. Comparable-store gains for all of fiscal year 1997 will be between 3 and 7%, says Michael Casey, Starbucks' chief financial officer.

Such signs of saturation are worrisome to investors, who have driven down the price of Starbucks shares to $32.12 (U.S.) from a previous high of $40.25 (U.S.). "Cannibalization" is only one of the factors that have eaten into sales growth. So has the small size of some stores: there's only so much coffee that can be sold from a 1000-square-foot space. Other stores are advancing in age, with some outlets in Seattle now almost 10 years old. Competitors are proliferating too, especially in urban areas. Starbucks' growth has also been hurt by a lacklustre merchandising effort that has left many of the same products, such as mugs and coffee makers, on display for years.

To be sure, Starbucks is hardly a company in decline. For its fiscal first quarter ended December 31, analysts expect Starbucks to report a net income of about $14.9 million, a 55% increase from the previous year's first quarter. Quarterly revenue is expected to rise 41% to $239 million. "As we add more stores, we increase our total business, but we cannibalize our existing stores," said Orin Smith, Starbucks' president and chief operating officer.

Starbucks executives say that the company's reputation reaches new markets even before the stores open. As a result, Starbucks' store launches have become steadily more successful. In 1995, new stores brought in an average of $700 000 in revenue in their first year, up from $427 000 in 1990.

One consumer research firm states that 50% of the population will consume coffee on a regular basis, while cautioning that the overall market for coffee isn't getting larger. Another analyst notes that "there are three billion cups of coffee drunk every day and 2.8 billion of them are rotten."

Starbucks plans to protect their brand's value by limiting their merchandising. However, they are now the official coffee for United Airlines and are considering a brand of coffee-flavoured ice cream.

SOURCE: David Bank, "Starbucks Finds Itself in Café Clash," *The Globe and Mail*, January 21, 1997. Reprinted with permission.

QUESTIONS

1. By what percent has the price of Starbucks' stock market shares declined?

2. By what percent have new stores' revenues increased from 1990 to 1995?

3. The article gives information about the results of this year's fiscal first quarter compared to last year's fiscal first quarter.

   (a) What was last year's first quarter net income?
   (b) What was last year's first quarter revenue?

4. If it is true that "there are three billion cups of coffee drunk every day and 2.8 billion of them are rotten," what percent of cups of coffee are *not* rotten?

5. Think about coffee shops in your community. If you were going to take on a Starbucks franchise or open a competitive store, such as a Second Cup shop, where would you locate it? Give your reasons.

CASE STUDY 3.2 EXCHANGING ON THE GO

Colin and Paulo, two students from Windsor, decided to go to Florida for their spring break. They pooled their money and found that they had $800 Canadian between them. They converted the Canadian dollars into American dollars and set off for Florida. It cost them one quarter of their money supply to get there. After two days of rain, they decided to move on to Mexico. A quick check of their wallets showed that they had spent another $200 American. They converted their remaining American dollars into Mexican pesos. The weather was fine in Mexico and everything seemed much cheaper.

When it was time to head for home, Colin and Paulo found that they had spent 1500 of their pesos. They phoned home for more money. Their parents sent a wire for $300 Canadian. When they added this to their cash on hand, Colin and Paulo were able to pay the hotel bill of 1460 pesos. They converted their remaining Mexican pesos into American dollars. The trip home through the United States cost them $50 American.

QUESTIONS

1. The currency cross rates in Table 3.4 were in effect for the duration of Colin and Paulo's trip. Assume they converted their remaining American dollars into Canadian dollars when they returned to Windsor. How much money (in Canadian dollars) did Colin and Paulo have left when they got home?

TABLE 3.4 Currency cross rates

	C$	US$	DM	Yen	£	Fr. fr.	Sw. fr.	A$	M. Peso
Canadian $	...	1.36495	0.80573	0.01106	2.18528	0.23877	0.93650	1.08875	0.17127
U.S. $	0.73263	...	0.59030	0.00810	1.60100	0.17493	0.68611	0.79765	0.12548
Deutschmark	1.24111	1.69405	...	0.01373	2.71217	0.29634	1.16230	1.35126	0.21256
Japanese yen	90.40	123.39	72.83	...	197.54	21.58	84.66	98.42	15.4828
British pnd.	0.45761	0.62461	0.36871	0.00506	...	0.10926	0.42855	0.49822	0.07837
French franc	4.18807	5.71650	3.37446	0.04633	9.15212	...	3.92213	4.55977	0.71729
Swiss franc	1.06780	1.45750	0.86036	0.01181	2.33346	0.25496	...	1.16257	0.18288
Australian $	0.91848	1.25368	0.74005	0.01016	2.00715	0.21931	0.86016	...	0.15731
Mexican peso	5.8387	7.96953	4.70442	0.06458	12.7592	1.39411	5.46794	6.35688	...

SUMMARY OF FORMULAE

Formula 3.1A

PERCENTAGE = RATE × BASE   The basic percentage relationship

or

NEW NUMBER = RATE × ORIGINAL NUMBER

Formula 3.1B

$$\text{RATE} = \frac{\text{PERCENTAGE}}{\text{BASE}} \text{ or } \frac{\text{NEW NUMBER}}{\text{ORIGINAL NUMBER}}$$

Formula for finding the rate percent when comparing a number (the percentage) to another number (the base or original number)

Formula 3.2

$$\text{ORIGINAL NUMBER} = \begin{array}{c} +\text{INCREASE} \\ -\text{DECREASE} \end{array} = \begin{array}{c} \text{NEW} \\ \text{NUMBER} \end{array}$$

The relationship to use with problems of increase or decrease (problems of change)

Formula 3.3

$$\text{RATE OF CHANGE} = \frac{\text{AMOUNT OF CHANGE}}{\text{ORIGINAL NUMBER}}$$

Formula for finding the rate of change (rate of increase or decrease)

Formula 3.4

$$\text{REAL INCOME} = \frac{\text{INCOME IN CURRENT DOLLARS}}{\text{CONSUMER PRICE INDEX}}$$

Formula for eliminating the effect of inflation on income

GLOSSARY

Base period   in an index, the period of time against which comparisons are made. The base period is arbitrarily selected, but it always has an index number of 100.

Consumer Price Index (CPI)   the index that shows the price change for a sample of goods and services that is used to indicate the price change for all goods and services. In Canada, the base year is 1986.

Cross-multiplication   a shortcut for solving proportions

Equivalent ratios in higher terms   ratios obtained by multiplying each term of a ratio by the same number

Exchange rate   the value of one nation's currency expressed in terms of another nation's currency

Index number   expresses the relative change in the value of an item at different points in time. One of the points in time is a *base period*, which is always defined to have a value of 100.

Marginal tax rate   rate at which your next dollar of earned income is taxed. Marginal tax rates tend to increase as earnings increase.

Nominal income   income stated in current dollars

Personal income tax   taxes imposed by the federal and provincial governments on the earned income of Canadian residents

Proportion   a statement of equality between two ratios

Purchasing power of the dollar   the reciprocal of the *Consumer Price Index.*

Ratio   a comparison by division of the relative values of numbers or quantities

Real income   income stated in base-period dollars.

Terms of a ratio   the numbers appearing in a ratio

4 Linear Systems

Most manufacturing companies produce more than one product. In deciding the quantities of each product to produce, management has to take into account the combination of production levels that will make the most efficient use of labour, materials, and transportation, and produce the highest level of profit. Most companies have so many factors to consider that they need sophisticated methods of evaluation. However, many situations like this can be simplified and solved. Suppose you were in the business of producing serving knives, forks, and spoons. If you cannot produce all the items because of limited manufacturing capacity, you would need to consider the relative profitability of each item to determine which combination of items to produce. You can define the variables, set up a system of linear equations and inequalities, and solve the system by graphical or algebraic methods to decide how to best allocate your resources.

Introduction

In many types of problems, the relationship between two or more variables can be represented by setting up linear equations or linear inequalities. Graphic as well as algebraic techniques are available to solve such problems.

OBJECTIVES

Upon completing this chapter, you will be able to do the following:

1. Graph linear equations in two variables in a set of rectangular coordinates.
2. Define the slope-intercept form of a linear equation and use it for graphing.
3. Graph linear inequalities in two variables in a set of rectangular coordinates.
4. Graph linear systems consisting of two or three linear relations in two variables.
5. Solve linear systems consisting of two simultaneous equations in two variables using the method of elimination by addition or subtraction.
6. Solve linear systems consisting of three simultaneous equations in three variables using the method of elimination by addition or subtraction.
7. Solve problems by setting up systems of linear equations in two or three variables.

4.1   GRAPHING LINEAR EQUATIONS

A. Graphing in a system of rectangular coordinates

A system of rectangular coordinates, as shown in Figure 4.1 below, consists of two straight lines that intersect at right angles in a plane. The *horizontal* line is called the **X axis** while the *vertical* line is called the **Y axis**. The point of intersection of the two axes is called the **origin**.

FIGURE 4.1   Rectangular Coordinates

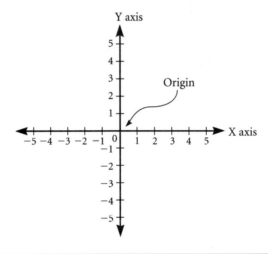

The two axes are used as number lines. By agreement, on the X axis the numbers are positive to the right of the origin and negative to the left. On the Y axis the numbers are positive above the origin and negative below the origin.

The position of any point relative to the pair of axes is defined by an *ordered pair* of numbers (x, y) such that the first number (the x value or x **coordinate**) always represents the directed distance of the point from the Y axis. The second number (the y value or y **coordinate**) always represents the directed distance of the point from the X axis.

The origin is identified by the ordered pair $(0, 0)$; that is, the coordinates of the origin are $(0, 0)$ since the distance of the point from either axis is zero.

As shown in Figure 4.2 on the next page, the point marked A is identified by the coordinates $(4, 3)$. That is, the directed distance of the point is four units to the right of the Y axis (its x value or x coordinate is $+4$), and the directed distance of the point is three units above the X axis (its y coordinate is $+3$). Note that the point may be found by counting four units to the right along the X axis and then moving three units up parallel to the Y axis.

FIGURE 4.2 **Locating a Point**

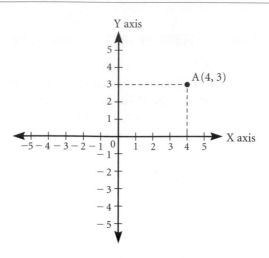

EXAMPLE 4.1A Determine the coordinates of the points A, B, C, D, E, F, G, and H as marked in the following diagram.

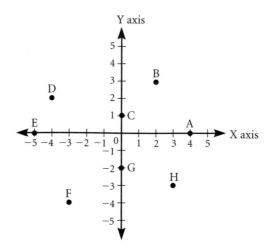

Solution

POINT		COORDINATES
A	$(4, 0)$	4 units to the right of the origin ($x = 4$) on the X axis ($y = 0$)
B	$(2, 3)$	2 units to the right ($x = 2$) and 3 units up ($y = 3$)
C	$(0, 1)$	on the Y axis ($x = 0$) 1 unit up ($y = 1$)
D	$(-4, 2)$	4 units to the left ($x = -4$) and 2 units up ($y = 2$)
E	$(-5, 0)$	5 units to the left ($x = -5$) on the X axis ($y = 0$)
F	$(-3, -4)$	3 units to the left ($x = -3$) and 4 units down ($y = -4$)
G	$(0, -2)$	on the Y axis ($x = 0$) 2 units down ($y = -2$)
H	$(3, -3)$	3 units to the right ($x = 3$) and 3 units down ($y = -3$)

To draw the graphs of linear relations, you must plot two or more points in a set of rectangular axes. To *plot* point (x, y), count the number of units represented by x along the X axis (to the right if x is positive, to the left if x is negative) and then count the number of units represented by y up or down (up if y is positive, down if y is negative).

EXAMPLE 4.1B

Plot the following points in a set of rectangular axes.

(i) $A(-3, 4)$

(ii) $B(2, -4)$

(iii) $C(-4, -4)$

(iv) $D(3, 3)$

(v) $E(-3, 0)$

(vi) $F(0, -2)$

Solution

(i) To plot point A, count 3 units to the left (x is negative) and 4 units up (y is positive).

(ii) To plot point B, count 2 units to the right (x is positive) and 4 units down (y is negative).

(iii) To plot point C, count 4 units to the left and 4 units down.

(iv) To plot point D, count 3 units to the right and 3 units up.

(v) To plot point E, count 3 units to the left and mark the point on the X axis since $y = 0$.

(vi) To plot point F, count 2 units down and mark the point on the Y axis since $x = 0$.

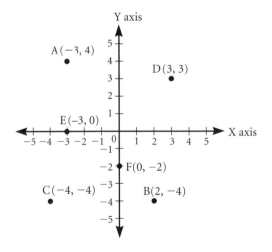

B. Constructing a table of values

To graph linear equations, plot a set of points whose coordinates *satisfy* the equation and then join the points.

A suitable set of points may be obtained by constructing a table of values. Substitute arbitrarily chosen values of x or y in the equation and compute the value of the second variable. The chosen value and the corresponding computed value form an ordered pair (x, y). A listing of such ordered pairs forms a table of values.

EXAMPLE 4.1C

Construct a table of values for

(i) $x = 2y$ for integral values of y from $y = +3$ to $y = -3$;

(ii) $y = 2x - 3$ for integral values of x from $x = -2$ to $x = +4$.

Solution

(i) To obtain the desired ordered pairs, substitute assumed values of y into the equation $x = 2y$.

$$
\begin{array}{ll}
y = +3 & x = 2(3) = 6 \\
y = +2 & x = 2(2) = 4 \\
y = +1 & x = 2(1) = 2 \\
y = 0 & x = 2(0) = 0 \\
y = -1 & x = 2(-1) = -2 \\
y = -2 & x = 2(-2) = -4 \\
y = -3 & x = 2(-3) = -6
\end{array}
$$

Listing the obtained ordered pairs gives the following table of values.

Table of values

x	6	4	2	0	−2	−4	−6
y	3	2	1	0	−1	−2	−3

— corresponding computed x values

— chosen y values

(ii) To obtain the desired ordered pairs, substitute assumed values of x into the equation $y = 2x - 3$.

$$
\begin{array}{ll}
x = -2 & y = 2(-2) - 3 = -4 - 3 = -7 \\
x = -1 & y = 2(-1) - 3 = -2 - 3 = -5 \\
x = 0 & y = 2(0) - 3 = 0 - 3 = -3 \\
x = 1 & y = 2(1) - 3 = 2 - 3 = -1 \\
x = 2 & y = 2(2) - 3 = 4 - 3 = +1 \\
x = 3 & y = 2(3) - 3 = 6 - 3 = +3 \\
x = 4 & y = 2(4) - 3 = 8 - 3 = +5
\end{array}
$$

Table of values

x	−2	−1	0	1	2	3	4
y	−7	−5	−3	−1	1	3	5

— chosen x values

— corresponding computed y values

Guidelines for constructing a table of values
1. Values may be chosen arbitrarily for either x or y.
2. The values chosen are usually integers.
3. Integers that yield an integer for the computed value are preferred.

EXAMPLE 4.1D Construct a table of values for the equation $3x - 2y = -3$. It should consist of five ordered pairs (x, y) such that x and y are integers.

Solution

(i) $y = 0$
$$3x - 2(0) = -3$$
$$3x = -3$$
$$x = -1$$

(ii) $x = 1$
$$3(1) - 2y = -3$$
$$-2y = -6$$
$$y = 3$$

(iii) $y = -3$
$$3x - 2(-3) = -3$$
$$3x = -9$$
$$x = -3$$

(iv) $x = 3$
$$3(3) - 2y = -3$$
$$-2y = -12$$
$$y = 6$$

(v) $x = -5$
$$3(-5) - 2y = -3$$
$$-2y = 12$$
$$y = -6$$

Table of values

x	-5	-3	-1	1	3
y	-6	-3	0	3	6

C. Graphing linear equations

To graph a linear equation, you need a minimum of two points. A third point is useful for checking purposes. To graph linear equations,
(1) *construct* a table of values consisting of at least two (preferably three) ordered pairs (x, y);
(2) *plot* the points in a system of rectangular axes;
(3) *join* the points by a straight line.

EXAMPLE 4.1E Graph each of the following equations.

(i) $x + y = 4$

(ii) $x - y = 5$

(iii) $4x + 3y = 12$

(iv) $2x - 3y = -6$

(v) $x = y$

(vi) $y = -2x$

Solution

(i) Equation: $x + y = 4$

Table of values

x	0	4	2
y	4	0	2

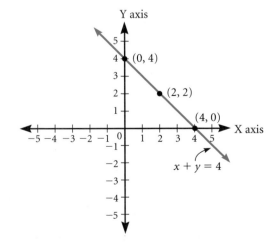

(ii) Equation: $x - y = 5$

Table of values

x	0	5	3
y	−5	0	−2

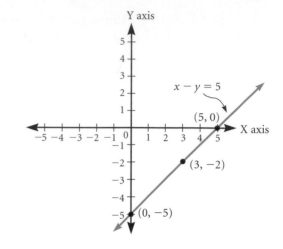

(iii) Equation: $4x + 3y = 12$

Table of values

x	0	3	6
y	4	0	−4

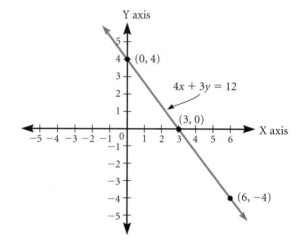

(iv) Equation: $2x - 3y = -6$

Table of values

x	0	−3	3
y	2	0	4

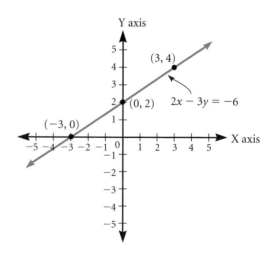

(v) Equation: $x = y$

Table of values

x	0	3	−3
y	0	3	−3

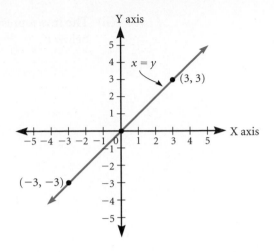

(vi) Equation: $y = -2x$

Table of values

x	0	2	−2
y	0	−4	4

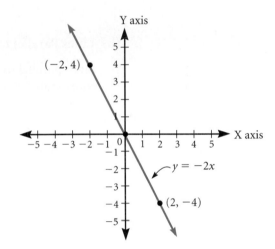

D. Special cases – lines parallel to the axes

(a) **Lines Parallel to the X axis**

Lines parallel to the X axis are formed by sets of points that all have the *same y* coordinates. Such lines are defined by the equation $y = b$ where b is any real number.

EXAMPLE 4.1F

Graph the lines represented by

(i) $y = 3$ (ii) $y = -3$

Solution

(i) The line represented by $y = 3$ is a line parallel to the X axis and three units above it.

(ii) The line represented by $y = -3$ is a line parallel to the X axis and three units below it.

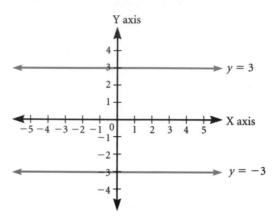

(b) **Lines Parallel to the Y axis**

Lines parallel to the Y axis are formed by sets of points that all have the same x coordinates. Such lines are defined by the equation $x = a$ where a is any real number.

EXAMPLE 4.1G

Graph the lines represented by

(i) $x = 3$ (ii) $x = -3$

Solution

(i) The line represented by $x = 3$ is a line parallel to the Y axis and three units to the right of it.

(ii) The line represented by $x = -3$ is a line parallel to the Y axis and three units to the left of it.

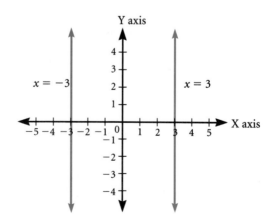

(c) **The Axes**

X axis The *y* coordinates of the set of points forming the X axis are zero. Thus the equation $y = 0$ represents the X axis.

Y axis The *x* coordinates of the set of points forming the Y axis are zero. Thus the equation $x = 0$ represents the Y axis.

E. The slope-intercept form of a linear equation

Every line has two important characteristics: its steepness, called the **slope**, and a point where the line intersects with the Y axis, called the **y-intercept**.

In more technical terms, **slope** is the ratio of the *rise* of a line to its *run*. The **rise** of a line is the distance along the Y axis between two points on a line. The **run** of a line is the distance along the X axis between the same two points on the line.

As shown in Figure 4.3 below, point A(1, 3) and point B(2, 1) lie on the line $2x + y = 5$. The *rise* between point A and point B is -2, since you must move 2 units down, parallel to the Y axis, when you move from point A to point B. The *run* between point A and point B is $+1$, since you must move 1 unit to the right, parallel to the X axis, when you move from point A to point B. The ratio $^{rise}/_{run}$ is $^{-2}/_{1}$, or -2.

FIGURE 4.3

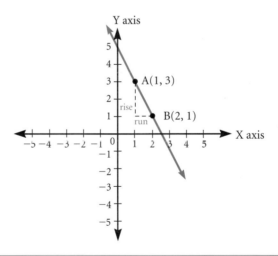

Notice that the slope of a line remains the same if you go from point B to point A. In the example above, the rise from point B to point A is 2 units up, or $+2$. The run is 1 unit to the left, or -1. The ratio $^{rise}/_{run}$ is $^{-2}/_{1}$, or -2, the same as was shown earlier.

For any straight line, the slope is the same for *any* two points on the line because a line has a constant steepness. Figure 4.4 shows an example of one line having a positive slope and another line having a negative slope.

FIGURE 4.4

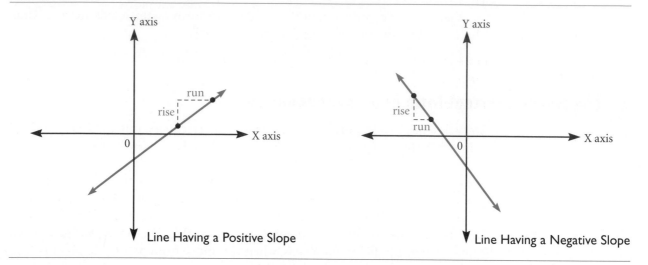

Line Having a Positive Slope

Line Having a Negative Slope

We know from Figure 4.3 that the slope of the line representing $2x + y = 5$ is -2. By rearranging the terms of this equation, we see that the equation of this line can be written $y = -2x + 5$. We say the line's equation is in the form $y = mx + b$. When a linear equation is in this form, it is easy to see that m, the coefficient of x, represents the slope of the line, which is -2 (or $^{-2}/_1$ or $^2/_{-1}$).

By substituting $x = 0$ into $y = -2x + 5$, we find that $y = 5$. You can see that the line $y = -2x + 5$ crosses the Y axis at the point $(0, 5)$ in Figure 4.3. In the linear equation $y = mx + b$, b is the y-intercept of the line.

The **slope-intercept form of a linear equation** is a linear equation expressed in the form $y = mx + b$.

$$\boxed{y = mx + b}$$ ———————————————— Formula 4.1

In any equation in the form $y = mx + b$, m is the slope and b is the y-intercept.

EXAMPLE 4.1H

Using algebra, find the slope and y-intercept of each of the following equations.

(i) $y = \dfrac{2}{3}x - 7$

(ii) $3x + 4y = -2$

Solution

(i) $y = \dfrac{2}{3}x - 7$ is already in the form $y = mx + b$.

Thus, slope $= ^2/_3$, since $m = ^2/_3$ in the equation $y = \dfrac{2}{3}x - 7$.

The y-intercept $= -7$, since $b = -7$ in the equation $y = \dfrac{2}{3}x - 7$.

(ii) $3x + 4y = -2$ must be expressed in the form $y = mx + b$.

$-3x + 3x + 4y = -3x - 2$ ———————— add $-3x$ to each side

$4y = -3x - 2$ ———————— simplify

$y = -\dfrac{3}{4}x - \dfrac{1}{2}$ ———————— slope-intercept form

Thus, slope $= -3/4$, since $m = -3/4$ in the equation $y = -\dfrac{3}{4}x - \dfrac{1}{2}$.

The y-intercept $= -1/2$, since $b = -1/2$ in the equation $y = -\dfrac{3}{4}x - \dfrac{1}{2}$.

Once you have found m and b, you can use the slope and y-intercept to graph a linear equation.

1. Graph the y-intercept, which is the point $(0, b)$.
2. Find another point on the line by using the slope. Beginning at the y-intercept, move up (if positive) or down (if negative) by the number of units in the rise (the numerator of the slope). Then move right (if positive) or left (if negative) by the number of units in the run (the denominator of the slope), and mark this point.
3. Draw a line through the point you just marked and the y-intercept to represent the linear equation.

EXAMPLE 4.11

Given the linear equation $6x + 2y = 8$,

(i) rearrange the equation into the slope-intercept form;

(ii) determine the values of m and b;

(iii) graph the equation.

Solution

(i)
$$6x + 2y = 8$$
$$-6x + 6x + 2y = -6x + 8 \quad\text{——— add } -6x \text{ to each side}$$
$$2y = -6x + 8 \quad\text{——— simplify}$$
$$y = -3x + 4 \quad\text{——— slope-intercept form}$$

(ii) $m = -3, b = 4$

(iii) Since $b = 4$, the y-intercept is 4, which is represented by the point $(0, 4)$. Since $m = -3$ (or $-3/1$), plot a second point on the graph by beginning at the point $(0, 4)$ and moving 3 units down and 1 unit to the right. (You could also move 3 units up and 1 unit to the left if you consider $m = -3$ to be $m = 3/-1$.) Draw the line that passes through these two points, as shown below.

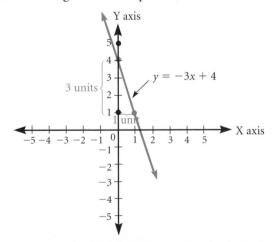

F. Special cases of the slope-intercept form of a linear equation

1. Lines Parallel to the X Axis

Recall from Section 4.1D that lines parallel to the X axis are defined by the equation $y = b$, where b is any real number. Since there is no mx in the equation $y = b$, the linear equation $y = b$ represents a line parallel to the X axis that crosses the Y axis at point b and has a slope of 0.

FIGURE 4.5

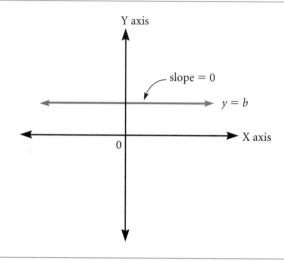

2. Lines Parallel to the Y Axis

Recall from Section 4.1D that lines parallel to the Y axis are defined by the equation $x = a$, where a is any real number. Since there is no y in the equation $x = a$, it cannot be expressed in the form $y = mx + b$. The equation $x = a$ represents a line parallel to the Y axis that crosses the X axis at point $(a, 0)$. Its slope is undefined.

FIGURE 4.6

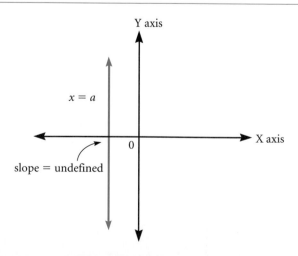

Exercise 4.1

A. Do each of the following.

1. Write the coordinates of the points A, B, C, D, E, F, G, and H marked in the diagram below.

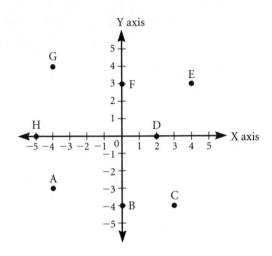

2. Plot the given sets of points in a system of rectangular axes.

(a) $A(-4, -5)$, $B(3, -2)$, $C(-3, 5)$, $D(0, -4)$, $E(4, 1)$, $F(-2, 0)$
(b) $K(4, -2)$, $L(-3, 2)$, $M(0, 4)$, $N(-2, -4)$, $P(0, -5)$, $Q(-3, 0)$

3. Construct a table of values for each of the following equations as shown.

(a) $x = y - 2$ for integral values of y from -3 to $+5$
(b) $y = 2x - 1$ for integral values of x from $+3$ to -2
(c) $y = 2x$ for integral values of x from $+3$ to -3
(d) $x = -y$ for integral values of y from $+5$ to -5

4. Using algebra, find the slope and y-intercept of the lines represented by each of the following equations.

(a) $4x + 5y = 11$
(b) $2y - 5x = 10$
(c) $1 - \frac{1}{2}y = 2x$
(d) $3y + 6 = 0$
(e) $\sqrt{2x - y} = 3$
(f) $0.15x + 0.3y - 0.12 = 0$
(g) $2 - \frac{1}{2}x = 0$
(h) $(x - 2)(y + 1) - xy = 2$

B. Graph each of the following equations.

1. $x - y = 3$
2. $x + 2y = 4$

3. $y = -x$
4. $x = 2y$

5. $3x - 4y - 12$
6. $2x + 3y = 6$

7. $y = -4$
8. $x = 5$

9. $y = 2x - 3$
10. $y = -3x + 9$

4.2   GRAPHING INEQUALITIES

A. Basic concepts and method

A straight line drawn in a plane divides the plane into two regions:

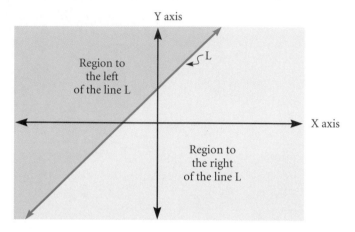

(a) the region to the left of the line drawn in the plane;
(b) the region to the right of the line drawn in the plane.

When a system of axes is introduced into the plane, each region consists of a set of points that may be represented by ordered pairs (x, y). Relative to the dividing line, the two sets of ordered pairs (x, y) that represent the points in the regions are defined by the two **inequalities** associated with the equation of the dividing line.

For the equation $x = 5$, the associated inequalities are $x < 5$ (x is less than 5) and $x > 5$ (x is greater than 5). For the equation $y = -3$, the associated inequalities are $y < -3$ and $y > -3$. For the equation $2x + 3y = 6$, the associated inequalities are $2x + 3y < 6$ and $2x + 3y > 6$.

Graphing an inequality means identifying the region that consists of the set of points whose coordinates satisfy the given inequality. To identify this region, use the following method.

1. *Draw* the graph of the equation associated with the inequality.
2. *Test* an arbitrarily selected point that is not a point on the line by substituting its coordinates in the inequality. The preferred point for testing is $(0, 0)$. If $(0, 0)$ is not available because the line passes through the origin, try the points $(0, 1)$ or $(1, 0)$.
3. (a) If substituting the coordinates of the selected point in the inequality yields a mathematical statement that is true, the selected point is a point in the region defined by the inequality. Thus, the region is identified as the area containing the selected point.
   (b) If substituting the coordinates of the selected point in the inequality yields a mathematical statement that is false, the selected point is not a point in the region defined by the inequality. Thus, the region defined by the inequality is the area that does not contain the point tested.

B. Graphing inequalities of the form $ax + by > c$ and $ax + by < c$

EXAMPLE 4.2A

Graph each of the following inequalities.

(i) $x - y > -3$

(ii) $3x + 2y < -8$

Solution

(i) The equation associated with the inequality $x - y > -3$ is $x - y = -3$.

Table of values

x	0	−3	2
y	3	0	5

Note: To show that the coordinates of the points on the line $x - y = -3$ do not satisfy the inequality, the graph of the equation is drawn as a broken line.

Since the line does not pass through the origin, the point $(0, 0)$ may be used for testing.

$$\text{Substituting } x = 0 \text{ and } y = 0 \text{ in the}$$
$$\text{inequality } x - y > -3 \text{ yields the statement}$$
$$0 - 0 > -3$$
$$0 > -3$$

Since the statement $0 > -3$ is true, the point $(0, 0)$ is a point in the region. The region defined by the inequality $x - y > -3$ is the area to the right of the line as shown in the diagram below.

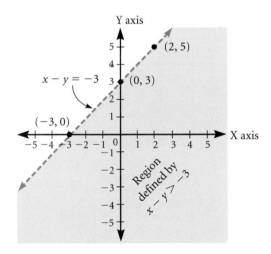

(ii) The equation associated with the inequality $3x + 2y < -8$ is $3x + 2y = -8$.

Table of values

x	0	−2	−4
y	−4	−1	2

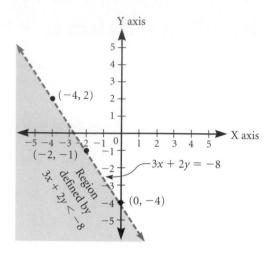

Testing the point $(0, 0)$

$$3(0) + 2(0) < -8$$
$$0 + 0 < -8$$
$$0 < -8$$

Since the statement $0 < -8$ is false, the point $(0, 0)$ is not a point in the region defined by $3x + 2y < -8$. The region defined by the inequality is the area to the left of the line as shown.

C. Graphing inequalities of the form $ax > by$ or $ax < by$

EXAMPLE 4.2B   Graph each of the following inequalities.

(i) $y \leq -x$ (ii) $3x < 2y$

Solution   (i) The equation associated with the inequality $y \leq -x$ is $y = -x$.

Table of values

x	0	3	-3
y	0	-3	3

Note: The inequality includes $y = -x$. Because the points on the line meet the condition stated, the graph of the equation is drawn as a solid line.

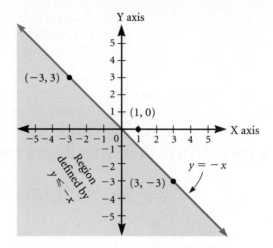

Since the line passes through the origin, the point $(0, 0)$ cannot be used for testing. Instead, we test $(1, 0)$.

Substituting $x = 1, y = 0$ in the
inequality $y < -x$ yields the statement
$$0 < -1$$

Since the statement $0 < -1$ is false, the point $(1, 0)$ is not a point in the region defined by $y \leq -x$. The region defined by the inequality is the area to the left of the line *including* the line.

(ii) The equation associated with the inequality $3x < 2y$ is $3x = 2y$.

Table of values

x	0	2	−2
y	0	3	−3

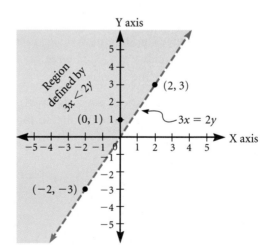

Since $(0, 0)$ is on the line, test $(0, 1)$.
Substituting $x = 0, y = 1$ in the
inequality $3x < 2y$ yields the statement
$$0 < 2$$

Since the statement $0 < 2$ is true, the point $(0, 1)$ is a point in the region defined by $3x < 2y$. The region defined by the inequality is the area to the left of the line as shown.

D. Graphing inequalities involving lines parallel to the axes

EXAMPLE 4.2C Graph each of the following inequalities.

(i) $x < 3$ (ii) $y \geq -3$

Solution (i) The equation associated with the inequality $x < 3$ is $x = 3$. The graph of $x = 3$ is a line parallel to the Y axis three units to the right.

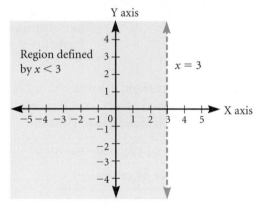

Test $(0, 0)$. Substituting $x = 0$ in the
inequality $x < 3$ yields the statement
$$0 < 3$$

Since the statement $0 < 3$ is true, $(0, 0)$ is a point in the region defined by the inequality $x < 3$. The region defined by the inequality is the region to the left of the line as shown.

(ii) The equation associated with the inequality $y \geq -3$ is $y = -3$. The graph of $y = -3$ is a line parallel to the X axis three units below it.

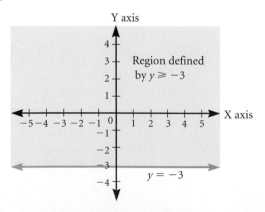

Test $(0, 0)$. Substituting $y = 0$ in the
inequality $y > -3$ yields the statement
$$0 > -3$$

Since the statement $0 > -3$ is true, $(0, 0)$ is a point in the region defined by
$y \geq -3$. The region defined by the inequality is the area above the line as shown.

Exercise 4.2

A. Graph each of the following inequalities.

1. $x + y > 4$

2. $x - y < -2$

3. $x - 2y \leq 4$

4. $3x - 2y \geq -10$

5. $2x < -3y$

6. $4y \geq 3x$

7. $x \geq -2$

8. $y < 5$

4.3 GRAPHING LINEAR SYSTEMS

A. Graphing systems of equations in two unknowns

Systems that consist of two linear equations in two variables may be solved by
drawing the graph of each equation. The graph of the system (or solution) is the
point where the two lines representing the equations intersect.

EXAMPLE 4.3A   Graph the linear system $x + y = 5$ and $x - y = 3$.

Solution

Table of values
for $x + y - 5$

x	0	5	2
y	5	0	3

Table of values
for $x - y = 3$

x	0	3	2
y	-3	0	-1

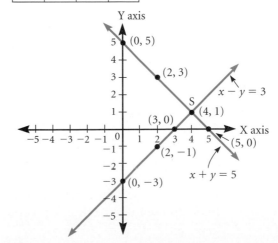

The graph of the system is S, the point of intersection of the two lines, whose coordinates apparently are (4, 1). The coordinates (4, 1) satisfy the equation of either line and are called the *solution* of the system.

EXAMPLE 4.3B   Graph the system $x = -2y$ and $y = 3$.

Solution

Table of values
for $x = -2y$

x	0	−4	4
y	0	2	−2

The graph of $y = 3$ is a line parallel to the X axis three units above it.

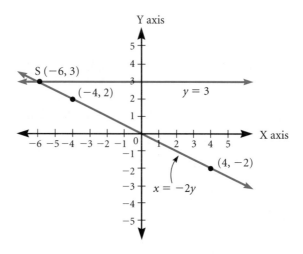

The graph of the system is S, the point of intersection of the two lines. The coordinates of S are apparently $(-6, 3)$ and represent the solution of the system.

EXAMPLE 4.3C   Graph the triangle formed by $3x + 4y = 12$, $3x + 2y = 0$, and $x = 2$.

Solution

Table of values
for $3x + 4y = 12$

x	0	4	−4
y	3	0	6

Table of values
for $3x + 2y = 0$

x	0	2	−2
y	0	−3	3

As shown in the diagram, the triangle ABC is formed by the intersection of pairs of lines representing the three equations.

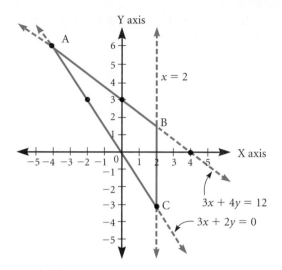

B. Graphing systems of linear inequalities

Systems consisting of two or more linear inequalities in two variables can be drawn by graphing each of the inequalities in the system. The graph of the system is the region *common* to all inequalities.

EXAMPLE 4.3D

Graph the region defined by $x > -2$ and $y > x - 3$.

Solution

The equation associated with the inequality $x > -2$ is $x = -2$. The graph of $x = -2$ is a line parallel to the Y axis and two units to the left of it. The substitution of 0 for x yields the true statement $0 > -2$. The point $(0, 0)$ is a point in the region defined by $x > -2$. The region defined by the inequality is the area to the right of the line.

The equation associated with the inequality $y > x - 3$ is $y = x - 3$. The graph of $y = x - 3$ is a line passing through the points $(3, 0)$ and $(0, -3)$. The substitution of $x = 0$ and $y = 0$ yields the statement $0 > 0 - 3$, or $0 > -3$. Since this statement is true, the point $(0, 0)$ is a point in the region defined by the inequality $y > x - 3$. The region defined by the inequality is the area to the left of the line $y = x - 3$.

The region defined by the two inequalities is the area formed by the intersection of the two regions. The common region is shown in the diagram.

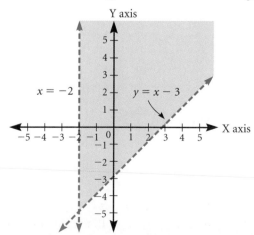

EXAMPLE 4.3E   Graph the region defined by $y \geq 0$, $4x + 5y \leq 20$, and $4x - 3y \geq -12$.

Solution   The equation associated with the inequality $y \geq 0$ is $y = 0$. The graph of $y = 0$ is the X axis. The region defined by the inequality $y \geq 0$ is the area above the X axis and includes the points forming the X axis.

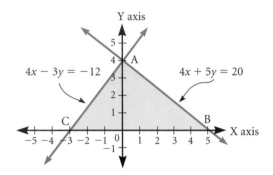

The equation associated with the inequality $4x + 5y \leq 20$ is $4x + 5y = 20$. The graph of the equation is the line passing through the points A(0, 4) and B(5, 0). The true statement $0 < 20$ shows that the origin is a point in the region defined by the inequality. The region defined by $4x + 5y \leq 20$ is the area to the left of the line and includes the line itself.

The equation associated with the inequality $4x - 3y \geq -12$ is $4x - 3y = -12$. The graph of this equation is the line passing through the points A(0, 4) and C(-3, 0). The true statement $0 > -12$ shows that the origin is a point in the region defined by the inequality. The region defined by $4x - 3y \geq -12$ is the area to the right of the line, including the line itself.

The region defined by the three inequalities is the area formed by the intersection of the three regions. It is the triangle ABC shown in the diagram.

Exercise 4.3

A. Solve each of the following linear systems graphically.

1. $x + y = 4$ and $x - y = -4$

2. $x - y = 3$ and $x + y = 5$

3. $x = 2y - 1$ and $y = 4 - 3x$

4. $2x + 3y = 10$ and $3x - 4y = -2$

5. $3x - 4y = 18$ and $2y = -3x$

6. $4x = -5y$ and $2x + y = 6$

7. $5x - 2y = 20$ and $y = 5$

8. $3y = -5x$ and $x = -3$

B. Graph the triangle formed by the following sets of equations.

1. $x = y, x = 4$, and $y = 0$

2. $y = -2x, y = 4$, and $x = 2$

3. $3x + 4y = 12, x = 0$, and $y = 0$

4. $x + y = -5, x - y = -5$, and $x = -2$

C. Graph the region defined by each of the following linear systems.

1. $y < 3$ and $x + y > 2$

2. $x - 2y < 4$ and $x > -3$

3. $3x - y \leq 6$ and $x + 2y > 8$

4. $5x > -3y$ and $2x - 5y \geq 10$

5. $2y - 3x \leq 9, x \leq 3$, and $y \geq 0$

6. $2x + y \leq 6, x \geq 0$, and $y \geq 0$

7. $y \geq -3x, y \leq 3$, and $2x - y \leq 6$

8. $2x \leq y, x \geq -3y$, and $x - 2y \geq -6$

4.4 ALGEBRAIC SOLUTION OF SYSTEMS OF LINEAR EQUATIONS IN TWO VARIABLES

A. Basic concept

Any linear system that consists of two equations in two variables can be solved graphically, as illustrated in Section 4.3. However, more efficient techniques are available. One of these techniques is based on eliminating one of the two variables from the system by addition or subtraction. This method is explained and illustrated in this text.

Solving a system of two equations requires finding a pair of values for the two variables that satisfies each of the two equations. The value of one of the two variables can be determined by first reducing the system of equations to one equation in one variable and solving this equation. The value of the variable obtained is then substituted into one of the original equations to find the value of the second variable.

Graphic and algebraic solution of systems of linear equations in two variables is used extensively when doing break-even analysis. Break-even analysis is explored further in Chapter 5.

B. Solving a system of two linear equations by addition or subtraction

If the coefficients of one variable are the *same* in both equations, the system can be reduced to one equation by addition or subtraction as follows.

(a) If the coefficients are numerically equal but opposite in sign, addition will eliminate the variable.

(b) If the coefficients are numerically equal and have the same sign, subtraction can eliminate the variable. Alternatively, one equation can be multiplied by -1; addition can then be used.

EXAMPLE 4.4A   Solve each of the following systems of equations.

(i) $x + y = 1$
    $x - y = 7$

(ii) $5x + 4y = 7$
    $3x - 4y = 17$

(iii) $2x + 3y = -2$
    $2x - 5y = -34$

(iv) $x - 3y = 2$
    $4x - 3y = -10$

Solution

(i) $x + y = 1$ ———————————— equation ①

        $x - y = 7$ ———————————— equation ②

       $2x\quad = 8$ ———————————— add ① and ② to eliminate y

           $x = 4$ *Note:* The coefficient of y in ① is 1; the coefficient of y in ② is -1. Since the coefficients are the same but opposite in sign, adding the two equations will eliminate the term in y.

     $4 + y = 1$ ———————————— substitute the value of x in ①

         $y = -3$

$\boxed{x = 4, y = -3}$ ———————————— **solution**

Check

in ① LS $= 4 + (-3) = 4 - 3 = 1$

      RS $= 1$

in ② LS $= 4 - (-3) = 4 + 3 = 7$

      RS $= 7$

(ii) $5x + 4y = 7$ ———————————— equation ①

       $3x - 4y = 17$ ———————————— equation ②

       $8x\quad = 24$ ———————————— add ① and ② to eliminate y

          $x = 3$

    $5(3) + 4y = 7$ ———————————— substitute 3 for x in ①

      $15 + 4y = 7$

            $4y = -8$

             $y = -2$

$\boxed{x = 3, y = -2}$ ———————————— **solution**

Check
in ① LS $= 5(3) + 4(-2) = 15 - 8 = 7$
　　RS $= 7$
in ② LS $= 3(3) - 4(-2) = 9 + 8 = 17$
　　RS $= 17$

(iii)　$2x + 3y = -2$ ————————— equation ①
　　　$\underline{2x - 5y = -34}$ ————————— equation ②

　　　　　$8y = 32$ ————————— subtract ② from ① to eliminate x
　　　　　　$y = 4$
　　　$2x + 3(4) = -2$ ————————— substitute 4 for y in ①
　　　$2x + 12 = -2$
　　　　　　$2x = -14$
　　　　　　　$x = -7$

$\boxed{x = -7, y = 4}$ ————————— **solution**

Check
in ① LS $= 2(-7) + 3(4) = -14 + 12 = -2$
　　RS $= -2$
in ② LS $= 2(-7) - 5(4) = -14 - 20 = -34$
　　RS $= -34$

(iv)　　$x - 3y = 2$ ————————— ①
　　　$4x - 3y = -10$ ————————— ②

　　　$-4x + 3y = 10$ ————————— ② multiplied by -1 to set up addition
　　　　$\underline{x - 3y = 2}$ ————————— ①
　　　　　$-3x = 12$ ————————— add
　　　　　　$x = -4$
　　　$-4 - 3y = 2$ ————————— substitute -4 for x in ①
　　　　　$-3y = 6$
　　　　　　$y = -2$

$\boxed{x = -4, y = -2}$ ————————— **solution**

Check
in ① LS $= -4 - 3(-2) = -4 + 6 = 2$
　　RS $= 2$
in ② LS $= 4(-4) - 3(-2) = -16 + 6 = -10$
　　RS $= -10$

C. Solving a system of two linear equations when the coefficients are not numerically equal

Sometimes numerical equality of one pair of coefficients must be *created* before addition or subtraction can be used to eliminate a variable. This equality is usually achieved by multiplying one or both equations by a number or numbers that make the coefficients of the variable to be eliminated numerically equal.

EXAMPLE 4.4B

Solve each of the following systems of equations.

(i) $x - 3y = -12$
$3x + y = -6$

(ii) $x + 4y = 18$
$2x + 5y = 24$

(iii) $3x - 4y = 8$
$4x + 5y = 21$

(iv) $6x - 5y + 70 = 0$
$4x = 3y - 44$

Solution

(i) $x - 3y = -12$ —————————— ①
$3x + y = -6$ —————————— ②

To eliminate the term in y, multiply equation ② by 3.

$9x + 3y = -18$ —————————— ② multiplied by 3
$x - 3y = -12$ —————————— ①
$10x\quad = -30$ —————————— add
$x = -3$

$-3 - 3y = -12$ —————————— substitute -3 for x in ①
$-3y = -9$
$y = 3$

$\boxed{x = -3, y = 3}$ ————————— **solution**

(ii) $x + 4y = 18$ —————————— ①
$2x + 5y = 24$ —————————— ②

To eliminate the term in x, multiply ① by 2.

$2x + 8y = 36$ —————————— ① multiplied by 2
$-2x - 5y = -24$ —————————— ② multiplied by -1 to set up addition
$3y = 12$ —————————— add
$y = 4$
$x + 4(4) = 18$ —————————— substitute 4 for y in ①
$x + 16 = 18$
$x = 2$

$\boxed{x = 2, y = 4}$ ————————— **solution**

(iii) $3x - 4y = 8$ —————————— ①
$4x + 5y = 21$ —————————— ②

To eliminate the term in y, multiply ① by 5 and ② by 4.

$15x - 20y = 40$ —————————— ① multiplied by 5
$16x + 20y = 84$ —————————— ② multiplied by 4
$31x\quad = 124$ —————————— add
$x = 4$

$$4(4) + 5y = 21 \quad \text{———————— substitute 4 for } x \text{ in ②}$$
$$16 + 5y = 21$$
$$5y = 5$$
$$y = 1$$

$$\boxed{x = 4, y = 1} \quad \text{———————— solution}$$

(iv) $6x - 5y + 70 = 0$ ———————— ①
$\underline{4x = 3y - 44}$ ———————— ②

Rearrange the two equations in the same order.

$6x - 5y = -70$ ———————— ①
$\underline{4x - 3y = -44}$ ———————— ②

To eliminate the term in y, multiply ① by 3 and ② by -5.

$18x - 15y = -210$ ———————— ① multiplied by 3
$\underline{-20x + 15y = 220}$ ———————— ② multiplied by -5
$-2x \qquad = 10$ ———————— add
$x = -5$
$6(-5) - 5y = -70$ ———————— substitute -5 for x in ①
$-30 - 5y = -70$
$-5y = -40$
$y = 8$

$$\boxed{x = -5, y = 8} \quad \text{———————— solution}$$

D. Solving linear systems in two variables involving fractions

When one or both equations contain decimal fractions or common fractions, it is best to eliminate the fractions by multiplying; then solve the system as shown in the previous examples.

EXAMPLE 4.4C   Solve each of the following systems of equations.

(i) $1.5x + 0.8y = 1.2$
$0.7x + 1.2y = -4.4$

(ii) $\dfrac{5x}{6} + \dfrac{3y}{8} = -1$

$\dfrac{2x}{3} - \dfrac{3y}{4} = -5$

Solution   (i) $1.5x + 0.8y = 1.2$ ———————— ①
$\underline{0.7x + 1.2y = -4.4}$ ———————— ②

To eliminate the decimals, multiply each equation by 10.

$$15x + 8y = 12 \qquad\qquad\qquad ③$$
$$7x + 12y = -44 \qquad\qquad\qquad ④$$

To eliminate the term in y, multiply ③ by 3 and ④ by 2.

$$45x + 24y = 36 \qquad\qquad\qquad ③ \text{ multiplied by 3}$$
$$14x + 24y = -88 \qquad\qquad\qquad ④ \text{ multiplied by 2}$$
$$31x \qquad\quad = 124 \qquad\qquad\qquad \text{subtract}$$
$$x = 4$$
$$15(4) + 8y = 12 \qquad\qquad\qquad \text{substitute 4 for } x \text{ in } ③$$
$$60 + 8y = 12$$
$$8y = -48$$
$$y = -6$$

$$\boxed{x = 4, y = -6} \qquad\qquad\qquad \textbf{solution}$$

(ii)
$$\frac{5x}{6} + \frac{3y}{8} = -1 \qquad\qquad\qquad ①$$
$$\frac{2x}{3} - \frac{3y}{4} = -5 \qquad\qquad\qquad ②$$

To eliminate the fractions, multiply ① by 24 and ② by 12.

$$\frac{24(5x)}{6} + \frac{24(3y)}{8} = 24(-1) \qquad\qquad ① \text{ multiplied by 24}$$
$$4(5x) + 3(3y) = -24$$
$$20x + 9y = -24 \qquad\qquad\qquad ③$$
$$\frac{12(2x)}{3} - \frac{12(3y)}{4} = 12(-5) \qquad\qquad ② \text{ multiplied by 12}$$
$$4(2x) - 3(3y) = -60$$
$$8x - 9y = -60 \qquad\qquad\qquad ④$$

To eliminate the term in y, add ③ and ④.

$$20x + 9y = -24 \qquad\qquad\qquad ③$$
$$8x - 9y = -60 \qquad\qquad\qquad ④$$
$$28x = -84$$
$$x = -3$$
$$20(-3) + 9y = -24 \qquad\qquad\qquad \text{substitute } -3 \text{ for } x \text{ in } ③$$
$$-60 + 9y = -24$$
$$9y = 36$$
$$y = 4$$

$$\boxed{x = -3, y = 4} \qquad\qquad\qquad \textbf{solution}$$

Exercise 4.4

A. Solve each of the following systems of equations and check your solutions.

1. $x + y = -9$
   $x - y = -7$

2. $x + 5y = 0$
   $x + 2y = 6$

3. $5x + 2y = 74$
   $7x - 2y = 46$

4. $2x + 9y = -13$
   $2x - 3y = 23$

5. $y = 3x + 12$
   $x = -y$

6. $3x = 10 - 2y$
   $5y = 3x - 38$

B. Solve each of the following systems of equations and check your solutions.

1. $4x + y = -13$
   $x - 5y = -19$

2. $6x + 3y = 24$
   $2x + 9y = -8$

3. $7x - 5y = -22$
   $4x + 3y = 5$

4. $8x + 9y = 129$
   $6x + 7y = 99$

5. $12y = 5x + 16$
   $6x + 10y - 54 = 0$

6. $3x - 8y + 44 = 0$
   $7x = 12y - 56$

C. Solve each of the following systems of equations.

1. $0.4x + 1.5y = 16.8$
   $1.1x - 0.9y = 6.0$

2. $6.5x + 3.5y = 128$
   $2.5x + 4.5y = 106$

3. $2.4x + 1.6y = 7.60$
   $3.8x + 0.6y = 7.20$

4. $2.25x + 0.75y = 2.25$
   $1.25x + 1.75y = 2.05$

5. $\dfrac{3x}{4} - \dfrac{2y}{3} = \dfrac{-13}{6}$
   $\dfrac{4x}{5} + \dfrac{3y}{4} = \dfrac{123}{10}$

6. $\dfrac{9x}{5} + \dfrac{5y}{4} = \dfrac{47}{10}$
   $\dfrac{2x}{9} + \dfrac{3y}{8} = \dfrac{5}{36}$

7. $\dfrac{x}{3} + \dfrac{2y}{5} = \dfrac{7}{15}$
   $\dfrac{3x}{2} - \dfrac{7y}{3} = -1$

8. $\dfrac{x}{4} + \dfrac{3y}{7} = \dfrac{-2}{21}$
   $\dfrac{2x}{3} + \dfrac{3y}{2} = \dfrac{-7}{36}$

4.5 SYSTEMS OF LINEAR EQUATIONS IN THREE VARIABLES

A. Solving by the method of elimination

Systems that consist of three linear equations in three variables can be solved by a process of elimination similar to the one used in Section 4.4.

The first step in the process involves reducing the system of three equations in three variables to a system of two equations in two variables. The same variable must be eliminated from two sets of equations to produce two equations in two variables. While any of the three variables may be eliminated, base the decision to eliminate a particular variable on ease of elimination.

The second step involves solving the new system by the method used in Section 4.4. Once the value of one variable has been obtained, the values of the second and third variables are obtained by successive substitution.

B. Worked examples

EXAMPLE 4.5A   Solve the system $x + y + z = 0$, $2x + 3y - z = -6$, and $5x - 3y + 2z = 21$.

Solution

$$x + y + z = 0 \qquad \text{①}$$
$$2x + 3y - z = -6 \qquad \text{②}$$
$$5x - 3y + 2z = 21 \qquad \text{③}$$

STEP 1   Eliminate z from the system and set up two equations in x and y.

(i) Eliminate z from ① and ② by adding.

$$x + y + z = 0$$
$$\underline{2x + 3y - z = -6}$$
$$3x + 4y \qquad = -6 \qquad \text{④}$$

(ii) Eliminate z from ② and ③.

$$2x + 3y - z = -6$$
$$\underline{5x - 3y + 2z = 21}$$

To eliminate z, multiply ② by 2 and add.

$$4x + 6y - 2z = -12 \qquad \text{② multiplied by 2}$$
$$\underline{5x - 3y + 2z = 21}$$
$$9x + 3y \qquad = 9 \qquad \text{⑤}$$

STEP 2   Now solve the new system consisting of ④ and ⑤.

$$3x + 4y = -6 \qquad \text{④}$$
$$\underline{9x + 3y = 9} \qquad \text{⑤}$$

To eliminate the term in x, multiply ④ by 3.

$$9x + 12y = -18 \qquad \text{④ multiplied by 3}$$
$$\underline{9x + 3y = 9}$$
$$9y = -27 \qquad \text{subtract}$$
$$y = -3$$

STEP 3   Substitute -3 for y in an equation that has two variables (equation ④ or ⑤).

$$3x + 4(-3) = -6 \qquad\qquad\qquad\text{substitute in ④}$$
$$3x - 12 = -6$$
$$3x = 6$$
$$x = 2$$

STEP 4   Substitute 2 for x and -3 for y in an equation that has three variables.

$$2 + (-3) + z = 0 \qquad\qquad\qquad\text{substitute in ①}$$
$$-1 + z = 0$$
$$z = 1$$

$$\boxed{x = 2, y = -3, z = 1}$$

Check
in ① LS $= 2 - 3 + 1 = 0$ $\qquad\qquad$ RS $= 0$
in ② LS $= 2(2) + 3(-3) - 1$
$\qquad\quad = 4 - 9 - 1$
$\qquad\quad = -6$ $\qquad\qquad\qquad\qquad$ RS $= -6$
in ③ LS $= 5(2) - 3(-3) + 2(1)$
$\qquad\quad = 10 + 9 + 2$
$\qquad\quad = 21$ $\qquad\qquad\qquad\qquad$ RS $= 21$

EXAMPLE 4.5B

Solve the system $3a + 4b - 2c = -28$, $5a - 3c = -19$, and $2a - 3b + c = 11$.

Solution

$$3a + 4b - 2c = -28 \qquad\qquad\qquad ①$$
$$5a \qquad\; - 3c = -19 \qquad\qquad\qquad ②$$
$$2a - 3b + \;\; c = 11 \qquad\qquad\qquad ③$$

Since ② has the two variables a and c, eliminate the variable b from the system to set up a second equation in a and c. This can be done by multiplying ① by 3 and ③ by 4.

$$9a + 12b - 6c = -84 \qquad\qquad\qquad ① \text{ multiplied by 3}$$
$$\underline{8a - 12b + 4c = 44} \qquad\qquad\quad ③ \text{ multiplied by 4}$$
$$17a \qquad\quad - 2c = -40 \qquad\qquad\qquad ④$$

Now solve the system in two variables consisting of ② and ④.

$$5a - 3c = -19 \qquad\qquad\qquad\qquad ②$$
$$\underline{17a - 2c = -40} \qquad\qquad\qquad\quad ④$$

To eliminate the term in c, multiply ② by 2 and ④ by -3.

$$10a - 6c = -38 \qquad\qquad\qquad ② \text{ multiplied by 2}$$
$$\underline{-51a + 6c = 120} \qquad\qquad\quad ④ \text{ multiplied by } -3$$
$$-41a \qquad\quad = 82$$
$$a = -2$$

Now substitute $a = -2$ in ② (one of the two equations in two variables).

$$5(-2) - 3c = -19$$
$$-10 - 3c = -19$$
$$-3c = -9$$
$$c = 3$$

Now substitute $a = -2, c = 3$ in ③ (one of the equations in three variables).

$$2(-2) - 3b + 3 = 11$$
$$-4 - 3b + 3 = 11$$
$$-3b = 12$$
$$b = -4$$

$$\boxed{a = -2, b = -4, c = 3}$$

Check

in ① LS $= 3(-2) + 4(-4) - 2(3)$
$\qquad = -6 - 16 - 6$
$\qquad = -28$ $\qquad\qquad\qquad\qquad$ RS $= -28$

in ② LS $= 5(-2) - 3(3)$
$\qquad = -10 - 9$
$\qquad = -19$ $\qquad\qquad\qquad\qquad$ RS $= -19$

in ③ LS $= 2(-2) - 3(-4) + 3$
$\qquad = -4 + 12 + 3$
$\qquad = 11$ $\qquad\qquad\qquad\qquad$ RS $= 11$

EXAMPLE 4.5C

Solve the system $3m + 2n = 4, 5m - 4k = 0,$ and $3n + 5k = 13$.

Solution

$$3m + 2n \qquad\quad = 4 \qquad\text{————————} ①$$
$$5m \qquad\ - 4k = 0 \qquad\text{————————} ②$$
$$3n + 5k = 13 \qquad\text{————————} ③$$

To set up a system of two equations in m and n, use ① and eliminate the term in k from ② and ③.

$$25m \qquad\quad - 20k = 0 \qquad\text{——————} ②\ \text{multiplied by 5}$$
$$\underline{12n + 20k \qquad\quad = 52} \qquad\text{——————} ③\ \text{multiplied by 4}$$
$$25m + 12n \qquad\quad = 52 \qquad\text{——————} ④$$

Now solve the system consisting of ① and ④.

$$3m +\ \ 2n = 4 \qquad\text{————————} ①$$
$$\underline{25m + 12n = 52} \qquad\text{————————} ④$$

To eliminate the term in n, multiply ① by -6.

$$\begin{array}{ll} -18m - 12n = -24 & \text{— ① multiplied by } -6 \\ \underline{25m + 12n = 52} & \\ 7m = 28 & \\ m = 4 & \end{array}$$

Substitute $m = 4$ in ①.

$$\begin{array}{l} 3(4) + 2n = 4 \\ 12 + 2n = 4 \\ 2n = -8 \\ n = -4 \end{array}$$

Substitute $m = 4$ in ②.

$$\begin{array}{l} 5(4) - 4k = 0 \\ -4k = -20 \\ k = 5 \end{array}$$

$$\boxed{m = 4, n = -4, k = 5}$$

Check

in ① LS $= 3(4) + 2(-4) = 12 - 8 = 4$ \qquad RS $= 4$
in ② LS $= 5(4) - 4(5) = 20 - 20 = 0$ \qquad RS $= 0$
in ③ LS $= 3(-4) + 5(5) = -12 + 25 = 13$ \qquad RS $= 13$

Exercise 4.5

A. Solve each of the following systems of equations and check your solutions.

1. $x + 2y - z = 0$
   $3x - 2y + 2z = -17$
   $5x + 3y - 4z = -25$

2. $4x - 3y + 2z = 43$
   $3x + 2y - 5z = -13$
   $6x - 5y + 3z = 66$

3. $7a + 3b + 5c = 181$
   $4a + 5b = 100$
   $8a + 2b + 3c = 149$

4. $5a + 9b + 8c = 389$
   $12a + 7b = 220$
   $6b + 9c = 321$

5. $9m + 8n = 12$
   $12n + 9k = 18$
   $7m + 12k = 20$

6. $5p + 9q = 6$
   $9p + 6r = 9$
   $5q + 10r = 5$

BUSINESS MATH NEWS BOX

SECOND PRIZE: A BRAND NEW AUDIT

The latest fund-raising lottery from the Canadian Opera Company has some ticket buyers hitting the high notes—in derision. The point of contention: the grand prize in this year's COC draw is a Ford Windstar worth $35 000. And it comes with a hitch—the winner pays the taxes. So if you're lucky enough to be an Ontario resident and you win the Windstar, you have to cough up an extra $5250. Meanwhile, back at the COC, a spokesperson said the tax on the van is "unfortunate" but the Windstar was a donation from Ford on the condition that the auto maker not be responsible for the taxes. Good thing the COC isn't giving away a Rolls-Royce Corniche convertible; the taxes would exceed $50 000.

QUESTIONS

1. What is the rate of tax being charged on the prize of a Ford Windstar?

2. What is the approximate value of a Rolls-Royce Corniche convertible?

3. How much tax would you have to pay if you won the Ford Windstar and lived in Manitoba, where the PST rate is 7%?

SOURCE: Adapted from David Menzies, "Second Prize: A Brand New Audit," *The Financial Post Magazine*, April 1995.

4.6   PROBLEM SOLVING

A. Problems leading to one equation in two variables

In many problems, the relationship between two or more variables can be represented by setting up linear equations. To find the solution to such problems, there must be as many equations as there are variables.

In the case of problems involving two variables, two equations are needed to obtain a solution. If only one equation can be set up, you can represent the relationship between the two variables graphically.

EXAMPLE 4.6A   A manufacturer processes two types of products through the Finishing Department. Each unit of Product A needs 20 time units in Finishing while each unit of Product B needs 30 time units. Per day, 1200 time units are available. Set up an equation that describes the relationship between the number of units of each product that can be processed daily in Finishing. Graph the relationship.

Solution   Let the number of units of Product A that can be processed daily be represented by x, and let the number of units of Product B be represented by y. Then the number of time units required per day for Product A is $20x$ and the number of time units for Product B is 30y. The total number of time units per day needed by both products is $20x + 30y$. Since 1200 time units are available,

$$20x + 30y = 1200$$

Graphic Representation

Table of values

x	60	0	30
y	0	40	20

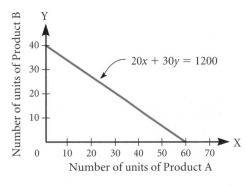

EXAMPLE 4.6B

The Olympic Swim Club rents pool facilities from the city at $2000 per month. Coaching fees and other expenses amount to $40 per swimmer per month. Set up an equation that describes the relationship between the number of swimmers and the total monthly cost of operating the swim club. Graph the relationship.

Solution

Let the number of swimmers be represented by x, and let the total monthly cost be represented by $\$y$. Then the monthly coaching fees and expenses are $\$40x$ and total monthly costs amount to $\$(2000 + 40x)$.

$$y = 2000 + 40x$$

Graphic Representation

Table of values

x	0	50	100
y	2000	4000	6000

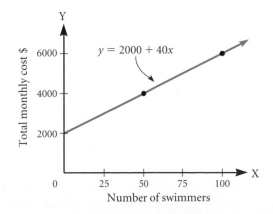

B. Problems leading to systems of equations

The problems in Chapter 2 were solved by using one variable, expressing all the information in terms of that variable, and setting up one equation. To solve many problems, using more than one variable and setting up a system of equations is necessary.

EXAMPLE 4.6C   The sum of two numbers is 64 and their difference is 10. Find the two numbers.

Solution   Let the greater number be x and the smaller number be y. Their sum is $x + y$ and their difference is $x - y$.

$$x + y = 64 \quad\text{———————————— ①}$$
$$\underline{x - y = 10 \quad\text{———————————— ②}}$$
$$2x \quad\ = 74$$
$$x = 37$$
$$37 + y = 64$$
$$y = 27$$

The larger number is 37 and the smaller number is 27.

Check
Sum, $37 + 27 = 64$
Difference, $37 - 27 = 10$

EXAMPLE 4.6D   Sheridan Service paid $240 for heat and power during January. If heat was $40 less than three times the cost of power, how much was the cost of heat for January? (See Chapter 2, Example 2.7C.)

Solution   Let the cost of heat be x, and the cost of power be y. The cost of heat and power together is $(x + y)$.

$$x + y = 240 \quad\text{———————————— ①}$$

Heat is represented by $(3y - 40)$.

$$x = 3y - 40 \quad\text{———————————— ②}$$
$$x - 3y = -40 \quad\text{———————————— ②}$$
$$\underline{x + \ y = 240 \quad\text{———————————— ①}}$$
$$-4y = -280 \quad\text{———————————— subtract}$$
$$y = 70$$
$$x + 70 = 240 \quad\text{———————————— substitute in ①}$$
$$x = 170$$

The cost of heat for January was $170.

EXAMPLE 4.6E

The Clarkson Soccer League has set a budget of $3840 for soccer balls. High quality game balls cost $36 each while lower quality practice balls cost $20 each. If 160 balls are to be purchased, how many balls of each type can be bought to exactly use up the budgeted amount? (See Chapter 2, Example 2.7D.)

Solution

Let the number of game balls be x;
let the number of practice balls be y;
then the total number of balls is $x + y$.

$$x + y = 160 \qquad \text{①}$$

The value of the x game balls is $36x$;
the value of the y practice balls is $20y$;
the total value of the balls is $(36x + 20y)$.

$$
\begin{aligned}
36x + 20y &= 3840 && \text{②} \\
-20x - 20y &= -3200 && \text{① multiplied by } -20 \\
\hline
16x &= 640 && \text{add} \\
x &= 40 \\
40 + y &= 160 && \text{substitute in ①} \\
y &= 120
\end{aligned}
$$

40 game balls and 120 practice balls can be bought.

EXAMPLE 4.6F

The Dutch Nook sells two brands of coffee—one for $7.90 per kilogram, the other for $9.40 per kilogram. If the store owner mixes twenty kilograms and intends to sell the mixture for $8.50 per kilogram, how many kilograms of each brand should she use to make the same revenue as if the two brands were sold unmixed?

Solution

Let the number of kilograms of coffee sold for $7.90 be x;
let the number of kilograms of coffee sold for $9.40 be y;
then the number of kilograms of coffee in the mixture is $x + y$.

$$x + y = 20 \qquad \text{① weight relationship}$$

The value of coffee in the mixture selling for $7.90 is $7.90x$;
the value of coffee in the mixture selling for $9.40 is $9.40y$;
the total value of the mixture is $(7.90x + 9.40y)$. Since each kilogram of mixture is to be sold at $8.50, the value is $8.50(20)$, or $170.

$$7.90x + 9.40y = 170.00 \qquad \text{② value relationship}$$

$$
\begin{aligned}
79x + 94y &= 1700 && \text{② multiplied by 10} \\
79x + 79y &= 1580 && \text{① multiplied by 79} \\
\hline
15y &= 120 && \text{subtract} \\
y &= 8 \\
x + 8 &= 20 && \text{substitute in ①} \\
x &= 12
\end{aligned}
$$

The store owner should mix 12 kg of coffee selling for $7.90 per kilogram with 8 kg of coffee selling for $9.40 per kilogram.

Check
Weight: $12 + 8 = 20$ kg
Value: $12 \times 7.90 + 8 \times 9.40 = 94.80 + 75.20 = \$170.00$

EXAMPLE 4.6G

The material cost of a product is $4 less than twice the cost of the direct labour, and the overhead is ⅚ of direct labour cost. If the total cost of the product is $157, determine the amount of each of the three elements of cost. (See Chapter 2, Example 2.7B.)

Solution

Let the cost of material be represented by x;
let the cost of direct labour be represented by y;
let the cost of overhead be represented by z;
then the total cost is $x + y + z$.

$$x + y + z = 157 \quad\text{————————————— ①}$$

Also, $4 less than twice the cost of direct labour is $2y - 4$.

$$x = 2y - 4 \quad\text{————————————— ②}$$

$\frac{5}{6}$ of direct labour cost is $\left(\frac{5}{6}\right)y$.

$$z = \frac{5y}{6} \quad\text{————————————— ③}$$

You can now solve this system of equations by using the process of elimination shown in Section 4.5. In this case, you can solve the system more directly by replacing x and z in ①.

$$(2y - 4) + y + \left(\frac{5y}{6}\right) = 157$$
$$12y - 24 + 6y + 5y = 942$$
$$23y = 966$$
$$y = 42$$

$$x = 2(42) - 4 \quad\text{————————————— substitute in ②}$$
$$x = 80$$
$$z = \frac{5(42)}{6} \quad\text{————————————— substitute in ③}$$
$$z = 35$$

Material cost is $80, labour cost is $42, and overhead is $35.

EXAMPLE 4.6H

A sum of money amounting to $12 consists of nickels, dimes, and quarters. If there are 95 coins in total and if the ratio of the number of nickels to the number of dimes is 8 to 5, how many of each type of coin make up the total?

Solution

Let the number of nickels be x;
let the number of dimes be y;
let the number of quarters be z;
then the total number of coins is $x + y + z$.

$$x + y + z = 95 \text{———————————} ①$$

The value of the x nickels is $\$0.05x$;
the value of the y dimes is $\$0.10y$;
the value of the z quarters is $\$0.25z$;
the total value of the coins is $\$(0.05x + 0.10y + 0.25z)$.

$$0.05x + 0.10y + 0.25z = 12 \text{—————} ②$$

The ratio of nickels to dimes is $x : y$ or $\dfrac{x}{y}$.

$$x : y = 8 : 5 \text{ or } \frac{x}{y} = \frac{8}{5} \text{—————} ③$$

To eliminate the fraction from ②, multiply by 20.

$$x + 2y + 5z = 240 \text{——————} ④$$

For a suitable order, cross-multiply the terms in ③ and rearrange them.

$$5x = 8y \text{—————————} \text{cross-multiplying in } ③$$
$$5x - 8y = 0 \text{—————————} ⑤$$

Now solve the system of equations numbered ①, ④, and ⑤.

$$x + y + z = 95 \text{—————} ①$$
$$x + 2y + 5z = 240 \text{—————} ④$$
$$\underline{5x - 8y = 0} \text{—————} ⑤$$

To eliminate the term in z from the system, multiply ① by 5 and subtract ④.

$$5x + 5y + 5z = 475$$
$$\underline{x + 2y + 5z = 240}$$
$$4x + 3y = 235 \text{—————} ⑥$$

Now solve the system in two variables.

$$5x - 8y = 0 \text{—————————} ⑤$$
$$4x + 3y = 235 \text{————————} ⑥$$

To eliminate the term in y from the system, multiply ⑤ by 3 and ⑥ by 8.

$$15x - 24y = 0$$
$$\underline{32x + 24y = 1880}$$
$$47x = 1880$$
$$x = 40$$

Substitute $x = 40$ in ⑤.

$$5(40) - 8y = 0$$
$$-8y = -200$$
$$y = 25$$

Substitute $x = 40$, $y = 25$ in ①.

$40 + 25 + z = 95$
$z = 30$

The sum of money consists of 40 nickels, 25 dimes, and 30 quarters.

Check
Number of coins: $40 + 25 + 30 = 95$
Value: $40 \times 0.05 + 25 \times 0.10 + 30 \times 0.25 = \$12.00$
Ratio of nickels to dimes: $40 : 25 = 8 : 5$

Exercise 4.6

A. Set up an equation that describes the relationship between the two variables in each of the following. Graph that relationship.

1. A manufacturer makes two types of products. Profit on Product A is $30 per unit while profit on Product B is $40 per unit. Budgeted monthly profit is $6000.

2. Smith Company manufactures two products. Product 1 requires three hours of machine time per unit while Product 2 requires four hours of machine time per unit. There are 120 hours of machine time available per week.

3. U-Save-Bucks tax consulting service rents space at $200 per week and pays the accounting personnel $4 per completed tax return.

4. George Bell is offered a position as a sales representative. The job pays a salary of $500 per month plus a commission of 10% on all sales.

B. Set up a system of simultaneous equations to solve each of the following problems.

1. The sum of two numbers is 24. If twice the larger number is three more than three times the smaller number, what are the two numbers?

2. The difference between seven times the first number and four times the second number is 12. The sum of three-fourths of the first number and two-thirds of the second number is 21. Find the two numbers.

3. Loblaws sells two brands of sauerkraut. Brand X sells for $2.25 per jar while the No-Name brand sells for $1.75 per jar. If 140 jars were sold for a total of $290, how many jars of each brand were sold?

4. Nancy's sales last week were $140 less than three times Andrea's sales. Together they sold $940. Determine how much each person sold last week.

5. Kaya and Fred agree to form a partnership. The partnership agreement requires that Fred invest $2500 more than two-thirds of what Kaya is to

invest. If the total investment in the partnership is to be $55 000, how much should each partner invest?

6. A Brush with Wood has been producing 2320 chairs a day working two shifts. The second shift has produced 60 chairs fewer than four-thirds of the number of chairs produced by the first shift. Determine the number of chairs each shift has produced.

7. An inventory of two types of floodlights showed a total of sixty lights valued at $2580. If Type A cost $40 each while Type B cost $50 each, how many of each type of floodlight were in inventory?

8. A machine requires four hours to make a unit of Product A and three hours to make a unit of Product B. Last month the machine operated for 200 hours producing a total of 60 units. How many units of each type of product did it produce?

9. Marysia has saved $8.80 in nickels, dimes, and quarters. If she has four nickels fewer than three times the number of dimes and one quarter more than three-fourths the number of dimes, how many coins of each type does Marysia have?

10. The local amateur football club spent $1475 on tickets to a professional football game. If the club bought ten more eight-dollar tickets than three times the number of twelve-dollar tickets, and three fewer fifteen-dollar tickets than four-fifths the number of twelve-dollar tickets, how many tickets of each type did the club buy?

REVIEW EXERCISE

1. Using algebra, find the slope and y-intercept of the line represented by each of the following equations.

   (a) $7x + 3y = 6$

   (b) $10y = 5x$

   (c) $\dfrac{2y - 3x}{2} = 4$

   (d) $1.8x + 0.3y - 3 = 0$

   (e) $\dfrac{1}{3}x = -2$

   (f) $11x - 33y = 99$

   (g) $xy - (x + 4)(y - 1) = 8$

   (h) $2.5y - 12.5 = 0$

2. Graph each of the following.

   (a) $2x - y = 6$

   (b) $3x + 4y = 0$

   (c) $5x + 2y = 10$

   (d) $y = -3$

   (e) $5y < -3x + 15$

   (f) $5x - 4y > 0$

   (g) $x > -2$

   (h) $3y < -4x - 12$

3. Graphically solve each of the following.

(a) $3x + y = 6$ and $x - y = 2$ (b) $x + 4y = -8$ and $3x + 4y = 0$

(c) $5x = 3y$ and $y = -5$ (d) $2x + 6y = 8$ and $x = -2$

4. Graph the regions defined by each of the following systems of inequalities.

(a) $y < 3x - 2$ and $y < 3$ (b) $y > -2x$ and $x < 4$

(c) $x \geq -2, y \geq 0$, and $3x + 4y \leq 12$ (d) $x \geq 0, y \geq -2$, and $5x + 3y \leq 15$

5. Solve each of the following systems of equations.

(a) $3x + 2y = -1$
$5x + 3y = -2$

(b) $4x - 5y = 25$
$3x + 2y = 13$

(c) $y = -10x$
$3y = 29 - x$

(d) $2y = 3x + 17$
$3x = 11 - 5y$

(e) $2x - 3y = 13$
$3x - 2y = 12$

(f) $2x = 3y - 11$
$y = 13 + 3x$

(g) $2a - 3b - 4c = 6$
$2a - b - c = 8$
$a + b - c = 0$

(h) $a + b + c = -4$
$3a - 5b = 0$
$8a + 4c = 0$

(i) $4a - 3b - 2c = 9$
$2a + 3b - 3c = -13$
$a - 2b + 4c = 15$

(j) $3a - 2b + 4c = 4$
$a + 3b - 3c = -8$
$2a + b - c = -6$

(k) $5m + 3n + 2k = 74$
$3m + 7n = 74$
$4m + 5k = 74$

(l) $\dfrac{3}{4}m + \dfrac{5}{8}n = \dfrac{3}{4}$
$\dfrac{6}{5}m + \dfrac{1}{3}k = \dfrac{21}{20}$
$\dfrac{5}{6}n + \dfrac{2}{3}k = \dfrac{5}{6}$

6. Write an equation describing the relationship between the two variables in each of the following problems and graph the relationship.

(a) Sun 'N' Ski Travel pays for radio advertising at the fixed rate of $1000 per week plus $75 per announcement during the week.

(b) The Bi-Products Company markets two products. Each unit of Product A requires five units of labour while each unit of Product B requires two units of labour. Two hundred units of labour are available per time period.

7. Set up a system of equations to solve each of the following problems.

(a) Find two numbers such that the sum of six times the first number and five times the second number is 93 and the difference between three-quarters of the first number and two-thirds of the second number is zero.

(b) The college theatre collected $1300 from the sale of 450 tickets. If the tickets were sold for $2.50 and $3.50 respectively, how many tickets were sold at each price?

(c) A jacket and two pairs of pants together cost $175. The jacket is valued at three times the price of one pair of pants. What is the value of the jacket?

(d) Three cases of White Bordeaux and five cases of Red Bordeaux together cost $438. Each case of Red Bordeaux costs $6 less than twice the cost of a case of White Bordeaux. Determine the cost of a case of each type.

(e) A product requires processing on three machines. Processing time on Machine A is three minutes less than four-fifths of the number of minutes on Machine B, and processing time on Machine C is five-sixths of the time needed on Machines A and B together. How many minutes' processing time is required on each machine if the total processing time on all three machines is 77 minutes?

(f) Last year, the total average monthly cost of heat, power, and water for Sheridan Service was $2010. This year's average is expected to increase by one-tenth over last year's average, and heat is expected to be $22 more than three-fourths the cost of power while water is expected to be $11 less than one-third the cost of power. How much should be budgeted on average for each month for each item?

(g) Widgits Unlimited has a promotional budget of $87 500. The budget is to be allocated to direct selling, TV advertising, and newspaper advertising according to a formula. This formula requires that the amount spent on TV advertising be $1000 more than three times the amount spent on newspaper advertising and that the amount spent on direct selling be three-fourths of the total spent on TV advertising and newspaper advertising combined. How should the budget be allocated?

(h) A cash box contains $74 made up of quarters, half-dollars, and one-dollar coins. How many coins of each type does the box contain if the number of half-dollar coins is one more than three-fifths of the number of one-dollar coins and the number of quarters is four times the number of one-dollar and half-dollar coins together?

SELF-TEST

1. Using algebra, find the slope and y-intercept of the line represented by each of the following questions.

(a) $4y + 11 = y$

(b) $\frac{2}{3}x - \frac{1}{9}y = 1$

(c) $x + 3y = 0$

(d) $-6y - 18 = 0$

(e) $13 - \frac{1}{2}x = 0$

(f) $ax + by = c$

2. Graphically solve each of the following systems of equations.

   (a) $y = -x - 2$ and $x - y = 4$ (b) $3x = -2y$ and $x = 2$

3. Graph the region defined by each of the following systems of inequalities.

   (a) $x < 3 - y$ and $y < 3$ (b) $xy \geq 0$, $y \geq -2$, and $3x + 2y \leq 12$

4. Solve each of the following systems of equations.

   (a) $6x + 5y = 9$ (b) $12 - 7x = 4y$
       $4x - 3y = 25$ $6 - 2y = 3x$

   (c) $5a - b + 4c = 5$ (d) $6a + b - 2c = 0$
       $2a + 3b + 5c = 2$ $4b - c = -13$
       $7a - 2b + 6c = 5$ $5a + 3c = 25$

5. Erica Lottsbriner invests $12 000 so that part earns interest at 8% per annum and part at 12% per annum. If the total annual interest on the investment is $1120, how much has Erica invested at each rate?

6. Jack and Jill divide a profit of $12 700. If Jack is to receive $2200 more than two-fifths of Jill's share, how much will Jill receive?

7. Direct distribution costs are to be allocated to three products based on sales value for an accounting period. Product A sells for $20 per unit, Product B for $15 per unit, and Product C for $10 per unit. Last month, the number of units of Product A was five-eighths the number of units of Product B, and the number of units of Product C was 16 less than three times the number of units of Product B. How much of the total direct distribution cost of $6280 is to be allocated to each product?

CHALLENGE PROBLEMS

1. Terry invested a total of $4500. A portion was invested at 4% and the rest was invested at 6%. The amount of Terry's annual return on each portion is the same. Find the average rate of interest Terry earned on the $4500.

2. Five times A's money added to B's money is more than $51.00. Three times A's money minus B's money is $21.00. If a represents A's money in dollars and b represents B's money in dollars, then which of the following is correct?

   (a) $a > 9, b = 6$

   (b) $a > 9, b < 6$

   (c) $a > 9, b > 6$

   (d) $a > 9$, but we can put no bounds on b

   (e) $2a = 3b$

CASE STUDY 4.1

FINDING THE RIGHT COMBINATION

Linda is a successful sales representative for a telecommunications company. Last month she closed a major sale worth $260 000. Her commission cheque arrived yesterday, and she saw that 40% of her cheque had been deducted for income taxes. She went out for dinner with her friend Cathy to celebrate. Commission at Linda's company is calculated as 6% of the first $100 000 of a sale, 8% of the next $100 000, and 10% of the amount over $200 000.

Linda decided to invest her commission in the stock market. At dinner, she asked Cathy, who is a stock broker, for advice. Cathy advised Linda that investing money is risky and Linda should be prepared to lose any money that she invests. So Linda decided to keep half of the money she received in the bank, and invest the other half in the stock market. Cathy gave Linda a set of reports on different companies to help her make her decision about which stocks to buy, and told Linda to call her the next day.

After dinner, Linda prepared the following summary of information from the reports Cathy gave her:

Company	Latest Selling Price per Share ($)	6-Month High/Low ($)
Indonesian Minerals Ltd.	2.50	57.50/2.50
Catalyst Biotech Inc.	20.00	20.00/1.10
Canada Power Corporation	25.00	25.25/24.50
Technet Communiciation Ltd.	10.00	12.00/8.00

QUESTIONS

1. How much money is Linda willing to invest in the stock market?

2. How many shares of each stock would she get if she invested equally in all four companies?

3. Linda decides to buy stock only in Catalyst Biotech Inc. and Technet Communication Ltd. How many shares of each will she get if she buys three times as many shares of Technet Communication Ltd. as she buys of Catalyst Biotech Inc.?

4. How many shares of each company will she get if she buys two shares of Canada Power Corporation for every three shares she buys of Technet Communication Ltd.?

5. How many shares of each company will Linda get if, for every share of Technet Communication Ltd. she buys, she buys two shares of Catalyst Biotech and five shares of Indonesian Minerals Ltd.?

CASE STUDY 4.2 WHAT TO PRODUCE?

The Wellington Cutlery Company produces serving knives, forks, and spoons that are sold in better department stores and gift shops.

As with most businesses, Wellington wants to produce a number of items, but it has limited production facilities. The company uses consumer demand forecasts and profitability of the products to choose among its production options.

The Wellington Cutlery Company operates one facility that can produce the three items of serving cutlery—knives, forks, and spoons. However, the company is able to produce only two items at a time due to limited production resources. The items of cutlery are sold as individual pieces, so Wellington Cutlery can base its production decision on factors such as maximum use of resources, maximum revenue, and minimum cost. The company does not have to produce equal numbers of forks, spoons, and knives, since they are not sold as sets.

Past experience has shown that it costs $5.50 to make a knife, $4.00 to make a fork, and $3.00 to make a spoon. Each knife can be sold for $9.50, each fork for $7.00, and each spoon for $5.25. Because of limitations in the manufacturing department, Wellington's capacity per hour is 1200 units if it produces only knives and forks. If the company produces only forks and spoons, the capacity per hour is 1600 units. If it produces only knives and spoons, the capacity per hour is 1300 units. The accountant has calculated the total manufacturing costs to be $5550 per hour for knives and forks, $5600 per hour for forks and spoons, and $5400 per hour for knives and spoons.

QUESTIONS

1. What number of knives, forks, and spoons can Wellington Cutlery Company manufacture per hour in each of the three manufacturing situations above?

2. (a) What is the percent markup from cost to selling price on a knife, a fork, and a spoon?
   (b) Based on these markups only, which pair of cutlery items should be produced to maximize profit?

3. (a) If Wellington Cutlery wants to make the maximum profit, should it produce knives and forks, forks and spoons, or knives and spoons?
   (b) How does your answer in part (a) compare to your answer in question 2(b)?

SUMMARY OF FORMULAE

Formula 4.1

$$y = mx + b$$

Slope-intercept form of a linear equation

GLOSSARY

Inequality a mathematical statement involving relationships between variables described as "greater than" or "less than"

Origin the point of intersection of the two axes in a system of rectangular coordinates

Rise the vertical distance (distance along the Y axis) between two points on a line or line segment

Run the horizontal distance (the distance along the X axis) between two points on a line or line segment

Slope measure of the steepness of a line; it is the ratio of the rise of a line to its run

slope-intercept form of a linear equation a linear equation expressed in the form $y = mx + b$

X axis the horizontal reference line in a system of rectangular coordinates

x coordinate the first number in an ordered pair of numbers. It describes the position of a point relative to the axes or the directed distance of a point from the vertical axis (Y axis).

Y axis the vertical reference line in a system of rectangular coordinates

y coordinate the second number in an ordered pair of numbers. It describes the position of a point relative to the axes or the directed distance of a point from the horizontal axis (X axis).

y-intercept the y coordinate of the point of intersection of a line and the Y axis

PART TWO

Mathematics of Business and Management

5 Business Applications – Depreciation and Break-even Analysis

Depreciation calculations and break-even analysis can be used in everyday situations. If you run a small business out of your home, such as an income tax or bookkeeping service, you are eligible to depreciate your computer and office furniture. This will reduce the income tax you pay on your business income. If you are in the market for a new car or other appliance, you can use break-even analysis to compare current costs to future savings. The concept of spending money to save money needs to be tempered with the time factor. A large box of cereal is not a bargain if it goes stale before you eat it. A new car that uses little gas doesn't save you money if you go broke paying for the new car.

Introduction

Depreciation is an accounting concept used by small and large businesses. It allows the cost of depreciable assets such as buildings, machinery, vehicles, furniture, and equipment to be allocated to accounting periods to properly measure net income and evaluate assets. As no single method of allocation is suitable for all depreciable assets under all circumstances, various methods of depreciation have been developed.

The main concern for owners and management in operating a business is profitability. To achieve or maintain a desired level of profitability, managers must make decisions that affect product mix, total revenue, and total cost.

A valuable tool in evaluating the potential effects of decisions on profitability is cost-volume-profit analysis. The most popular approach to cost-volume-profit analysis is called **break-even analysis**.

Appendix II contains a more extensive consideration of cost-profit-volume analysis as well as an introduction to linear programming, which is a useful mathematical tool in making decisions regarding product mix to maximize total profit.

OBJECTIVES

Upon completing this chapter, you will be able to do the following:

1. Compute the depreciation and the book value for an asset in each year of its life.

2. Construct depreciation schedules using averaging methods (straight-line, units of product, service hours), sum-of-the-years-digits method, and declining balance methods (simple, complex, constant percentage).
3. Construct detailed break-even charts and compute break-even values.

5.1 DEPRECIATION

A. Basic concepts and methods

The useful life of physical assets such as plant, machinery, and equipment that are used to produce goods and services is limited due to physical deterioration, wear and tear, decay, and obsolescence. As a result, such assets lose their value over a period of time. From an accounting point of view, this loss in value, **depreciation**, is treated as an *expense* of operating a business.

To make provision for this expense, various systematic methods to record the expiration of the usefulness of such assets have been developed. Recording depreciation is a process of allocating the original cost of assets to the accounting periods that benefit from the use of the assets.

Whatever *method of depreciation* is used, certain aspects are common to all.

1. The **original cost** of the asset including all necessary and reasonable expenditures to ready the asset for its intended purpose.
2. The **residual value** (**scrap value**, **salvage value**, **trade-in value**) at the time the asset has lost its usefulness.
3. The **wearing value**, or the total amount of depreciation over the useful life of the asset; that is, the difference between the original cost and the residual value of the asset.
4. The **useful life** of the asset (usually stated in years).
5. The **accumulated depreciation**—the total depreciation allocated at any point in the life of the asset to expired accounting periods.
6. The **book value** or net value of the asset at any point in the life of the asset; that is, the difference between the original cost and the accumulated depreciation.
7. **Depreciation schedules** showing the details of allocating the cost of the asset to the various accounting periods.

No single method of allocating the wearing value is suitable for all depreciable assets. Instead, the various assumptions about how the loss in value should be allocated to accounting periods have led to the development of a variety of **methods of depreciation**.

Of the methods available, the following are described in this chapter:

(a) **Allocation on the Basis of Averages**

1. Straight Line
2. Service Hours
3. Units of Product

(b) Allocation Based on a Diminishing Charge per Year

1. Sum-of-the-years-digits
2. Declining balance:
   (i) Simple declining balance
   (ii) Complex declining balance
   (iii) Constant percentage

B. Methods of allocating depreciation based on an average

Methods of depreciation in this category are based on the assumption that the loss in value (depreciation) is the same for each unit of useful life of the asset, such as time period, service hour, or unit of product.

1. The Straight-Line Method of Depreciation

This method is the simplest. It is based on the assumption that the loss in value is the same for equal time periods (usually years). The depreciation per time period is found by dividing the total wearing value by the number of time periods in the life of the asset. Since the wearing value is the difference between the original cost and the residual value, the yearly depreciation is

$$\text{YEARLY DEPRECIATION} = \frac{\text{ORIGINAL COST} - \text{RESIDUAL VALUE}}{n}$$

where n = the number of years in the life of the asset

———— Formula 5.1

EXAMPLE 5.1A   A machine costing $20 000.00 has a salvage value of $3200.00 after five years. Use the straight-line method to

(i) compute the yearly depreciation expense;

(ii) determine the depreciation expense in Year 4;

(iii) construct a depreciation schedule.

Solution

(i) The original cost = 20 000.00;
the residual value = 3200.00;
the wearing value is 20 000.00 − 3200.00 = 16 800.00;
the life of the asset (in years) = 5.
Yearly depreciation expense is $\dfrac{16\ 800.00}{5}$ = $3360.00.

(ii) The depreciation expense in Year 4 = $3360.00.

(iii) *Depreciation schedule (straight-line method)*

End of Year	Annual Depreciation Expense	Accumulated Depreciation	Book Value
0			20 000.00
1	3 360.00	3 360.00	16 640.00
2	3 360.00	6 720.00	13 280.00
3	3 360.00	10 080.00	9 920.00
4	3 360.00	13 440.00	6 560.00
5	3 360.00	16 800.00	3 200.00
Total	16 800.00		

Explanations of the schedule

1. The annual depreciation expense is the same for each year and totals the wearing value of $16 800.00.
2. The accumulated depreciation is a running total of the annual depreciation. After five years, it equals the wearing value.
3. The book value diminishes each year by the annual depreciation expense. After five years, it must equal the salvage value of $3200.00.

2. The Service-Hours Method of Depreciation

The underlying assumption for this method is similar to that for the straight-line method. However, this method is based on the number of useful service hours in the life of the asset.

$$\text{DEPRECIATION PER SERVICE HOUR} = \frac{\text{ORIGINAL COST} - \text{RESIDUAL VALUE}}{n}$$

where n = the number of service hours in the life of the asset

— **Formula 5.2**

The depreciation expense for a time period (such as a year) is found by multiplying the number of service hours in the time period by the depreciation per service hour.

EXAMPLE 5.1B

Assuming that the useful life of the machine in Example 5.1A is 9600 hours, use the service-hours method to

(i) determine the depreciation expense per service hour;

(ii) determine the depreciation expense in Year 4 if the number of service hours in Year 4 is 1880;

(iii) construct a depreciation schedule if the service hours per year for the five years are respectively 2000, 1960, 1840, 1880, and 1920.

Solution

(i) The original cost = 20 000.00;
the residual value = 3200.00;
the wearing value is 20 000.00 − 3200.00 = 16 800.00;
the life of the asset (in number of service hours) = 9600.
The depreciation per service hour is $\dfrac{16\,800.00}{9600} = \$1.75$.

(ii) Depreciation in Year 4 is 1.75(1880) = $3290.00.

(iii) *Depreciation schedule (service-hours method)*

End of Year	Annual Depreciation Expense		Accumulated Depreciation	Book Value
0				20 000.00
1	1.75(2000) =	3 500.00	3 500.00	16 500.00
2	1.75(1960) =	3 430.00	6 930.00	13 070.00
3	1.75(1840) =	3 220.00	10 150.00	9 850.00
4	1.75(1880) =	3 290.00	13 440.00	6 560.00
5	1.75(1920) =	3 360.00	16 800.00	3 200.00
Total		16 800.00		

3. The Units-of-Product Method

This method is based on the assumption that the loss in value is the same per unit of product.

$$\frac{\text{DEPRECIATION PER}}{\text{SERVICE HOUR}} = \frac{\text{ORIGINAL COST} - \text{RESIDUAL VALUE}}{n}$$

— Formula 5.3

where n = the number of product units in the life of the asset

The depreciation expense for a time period (such as a year) is found by multiplying the number of product units in the time period by the depreciation per unit.

EXAMPLE 5.1C

Assuming that the machine in Example 5.1A can make 240 000 units of product during its useful life, use the units-of-product method to

(i) determine the depreciation expense per unit of product;

(ii) determine the depreciation in Year 4 if the number of units of product in Year 4 is 46 400;

(iii) construct a depreciation schedule if the number of units of product during each of the five years is respectively 50 800, 49 200, 46 700, 46 400, and 46 900.

Solution

(i) The original cost = 20 000.00;
the residual value = 3200.00;
the wearing value is 20 000.00 − 3200.00 = 16 800.00;
the life of the asset (in number of units of product) = 240 000.

The depreciation per unit of product is $\dfrac{16\ 800.00}{240\ 000} = \$0.07$.

(ii) The depreciation in Year 4 is 0.07(46 400) = $3248.00.

(iii) *Depreciation schedule (units-of-product method)*

End of Year	Annual Depreciation Expense		Accumulated Depreciation	Book Value
0				20 000.00
1	0.07(50 800) =	3 556.00	3 556.00	16 444.00
2	0.07(49 200) =	3 444.00	7 000.00	13 000.00
3	0.07(46 700) =	3 269.00	10 269.00	9 731.00
4	0.07(46 400) =	3 248.00	13 517.00	6 483.00
5	0.07(46 900) =	3 283.00	16 800.00	3 200.00
Total		16 800.00		

C. Methods of allocating depreciation as a diminishing charge per year

Methods of depreciation in this category are based on the assumption that the loss in value is highest in the first year and then diminishes yearly during the useful life of an asset.

1. The Sum-of-the-Years-Digits Method

This method assumes that the loss in value diminishes by a constant amount from year to year. First, the number of parts into which the wearing value is to be divided must be determined. This number is the sum of the digits corresponding to the years in the life of the asset in sequential order starting with 1. Proportional parts of the total depreciation expense are then assigned to each year in reverse order of the digits.

EXAMPLE 5.1D

Assume that the machine in Example 5.1A is depreciated by the sum-of-the-years-digits method.

(i) Determine the depreciation for each year.

(ii) Construct a depreciation schedule.

Solution   (i) The original cost = 20 000.00;
the residual value = 3200.00;
the wearing value is 20 000.00 − 3200.00 = 16 800.00;
the life of the asset (in years) = 5.

The yearly depreciation is determined by following the steps outlined below.

Year in Life of Asset	Digit Identifying Year	Proportional Part of Wearing Value Assigned to Year	Yearly Depreciation Expense
One	1	5	5(1120.00) = 5600.00
Two	2	4	4(1120.00) = 4480.00
Three	3	3	3(1120.00) = 3360.00
Four	4	2	2(1120.00) = 2240.00
Five	5	1	1(1120.00) = 1120.00

Sum of the digits   15

Value of each of the 15 parts is $\dfrac{16\ 800.00}{15} = 1120.00$

STEP 1   Identify each year in the life of the asset by a digit in sequential order starting with 1, i.e., 1, 2, 3, 4, 5.

STEP 2   Assign to each year proportional parts of the total wearing value in *reverse* order of the digits identifying the years, i.e., 5, 4, 3, 2, 1.

STEP 3   Determine the sum of the years-digits: $1 + 2 + 3 + 4 + 5 = 15$. Since the sum of the years-digits is always the sum of an arithmetic progression formed by the first n whole numbers, it can be more conveniently determined by using the formula

$$S_n = \frac{n(n + 1)}{2}$$

$$S_5 = \frac{5(5 + 1)}{2} = 15$$

STEP 4   Compute the value of each of the 15 parts of the wearing value.

$$\frac{16\ 800.00}{15} = \$1120.00$$

STEP 5   Determine the yearly depreciation by multiplying the value of one part ($1120.00) by the number of parts assigned to each year.

An algebraic approach can replace the arithmetic approach shown above.

$nk + (n − 1)k + (n − 2)k + \ldots + 3k + 2k + k =$ Wearing Value
$n =$ the digit identifying the last year in the life of the asset

$$k = \text{the value of one of the } \frac{n(n+1)}{2} \text{ proportional parts}$$

$$k[n + (n-1) + (n-2) + \ldots + 3 + 2 + 1] = \text{Wearing Value}$$

$$k\left[\frac{n(n+1)}{2}\right] = \text{Wearing Value}$$

$$k = \frac{\text{WEARING VALUE}}{\frac{n(n+1)}{2}} \quad\text{—— Formula 5.4}$$

In this example, $5k + 4k + 3k + 2k + k = 16\ 800.00$

or, directly by formula, $k = \dfrac{16\ 800.00}{\frac{5(5+1)}{2}} = \dfrac{16\ 800.00}{15} = \$1120.00$

(ii) *Depreciation schedule (sum-of-the-years-digits method)*

End of Year	Parts	Annual Depreciation Expense	Accumulated Depreciation	Book Value
0				20 000.00
1	5	5 600.00	5 600.00	14 400.00
2	4	4 480.00	10 080.00	9 920.00
3	3	3 360.00	13 440.00	6 560.00
4	2	2 240.00	15 680.00	4 320.00
5	1	1 120.00	16 800.00	3 200.00
Total	15	16 800.00		

2. Declining-Balance Methods

In these methods, the depreciation for a particular year is based on the book value at the end of the previous year and is calculated over the years at a constant rate. Three variations are used.

(a) The simple declining-balance method
(b) The complex declining-balance method
(c) The constant-percentage method

All three methods work in basically the same way and differ only in how the rate of depreciation, d, is determined.

(a) The Simple Declining-Balance Method

When this variation of the declining-balance methods is used, the rate of depreciation is determined by

$$d = 2 \times \frac{1}{n}$$

where n = the number of years in the life of the asset

—— Formula 5.5

No consideration is given to the residual value until the final year in the life of the asset or until the book value drops below the residual value.

EXAMPLE 5.1E

Assume that the machine in Example 5.1A is depreciated by the simple declining-balance method.

(i) Determine the rate of depreciation.

(ii) Compute the depreciation for Year 4.

(iii) Construct a depreciation schedule.

Solution

(i) The rate of depreciation is $2\left(\frac{1}{5}\right) = \frac{2}{5} = 40\%$

(ii)

Original book value	20 000.00
Depreciation in Year 1: 40% of 20 000.00	8 000.00
Book Value End of Year 1	12 000.00
Depreciation in Year 2: 40% of 12 000.00	4 800.00
Book Value End of Year 2	7 200.00
Depreciation in Year 3: 40% of 7200.00	2 880.00
Book Value End of Year 3	4 320.00

Ordinarily, the depreciation for Year 4 would be computed as 40% of 4320.00 = 1728.00. However, when $1728.00 is subtracted from $4320.00, the result is smaller than the residual value of $3200.00. When this happens, the depreciation is the difference between the previous book value and the residual value; that is, the depreciation for Year 4 is 4320.00 − 3200.00 = $1120.00. The depreciation for Year 5 is zero, because the accumulated depreciation at the end of Year 4 equals the residual value.

(iii) *Depreciation schedule (simple declining-balance method)*

End of Year	Annual Depreciation Expense		Accumulated Depreciation	Book Value
0				20 000.00
1	0.40(20 000.00) =	8 000.00	8 000.00	12 000.00
2	0.40(12 000.00) =	4 800.00	12 800.00	7 200.00
3	0.40(7200.00) =	2 880.00	15 680.00	4 320.00
4	4320.00 − 3200.00 =	1 120.00	16 800.00	3 200.00
5	3200.00 − 3200.00 =	0.00	16 800.00	3 200.00
Total		16 800.00		

Alternative Approach to Part (ii)

In part (ii), the successive book values were obtained by subtracting the amount of depreciation for each year. Alternatively, the book value can be determined by multiplying the value at the beginning of the year by net factor $1 - 0.40 = 0.60$.

Book value at the end of Year 1 = 20 000.00(0.60) = 12 000.00;
Book value at the end of Year 2 = 12 000.00(0.60) = 7 200.00;
Book value at the end of Year 3 =   7200.00(0.60) = 4 320.00.

This approach permits the book value to be determined directly at any time by multiplying the original book value by the product of the net factors. For the book value at the end of Year 3, the product of the net factors = $(0.60)(0.60)(0.60)$.

The book value at the end of Year 3

$$
\begin{aligned}
&= 20\ 000.00(0.60)(0.60)(0.60) \\
&= 20\ 000.00(0.60)^3 \\
&= 20\ 000.00(0.216) \\
&= \$4320.00
\end{aligned}
$$

EXAMPLE 5.1F

Equipment costing $36 000.00 with a scrap value of $4300.00 is depreciated over twenty years by the simple declining-balance method. Determine the depreciation in Year 8.

Solution

The original cost = 36 000.00;

the rate of depreciation = $2\left(\dfrac{1}{20}\right) = \dfrac{1}{10} = 0.10 = 10\%$;

the net factor = $1 - 0.10 = 0.90$.

Since the depreciation in Year 8 is 10% of the previous book value, we need to determine the book value after seven years. During each of the first seven years, depreciation of 10% has been taken from the successive book values starting with the original book value.

Using the net factor approach, the book value after seven years

$$
\begin{aligned}
&= 36\ 000.00(0.90)(0.90)(0.90)(0.90)(0.90)(0.90)(0.90) \\
&= 36\ 000.00(0.90)^7 \\
&= 36\ 000.00(0.4782969) \\
&= \$17\ 218.69
\end{aligned}
$$

The depreciation in Year 8 is $0.10(17\ 218.69) = \$1721.87$.

(b) The Complex Declining-Balance Method

While the simple declining-balance method ignores any residual value in establishing the rate of depreciation, the complex variation takes the residual value into account by using the following formula to determine the rate of depreciation.

$$d = 1 - \sqrt[n]{\frac{\text{RESIDUAL VALUE}}{\text{ORIGINAL COST}}}$$

where n = the number of years in the life of the asset

———— **Formula 5.6**

Development of Formula 5.6

Let the original cost be represented by C; let the residual value after n years be represented by T_n; let the book value after n years be represented by B_n; let the number of years in the life of the asset be represented by n; and let the rate of depreciation that will reduce the original cost to the residual value in n years be represented by d.

Then the book value after

one year	$B_1 = C - Cd = C(1 - d)$
two years	$B_2 = B_1 - B_1 d = B_1(1 - d) = C(1 - d)(1 - d) = C(1 - d)^2$
three years	$B_3 = B_2 - B_2 d = B_2(1 - d) = C(1 - d)^2(1 - d) = C(1 - d)^3$
four years	$B_4 = C(1 - d)^4$
five years	$B_5 = C(1 - d)^5$
n years	$B_n = C(1 - d)^n$

However, after n years $B_n = T_n$:

$$T_n = C(1 - d)^n$$

$$\frac{T_n}{C} = (1 - d)^n \qquad\text{———— divide both sides by C}$$

$$\sqrt[n]{\frac{T_n}{C}} = 1 - d \qquad\text{———— take the } n\text{th root}$$

$$d = 1 - \sqrt[n]{\frac{T_n}{C}} = 1 - \sqrt[n]{\frac{\text{RESIDUAL VALUE}}{\text{ORIGINAL COST}}}$$

EXAMPLE 5.1G

Assuming that the machine in Example 5.1A is depreciated by the complex declining-balance method,

(i) determine the rate of depreciation;

(ii) compute the depreciation in Year 4;

(iii) construct a depreciation schedule.

Solution

(i) The original cost = 20 000.00;
the residual value = 3200.00;
the life of the asset (in years) = 5.

$$d = 1 - \sqrt[5]{\frac{3200.00}{20\,000.00}} = 1 - \sqrt[5]{0.16} = 1 - 0.6931448 = 0.3068552$$

The rate of depreciation d = 30.68552%.

(ii) The book value after three years

$$= 20\,000.00(1 - 0.3068552)^3$$
$$= 20\,000.00(0.6931448)^3$$
$$= 20\,000.00(0.3330213)$$
$$= \$6660.43$$

The depreciation in Year 4 is $6660.43(0.3068552) = \$2043.79$.

(iii) *Depreciation schedule (complex declining-balance method)*

End of Year	Annual Depreciation Expense	Accumulated Depreciation	Book Value
0			20 000.00
1	6 137.10	6 137.10	13 862.90
2	4 253.90	10 391.00	9 609.00
3	2 948.57	13 339.57	6 660.43
4	2 043.79	15 383.36	4 616.64
5	1 416.64	16 800.00	3 200.00
Total	16 800.00		

(c) The Constant-Percentage Method

This variation of the declining-balance methods is based on an arbitrarily established yearly rate of depreciation. It is the method commonly used for income tax purposes when computing capital cost allowance.

Under the regulations of the Income Tax Act, a capital cost allowance may be claimed for depreciable business assets according to their classification at a maximum rate established for each classification.

The most common classes are

Class 3   Buildings—maximum rate 3%;
Class 8   Machinery and Equipment—maximum rate 20%;
Class 10 Cars, trucks, vans, tractors, contractor's equipment—maximum rate 30%.

EXAMPLE 5.1H   Assuming that the machine in Example 5.1A falls into Class 8, develop a capital cost allowance schedule for the five years at the maximum allowable rate.

Solution   The original cost = 20 000.00;
the residual value = 3200.00;
the life of the asset (in years) = 5;
the maximum allowable rate = 20%.

Capital cost allowance schedule

End of Year	Annual Capital Cost Allowance	Accumulated Capital Cost Allowance	Book Value
0			20 000.00
1	4 000.00	4 000.00	16 000.00
2	3 200.00	7 200.00	12 800.00
3	2 560.00	9 760.00	10 240.00
4	2 048.00	11 808.00	8 192.00
5	1 638.40	13 446.40	6 553.60
Total	13 446.40		

Note: The depreciated value of the machine after five years is well above its estimated residual value at that time. The tax implications of this situation are beyond the scope of this text and are not considered here.

D. Finding the book value and yearly depreciation without a depreciation schedule

The book value after a given number of years or the depreciation in any particular year can be determined without constructing a depreciation schedule when using any of the methods illustrated.

EXAMPLE 5.1I   Equipment costing $35 720.00 has an estimated trade-in value of $1400.00 after fifteen years. Find (a) the book value after nine years and (b) the depreciation charge in Year 10 using

  (i) the straight-line method;

 (ii) the sum-of-the-years-digits method;

(iii) the simple declining-balance method;

(iv) the complex declining-balance method.

Solution   The original cost = 35 720.00;
the residual value = 1400.00;
the wearing value is 35 720.00 − 1400.00 = 34 320.00;
$n = 15$.

  (i) *Straight-Line Method*

The yearly depreciation is $\dfrac{34\ 320.00}{15}$ = $2288.00.

The accumulated depreciation after nine years is 2288.00(9) = $20 592.00.

(a) The book value after nine years is 35 720.00 − 20 592.00 = $15 128.00.

(b) The depreciation in Year 10 (as in any year) = $2288.00.

(ii) *Sum-of-the-Years-Digits Method*

The number of parts into which the wearing value is to be divided is $\frac{(15)(16)}{2} = 120$.

The value of each part is $\frac{34\,320}{120} = \$286.00$.

The sum of the number of parts assigned to the first nine years
$= 15 + 14 + 13 + 12 + 11 + 10 + 9 + 8 + 7$
$= 120 - $ sum of the parts in the remaining six years
$= 120 - \frac{6(7)}{2} = 120 - 21 = 99$

The accumulated depreciation for the first nine years $= 99(286.00)$
$= \$28\,314.00$

(a) The book value after nine years is $35\,720.00 - 28\,314.00 = \$7406.00$

(b) Since Year 10 is the first of the remaining six years, six parts are assigned; the depreciation in Year 10 is $6(286.00) = \$1716.00$.

(iii) *Simple Declining-Balance Method*

The rate of depreciation is $2\left(\frac{1}{15}\right) = 0.1333333 = 13.33333\%$.

(a) The book value after nine years
$= 35\,720.00(1 - 0.1333333)^9$———————— see Example 5.1E
$= 35\,720.00(0.8666667)^9$
$= 35\,720.00(0.2758475)$
$= \$9853.27$

(b) The depreciation in Year 10 is $9853.27(0.1333333) = \$1313.77$.

(iv) *Complex Declining-Balance Method*

$\text{Rate} = 1 - \sqrt[15]{\frac{1400.00}{35\,720.00}} = 1 - 0.8057762 = 0.1942238 = 19.42238\%$

(a) The book value after nine years
$= 35\,720.00(1 - 0.1942238)^9$
$= 35\,720.00(0.8057762)^9$
$= 35\,720.00(0.1431957)$
$= \$5114.95$

(b) The depreciation in Year 10 is $5114.95(0.1942238) = \$993.45$.

E. Computer application—depreciation schedules

Many of the problems dealt with in this text can be solved by computers. Spreadsheet programs like Excel and Lotus 1-2-3 make creating lengthy depreciation schedules much easier. Once a depreciation schedule has been created in a spreadsheet, you can change things like the original cost or residual value of an asset and see immediately the effect of the change on the depreciation schedule, without inputting all the formulae again. While the procedures that follow are generic, the formulae in the diagram were created using the Excel spreadsheet program. Modify these procedures if your spreadsheet program requires different instructions.

EXAMPLE 5.1J

Create a depreciation schedule using the straight-line method for a machine costing $20 000.00 that has a salvage value of $3200.00 after five years. (This is Example 5.1A from page 200.)

Solution

STEP 1   Open a new spreadsheet file. Enter the labels and formulae shown in the diagram below. For the labels in row 1, widen the columns to display the long titles, or shorten the titles, as shown below. (In Excel, you can widen columns by going to the Format menu, choosing Column, then choosing Width. Type numbers until you get the column width you want. You can also widen columns by placing the cursor between columns until the cursor changes to a double-pointed arrow. Drag the side of the column to the desired width.)

To reduce inputting time and avoid inputting errors, copy the formulae in cells B4, C3, and D3 into the cells below. (In Excel, you can go to the Edit menu and choose Copy. Then highlight the cell or cells you want to copy into. Go to the Edit menu and choose Paste. You can also copy formulae by going to the Edit menu and choosing Fill, then Down.) Since we know the machine has an expected useful life of five years, create the depreciation schedule so that it displays five years of depreciation.

	A	B	C	D	E	F
			Workbook 1			
1	End of year	Annual depr. expense	Accumulated depr.	Book value	Residual value	n
2	0					
3	1	= (D2 − E2)/F2	= C2 + B3	= D2 − B3		
4	2	= B3	= C3 + B4	= D3 − B4		
5	3	= B4	= C4 + B5	= D4 − B5		
6	4	= B5	= C5 + B6	= D5 − B6		
7	5	= B6	= C6 + B7	= D6 − B7		
8						

Note that this spreadsheet can be used for any asset having a useful life of five years that is depreciated using the straight-line method. Because the formulae are all linked together, just change the numbers in cells D2, E2, and F2 for each new asset.

STEP 2   Input the following information required to generate the depreciation schedule for this machine. In cell D2, enter **20000** (the cost of the machine). In cell E2, enter **3200** (the residual value), and in cell F2, enter **5** (the life of the asset). Hit the Enter key.

STEP 3   You can display the total annual depreciation expense (the contents of column B) by entering **Total** in cell A8 and entering a formula in cell B8 to add the contents of cells B3 to B7. (In Excel, this formula is **=SUM(B3:B7)**, or you can use the Σ icon on the Toolbar.)

Your spreadsheet should look similar to the depreciation schedule on page 201.

You can create depreciation schedules for other methods of depreciation using a spreadsheet program. The key is to create the correct equations, based on the formulae in this chapter. Always test your spreadsheet by calculating the first two or three years of depreciation and accumulated depreciation by hand, to ensure the spreadsheet-generated results are correct.

Exercise 5.1

A. For each of the following, construct a depreciation schedule using the indicated methods of depreciation.

1. Equipment with an original book value of $40 000 is estimated to have a scrap value of $5000 after ten years. The number of service hours for each of the first four years will be 2025, for each of the next three years 1990, and for each of the last three years 1775. For each of the first four years, the number of units of product is expected to be 10 750, for each of the next three years 9800, and for each of the last three years 9200. For income tax purposes, the equipment is grouped into Class 8. Construct a depreciation schedule using

    (a) the straight-line method;
    (b) the service-hours method;
    (c) the units-of-product method;
    (d) the sum-of-the-years-digits method;
    (e) the simple declining-balance method;
    (f) the complex declining-balance method;
    (g) the constant-percentage method.

2. A combine costing $32 000 has a trade-in value of $5000 after eight years. Construct a depreciation schedule using

    (a) the straight-line method;
    (b) the sum-of-the-years-digits method;
    (c) the simple declining-balance method;
    (d) the complex declining-balance method.

B. Answer the following questions.

1. A building costing $560 000 is estimated to have a life of 40 years and a salvage value of $68 000. Compute the book value after 15 years and the depreciation charge in Year 16 for

    (a) the straight-line method;
    (b) the sum-of-the-years-digits method;
    (c) the simple declining-balance method;
    (d) the complex declining-balance method.

2. Heavy machinery costing $150 000 with a scrap value of $13 500 is estimated to have a life of 25 years. Compute the book value after 10 years and the depreciation charge in Year 11 for

   (a) the straight-line method;
   (b) the sum-of-the-years-digits method;
   (c) the simple declining-balance method;
   (d) the complex declining-balance method.

BUSINESS MATH NEWS BOX

MEET THE NEW BOSS

The ranks of the self-employed continue to increase. StatsCan says that 2.2 million Canadians earned at least some income from self-employment in 1994, a 5.9 percent jump over the previous year. Among urban centres, Olds, Alberta, had the largest proportion of self-employed people—20 percent.

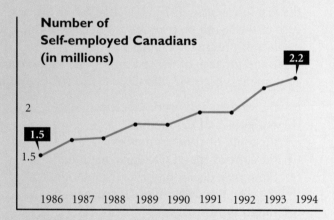

Source: Statistics Canada

QUESTIONS

1. What was the average number of people who were self-employed over the period from 1986 to 1994?

2. Given the data for 1994, about how many people were self-employed in 1993?

3. Use an atlas or other source to find the approximate number of self-employed people in Olds, Alberta.

4. If you were to be self-employed, what type of business would you start?

SOURCE: Adapted from *Maclean's Magazine*, September 9, 1996, p. 37.

5.2 BREAK-EVEN ANALYSIS

A. Cost-volume-profit relationships

A primary function of accounting is the collection of cost and revenue data. These data are then used to examine the existing relationships between cost behaviour and revenue behaviour.

Any analysis, whether graphic or algebraic, makes certain assumptions about the behaviour of costs and revenue. In its simplest form, cost-volume-profit analysis makes the following assumptions.

1. Revenue per unit of output is constant. Total revenue varies directly with volume.
2. Costs can be classified as either fixed or variable.
3. **Fixed costs** remain constant over the time period considered for all levels of output. Examples of costs in this category are depreciation, rent, property taxes, and supervision and management salaries. Since fixed costs are constant in total, they vary per unit of output. They decrease per unit of output as volume increases and increase per unit of output as volume decreases.
4. **Variable costs** are constant per unit of output regardless of volume. They fluctuate in total amount as volume fluctuates. Examples of costs in this category are direct material costs, direct labour costs, and sales commissions.

The above assumptions present a simplified view of the real world. Fixed costs are not constant across all levels of output; instead they tend to change in a step-like manner. Per unit variable costs are not always constant; they are often influenced by economies of scale. Costs cannot be rigidly classified into fixed costs and variable costs. Rather, many costs are semi-variable; that is, they contain a fixed component as well as a variable component. However, for purposes of an uncomplicated introductory analysis, these assumptions serve a useful purpose.

Using these simplified assumptions, the behaviour of revenue and the behaviour of costs may be represented graphically by straight-line diagrams as shown in Figures 5.1 and 5.2.

FIGURE 5.1   Revenue Behaviour

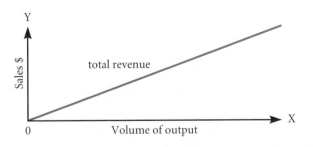

FIGURE 5.2   **Cost Behaviour**

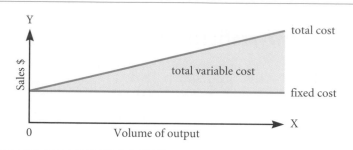

B. Break-even chart

The break-even approach to cost-volume-profit analysis focuses on profitability. It is specifically concerned with identifying the level of output at which the business neither makes a profit nor sustains a loss, that is, the level of output at which

$$\text{NET INCOME} = 0$$

The level of output at which NET INCOME = 0 is called the **break-even point** and is obtained from the relationship

$$\text{TOTAL REVENUE} = \text{TOTAL COST}$$

In addition, the following relationships are useful.

$$\text{TOTAL REVENUE} = \text{VOLUME} \times \text{UNIT REVENUE}$$

$$\text{TOTAL VARIABLE COST} = \text{VOLUME} \times \text{VARIABLE COST PER UNIT}$$

$$\text{TOTAL COST} = \text{FIXED COST} + \text{TOTAL VARIABLE COST}$$

The relationship between revenue and costs at different levels of output may be portrayed graphically by showing revenue behaviour (Figure 5.1) and cost behaviour (Figure 5.2) on the same graph. The resulting graph shows the break-even point and is known as a **break-even chart** (see Figure 5.3).

Notes on the charts
1. The horizontal axis represents volume of output either as a number of units or as a percent of capacity. The vertical axis represents dollar values (sales revenue). The origin is at zero—zero volume and zero dollars.
2. The total revenue line is drawn by plotting two or more total revenue points (one of which is always the origin) and joining them.
3. The fixed cost line is drawn parallel to the horizontal axis from the point on the vertical axis that represents total fixed cost dollars.
4. The total cost line is drawn by plotting two or more total cost points (one of which is always the point at which the fixed cost line starts on the vertical axis) and joining them.
5. The point at which the total revenue line and the total cost line intersect is the break-even point.

FIGURE 5.3   Break-even Chart

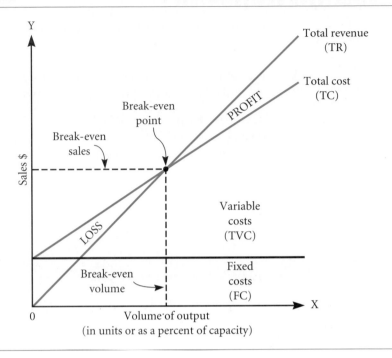

6. The point of intersection on the horizontal axis of the perpendicular drawn from the break-even point to the horizontal axis indicates the break-even volume in units or as a percent of capacity.

7. The point of intersection on the vertical axis of the perpendicular drawn from the break-even point to the vertical axis indicates the break-even volume in dollars (Sales $).

8. The area between the horizontal axis and the fixed cost line represents the fixed cost in dollars.

9. The area between the fixed cost line and the total cost line represents the total variable cost in dollars for all levels of operations.

10. The area between the total revenue line and the total cost line to the left of the break-even point represents the loss area, that is, where total revenue is less than total cost.

11. The area between the total cost line and the total revenue line to the right of the break-even point represents the profit area, that is, where total revenue is greater than total cost.

The graphic approach of a break-even chart is complemented by an algebraic approach that uses the relationship Total Revenue = Total Cost.

Both approaches are illustrated in the examples that follow. Two distinct situations may be encountered depending on the accounting data that are available. In the first situation, illustrated in Section C, the accounting information is in units. In the second situation, illustrated in Section D, the accounting information is in total dollars.

C. Break-even analysis—Case 1

The available accounting data are in units.

EXAMPLE 5.2A

Market research for a new product indicates that the product can be sold at $50.00 per unit. Cost analysis provides the following information.

Fixed cost per period = $8640.00
Variable cost per unit = $30.00
Production capacity per period = 900 units

Perform a break-even analysis. Provide

 (i) an algebraic statement of

    (a) the total revenue,
    (b) the total cost;

 (ii) a detailed break-even chart;

(iii) computation of the break-even point

    (a) in units,
    (b) as a percent of capacity,
    (c) in dollars.

Solution

 (i) Let the volume in units be X.

    (a)   Total revenue, TR = Volume × Unit revenue
       = (X)(50.00)
       = 50.00X
       Total revenue, TR = 50X.

    (b)   Total variable cost = Volume × Variable cost per unit
       = (X)(30.00)
       = 30.00X
       Total cost, TC = Fixed cost + Total variable cost
       = 8640.00 + 30.00X
       Total cost, TC = 8640 + 30X.

 (ii) *Break-even Chart*
You can draw the break-even chart by graphing the **revenue function**, TR = 50X, and the **cost function**, TC = 8640 + 30X.
    Since capacity is 900 units, the horizontal scale needs to allow for X values up to 900. The vertical scale must allow for maximum sales dollars of (900)(50) = 45 000.

Graphing the Revenue Function, TR = 50X
To graph the revenue function, assume at least two values of X and compute the corresponding value of TR.

For X = 0, TR = (50)(0) = 0 ──────────→ Graph point (0, 0)
For X = 900, TR = (50)(900) = 45 000 ──────→ Graph point (900, 45 000)

While any value of X may be used, the two values selected are the preferred values. They represent the two extreme values (minimum and maximum volume) for the example.

Graphing the Cost Function, TC = 8640 + 30X

Assume two values of X and compute the corresponding value of TC.

For X = 0, TC = 8640 + 30(0) = 8640 ──────→ Graph point (0, 8640)
For X = 900, TC = 8640 + 30(900)
                = 8640 + 27 000 = 35 640 ──→ Graph point (900, 35 640)

FIGURE 5.4   Break-even Chart for Example 5.2A

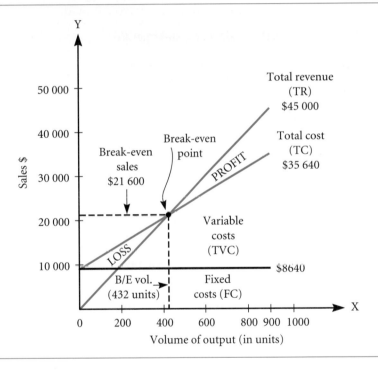

(iii) To determine the break-even point, use the break-even relationship.

Total Revenue, TR = Total Cost, TC
$$50X = 8640 + 30X$$
$$20X = 8640$$
$$X = 432$$

(a) The break-even volume in units is 432.

(b) As a percent of capacity, the break-even volume is $\dfrac{432}{900} = 0.48 = 48\%$.

(c) The break-even volume in dollars = (432)(50) = \$21 600.

D. Break-even analysis—Case 2

The available accounting data are in total dollars.

EXAMPLE 5.2B

The following information is available about the operations of the King Corp. for the current year.

Sales		$40 000
Fixed costs	$12 600	
Variable costs	16 000	
Total cost		28 600
Net income		$11 400

Capacity is a sales volume of $60 000.

Perform a break-even analysis. Provide

(i) an algebraic statement of

  (a) the revenue function,
  (b) the cost function;

(ii) a detailed break-even chart;

(iii) computation of the break-even point

  (a) in sales dollars,
  (b) as a percent of capacity.

Solution

(i) When the data are in terms of dollars rather than units, express the functions in terms of sales volume.

Let X represent the sales volume in dollars.

(a) The revenue function is Total Revenue, TR = X.
(b) Since variable costs are directly related to sales volume, they can be expressed as a percent of sales volume.
    In this example, total variable costs are $16 000 for a sales volume of $40 000.

$$\frac{\text{Total Variable Cost}}{\text{Total Revenue}} = \frac{16\ 000}{40\ 000} = 0.40 = 40\%$$

Total Variable Cost = 40% of Total Revenue = 0.40 TR

The cost function is TC = 12 600 + 0.40 TR
         or TC = 12 600 + 0.40X

(ii) When the accounting data are in terms of total dollars, the horizontal axis represents output in terms of percent of sales capacity. Subdivide the horizontal scale to allow percent sales levels up to 100%. The vertical scale must allow for the maximum sales level of $60 000.

Graphing the Revenue Function, TR = X

To graph the revenue function, assume at least two sales volume levels expressed as a percent of capacity.

For X = 0,   TR = 0 ⎯⎯⎯⎯⎯⎯→ Graph point (0, 0)
For X = 60 000, TR = 60 000 ⎯⎯⎯⎯→ Graph point (60 000, 60 000)

The line joining the two points represents the revenue function.

Graphing the Cost Function, TC = 12 600 + 0.40X

Assume two sales volume levels and compute TC.

For X = 0,   TC = 12 600 + 0.40(0)
                         = 12 600 ⎯⎯⎯⎯→ Graph point (0, 12 600)

For X = 60 000, TC = 12 600 + 0.40(60 000)
                         = 12 600 + 24 000
                         = 36 600 ⎯⎯⎯→ Graph point (60 000, 36 600)

FIGURE 5.5   Break-even Chart for Example 5.2B

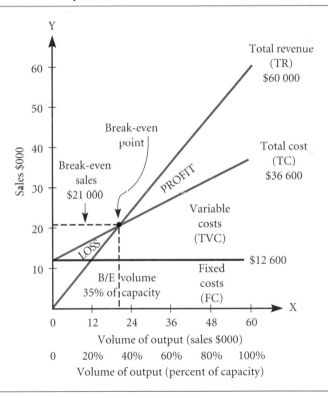

(iii) The break-even point is given by

$$X = 12\ 600 + 0.40X$$
$$0.60X = 12\ 600$$
$$X = 21\ 000$$

(a) The break-even volume in dollars is $21 000.

(b) The break-even point is $\dfrac{21\,000}{60\,000} = 35\%$ of sales capacity.

E. Finding the break-even point by using unit contribution

As an alternative to using the break-even relationship, Total Revenue = Total Cost, we can use the concept of contribution margin per unit to determine break-even volume:

$$\begin{array}{c} \text{CONTRIBUTION MARGIN} \\ \text{PER UNIT} \end{array} = \begin{array}{c} \text{SELLING PRICE} \\ \text{PER UNIT} \end{array} - \begin{array}{c} \text{VARIABLE COST} \\ \text{PER UNIT} \end{array}$$

$$\text{BREAK-EVEN VOLUME} = \dfrac{\text{FIXED COST}}{\text{UNIT CONTRIBUTION MARGIN}}$$

EXAMPLE 5.2C

Use contribution margin per unit to determine the break-even volume for Example 5.2A.

Solution

Fixed cost = $8640.00;
Selling price per unit = $50.00;
Variable cost per unit = $30.00.
Contribution margin per unit = 50.00 − 30.00 = $20.00

$$\text{Break-even volume} = \dfrac{\text{FIXED COST}}{\text{CONTRIBUTION MARGIN}} = \dfrac{8640.00}{20.00} = 432$$

Break-even volume is 432 units.

EXAMPLE 5.2D

Use contribution margin per unit to determine the break-even volume for Example 5.2B.

Solution

Fixed cost = $12 600.00;
When the sales volume is given in total dollars, the selling price per unit = $1.00;
Variable cost per unit = 40% of $1.00 = $0.40.
Contribution margin = 1.00 − 0.40 = $0.60.

$$\text{Break-even volume} = \dfrac{12\,600.00}{0.60} = 21\,000.00.$$

Break-even volume is a sales volume of $21 000.

Exercise 5.2

A. For each of the following, perform a break-even analysis showing

(a) an algebraic statement of
   (i) the revenue function,
   (ii) the cost function;

(b) a detailed break-even chart;

(c) computation of the break-even point
   (i) in units (if applicable),
  (ii) as a percent of capacity,
 (iii) in sales dollars.

1. Engineering estimates show that the variable cost of manufacturing a new product will be $35 per unit. Based on market research, the selling price of the product is to be $120 per unit and variable selling expense is expected to be $15 per unit. The fixed costs applicable to the new product are estimated to be $2800 per period and capacity per period is 100 units.

2. A firm manufactures a product that sells for $12.00 per unit. Variable cost per unit is $8.00 and fixed cost per period is $1200. Capacity per period is 1000 units.

3. The following data pertain to the operating budget of Matt Mfg.

Sales		$720 000
Fixed cost	$220 000	
Total variable cost	324 000	544 000
Net income		$176 000

Capacity is a sales volume of $800 000 per period.

4. Harrow Seed and Fertilizer has compiled the following estimates for operations.

Sales		$120 000
Fixed cost	$43 200	
Variable costs	48 000	91 200
Net income		$ 28 800

Capacity is a sales volume of $150 000.

REVIEW EXERCISE

1. A machine costing $12 000 has a trade-in value of $2460 after eight years. Construct a depreciation schedule using

   (a) the sum-of-the-years-digits method;

   (b) the simple declining-balance method;

   (c) the complex declining-balance method.

2. Equipment with an original cost of $32 000 has an estimated life of 25 years and a scrap value of $480. Compute the book value after 20 years and the depreciation charge in Year 21 using

(a) the straight-line method;

(b) the sum-of-the-years-digits method;

(c) the simple declining-balance method;

(d) the complex declining-balance method.

3. A machine with an original cost of $9160 has a trade-in value of $2230 after six years. Construct a depreciation schedule using the sum-of-the-years-digits method.

4. A building has an original cost of $80 000, a life of 25 years, and a salvage value of $8500. Find the book value of the building after fifteen years using the simple declining-balance method.

5. A turbine costing $75 000 has a life of twenty years and a scrap value of $3500. Determine the depreciation in Year 12 using the complex declining-balance method.

6. The lighting division of Universal Electric Company plans to introduce a new street light based on the following accounting information.

   Fixed costs per period are $3136; variable cost per unit is $157; selling price per unit is $185; and capacity per period is 320 units.

   (a) Draw a detailed break-even chart.

   (b) Compute the break-even point
       (i) in units;
       (ii) as a percent of capacity;
       (iii) in dollars.

   (c) Determine the break-even point as a percent of capacity
       (i) if fixed costs are reduced to $2688;
       (ii) if fixed costs increase to $4588 and variable costs are reduced to 80% of the selling price;
       (iii) if the selling price is reduced to $171.

7. The following information is available from the accounting records of Eva Corporation.

   Fixed costs per period are $4800. Sales volume for the last period was $19 360 and variable costs were $13 552. Capacity per period is a sales volume of $32 000.

   (a) Draw a detailed break-even chart.

   (b) Compute the break-even point
       (i) in dollars;
       (ii) as a percent of capacity.

(c) Determine the break-even point
  (i) if fixed costs are decreased by $600;
  (ii) if fixed costs are increased to $5670 and variable costs are changed to 55% of sales.

8. The operating budget of the Bea Company contains the following information.

Sales at 80% of capacity		$400 000
Fixed costs	$105 000	
Variable costs	260 000	365 000
Net income		$ 35 000

(a) Draw a detailed break-even chart.

(b) Compute the break-even point
  (i) as a percent of capacity;
  (ii) in dollars.

(c) Determine the break-even point in dollars if fixed costs are reduced by $11 200 while variable costs are changed to 72% of sales.

9. A manufacturer of major appliances provides the following information about the operations of the refrigeration division.

Fixed costs per period are $26 880; variable costs per unit are $360; selling price per unit is $640; and capacity is 150 units.

(a) Compute the break-even point
  (i) in units;
  (ii) as a percent of capacity;
  (iii) in dollars.

(b) Determine the break-even point in dollars if fixed costs are increased to $32 200.

(c) Determine the break-even point as a percent of capacity if fixed costs are reduced to $23 808 while variable costs are increased to 60% of sales.

SELF-TEST

1. An asset costing $85 000 has an expected salvage value of $5000 after sixteen years. Compute the book value of the asset after ten years using the straight-line method.

2. Equipment costing $25 000 has an estimated disposal value of $1600 after twelve years. What is the book value of the asset after seven years by the sum-of-the-years-digits method?

3. A vault has been installed at a cost of $45 000 and is expected to have a residual value of $2500 after twenty years. Determine the depreciation charge in Year 15 using the complex declining-balance method.

4. The Superior CD Company sells CDs for $10 each. Manufacturing cost is $2.60 per CD; marketing costs are $2.40 per CD; and royalty payments are 20% of the selling price. The fixed cost of preparing the CDs is $18 000. Capacity is 15 000 CDs.

(a) Draw a detailed break-even chart.

(b) Compute the break-even point
     (i) in units;
     (ii) in dollars;
     (iii) as a percent of capacity.

(c) Determine the break-even point in units if fixed costs are increased by $1600 while manufacturing cost is reduced $0.50 per album.

(d) Determine the break-even point in units if the selling price is increased by 10% while fixed costs are increased by $2900.

5. The management of Lambda Corporation has received the following forecast for the next year.

Sales revenue		$600 000
Fixed costs	$275 000	
Variable costs	270 000	545 000
Net income		$ 55 000

Capacity is a sales volume of $800 000.

(a) Compute the break-even point
     (i) in dollars;
     (ii) as a percent of capacity.

(b) Determine the break-even volume in dollars if fixed costs are increased by $40 000 while variable costs are held to 40% of sales.

CHALLENGE PROBLEMS

1. A company's new minivan costs $18 720. It has an estimated useful life of 6 years and an estimated scrap value of $1500. Prepare a chart comparing the straight-line, complex declining-balance, and sum-of-the-years-digits methods of depreciation for the minivan. Which method would you recommend if the company wanted to take the maximum amount of depreciation expense in the first three years?

2. An aluminum company uses a highly mechanized production process to produce brackets for the automotive industry. The company's profit function in millions of dollars for x million brackets is $P = 0.7x - 24.5$. The cost function is $C = 0.9x + 24.5$. Find the break-even point in millions of units.

CASE STUDY 5.1 — PLANNING FOR PRODUCTION

Fred Gardiner has decided to expand his garden supply manufacturing business. He has an available factory site that is presently costing him $40 000 per year in taxes and maintenance. He has made a deal with Stellar Supply Company to provide him with the necessary material to produce 1000 garden hoses. Stellar has agreed to supply the material for $6000 less 2% for quantity discount. Fred's shop steward has informed him that labour costs to make the capacity 1000 garden hoses will amount to $10 000.

QUESTIONS

1. Fred expects that it will take 3 months to produce the garden hoses, and he intends to market them at $29.99 per hose. How many hoses must Fred sell to break even?

2. What is the break-even point as a percent of capacity?

3. If Fred sells all 1000 hoses, how much profit can he expect to make based on the costs listed above?

4. Fred has been informed that the union has negotiated a 5% wage increase.

   (a) What effect will the wage increase have on the break-even point?

   (b) What effect will the wage increase have on Fred's profit?

CASE STUDY 5.2 — CALCULATING CAR COSTS

Roy is concerned about the high cost of the gasoline that his current car consumes. He is considering purchasing a new car. He realizes that he must take into account the purchase price of the new car as well as the savings in gasoline costs to determine when he would be saving money by having a new car.

Roy designed a mathematical formula to calculate the number of years he must drive the new car. He used the following variables in his formula:

y = the number of years Roy must own the new car
m = the gasoline used by the current car, measured in kilometres per litre
n = the gasoline used by the new car, measured in kilometres per litre
c = the net cost of the new car (purchase price of the new car − trade-in value of the old car)
d = the average number of kilometres driven per year
p = the price of gasoline per litre
x = the number of years to break even

Roy decided the "current car–new car" relationship could be expressed as follows:

Cost of gasoline for current car during break-even period	=	Cost of gasoline for new car during break-even period	+	Net cost of new car

QUESTIONS

1. Using the variables defined by Roy, what is the expression for each side of the "current car–new car" relationship?

2. What is the general formula for the break-even period for the "current car–new car" relationship?

3. What is the break-even period if Roy's current car has a trade-in value of $8000 and gets 6 km/L. Gasoline prices in Roy's neighbourhood average 60¢/L. Assume Roy drives an average of 30 000 km/year.

4. Assume that the price of gasoline can vary by ±25% from the price of 60¢/L.

   (a) How does the break-even period change when the price of gasoline declines by 25%?

   (b) How does the break-even period change when the price of gasoline increases by 25%?

5. What is the expected break-even period if Roy buys a car costing $17 000 with an expected gas consumption of 15 km/L if the average price is (a) 60¢/L (b) 51¢/L (c) 75¢/L?

6. What assumptions did you make when you solved these problems? What cost factors have not been considered?

SUMMARY OF FORMULAE

Formula 5.1

$$\text{YEARLY DEPRECIATION} = \frac{\text{ORIGINAL COST} - \text{RESIDUAL VALUE}}{n}$$

Formula for finding the yearly depreciation when using the straight-line method

where n = the number of years in the life of the asset

Formula 5.2

$$\text{DEPRECIATION PER SERVICE HOUR} = \frac{\text{ORIGINAL COST} - \text{RESIDUAL VALUE}}{n}$$

Formula for finding the depreciation per service hour when using the service-hours method

where n = the number of service hours in the life of the asset

Formula 5.3

$$\text{DEPRECIATION PER UNIT OF PRODUCT} = \frac{\text{ORIGINAL COST} - \text{RESIDUAL VALUE}}{n}$$

Formula for finding the depreciation per unit of product when using the units-of-product method

where n = the number of product units in the life of the asset

Formula 5.4

$$k = \frac{\text{WEARING VALUE}}{\dfrac{n(n + 1)}{2}}$$

Formula for finding the value of one part (constant of proportion) when using the sum-of-the-years-digits method

where Wearing Value = $\dfrac{\text{Original Cost} - \text{Residual Value}}{}$

Formula 5.5

$$d = 2 \times \frac{1}{n}$$

Formula for finding the rate of depreciation when using the simple declining-balance method

where n = the number of years in the life of the asset

Formula 5.6

$$d = 1 - \sqrt[n]{\frac{\text{RESIDUAL VALUE}}{\text{ORIGINAL COST}}}$$

Formula for finding the rate of depreciation when using the complex declining-balance method

GLOSSARY

Accumulated depreciation   the total depreciation allocated to expired accounting periods at any point in the life of an asset

Book value   the net value of an asset at any point in its life; the difference between the original cost and the accumulated depreciation

Break-even analysis   a method of determining the level of output at which a business neither makes a profit nor sustains a loss

Break-even chart   a graphic representation of cost-volume-profit relationships used to identify the break-even point

Break-even point   the level of output at which net income is zero

Cost function   an algebraic expression stating the relationship between cost and volume

Depreciation   loss in value of an asset due to physical deterioration, wear and tear, decay, or obsolescence

Depreciation schedule   chart showing how the loss in an asset's value is allocated to the various accounting periods

Fixed costs   costs that remain constant for the time period for all levels of output considered

Methods of depreciation   systematic ways of allocating depreciation to accounting periods

Original cost   the price originally paid for an asset, including the necessary and reasonable costs incurred in readying the asset for its intended purpose

Residual value   the value of an asset when it has lost its usefulness or is disposed of

Revenue function   an algebraic expression representing the behaviour of revenue

Salvage value   see *Residual value*

Scrap value   see *Residual value*

Trade-in value   see *Residual value*

Useful life   the period of time an asset is expected to be used for its intended purpose; it is usually stated in years, but can also be stated in hours or in units of output

Variable costs   costs that are constant per unit of output regardless of volume; they fluctuate in total amount as volume fluctuates

Wearing value   the total depreciation over the life of an asset; the difference between original cost and residual value

6

Trade Discount, Cash Discount, Markup, and Markdown

Suppose you were the owner of a furniture manufacturing company. You purchase your raw materials from suppliers, who offer their goods to you at a *list*, or catalogue price. You might receive a *trade discount* if you pay for the materials promptly or if you purchase the materials in bulk. When you sell your furniture to furniture retailers, you offer your furniture at a list, or catalogue, price and you might offer a discount for prompt payment or bulk purchases. As you can see, we need to be careful, since the same terms are used by different companies to represent different dollar amounts.

Introduction

A product typically passes through a number of stages of the *merchandising chain* on its way from a raw material to a product purchased by the consumer.

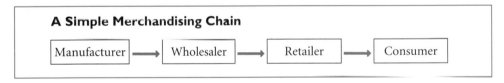

A Simple Merchandising Chain

Manufacturer → Wholesaler → Retailer → Consumer

A simple merchandising chain may include manufacturers, wholesalers, and retailers, all of whom must make a profit on the product to remain in business. As the product is purchased and resold along the chain, each member adds a *markup* that increases the price of the product. Sometimes a member offers a discount in order to sell more product or to encourage prompt payment for the product. When the product is sold to the consumer, it may be *marked down* in price in response to competitors' prices or other economic conditions.

This chapter deals with trade discount, cash discount, markup, and markdown.

OBJECTIVES

Upon completing this chapter, you will be able to do the following:

1. **Solve problems involving trade discounts.**
2. **Calculate equivalent single rates of discount for discount series, and solve problems involving discount series.**
3. **Apply the three most commonly used methods of cash discount.**

   4. **Solve problems involving markup based on either cost or selling price.**
   5. **Solve pricing problems involving markup, markdown, and discounts.**

6.1   TRADE DISCOUNT

A. Basic concepts and computations

The merchandising chain is made up of retailers, wholesalers, distributors, and manufacturers. Merchandise is usually bought and sold among the members of the chain on credit terms. The prices quoted to other members often involve *trade discounts*. A **trade discount** is a reduction of a catalogue or **list price** and is usually stated as a percent of the catalogue or list price.

Trade discounts are used by manufacturers, wholesalers, and distributors as pricing tools for a number of reasons. The most important reasons are

(a) to facilitate the establishment of price differentials for different groups of customers;

(b) to facilitate the communication of changes in prices;

(c) to reduce the cost of making changes in prices.

When computing trade discounts, keep in mind that the rate of discount is based on the list price.

$$\text{AMOUNT OF DISCOUNT} = \text{RATE OF DISCOUNT} \times \text{LIST PRICE} \qquad \text{——— Formula 6.1}$$

The amount of discount is then subtracted from the list price. The remainder is the **net price**.

$$\text{NET PRICE} = \text{LIST PRICE} - \text{AMOUNT OF TRADE DISCOUNT} \qquad \text{——— Formula 6.2}$$

EXAMPLE 6.1A   An item listed at $80.00 is subject to a trade discount of 25%.

Compute   (i) the amount of discount;

(ii) the net price.

Solution
   (i) Amount of discount = Rate of discount × List price
   $$= (0.25)(80.00) = \$20.00$$

   (ii) Net price = List price − Trade discount
   $$= 80.00 - 20.00 = \$60.00$$

B. The net factor approach to computing the net price

Instead of computing the amount of discount and then deducting this amount from the list price, the net price can be found by using the more efficient net factor approach developed in the following illustration.

Referring back to Example 6.1A, the solution can be restated as follows.

List price	$80.00
Less trade discount 25% of 80.00	20.00
Net price	$60.00

Since the discount is given as a percent of the list price, the three dollar values may be stated as percents of list price.

List price	$80.00	⟶ 100% of List price
Less trade discount	$20.00	⟶ 25% of List price
Net price	$60.00	⟶ 75% of List price

Note: The "75%," called the **Net Price Factor** or **Net Factor** (in abbreviated form, **NPF**) is obtained by deducting the 25% discount from 100%.

$$\text{NET PRICE FACTOR (NPF)} = 100\% - \% \text{ DISCOUNT}$$ ———— **Formula 6.3A**

The resulting relationship between net price and list price may be stated generally.

$$\text{NET PRICE} = \text{NET PRICE FACTOR (NPF)} \times \text{LIST PRICE}$$ ———— **Formula 6.4A**

The two relationships represented by Formulae 6.3A and 6.4A can be restated in algebraic terms:

Convert the % discount into its decimal equivalent represented by d and express 100% by its decimal equivalent 1.

$$\text{NET PRICE FACTOR} = 1 - d$$ ———— **Formula 6.3B**

Let the list price be represented by L and let the net price be represented by N.

$$N = (1 - d)L \quad \text{or} \quad N = L(1 - d)$$ ———— **Formula 6.4B**

EXAMPLE 6.1B   Find the net price for

(i) list price $36.00 less 15%;

(ii) list price $125.64 less 37.5%;

(iii) list price $86.85 less 33⅓%;

(iv) list price $49.98 less 16⅔%.

Solution

(i) Net price = Net price factor × List price ——— using Formula 6.4A
$$= (100\% - 15\%)(36.00)$$ ——— using Formula 6.3A
$$= (85\%)(36.00)$$ ——— subtract
$$= (0.85)(36.00)$$ ——— convert the percent into
$$= \$30.60$$ a decimal

(ii) Net price = $(1 - d)$L ——— using Formula 6.4B
$$= (1 - 0.375)(125.64)$$ ——— 37.5% = 0.375
$$= (0.625)(125.64)$$
$$= \$78.53$$

(iii) Net price = $(100\% - 33\frac{1}{3}\%)(86.85)$ ——— using Formula 6.3A
$$= (66\frac{2}{3}\%)(86.85)$$
$$= (0.6666667)(86.85)$$ ——— use a sufficient number
$$= \$57.90$$ of decimals

(iv) Net price = $(1 - 0.1\dot{6})(49.98)$ ——— using Formula 6.4B
$$= (0.8\dot{3})(49.98)$$
$$= (0.8333333)(49.98)$$ ——— use a sufficient number
$$= \$41.65$$ of decimals

C. Discount series

If a list price is subject to two or more discounts, these discounts are called a **discount series**. A manufacturer may offer two or more discounts to different members of the merchandising chain. For example, a chain member closest to the consumer might be offered additional discounts, since there are fewer chain members who must make a profit on an item. If the manufacturer wants to encourage large-volume orders or early orders of seasonal items, it may offer additional discounts. For example, a manufacturer might offer a store a 5% discount on orders over 1000 items and an additional discount of 6% for ordering Christmas items in April. It may also offer additional discounts to compensate for advertising, promotion, and service costs handled by merchandising chain members. (Today, discount series are becoming less common as more retailers and large buying groups buy directly from the manufacturer, bypassing chain members to keep prices low. These buyers demand the best price. They are not concerned with whether the best price is due to a discount series, a single large discount, or any other price-setting method.)

When computing the net price, the discounts making up the discount series are applied to the list price successively. The net price resulting from the first discount becomes the list price for the second discount; the net price resulting from the second discount becomes the list price for the third discount; and so on. In fact, finding the net price when a list price is subject to a discount series consists of solving as many discount problems as there are discounts in the discount series.

EXAMPLE 6.1C

An item listed at $150.00 is subject to the discount series 20%, 10%, 5%. Determine the net price.

Solution

List price	$150.00	⎫
Less first discount 20% of 150.00	30.00	⎬ ——— Problem 1
Net price after first discount	$120.00	⎫
Less second discount 10% of 120.00	12.00	⎬ ——— Problem 2
Net price after second discount	$108.00	⎭
Less third discount 5% of 108.00	5.40	⎫ ——— Problem 3
Net price	$102.60	⎭

Because the solution to Example 6.1C consists of three problems involving a simple discount, the net price factor approach can be used to solve it or any problem involving a series of discounts.

Problem 1 Net price after the first discount
$$= \text{NPF for 20\% discount} \times \text{Original list price}$$
$$= (1 - 0.20)(150.00)$$
$$= (0.80)(150.00)$$
$$= \$120.00$$

Problem 2 Net price after the second discount
$$= \text{NPF for 10\% discount} \times \text{Net price after the first discount}$$
$$= (1 - 0.10)(120.00)$$
$$= (0.90)(120.00)$$
$$= (0.90)(0.80)(150.00)$$
$$= \$108.00$$

Problem 3 Net price after the third discount
$$= \text{NPF for 5\% discount} \times \text{Net price after the second discount}$$
$$= (1 - 0.05)(108.00)$$
$$= (0.95)(108.00)$$
$$= (0.95)(0.90)(0.80)(150.00)$$
$$= \$102.60$$

The final net price of $102.60 is obtained from
$$(0.95)(0.90)(0.80)(150.00)$$
$$= (0.80)(0.90)(0.95)(150.00) \quad \text{——— the order of the factors may be rearranged}$$
$$= \text{NPF for 20\%} \times \text{NPF for 10\%} \times \text{NPF for 5\%} \times \text{Original list price}$$
$= $ Product of the NPFs for the discounts in the discount series $\times$ Original list price
$= $ Net price factor for the discount series $\times$ Original list price

This result may be generalized to find the net price for a list price subject to a discount series.

NPF FOR THE DISCOUNT SERIES = NPF FOR THE FIRST DISCOUNT × NPF FOR THE SECOND DISCOUNT × ... × NPF FOR THE LAST DISCOUNT

——— **Formula 6.5A**

$$\boxed{\text{NET PRICE} = \frac{\text{NPF FOR THE DISCOUNT SERIES}}{} \times \text{LIST PRICE}} \quad \text{———————— Formula 6.6A}$$

The two relationships represented by Formulae 6.5A and 6.6A can be restated in algebraic terms.

Let the net price be represented by N,
the original list price by L,
the first rate of discount by d_1,
the second rate of discount by d_2,
the third rate of discount by d_3, and
the last rate of discount by d_n.

Then Formula 6.5A can be shown as

$$\boxed{\frac{\text{NPF FOR A}}{\text{DISCOUNT SERIES}} = (1 - d_1)(1 - d_2)(1 - d_3) \ldots (1 - d_n)} \quad \text{——— Formula 6.5B}$$

and Formula 6.6A can be shown as

$$\boxed{\text{NET PRICE} = (1 - d_1)(1 - d_2)(1 - d_3) \ldots (1 - d_n)L} \quad \text{——— Formula 6.6B}$$

EXAMPLE 6.1D   Determine the net price for

(i)   an office desk listed at $440.00 less 25%, 15%, 2%;

(ii) a power drill listed at $180.00 less 30%, 12.5%, 5%, 5%;

(iii) a home computer listed at $1260.00 less 33⅓%, 16⅔%, 2.5%;

(iv) an electronic chessboard listed at $1225.00 less 66⅔%, 8⅓%.

Solution   (i) Net price = NPF for the discount series × list price —— using Formula 6.6A
$$= (1 - 0.25)(1 - 0.15)(1 - 0.02)(440.00)$$
$$= (0.75)(0.85)(0.98)(440.00)$$
$$= \$274.89$$

(ii) Net price = $L(1 - d_1)(1 - d_2)(1 - d_3)(1 - d_4)$ ———— using Formula 6.6B
$$= 180.00(1 - 0.30)(1 - 0.125)(1 - 0.05)(1 - 0.05)$$
$$= 180.00(0.70)(0.875)(0.95)(0.95)$$
$$= \$99.50$$

(iii) Net price = $1260.00(1 - 0.3\dot{3})(1 - 0.1\dot{6})(1 - 0.025)$
$$= 1260.00(0.6\dot{6})(0.8\dot{3})(0.975)$$
$$= 1260.00(0.6666667)(0.8333333)(0.975)$$
$$= \$682.50$$

(iv) Net price = $(1 - 0.6\dot{6})(1 - 0.08\dot{3})(1225.00)$
$$= (0.3\dot{3})(0.91\dot{6})(1225.00)$$
$$= (0.3333333)(0.9166667)(1225.00)$$
$$= \$374.31$$

D. Computing rates of discount

Since the rate of trade discount is based on a list price, computing a rate of discount involves comparing the amount of discount to the list price.

$$\text{RATE OF TRADE DISCOUNT} = \frac{\text{AMOUNT OF DISCOUNT}}{\text{LIST PRICE}}$$ ——— **Formula 6.7**

EXAMPLE 6.1E   Find the rate of discount for

   (i)   skis listed at $280.00 less a discount of $67.20;

   (ii) ski gloves listed at $36.80 whose net price is $23.92;

   (iii) ski sweaters whose net price is $55.68 after a discount of $40.32.

Solution

   (i) Rate of discount $= \dfrac{\text{Amount of discount}}{\text{List price}} = \dfrac{67.20}{280.00} = 0.24 = 24\%$

   (ii) Amount of discount = List price − Net price = 36.80 − 23.92 = $12.88

   Rate of discount $= \dfrac{\text{Amount of discount}}{\text{List price}} = \dfrac{12.88}{36.80} = 0.35 = 35\%$

   (iii) Since Amount of discount = List price − Net price,

   List price = Net price + Amount of discount = 55.68 + 40.32 = $96.00

   Rate of discount $= \dfrac{\text{Amount of discount}}{\text{List price}} = \dfrac{40.32}{96.00} = 0.42 = 42\%$

EXAMPLE 6.1F   A manufacturer sells skidoos to dealers at a list price of $2100.00 less 40%, 10%, 5%. Determine

   (i) the amount of discount;

   (ii) the single rate of discount.

Solution

   (i) Net price = NPF × List price
      = (1 − 0.40)(1 − 0.10)(1 − 0.05)(2100.00)
      = (0.60)(0.90)(0.95)(2100.00)
      = $1077.30

   Amount of discount = List price − Net price
      = 2100.00 − 1077.30 = $1022.70

   (ii) Rate of discount $= \dfrac{\text{Amount of discount}}{\text{List price}} = \dfrac{1022.70}{2100.00} = 0.487 = 48.7\%$

Note: Taking off a single discount of 48.7% has the *same* effect as using the discount series 40%, 10%, 5%. That is, the single discount of 48.7% is equivalent to the discount series 40%, 10%, 5%. Caution: The sum of the discounts in the series, 40% + 10% + 5% or 55%, is *not* equivalent to the single discount.

E. Single equivalent rates of discount

For every discount series, a **single equivalent rate of discount** exists. You can find this equivalent rate by choosing a suitable list price and computing first the amount of discount and then the rate of discount.

EXAMPLE 6.1G   Find the single equivalent rate of discount for the discount series 30%, 8%, 2%.

Solution   Assume a list price of $1000.00.

Net price = NPF for the series × List price
$$= (0.70)(0.92)(0.98)(1000.00)$$
$$= (0.63112)(1000.00)$$
$$= \$631.12$$

Amount of discount = $1000.00 - 631.12 = \$368.88$

Single equivalent rate of discount $= \dfrac{368.88}{1000.00} = 0.36888 = 36.888\%$

Note: The net price factor for the series $= (0.70)(0.92)(0.98) = 0.63112$, and $1 - 0.63112 = 0.36888$. Therefore, you can find the single equivalent rate of discount by subtracting the net price factor for the series from 1.

> SINGLE EQUIVALENT RATE OF DISCOUNT FOR A DISCOUNT SERIES
> $= 1 -$ NPF FOR THE DISCOUNT SERIES
> $= 1 - [(1 - d_1)(1 - d_2)(1 - d_3) \dots (1 - d_n)]$ — **Formula 6.8**

EXAMPLE 6.1H   Determine the single equivalent rate of discount for each of the following discount series.

(i) 25%, 20%, 10%

(ii) 30%, 12.5%, 2.5%

(iii) $33\frac{1}{3}\%$, 15%, 5%, 5%

Solution   (i) Single equivalent rate of discount
$$= 1 - (1 - 0.25)(1 - 0.20)(1 - 0.10) \quad\text{——— using Formula 6.8}$$
$$= 1 - (0.75)(0.80)(0.90)$$
$$= 1 - 0.540000$$
$$= 0.46$$
$$= 46\%$$

(ii) Single equivalent rate of discount
$$= 1 - (1 - 0.30)(1 - 0.125)(1 - 0.025)$$
$$= 1 - (0.70)(0.875)(0.975)$$
$$= 1 - 0.5971875$$
$$= 0.4028125$$
$$= 40.28125\%$$

   (iii) Single equivalent rate of discount

$$= 1 - (1 - 0.3\dot{3})(1 - 0.15)(1 - 0.05)(1 - 0.05)$$
$$= 1 - (0.6\dot{6})(0.85)(0.95)(0.95)$$
$$= 1 - 0.5114167$$
$$= 0.4885833$$
$$= 48.85833\%$$

Note: When computing or using single equivalent rates of discount, use a sufficient number of decimals to ensure an acceptable degree of accuracy.

EXAMPLE 6.1I

Determine the amount of discount for each of the following list prices subject to the discount series 40%, 12.5%, 8⅓%, 2%.

(i) $625.00

(ii) $786.20

(iii) $1293.44

Solution

Single equivalent rate of discount
$$= 1 - (1 - 0.40)(1 - 0.125)(1 - 0.08\dot{3})(1 - 0.02)$$
$$= 1 - (0.60)(0.875)(0.91\dot{6})(0.98)$$
$$= 1 - 0.4716250$$
$$= 0.528375$$
$$= 52.8375\%$$

  (i) Amount of discount $= $ Rate of discount $\times$ List price
$$= (0.528375)(625.00)$$
$$= \$330.23$$

  (ii) Amount of discount $= (0.528375)(786.20)$
$$= \$415.41$$

  (iii) Amount of discount $= (0.528375)(1293.44)$
$$= \$683.42$$

F. Additional problems

EXAMPLE 6.1J

The local hardware store has listed a power saw for $136.00 less 30%. A catalogue store in a nearby shopping mall lists the same model for $126.00 less 20%, less an additional 15%. What additional discount must the hardware store give to meet the catalogue store price?

Solution

Hardware store net price $= 136.00(0.70)$	$95.20
Catalogue store price $= 126.00(0.80)(0.85)$	85.68
Additional discount needed	$ 9.52

$$\text{Additional rate of discount needed} = \frac{9.52}{95.20}$$
$$= 0.10$$
$$= 10\%$$

EXAMPLE 6.1K

A manufacturer can cover its cost and make a reasonable profit if it sells an article for $63.70. At what price should the article be listed so that a discount of 30% can be allowed?

Solution

Let the list price be represented by $L.
The net price factor is 0.70 and the net price is $63.70.

$$63.70 = 0.70 \text{ L} \quad\text{————————————— using Formula 6.4A}$$

$$L = \frac{63.70}{0.70} = \$91.00$$

The article should be listed at $91.00.

EXAMPLE 6.1L

Redden Distributors bought a shipment of personal computers for $477.36 each. At what price were the computers listed if the list price was subject to discounts of 15%, 10%, 4%?

Solution

Let the list price be $L.
The net price factor is $(0.85)(0.90)(0.96)$ ——— using Formula 6.5A
The net price is $477.36.

$$477.36 = (0.85)(0.90)(0.96)L$$

$$L = \frac{477.36}{(0.85)(0.90)(0.96)} = \$650.00$$

The computers were listed at $650.00.

Exercise 6.1

A. For each of the following 12 questions, find the missing value or values represented by the question marks.

	Rate of Discount	List Price	Net Price	Single Equivalent Rate of Dscount
1.	45%	$24.60	?	Not applicable
2.	16⅔%	$184.98	?	Not applicable
3.	37.5%	?	$84.35	Not applicable
4.	22%	?	$121.29	Not applicable
5.	?	$76.95	$51.30	Not applicable
6.	?	$724.80	$616.08	Not applicable
7.	25%, 10%	$44.80	?	?
8.	33⅓%, 5%	$126.90	?	?
9.	40%, 12.5%, 2%	$268.00	?	?
10.	20%, 16⅔%, 3%	$72.78	?	?
11.	35%, 33⅓%, 10%	?	$617.50	?
12.	20%, 20%, 10%	?	$53.28	?

B. Answer each of the following questions.

1. A patio chair is listed for $240.00 less 30%, 20%, 5%.

   (a) What is the net price?
   (b) How much is the amount of discount allowed?
   (c) What is the exact single rate of discount that was allowed?

2. A power saw is listed for $174.00 less 16⅔%, 10%, 8%.

   (a) What is the net price?
   (b) How much is the amount of discount allowed?
   (c) What is the exact single rate of discount that was allowed?

3. A motorcycle listed for $975.00 is sold for $820.00. What is the rate of discount that was allowed?

4. A washer-dryer combination listed at $1136.00 has a net price of $760.00. What is the rate of discount?

5. Compute the equivalent single rate of discount for each of the following discount series.

   (a) 30%, 12.5%
   (b) $33\frac{1}{3}$%, 20%, 3%

6. Determine the equivalent single rate of discount for each of the following series of discounts.

   (a) $16\frac{2}{3}$%, 7.5%
   (b) 25%, $8\frac{1}{3}$%, 2%

7. A 16⅔% discount allowed on a silk shirt amounted to $14.82. What was the net price?

8. A store advertises a discount of $44.24 on winter boots. If the discount is 35%, for how much were the boots sold?

9. A distributor lists an item for $85.00 less 20%. To improve lagging sales, the price of the item is to be reduced to $57.80. What additional rate of discount should be offered?

10. Crosstown Jewellers sells watches for $340.00 less 25%. Its competitors across the street offer the same type of watch for $360.00 less 30%, 15%. What additional rate of discount must Crosstown offer to meet the competitors' price?

11. The net price of a freezer after a discount of 16⅔% is $355.00. What is the list price?

12. The net price of an article is $63.31. What is the list price if a discount of 35% was allowed?

13. Arrow Manufacturing offers discounts of 25%, 12.5%, 4% on a line of products. For how much should an item be listed if it is to be sold for $113.40?

14. What is the list price of an article that is subject to discounts of 33⅓%, 10%, 2% if the net price is $564.48?

6.2 CASH DISCOUNT

A. Basic concepts

Goods among manufacturers, wholesalers, distributors, and retailers are usually sold on credit rather than for cash. To encourage prompt payment, many businesses offer a reduction in the amount of the invoice. This reduction is called a **cash discount**.

Cash discounts are offered in a variety of ways. The three most commonly used methods are

1. **ordinary dating**;
2. **end-of-the-month (or proximo) dating**;
3. **receipt-of-goods dating**.

The invoice's terms of payment specify the method and size of cash discount. Regardless of the method used, all **payment terms** have three things in common.

1. The **rate of discount** is stated as a percent of the net amount of the invoice. The net amount of the invoice is the amount after trade discounts are deducted.
2. The **discount period** is stipulated. The cash discount applies during this time period only.
3. The **credit period** is stipulated. The invoice must be paid during this time period.

If payment is not made during the stipulated discount period, the net amount of the invoice is to be paid by the end of the credit period. This date, called the *due date*, is either stipulated by the terms of payment or implied by the prevailing business practice. If payment is not made by the due date, the account is overdue and might be subject to late payment charges.

In dealing with cash discounts, the major new problem is how to interpret the terms of payment. Otherwise, the mathematics of working with cash discounts is similar to that used in working out trade discounts.

B. Ordinary dating

The most frequently used method of offering a cash discount is ordinary dating and the most commonly used payment terms are *2/10, n/30* (read *two ten, net thirty*).

This payment term means that if payment is made *within* ten days of the date of the invoice, a discount of 2% may be deducted from the net amount of the invoice. Otherwise, payment of the net amount of the invoice is due within thirty days. (See Figure 6.1.)

EXAMPLE 6.2A   Determine the payment needed to settle an invoice of $950.00 dated September 22, terms 2/10, n/30, if the invoice is paid

(i) on October 10;   (ii) on October 1.

FIGURE 6.1   Interpretation of Payment Terms

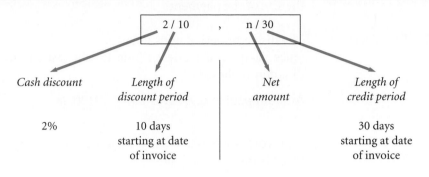

Solution   The terms of the invoice indicate a credit period of 30 days and state that a 2% discount may be deducted from the invoice amount of $950.00 if the invoice is paid within ten days of the invoice date of September 22. The applicable time periods and dates are shown in Figure 6.2.

FIGURE 6.2   Discount and Credit Periods—Example 6.2A, Ordinary Dating

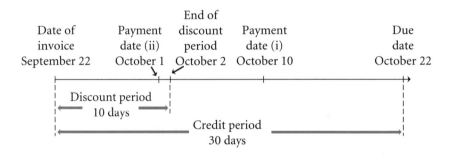

Ten days after September 22 is October 2. The discount period ends October 2.

(i)   Payment on October 10 is beyond the last day for taking the discount. The discount cannot be taken. The full amount of the invoice of $950.00 must be paid.

(ii)   October 1 is within the discount period; the 2% discount can be taken.

$$\text{Amount paid} = \text{Net amount} - 2\% \text{ of the net amount}$$
$$= 950.00 - 0.02(950.00)$$
$$= 950.00 - 19.00$$
$$= \$931.00$$

Alternatively, using the net price factor approach,

$$\text{Amount paid} = \text{NPF for a 2\% discount} \times \text{Net amount}$$
$$= 0.98(950.00)$$
$$= \$931.00$$

EXAMPLE 6.2B

An invoice of $2185.65 dated May 31, terms 3/15, n/60, is paid on June 15. What is the size of the payment?

Solution

The discount period ends June 15.
Since payment is made on June 15 (the last day for taking the discount), the 3% discount is allowed.

Amount paid = 0.97(2185.65) = $2120.08

EXAMPLE 6.2C

An invoice for $752.84 dated March 25, terms 5/10, 2/30, n/60, is paid on April 20. What is the amount paid?

Solution

The payment terms state that

(i) a 5% discount may be taken within ten days of the invoice date (up to April 4); or

(ii) a 2% discount may be taken within 30 days of the invoice date (after April 4 but no later than April 24); or

(iii) the net amount is due within 60 days of the invoice date if advantage is not taken of the cash discounts offered.

FIGURE 6.3 **Discount and Credit Periods—Example 6.2C, Ordinary Dating**

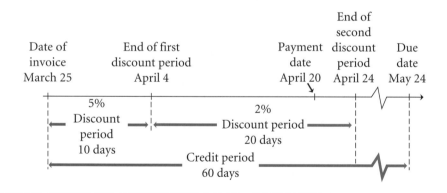

The 5% cash discount is *not* allowed; payment on April 20 is after the end of the discount period for the 5% discount. However, the 2% discount *is* allowed since payment on April 20 is within the 30 day period for the 2% discount.

Amount paid = 0.98(752.84) = $737.78

EXAMPLE 6.2D

Three invoices with terms 5/10, 3/20, n/60 are paid on November 15. The invoices are for $645.00 dated September 30, $706.00 dated October 26, and $586.00 dated November 7. What is the total amount paid?

Solution

Invoice Dated	End of Discount Period		Discount Allowed	Amount Paid	
	For 5%	For 3%			
Sept. 30	Oct. 10	Oct. 20	None		$ 645.00
Oct. 26	Nov. 5	Nov. 15	3%	0.97(706.00)	684.82
Nov. 7	Nov. 17	Nov. 27	5%	0.95(586.00)	556.70
				Amount paid	$1886.52

C. End-of-the-month or proximo dating

End-of-the-month dating is shown in the terms of payment by the abbreviation E.O.M. (*end of month*), such as in 2/10, n/30 E.O.M. The abbreviation E.O.M. means that the discount may be taken within the stipulated number of days following the end of the month shown in the invoice date. The abbreviation has the effect of shifting the invoice date to the last day of the month. The abbreviation "prox." (meaning "in the following month") has a similar effect.

Commonly, in end-of-the-month dating, the credit period (such as n/30) is not stated. In our example, "2/10, n/30 E.O.M." would be written "2/10 E.O.M." In this case, it is understood that the end of the credit period (the due date) is *twenty* days after the last day for taking the discount.

EXAMPLE 6.2E

An invoice for $1233.95 dated July 16, terms 2/10 E.O.M., is paid on August 10. What is the amount paid?

Solution

The abbreviation E.O.M. means that the invoice is to be treated as if the invoice date were July 31. Therefore, the last day for taking the discount is August 10.

Amount paid = 0.98(1233.95) = $1209.27

FIGURE 6.4   Discount and Credit Periods—Example 6.2E, End-of-the-Month Dating

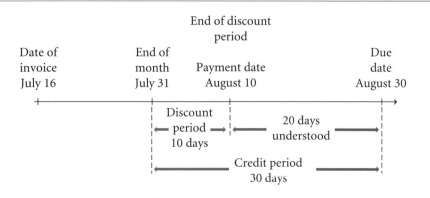

D. Receipt-of-goods dating

When the abbreviation R.O.G. (*receipt of goods*) appears in the terms of payment, as in 2/10, n/30 R.O.G., the last day for taking the discount is the stipulated number of days after the date the merchandise is received rather than the invoice date. This method of offering a cash discount is used when the transportation of the goods takes a long time, as in the case of long-distance overland shipments by rail or truck, or shipments by boat.

EXAMPLE 6.2F

Hansa Import Distributors has received an invoice of $8465.00 dated May 10, terms 3/10, n/30 R.O.G., for a shipment of cuckoo clocks that arrived on July 15. What is the last day for taking the cash discount and how much is to be paid if the discount is taken?

Solution

The last day for taking the discount is ten days after receipt of the shipment, that is, July 25.

Amount paid $= 0.97(8465.00) = \$8211.05$

FIGURE 6.5 **Discount and Credit Periods—Example 6.2F, Receipt-of-Goods Dating**

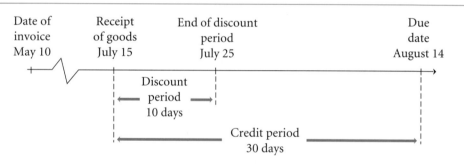

E. Partial payments and additional problems

The problem of a cash discount for a **partial payment** arises when a business pays *part* of an invoice within the discount period. In such cases, the purchaser is entitled to the cash discount on the partial amount paid.

EXAMPLE 6.2G

Sheridan Service has received an invoice of $2780.00 dated August 18, terms 2/10 E.O.M. What payment must be made on September 10 to reduce the debt

(i) by $1000.00?

(ii) to $1000.00?

Solution   Since the terms of payment involve end-of-month dating, the last day for taking the cash discount is September 10. The discount of 2% may be taken off the partial payment.

(i) Reducing the debt by $1000.00 requires paying $1000.00 less the discount.

Amount paid = $1000.00(0.98) = \$980.00$

(ii) Reducing the debt to $1000.00 requires paying ($2780.00 − 1000.00), that is, $1780.00 less the discount.

Amount paid = $1780.00(0.98) = \$1744.40$

EXAMPLE 6.2H   A cheque for $1480.22 was received on June 24 in full payment of an invoice dated June 14, terms 3/10, n/30. What was the net amount of the invoice?

Solution   Since the payment was made by the last day of the discount period, the purchaser was entitled to the 3% cash discount. The payment of $1480.22 is the amount left *after* taking 3% off the net invoice amount.

Let the net invoice amount be x.

Amount paid = NPF × Net amount of invoice

$$1480.22 = 0.97x$$

$$x = \frac{1480.22}{0.97} = \$1526.00$$

The net amount of the invoice was $1526.00.

EXAMPLE 6.2I   Applewood Supplies received a payment of $807.50 from Sheridan Service on October 10 on an invoice of $2231.75 dated September 15, terms 5/10 prox.

(i) For how much should Applewood credit Sheridan Service's account for the payment?

(ii) How much does Sheridan Service still owe on the invoice?

Solution   Since the payment terms involve proximo dating, the payment is within the discount period. Sheridan Service is entitled to the 5% discount on the partial payment. The amount of $807.50 represents a partial payment reduced by 5%.

Let the credit allowed be x.

Amount paid = NPF × Credit allowed

$$807.50 = 0.95x$$

$$x = \frac{807.50}{0.95} = \$850.00$$

(i) Applewood should credit the account of Sheridan Service with $850.00.

(ii) Sheridan Service still owes ($2231.75 − 850.00) = \$1381.75$.

Exercise 6.2

A. Determine the amount paid to settle each of the following 8 invoices on the date indicated.

	Invoice Amount	Payment Terms	Date of Invoice	Date Goods Received	Date Paid
1.	$640.00	2/10, n/30	Aug. 10	Aug. 11	Sept. 9
2.	$1520.00	3/15, n/60	Sept. 24	Sept. 27	Oct. 8
3.	$783.95	3/10, 1/20, n/60	May 18	May 20	June 5
4.	$1486.25	5/10, 2/30, n/60	June 28	June 30	July 8
5.	$1160.00	2/10 E.O.M.	Mar. 22	Mar. 29	April 10
6.	$920.00	3/15 E.O.M.	Oct. 20	Oct. 30	Nov. 12
7.	$4675.00	2/10 R.O.G.	April 15	May 28	June 5
8.	$2899.65	4/20 R.O.G.	July 17	Sept. 21	Oct. 10

B. Determine the missing values for each of the following 6 invoices. Assume that a partial payment was made on each of the invoices by the last day for taking the cash discount.

	Amount of Invoice	Payment Terms	Amount of Credit for Payment	Net Payment Received	Invoice Balance Due
1.	$1450.00	3/10, n/30	$600.00	?	?
2.	$3126.54	2/10 E.O.M.	$2000.00	?	?
3.	$964.50	5/20 R.O.G.	?	?	$400.00
4.	$1789.95	4/15, n/60	?	?	$789.95
5.	$1620.00	3/20 E.O.M.	?	$785.70	?
6.	$2338.36	2/10 R.O.G.	?	$1311.59	?

C. Answer the following questions.

1. Santucci Appliances received an invoice dated August 12 with terms 3/10 E.O.M. for the items listed below:

   5 G.E. refrigerators at $980.00 each less 25%, 5%;
   4 Inglis dishwashers at $696.00 each less $16\frac{2}{3}$%, 12.5%, 4%.

   (a) What is the last day for taking the cash discount?
   (b) What is the amount due if the invoice is paid on the last day for taking the discount?
   (c) What is the amount of the cash discount if a partial payment is made such that a balance of $2000.00 remains outstanding on the invoice?

2. Import Exclusives Ltd. received an invoice dated May 20 from Dansk Specialities of Copenhagen with terms 5/20 R.O.G. for:

> 100 teak trays at $34.30 each;
> 25 teak icebuckets at $63.60 each;
> 40 teak salad bowls at $54.50 each.

All items are subject to trade discounts of 33⅓%, 7½%, 5%.

(a) If the shipment was received on June 28, what is the last day of the discount period?

(b) What is the amount due if the invoice is paid in full on July 15?

(c) If a partial payment only is made on the last day of the discount period, what amount is due to reduce the outstanding balance to $2500.00?

3. What amount must be remitted if invoices dated July 25 for $929.00, August 10 for $763.00, and August 29 for $864.00, all with terms 3/15 E.O.M., are paid together on September 12?

4. The following invoices, all with terms 5/10, 2/30, n/60, were paid together on May 15. Invoice No. 234 dated March 30 is for $394.45; invoice No. 356 dated April 15 is for $595.50; and invoice No. 788 dated May 10 is for $865.20. What amount was remitted?

5. An invoice for $5275.00 dated November 12, terms 4/10 E.O.M., was received on November 14. What payment must be made on December 10 to reduce the debt to $3000.00?

6. What amount will reduce the amount due on an invoice of $1940.00 by $740.00 if the terms of the invoice are 5/10, n/30 and the payment was made during the discount period?

7. Sheridan Service received an invoice dated September 25 from Wolfedale Automotive. The invoice amount was $2540.95, and the payment terms were 3/10, 1/20, n/30. Sheridan Service made a payment on October 5 to reduce the balance due by $1200.00, made a second payment on October 15 to reduce the balance to $600.00, and paid the remaining balance on October 25.

(a) How much did Sheridan Service pay on October 5?

(b) How much did it pay on October 15?

(c) What was the amount of the final payment on October 25?

8. The Ski Shop received an invoice for $9600.00 dated August 11, terms 5/10, 2/30, n/90, for a shipment of skis. The Ski Shop made two partial payments.

(a) How much was paid on August 20 to reduce the unpaid balance to $7000.00?

(b) How much was paid on September 10 to reduce the outstanding balance by $3000.00?

(c) What is the remaining balance on September 10?

9. Jelinek Sports received a cheque for $1867.25 in partial payment of an invoice owed by The Ski Shop. The invoice was for $5325.00 with terms 3/20 E.O.M. dated September 15, and the cheque was received on October 18.

   (a) With how much should Jelinek Sports credit the account of The Ski Shop?
   (b) How much does The Ski Shop still owe Jelinek?

10. Darrigo Grape received an invoice for $13 780 dated September 28, terms 5/20 R.O.G., from Nappa Vineyards for a carload of grape juice received October 20. Darrigo made a partial payment of $5966.00 on November 8.

   (a) By how much did Darrigo reduce the amount due on the invoice?
   (b) How much does Darrigo still owe?

6.3 PRICING TERMINOLOGY

As you make your way through the merchandising chain, you will find many of the same terms used to represent different things, depending on where you are in the chain. As shown in Figure 6.6, the terms *markup*, *list price*, and *trade discount* are used throughout the merchandising chain.

If you are a manufacturer or supplier, you might mark up an item to create a list, or catalogue, price. If you want to sell the item to a wholesaler for less than list price, you might offer a trade discount. The wholesaler would add a mark-up to create a list price at which it offers the item to the retailer. The wholesaler could offer the retailer a trade discount to sell the item for less than the list price. The retailer would then add a markup and offer the item to the consumer at a regular selling price, or list price. The retailer might offer a markdown on the item to sell the item for less than the regular selling price.

For any particular situation, first identify where you are in the merchandising chain. You will then be able to understand and apply these terms correctly.

DID YOU KNOW?

Companies often offer credit terms of "2/10, n/30" to their customers. This means that if payment is made within 10 days of the invoice date, the customer can deduct 2% from the invoice amount. In this case, the discount period is 10 days. Did you know that companies will sometimes extend the discount period? They might do this to match competitors' discount periods or to encourage purchase of seasonal or slow-moving products. The extended discount period would be identified by adding "extra," "ex," or "X" to the regular discount period on the invoice. For example, adding 30 days to the regular discount period would appear as "2/10—30 extra" on the invoice. It would *not* appear as "2/40" because the company wants to indicate that it is granting a special discount period to a particular customer.

FIGURE 6.6   **Pricing Terminology Used in the Merchandising Chain**

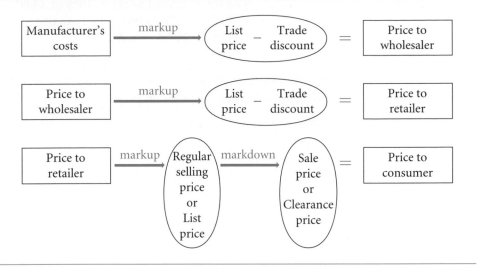

6.4   MARKUP

A. Basic concepts and calculations

The primary purpose of operating a business is to generate profits. Businesses engaged in merchandising generate profits through their buying and selling activities. The amount of profit depends on many factors, one of which is the pricing of goods. The selling price must cover

(i) the cost of buying the goods;

(ii) the operating expenses (or overhead) of the business;

(iii) the profit required by the owner to stay in business.

SELLING PRICE $=$ COST OF BUYING $+$ EXPENSES $+$ PROFIT

$$S = C + E + P \quad \text{————— Formula 6.9A}$$

EXAMPLE 6.4A   Sheridan Service buys a certain type of battery for $84.00 each. Operating expenses of the business are 25% of cost and the owner requires a profit of 10% of cost. For how much should Sheridan sell the batteries?

Solution

$$\begin{aligned}
\text{Selling price} &= \text{Cost of buying} + \text{Expenses} + \text{Profit} \\
&= 84.00 + 25\% \text{ of } 84.00 + 10\% \text{ of } 84.00 \\
&= 84.00 + 0.25(84.00) + 0.10(84.00) \\
&= 84.00 + 21.00 + 8.40 \\
&= \$113.40
\end{aligned}$$

Sheridan should sell the batteries for $113.40 to cover the cost of buying, the operating expenses, and the required profit.

Note: In example 6.4A, the selling price is $113.40 while the cost is $84.00. The difference between selling price and cost $= 113.40 - 84.00 = \$29.40$. This difference covers operating expenses of $21.00 and a profit of $8.40 and is known as **markup**, **margin,** or **gross profit**.

> MARKUP = EXPENSES + PROFIT

> $M = E + P$ ———————————————— **Formula 6.10**

Using this relationship between markup, expenses, and profit, the relationship stated in Formula 6.9 becomes

> SELLING PRICE = COST OF BUYING + MARKUP

> $S = C + M$ ———————————————— **Formula 6.9B**

The following diagram illustrates the relationships among cost of buying (C), markup (M), operating expenses (E), profit (P), and selling price (S) established in Formulae 6.9A, 6.9B, and 6.10.

FIGURE 6.7

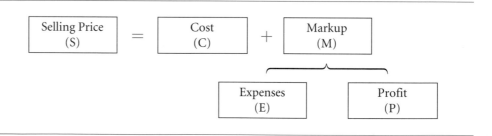

EXAMPLE 6.4B

Friden Business Machines bought two types of electronic calculators for resale. Model A cost $42.00 and sells for $56.50. Model B cost $78.00 and sells for $95.00. Business overhead is 24% of cost. For each model, determine

(i)   the markup (or gross profit);

(ii) the operating expenses (or overhead);

(iii) the profit.

Solution

Model A	Model B

(i)
$$C + M = S$$
$$42.00 + M = 56.50$$
$$M = 56.50 - 42.00$$
$$M = \$14.50$$
The markup on Model A is $14.50.

$$C + M = S \text{——— using Formula 6.9B}$$
$$78.00 + M = 95.00$$
$$M = 95.00 - 78.00$$
$$M = \$17.00$$
The markup on Model B is $17.00.

(ii) Expenses (or overhead)
$$= 24\% \text{ of } 42.00$$
$$= 0.24(42.00)$$
$$= \$10.08$$
Overhead for Model A is $10.08.

Expenses (or overhead)
$$= 24\% \text{ of } 78.00$$
$$= 0.24(78.00)$$
$$= \$18.72$$
Overhead for Model B is $18.72.

(iii)
$$E + P = M$$
$$10.08 + P = 14.50$$
$$P = 14.50 - 10.08$$
$$P = \$4.42$$
Profit on Model A is $4.42.

$$E + P = M \text{——— using Formula 6.10}$$
$$18.72 + P = 17.00$$
$$P = 17.00 - 18.72$$
$$P = -\$1.72$$
Profit on Model B is −$1.72, that is, a loss of $1.72.

EXAMPLE 6.4C

A ski shop bought 100 pairs of skis for $105.00 per pair and sold 60 pairs for the regular selling price of $295.00 per pair. The remaining skis were sold during a clearance sale for $180.00 per pair. Overhead is 40% of the regular selling price. Determine

(i)   the markup, the overhead, and the profit per pair of skis sold at the regular selling price;

(ii) the markup, the overhead, and the profit per pair of skis sold during the clearance sale;

(iii) the total profit realized.

Solution

(i) *At regular selling price*

Markup

$$C + M = S$$
$$105.00 + M = 295.00$$
$$M = \$190.00$$

(ii) *At clearance price*

Markup

$$C + M = S$$
$$105.00 + M = 180.00$$
$$M = \$75.00$$

(i) *At regular selling price (continued)*	(ii) *At clearance price (continued)*

Overhead

E = 40% of Regular selling price
  = 0.40(295.00)
  = $118.00

Overhead

E = 40% of Regular selling price
  = 0.40(295.00)
  = $118.00

Profit

$E + P = M$
118.00 + P = 190.00
    P = $72.00

Profit

$E + P = M$
118.00 + P = 75.00
    P = −$43.00

(iii) Profit from sale of 60 pairs
    at regular selling price = 60(72.00) $4320.00
    Profit from sale of 40 pairs
    during clearance sale = 40(−43.00)   −1720.00
                            Total profit $2600.00

B. Rate of markup

A markup may be stated in one of two ways:

1. As a percent of cost.
2. As a percent of selling price.

The method used is usually determined by the way in which a business keeps its records. Since most manufacturers keep their records in terms of cost, they usually calculate markup as a percent of cost. Since most department stores and other retailers keep their records in terms of selling price, they usually calculate markup as a percent of selling price.

Computing the rate of markup involves comparing the amount of markup to a base amount. Depending on the method used, the base amount is either the cost or the selling price. Since the two methods produce different results, great care must be taken to note whether the markup is based on the cost or on the selling price.

$$\text{RATE OF MARKUP BASED ON COST} = \frac{\text{MARKUP}}{\text{COST}} = \frac{M}{C} \qquad \text{———— Formula 6.11}$$

$$\frac{\text{RATE OF MARKUP BASED}}{\text{ON SELLING PRICE}} = \frac{\text{MARKUP}}{\text{SELLING PRICE}} = \frac{M}{S} \qquad \text{———— Formula 6.12}$$

EXAMPLE 6.4D Compute (a) the missing value (cost, selling price, markup), (b) the rate of markup based on cost, and (c) the rate of markup based on selling price for each of the following.

  (i) cost, $60.00; selling price, $75.00

 (ii) cost, $48.00; markup, $16.00

(iii) selling price, $88.00; markup, $33.00

(iv) cost, \$8.00; markup, \$8.00

(v) selling price, \$24.00; markup, \$18.00

Solution

	(a) Missing Value	(b) Rate of Markup Based on Cost	(c) Rate of Markup Based on Selling Price
(i)	Markup = 75.00 − 60.00 = \$15.00	$\frac{15}{60} = 0.25 = 25\%$	$\frac{15}{75} = 0.20 = 20\%$
(ii)	Selling price = 48.00 + 16.00 = \$64.00	$\frac{16}{48} = \frac{1}{3} = 33\frac{1}{3}\%$	$\frac{16}{64} = 0.25 = 25\%$
(iii)	Cost = 88.00 − 33.00 = \$55.00	$\frac{33}{55} = 0.60 = 60\%$	$\frac{33}{88} = 0.375 = 37.5\%$
(iv)	Selling price = 8.00 + 8.00 = \$16.00	$\frac{8}{8} = 1.00 = 100\%$	$\frac{8}{16} = 0.50 = 50\%$
(v)	Cost = 24.00 − 18.00 = \$6.00	$\frac{18}{6} = 3.00 = 300\%$	$\frac{18}{24} = 0.75 = 75\%$

C. Finding the cost or selling price

When the rate of markup is given and either the cost or the selling price is known, the missing value can be found using Formula 6.9B.

$$\boxed{\text{COST} + \text{MARKUP} = \text{SELLING PRICE}} \qquad \boxed{C + M = S}$$

When using this formula, pay special attention to the base of the markup, that is, whether it is based on cost or based on selling price.

EXAMPLE 6.4E

What is the selling price of an article costing \$72.00 if the mark-up is

(i) 40% of cost?

(ii) 40% of the selling price?

Solution

(i)
$$C + M = S \qquad \text{——————— using Formula 6.9B}$$
$$C + 40\% \text{ of } C = S \qquad \text{——————— replacing M by 40\% of C is the crucial}$$
$$72.00 + 0.40(72.00) = S \qquad \text{step in the solution}$$
$$72.00 + 28.80 = S$$
$$S = \$100.80$$

If the markup is 40% based on cost, the selling price is \$100.80.

(ii)
$$C + M = S$$
$$C + 40\% \text{ of } S = S$$
$$72.00 + 0.40S = S$$
$$72.00 = S - 0.40S$$
$$72.00 = 0.60S$$
$$S = \frac{72.00}{0.60}$$
$$S = \$120.00$$

If the markup is 40% based on selling price, the selling price is $120.00.

Note: In problems of this type, replace M by X% of C or X% of S before using specific numbers. This approach is used in the preceding problem and in the following worked examples.

EXAMPLE 6.4F   What is the cost of an article selling for $65.00 if the markup is

(i) 30% of selling price?   (ii) 30% of cost?

Solution   (i)
$$C + M = S$$
$$C + 30\% \text{ of } S = S \quad\text{——————— replace M by 30\% of S}$$
$$C + 0.30(65.00) = 65.00$$
$$C + 19.50 = 65.00$$
$$C = 65.00 - 19.50$$
$$C = \$45.50$$

If the markup is 30% based on selling price, the cost is $45.50.

(ii)
$$C + M = S$$
$$C + 30\% \text{ of } C = S \quad\text{——————— replace M by 30\% of C}$$
$$C + 0.30C = 65.00$$
$$1.30C = 65.00$$
$$C = \frac{65.00}{1.30}$$
$$C = \$50.00$$

If the markup is 30% based on cost, the cost is $50.00.

EXAMPLE 6.4G   Find the missing value in each of the following.

	(i)	(ii)	(iii)	(iv)	(v)
Cost	$45.00	$84.00	?	?	?
Selling price	?	?	$3.24	$23.10	$42.90
Markup based on cost	$33\frac{1}{3}\%$	?	?	37.5%	50%
Markup based on selling price	?	40%	$16\frac{2}{3}\%$	?	?

Solution

(i)
$$C + M = S$$
$$C + 33\tfrac{1}{3}\% \text{ of } C = S$$
$$45.00 + \tfrac{1}{3}(45.00) = S$$
$$45.00 + 15.00 = S$$
$$S = \$60.00$$

Markup based on selling price $= \dfrac{15}{60} = 0.25 = 25\%$

(ii)
$$C + M = S$$
$$C + 40\% \text{ of } S = S$$
$$84.00 + 0.40S = S$$
$$84.00 = 0.60S$$
$$S = \dfrac{84.00}{0.60}$$
$$S = \$140.00$$

Markup based on cost $= \dfrac{140.00 - 84.00}{84.00} = \dfrac{56.00}{84.00} = 0.6666667 = 66\tfrac{2}{3}\%$

(iii)
$$C + M = S$$
$$C + 16\tfrac{2}{3}\% \text{ of } S = S$$
$$C + \tfrac{1}{6}(3.24) = 3.24$$
$$C + 0.54 = 3.24$$
$$C = \$2.70$$

Markup based on cost $= \dfrac{3.24 - 2.70}{2.70} = \dfrac{0.54}{2.70} = 0.20 = 20\%$

(iv)
$$C + M = S$$
$$C + 37.5\% \text{ of } C = S$$
$$C + 0.375C = 23.10$$
$$1.375C = 23.10$$
$$C = \dfrac{23.10}{1.375}$$
$$C = \$16.80$$

Markup based on selling price $= \dfrac{23.10 - 16.80}{23.10} = \dfrac{6.30}{23.10} = 0.2727273 \cong 27.27\%$

(The symbol $\cong$ means "approximately equal to.")

(v)
$$C + M = S$$
$$C + 50\% \text{ of } C = S$$
$$C + 0.50C = 42.90$$
$$1.50C = 42.90$$
$$C = \$28.60$$

Markup based on selling price $= \dfrac{42.90 - 28.60}{42.90} = \dfrac{14.30}{42.90} = 0.3333333 = 33\tfrac{1}{3}\%$

EXAMPLE 6.4H   The Beaver Ski Shop sells ski vests for $98.00. The markup based on cost is 75%.

(i) What did the Beaver Ski Shop pay for each vest?

(ii) What is the rate of markup based on the selling price?

Solution

(i)
$$C + M = S$$
$$C + 75\% \text{ of } C = S$$
$$C + 0.75C = 98.00$$
$$1.75C = 98.00$$
$$C = 56.00$$

The Beaver Ski Shop paid $56.00 for each vest.

(ii) Rate of markup based on selling price $= \dfrac{\text{Markup}}{\text{Selling price}}$

$$= \dfrac{98.00 - 56.00}{98.00}$$

$$= \dfrac{42.00}{98.00} = 0.4285714 \cong 42.86\%$$

EXAMPLE 6.4I   Sheridan Service bought four Michelin tires from a wholesaler for $343.00 and sold the tires at a markup of 30% of the selling price.

(i) For how much were the tires sold?

(ii) What is the rate of markup based on cost?

Solution

(i)
$$C + M = S$$
$$C + 30\% \text{ of } S = S$$
$$343.00 + 0.30S = S$$
$$343.00 = 0.70S$$
$$S = 490.00$$

Sheridan sold the tires for $490.00.

(ii) Rate of markup based on cost $= \dfrac{\text{Markup}}{\text{Cost}}$

$$= \dfrac{490.00 - 343.00}{343.00}$$

$$= \dfrac{147.00}{343.00} = 0.4285714 \cong 42.86\%$$

EXAMPLE 6.4J   The gross profit on each of two articles is $25.80. If the rate of markup for Article A is 40% of cost while the rate for Article B is 40% of the selling price of markup, determine the cost and the selling price of each.

Solution

For Article A
Gross profit (or Markup) = 40% of Cost
$$25.80 = 0.40C$$
$$C = 64.50$$

The cost of Article A is $64.50.
The selling price is 64.50 + 25.80 = $90.30.

For Article B

Gross profit (or Markup) = 40% of Selling price

$$25.80 = 0.40S$$
$$S = 64.50$$

The selling price of Article B is $64.50.
The cost = 64.50 − 25.80 = $38.70.

Exercise 6.4

A. For each of the following 6 questions, determine

   (a) the amount of markup;
   (b) the amount of overhead;
   (c) the profit or loss realized on the sale;
   (d) the rate of markup based on cost;
   (e) the rate of markup based on selling price.

	Cost	Selling Price	Overhead
1.	$24.00	$30.00	16% of Cost
2.	$72.00	$96.00	15% of Selling price
3.	$52.50	$87.50	36% of Selling price
4.	$42.45	$67.92	60% of Cost
5.	$27.00	$37.50	34% of Selling price
6.	$36.00	$42.30	21% of Cost

B. For each of the following 12 questions, compute the missing values represented by the question marks.

	Cost	Selling Price	Markup	Rate of Markup Based on Cost	Rate of Markup Based on Selling Price
1.	$25.00	$31.25	?	?	?
2.	$63.00	$84.00	?	?	?
3.	$64.00	?	$38.40	?	?
4.	?	$162.00	$27.00	?	?
5.	$54.25	?	?	40%	?
6.	?	$94.50	?	?	30%
7.	?	$66.36	?	50%	?
8.	?	$133.25	?	66⅔%	?
9.	$31.24	?	?	?	60%
10.	$87.74	?	?	?	33⅓%
11.	?	?	$22.26	?	16⅔%
12.	?	?	$90.75	125%	?

C. Answer each of the following questions.

1. Windsor Hardware buys outdoor lights for $5.00 per dozen less 20%, 20%. The store's overhead is 45% of cost and the required profit is 15% of cost. For how much per dozen should the lights be sold?

2. A merchant buys an item listed at $96.00 less 33⅓% from a distributor. Overhead is 32% of cost and profit is 27.5% of cost. For how much should the item be retailed?

3. Aldo's Shoes bought a shipment of 200 pairs of women's shoes for $42.00 per pair. The store sold 120 pairs at the regular selling price of $125.00 per pair, 60 pairs at a clearance sale at a discount of 40%, and the remaining pairs during an inventory sale at a price that equals cost plus overhead (i.e., a break-even price). The store's overhead is 50% of cost.

    (a) What was the price at which the shoes were sold during the clearance sale?
    (b) What was the price during the inventory sale?
    (c) What was the total profit realized on the shipment?
    (d) What was the average rate of markup based on cost that was realized on the shipment?

4. The Pottery bought 600 pans auctioned off en bloc for $4950.00. This means that each pan has the same cost. On inspection, the pans were classified as normal quality, seconds, and substandard. The 360 normal-quality pans were sold at a markup of 80% of cost, the 190 pans classified as seconds were sold at a markup of 20% of cost, and the pans classified as substandard were sold at 80% of their cost.

    (a) What was the unit price at which each of the three classifications was sold?
    (b) If overhead is 33⅓% of cost, what was the amount of profit realized on the purchase?
    (c) What was the average rate of markup based on the selling price at which the pans were sold?

5. Tennis racquets were purchased for $55.00 less 40% (for purchasing more than 100 items), and less a further 25% (for purchasing the racquets in October). They were sold for $54.45.

    (a) What is the markup as a percent of cost?
    (b) What is the markup as a percent of selling price?

6. A dealer bought personal computers for $1240.00 less 50%, 10%. They were sold for $1395.00.

    (a) What was the markup as a percent of cost?
    (b) What was the markup as a percent of selling price?

7. The Bargain Bookstore makes a gross profit of $3.42 on a textbook. The store's markup is 15% of cost.

    (a) For how much did the bookstore buy the textbook?
    (b) What is the selling price of the textbook?
    (c) What is the rate of markup based on the selling price?

8. An appliance store sells electric kettles at a markup of 18% of the selling price. The store's margin on a particular model is $6.57.

   (a) What was the cost of the kettles to the store?
   (b) For how much does the store sell the kettles?
   (c) What is the percent markup based on cost?

9. The markup on an item selling for $74.55 is 40% of cost.

   (a) What is the cost of the item?
   (b) What is the rate of markup based on the selling price?

10. Sheridan Service sells oil at a markup of 40% of the selling price. If Sheridan paid $0.99 per litre of oil,

    (a) what is the selling price per litre?
    (b) what is the rate of markup based on cost?

11. The Ski Shop purchased ski poles for $12.80 per pair. The poles are marked up 60% of the selling price.

    (a) For how much does The Ski Shop sell a pair of ski poles?
    (b) What is the percent markup based on cost?

12. Neal's Photographic Supplies sells a Pentax camera for $444.98. The markup is 90% of cost.

    (a) How much does the store pay for this camera?
    (b) What is the rate of markup based on selling price?

6.5 MARKDOWN

A. Basic concepts and calculations

A **markdown** is a reduction in the price of an article sold to the consumer. As you recall from Figure 6.6, markdowns are used for a variety of purposes, such as sales promotions, meeting competitors' prices, reducing excess inventories, clearing out seasonal merchandise, and selling off discontinued items. A markdown, unlike a markup, is always stated as a percent of the price to be reduced and is computed as if it were a discount.

FIGURE 6.8

While markdowns are simple to calculate, the rather wide variety of terms used to identify both the price to be reduced (such as *selling price*, *regular selling price*, *list price*, *marked price*, *price tag*) and the reduced price (such as *sale price* or *clearance price*) introduces an element of confusion. In this text, we use *regular selling price* to describe the price to be reduced and *sale price* to describe the reduced price.

In general,

$$\boxed{\text{SALE PRICE} = \text{REGULAR SELLING PRICE} - \text{MARKDOWN}}$$

However, since the markdown is a percent of the regular selling price, the net price factor approach used with discounts is applicable (see Formula 6.4A).

$$\boxed{\begin{array}{c} \text{SALE PRICE} = \text{NPF} \times \text{REGULAR SELLING PRICE} \\ \text{where NPF} = 100\% - \% \text{ markdown} \end{array}}$$

EXAMPLE 6.5A

A ski suit with a regular selling price of $280.00 is marked down 45% during Beaver Ski Shop's annual clearance sale. What is the sale price of the ski suit?

Solution

Sale price = Regular selling price − Markdown
= 280.00 − 45% of 280.00
= 280.00 − 0.45(280.00)
= 280.00 − 126.00
= $154.00

Alternatively
Sale price = NPF × Regular selling price
= (100% − 45%)(280.00)
= 0.55(280.00)
= $154.00

The ski suit sold for $154.00.

EXAMPLE 6.5B

Solomon 555 ski bindings bought for $57.75 were marked up 45% of the selling price. When the binding was discontinued, it was marked down 40%. What was the sale price of the binding?

Solution

First determine the regular selling price.

C + M = S
C + 45% of S = S
57.75 + 0.45S = S
57.75 = 0.55S
S = $105.00

The regular selling price is $105.00.

Sale price = Regular selling price − Markdown
= 105.00 − 40% of 105.00
= 105.00 − 42.00
= $63.00

Alternatively

Sale price = NPF × Regular selling price
$$= 0.60 \times 105.00$$
$$= \$63.00$$

The sale price is $63.00.

EXAMPLE 6.5C   Lund Sporting Goods sold a bicycle regularly priced at $195.00 for $144.30.

(i) What is the amount of markdown?

(ii) What is the rate of markdown?

Solution   (i) Markdown = Regular selling price − Sale price
$$= 195.00 - 144.30$$
$$= \$50.70$$

(ii) Rate of markdown $= \dfrac{\text{Markdown}}{\text{Regular selling price}}$

$$= \frac{50.70}{195.00} = 0.26 = 26\%$$

BUSINESS MATH NEWS BOX

BUY MORE TO SAVE MORE

You saw the advertisement above in the newspaper, so you have gone shopping at this store. You have found three suits that you like equally and are interested in buying. Their retail prices are $375, $400, and $439.

QUESTIONS

1. If you could buy only one suit, which one would you choose? How much money would you save?

2. If you could buy only two suits, which two would you buy? What would be the amount of your bill (before taxes)? How much money would you save?

3. If you could buy all three suits, what would be the amount of your bill (before taxes)? How much money would you save?

4. Do you think it is worth spending the extra money to get the extra savings? As consumers, this is something we all need to consider when faced with a sale.

B. Pricing strategies

The pricing relationship, Selling price = Cost + Expense + Profit (S = C + E + P), plays an important role in pricing. It describes how big a markup is needed to cover overhead and a reasonable profit, and how large a markdown can be tolerated. One pricing strategy is to set a selling price based on the business's "internal" factors—actual costs and expenses, and a desired profit level. However, pricing decisions must often be based on "external" market factors—competitors' prices, consumers' sensitivity to a high price, economic conditions that affect interest rates and income available for purchases, and so on. Often, selling prices must be marked down more than anticipated in response to market conditions, leading to less-than-desired profit levels. Use the pricing relationship S = C + E + P as a guide to determine the effect of markdown decisions on the operations of a business.

The cost of buying an article plus the overhead represents the **total cost**, or handling cost, of the article.

> TOTAL COST = COST OF BUYING + OVERHEAD

If an article is sold at a price that equals the **total cost**, the business makes no profit nor does it suffer a loss. This price is called the break-even point and is discussed in Chapter 5. Any business, of course, prefers to sell at least at a break-even price. If the price is insufficient to recover the total cost, the business will suffer an operating loss. If the price does not even cover the cost of buying, the business suffers an absolute loss. To determine the profit or loss, the following accounting relationship is used.

> PROFIT = REVENUE − TOTAL COST

EXAMPLE 6.5D   During its annual Midnight Madness Sale, The Ski Shop sold a pair of ski boots, regularly priced at $245.00, at a discount of 40%. The boots cost $96.00 and expenses are 26% of the regular selling price.

(i) For how much were the ski boots sold?

(ii) What was the total cost of the ski boots?

(iii) What operating profit or loss was made on the sale?

Solution

(i) Sale price $= 0.60(245.00) = \$147.00$

(ii) Total cost $=$ Cost of buying $+$ Expenses

$= 96.00 + 0.26(245.00)$

$= 96.00 + 63.70$

$= \$159.70$

(iii) Profit $=$ Revenue $-$ Total cost

$= 147.00 - 159.70$

$= -\$12.70$ (a loss)

Since the total cost was higher than the revenue received from the sale of the ski boots, The Ski Shop had an operating loss of $12.70.

EXAMPLE 6.5E

The Cook Nook paid $115.24 for a set of dishes. Expenses are 18% of selling price and the required profit is 15% of selling price. During an inventory sale, the set of dishes was marked down 30%.

(i) What was the sale price?

(ii) What was the operating profit or loss?

Solution

(i) First determine the selling price (or regular selling price).

Selling price $=$ Cost $+$ Expenses $+$ Profit

$S = C + 18\%$ of $S + 15\%$ of S

$S = C + 0.18S + 0.15S$

$S = 115.24 + 0.33S$

$0.67S = 115.24$

$S = \dfrac{115.24}{0.67} = \$172.00$

Sale price $=$ Selling price $-$ Markdown

$= S - 30\%$ of S

$= S - 0.30S$

$= 0.70S$

$= 0.70(172.00)$

$= \$120.40$

The sale price is $120.40.

(ii) Total cost $=$ Cost of buying $+$ Expenses

$= C + 18\%$ of S

$= 115.24 + 0.18(172.00)$

$= 115.24 + 30.96$

$= \$146.20$

Profit = Revenue − Total cost
$$= 120.40 − 146.20$$
$$= −\$25.80$$

The dishes were sold at an operating loss of $25.80.

EXAMPLE 6.5F

The Winemaker sells California concentrate for $22.50. The store's overhead is 50% of cost and the owners require a profit of 30% of cost.

(i)   For how much does The Winemaker buy the concentrate?

(ii) What is the break-even price?

(iii) What is the highest rate of markdown at which the store will still break even?

(iv) What is the highest rate of discount that can be advertised without incurring an absolute loss?

Solution

(i)   S = C + E + P
        S = C + 50% of C + 30% of C
        S = C + 0.50C + 0.30C
    22.50 = 1.80C
        $C = \dfrac{22.50}{1.80} = \$12.50$

The Winemaker bought the concentrate for $12.50.

(ii) Total cost = C + 50% of C
                = 1.50C
                = 1.50(12.50)
                = $18.75

To break even, the concentrate must be sold for $18.75.

(iii) To break even, the maximum markdown is 22.50 − 18.75 = $3.75.
Rate of markdown $= \dfrac{3.75}{22.50} = 0.1666667 = 16\tfrac{2}{3}\%$

The highest rate of markdown to break even is $16\tfrac{2}{3}\%$.

(iv) The lowest price at which the concentrate can be offered for sale without incurring an absolute loss is the cost at which the concentrate was bought, that is, $12.50. The maximum amount of discount = 22.50 − 12.50 = $10.00.
Rate of discount $= \dfrac{10.00}{22.50} = 0.4444444 = 44\tfrac{4}{9}\%$

The maximum rate of discount that can be advertised without incurring an absolute loss is $44\tfrac{4}{9}\%$.

EXAMPLE 6.5G

Big Sound Electronics bought stereo equipment for $960.00 less 30%, 15%. Big Sound marks all merchandise at a regular selling price that allows the store to offer a discount of 20% while still making its usual profit of 15% of discounted regular selling price. Overhead is 25% of discounted regular selling price. During its annual mid-summer sale, the usual discount of 20% was replaced by a markdown of 45%. What operating profit or loss was made when the equipment was sold?

Solution   Complex problems of this type are best solved by a systematic approach. Consider the given information step by step. The following computations are necessary to determine the profit.

   (i)   the cost (or purchase price) to the store;

   (ii) the discounted regular selling price required to cover cost, expenses, and the usual profit;

   (iii) the regular selling price from which the 20% discount is offered;

   (iv) the mid-summer sale price;

   (v)   the total cost (cost and expenses);

   (vi) the operating profit or loss.

Step-by-Step Computations

   (i)   Cost = NPF $\times$ List price = 0.70(0.85)(960.00) = \$571.20

   (ii) Let the discounted regular selling price be S.

$$S = C + E + P$$
$$S = C + 25\% \text{ of } S + 15\% \text{ of } S$$
$$S = C + 0.25S + 0.15S$$
$$S = 571.20 + 0.40S$$
$$0.60S = 571.20$$
$$S = \frac{571.20}{0.60} = \$952.00$$

The discounted regular selling price is \$952.00.

   (iii) Regular selling price $-$ Discount = Discounted regular selling price

Let the regular selling price be \$x.

$$x - 20\% \text{ of } x = 952.00$$
$$x - 0.20x = 952.00$$
$$0.80x = 952.00$$
$$x = \frac{952.00}{0.80} = \$1190.00$$

The regular selling price was \$1190.00.

   (iv) Mid-summer sale price = Regular selling price $-$ Markdown
$$= 1190.00 - 45\% \text{ of } 1190.00$$
$$= 1190.00 - 0.45(1190)$$
$$= 1190.00 - 535.50$$
$$= \$654.50$$

   (v)   Total cost = Cost of buying + Overhead
$$= C + 25\% \text{ of } S$$
$$= 571.20 + 0.25(952.00)$$
$$= 571.20 + 238.00$$
$$= \$809.20$$

   (vi) Profit = Revenue $-$ Total cost
$$= 654.50 - 809.20$$
$$= -\$154.70$$

The equipment was sold at an operating loss of \$154.70.

EXAMPLE 6.5H

Magder's Furniture Emporium bought a dining room suite that must be retailed for $5250.00 to cover the wholesale price, overhead of 50% of the wholesale price, and a normal profit of 25% of the wholesale price. The suite is marked at a regular selling price so that the store can allow a 20% discount and still receive the required retail price.

When the suite remained unsold, the store owner decided to mark the suite down for an inventory clearance sale. To arrive at the rate of markdown, the owner decided that the store's profit would have to be no less than 10% of the normal profit and that part of the markdown would be covered by reducing the commission paid to the salesperson. The normal commission (which accounts for 40% of the overhead) was reduced by $33\frac{1}{3}$%.

What is the maximum rate of markdown that can be advertised instead of the usual 20%?

Solution

STEP 1

Determine the cost, referred to above as the wholesale price.

Let the retail price be S.

$$S = C + E + P$$
$$S = C + 50\% \text{ of } C + 25\% \text{ of } C$$
$$S = C + 0.50C + 0.25C$$
$$5250.00 = 1.75C$$
$$C = \frac{5250.00}{1.75} = \$3000.00$$

STEP 2

Determine the regular selling price.

Let the regular selling price be $x.

$$\text{Regular selling price} - \text{Discount} = \text{Retail price}$$
$$x - 20\% \text{ of } x = 5250.00$$
$$x - 0.20x = 5250.00$$
$$0.80x = 5250.00$$
$$x = \frac{5250.00}{0.80} = \$6562.50$$

STEP 3

Determine the required profit.

$$\text{Normal profit} = 25\% \text{ of Cost (or Wholesale price)}$$
$$= 0.25(3000.00)$$
$$= \$750.00$$

$$\text{Required profit} = 10\% \text{ of Normal profit}$$
$$= 0.10(750.00)$$
$$= \$75.00$$

STEP 4

Determine the amount of overhead to be recovered.

$$\text{Normal overhead} = 50\% \text{ of Cost (or Wholesale price)}$$
$$= 0.50(3000.00)$$
$$= \$1500.00$$

Normal commission = 40% of Normal overhead
$$= 0.40(1500.00)$$
$$= \$600.00$$

Reduction in overhead = $33\frac{1}{3}$% of commission

$$= \frac{1}{3}(600.00)$$

$$= \$200.00$$

Overhead to be recovered = $1500.00 - 200.00 = \$1300.00$

STEP 5   Determine the inventory clearance sale price.

Inventory clearance sale price = Cost + Overhead + Profit
$$= 3000.00 + 1300.00 + 75.00$$
$$= \$4375.00$$

STEP 6   Determine the amount of markdown.

Markdown = Regular selling price − Inventory clearance sale price
$$= 6562.50 - 4375.00$$
$$= \$2187.50$$

STEP 7   Determine the rate of markdown.

Rate of markdown $= \dfrac{\text{Amount of markdown}}{\text{Regular selling price}}$

$$= \frac{2187.50}{6562.50}$$

$$= 0.3333333$$

$$= 33\frac{1}{3}\%$$

Instead of the usual 20%, the store can advertise a markdown of $33\frac{1}{3}$%.

Exercise 6.5

A. Compute the values represented by question marks. Assume that all items carry a regular selling price such that a discount may be allowed to obtain the sale price. At the end of the season, a markdown is taken on the regular selling price to obtain the clearance sale price.

	Cost (C)	Markup	Sale Price (S)	Discount	Regular Selling Price	Mark-Down	Clearance Sale Price
1.	$51.00	25% of S	?	20%	?	26%	?
2.	?	50% of C	$105.00	25%	?	?	$84.00
3.	$40.00	? of C	?	$16\frac{2}{3}$%	$144.00	?	$90.00
4.	$29.16	? of S	?	10%	$72.00	35%	?
5.	?	60% of C	$72.80	?	?	36%	$61.60
6.	?	$33\frac{1}{3}$% of C	?	16%	?	40%	$45.00

B. Compute the values represented by question marks for each of the following 6 questions.

	Regular Selling Price (S)	Markdown	Sale Price	Cost (C)	Overhead	Total Cost	Operating Profit (Loss)
1.	$85.00	40%	?	$42.00	20% of S	?	?
2.	?	$33\frac{1}{3}$%	$42.00	$34.44	12% of S	?	?
3.	?	35%	$62.66	?	25% of S	$54.75	?
4.	$72.80	$12\frac{1}{2}$%	?	$54.75	20% of C	?	?
5.	?	25%	$120.00	$105.00	? of S	?	($4.20)
6.	$92.40	$16\frac{2}{3}$%	?	?	15% of C	?	$8.46

C. Answer each of the following questions.

1. A cookware set that cost a dealer $440.00 less 55%, 25% is marked up to a regular selling price of 180% of cost. For quick sale, the cookware was reduced 45%.

   (a) What is the sale price?
   (b) What rate of markup based on cost was realized?

2. A gas barbecue cost a retailer $420.00 less 33⅓%, 20%, 5%. It carries a regular selling price on its price tag at a markup of 60% of the regular selling price. During the end-of-season sale, the barbecue is marked down 45%.

   (a) What is the end-of-season sale price?
   (b) What rate of markup based on cost will be realized during the sale?

3. Bargain City clothing store purchased raincoats for $36.75. The store requires a gross profit of 30% of the sale price. What regular selling price should be marked on the raincoats if the store wants to offer a 25% discount without reducing its gross profit?

4. The Outdoor Shop buys tents for $264.00 less 25% for buying more than 20 tents. The store operates on a margin of 33⅓% of the sale price and advertises that all merchandise is sold at a discount of 20% of the regular selling price. What is the regular selling price of the tents?

5. The Stereo Shop sold a radio regularly priced at $125.00 for $75.00. The radio was originally purchased for $120.00 less 33⅓%, 15%. The store's overhead is 12% of the regular selling price.

   (a) What was the rate of markdown at which the radio was sold?
   (b) What was the operating profit or loss?
   (c) What rate of markup based on cost was realized?
   (d) What was the rate of markup based on the sale price?

6. An automatic dishwasher cost a dealer $620.00 less 37½%, 4%. It is regularly priced at $558.00. The dealer's overhead is 15% of the regular selling price and the dishwasher was cleared out for $432.45.

   (a) What was the rate of markdown at which the dishwasher was sold?
   (b) What is the regular markup based on selling price?
   (c) What was the operating profit or loss?
   (d) What rate of markup based on cost was realized?

7. A jewellery store paid $36.40 for a watch. Store expenses are 24% of regular selling price and the normal net profit is 20% of regular selling price. During a Special Bargain Day Sale, the watch was sold at a discount of 30%. What operating profit or loss was realized on the sale?

8. A hardware store paid $33.45 for a set of cookware. Overhead is 15% of the regular selling price and profit is 10% of the regular selling price. During a clearance sale, the set was sold at a markdown of 15%. What was the operating profit or loss on the sale?

9. A clothing store buys shorts for $24.00 less 40% for buying over 50 pairs, and less a further 16⅔% for buying last season's style. The shorts are marked up to cover overhead of 25% of cost and a profit of 33⅓% of cost.

   (a) What is the regular selling price of the shorts?
   (b) What is the maximum amount of markdown to break even?
   (c) What is the rate of markdown if the shorts are sold at the break-even price?

10. Furniture City bought chairs for $75.00 less 33⅓%, 20%, 10%. The store's overhead is 75% of cost and normal profit is 25% of cost.

    (a) What is the regular selling price of the chairs?
    (b) At what price can the chairs be put on sale so that the store incurs an operating loss of no more than 33⅓% of the overhead?
    (c) What is the maximum rate of markdown at which the chairs can be offered for sale in part (b)?

11. The Blast bought stereo equipment listed at $900.00 less 60%, 16⅔%. Expenses are 45% of the regular selling price and normal profit is 15% of the regular selling price. The store decided to change the regular selling price so that it could advertise a 37.5% discount while still maintaining its usual markup. During the annual inventory sale, the unsold equipment was marked down 55%. What operating profit or loss was realized on the equipment sold during the sale?

12. Lund's Pro Shop purchased sets of golf clubs for $500.00 less 40%, 16⅔%. Expenses are 20% of the regular selling price and the required profit is 17.5% of the regular selling price. The store decided to change the regular selling price so that it could offer a 36% discount without affecting its margin. At the end of the season, the unsold sets were advertised at a discount of 54%. What operating profit or loss was realized on the sets sold at the end of the season?

272 CHAPTER 6

13. Big Boy Appliances bought self-cleaning ovens for $900.00 less 33⅓%, 5%. Expenses are 15% of the regular selling price and profit is 9% of the regular selling price. For competitive reasons, the store marks all merchandise with a new regular selling price so that a discount of 25% can be advertised without affecting the margin. To promote sales, the ovens were marked down 40%. What operating profit or loss did the store make on the ovens sold during the sales promotion?

14. Blue Lake Marina sells a make of cruiser for $16 800.00. This regular selling price covers overhead of 15% of cost and a normal profit of 10% of cost. The cruisers were marked with a new regular selling price so that the marina can offer a 20% discount while still maintaining its regular gross profit. At the end of the boating season, the cruiser was marked down. The marina made 25% of its usual profit and reduced the usual commission paid to the sales personnel by 33⅓%. The normal commission accounts for 50% of the normal overhead. What was the rate of markdown?

REVIEW EXERCISE

1. A tool box is listed for $56.00 less 25%, 20%, 5%.

   (a) What is the net price of the tool box?

   (b) What is the amount of discount?

   (c) What is the single rate of discount that was allowed?

2. Compute the exact rate of discount allowed on a lawn mower that lists for $168.00 and is sold for $105.00.

3. Determine the exact single rate of discount equivalent to the discount series 35%, 12%, 5%.

4. A 40% discount allowed on an article amounts to $1.44. What is the net price?

5. Baton Construction Supplies has been selling wheelbarrows for $112.00 less 15%. What additional discount percent must the company offer to meet a competitor's price of $80.92?

6. A freezer was sold during a clearance sale for $387.50. If the freezer was sold at a discount of 16⅔%, what was the list price?

7. The net price of a snow shovel is $20.40 after discounts of 20%, 15%. What is the list price?

8. On May 18, an invoice dated May 17 for $4000.00 less 20%, 15%, terms 5/10 E.O.M., was received by Aldo Distributors.

(a) What is the last day of the discount period?

(b) What is the amount due if the invoice is paid within the discount period?

9. What amount must be remitted if the following invoices, all with terms 5/10, 2/30, n/60, are paid together on December 8?

   Invoice No. 312 dated November 2 for $923.00
   Invoice No. 429 dated November 14 for $784.00
   Invoice No. 563 dated November 30 for $873.00

10. Delta Furnishings received an invoice dated May 10 for a shipment of goods received June 21. The invoice was for $8400.00 less $33\frac{1}{3}\%$, $12\frac{1}{2}\%$ with terms 3/20 R.O.G. How much must Delta pay on July 9 to reduce its debt

    (a) by $2000.00?

    (b) to $2000.00?

11. The Peel Trading Company received an invoice dated September 20 for $16 000.00 less 25%, 20%, terms 5/10, 2/30, n/60. Peel made a payment on September 30 to reduce the debt to $5000.00 and a payment on October 20 to reduce the debt by $3000.00.

    (a) What amount must Peel remit to pay the balance of the debt at the end of the credit period?

    (b) What is the total amount paid by Peel?

12. Emco Ltd. received an invoice dated May 5 for $4000.00 less 15%, $7\frac{1}{2}\%$, terms 3/15 E.O.M. A cheque for $1595.65 was mailed by Emco on June 15 as part payment of the invoice.

    (a) By how much did Emco reduce the amount due on the invoice?

    (b) How much does Emco still owe?

13. Homeward Hardware buys cat litter for $6.00 less 20% per bag. The store's overhead is 45% of cost and the owner requires a profit of 20% of cost.

    (a) For how much should the bags be sold?

    (b) What is the amount of markup included in the selling price?

    (c) What is the rate of markup based on selling price?

    (d) What is the rate of markup based on cost?

    (e) What is the break-even price?

    (f) What operating profit or loss is made if a bag is sold for $6.00?

14. A retail store realizes a gross profit of $31.50 if it sells an article at a margin of 35% of the selling price.

(a) What is the regular selling price?

(b) What is the cost?

(c) What is the rate of markup based on cost?

(d) If overhead is 28% of cost, what is the break-even price?

(e) If the article is sold at a markdown of 24%, what is the operating profit or loss?

15. Using a markup of 35% of cost, a store priced a book at $8.91.

(a) What was the cost of the item?

(b) What is the markup as a percent of selling price?

16. A bicycle helmet costing $54.25 was marked up to realize a gross profit of 30% of the selling price.

(a) What was the selling price?

(b) What was the gross profit as a percent of cost?

17. A bedroom suite that cost a dealer $1800.00 less 37.5%, 18% carries a price tag with a regular selling price at a markup of 120% of cost. For quick sale, the bedroom suite was marked down 40%.

(a) What was the sale price?

(b) What rate of markup based on cost was realized?

18. Gino's purchased men's suits for $195.00 less 33⅓%. The store operates at a normal gross profit of 35% of regular selling price. The owner marks all merchandise with new regular selling prices so that the store can offer a 16⅔% discount. What is the new regular selling price?

19. An appliance store sold G.E. coffee makers for $22.95 during a promotional sale. The store bought the coffee makers for $36.00 less 40%, 15%. Overhead is 25% of the regular selling price.

(a) If the store's markup is 40% of the regular selling price, what was the rate of markdown?

(b) What operating profit or loss was made during the sale?

(c) What rate of markup based on cost was realized?

20. Harvey and Billnot buy shirts for $21.00 less 25%, 20%. The shirts are priced at a regular selling price to cover expenses of 20% of selling price and a profit of 17% of selling price. For a special weekend sale, shirts were marked down 20%.

(a) What was the operating profit or loss on the shirts sold during the weekend sale?

(b) What rate of markup was realized based on the sale price?

21. A jewellery store paid a unit price of $250.00 less 40%, 16⅔%, 8% for a shipment of designer watches. The store's overhead is 65% of cost and the normal profit is 55% of cost.

    (a) What is the regular selling price of the watches?

    (b) What is the sale price for the store to break even?

    (c) What is the rate of markdown to sell the watches at the break-even price?

22. Sight and Sound bought large-screen colour TV sets for $1080.00 less 33⅓%, 8⅓%. Overhead is 18% of regular selling price and required profit is 15⅓% of regular selling price. The TV sets were marked at a new regular selling price so that the store was able to advertise a discount of 25% while still maintaining its margin. To clear the inventory, the remaining TV sets were marked down 37½%.

    (a) What operating profit or loss is realized at the clearance price?

    (b) What is the realized rate of markup based on cost?

23. Ward Machinery lists a log splitter at $1860.00 less 33⅓%, 15%. To meet competition, Ward wants to reduce its net price to $922.25. What additional percent discount must Ward allow?

24. West End Appliances bought bread makers for $180.00 less 40%, 16⅔%, 10%. The store's overhead is 45% of regular selling price and the profit required is 21¼% of regular selling price.

    (a) What is the break-even price?

    (b) What is the maximum rate of markdown that the store can offer to break even?

    (c) What is the realized rate of markup based on cost if the bread makers are sold at the break-even price?

25. A merchant realizes a markup of $42.00 by selling an article at a markup of 37.5% of cost.

    (a) What is the regular selling price?

    (b) What is the rate of markup based on the regular selling price?

    (c) If the merchant's expenses are 17.5% of the regular selling price, what is the break-even price?

    (d) If the article is reduced for sale to $121.66, what is the rate of markdown?

26. The Knit Shoppe bought 250 sweaters for $3100.00; 50 sweaters were sold at a markup of 150% of cost and 120 sweaters at a markup of 75% of cost; 60 of the sweaters were sold during a clearance sale for $15.00 each and the remaining sweaters were disposed of at 20% below cost. Assume all sweaters had the same cost.

(a) What was the markup realized on the purchase?

(b) What was the percent markup realized based on cost?

(c) What was the gross profit realized based on selling price?

SELF-TEST

1. Determine the net price of an article listed at $590.00 less 37.5%, 12.5%, $8\frac{1}{3}$%.

2. What rate of discount has been allowed if an item that lists for $270.00 is sold for $168.75?

3. Compute the single discount percent equivalent to the discount series 40%, 10%, $8\frac{1}{3}$% (the rate must be exact).

4. Discount Electronics lists an article for $1020.00 less 25% and 15%. A competitor carries the same article for $927.00 less 25%. What further discount (correct to the nearest $\frac{1}{10}$ of 1%) must the competitor allow so that its net price is the same as Discount's?

5. What amount must be remitted if the following invoices, all with terms 4/10, 2/30, n/60, are paid on May 10?

   $850.00 less 20%, 10% dated March 21
   $960.00 less 30%, $16\frac{2}{3}$% dated April 10
   $1040.00 less $33\frac{1}{3}$%, 25%, 5% dated April 30

6. An invoice for $3200.00, dated March 20, terms 3/10 E.O.M., was received March 23. What payment must be made on April 10 to reduce the debt to $1200.00?

7. On January 15, Sheridan Service received an invoice dated January 14, terms 4/10 E.O.M., for $2592.00. On February 9, Sheridan Service mailed a cheque for $1392.00 in partial payment of the invoice. By how much did Sheridan Service reduce its debt?

8 What is the regular selling price of an item bought for $1270.00 if the markup is 20% of the regular selling price?

9. The regular selling price of merchandise sold in a store includes a markup of 40% based on the regular selling price. During a sale, an item that cost the store $180.00 was marked down 20%. For how much was the item sold?

10. The net price of an article is $727.20 after discounts of 20% and 10% have been allowed. What was the list price?

11. An item that cost the dealer $350 less 35%, 12.5% carries a regular selling price on the tag at a markup of 150% of cost. For quick sale, the item was reduced 30%. What was the sale price?

12. Find the cost of an item sold for $1904.00 to realize a markup of 40% based on cost.

13. An article cost $900.00 and sold for $2520.00. What was the percent markup based on cost?

14. A gross profit of $90.00 is made on a sale. If the gross profit was 45% based on selling price, what was the cost?

15. An appliance shop reduces the price of an appliance for quick sale from $1560.00 to $1195.00. Compute the markdown correct to the nearest $\frac{1}{100}$ of 1%.

16. An invoice shows a net price of $552.44 after discounts of $33\frac{1}{3}$%, 20%, $8\frac{1}{3}$%. What was the list price?

17. A retailer buys an appliance for $1480.00 less 25%, 15%. The store marks the merchandise at a regular selling price to cover expenses of 40% of the regular selling price and a net profit of 10% of the regular selling price. During a clearance sale, the appliance was sold at a markdown of 45%. What was the operating profit or loss?

18. Discount Electronics buys stereos for $830.00 less 37.5%, 12.5%. Expenses are 20% of the regular selling price and the required profit is 15% of the regular selling price. All merchandise is marked with a new regular selling price so that the store can advertise a discount of 30% while still maintaining its regular markup. During the annual clearance sale, the new regular selling price of unsold items is marked down 50%. What operating profit or loss does the store make on items sold during the sale?

CHALLENGE PROBLEMS

1. Rose Bowl Florists buys and sells roses only by the complete dozen. The owner buys 12 dozen fresh roses daily for $117. He knows that 10% of the roses will wilt before they can be sold. What price per dozen must Rose Bowl Florists charge for its saleable roses to realize a 55% markup based on selling price?

2. A merchant bought some goods at a discount of 25% of the list price. She wants to mark them at a regular selling price so that she can give a discount of 20% of the regular selling price and still make a markup of 25% of the sale price.

   (a) At what percent of the list price should she mark the regular selling price of the goods?

   (b) Suppose the merchant decides she must make a markup of 25% of the cost price. At what percent of the list price should she mark the regular selling price of the goods?

3. On April 13, a stereo store received a new sound system with a list price of $2500 from the manufacturer. The stereo store received a trade discount of 25%. The invoice, with terms 2/10, n/30, arrived on the same day as the sound system. The owner of the store marked up the sound system by 60% of the invoice amount (before cash discount) to cover overhead and profits. The owner paid the invoice on April 20. How much extra profit will be made on the sale, as a percent of the regular selling price, due to the early payment of the invoice?

CASE STUDY 6.1   FOCUSING ON PRICES

Elliot's Drug Store is a small independent drug store. It has a small-but-progressive camera department. Since Elliot's does not sell very many cameras in a year, it only keeps a small number in stock. Elliot's has just ordered five of the new auto-focus or "idiot-proof" cameras from Kodak. Elliot's owner has been told that the cost of each camera will be $190, with terms 2/10, n/30. The Manufacturer's Suggested Retail Price (MSRP) of each camera is $425. Elliot's owner calculates that the overhead is 40% of the MSRP and that the desired profit is 15% of the MSRP.

Zellers has a large camera shop in its store in the mall in this same town. It has ordered 50 of these same cameras from Kodak. Zellers has been offered both a cash discount and a quantity discount on the list price of $190. The cash discount is 3/15, n/30, while the quantity discount is 4%. Zellers estimates its overhead is 20% of the MSRP and it would like to make a profit of 30% of the MSRP.

QUESTIONS

1. What is the cost per camera (ignoring taxes) for Elliot's Drug Store and for Zellers?

2. For each store, what is the minimum selling price required to cover cost, overhead, and desired profits?

3. If Elliot's and Zellers sell the camera at the MSRP, how much extra profit will each store make
   (a) in dollars?
   (b) as a percent of MSRP?

4. What rate of a markdown from MSRP can Zellers offer to cover its overhead and make its originally intended profit?

CASE STUDY 6.2 PUTTING A PRICE ON THE TABLE

Hanover Furniture Company manufactures furniture but is well known for its stylish dining room suites. Hanover has found that there is a lot of confusion surrounding the term *list price*. There is the list price at which Hanover offers its product to the furniture stores. These furniture retailers expect to get a discount on this list price because they pay their bills early, or they order large quantities, or they offer a prestigious location for selling Hanover's excellent dining room suites. Hanover also has a list price or Manufacturer's Suggested Retail Price (MSRP) at which it would like to see its product sold. Hanover feels that this MSRP is a fair price in comparison with competitive suites and will bring a good return to both retailer and manufacturer. Most retailers, of course, would like to advertise the list price (MSRP) less a discount so that consumers will feel that they are getting a bargain. To resolve this problem, Hanover has decided to offer its dining room suites to retail outlets at the MSRP and offer a larger trade discount.

Putting its new policy into practice, Hanover has offered its newest dining room suite to McKay's Furniture Store for a list price (MSRP) of $1025, less a trade discount of 40%. McKay's will now advertise the suite as $1025 less 20%.

QUESTIONS

1. For how much did McKay's purchase the dining room suite?

2. What is McKay's selling price?

3. If McKay's sells at this price, what will be the rate of markup based on cost?

4. McKay's discovers that Becker Furniture, across town, is advertising a similar dining room suite for $779. By what additional percent must McKay's mark down its suite to match this price?

5. If McKay's marks down its suite to match the Becker Furniture advertised price, what rate of markup based on cost will McKay's make?

SUMMARY OF FORMULAE

Formula 6.1

$$\frac{\text{AMOUNT}}{\text{OF DISCOUNT}} = \frac{\text{RATE OF}}{\text{DISCOUNT}} \times \text{LIST PRICE}$$

Finding the amount of discount when the list price is known

Formula 6.2

$$\text{NET PRICE} = \text{LIST PRICE} - \frac{\text{AMOUNT OF}}{\text{TRADE DISCOUNT}}$$

Finding the net amount when the amount of discount is known

Formula 6.3A

$$\frac{\text{NET PRICE}}{\text{FACTOR (NPF)}} = 100\% - \% \text{ DISCOUNT}$$

Finding the net price factor (NPF)

Formula 6.3B

$$\text{NET PRICE FACTOR (NPF)} = (1 - d)$$

where d = rate of discount in decimal form

Restatement of Formula 6.3A in algebraic terms

Formula 6.4A

$$\text{NET PRICE} = \frac{\text{NET PRICE}}{\text{FACTOR (NPF)}} \times \text{LIST PRICE}$$

Finding the net amount directly without computing the amount of discount

Formula 6.4B

$$N = (1 - d)L \quad \text{or} \quad N = L(1 - d)$$

Restatement of Formula 6.4A in algebraic terms

Formula 6.5A

$$\frac{\text{NET PRICE FACTOR}}{\text{(NPF) FOR}} = \frac{\text{NPF FOR THE}}{\text{FIRST DISCOUNT}} \times \frac{\text{NPF FOR THE}}{\text{SECOND DISCOUNT}} \times \ldots \times \frac{\text{NPF FOR THE}}{\text{LAST DISCOUNT}}$$

Formula 6.5B

$$\text{NPF FOR A DISCOUNT SERIES} = (1 - d_1)(1 - d_2)(1 - d_3) \ldots (1 - d_n)$$

Formula 6.6A

$$\text{NET PRICE} = \frac{\text{NET PRICE FACTOR FOR}}{\text{THE DISCOUNT SERIES}} \times \text{LIST PRICE}$$

Finding the net amount directly when a list price is subject to a series of discounts

Formula 6.6B

$$\frac{\text{NET}}{\text{PRICE}} = (1 - d_1)(1 - d_2)(1 - d_3) \ldots (1 - d_n)L$$

Restatement of Formula 6.6A in algebraic terms

Formula 6.7

$$\frac{\text{RATE OF}}{\text{TRADE DISCOUNT}} = \frac{\text{AMOUNT OF DISCOUNT}}{\text{LIST PRICE}}$$

Finding the rate of discount

Formula 6.8

SINGLE EQUIVALENT RATE OF DISCOUNT
FOR A DISCOUNT SERIES

$$= 1 - \text{NPF FOR THE DISCOUNT SERIES}$$

$$= 1 - [(1 - d_1)(1 - d_2)(1 - d_3) \ldots (1 - d_n)]$$

Finding the single rate of discount that has the same effect as a given series of discounts

Formula 6.9A

$$\text{SELLING PRICE} = \text{COST} + \text{EXPENSES} + \text{PROFIT}$$

or

$$S = C + E + P$$

Basic relationship between selling price, cost, operating expenses (or overhead), and profit

Formula 6.9B

$$\text{SELLING PRICE} = \text{COST} + \text{MARKUP}$$

or

$$S = C + M$$

Formula 6.10

$$\text{MARKUP} = \text{EXPENSES} + \text{PROFIT}$$

or

$$M = E + P$$

Relationship between markup, operating expenses (or overhead), and profit

Formula 6.11

$$\text{RATE OF MARKUP BASED ON COST} = \frac{\text{MARKUP}}{\text{COST}} = \frac{M}{C}$$

Finding the rate of markup as a percent of cost

Formula 6.12

$$\text{RATE OF MARKUP BASED ON SELLING PRICE} = \frac{\text{MARKUP}}{\text{SELLING PRICE}} = \frac{M}{S}$$

Finding the rate of markup as a percent of selling price

GLOSSARY

Cash discount a reduction in the amount of an invoice

Credit period the time period at the end of which an invoice has to be paid

Discount a reduction from the original price

Discount period the time period during which a cash discount applies

Discount series two or more discounts taken off a list price in succession

End-of-month dating payment terms based on the last day of the month in which the invoice is dated

Gross profit see *Markup*

List price price printed in a catalogue or in a list of prices

Margin see *Markup*

Markdown a reduction in the price of an article sold to the consumer

Markup   the difference between the cost of merchandise and the selling price

Net factor   see *Net price factor*

Net price   the difference between a list price and the amount of discount

Net price factor (NPF)   the difference between 100% and a percent discount— the net price expressed as a fraction of the list price

Ordinary dating   payment terms based on the date of an invoice

Payment terms   a statement of the conditions under which a cash discount may be taken

Partial payment   part payment of an invoice

Proximo dating   see *End-of-month dating*

Rate of discount   a reduction in price expressed as a percent of the original price

Receipt-of-goods dating   payment terms based on the date the merchandise is received

Regular selling price   the price of an article sold to the consumer before any markdown is applied

Sale price   the price of an article sold to the consumer after a markdown has been applied

Single equivalent rate of discount   the single rate of discount that has the same effect as a specific series of discounts

Total cost   the cost at which merchandise is bought plus the overhead

Trade discount   a reduction of a catalogue or list price

7 Simple Interest

We all make informal, short-term loans in our daily lives. We've all borrowed or lent coffee money, parking money, or a few dollars to friends. We expect to repay and be repaid, but often we don't give a thought to interest.

Formal loans are another matter. We have to take into account the size of the loan, the length of time between the loan and repayment dates, and the interest rate.

We should think of interest rates in other situations as well. For example, many companies selling home and auto insurance now offer the option of paying premiums in instalments. In this situation, one factor we should consider is the interest you miss earning if you pay your whole bill now. Are you better off paying the whole bill now, or should you pay a part now and a part later?

Introduction

As we know from our daily lives, the use of money as a means of exchange has led to the practice of lending and borrowing money. Lenders usually require compensation for their services in the form of interest. The amount of such interest is based on three factors: the amount of money borrowed, the rate of interest at which it is borrowed, and the time period for which it is borrowed.

OBJECTIVES

Upon completing this chapter, you will be able to do the following:

1. Interpret the letter symbols used in the formula $I = Prt$.
2. Determine the exact time in days between two dates.
3. Compute the exact simple interest by means of the formula $I = Prt$.
4. Find the principal, rate, or time using the formula $I = Prt$.
5. Use the formula $S = P(1 + rt)$ to find the future value (or maturity value) when the principal, rate, and time are given.
6. Use the formula $P = \dfrac{S}{1 + rt}$ to compute the principal (or present value) when the maturity value, rate, and time are given.
7. Compute equivalent values for specified focal dates.

7.1   BASIC CONCEPTS AND FORMULA

A. Formula

Interest is the rent charged for the use of money. The amount of **simple interest** is determined by the relationship Interest = Principal × Rate × Time

$$I = Prt$$ ——————————————— Formula 7.1A

where I is the amount of interest earned, measured in dollars and cents;
     P is the principal sum of money earning the interest, measured in dollars and cents:
     r is the simple annual (yearly) rate of interest, expressed as a decimal;
     t is the time period in years.

Simple interest is often used between friends, and in short-term loans from financial institutions and insurance companies.

B. Matching r and t

While the time may be stated in days, months, or years, the rate of interest is a yearly charge unless otherwise stated. In using the simple interest formula, it is imperative that the time t corresponds to the interest rate r. Months or days often need to be converted into years.

EXAMPLE 7.1A   State r and t for each of the following.

  (i) Rate 9%; time 3 years

 (ii) Rate 8.5%; time 18 months

(iii) Rate 11¼%; time 243 days

Solution

  (i) The annual rate $r = 9\% = 0.09$
     The time in years $t = 3$

 (ii) The annual rate $r = 8.5\% = 0.085$
     The time in years $t = \dfrac{18}{12}$

     Note: To convert months into years, divide by 12.

(iii) The annual rate $r = 11.25\% = 0.1125$
     The time in years $t = \dfrac{243}{365}$

     Note: To convert days into years, divide by 365.

Exercise 7.1

A. State r and t for each of the following.

1. Rate is $12\frac{1}{2}\%$; time is $1\frac{1}{4}$ years

2. Rate is $9\frac{3}{4}\%$; time is 21 months

3. Rate is 10.25%; time is 165 days

4. Rate is $15\frac{1}{2}\%$; time is 332 days

7.2 DETERMINING THE NUMBER OF DAYS

A. Counting exact time

The **interest period** is the time period for which interest is charged. When the interest period involves two dates, the number of days between the two dates (the **exact time**) must be determined. In counting the number of days, the traditional practice was to count the ending date but *not* the starting date. However, the current practice, associated with the computerization of interest calculation, is to count the starting date but *not* the ending date. While in most cases the end result is the same, there are situations in which slightly different answers result, depending on the method used. This text will use the current method of counting the starting date.

Counting days requires knowing the order of the twelve months in the year and the number of days in each month. The number of days in each of the twelve months in order (ignoring leap years) is listed below.

1.	January	31	2.	February	28	3.	March	31
4.	April	30	5.	May	31	6.	June	30
7.	July	31	8.	August	31	9.	September	30
10.	October	31	11.	November	30	12.	December	31

One way to remember the number of days in each month is to recall the following nursery rhyme:

Thirty days hath September,
April, June, and November.
All the rest have thirty-one,
Excepting February alone,
Which has but twenty-eight days clear
And twenty-nine in each leap year.

EXAMPLE 7.2A   Find the number of days between January 30 and June 1.

Solution   The starting date is January 30 —————————— to be counted
The ending date is June 1 —————————— do *not* count

$$\text{Number of days} \begin{array}{llr} \text{January} & 2 & \underline{\hspace{2cm}} \; (31 - 29) \\ \text{February} & 28 & \\ \text{March} & 31 & \\ \text{April} & 30 & \\ \text{May} & 31 & \\ \text{June} & \underline{0} & \\ \text{TOTAL} & \underline{\underline{122}} & \end{array}$$

EXAMPLE 7.2B Find the number of days between November 12, 1998, and May 5, 1999.

Solution

The starting date is November 12 —————— to be counted
The ending date is May 5 —————— do *not* count

$$\text{Number of days} \begin{array}{llr} \text{November 1998} & 19 & \underline{\hspace{1cm}} \; (30 - 11) \\ \text{December} & 31 & \\ \text{January 1999} & 31 & \\ \text{February} & 28 & \\ \text{March} & 31 & \\ \text{April} & 30 & \\ \text{May} & \underline{4} & \\ \text{TOTAL} & \underline{\underline{174}} & \end{array}$$

B. Using a table

Exact time can also be obtained from a table listing the number of each day of the year. (See Table 7.1.) When using such a table, take care to distinguish between two cases:

(i) the starting date and the ending date are in the *same* year;

(ii) the ending date is in the year *following* the starting date or in a later year.

EXAMPLE 7.2C Find the number of days between May 29 and August 3.

Solution

The starting date is May 29 ————————→ Day 149
The ending date is August 3 ————————→ Day $\underline{215}$

The difference in days is $(215 - 149)$ $\qquad\qquad \underline{\underline{66}}$

EXAMPLE 7.2D Find the number of days between September 1, 2001, and April 1, 2002.

Solution

The starting date is September 1, 2001 ————→ Day 244
Number of days in 2001 is 365
Number of days remaining in 2001 is $(365 - 244) =$ $\quad$ 121
The ending date is April 1, 2002 ————————→ Day 91
The total number of days is $(121 + 91) =$ $\qquad$ 212

TABLE 7.1 The Number of Each Day of the Year

Day of Month	Jan.	Feb.	Mar.	Apr.	May	June	July	Aug.	Sept.	Oct.	Nov.	Dec.	Day of Month
1	1	32	60	91	121	152	182	213	244	274	305	335	1
2	2	33	61	92	122	153	183	214	245	275	306	336	2
3	3	34	62	93	123	154	184	215	246	276	307	337	3
4	4	35	63	94	124	155	185	216	247	277	308	338	4
5	5	36	64	95	125	156	186	217	248	278	309	339	5
6	6	37	65	96	126	157	187	218	249	279	310	340	6
7	7	38	66	97	127	158	188	219	250	280	311	341	7
8	8	39	67	98	128	159	189	220	251	281	312	342	8
9	9	40	68	99	129	160	190	221	252	282	313	343	9
10	10	41	69	100	130	161	191	222	253	283	314	344	10
11	11	42	70	101	131	162	192	223	254	284	315	345	11
12	12	43	71	102	132	163	193	224	255	285	316	346	12
13	13	44	72	103	133	164	194	225	256	286	317	347	13
14	14	45	73	104	134	165	195	226	257	287	318	348	14
15	15	46	74	105	135	166	196	227	258	288	319	349	15
16	16	47	75	106	136	167	197	228	259	289	320	350	16
17	17	48	76	107	137	168	198	229	260	290	321	351	17
18	18	49	77	108	138	169	199	230	261	291	322	352	18
19	19	50	78	109	139	170	200	231	262	292	323	353	19
20	20	51	79	110	140	171	201	232	263	293	324	354	20
21	21	52	80	111	141	172	202	233	264	294	325	355	21
22	22	53	81	112	142	173	203	234	265	295	326	356	22
23	23	54	82	113	143	174	204	235	266	296	327	357	23
24	24	55	83	114	144	175	205	236	267	297	328	358	24
25	25	56	84	115	145	176	206	237	268	298	329	359	25
26	26	57	85	116	146	177	207	238	269	299	330	360	26
27	27	58	86	117	147	178	208	239	270	300	331	361	27
28	28	59	87	118	148	179	209	240	271	301	332	362	28
29	29		88	119	149	180	210	241	272	302	333	363	29
30	30		89	120	150	181	211	242	273	303	334	364	30
31	31		90		151		212	243		304		365	31

Note: In leap years, February 29 becomes day 60 and the numbers in the table increase by 1 for all following days.

C. Leap years

Leap years are evenly divisible by 4, such as 1988, 1992, and 1996. An extra day is added to February if a year is a **leap year**. However, a centennial year is not a leap year unless the number is *evenly* divisible by 400. This means that the year 1900 was not a leap year but the year 2000 is. It will have the extra day.

EXAMPLE 7.2E   Find the number of days between December 12, 1999, and April 1, 2000,

(i) by counting;

(ii) by using Table 7.1.

Solution   (i) The starting date is December 12, 1999
        The ending date is April 1, 2000

Number of days	December 1999	20	—————— (31 − 11)
	January 2000	31	
	February	29	—————— Leap year
	March	31	
	April	0	
	TOTAL	111	

(ii) The starting date is December 12, 1999 —————————→ Day 346
        The number of days in 1999 is 365
        The number of days remaining in 1999 is (365 − 346) =   19
        The ending date is April 1, 2000 —————————→ Day 92
        (for a leap year, increase the table number 91 by 1 to 92)
                                        TOTAL = 19 + 92 = 111

Exercise 7.2

A. Determine the exact time by counting days for each of the following.

1. January 18, 1998, to May 10, 1998

2. August 30, 2000, to April 1, 2001

3. November 1, 1999, to April 15, 2000

4. December 24, 2000, to February 5, 2002

B. Determine the exact time using a table. (See Table 7.1.)

1. April 1, 1999, to December 1, 1999

2. July 30, 1998, to March 30, 1999

3. April 5, 1999, to March 11, 2000

4. August 25, 1998, to May 20, 2000

7.3   COMPUTING THE AMOUNT OF INTEREST

If the principal, rate, and time are known, the amount of interest can be determined by the formula $I = Prt$.

A.

EXAMPLE 7.3A

Compute the amount of interest for

(i) $3600.00 at 9% p.a. (per annum) for 3 years;

(ii) $5240.00 at 10.5% p.a. for 16 months;

(iii) $1293.60 at 11.75% p.a. for 215 days.

Solution

(i) $P = 3600.00; r = 9\% = 0.09; t = 3$
  $I = Prt = (3600.00)(0.09)(3) = \$972.00$

(ii) $P = 5240.00; r = 10.5\% = 0.105; t = 16 \text{ months} = \dfrac{16}{12}$

  $I = Prt = (5240.00)(0.105)\left(\dfrac{16}{12}\right) = \$733.60$

(iii) $P = 1293.60; r = 11.75 = 0.1175; t = 215 \text{ days} = \dfrac{215}{365}$

  $I = Prt = (1293.60)(0.1175)\left(\dfrac{215}{365}\right) = \$89.53$

B.

EXAMPLE 7.3B

Find the amount of interest earned by $785.95 invested at 9.25% from January 30, 2001, to April 21, 2001.

Solution

Number of days			
	January	2	—— (31 − 29)
	February	28	
	March	31	
	April	20	
	TOTAL	81	

$P = 785.95; r = 9.25\% = 0.0925; t = \dfrac{81}{365}$

$I = (785.95)(0.0925)\left(\dfrac{81}{365}\right) = \$16.13$

C.

EXAMPLE 7.3C

Compute the amount of interest on $1240.00 earning 10.75% p.a. from September 30, 1999, to May 15, 2000.

Solution

The starting date is September 30, 1999 ⟶ Day 273
The number of days remaining in 1999 is (365 − 273) =   92
The ending date is May 15, 2000 (Day 135 + 1)   136 —— Leap year
                                         TOTAL   228

$$P = 1240.00;\ r = 10.75\% = 0.1075;\ t = \frac{228}{365}$$

$$I = (1240.00)(0.1075)\left(\frac{228}{365}\right) = \$83.27$$

Note: 365 is used to convert the number of days into years even if the year involved is a leap year.

Exercise 7.3

A. Compute the amount of interest for each of the following.

1. $4000.00 at $10\frac{1}{2}\%$ for $2\frac{1}{4}$ years

2. $645.00 at $6\frac{1}{4}\%$ for $1\frac{3}{4}$ years

3. $1660 at 9.75% for 16 months

4. $742.40 at 10.9% for 9 months

5. $980.00 at 11.5% for 244 days

6. $465.40 at 12.4% for 163 days

B. Compute the exact interest for each of the following.

1. $275.00 at 9.25% from November 30, 2000, to May 5, 2001

2. $1090.60 at 7.8% from October 12, 1999, to April 24, 2000

3. $424.23 at $12\frac{3}{4}\%$ from April 4, 1999, to November 4, 1999

4. $724.85 at 10.4% from August 30, 1998, to March 30, 1999

7.4 FINDING THE PRINCIPAL, RATE, OR TIME

A. Problems derived from the simple interest formula

The simple interest formula $I = Prt$ contains the four variables I, P, r, and t. If any *three* of the four are given, the value of the unknown variable can be computed by substituting the known values in the formula or by solving for the unknown variable first and then substituting in the resulting derived formula.

The three derived formulae are

(i) to find the principal P,

$$\boxed{P = \frac{I}{rt}}$$ ———————————————— **Formula 7.1B**

(ii) to find the rate of interest r,

$$r = \frac{I}{Pt}$$ —————————————— **Formula 7.1C**

(iii) to find the time period t,

$$t = \frac{I}{Pr}$$ —————————————— **Formula 7.1D**

Note:

(a) In Formula 7.1C, if the time period t is expressed in *years*, the value of r represents an *annual* rate of interest in decimal form.

(b) In Formula 7.1D, if the rate of interest r is an *annual* rate, the value of t represents *years* in decimal form.

B. Finding the principal

If the amount of interest, the rate of interest, and the time period are known, the principal can be determined.

EXAMPLE 7.4A   What principal will earn interest of $57.40 at 10.25% in 8 months?

Solution $I = 57.40; \quad r = 10.25\%; \quad t = \dfrac{8}{12}$

(i) Using the formula $I = Prt$,

$57.40 = (P)(0.1025)\left(\dfrac{8}{12}\right)$ ——————— by substitution

$57.40 = (P)(0.0683333)$ ——————— $(0.1025)\left(\frac{8}{12}\right)$

$P = \dfrac{57.40}{0.0683333}$ ——————— divide 57.40 by the coefficient of P

$= \$840.00$

(ii) Using the derived formula $P = \dfrac{I}{rt}$,

$P = \dfrac{57.40}{(0.1025)\left(\frac{8}{12}\right)}$ ——————— by substitution

$= \dfrac{(57.40)(12)}{(0.1025)(8)}$ ——————— move the 12 into the numerator

$= \$840.00$

Note:

(1) When the time is given in months, the formula may be modified to

$$P = \frac{(I)(12)}{(r)(t \text{ in months})}$$

(2) When the time is given in days, the formula may be modified to

$$P = \frac{(I)(365)}{(r)(t \text{ in days})}$$

EXAMPLE 7.4B Determine the sum of money that must be invested for 245 days at 9.75% to earn $71.99.

Solution $I = 71.99; \quad r = 9.75\% = 0.0975; \quad t = \dfrac{245}{365}$

(i) Using the formula I = Prt,

$$71.99 = (P)(0.0975)\left(\frac{245}{365}\right)$$

$$71.99 = (P)(0.0654452)$$

$$P = \frac{71.99}{0.0654452}$$

$$= \$1100.00$$

(ii) Using the derived formula $P = \dfrac{I}{rt}$,

$$P = \frac{71.99}{(0.0975)\left(\frac{245}{365}\right)}$$

$$= \frac{(71.99)(365)}{(0.0975)(245)} \qquad\text{—————— move the 365 into the numerator}$$

$$= \$1100.00$$

C. Finding the rate

If the amount of interest, the principal, and the time period are known, the rate of interest can be determined.

EXAMPLE 7.4C Find the annual rate of interest required for $744.00 to earn $75.95 in 14 months.

Solution $I = 75.95; \quad P = 744.00; \quad t = \dfrac{14}{12}$

(i) Using the formula I = Prt,

$$75.95 = (744)(r)\left(\frac{14}{12}\right)$$

$$75.95 = (868)(r)$$

$$r = \frac{75.95}{868}$$

$$= 0.0875$$

$$= 8.75\% \qquad\text{——————— convert to a percent}$$

(ii) Using the derived formula $r = \dfrac{I}{Pt}$,

$$r = \frac{75.95}{(744.00)\left(\frac{14}{12}\right)}$$

$$= \frac{(75.95)(12)}{(744.00)(14)}$$

$$= 0.0875$$

$$= 8.75\%$$

Note:

(1) When the time is given in months, the formula may be modified to

$$r = \frac{(I)(12)}{(P)(t \text{ in months})}$$

(2) When the time is given in days, the formula may be modified to

$$r = \frac{(I)(365)}{(P)(t \text{ in days})}$$

EXAMPLE 7.4D Find the yearly rate of interest on a principal of $1600.00 earning interest of $59.18 in 120 days.

Solution $I = 59.18;\quad P = 1600.00;\quad t = \dfrac{120}{365}$

(i) Using the formula $I = Prt$,

$$59.18 = (1600.00)(r)\left(\frac{120}{365}\right)$$

$$59.18 = (526.0274)(r)$$

$$r = \frac{59.18}{526.0274}$$

$$= 0.1125$$

$$= 11.25\%$$

(ii) Using the derived formula $r = \dfrac{I}{Pt}$,

$$r = \frac{59.18}{(1600.00)\left(\frac{120}{365}\right)}$$

$$= \frac{(59.18)(365)}{(1600.00)(120)}$$

$$= 0.1125$$

$$= 11.25\%$$

D. Finding the time

If the amount of interest, the principal, and the rate of interest are known, the time period can be determined.

EXAMPLE 7.4E Find the number of years required for $745.00 to earn $178.80 simple interest at 8% p.a.

Solution $I = 178.80;\quad P = 745.00;\quad r = 8\% = 0.08$

(i) Using the formula $I = Prt$,

$$178.80 = (745.00)(0.08)(t)$$

$$178.80 = (59.60)(t)$$

$$t = \frac{178.80}{59.60}$$

$$= 3.00 \text{ (years)}$$

(ii) Using the derived formula $t = \dfrac{I}{Pr}$,

$$t = \frac{178.80}{(745.00)(0.08)}$$

$$= 3.00 \text{ (years)}$$

Note:

(1) The value of t in the formula $I = Prt$ will be in years. If the time period is to be stated in months or in days, it is necessary to multiply the initial value of t by 12 for months or 365 for days.

(2) If the time is to be shown in months, the derived formula may be modified to

$$t = \frac{(I)(12)}{Pr}$$

(3) If the time is to be shown in days, the derived formula may be modified to

$$t = \frac{(I)(365)}{Pr}$$

EXAMPLE 7.4F

Determine the number of months required for a deposit of $1320.00 to earn $51.70 interest at 11.75%.

Solution

$I = 51.70; \quad P = 1320.00; \quad r = 11.75\% = 0.1175$

(i) Using the formula $I = Prt$,

$51.70 = (1320.00)(0.1175)(t)$

$51.70 = (155.10)(t)$

$$t = \frac{51.70}{155.10}$$

$= 0.3333333 \text{ years}$

$= (0.3333333)(12) \text{ months}$

$= 4 \text{ months}$

(ii) Using the derived formula $t = \dfrac{I}{Pr}$,

$$t = \frac{51.70}{(1320.00)(0.1175)} \text{ years}$$

$$= \frac{(51.70)(12)}{(1320.00)(0.1175)} \text{ months}$$

$= 4 \text{ months}$

EXAMPLE 7.4G

How many days are needed for $1500.00 to earn $69.04 at 10.5% p.a.?

Solution

$I = 69.04; \quad P = 1500.00; \quad r = 10.5\% = 0.105$

(i) Using the formula $I = Prt$,

$69.04 = (1500.00)(0.105)(t)$

$69.04 = (157.50)(t)$

$$t = \frac{69.04}{157.50}$$
$$= 0.4383492 \text{ years}$$
$$= (0.4383492)(365) \text{ days}$$
$$\cong 160 \text{ days}$$

(ii) Using the derived formula $t = \dfrac{I}{Pr}$,

$$t = \frac{69.04}{(1500.00)(0.105)} \text{ years}$$
$$= \frac{(69.04)(365)}{(1500.00)(0.105)} \text{ days}$$
$$\cong 160 \text{ days}$$

Exercise 7.4

A. Determine the missing value for each of the following.

	Interest	Principal	Rate	Time
1.	$67.83	?	9.5%	7 months
2.	$256.25	?	10.25%	250 days
3.	$215.00	$2400.00	?	10 months
4.	$53.40	$750.00	?	315 days
5.	$136.34	$954.00	12.25%	? (months)
6.	$52.64	$1295.80	9.75%	? (months)
7.	$15.30	$344.75	11.25%	? (days)
8.	$68.96	$830.30	10.75%	? (days)

B. Find the value indicated for each of the following.

1. Find the principal that will earn $148.32 at 6.75% in 8 months.

2. Determine the deposit that must be made to earn $39.27 in 225 days at 11%.

3. A loan of $880.00 can be repaid in 15 months by paying the principal sum borrowed plus $104.50 interest. What was the rate of interest charged?

4. At what rate of interest will $1387.00 earn $63.84 in 200 days?

5. In how many months will $1290.00 earn $100.51 interest at $8\frac{1}{2}$%?

6. Determine the number of days it will take $564.00 to earn $15.09 at $7\frac{3}{4}$%.

DID YOU KNOW?

Only in February

Did you know that, in 1984, February 1 fell on a Wednesday and February 29 fell on a Wednesday? February 1984 had five Wednesdays. Do you know when that will happen again?

Only in a leap year is it possible to have five Wednesdays in February. Seven leap years have to go by before this situation can occur again, because in each of the leap years, February 29 would fall on a different weekday. February will have five Wednesdays again in 2012.

7. What principal will earn $39.96 from June 18, 1999, to December 15, 1999, at 9.25%?

8. What rate of interest is required for $740.48 to earn $42.49 interest from September 10, 1999, to March 4, 2000?

9. Philip wants to supplement his pension by $2000 per month with income from his investments. His investments pay him monthly and earn 6% p.a. What value of investments must Philip have in his portfolio to generate enough interest to give him his desired income?

7.5 THE FUTURE VALUE (MATURITY VALUE) OF A SUM OF MONEY

A. Basic concept

When you borrow money, you are obligated to repay both the sum borrowed (the principal) and any interest due. Therefore, the **future value of a sum of money** (or **maturity value**) is the value obtained by adding the original principal and the interest due.

$$\text{FUTURE VALUE (OR MATURITY VALUE)} = \text{PRINCIPAL} + \text{INTEREST}$$
$$S = P + I$$

—— Formula 7.2

EXAMPLE 7.5A   Determine the future value (maturity value), principal, or interest as indicated.

(i) The principal is $2200.00 and the interest is $240.00. Find the future value (maturity value).

Solution
$P = 2200.00;\quad I = 240.00$

$S = P + I$
$ = 2200.00 + 240.00$
$ = \$2440.00$

The future value is $2440.00.

(ii) The principal is $850.00 and the future value (maturity value) is $920.00. Find the interest.

Solution
$P = 850.00;\quad S = 920.00$

$$S = P + I$$
$$920.00 = 850.00 + I$$
$$920.00 - 850.00 = I$$
$$I = \$70.00$$

The amount of interest is $70.00.

(iii) The future value (maturity value) is $430.00 and the interest is $40.00. Find the principal.

Solution

$S = 430.00;   I = 40.00$

$$S = P + I$$
$$430.00 = P + 40.00$$
$$430.00 - 40.00 = P$$
$$P = \$390.00$$

The principal is $390.00.

B. The future value formula $S = P(1 + rt)$

The formulae $I = Prt$ and $S = P + I$ are combined to obtain the future value (maturity value) formula for simple interest.

$S = P + I$

$S = P + Prt$ ——————————————— substitute Prt for I

$S = P(1 + rt)$ ——————————————— take out the common factor P

$\boxed{S = P(1 + rt)}$ ——————————————— **Formula 7.3A**

EXAMPLE 7.5B

Find the future value (maturity value) of an investment of $720.00 earning 11% p.a. for 146 days.

Solution

$P = 720.00;   r = 11\% = 0.11;   t = \dfrac{146}{365}$

$S = P(1 + rt)$

$= (720.00)\left[1 + (0.11)\left(\dfrac{146}{365}\right)\right]$

$= (720.00)(1 + 0.044)$

$= (720.00)(1.044)$

$= \$751.68$

The future value of the investment is $751.68.

EXAMPLE 7.5C

Find the maturity value of a deposit of $1250.00 invested at 9.75% p.a. from October 15, 1997, to May 1, 1998.

Solution

The time period in days $= 17 + 30 + 31 + 31 + 28 + 31 + 30 + 0 = 198$.
Using Table 7.1, the time period in days $= (\text{Dec. } 31 - \text{Oct. } 15) + \text{May } 1 = (365 - 288) + 121 = 77 + 121 = 198$.

$P = 1250.00;   r = 9.75\% = 0.0975;   t = \dfrac{198}{365}$

$$S = P(1 + rt)$$
$$= (1250.00)\left[1 + (0.0975)\left(\frac{198}{365}\right)\right]$$
$$= (1250.00)(1 + 0.0528904)$$
$$= (1250.00)(1.0528904)$$
$$\cong \$1316.11$$

The maturity value of the deposit is about $1316.11.

Exercise 7.5

A. Use the future value (maturity value) formula to answer each of the following.

1. Find the future value of $480.00 at 12½% for 220 days.

2. Find the maturity value of $732.00 invested at 9.8% from May 20, 1998, to November 23, 1998.

3. Compute the future value of $820.00 over 9 months at 11¾%.

4. What payment is required to pay off a loan of $1200.00 at 7% fourteen months later?

7.6 PRESENT VALUE

A. Finding the principal when the future value (maturity value) is known

The formula $S = P(1 + rt)$ permits the calculation of the principal when the maturity value, the rate, and the time are given.

EXAMPLE 7.6A   Find the principal that will amount to $1294.50 in 9 months at 10.5% per annum.

Solution $S = 1294.50; \quad r = 10.5\% = 0.105; \quad t = \dfrac{9}{12}$

$$S = P(1 + rt) \text{ ———————— use the future value formula when S is known}$$
$$1294.50 = (P)\left[1 + (0.105)\left(\frac{9}{12}\right)\right]$$
$$1294.50 = (P)(1 + 0.07875)$$
$$1294.50 = (P)(1.07875)$$
$$P = \frac{1294.50}{1.07875}$$
$$P = \$1200.00$$

The principal is $1200.00.

EXAMPLE 7.6B   What sum of money must be invested on January 31, 2000, to amount to $7700.00 on August 18, 2000, at 10% p.a.?

Solution   The time period in days $= 1 + 29(\text{leap year}) + 31 + 30 + 31 + 30 + 31 + 17 = 200$

$$S = 7700.00; \quad r = 10\% = 0.10; \quad t = \frac{200}{365}$$

$$7700.00 = (P)\left[1 + (0.10)\left(\frac{200}{365}\right)\right] \quad \text{——— using Formula 7.3A}$$

$$7700.00 = (P)(1 + 0.0547945)$$

$$7700.00 = (P)(1.0547945)$$

$$P = \frac{7700.00}{1.0547945}$$

$$P = \$7300.00$$

Note:

(1) The total interest earned is $\$7700 - \$7300 = \$400.00$.

(2) The daily amount of interest is $\dfrac{\$400.00}{200} = \$2.00$.

B. The present value concept and formula

When interest is paid for the use of money, the value of any sum of money subject to interest changes with time. This change is called the **time value of money**.

To illustrate the concept of time value of money, Example 7.6B is represented on the time graph shown in Figure 7.1.

FIGURE 7.1   **Time Graph for Example 7.6B**

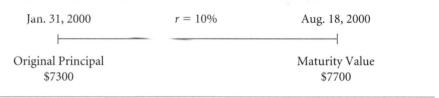

Jan. 31, 2000	$r = 10\%$	Aug. 18, 2000
Original Principal $7300		Maturity Value $7700

As shown, the original principal of $7300 will grow to $7700 at 10% in 200 days. The original principal earns $400 interest in 200 days; that is, the original principal of $7300 will grow by $2.00 per day. Accordingly, the value of the investment changes day by day. The future value (or maturity value) of $7300 is $7700 on August 18, 2000, at 10% p.a. On January 31, 2000, the $7300 principal is known as the *present value* of the August 18 $7700. *The* **present value** *of an amount at any given time is the principal needed to grow to that amount at a given rate of interest over a given period of time.*

Since the problem of finding the present value is equivalent to finding the principal when the future value, rate, and time are given, the future value formula $S = P(1 + rt)$ applies. However, as the problem of finding the present value of an amount is one of the frequently recurring problems in financial analysis, it is useful to solve the future value formula for P to obtain the present value formula.

$$S = P(1 + rt) \text{——————— starting with the future value formula}$$

$$\frac{S}{(1 + rt)} = \frac{P(1 + rt)}{(1 + rt)} \text{————— divide both sides by } (1 + rt)$$

$$\frac{S}{(1 + rt)} = P \text{————— reduce the fraction } \tfrac{(1 + rt)}{(1 + rt)} \text{ to } 1$$

This is the present value formula for simple interest.

$$\boxed{P = \frac{S}{1 + rt}} \text{————— Formula 7.3B}$$

EXAMPLE 7.6C Find the present value of an investment, eight months before the maturity date, that earns interest at 12% p.a. and has a maturity value of $918.00.

FIGURE 7.2 **Time Graph for Example 7.6C**

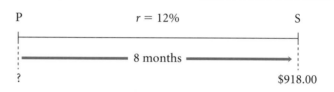

Solution $S = 918.00; \quad r = 12\% = 0.12; \quad t = \dfrac{8}{12}$

$$P = \frac{S}{1 + rt}$$

$$P = \frac{918.00}{1 + (0.12)\left(\frac{8}{12}\right)} \text{————— using Formula 7.3B}$$

$$= \frac{918.00}{1 + 0.08}$$

$$= \frac{918.00}{1.08}$$

$$= \$850.00$$

The present value of the investment is $850.00.

EXAMPLE 7.6D Find the sum of money that, deposited in an account on April 1, will grow to $674.73 by September 10 at 10.75% p.a.

Solution The time in days = 30 + 31 + 30 + 31 + 31 + 9 = 162

$$S = 674.73; \quad r = 10.75\% = 0.1075; \quad t = \frac{162}{365}$$

$$P = \frac{674.73}{1 + (0.1075)\left(\frac{162}{365}\right)}$$

$$= \frac{674.73}{1 + 0.0477123}$$

$$= \frac{674.73}{1.0477123}$$

$$= \$644.00$$

The sum of money is $644.00.

Exercise 7.6

A. Find the principal and the missing value in each of the following.

	Future Value (maturity value)	Interest Amount	Interest Rate	Time
1.	$305.90	?	12%	15 months
2.	$729.30	$117.30	?	20 months
3.	?	$29.67	8.6%	8 months
4.	?	$27.11	9.5%	240 days
5.	$2195.10	$170.10	10.5%	?
6.	$1035.38	?	7.5%	275 days

B. Solve each of the following.

1. What principal will have a future value of $1276.99 at 10.8% in 5 months?

2. What sum of money will accumulate to $489.04 in 93 days at 11.6%?

3. Determine the present value of a debt of $1760.00 due in four months if interest at 9¾% is allowed.

4. Find the present value of a debt of $460.00 ninety days before it is due if money is worth 6.5%.

BUSINESS MATH NEWS BOX

PERFORMANCES IN PERSPECTIVE: THE TSE 300 AND S&P 500

Nineteen ninety-six was a stellar year for both the Canadian and U.S. stock markets, as measured by the Toronto Stock Exchange 300 Composite Stock Index (TSE 300) and the Standard and Poor's Composite Index of 500 Stocks (S&P 500), respectively. The total return of the TSE 300 was 28.35% and that of the S&P 500 was 22.96%.

These gains are substantial, but it's important to keep any year's market performance in perspective. While past performance is no indication of future returns, a look at what the market has tended to do in the past can help investors set realistic expectations for the coming years.

The TSE 300 topped 20% only thirteen times between 1957 and 1996. More often than not, years of above-average performance are often followed by returns that are closer to the long-term average. The chart below shows the returns of the TSE 300 for eight of the years after which the TSE 300 advanced by more than 20%. A similar pattern holds true for the S&P 500. History suggests that the markets may not sustain the kind of returns in 1997 that they did in 1996, although there are no guarantees.

Don't panic if the market undergoes a temporary correction. A decline of 5% after a rise of 30% still leaves a net gain of 23.5%. Staying invested positions you to enjoy the returns equity markets offer over time.

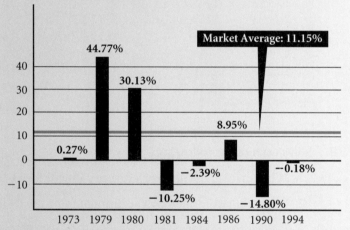

TSE 300 in Years Following a Gain of 20% or More

The returns of the TSE 300 following years in which it advanced by more than 20% were—on the whole—below the market average.

QUESTIONS

1. What was the average annual return of the TSE 300 for the eight years shown on the graph?

2. Is it true that "A decline of 5% after a rise of 30% still leaves a net gain of 23.5%"? Check this statement using your own numbers.

3. What was the average difference between the TSE 300 return and the market average for the eight years shown on the graph?

4. Based on the graph, is it generally a good thing for the market when the TSE 300 advances more than 20% in one year?

7.7 EQUIVALENT VALUES

A. Dated values

If a sum of money is subject to a rate of interest, it will grow over time. Thus, the value of the sum of money changes with time. This change is known as the time value of money.

For example, a sum of $1000.00 invested today at 8% p.a. simple interest has a value of $1000.00 today, $1020.00 in three months, $1040.00 in six months, and $1080.00 in one year.

The value of the original sum at any particular time is a **dated value** of that sum. The dated value combines the original sum with the interest earned up to the dated value date. Each dated value at a different time is equivalent to the original sum of money. The table below shows four dated values for $1000.00 invested at 8% p.a. The longer the time is from today, the greater is the dated value. This is so because interest has been earned on the principal over a longer time period.

Time	Dated Value
Today	$1000.00
3 months from today	$1020.00
6 months from today	$1040.00
1 year from today	$1080.00

Consider the case of an obligation of $500.00 that is payable today. Suppose the debtor requests an extension of four months to pay off the obligation. How much should he expect to pay in four months' time if money is worth 9% p.a.?

Since the lender could invest the $500.00 at 9% p.a., the debtor should be prepared to pay the dated value. This dated value includes interest for the additional four-month time period. It represents the amount to which the $500.00 will grow in four months (the future value) and is found using Formula 7.3A.

$$S = P(1 + rt)$$
$$= 500.00\left[1 + (0.09)\left(\frac{4}{12}\right)\right]$$
$$= 500.00(1 + 0.03)$$
$$= \$515.00$$

Now consider the case of an obligation of $1045.00 due six months from now. Suppose the debtor offers to pay the debt today. How much should the payment be if money is worth 9% p.a.?

Since the lender could invest the payment at 9% p.a., the payment should be the sum of money that will grow to $1045.00 in six months at 9% p.a. By definition, this sum of money is the present value of the $1045.00. The present value represents today's dated value of the $1045.00 and is found using Formula 7.3B.

$$P = \frac{S}{1 + rt}$$

$$= \frac{1045.00}{1 + (0.09)\left(\frac{6}{12}\right)}$$

$$= \frac{1045.00}{1 + 0.045}$$

$$= \$1000.00$$

Because of the time value of money, sums of money given at different times are *not* directly comparable. For example, imagine you are given a choice between $2000.00 today and $2200.00 one year from now. It does not automatically follow, from the point of view of investing money, that either the larger sum of money or the chronologically earlier sum of money is preferable.

To make a rational choice, we must allow for the rate of interest money can earn and choose a comparison date or **focal date** to obtain the dated values of the sums of money at a specific time.

Dated values at the *same* time are directly comparable and may be obtained for simple interest by using either the future value (or maturity value) formula, Formula 7.3A, $S = P(1 + rt)$, or the present value formula, Formula 7.3B, $P = \frac{S}{1 + rt}$.

B. Choosing the appropriate formula

The choice of which formula to use for finding dated values depends on the due date of the sum of money relative to the selected focal (or comparison) date.

(a) If the due date falls before the focal date, use the future value (or maturity value) formula.

FIGURE 7.3 **When to Use the Future Value (or Maturity Value) Formula**

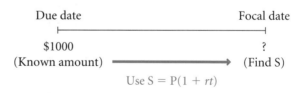

Explanation of diagram: We are looking for a future value relative to the given value. This future value will be higher than the known value by the interest that accumulates on the known value from the due date to the focal date. Because this is a future value problem (note that the arrow points to the right), the future value (or maturity value) formula $S = P(1 + rt)$ applies.

(b) If the due date falls after the focal date, use the present value formula.

FIGURE 7.4 **When to Use the Present Value Formula**

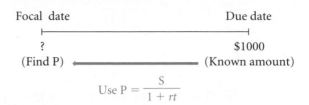

Focal date   Due date

? $1000

(Find P)   (Known amount)

$$\text{Use } P = \frac{S}{1 + rt}$$

Explanation of diagram: We are looking for an earlier value relative to the given value. This earlier value will be less than the given value by the interest that would accumulate on the unknown earlier value from the focal date to the due date. We are, in fact, looking for the principal that will grow to the given value. Because this is a present value problem (note that the arrow points to the left), the present value formula $P = \dfrac{S}{1 + rt}$ is appropriate.

C. Finding the equivalent single payment

EXAMPLE 7.7A   A debt can be paid off by payments of $872.00 one year from now and $1180.00 two years from now. Determine the single payment now that would settle the debt. Allow for simple interest at 9% p.a.

Solution   See Figure 7.5 for the graphic representation of the dated values. Refer to Figures 7.3 and 7.4 to determine which formula is appropriate.

FIGURE 7.5 **Graphic Representation of the Dated Values**

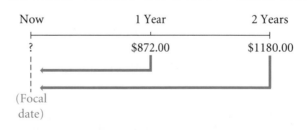

Now   1 Year   2 Years

? $872.00 $1180.00

(Focal
date)

Since the focal date is *earlier* relative to the dates for the given sums of money (the arrows point to the left), the present value formula $P - \dfrac{S}{1 + rt}$ is appropriate.

(i) The dated (present) value of the $872.00 at the focal date

$$P = \frac{872.00}{1 + (0.09)(1)}$$

$$= \frac{872.00}{1.09}$$

$$= 800.00$$

(ii) The dated (present) value of the $1180.00 at the focal date

$$P = \frac{1180.00}{1 + (0.09)(2)} = \frac{1180.00}{1.18} = 1000.00$$

(iii) Single payment required now = 800.00 + 1000.00 = $1800.00

EXAMPLE 7.7B   Debt payments of $400 due today, $500 due in five months, and $618 due in one year are to be combined into a single payment to be made nine months from now with interest allowed at 12% p.a.

Solution

FIGURE 7.6   Graphic Representation of the Dated Values

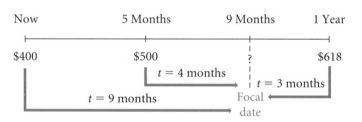

Since the focal date is in the *future* relative to the $400 now and the $500 five months from now (the arrows point to the right), the future value formula $S = P(1 + rt)$ is appropriate for these two amounts. However, since the focal date is *earlier* relative to the $618 one year from now (the arrow points to the left), the present value formula $P = \dfrac{S}{1 + rt}$ is appropriate for this amount.

(i) The dated (future) value of $400 at the focal date

$$P = 400.00; \quad r = 12\% = 0.12; \quad t = \frac{9}{12}$$

$$S = 400\left[1 + (0.12)\left(\frac{9}{12}\right)\right] = 400(1 + 0.09) = 400(1.09) = 436.00$$

(ii) The dated (future) value of $500 at the focal date

$$P = 500.00; \quad r = 12\% = 0.12; \quad t = \frac{4}{12}$$

$$S = 500\left[1 + (0.12)\left(\frac{4}{12}\right)\right] = 500(1 + 0.04) = 500(1.04) = 520.00$$

(iii) The dated (present) value of $618 at the focal date

$$S = 618.00; \quad r = 12\% = 0.12; \quad t = \frac{3}{12}$$

$$P = \frac{618.00}{1 + (0.12)\left(\frac{3}{12}\right)} = \frac{618.00}{1 + 0.03} = \frac{618.00}{1.03} = 600.00$$

(iv) The single payment needed = 436.00 + 520.00 + 600.00 = $1556.00

D. Finding the value of two or more equivalent payments

The **equivalent values** (the dated values of an original sum of money) obtained when using simple interest formulae are influenced by the choice of focal date. Although the differences in the values obtained are small, the parties to the financial transaction need to agree on the focal date.

EXAMPLE 7.7C   Debts of $400.00 due now and $700.00 due in 5 months are to be settled by a payment of $500.00 in 3 months and a final payment in 8 months. Determine the value of the final payment at 6% p.a. with a focal date 8 months from now.

Solution   Let the value of the final payment be $x.

(i) Represent the data given in a time diagram.

FIGURE 7.7   **Graphic Representation of Data**

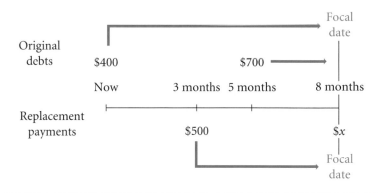

(ii) Dated value of the original debts

(a) The value at the focal date of the $400 due 8 months before the focal date is found by using the future value formula.

$$S = 400\left[1 + (0.06)\left(\frac{8}{12}\right)\right] = 400(1 + 0.04) = 400(1.04) = \$416.00$$

(b) The value at the focal date of the $700 due 3 months before the focal date is found by using the future value formula.

$$S = 700\left[1 + (0.06)\left(\frac{3}{12}\right)\right] = 700(1 + 0.015) = 700(1.015) = \$710.50$$

(iii) Dated value of the replacement payments

(a) The value at the focal date of the $500 payment made 5 months before the focal date is found by using the future value formula.

$$S = 500\left[1 + (0.06)\left(\frac{5}{12}\right)\right] = 500(1 + 0.025) = 500(1.025) = \$512.50$$

(b) The value at the focal date of the final payment is $x (no adjustment for interest is necessary for a sum of money located at the focal date).

(iv) The **equation of values** at the focal date is now set up by matching the dated values of the original debts to the dated values of the replacement payments.

> THE SUM OF THE DATED VALUES OF THE REPLACEMENT PAYMENTS =
> THE SUM OF THE DATED VALUES OF THE ORIGINAL DEBTS

$$500\left[1 + (0.06)\left(\frac{5}{12}\right)\right] + x = 400\left[1 + (0.06)\left(\frac{8}{12}\right)\right] + 700\left[1 + (0.06)\left(\frac{3}{12}\right)\right]$$

$$512.50 + x = 416.00 + 710.50$$
$$512.50 + x = 1126.50$$
$$x = 1126.50 - 512.50$$
$$x = 614.00$$

The final payment to be made in 8 months is $614.00.

EXAMPLE 7.7D Debts of $2000 due 60 days ago and $1800 due in 30 days are to be settled by three equal payments due now, 60 days from now, and 120 days from now. Find the size of the equal payments at 10% p.a. The agreed focal date is now.

Solution Let the size of the equal payments be $x.

(i) Graphic representation of data

FIGURE 7.8 **Graphic Representation of Data**

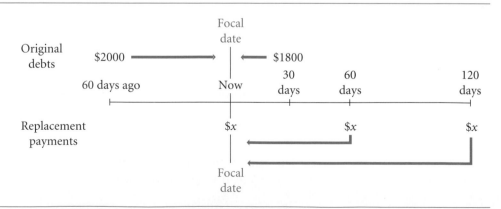

(ii) Dated value of the original debts at the focal date

(a) Because the $2000 debt is due 60 days before the focal date, the future value formula is appropriate.

$$S = 2000\left[1 + (0.10)\left(\frac{60}{365}\right)\right] = 2000(1 + 0.0164384) = \$2032.88$$

(b) Because the $1800 debt is due 30 days after the focal date, the present value formula is appropriate.

$$P = \frac{1800}{1 + (0.10)\left(\frac{30}{365}\right)} = \frac{1800}{1 + 0.0082192} = \$1785.33$$

(iii) Dated value of the replacement payments at the focal date

(a) Since the first payment is to be made at the focal date, its value is $x.

(b) Because the second payment is to be made 60 days after the focal date, the present value formula is appropriate.

$$P = \frac{x}{1 + (0.10)\left(\frac{60}{365}\right)} = \frac{x}{1 + 0.0164384}$$

$$- \frac{1}{1.0164384}\,(x) = \$0.9838275x$$

(c) Because the third payment is to be made 120 days after the focal date, the present value formula is appropriate.

$$P = \frac{x}{1 + (0.10)\left(\frac{120}{365}\right)} = \frac{x}{1 + 0.0328767}$$

$$= \frac{1}{1.0328767}\,(x) = \$0.9681698x$$

(iv) The equation of values (dated value of the replacement payments = dated value of the original debts)

$$x + 0.9838275x + 0.9681698x = 2032.88 + 1785.33$$
$$2.9519973x = 3818.21$$
$$x = \frac{3818.21}{2.9519973}$$
$$x = 1293.43$$

The size of each of the three equal payments is $1293.43.

EXAMPLE 7.7E

Two debts, one of $4000 due in three months with interest at 8% and the other of $3000 due in eighteen months with interest at 10%, are to be discharged by making two equal payments. What is the size of the equal payments if the first is due one year from now, the second two years from now, money is worth 12%, and the chosen focal date is one year from now?

Solution

Let the size of the equal payments be $x.

(i) Graphic representation of data

FIGURE 7.9   Graphic Representation of Data

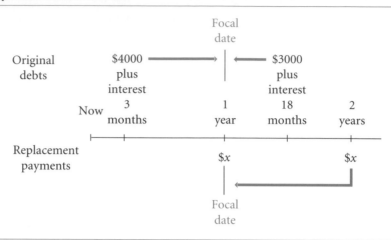

(ii) Maturity value of the original debts

Since the two original debts are interest bearing, their maturity values need to be determined first so that the principal *and* interest of these original debts are discharged by the two equal payments.

(a) For the $4000 debt: P = 4000; r = 8% = 0.08; $t = \dfrac{3}{12}$

Maturity value, S = $4000\left[1 + (0.08)\left(\dfrac{3}{12}\right)\right]$ = 4000(1.02) = $4080

(b) For the $3000 debt: P = 3000; r = 10% = 0.10; $t = \dfrac{18}{12}$

Maturity value, S = $3000\left[1 + (0.10)\left(\dfrac{18}{12}\right)\right]$ = 3000(1.15) = $3450

(iii) Dated value of the money value of the original payments at 12%

(a) Because the maturity value of $4080 is due 9 months before the focal date, the future value formula is appropriate.

$$S = 4080\left[1 + (0.12)\left(\dfrac{9}{12}\right)\right] = 4080(1.09) = \$4447.20$$

(b) Because the maturity value of $3450 is due 6 months after the focal date, the present value formula is appropriate.

$$P = \dfrac{3450}{1 + (0.12)\left(\frac{6}{12}\right)} = \dfrac{3450}{1.06} = \$3254.72$$

(iv) Dated value of the replacement payments

(a) Since the first replacement payment is made at the focal date, its value is $x.

(b) Because the second replacement payment is made 12 months after the focal date, the present value formula is appropriate.

$$P = \dfrac{x}{1 + (0.12)\left(\frac{12}{12}\right)} = \dfrac{x}{1.12} = 0.8928571x$$

(v) The equation of values

$$x + 0.8928571x = 4447.20 + 3254.72$$
$$1.8928571x = 7701.92$$
$$x = \frac{7701.92}{1.8928571}$$
$$x = 4068.94$$

The size of the equal payments is about $4068.94.

E. Loan repayments

Loans by financial institutions to individuals are usually repaid by **blended payments**, which are equal periodic payments that include payment of interest and repayment of principal. To repay the loan, the sum of the present values of the periodic payments must equal the original principal. The concept of equivalent values is used to determine the size of the blended payments.

EXAMPLE 7.7F   A loan of $2000 made at 8.5% p.a. is to be repaid in four equal payments due at the end of the next four quarters respectively. Determine the size of the quarterly payments if the agreed focal date is the date of the loan.

Solution   Let the size of the equal quarterly payments be represented by $x.

(i) Graphic representation of data

FIGURE 7.10   Graphic Representation of Data

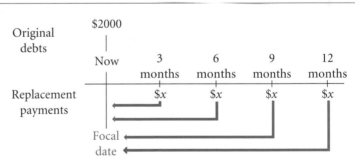

(ii) Dated value of debt at the focal date is $2000.00.

(iii) Dated value of payments at the focal date
The payments are due 3, 6, 9, and 12 months after the focal date respectively.
Their values are

(a) $P_1 = \dfrac{x}{1 + (0.085)\left(\frac{3}{12}\right)} = \dfrac{x}{1 + 0.02125} = \dfrac{1}{1.02125}(x) = 0.9791922x$

(b) $P_2 = \dfrac{x}{1 + (0.085)\left(\frac{6}{12}\right)} = \dfrac{x}{1 + 0.0425} = \dfrac{1}{1.0425}(x) = 0.9592326x$

(c) $P_3 = \dfrac{x}{1 + (0.085)\left(\frac{9}{12}\right)} = \dfrac{x}{1 + 0.06375} = \dfrac{1}{1.06375}(x) = 0.9400705x$

(d) $P_4 = \dfrac{x}{1 + (0.085)\left(\frac{12}{12}\right)} = \dfrac{x}{1 + 0.085} = \dfrac{1}{1.085}(x) = 0.9216590x$

(iv) $0.9791922x + 0.9592326x + 0.9400705x + 0.9216590x = 2000.00$

$$3.8001543x = 2000.00$$

$$x = 526.29$$

The size of the quarterly payment is about \$526.29.

Exercise 7.7

A. Find the equivalent replacement payments indicated for each of the following debts.

	Original Debt	Replacement Payment	Focal Date	Rate
1.	$800 due today	In full	4 months from today	11%
2.	$1200 due 3 months ago	In full	Today	12%
3.	$600 due in 2 months	In full	7 months from today	7%
4.	$900 due in 8 months	In full	2 months from today	10%
5.	$500 due 4 months ago, $600 due in 2 months	In full	Today	12%
6.	$800 due today, $700 due in 2 months	In full	4 months from today	9%
7.	$2000 due today	$1200 in 3 months and the balance in 6 months.	Today	12%
8.	$400 due 1 month ago, $600 due in 3 months	$500 today and the balance in 6 months.	Today	8%
9.	$1200 due today	Two equal payments due in 3 and 6 months	Today	10%
10.	$1800 due 30 days ago	Three equal payments due today, in 30 days, and in 60 days.	Today	9%
11.	$1500 due 4 months ago. $1200 due in 8 months with 10% interest.	$700 due now and two equal payments due in 6 months and in 12 months.	Today	12%
12.	$2000 due in 6 months with interest at 8%. $1600 due in 2 years with interest at 7%.	Three equal payments due in 6, 12, and 18 months respectively.	1 year from today	11%

B. Solve each of the following problems.

1. Debt payments of $600 each are due 3 months and 6 months from now respectively. If interest at 10% is allowed, what single payment is required to settle the debt today?

2. A loan payment of $1000 was due 60 days ago and another payment of $1200 is due 30 days from now. What single payment 90 days from now will pay off the two obligations if interest is to be 12% and the agreed focal date is 90 days from now?

3. Loans of $400 due 3 months ago and $700 due today are to be repaid by a payment of $600 one month from today and the balance 4 months from today. If money is worth 6% and the agreed focal date is one month from today, what is the size of the final payment?

4. Two obligations of $800 each, due 60 days ago and 30 days ago respectively, are to be settled by two equal payments to be made today and 60 days from now respectively. If interest allowed is 9.75% and the agreed focal date is today, what is the size of the equal payments?

5. A loan of $4000 is to be repaid by 3 equal payments due in 4, 8, and 12 months from now respectively. Determine the size of the equal payments at 12% with a focal date of today.

6. A loan of $1500 taken out on March 1 requires equal payments on April 30, June 20, and August 10, and a final payment of $400 on September 30. If the focal date is September 30, what is the size of the equal payments at $8\frac{3}{4}$%?

7. Two debt payments, the first $800 due today, the second $1000 due nine months from now with interest at 9%, are to be settled by two equal payments due in three and six months respectively. Determine the size of the equal payments if money is worth 11% and the agreed focal date is today. Remember to find the maturity value of the original debts first.

8. Payments of $1200 due one year ago and $1500 due with interest of 10% in nine months are to be settled by three equal payments due today, six months from now, and one year from now at 11.5%. Determine the size of the equal payments if the agreed focal date is one year from today.

REVIEW EXERCISE

1. Determine the exact time for

   (a) April 25 to October 14;

   (b) July 30 to February 1.

2. Compute the amount of interest for

   (a) $1975.00 at 5.5% for 215 days;

   (b) $844.65 at 8.25% from May 30 to January 4.

3. What principal will earn

   (a) $83.52 interest at 12% in 219 days?

   (b) $34.40 interest at 9¾% from October 30, 1998, to June 1, 1999?

4. Answer each of the following.

   (a) What was the rate of interest if the interest on a loan of $675 for 284 days was $39.39?

   (b) How long will it take for $2075 to earn $124.29 interest at 8¼% p.a.? (State your answer in days.)

   (c) If $680 is worth $698.70 after three months, what interest rate was charged?

   (d) How many months will it take $750 to grow to $795 at 7.2% p.a.?

5. Solve each of the following.

   (a) What principal will have a maturity value of $665.60 at 10% in 146 days?

   (b) What is the present value of $6300 due in 16 months at 7¾%?

6. What principal will earn $61.52 at 11.75% in 156 days?

7. What sum of money will earn $148.57 from September 1, 1998, to April 30, 1999, at 7.5%?

8. At what rate of interest must a principal of $1435.00 be invested to earn interest of $45.46 in 125 days?

9. At what rate of interest will $1500.00 grow to $1562.04 from June 1 to December 1?

10. In how many months will $2500.00 earn $182.29 interest at 12.5%?

11. In how many days will $3100.00 grow to $3195.72 at 5.75%?

12. Compute the accumulated value of $4200.00 at 11.5% after eleven months.

13. What is the amount to which $1550.00 will grow from June 10 to December 15 at 6.5%?

14. What sum of money will accumulate to $1516.80 in eight months at 8%?

15. What principal will amount to $3367.28 if invested at 9% from November 1, 1999, to May 31, 2000?

16. What is the present value of $3780.00 due in nine months if interest is 12%?

17. Find the present value on June 1 of $1785.00 due on October 15 if interest is 7.5%.

18. Debt payments of $1750.00 and $1600.00 are due four months from now and nine months from now respectively. What single payment is required to pay off the debt today if interest is 11.5%?

19. A loan payment of $1450.00 was due 45 days ago and a payment of $1200.00 is due in 60 days. What single payment made 30 days from now is required to settle the two payments if interest is 9% and the agreed focal date is 30 days from now?

20. Debt obligations of $800.00 due two months ago and $1200.00 due in one month are to be repaid by a payment of $1000.00 today and the balance in three months. What is the size of the final payment if interest is 7.75% and the agreed focal date is one month from now?

21. An obligation of $10 000.00 is to be repaid by equal payments due in 60 days, 120 days, and 180 days respectively. What is the size of the equal payments if money is worth 7.5% and the agreed focal date is today?

22. Payments of $4000 each due in four, eight, and twelve months from now are to be settled by five equal payments due today, three months from now, six months from now, nine months from now, and twelve months from now. What is the size of the equal payments if interest is 12.75% and the agreed focal date is today?

23. A loan of $5000.00 due in one year is to be repaid by three equal payments due today, six months from now, and one year from now respectively. What is the size of the equal payments if interest is 9.5% and the agreed focal date is today?

24. Three debts, the first for $1000 due two months ago, the second for $1200 due in 2 months, and the third for $1400 due in 4 months, are to be paid by a single payment today. How much is the single payment if money is worth 11.5% p.a. and the agreed focal date is today?

25. Debts of $700 due three months ago and of $1000 due today are to be paid by a payment of $800 in two months and a final payment in five months. If 9% interest is allowed and the focal date is five months from now, what is the size of the final payment?

26. A loan of $3000 is to be repaid in three equal instalments due 90, 180, and 300 days respectively after the date of the loan. If the focal date is the date of the loan and interest is 10.9% p.a., find the size of the instalments.

27. Three debts, the first for $2000 due three months ago, the second for $1500 with interest of 7.5% due in nine months, and the third for $1200 with interest of 10.5% due in eighteen months, are to be paid in three equal instalments due today, six months from now, and one year from now respectively. If money is worth 8.5% and the agreed focal date is today, determine the size of the equal payments. (Find the maturity values of the original debts first.)

28. A debt of $6500 is to be settled by four equal payments due today, and one year, two years, and three years from now respectively. Determine the size of the equal payments if money is worth 10% and the agreed focal day is today.

SELF-TEST

1. Find the amount of interest earned by $1290.00 at 10.5% p.a. in 173 days.

2. In how many months will $8500.00 grow to $8818.75 at 5% p.a.?

3. What interest rate is paid if the interest on a loan of $2500.00 for 6 months is $81.25?

4. What principal will have a maturity value of $10 000.00 at 8.25% p.a. in 3 months?

5. What is the amount to which $5500.00 will grow at 8.75% p.a. in 10 months?

6. What principal will earn $67.14 interest at 6.25% p.a. for 82 days?

7. What is the present value of $5000.00 due at 7.25% p.a. in 243 days?

8. What rate of interest is paid if the interest on a loan of $2500.00 is $96.06 from November 14, 1998, to May 20, 1999?

9. How many days will it take for $8500.00 to earn $689.72 at 8.25% p.a.?

10. What principal will earn $55.99 interest at 9.75% p.a. from February 4, 2000, to July 6, 2000?

11. What sum of money will accumulate to $7500.00 at 11.75% p.a. in 88 days?

12. Find the amount of interest on $835.00 at 7.5% p.a. from October 9, 1999, to August 4, 2000.

13. A loan of $3320.00 is to be repaid by 3 equal payments due in 92 days, 235 days, and 326 days respectively. Determine the size of the equal payments at 8.75% p.a. with a focal date today.

14. Debt payments of $1725.00 due today, $510.00 due in 75 days, and $655.00 due in 323 days are to be combined into a single payment to be made 115 days from now. What is that single payment if money is worth 8.5% p.a. and the agreed focal date is 115 days from now?

15. Debt payments of $1010.00 due 5 months ago and $1280.00 due today are to be repaid by a payment of $615.00 in 4 months and the balance in 7 months. If money is worth 7.75% p.a. and the agreed focal date is in 7 months, what is the size of the final payment?

16. A debt of $1310.00 due 5 months ago and a second debt of $1225.00 due in 3 months with interest at 12% p.a. are to be settled by two equal payments due now and 7 months from now respectively. Find the size of the equal payments at 10.25% p.a. with the agreed focal date now.

CHALLENGE PROBLEMS

1. Nora borrowed $3750 on September 28, 1999, at 9% p.a. simple interest, to be repaid on October 31, 2000. She has the option of making payments toward the loan before the due date. Nora paid $635 on February 17, 2000, $825 on July 2, 2000, and $750 on October 1, 2000. Find the payment required to pay off the debt on the agreed focal date of October 31, 2000.

2. A supplier will give you a discount of 3% if an invoice is paid 60 days before its due date. Suppose you want to take advantage of this discount but need to borrow the money. You plan to pay back the loan in 60 days. What is the highest annual simple interest rate at which you can borrow the money and still save by paying the invoice 60 days before its due date? (Express your answer to two decimal places.)

CASE STUDY 7.1   LOANS, LOANS, LOANS

Nearing the end of the school year, Harry finds he is running short of funds. He needs to take out some loans to get through the rest of the school year until his summer job begins. This morning, Harry went to the Royal Bank and negotiated a loan of $2500 at 8.25% p.a. simple interest, to be repaid in full four months from now. He then went to his credit union, where he was able to get another loan of $2750 at 9.75% p.a. simple interest. The credit union is giving him 10 months to repay the loan.

On his way home from negotiating the loans, Harry's car broke down. After paying for the car repairs, he realized that he will not be able to pay his Royal Bank loan due in four months.

That same day, Harry went to The Helpful Loan Company and negotiated a third loan. The loan agreement provides for two advances to cover the maturity values of the Royal Bank and credit union loans when they come due. The agreement requires Harry to make two equal payments, the first due one year from today and the second due two years from today. The simple interest rate on the loan is 11.85% p.a.

QUESTIONS

1. What are the maturity values of the Royal Bank and credit union loans on their original repayment dates?

2. If the focal date for the third loan is one year from now, what is the size of the equal payments Harry must make one year and two years from now?

3. Suppose Harry had negotiated with the Royal Bank to pay the maturity value of the loan one year from now and with the Credit Union to repay the maturity value two years from now. How much would Harry have saved assuming rates to remain unchanged?

CASE STUDY 7.2

PAY NOW OR PAY LATER?

Buying insurance is a way of protecting yourself against unexpected financial loss during some future period of time. To obtain an insurance policy, you generally have to pay at least a portion of the cost (or premium) at the outset to ensure coverage is in place.

The Larondes are renewing their house insurance for the coming year. They will receive coverage for the next twelve months. Along with the invoice for the premium, Canmore Insurance Company sent a brochure outlining the three payment plans customers can use to pay their premiums.

Canmore's Plan One is for customers to pay the premium for the whole year at the beginning of the policy term.

Plan Two allows customers to pay the annual premium in three instalments. The first instalment is one-third of the annual premium plus a $10 service charge. It is due on the starting date of the policy term. The second and third instalments are each one-third of the annual premium. No service charges are added to either of these instalments. The second instalment is due in four months and the third instalment is due in eight months.

Plan Three allows customers to pay the total premium in eleven instalments. The total premium is calculated as the annual premium plus a 3% service charge. The first payment is due at the beginning of the policy period and is $2/12$ of the total premium. The remaining $10/12$ of the total premium is divided into ten equal instalments. Each instalment is paid on the first day of the month, beginning with month two.

The Larondes paid their house insurance bill using Plan One. However, they realize that they are missing out on interest they could have earned on this money when they pay the whole year's premium at the beginning of the policy term. They consider this to be the "cost" of paying their bill in one lump sum. The Larondes are interested in knowing the cost of their insurance payment options.

QUESTIONS

1. Suppose the Larondes' annual premium was $900 (ignore all taxes), and they could earn 3.5% p.a. simple interest on their money over the next year. Assume the first premium payment is due today (the first day of the insurance policy term) and the focal date is one year from today. What is the cost to the Larondes of paying their insurance using each of the three payment plans?

2. Suppose the Larondes' annual premium was $600 and they could earn 4¼% p.a. simple interest on their money over the next year. Calculate again the cost to the Larondes of each of the three payment plans.

3. Suppose the Larondes expect to earn 5% p.a. simple interest on any money they invest in the first two months of this year, and 4% p.a. simple interest on any money they invest during the rest of this year. Assume the annual premium is $600, the first premium payment is due today, and the focal date is one year from today. Which option—Plan One, Plan Two, or Plan Three—will have the least cost for the Larondes?

4. Examine an insurance policy of your own or of a family member. Find out what you could earn on your money at today's rates of interest. What is the cost of this insurance policy if you pay the annual premium at the beginning of the policy term? Make the focal date the last day of the policy term.

SUMMARY OF FORMULAE

Formula 7.1A

$I = Prt$

Finding the amount of interest when the principal, the rate, and the time are known

Formula 7.1B

$P = \dfrac{I}{rt}$

Finding the principal directly when the amount of interest, the rate of interest, and the time are known

Formula 7.1C

$r = \dfrac{I}{Pt}$

Finding the rate of interest directly when the amount of interest, the principal, and the time are known

Formula 7.1D

$$t = \frac{I}{Pr}$$

Finding the time directly when the amount of interest, the principal, and the rate of interest are known

Formula 7.2

$$S = P + I$$

Finding the future value (maturity value) when the principal and the amount of interest are known

Formula 7.3A

$$S = P(1 + rt)$$

Finding the future value (maturity value) at simple interest directly when the principal, rate of interest, and time are known

Formula 7.3B

$$P = \frac{S}{1 + rt}$$

Finding the present value at simple interest when the future value (maturity value), the rate of interest, and the time are known

GLOSSARY

Blended payments   equal periodic payments that include payment of interest and repayment of principal, usually paid by individuals to financial institutions

Dated value   the value of a sum of money at a specific time relative to its due date, including interest

Equation of values   the equation obtained when matching the dated values of the original payments at an agreed focal date to the dated values of the replacement payments at the same focal date

Equivalent values   the dated values of an original sum of money

Exact time   the period in days between two calendar dates

Focal date   a specific time chosen to compare the time value of one or more dated sums of money

Future value of a sum of money   the value obtained when the amount of interest is added to the original principal

Interest   rent paid for the use of money

Interest period   the time period for which interest is charged

Leap year   a year with an extra day in February

Maturity value   see *Future value of a sum of money*

Present value   the principal that grows to a given future value (maturity value) over a given period of time at a given rate of interest

Simple interest   interest calculated on the original principal by the formula $I = Prt$, and paid only when the principal is repaid

Time value of money   a concept of money value that allows for a change in the value of a sum of money over time if the sum of money is subject to a rate of interest

8 Simple Interest Applications

O ften we borrow money for less than one year. For example, we might borrow money at a lower interest rate to pay off higher-rate credit card debts. A business might borrow money to pay for products now, and repay the loan with money collected from customers later.

The methods for borrowing money for less than one year have changed significantly in the last few years. Promissory notes have been used for a long time. What is new is the growing use of demand loans and lines of credit. Financial institutions are making it easier for us to borrow money and they are making it more convenient to repay what we borrow.

Introduction

Individuals, as well as businesses, often encounter situations that involve the application of simple interest. Simple interest calculation is usually restricted to financial instruments subject to time periods of less than one year. In this chapter we apply simple interest to short-term promissory notes, treasury bills, lines of credit, and demand loans.

OBJECTIVES

Upon completing this chapter, you will be able to do the following:

1. Define promissory notes and related terms such as maker, payee, face value, term of a note, three days of grace, due date, interest period, and maturity value.
2. Determine the maturity value of interest-bearing notes by using the formula $S = P(1 + rt)$.
3. Determine the present value of promissory notes and treasury bills.
4. Discount promissory notes and treasury bills using simple discount.
5. Compute interest and balances for demand loans and lines of credit.
6. Construct repayment schedules for loans using blended payments.

8.1 PROMISSORY NOTES—BASIC CONCEPTS AND COMPUTATIONS

A. Nature of promissory notes and illustration

A **promissory note** is a written promise by one party to pay a certain sum of money, with or without interest, at a specific date or on demand, to another party. (See the illustration that follows.)

FIGURE 8.1   **Promissory Note Illustrated**

> $650.00   MISSISSAUGA, ONTARIO   OCTOBER 30, 1998
>
> ___FOUR MONTHS___ after date ___I___ promise to pay to the order of
> CREDIT VALLEY NURSERY
> SIX-HUNDRED-FIFTY AND 00/100 ···················· Dollars
> at   SHERIDAN CREDIT UNION LIMITED   for value received
> with interest at ___10.5%___ per annum.
>
>   Signed ___D. Peel___

This is an **interest-bearing promissory note** because it is a note subject to the rate of interest stated on the face of the note.

B. Related terms explained

The following information is directly available in the promissory note (see items a, b, c, d, e, f below) or can be determined (see items g, h, i, j).

(a) The **maker** of the note is the party making the promise to pay.——— (D. Peel)

(b) The **payee** of the note is the party to whom the promise to pay is made. ————————— (Credit Valley Nursery)

(c) The **face value** of the note is the sum of money (principal) specified. ————————————— ($650.00)

(d) The **rate of interest** is stated as a simple annual rate based on the face value. ————————— (10.5%)

(e) The **issue date** is the date on which the note was made. ————————————————— (October 30, 1998)

(f) The **term** of the note is the length of time before the note matures (becomes payable). ————— (four months)

(g) The **due date** or **date of maturity** is the date on which the note is to be paid. ————————— (See Subsection C)

(h) The **interest period** is the time period from the date of issue to the legal due date. ————— (See Subsection C)

(i) The **amount of interest** is payable together with the face value on the legal due date. ————— (See Subsection C)

(j) The **maturity value** is the amount payable on the due date (face value plus interest). ————— (See Subsection C)

This is an **interest-bearing promissory note** because it is a note subject to the rate of interest stated on the face of the note.

The Canadian law relating to promissory notes adds **three days of grace** to the term of the note to obtain the **legal due date** (Bills of Exchange Act, Section 42). This is to allow for the situation of the repayment date falling on the Saturday of a long weekend. In this case, without three days of grace, you would either have to pay the note early, or take a penalty for paying three days late. Therefore, three days are added to the due date of a promissory note. Interest must be paid for those three days of grace, but there is no late payment penalty and your credit rating remains good. Today, with electronic banking, you can arrange to pay your note at any time, even on the weekend, so you may not need the three days of grace. If you decide not to include the three days of grace, write "No Grace Days" on the note when you negotiate the loan.

C. Computed values

EXAMPLE 8.1A   For the promissory note illustrated in Figure 8.1, determine

(i)   the due date;

(ii)   the interest period;

(iii)   the amount of interest;

(iv)   the maturity value.

Solution   (i)   *Finding the due date*
Add three days of grace to the term of the note to obtain the legal due date. Since calendar months vary in length, the month in which the term ends does not necessarily have a date that corresponds to the date of issue. In such cases, the last day of the month is used as the end of the term of the note. Three days of grace are added to that date to determine the legal due date. (Throughout this chapter, we have included three days of grace in the exercises. However, as we pointed out earlier, electronic banking has reduced the need for three days of grace.)

With reference to the promissory note in Figure 8.1,

> the date of issue is October 30, 1998
> the term of the note is four months
> the month in which the term ends is February, 1999
> the end of the term is February 28 (since February has no day corresponding to day 30, the last day of the month is used to establish the end of the term of the note)
> the legal due date (adding 3 days) is March 3.

(ii)   *Determining the interest period*
If the note bears interest, the interest period covers the number of days from the date of issue of the note to the legal due date. (Remember to count the first day but not the last day of the interest period.)

October 30 to March 3 $(2 + 30 + 31 + 31 + 28 + 2) = 124$ days

(iii) *Computing the amount of interest*
The interest payable on the note is the simple interest based on the face value of the note for the interest period at the stated rate. It is found using the simple interest formula

$$\boxed{I = Prt} \quad \text{——————————— Formula 7.1A}$$

$$I = (650.00)(0.105)\left(\frac{124}{365}\right) = \$23.19$$

(iv) *Finding the maturity value of the note*
The maturity value of the promissory note is the total amount payable at the legal due date.

Face value + Interest = 650.00 + 23.19 = $673.19

Exercise 8.1

A. Determine each of the items listed from the information provided in the promissory note below.

$530.00	OAKVILLE, ONTARIO	DECEMBER 30, 1998

FIVE MONTHS   after date   I   promise to pay

to the order of   JANE WELTON

FIVE-HUNDRED-THIRTY and 00/100 ······················ Dollars

at   SHERIDAN CENTRAL BANK   for value received

with interest at   8.5%   per annum.

Signed   *E. Salt*

1. Date issued
2. Legal due date
3. Face value
4. Interest rate
5. Interest period (days)
6. Amount of interest
7. Maturity value

B. For each of the following notes, determine

(a) the legal due date;
(b) the interest period (in days);
(c) the amount of interest;
(d) the maturity value.

1. The face value of a five-month, 12% note dated September 30, 1999, is $840.

2. A note for $760 dated March 20, 2000, with interest at 7% per annum, is issued for 120 days.

3. A sixty-day, 10.5% note for $1250 is issued January 31, 2000.

4. A four-month, 11% note for $2000 is issued July 31, 1999.

8.2   MATURITY VALUE OF PROMISSORY NOTES

A. Using the formula S = P(1 + rt)

Since the maturity value of a promissory note is the principal (face value) plus the interest accumulated to the legal due date, the future value formula for simple interest will determine the maturity value directly.

$$S = P(1 + rt)$$ ———————————— **Formula 7.3A**

S = maturity value of the promissory note;
P = the face value of the note;
r = the rate of interest on the note;
t = the interest period (the number of days between the *date of issue* and the *legal due date*).

B. Worked examples

EXAMPLE 8.2A   For the promissory note illustrated in Figure 8.1, determine the maturity value using the future value formula S = P(1 + *rt*).

Solution $P = 650.00; \quad r = 0.105; \quad t = \dfrac{124}{365}$

$S = 650.00\left[1 + (0.105)\left(\dfrac{124}{365}\right)\right] = 650.00(1 + 0.0356712) = \$673.19$

EXAMPLE 8.2B   Find the maturity value of an $800, six-month note with interest at 9.5% dated May 31.

Solution   The date of issue is May 31;
the term of the note is six months;
the term ends November 30;
the legal due date is December 3;
the interest period (May 31 to December 3) has 186 days.

$P = 800.00; \quad r = 0.095; \quad t = \dfrac{186}{365}$

$S = 800.00\left[1 + (0.095)\left(\dfrac{186}{365}\right)\right] = 800.00(1 + 0.0484110) = \$838.73$

EXAMPLE 8.2C   Determine the maturity value of a ninety-day, $750 note dated December 15, 1999, with interest at 11%.

Solution   The date of issue is December 15, 1999;
the term is 90 days;
the term ends March 14, 2000 (from 90 days take away 16 days remaining in December, 31 days for January, 29 days for February, 2000 being a leap year, which leaves 14 days for March);

the legal due date (adding the three days of grace) is March 17;
the interest period (December 15 to March 17) has 93 days.

$$P = 750.00; \quad r = 0.11; \quad t = \frac{93}{365}$$

$$S = 750.00\left[1 + (0.11)\left(\frac{93}{365}\right)\right] = 750.00(1 + 0.0280274) = \$771.02$$

Exercise 8.2

A. Use the future value formula to compute the maturity value of each of the following promissory notes.

1. A four-month, 11.5% note for $620 is issued May 25.

2. A $350 note is issued on October 30 at 10.5% for 90 days.

3. A 150-day note for $820 with interest at 5% is dated June 28.

4. A seven-month, $420 note dated November 1, 1999, earns interest at 9.5%.

8.3   PRESENT VALUE OF PROMISSORY NOTES

A. Finding the face value

The face value (or principal) of promissory notes can be obtained by solving the future value formula S = P(1 + rt) for P, that is, by using the present value formula

$$P = \frac{S}{1 + rt}$$ ──────── **Formula 7.3B**

P = the face value (or present value) of the note at the date of issue;
S = the maturity value;
r = the rate of interest;
t = the interest period.

EXAMPLE 8.3A   A five-month note dated January 31, 1999, and bearing interest at 12% p.a. has a maturity value of $567.16. Find the face value of the note.

Solution

FIGURE 8.2   **Graphic Representation of Data**

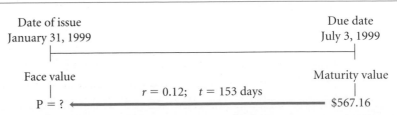

Date of issue — January 31, 1999 ... Due date — July 3, 1999

Face value   P = ?   r = 0.12;   t = 153 days   Maturity value $567.16

The term of the note ends June 30;
the legal due date is July 3;
the interest period (January 31 to July 3) has 153 days.

$$S = 567.16; \quad r = 0.12; \quad t = \frac{153}{365}$$

$$P = \frac{567.16}{1 + (0.12)\left(\frac{153}{365}\right)} = \frac{567.16}{1 + 0.0503014} = \$540.00$$

B. Present value of promissory notes

The **present value of a promissory note** is its value any time before the due date, allowing for the rate money is worth. That is, it is the present value of the maturity value of the promissory note.

To determine the present value, we need to know the maturity value of the note. In computing the maturity value and the present value, we must consider *two* rates of interest:

(a) the rate of the interest stated on the promissory note. This is the rate needed to determine the maturity value;

(b) the rate money is worth. This rate is needed to determine the present value of the note at the date specified (the focal date).

As the two rates are likely to be *different*, take care in using them.

EXAMPLE 8.3B A seven-month note for $1500 is issued on March 31 bearing interest at 9%. Find the present value of the note on the date of issue if money is worth 12%.

Solution (i) First, determine the *maturity value* of the note. Use the date of issue as the focal date.

The term of the note ends October 31;
the legal due date is November 3;
the interest period (March 31 to November 3) has 217 days.

FIGURE 8.3   Graphic Representation of Data

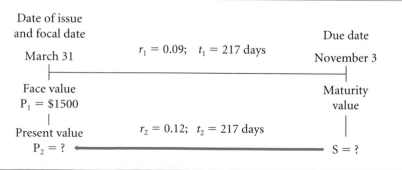

Date of issue
and focal date   Due date

March 31 $r_1 = 0.09; \quad t_1 = 217$ days   November 3

Face value   Maturity
$P_1 = \$1500$ value

Present value $r_2 = 0.12; \quad t_2 = 217$ days
$P_2 = ?$ ⟵ $S = ?$

$$P_1 = 1500.00; \quad r_1 = 0.09; \quad t_1 = \frac{217}{365}$$

$$S = 1500\left[1 + (0.09)\left(\frac{217}{365}\right)\right] = 1500(1 + 0.0535069) = \$1580.26$$

(ii) Second, use the maturity value found in part (i) to determine the *present value* at the specified date.

The focal date (date of issue) is March 31;

the legal due date is November 3;

the interest period (March 31 to November 3) has 217 days.

$$S = 1580.26; \quad r_2 = 0.12; \quad t_2 = \frac{217}{365}$$

$$P_2 = \frac{1580.26}{1 + (0.12)\left(\frac{217}{365}\right)} = \frac{1580.26}{1 + 0.0713425} = \$1475.03$$

Note: The present value at the date of issue is less than the face value of the note because the interest rate on the note (9.0%) is less than the rate money is worth (12.0%).

EXAMPLE 8.3C   Find the present value on the date of issue of a non-interest-bearing $950, three-month promissory note dated April 30 if money is worth 8.5%.

Solution

FIGURE 8.4   **Graphic Representation of Data**

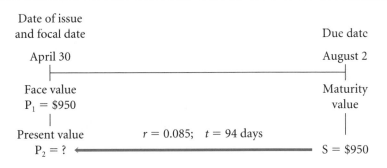

The term of the note ends July 30;

the legal due date is August 2;

the interest period (April 30 to August 2) has 94 days.

If a promissory note is **non-interest-bearing**, the maturity value of the note is the same as the face value of the note.

The maturity value of the note is the face value—$950.00.

$$S = 950.00; \quad r = 0.085; \quad t = \frac{94}{365}$$

$$P = \frac{950.00}{1 + (0.085)\left(\frac{94}{365}\right)} = \frac{950.00}{1 + 0.0218904} = \$929.65$$

EXAMPLE 8.3D A 180-day note for $2000 with interest at 15% is dated September 18, 2000. Find the value of the note on December 1, 2000, if money is worth 11.5%.

Solution
(i) Find the maturity value of the note.
The 180-day term ends March 17, 2001;
the legal due date is March 20, 2001;
the interest period (September 18 to March 20) has 183 days.

FIGURE 8.5   Graphic Representation of Data

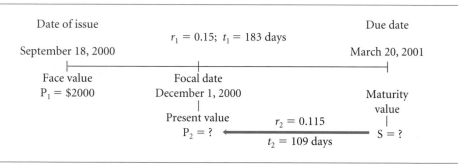

$$P_1 = 2000; \quad r_1 = 0.15; \quad t_1 = \frac{183}{365}$$

$$S = 2000\left[1 + (0.15)\left(\frac{183}{365}\right)\right] = 2000(1 + 0.0752055) = \$2150.41$$

(ii) Find the present value.
The focal date is December 1, 2000;
the interest period (December 1 to March 20) has 109 days.

$$S = 2150.41; \quad r_2 = 0.115; \quad t_2 = \frac{109}{365}$$

$$P_2 = \frac{2150.41}{1 + (0.115)\left(\frac{109}{365}\right)} = \frac{2150.41}{1 + 0.0343425} = \$2079.01$$

EXAMPLE 8.3E Find the value of a non-interest-bearing $400, 120-day note dated March 2 on May 15 if money is worth 9%.

Solution
The 120-day term ends June 30;
the legal due date is July 3;
the focal date is May 15;
the interest period (May 15 to July 3) has 49 days;
the maturity value of the note is its face value, $400.00.

FIGURE 8.6   **Graphic Representation of Data**

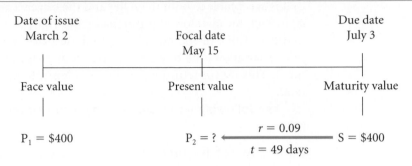

$$S = 400.00; \quad r = 0.09; \quad t = \frac{49}{365}$$

$$P_2 = \frac{400.00}{1 + (0.09)\left(\frac{49}{365}\right)} = \frac{400.00}{1 + 0.0120822} = \$395.22$$

Exercise 8.3

A. Compute the face value of each of the following promissory notes.

  1. A six-month note dated April 9 with interest at 9% has a maturity value of $475.87.

  2. The maturity value of a 150-day 12.5% note dated March 25 is $1641.74.

B. Find the present value, on the date indicated, of each of the following promissory notes:

  1. a non-interest-bearing note for $1200 issued August 10 for three months if money is worth 11%, on the date of issue;

  2. a non-interest-bearing note for $750 issued February 2, 2000, for 180 days if money is worth 12.5%, on June 1, 2000;

  3. a sixty-day, 11% note for $1600 issued October 28 if money is worth 9%, on November 30;

  4. a four-month note for $930 dated April 1 with interest at 6.5% if money is worth 8%, on June 20.

8.4   THE SIMPLE DISCOUNT METHOD OF DISCOUNTING PROMISSORY NOTES

A. Discounting promissory notes

Promissory notes are negotiable; that is, they can be transferred or sold by one party (the holder of the note) to another party (the buyer or investor). The act of selling or buying a promissory note is called **discounting**.

Discounting a promissory note involves the valuation of a financial obligation that is acceptable to both the seller and the buyer. The buyer of the promissory note is, in fact, an investor who purchases the right to receive a future payment—the maturity value of the note. The purchase price of the promissory note will be a price that allows the buyer to realize an appropriate rate of return on the investment. This rate of return is the rate of interest to be used to discount a promissory note.

The following terms are important in computing the discounted value of a note.

(a) The **rate of discount** is the rate of interest to be used in discounting.
(b) The **date of discount** is the date on which the discounting takes place.
(c) The **discount period** is the time period from the date of discount to the legal due date.
(d) The **proceeds** of the note is the amount the buyer pays.
(e) The **amount of discount** is the difference between the maturity value and the proceeds of the note.

B. Simple discount

Valuation of a promissory note at a specific date is done by using the **simple discount** method. The value (proceeds) of a promissory note is the present value of the note at the date of discount using the rate of discount. The present value formula

$$P = \frac{S}{(1 + rt)} \text{ applies:}$$

P is the proceeds of the note;
S is the maturity value;
r is the discount rate to be used;
t is the discount period.

Using this formula means that the amount of discount is the same as the amount of simple interest based on the present value of the note on the date of discount. That is, discounting promissory notes by the simple discount method requires the same formulae and computations used in subsections 8.3A and B.

C. Discounting non-interest-bearing notes

EXAMPLE 8.4A | A two-month, non-interest-bearing promissory note for $700.00 is dated June 30. Find the proceeds of the note and the amount of discount if the note is discounted on July 31 at 9%.

Solution | The maturity value is the face value of the note, $700.00;
the term of the note ends August 30;
the legal due date of the note is September 2;
the discount date is July 31;
the discount period (July 31 to September 2) has 33 days.

$$S = 700.00; \quad r = 0.09; \quad t = \frac{33}{365}$$

$$P = \frac{700.00}{1 + (0.09)\left(\frac{33}{365}\right)} = \frac{700.00}{1 + 0.008137} = \$694.35$$

The proceeds of the note on July 31 are $694.35.
The amount of simple discount (simple interest) is $(700.00 - 694.35) = \$5.65$.

Note: The buyer of the promissory note invests $694.35 for 33 days and will make 9% p.a. simple interest. This figure can be verified by computing the amount of simple interest.

$$I = Prt = (694.35)(0.09)\left(\frac{33}{365}\right) = \$5.65$$

D. Discounting interest-bearing notes

EXAMPLE 8.4B   A 150-day, 8% promissory note for $1200 dated October 28, 1999, is sold January 31, 2000, to yield 11%. Determine the proceeds of the note and the amount of discount.

Solution   (i) *Diagram*
The information needed in discounting interest-bearing notes is essentially the same as the information used in computing the present value of such notes. See Figure 8.7.

FIGURE 8.7   Graphic Representation of Data

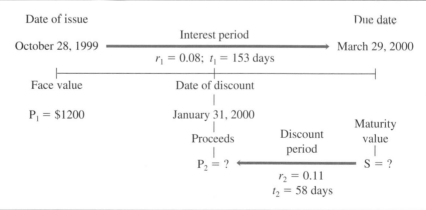

(ii) *Find the maturity value*
The 150-day term of the note ends March 26 (note that 2000 is a leap year; February has 29 days);
the legal due date is March 29;
the interest period (October 28 to March 29) has 153 days.

$$P_1 = 1200; \quad r_1 = 0.08; \quad t_1 = \frac{153}{365}$$

$$S = 1200\left[1 + (0.08)\left(\frac{153}{365}\right)\right] = 1200(1 + 0.0335342) = \$1240.24$$

(iii) *Find the proceeds* (present value on January 31, 2000)
The date of discount is January 31, 2000;
the discount period (January 31 to March 29) has 58 days.

$$S = 1240.24; \quad r_2 = 0.11; \quad t_2 = \frac{58}{365}$$

$$P_2 = \frac{1240.24}{1 + (0.11)\left(\frac{58}{365}\right)} = \frac{1240.24}{1 + 0.0174795} = \$1218.93$$

The proceeds of the note on January 31, 2000, are $1218.93.
The amount of simple discount is 1240.24 − 1218.93 = $21.31. This figure is the same amount as the simple interest on $1218.93 at 11% for 58 days [found by $(1218.93)(0.11)\left(\frac{58}{365}\right)$].

Exercise 8.4

A. Find the proceeds and the amount of discount for each of the following using the simple discount method.

1. A 90-day non-interest-bearing note for $1000 dated May 1 is discounted June 10 at 7.5%.

2. A five-month non-interest-bearing note for $680 issued December 2, 2000, is discounted at 12% on February 15, 2001.

3. A three-month $850 note with interest at 9% dated June 1 is discounted at 11.5% on July 20.

4. A 120-day note for $1300 with interest at 10.5% issued August 12 is discounted September 30 at 8%.

8.5 APPLICATIONS—TREASURY BILLS

Treasury bills (or **T-bills**) are promissory notes issued by the federal government and most provincial governments to meet short-term financing requirements.

Government of Canada T-bills are for terms of 91 days, 182 days, and 364 days. There are no days of grace with T-bills. T-bills are auctioned by the Bank of Canada on behalf of the federal government. They are available in denominations of $1000, $5000, $25 000, $100 000, and $1 000 000. T-bills are bought at the auction mainly by chartered banks and investment dealers for resale to other investors, such as smaller financial institutions, corporations, mutual funds, and individuals.

T-bills are promissory notes that do not carry an interest rate. The issuing government guarantees payment of the face value at maturity. The investor purchases T-bills at a discounted price reflecting a rate of return that is determined by current market conditions. The discounted price is determined by computing the present value of the T-bills using the simple discount method. This is the same method used to find the discounted value of a promissory note.

EXAMPLE 8.5A

An investment dealer bought a 91-day Canada T-bill to yield an annual rate of return of 3.08%.

(i) What was the price paid by the investment dealer for a T-bill with a face value of $100 000?

(ii) The investment dealer resold the $100 000 T-bill the same day to an investor to yield 2.98%. What was the investment dealer's profit on the transaction?

Solution

(i) *Find the purchase price, P_1*
The maturity value is the face value of the T-bill, $100 000.00; the discount period has 91 days (no days of grace are allowed on T-bills).

$$S = 100\,000.00; \quad r_1 = 0.0308; \quad t_1 = \frac{91}{365}$$

$$P_1 = \frac{S}{1 + r_1 t_1} = \frac{100\,000.00}{1 + 0.0308\left(\frac{91}{365}\right)} = \frac{100\,000.00}{1 + 0.0076789} = \frac{100\,000.00}{1.0076789}$$

$$= 99\,237.96$$

The investment dealer paid $99 237.96 for a $100 000 T-bill.

(ii) *Find the resale price, P_2*

$$S = 100\,000.00; \quad r_2 = 0.0298; \quad t_2 = \frac{91}{365}$$

$$P_2 = \frac{100\,000.00}{1 + 0.0298\left(\frac{91}{365}\right)} = \frac{100\,000.00}{1 + 0.0074296} = 99\,262.52$$

Investment dealer's profit = Resale price − Price paid by dealer
$$= P_2 - P_1$$
$$= 99\,262.52 - 99\,237.96 = 24.56$$

The investment dealer's profit on the transaction was $24.56.

EXAMPLE 8.5B

An investor purchased $250 000 in 364-day T-bills 315 days before maturity to yield 4.34%. He sold the T-bills 120 days later to yield 3.92%.

(i) How much did the investor pay for the T-bills?

(ii) For how much did the investor sell the T-bills?

(iii) What rate of return did the investor realize on the investment?

Solution

(i) *Find the purchase price of the T-bills, P_1*

$$S = 250\,000.00; \quad r_1 = 0.0434; \quad t_1 = \frac{315}{365}$$

$$P_1 = \frac{250\,000.00}{1 + 0.0434\left(\frac{315}{365}\right)} = \frac{250\,000.00}{1 + 0.0374548} = 240\,974.35$$

The investor paid $240 974.35.

(ii) *Find the selling price of the T-bills, P_2*
The time to maturity at the date of sale is 195 days (315 − 120).

$$S = 250\,000.00; \quad r_2 = 0.0392; \quad t_2 = \frac{195}{365}$$

$$P_2 = \frac{250\,000.00}{1 + 0.0392\left(\frac{195}{365}\right)} = \frac{250\,000.00}{1 + 0.0209425} = 244\,871.77$$

The investor sold the T-bills for 244 871.77.

(iii) The investment of $240 974.35 grew to $244 871.77 in 120 days.
To compute the rate of return, use the future value formula (Formula 7.3A).

$$P = 240\,974.35; \quad S = 244\,871.77; \quad t = \frac{120}{365}$$

$$S = P(1 + rt)$$

$$244\,871.77 = 240\,974.35\left[1 + r\left(\frac{120}{365}\right)\right]$$

$$\frac{244\,871.77}{240\,974.35} = 1 + \left(\frac{120}{365}\right)r$$

$$1.01617359 = 1 + 0.3287671r$$

$$0.01617359 = 0.3287671r$$

$$\frac{0.01617359}{0.3287671} = r$$

$$r = 0.04919 = 4.92\%$$

The investor realized a rate of return of about 4.92%.

Alternatively
The gain realized represents the interest.

$$I = 244\,871.77 - 240\,974.35 = 3897.42$$

Using the formula $r = \dfrac{I}{Pt}$,

$$r = \frac{3897.42}{240\,974.35\left(\frac{120}{365}\right)} = \frac{3897.42}{79\,224.4438} = 0.04919 = 4.92\%$$

Exercise 8.5

A. Answer each of the following questions.

1. What is the price of a 182-day, $100 000 Government of Canada treasury bill that yields 3.16% per annum?

2. An investment dealer bought a 182-day Government of Canada treasury bill at the price required to yield an annual rate of return of 5.655%.

   (a) What was the price paid by the investment dealer if the T-bill has a face value of $1 000 000?

   (b) Later the same day, the investment dealer sold this T-bill to a large corporation to yield 5.605%. What was the investment dealer's profit on this transaction?

3. An investment dealer acquired a $5000, 91-day Province of Alberta treasury bill on its date of issue at a price of $4913.45. What was the annual rate of return?

4. An investor purchased a 91-day, $100 000 T-bill on its issue date for $99 024.56. After holding it for 42 days, she sold the T-bill for a yield of 3.725%.

(a) What was the original yield of the T-bill?

(b) For what price was the T-bill sold?

(c) What rate of return (per annum) did the investor realize while holding this T-bill?

5. On April 1, $25 000 364-day treasury bills were auctioned off to yield 4.872%.

(a) What is the price of each $25 000 T-bill on April 1?

(b) What is the yield rate on August 15 if the market price is $24 205.50?

(c) Calculate the market value of each $25 000 T-bill on October 1 if the rate of return on that date is 4.545%.

(d) What is the rate of return realized if a $25 000 T-bill purchased on April 1 is sold on November 20 at a market rate of 4.625%?

8.6   DEMAND LOANS

A. Nature of demand loans

A **demand loan** is a loan for which repayment, in full or in part, may be required at any time, or made at any time. The financial instrument representing a demand loan is called a **demand note**.

When borrowing on a demand note, the borrower receives the full face value of the note. The lender may demand payment of the loan in full or in part at any time. Conversely, the borrower may repay all of the loan or any part at any time without notice and without interest penalty. Interest, based on the unpaid balance, is usually payable monthly. The interest rate on such loans is normally not fixed for the duration of the loan but fluctuates with market conditions. Thus the total interest cost cannot be predicted with certainty. Note that the method of counting days is to count the first day but not the last.

B. Examples

EXAMPLE 8.6A   Penny Rose borrowed $1200.00 from the Royal Bank on a demand note. She agreed to repay the loan in six equal monthly instalments and also authorized the bank to collect interest monthly from her bank account at 9% p.a. calculated on the unpaid balance. What will the loan cost?

Solution

$$\text{Monthly payment of principal} = \frac{1200.00}{6} = \$200.00$$

$$\text{Monthly rate of interest} = \frac{9\%}{12} = 0.75\%$$

Month	Loan Amount Owing During Month		Interest Collected for Month	
1	$1200.00	——— Original	$9.00	——— (1200)(0.0075)
2	$1000.00	——— 1200 − 200	$7.50	——— (1000)(0.0075)
3	$ 800.00	——— 1000 − 200	$6.00	——— (800)(0.0075)
4	$ 600.00	——— 800 − 200	$4.50	——— (600)(0.0075)
5	$ 400.00	——— 600 − 200	$3.00	——— (400)(0.0075)
6	$ 200.00	——— 400 − 200	$1.50	——— (200)(0.0075)
	Total interest cost	——————→	$31.50	

EXAMPLE 8.6B

On August 17, Sheridan Toy Company borrowed $30 000.00 from Peel Credit Union on a demand note to finance its inventory. Interest on the loan, calculated on the daily balance, is charged against the borrower's current account on the 17th of each month while the loan is in force. The company makes a payment of $5000.00 on September 24, makes a further payment of $10 000.00 on October 20, and pays the balance on December 10. The interest on demand loans on August 17 was 8% p.a. The rate was changed to 9% effective October 1, to 10.5% effective November 1, and to 10% effective December 1. Determine the cost of financing the loan.

Solution

Payment Date	Interest Period	Principal	Rate	Amount of Interest Due	
Sept. 17	Aug. 17–Sept. 17	$30 000.00	8.0%	$203.84	— $(30\ 000)(0.08)\left(\frac{31}{365}\right)$
Oct. 17	Sept. 17–Sept. 24	$30 000.00	8.0%	46.03	— $(30\ 000)(0.08)\left(\frac{7}{365}\right)$
	Sept. 24–Sept. 30*	$25 000.00	8.0%	38.36	— $(25\ 000)(0.08)\left(\frac{7}{365}\right)$
	Oct. 1–Oct. 17	$25 000.00	9.0%	98.63	— $(25\ 000)(0.09)\left(\frac{16}{365}\right)$
				$183.02	
Nov. 17	Oct. 17–Oct. 20	$25 000.00	9.0%	$ 18.49	— $(25\ 000)(0.09)\left(\frac{3}{365}\right)$
	Oct. 20–Oct. 31*	$15 000.00	9.0%	44.38	— $(15\ 000)(0.09)\left(\frac{12}{365}\right)$
	Nov. 1–Nov. 17	$15 000.00	10.5%	69.04	— $(15\ 000)(0.105)\left(\frac{16}{365}\right)$
				$131.91	
Dec. 10	Nov. 17–Nov. 30*	$15 000.00	10.5%	$ 60.41	— $(15\ 000)(0.105)\left(\frac{14}{365}\right)$
	Dec. 1–Dec. 10	$15 000.00	10.0%	36.99	— $(15\ 000)(0.10)\left(\frac{9}{365}\right)$
				$ 97.40	
	Total cost of financing	————→		$616.17	

*Inclusive

c. Partial payments

Demand loans and similar debts are sometimes paid off by a series of **partial payments**. The commonly used approach to dealing with this type of loan repayment, called the **declining balance method**, requires that each partial payment is applied first to the accumulated interest. Any remainder is then used to reduce the outstanding principal. Thus, interest is always calculated on the unpaid balance and the new unpaid balance is determined after each partial payment.

The following step-by-step procedure is useful in dealing with such problems.

(a) Compute the interest due to the date of the partial payment.

(b) Compare the interest due computed in part (a) with the partial payment received and do part (c) if the partial payment is greater than the interest due or do part (d) if the partial payment is less than the interest due.

(c) *Partial payment greater than interest due*
   (i) Deduct the interest due from the partial payment.
   (ii) Deduct the remainder in part (i) from the principal balance to obtain the new unpaid balance.

(d) *Partial payment less than interest due*
   In this case, the partial payment is not large enough to cover the interest due.
   (i) Deduct the partial payment from the interest due to determine the unpaid interest due at the date of the principal payment.
   (ii) Keep a record of this balance and apply any future partial payments to this unpaid interest first.

EXAMPLE 8.6C

On April 20, Bruce borrowed $4000.00 at 11% on a note requiring payment of principal and interest on demand. Bruce paid $600.00 on May 10 and $1200.00 on July 15. What payment is required on September 30 to pay the note in full?

Solution

April 20
Original loan balance ⟶ $4000.00

May 10
Deduct
   First partial payment ⟶ $ 600.00
   Less interest
      April 20–May 10 ⟶ $\underline{\quad 24.11\quad}$ —— $(4000)(0.11)\left(\frac{20}{365}\right)$
                     575.89
Unpaid balance ⟶ $3424.11

July 15
Deduct
   Second partial payment ⟶ $1200.00
   Less interest
      May 10–July 15 ⟶ $\underline{\quad 68.11\quad}$ —— $(3424.11)(0.11)\left(\frac{66}{365}\right)$
                  1131.89
Unpaid balance ⟶ $2292.22

September 30
Add
    Interest
        July 15–Sept. 30 ————————————→ <u>53.19</u> — $(2292.22)(0.11)\left(\frac{77}{365}\right)$
Payment required to pay
    to pay the note in full ————————→ <u>$2345.40</u>

EXAMPLE 8.6D

The Provincial Bank lent $20 000.00 to the owner of the Purple Pelican on April 1 for commercial improvements. The loan was secured by a demand note subject to a variable rate of interest. This rate was 10% on April 1. The rate of interest was raised to 12% effective August 1 and reduced to 11% effective November 1. Partial payments, applied to the loan by the declining balance method, were made as follows: June 10, $1000.00; September 20, $500.00; November 15, $1200.00. How much interest is due to the Provincial Bank on December 31?

Solution

April 1
Original loan balance ————————————→ $20 000.00

June 10
Deduct
    First partial payment ———→ $1000.00
    Less interest
        April 1–June 10 ———→ <u>383.56</u> ————— $(20\,000.00)(0.10)\left(\frac{70}{365}\right)$
                                  616.44
    Unpaid loan balance ———————→ $19 383.56

September 20
Deduct
    Second partial payment ———→ $ 500.00
    Less interest
        June 10–Sept. 20
        June 10–July 31 → $276.15 ——————— $(19\,383.56)(0.10)\left(\frac{52}{365}\right)$
          (inclusive)
        Aug. 1–Sept. 20 → <u>$318.63</u> <u>594.78</u> ——————— $(19\,383.56)(0.12)\left(\frac{50}{365}\right)$
    Unpaid interest to Sept. 20 ———→ $ 94.78
    Unpaid loan balance ————————→ $19 383.56

November 15
    Third partial payment ———→ $1200.00
    Less interest
        Unpaid interest
        to Sept. 20 ———→ $ 94.78 ——————— (see above)
        Sept. 20–Oct. 31 → 267.65 ——————— $(19\,383.56)(0.12)\left(\frac{42}{365}\right)$
        (inclusive)
        Nov. 1–Nov. 15 → <u>81.78</u> ——————— $(19\,383.56)(0.11)\left(\frac{14}{365}\right)$
                          <u>444.21</u>
                                    755.79
    Unpaid loan balance ————————→ $18 627.77

December 31
Interest due
Nov. 15–Dec. 31 ⟶ $ 258.24 ⟶ $(18\,627.77)(0.11)\left(\frac{46}{365}\right)$

Exercise 8.6

A. Determine the total interest cost for each of the following loans.

1. Jean-Luc borrowed $1500.00 from his bank secured by a demand note. He agreed to repay the loan in five equal monthly instalments and authorized the bank to collect the interest monthly from his bank account at 9.0% per annum calculated on the unpaid balance.

2. Jamie borrowed $900.00 from the Essex District Credit Union. The line of credit agreement provided for repayment of the loan in four equal monthly payments plus interest at 12% per annum calculated on the unpaid balance.

3. Erindale Automotive borrowed $8000.00 from the Bank of Montreal on a demand note on May 10. Interest on the loan, calculated on the daily balance, is charged to Erindale's current account on the 10th of each month. Erindale made a payment of $2000.00 on July 20, a payment of $3000.00 on October 1, and repaid the balance on December 1. The rate of interest on the loan on May 10 was 8% per annum. The rate was changed to 9.5% on August 1 and to 8.5% on October 1.

4. The Tomac Swim Club arranged short-term financing of $12 500.00 on July 20 with the Bank of Commerce and secured the loan with a demand note. The club repaid the loan by payments of $6000.00 on September 15, $3000.00 on November 10, and the balance on December 30. Interest, calculated on the daily balance and charged to the club's current account on the last day of each month, was at 9.5% per annum on July 20. The rate was changed to 8.5% effective September 1 and to 9% effective December 1.

B. Use the declining balance method to answer each of the following.

1. A loan of $6000.00 made at 11% per annum on March 10 is repaid in full on November 15. A payment of $2000.00 was made on June 30 and of $2500.00 on September 5. What was the final payment?

2. D. Slipp borrowed $15 000.00 on August 12. She paid $6000.00 on November 1, $5000.00 on December 15, and the balance on February 20. The rate of interest on the loan was 10.5%. How much did she pay on February 20?

3. The Continental Bank made a loan of $20 000.00 on March 25 to Dr. Hirsch to purchase equipment for her office. The loan was secured by a demand loan subject to a variable rate of interest which was 7% on March 25. The rate of interest was raised to 8.5% effective July 1 and to 9.5% effective September 1. Dr. Hirsch made partial payments on the loan as follows: $600.00 on May 15; $800.00 on June 30; and $400.00 on October 10. The terms of the note require payment of any accrued interest on October 31. How much must Dr. Hirsch pay on October 31?

4. Dirk Ward borrowed $12 000.00 for investment purposes on May 10 on a demand note providing for a variable rate of interest and payment of any accrued interest on December 31. He paid $300.00 on June 25, $150 on September 20, and $200.00 on November 5. How much is the accrued interest on December 31 if the rate of interest was 9.5% on May 10, 8% effective August 1, and 6.5% effective November 1?

8.7 APPLICATIONS—PERSONAL LINES OF CREDIT

A personal line of credit combines features of a demand loan and a credit card. A **personal line of credit** is a preapproved loan amount issued by a bank, trust company, or credit union that can be used by an individual for any purpose. As with a credit card, a minimum repayment of the amount borrowed must be made each month. As with a demand loan, the borrower can repay any amount at any time. Any repayment is applied first to the interest and then to the principal. In general, the rate of interest charged for money borrowed on a line of credit is lower than the rate of interest charged on most credit cards. Interest is charged only for the days money is borrowed on the line of credit. The interest rate can change over time.

An **unsecured line of credit** is a line of credit with no assets promised to the lender to cover non-payment of the loan. Since no security is offered to the lender, the limit of an unsecured line of credit depends on the individual's credit rating and past relationship with the lender.

A **secured line of credit** is a line of credit with assets promised to the lender to cover non-payment of the loan. For example, homeowners might pledge the value of their home, i.e., their home equity, to secure a line of credit. In general, the limit of a secured line of credit is higher than the limit of an unsecured one. Furthermore, the interest rate of a secured line of credit is lower than the interest rate of an unsecured one.

Lines of credit secured by home equity are becoming quite popular and are used by some borrowers as an alternative to mortgages. Home equity lines of credit provide access to larger credit limits.

EXAMPLE 8.7A   Suppose you have a line of credit and receive the following statement of account for the month of February.

Date	Transaction Description	Deposit	Withdrawal	Balance
Feb 01	Balance			−600.00
04	Cheque 262		500.00	−1100.00
10	Deposit	2050.00		950.00
16	Withdrawal—Hydro		240.00	710.00
20	Cheque 263		1000.00	−290.00
22	Withdrawal—Cable TV		80.00	−370.00
27	Withdrawal—Insurance		150.00	−520.00
28	Interest earned	?		
	Line of credit interest		?	
	Overdraft interest		?	
	Service charge		?	

Note: "−" indicates a negative balance.

The limit on your line of credit is $1000. You receive daily interest of 3% p.a. on positive balances and pay daily interest of 10% p.a. on *negative (line of credit) balances*. Overdraft interest is 24% p.a. on the daily amount exceeding your line of credit limit. There is a service charge of $5.00 for each transaction causing an overdraft or adding to an overdraft.

Determine

(i) the amount of interest earned;

(ii) the amount of interest charged on the line of credit;

(iii) the amount of interest charged on overdrafts;

(iv) the amount of the service charge;

(v) the account balance on February 28.

Solution

(i) Interest earned (on positive balances)

February 10 to February 15 inclusive: 6 days at 3% on $950.00

$$I = 950.00(0.03)\left(\frac{6}{365}\right) = \$0.47$$

February 16 to February 19 inclusive: 4 days at 3% on $710.00

$$I = 710.00(0.03)\left(\frac{4}{365}\right) = \$0.23$$

Total interest earned = 0.47 + 0.23 = $0.70

(ii) Line of credit interest charged (on negative balances up to $1000.00)

February 1 to February 3 inclusive: 3 days at 10% on $600.00

$$I = 600.00(0.10)\left(\frac{3}{365}\right) = \$0.49$$

February 4 to February 9 inclusive: 6 days at 10% on $1000.00

$$I = 1000.00(0.10)\left(\frac{6}{365}\right) = \$1.64$$

February 20 to February 21 inclusive: 2 days at 10% on $290.00

$$I = 290.00(0.10)\left(\frac{2}{365}\right) = \$0.16$$

February 22 to February 26 inclusive: 5 days at 10% on $370.00

$$I = 370.00(0.10)\left(\frac{5}{365}\right) = \$0.51$$

February 27 to February 28 inclusive: 2 days at 10% on $520.00

$$I = 520.00(0.10)\left(\frac{2}{365}\right) = \$0.28$$

Total line of credit interest charged
$$= 0.49 + 1.64 + 0.16 + 0.51 + 0.28 = \$3.08$$

(iii) Since your line of credit limit is $1000.00, overdraft interest is charged on the amount in excess of a negative balance of $1000.00. You were in overdraft from February 4 to February 9 inclusive in the amount of $100.00.

$$\text{Overdraft interest} = 100.00(0.24)\left(\frac{6}{365}\right) = \$0.39$$

(iv) You had one transaction causing an overdraft or adding to an overdraft.

Service charge $= 1(5.00) = \$5.00$

(v) The account balance on February 28

$$= -520.00 + 0.70 - 3.08 - 0.39 - 5.00 = -\$527.77$$

Exercise 8.7

A. Determine the missing information for each of the following lines of credit.

1. Suppose you have a line of credit and receive the following statement for the month of March.

Date	Transaction Description	Deposit	Withdrawal	Balance
Feb 28	Balance			−527.71
Mar 02	Cheque 264		600.00	−1127.71
05	Cheque 265		300.00	−1427.71
10	Deposit	2000.00		572.29
16	Withdrawal—Hydro		265.00	307.29
20	Cheque 266		1000.00	−692.71
22	Withdrawal—Cable TV		83.50	−776.21
27	Withdrawal—Insurance		165.00	−941.21
31	Interest earned	?		
	Line of credit interest		?	
	Overdraft interest		?	
	Service charge		?	?

Note: "−" indicates a negative balance.

The limit on your line of credit is $1000. You receive daily interest of 3.5% p.a. on positive balances and pay daily interest of 11% p.a. on negative (line of credit) balances. Overdraft interest is 24% p.a. on the daily amount exceeding your line of credit limit. There is a service charge of $5.00 for each transaction causing an overdraft or adding to an overdraft.

(a) Calculate the amount of interest earned.

(b) Calculate the amount of interest charged on the line of credit.

(c) Calculate the amount of interest charged on overdrafts.

(d) Calculate the amount of the service charge.

(e) What is the account balance on March 31?

2. Lorenzo has a line of credit secured by the equity in his home. The limit on his line of credit is $45 000. Transactions for the period April 1 to September 30 are shown below. Lorenzo owed $25 960.06 on his line of credit on April 1.

Date	Principal Withdrawal	Principal Payment	Interest Payment	Balance
Apr 01				−25 960.06
30		200.00	?	
May 23	5 000.00			
31		200.00	?	
Jun 30		200.00	?	
July 19	5 000.00			
31		200.00	?	
Aug 05	10 500.00			
31		200.00	?	
Sept 30		200.00	?	

Note: "−" indicates a negative balance.

The line of credit agreement requires regular payment of $200.00 on the principal plus interest (including overdraft interest) by electronic transfer after closing on the last day of each month. Overdraft interest is 24% p.a. The line of credit interest is variable. It was 6.00% on April 1, 5.50% effective June 20, and 5.00% effective September 10.

(a) Calculate the interest payments on April 30, May 31, June 30, July 31, August 31, and September 30.

(b) What is the account balance on September 30?

BUSINESS MATH NEWS BOX

EXPLORING PERSONAL LINES OF CREDIT

Canada Trust recently distributed the information shown below. "PowerLine" is the trademark for Canada Trust's personal line of credit, and "PowerCheques" are the cheques used to pay bills with money from the PowerLine.

Consolidate high-interest credit cards with your PowerCheques
Use the enclosed PowerCheques to consolidate balances from your credit cards and loans onto your PowerLine. Here's a sampling of how much your PowerLine line of credit can help you save in just 6 months:

Your Balance	Some Department Store Cards 28.8%	Other Credit Cards 18.9%	Canada Trust PowerLine Unsecured 9%	In Just 6 Months You Can Save Up To
$6500	$936	$614	$292	$644
$4000	$576	$378	$180	$396
$2500	$360	$236	$112	$248

(Savings based on the rates remaining the same for 6 months. Calculations rounded down to nearest dollar. Rates subject to change without notice.)

QUESTIONS

1. In the table above, calculations have been rounded down to the nearest dollar. Recalculate the figures in the last row of the table for the balance of $2500, rounding to two decimal places. What effect does rounding have on the six-month savings (the balance in column 5)?

2. Suppose you had a balance of $5000 on a credit card charging interest at a rate of 17.25%. Suppose you consolidated this balance onto the unsecured PowerLine, which charges interest at a rate of 9%. How much interest would you save in six months?

3. Suppose you used money from your unsecured PowerLine to make an RRSP contribution of $3000. For the first two months, the PowerLine had an interest rate of 9%. The rate then increased to 9.5% for the next four months. How much interest would you have paid on the $3000 balance after six months?

8.8 LOAN REPAYMENT SCHEDULES

A. Purpose

In the case of loans repaid in fixed instalments (often called a **blended payment**), the constant periodic payment is first applied to pay the accumulated interest. The remainder of the payment is then used to reduce the unpaid balance of the principal.

FIGURE 8.8   **Statement of Disclosure**

STATEMENT OF DISCLOSURE
(COST OF LOAN AND ANNUAL INTEREST RATE)   PURSUANT TO THE CONSUMER PROTECTION ACT

Name of Credit Union _____ *SHERIDAN* _____   Account No. ____ *2000* ____

1) Balance of existing loan (if any) $ ____ *2000.00* ____   4) Cost of Borrowing expressed in dollars and cents
(Interest calculated on full amount of loan (Item 3) $ __ *1473.00*

2) Add new amount loaned $ ____ *4000.00* ____   5) Annual Interest Rate charged (calculated in accordance with the Consumer Protection Act)   ___ *9* ___ %

3) Full amount of loan $ ____ *6000.00* ____

6) If any charge is made to the borrower in addition to interest herein noted, it must be disclosed here. $ _____
(Description) ....
Frequency of instalments ___ *60 MONTHS* ___ Amount of instalments $ *124.55* First instalment due _____ 19 ___

I, the undersigned, acknowledge receipt of this statement of cost of loan and annual interest rate, prior to the advance of the credit.

DATE _____   X ....
SIGNATURE OF BORROWER

COMPLETE IN DUPLICATE   NOTE: Where more than one maker or co-maker, separate Disclosure Forms should
Original to Borrower   be signed for individually.

Courtesy Peel Sheridan Dufferin Educational Credit Union Limited

While lenders are obliged to disclose to the borrower the total cost of borrowing as well as the interest rate (see Figure 8.8), a detailed statement of the cost of borrowing as well as the effect of the periodic payments on the principal may be obtained by constructing a **loan repayment schedule**, or an **amortization schedule**.

The information usually contained in such a schedule includes

(**a**) the payment number or payment date;
(**b**) the amount paid at each payment date;
(**c**) the interest paid by each payment;
(**d**) the principal repaid by each payment;
(**e**) the unpaid loan balance after each payment.

Figure 8.9 provides a possible design for such schedules and the same design is used in the solution to Example 8.8A.

FIGURE 8.9   Basic Design of a Loan Repayment Schedule

① Payment Number	② Balance Before Payment	③ Amount Paid	④ Interest Paid	⑤ Principal Repaid	⑥ Balance After Payment

B. Construction of loan repayment schedules illustrated

EXAMPLE 8.8A   You borrowed $1600.00 from Sheridan Credit Union at 9% p.a. and agreed to repay the loan in monthly instalments of $300.00 each, such payments to cover interest due and repayment of principal. Use the design shown in Figure 8.9 to construct a complete repayment schedule including the totalling of Columns ③, ④, and ⑤ ("Amount paid," "Interest paid," and "Principal repaid").

Solution   See Figure 8.10 and the explanatory notes that follow.

FIGURE 8.10   Loan Repayment Schedule for Example 8.8A

① Payment Number	② Balance Before Payment	③ Amount Paid (1)	④ Interest Paid (2)	⑤ Principal Repaid (3)	⑥ Balance After Payment (4)
0					1600.00 (5)
1	1600.00	300.00	12.00 (6)	288.00 (7)	1312.00 (8)
2	1312.00	300.00	9.84 (9)	290.16 (10)	1021.84 (11)
3	1021.84	300.00	7.66	292.34	729.50
4	729.50	300.00	5.47	294.53	434.97
5	434.97	300.00	3.26	296.74	138.23 (12)
6	138.23	139.27 (15)	1.04 (14)	138.23 (13)	0.00
Totals (16)		1639.27 (18)	39.27 (19)	1600.00 (17)	

Explanatory notes

(1) The Amount Paid shown in column ③ is the agreed-upon monthly payment of $300.00.

·(2) The Interest Paid shown in column ④ is at 9% per annum. This figure is converted into a periodic (monthly) rate of $9\%/12$ (0.75% per month) to facilitate the computation of the monthly amount of interest paid. (See notes (6) and (9).)

(3) The amount of Principal Repaid each month shown in column ⑤ is found by subtracting the Interest Paid for the month (column ④) from the Amount Paid for the month (column ③). (See notes (7) and (10).)

(4) The Balance After Payment for a month shown in column ⑥ is found by subtracting the Principal Repaid for the month (column ⑤) from the Balance Before Payment for the month (column ②) OR from the previous Balance After Payment figure (column ⑥). (See notes (8) and (11).)

(5) The original loan balance of $1600.00 is introduced as the starting amount for the schedule and is the only amount shown in Line 0.

(6) Interest paid in Payment number 1
$$= 0.75\% \text{ of } 1600.00 = (0.0075)(1600.00) = \$12.00$$

(7) Principal Repaid by Payment number 1
$$= 300.00 - 12.00 = \$288.00$$

(8) Balance After Payment for Payment number 1
$$= 1600.00 - 288.00 = \$1312.00$$

(9) Interest Paid in Payment number 2
$$= 0.75\% \text{ of } 1312.00 = (0.0075)(1312.00) = \$9.84$$

(10) Principal Repaid by Payment number 2
$$= 300.00 - 9.84 = \$290.16$$

(11) Balance After Payment for Payment number 2
$$= 1312.00 - 290.16 = \$1021.84$$

(12) The Balance After Payment for Payment number 5 of $138.23 is smaller than the regular monthly payment of $300.00. The next payment need only be sufficient to pay the outstanding balance of $138.23 plus the interest due. (See notes (13), (14), and (15).)

(13) Principal Repaid in Payment number 6 must be $138.23 to pay off the outstanding loan balance.

(14) Interest Paid in Payment number 6 is the interest due on $138.23 = 0.75% of $138.23 = (0.0075)(138.23) = \$1.04$.

(15) Amount paid in Payment number 6
$$= 138.23 + 1.04 = \$139.27.$$

(16) The Totals of columns ③, ④, and ⑤ serve as a check of the arithmetic accuracy of the payment schedule. (See notes (17), (18), and (19).)

(17) Principal Repaid, the total of column ⑤, must equal the original loan balance of $1600.00.

(18) Amount Paid, the total of column ③, must equal the total of all the payments made (five payments of $300.00 each plus the final payment of $139.27).

(19) Interest paid, the total of column ④, must be the difference between the totals of columns ③ and ⑤ = 1639.27 − 1600.00 = $39.27.

c. Computer application—loan repayment schedule

Spreadsheet programs like EXCEL and Lotus 1-2-3 make creating loan repayment schedules much easier. Once you create a loan repayment schedule in a spreadsheet, you can change the loan amount or repayment instalments and see immediately the effect of the change on the loan repayment schedule, without inputting all the formulae again. The procedures that follow are general instructions for creating Figure 8.10 in a spreadsheet. The formulae in the spreadsheet diagram were created using EXCEL. Many other spreadsheet programs work in a similar way. Modify the procedures below if your spreadsheet program requires different instructions.

STEP 1 To create Figure 8.10 in a spreadsheet, open a new spreadsheet file. Enter the labels, formulae, and numbers shown in the diagram below. To display the labels in row 1, you can widen the columns (as shown below) or shorten the labels. (In EXCEL, you can widen columns by going to the Format menu, choosing Column, then choosing Width. Type numbers until you get the column width you want. You can also widen columns by placing the cursor between columns until the cursor changes to a double-pointed arrow. Drag the side of the column until you get the column width you want.)

To reduce inputting time and avoid inputting errors, copy as many formulae and numbers as possible within the spreadsheet. (To copy and paste formulae and numbers in EXCEL, click on the cell you want to copy. Go to the Edit menu and choose Copy. Then highlight the cell or cells you want to copy into. Go to the Edit menu and choose Paste. You can also copy formulae into the cells below a particular cell. Highlight the particular cell and all the cells below it that you want to fill. Go to the Edit menu, choose Fill, then choose Down.) The numbers and formulae in cells B3, C3, D3, E3, and F3 can be copied into many of the cells that appear below these cells. Notice that the formulae in cells C3 and D3 include **G2** and **G4** respectively. In EXCEL, the $ symbols are required for *absolute cell references*. This is to make sure that when you copy the formulae in cells C3 and D3, the new formulae you create will always link to cells G2 and G4.

FIGURE 8.11

	A	B	C	D	E	F	G
				Workbook 1			
		A	**B**	**C**	**D**	**E**	**F**	**G**
1	Payment	Balance before payment	Amount paid	Interest paid	Principal repaid	Balance	
2	0					1600.00	300.00
3	1	= F2	= G2	= G4*B3	= C3–D3	= B3–E3	
4	2	= F3	= G2	= G4*B4	= C4–D4	= B4–E4	= 0.09/12
5	3	= F4	= G2	= G4*B5	= C5–D5	= B5–E5	
6	4	= F5	= G2	= G4*B6	= C6–D6	= B6–E6	
7	5	= F6	= G2	= G4*B7	= C7–D7	= B7–E7	
8	6	= F7	= D8+E8	= G4*B8	= B8	= B8–E8	
9	Totals		= SUM(C3:C8)	= SUM(D3:D8)	= SUM(E3:E8)		

STEP 2   To make the spreadsheet easier to read, format the numbers to two decimal places. (In EXCEL, change the format by highlighting cells B3 to F9. Go to the Format menu, choose Cells, then choose **0.00** from the Number section.)

STEP 3   Notice the formulae that are entered in cells C8, D8, and E8. They calculate the principal and interest required to pay off the outstanding loan balance. For an explanation of these amounts, refer to explanatory notes 13, 14, and 15 on page 349.

STEP 4   Notice the formulae entered in cells C9, D9, and E9. The sum in cell C9 must equal the total of all the payments made (five payments of $300.00 each plus the final payment of $139.27). The sum in cell D9 is the total interest paid, and must be the difference between cells C9 (total payments made) and E9 (the principal). The sum in cell E9 is the total principal repaid and must equal the loan amount of $1600.00 entered in cell F2.

Now that you have created the loan repayment schedule in a spreadsheet, it is easy to change aspects of the loan and see the effects quickly. Suppose the interest rate was changed from 9% p.a. to 10% p.a. You can reflect this change in the spreadsheet loan repayment schedule by changing the formula in cell G4 to = **0.10/12**. (If you do this, you should see 143.77 in cell C8, representing the new final payment.)

To then reflect a repayment amount of $325 instead of $300, change the number in cell G2 to **325**. (If you do this, you should see 15.61 in cell C8, representing the new final payment.) Suppose the loan principal then changed from $1600 to $1800. To reflect the change, enter 1800 in cell F2. (If you do this, you should see 225.82 in cell C8, representing the new final payment.)

Exercise 8.8

A. Use the design shown in Figure 8.9 to construct a complete repayment schedule including the totalling of the Amount Paid, Interest Paid, and Principal Repaid columns for each of the following loans.

1. Carla borrowed $1200.00 from the Royal Bank at 8.5% per annum calculated on the monthly unpaid balance. She agreed to repay the loan in blended payments of $180.00 per month.

2. On March 15, Julio borrowed $900.00 from Sheridan Credit Union at 7.5% per annum calculated on the daily balance. He gave the Credit Union six cheques for $135.00 dated the 15th of each of the next six months starting April 15 and a cheque dated October 15 for the remaining balance to cover payment of interest and repayment of principal.

REVIEW EXERCISE

1. A four-month promissory note for $1600.00 dated June 30 bears interest at 6.5%.

(a) What is the due date of the note?

(b) What is the amount of interest payable at the due date?

(c) What is the maturity value of the note?

2. Determine the maturity value of a 120-day note for $1250.00 dated May 23 and bearing interest at 5.75%.

3. Compute the face value of a 90-day note dated September 10 bearing interest at 9.25% whose maturity value is $767.68.

4. The maturity value of a seven-month promissory note issued July 31, 2000, is $3275.00. What is the present value of the note on the date of issue if interest is 7.75%?

5. Compute the maturity value of a 150-day, 12% promissory note with a face value of $5000.00 dated August 5.

6. What is the face value of a three-month promissory note dated November 30, 1999, with interest at 11.5 percent if its maturity value is $967.84?

7. A 90-day, $800 promissory note was issued July 31 with interest at 8%. What is the present value of the note on October 20?

8. An $1850, four-month promissory note with interest at 7.5% issued June 1 is discounted on August 28 at 10.5%. Find the amount of discount and the proceeds of the note using the simple discount method.

9. Determine the present value on the date of issue of a non-interest-bearing promissory note for $1300 dated March 10 for four months if money is worth 9.5%.

10. Find the proceeds and the discount of a five-month, $700 promissory note dated September 6 with interest at 5.5% discounted on November 28 at 8.5% by the simple discount method.

11. An investment dealer paid $24 256.25 to acquire a $25 000.00 182-day Government of Canada treasury bill at the weekly auction. What was the rate of return on this T-bill?

12. Government of Alberta 364-day T-bills with a face value of $1 000 000 were purchased on April 7 for $944 470. The T-bills were sold on May 16 for $953 500.

    (a) What was the market yield rate on April 7?

    (b) What was the yield rate on May 16?

    (c) What was the rate of return realized?

13. Tryman borrowed $10 000 on March 10 on a demand note. The loan was repaid by payments of $3000 on June 20, $4000 on September 1, and the balance on November 15. Interest, calculated on the daily balance and charged to Tryman's current account on the last day of each month, was at 9% on March 10 but was changed to 10% effective June 1 and to 8% effective October 1. How much did the loan cost?

14. Quick Print Press borrowed $20 000 from the Provincial Bank on May 25 at 7.5% and secured the loan by signing a promissory note subject to a variable rate of interest. Quick Print made partial payments of $5000 on July 10 and $8000 on September 15. The rate of interest was increased to 8% effective August 1 and to 8.5% effective October 1. What payment must Quick Print make on October 31 if, under the terms of the loan agreement, any interest accrued as of October 31 is to be paid on October 31?

15. Muriel has a line of credit with a limit of $10 000.00. She owed $8195.00 on July 1. Principal withdrawals for the period July 1 to November 30 were $3000.00 on August 20 and $600.00 on October 25. The line of credit agreement requires regular payments of $300.00 on the 15th day of each month. Muriel has made all required payments. Interest (including overdraft interest) is charged to the account on the last day of each month. The interest rate was 10% on July 1, but was changed to 9.5% effective September 15. Overdraft interest is 24% for any balance in excess of $10 000.00.

    (a) Calculate the interest charges on July 31, August 31, September 30, October 31, and November 30.

    (b) Calculate the account balance on November 30.

16. You borrowed $3000 at 9% per annum calculated on the unpaid monthly balance and agreed to repay the principal together with interest in monthly payments of $500 each. Construct a complete repayment schedule.

SELF-TEST

1. For the following promissory note, determine the amount of interest due at maturity.

$565.00   TORONTO, ONTARIO   JANUARY 10, 2000

_____FIVE MONTHS_____ after date __we__ promise to pay to the order of

WILSON LUMBER COMPANY

EXACTLY FIVE-HUNDRED-SIXTY-FIVE and 00/100 --------------- Dollars

at _____WILSON LUMBER COMPANY_____   for value received

with interest at __8.25%__ per annum.

Due _____   (seal) _____

                            (seal) _____

---

2. Find the maturity value of a $1140.00, 7.75%, 120-day note dated February 19, 1999.

3. Determine the face value of a four-month promissory note dated May 20, 1998, with interest at 11.5% p.a. if the maturity value of the note is $1206.05.

4. Find the present value of a non-interest-bearing seven-month promissory note for $1800 dated August 7, 2001, on December 20, 2001, if money is then worth 8.75%.

5. A 180-day note dated September 14, 2000, is made at 9.25% for $1665.00. What is the present value of the note on October 18, 2000, if money is worth 10.5%?

6. What is the price of a 91-day, $25 000 Government of Canada treasury bill that yields 3.28% per annum?

7. An investor purchased a 182-day, $100 000 T-bill on its issue date. It yielded 3.85%. The investor held the T-bill for 67 days, then sold it for $98 853.84.

   (a) What was the original price of the T-bill?

   (b) When the T-bill was sold, what was its yield?

8. The owner of Jane's Boutique borrowed $6000.00 from Halton Community Credit Union on June 5. The loan was secured by a demand note with interest calculated on the daily balance and charged to the store's account on the 5th day of each month. The loan was repaid by payments of $1500.00 on July 15, $2000.00 on October 10, and $2500.00 on December 30. The rate of interest charged by the credit union was 8.5% on June 5. The rate was changed to 9.5% effective July 1 and to 10% effective October 1. Determine the total interest cost on the loan.

9. Herb's Restaurant borrowed $24 000.00 on March 1 on a demand note providing for a variable rate of interest. While repayment of principal is open, any accrued interest is to be paid on November 30. Payments on the loan were made as follows: $600.00 on April 15, $400.00 on July 20, and $400.00 on October 10. The rate of interest was 7% on March 1 but was changed to 8.5% effective August 1 and to 7.5% effective November 1. Using the declining balance method to record the partial payments, determine the accrued interest on November 30.

10. Jingyi has a line of credit from her local bank with a limit of $10 000.00. On March 1, she owed $7265.00. From March 1 to June 30, she withdrew principal amounts of $3000.00 on April 10 and $500.00 on June 20. According to the line of credit agreement, Jingyi must make a regular payment of $200.00 on the 15th of each month. She has made these payments. Interest (including overdraft interest) is charged to the account on the last day of each month. On March 1, the interest rate was 9%, but it was changed to 8.5% effective May 15. Overdraft interest is 22% for any balance in excess of $10 000.00.

(a) Calculate the interest charges on March 31, April 30, May 31, and June 30.

(b) What is the account balance on June 30?

11. Use the design shown in Figure 8.9 to construct a complete repayment schedule, including the totalling of the Amount Paid, Interest Paid, and Principal Repaid columns, for a loan of $4000 repaid in monthly instalments of $750.00 each including interest of 6.5% per annum calculated on the unpaid balance.

CHALLENGE PROBLEMS

1. Mike Kornas signed a 12-month, 11% p.a. simple interest promissory note for $12 000 with MacDonald's Furniture. After 100 days, MacDonald's Furniture sold the note to the Royal Bank at a discount rate of 13% p.a. Royal Bank resold the note to Friendly Finance Company 25 days later at a discount rate of 9% p.a. Find the gain or loss on this note for each company and bank involved.

2. A father wanted to show his son what it might be like to borrow money from a financial institution. When his son asked if he could borrow $120, the father lent him the money and set up the following arrangements. He charged his son $6 for the loan of $120. The son therefore received $114 and agreed to pay his father 12 instalments of $10 a month, beginning one month from today, until the loan was repaid. Find the approximate rate of simple interest the father charged on this loan.

CASE STUDY 8.1 THE BUSINESS OF BORROWING

Magnusson's Computer Store agrees to purchase some new computer monitors costing $5000 plus 7% GST. Doug Magnusson, the store's owner, was informed that if he paid cash on receipt of the goods he could take a cash discount of 4% of the invoice price before GST. GST would then be added to the new invoice price. Doug would like to take advantage of this discount, but the store is short of cash right now. A number of customers are expected to pay their invoices in the next 30 to 60 days.

Doug went to his bank manager to negotiate a short-term loan to pay for the monitors when they arrive and take advantage of the cash discount. The bank manager suggested a 90-day non-interest-bearing promissory note discounted at an annual rate of 9% charged on the face value. Doug agreed to the note and suggested that the three days of grace should be added to give him more repayment flexibility.

QUESTIONS

1. What is the face value of the 90-day promissory note using three days of grace for the goods including GST?

2. Suppose Doug decides he does not need the three days of grace. What effect would this have on the face value of the note?

3. Doug later discussed his situation with a friend, who suggested that Doug could have negotiated a short-term loan for 90 days instead of using a promissory note. What is the highest annual simple interest rate at which Doug could have borrowed the money and still saved by taking the cash discount?

4. (a) Which financing option would have been cheaper—a 90-day non-interest-bearing promissory note discounted at 9% or a 90-day demand loan at 9%?

   (b) How much would Doug have saved by using the cheaper option?

CASE STUDY 8.2　DEALING WITH DEBT

Don and Rosemary Schaus were concerned about their high debts. They borrowed money from their bank to purchase their house, car, and computer. They must make regular monthly payments for these three loans. For some of their other expenses, they also owe $4000 to MasterCard and $3500 to VISA. Don and Rosemary decided to meet with a consumer credit counsellor to gain control of their debts.

The consumer credit counsellor explained to Don and Rosemary the details of their loans and credit card debts. Don and Rosemary were shocked to discover that whereas their computer and car loans had an interest rate of 9.0% p.a., their credit cards had an interest rate of 17.5% p.a. The counsellor pointed out that the interest rate on their three loans was reasonable. However, because the interest rate on the credit cards was so high, she advised Don and Rosemary to borrow money at a lower interest rate and pay off the credit card debts.

The credit counsellor suggested that they should consider obtaining a line of credit. She explained that the rate of interest on the line of credit would likely be a few percentage points higher than the prime rate, but much lower than the rate of interest charged on credit card balances. Don and Rosemary would have to make a minimum payment every month, similar to a credit card, that would be applied to pay all the interest and a portion of the principal balance owing on the line of credit. The line of credit would allow them to make monthly payments higher than the minimum so that they could pay as much toward the principal balance as they could afford. Due to the much lower interest rate on a line of credit compared to a typical credit card, the money they would save on interest each month could be paid toward the principal. A line of credit appealed to Don and Rosemary. It helped them feel more in control of their finances and gave them the resolve to pay off their credit card debts.

The next day, Don and Rosemary met with their bank manager and were approved for a $10 000.00 line of credit. Immediately, they paid off the $4000.00 owed to MasterCard and the $3500.00 owed to VISA with money from the line of credit. They then decided to pay off the line off credit over the next ten months by making monthly payments equal to one-tenth of the original line of credit balance plus the simple interest owed on the remaining line of credit balance. The simple interest rate on the line of credit is expected to be 8.25% over the next ten months. Don and Rosemary agreed to cut up their credit cards and not charge any more purchases until they had paid off their line of credit.

QUESTIONS

1. Suppose Don and Rosemary pay off their credit cards with their line of credit on April 20. They will make their monthly payments on the 20th of each month, beginning in May. Create a schedule showing their monthly payments for the next ten months. How much interest will they pay using this repayment plan?

2. Suppose Don and Rosemary had not gotten a line of credit but keep their credit cards. They decided not to make any more credit card purchases. Instead, they made monthly payments equal to one-tenth of the original credit card balance plus the simple interest owed on the remaining credit card balance. They will make their monthly payments on the 20th of each month, beginning in May. Create a schedule showing their monthly payments for the next ten months. How much interest would they have paid using this repayment plan?

3. How much money did Don and Rosemary save on interest by getting the line of credit?

4. What are the requirements for obtaining a line of credit from your financial institution?

SUMMARY OF FORMULAE

Formula 7.1A
$$I = Prt$$

Finding the amount of interest on promissory notes

Formula 7.3A
$$S = P(1 + rt)$$

Finding the maturity value of promissory notes directly

Formula 7.3B
$$P = \frac{S}{1 + rt}$$

Finding the present value of promissory notes or treasury bills given the maturity value

GLOSSARY

Amortization schedule   see *Loan repayment schedule*

Amount of discount   the difference between the maturity value of a promissory note and its proceeds when discounted

Amount of interest   interest, in dollars and cents, payable to the payee on the legal due date

Blended payments   the usual method of repaying a personal consumer loan by fixed periodic (monthly) payments that cover payment of interest and repayment of principal

Date of discount   the date on which a promissory note is bought or sold

Date of issue   the date on which a promissory note is made

Date of maturity   see *Legal due date*

Declining balance method   the commonly used approach to applying partial payments to demand loans whereby each partial payment is first applied to pay the interest due and then applied to the outstanding principal

Demand loan   a loan for which repayment in full or in part may be required at any time or made at any time

Demand note   the financial instrument representing a demand loan

Discount   see *Amount of discount*

Discounting   the act of buying or selling promissory notes

Discount period   the time, in days, from the date of discount to the legal due date

Due date   see *Legal due date*

Face value   the sum of money specified on the promissory note

Interest-bearing promissory notes   notes subject to the rate of interest stated on the note

Interest period   the time, in days, from the date of issue to the legal due date for promissory notes

Issue date   see *Date of issue*

Legal due date   the date on which the promissory note is to be paid; it includes three days of grace unless "No Grace Days" is written on the promissory note

Line of credit   see *Personal line of credit*

Loan repayment schedule   a detailed statement of instalment payments, interest cost, repayment of principal, and outstanding balance of principal for an instalment plan

Maker the party making the promise to pay by signing the promissory note

Maturity value the amount (face value plus interest) that must be paid on the legal due date to honour the note

Non-interest-bearing promissory notes notes that do not require the payment of interest (the maturity value of such notes is the same as their face value)

Partial payments a series of payments on a debt

Payee the party to whom the promise to pay is made

Personal line of credit a preapproved loan amount issued by a financial institution for use by an individual at any time for any purpose; interest is charged only for the time money is borrowed on the line of credit; a minimum monthly payment is required (similar to a credit card); the interest rate can change over time

Present value of a promissory note the value of a promissory note at a specified date before the legal due date determined on the basis of a specified rate of interest or rate of discount or the rate money is worth

Proceeds the sum of money for which a promissory note is bought or sold at the date of discount

Promissory note a written promise to pay a specified sum of money after a specified period of time or on demand, with or without interest as specified

Rate money is worth the prevailing rate of interest

Rate of discount the rate used to determine the proceeds of a promissory note

Rate of interest the simple annual rate of interest based on the face value

Secured line of credit a line of credit with assets pledged as security

Simple discount the method of discounting promissory notes using the present value approach (simple interest) to determine the proceeds; the amount of discount deducted from the maturity value to find the proceeds when using the simple discount method

T-bills see *Treasury bills*

Term of a promissory note the time period for which the note was written (in days or months)

Three days of grace the number of days added to the term of a note in Canada to determine its legal due date

Treasury bills promissory notes issued at a discount from their face values by the federal government and most provincial governments to meet short-term financing requirements (the maturity value of treasury bills is the same as their face value)

Unsecured line of credit a line of credit where no assets are pledged by the borrower to the lender to cover non-payment of the line of credit

PART THREE

Mathematics of Finance and Investment

9

Compound Interest—Future Value and Present Value

In today's world of computerized banking and electronic calculations, compound interest is very common. Under compound interest, you earn interest that is added on a principal, and the interest is then added to form a new principal. You then earn interest on this new, higher principal. This is what is meant by the expression "earning interest on interest."

Compound interest formulae contain exponents. Before the arrival of calculators, long, complicated tables were required to calculate compound interest amounts. Therefore, in the past, financial institutions often offered only one type of savings account in which interest was compounded only once or twice a year. Today, however, calculators and computers have made it very easy to calculate compound interest amounts for all sorts of interest rates and time periods. Therefore, financial institutions now offer many types of savings accounts paying compound interest. To decide which account is best for you, you have to understand how compound interest works.

Introduction

Under the compound interest method, interest is added periodically to the principal. As we did with simple interest, we use compound interest formulae to determine future values and present values. The compound interest formulae contain the compounding factor $(1 + i)^n$. The arithmetic difficulties associated with computing the numerical value of $(1 + i)^n$ have disappeared with the availability of electronic calculators equipped with an exponential function (universal power key and universal root key).

OBJECTIVES

Upon completing this chapter, you will be able to do the following:

1. Determine the rate per compounding period *i* and the number of compounding periods *n*, set up the compounding factor $(1 + i)^n$ in exponential form, and compute the numerical value of $(1 + i)^n$.

2. Use the future value formula for a compound amount $S = P(1 + i)^n$ to compute future values, including problems involving changes in rate of interest and principal.

3. Use the present value formula $P = \dfrac{S}{(1 + i)^n}$ to compute the present value of future sums of money.
4. Discount long-term promissory notes.
5. Solve problems involving equations of value.

9.1   BASIC CONCEPTS AND COMPUTATIONS

A. Basic procedure for computing compound interest

The term **compound interest** refers to a procedure for computing interest whereby the interest for a specified time period is added to the original principal. The resulting amount becomes the new principal for the next time period. The interest earned in earlier periods earns interest in future periods.

The compound interest method is generally used to calculate interest for long-term investments. The amount of compound interest for the first interest period is the same as the amount of simple interest, but for further interest periods the amount of compound interest becomes increasingly greater than the amount of simple interest.

The basic procedure for computing compound interest and the effect of compounding is illustrated in Table 9.1. The table also provides a comparison of compound interest and simple interest for an original principal of $10 000.00 invested at 10% per annum for six years.

TABLE 9.1   **Compound Interest Versus Simple Interest for a Principal of $10 000.00 Invested at 10% per Annum for 6 Years**

Year		At Compound Interest		At Simple Interest	
		Interest Computation	Amount	Interest Computation	Amount
	Original Principal		10 000.00		10 000.00
1	Add Interest	(0.10)(10 000.00)	1 000.00	(0.10)(10 000.00)	1 000.00
	Amount End Year 1		11 000.00		11 000.00
2	Add Interest	(0.10)(11 000.00)	1 100.00	(0.10)(10 000.00)	1 000.00
	Amount End Year 2		12 100.00		12 000.00
3	Add Interest	(0.10)(12 100.00)	1 210.00	(0.10)(10 000.00)	1 000.00
	Amount End Year 3		13 310.00		13 000.00
4	Add Interest	(0.10)(13 310.00)	1 331.00	(0.10)(10 000.00)	1 000.00
	Amount End Year 4		14 641.00		14 000.00
5	Add Interest	(0.10)(14 641.00)	1 464.10	(0.10)(10 000.00)	1 000.00
	Amount End Year 5		16 105.10		15 000.00
6	Add Interest	(0.10)(16 105.10)	1 610.51	(0.10)(10 000.00)	1 000.00
	Amount End Year 6		17 715.61		16 000.00

The method of computation used in Table 9.1 represents the step-by-step approach used in maintaining a savings account record. It is sometimes called the *bankbook method* of computing compound interest. Note that the amount of interest is determined for each interest period based on the previous balance and is then added to that balance.

Note the following about the end results after six years.

	At compound interest	At simple interest
Amount after six years	$17 715.61	$16 000.00
Less original principal	10 000.00	10 000.00
Amount of interest	$ 7 715.61	$ 6 000.00

In this case, the compound interest exceeds the simple interest by $1715.61. This difference represents the amount of interest earned by interest added to the principal at the end of each compounding period.

B. Computer application–Accumulation of principal using a spreadsheet

Table 9.1 shows the accumulation of $10 000.00 principal and compound interest at 10% per annum for six years. Spreadsheet programs like EXCEL or Lotus can be used to create the compound interest data in Table 9.1. The advantage of a spreadsheet is that once these data are created in the spreadsheet, you can change the principal, interest rate, or number of years of accumulation and see immediately the effects on the final balance, without inputting all the formulae again.

The procedures that follow are general instructions for creating the compound interest data in Table 9.1. The formulae in the spreadsheet diagram were created using EXCEL. Modify the procedures if your spreadsheet program requires different instructions.

STEP I　To create the compound interest data from Figure 9.1 in a spreadsheet, open a new spreadsheet file. Enter the labels, formulae, and numbers shown in the diagram below. To display the labels in row 1, you can widen the columns or shorten the labels. (In EXCEL, you can widen columns by going to the Format menu, choosing Column, then choosing Width. Type numbers until you get the column width you want. You can also widen columns by placing the cursor between columns until the cursor changes to a double-pointed arrow. Drag the side of the column until you get the column width you want.)

Workbook 1

	A	B	C	D	E
1	Year	Amount, beginning of year	Interest	Amount, end of year	0.10
2	1	10000	= B2*E1	= B2+C2	
3	2	= D2	= B3*E1	= B3+C3	
4	3	= D3	= B4*E1	= B4+C4	
5	4	= D4	= B5*E1	= B5+C5	
6	5	= D5	= B6*E1	= B6+C6	
7	6	= D6	= B7*E1	= B7+C7	

To reduce inputting time and avoid inputting errors, copy as many formulae and numbers as possible within the spreadsheet. Since the interest rate is used repeatedly, set up the interest rate in a special cell (such as cell E1). This will eliminate the need to change the formulae in column C. Copy the formula in cell B3 into the four cells below it (cells B4 to B7). Copy the formulae in cells C2 and D2 into the five cells below them. (To copy and paste formulae and numbers in EXCEL, click with the mouse on the cell you want to copy. Go to the Edit menu and choose Copy. Then highlight the cells you want to copy into. Go to the Edit menu and choose Paste. You can also copy formulae into the cells below a particular cell. Highlight the particular cell and all the cells below it that you want to fill. Go to the Edit menu, choose Fill, then choose Down.)

STEP 2   To make the spreadsheet easier to read, format the numbers to two decimal places. (In EXCEL, change the format by highlighting cells B2 to D7. Go to the Format menu, choose Cells, then choose **0.00** from the Number section.)

When you have finished your spreadsheet, you should see interest of $1610.51 in cell C7 and an amount of $17 715.61 in cell D7. Make sure that the interest amounts in column C of the spreadsheet match the compound interest computations in Table 9.1.

Now that you have created the spreadsheet, it is easy to make changes to it and see the effects of the changes. For example, you can change the principal from $10 000.00 to $20 000.00 by typing **20 000** in cell B2. (If you do this, you should see $35 431.22 in cell D7, representing the compounded amount of $20 000.00 at 10% p.a. after six years.) You can then change the rate of compound interest from 10% to 12% by entering 0.12 in cell E1. (If you do this, you should see $39 476.45 in cell D7, representing the new compounded amount of $20 000.00 at 12% p.a. after six years.) You can also then change the number of interest periods from six years to ten years. First, type the numbers **7** to **10** in cells A8 to A11. Then copy the formulae from row 7 into rows 8 to 11. (If you do this, you should see $62 116.96 in cell D11, representing the new compounded amount of $20 000.00 at 12% p.a. after ten years.)

C. The future value formula for compound interest

While the bankbook method is useful in maintaining a savings account record, it is impractical for computational purposes. As in the case of simple interest, the **future value** or **maturity value** of a loan or investment can be found by using the future value formula.

For simple interest, the future value formula is S = P(1 + rt), Formula 7.3A.

For compound interest, the formula for the **future value** is

$$S = P(1 + i)^n$$ ———————— **Formula 9.1A**

S = the future or maturity value;
P = the original principal;
i = the periodic rate of interest;
n = the number of compounding periods for the term of the loan or investment.

The results of Table 9.1 could have been obtained by using the two future value formulae.

For simple interest: $P = 10\,000.00$; $\quad r = 0.10$; $\quad t = 6$

$$
\begin{aligned}
S = P(1 + rt) &= 10\,000.00[1 + (0.10)(6)] \\
&= 10\,000.00(1 + 0.60) \\
&= 10\,000.00(1.60) \\
&= \$16\,000.00
\end{aligned}
$$

For compound interest: $P = 10\,000.00$; $\quad i = 0.10$; $\quad n = 6$

$$
\begin{aligned}
S = P(1 + i)^n &= 10\,000.00(1 + 0.10)^6 \\
&= 10\,000.00(1.10)^6 \\
&= 10\,000.00(1.10)(1.10)(1.10)(1.10)(1.10)(1.10) \\
&= 10\,000.00(1.771561) \\
&= \$17\,715.61
\end{aligned}
$$

When using the compound interest formula, determining the factor $(1 + i)^n$ is the main computational problem. The value of this factor, called the **compounding factor** or **accumulation factor**, depends on the values of i and n.

D. Determining the periodic rate of interest

The value of i, the periodic rate of interest, is determined from the stated rate of interest to be used in the compounding situation. The stated rate is called the **nominal rate of interest**. Since the nominal rate of interest is usually stated as an annual rate, the value of i depends on the **compounding** (or **conversion**) **frequency** per year. The value of i is obtained by dividing the nominal annual rate by the number of **compounding** (or **conversion**) **periods** per year.

$$
\text{PERIODIC RATE OF INTEREST, } i = \frac{\text{NOMINAL (ANNUAL) RATE}}{\substack{\text{NUMBER OF COMPOUNDING} \\ \text{(CONVERSION) PERIODS PER YEAR}}}
$$

The compounding (conversion) periods commonly used in business and finance cover a number of months, usually an exact divisor of twelve, and are listed in Table 9.2.

TABLE 9.2   Commonly Used Compounding Frequencies and Conversion Periods

Compounding (Conversion) Frequency	Length of Compounding (Conversion) Period	Number of Compounding (Conversion) Periods per Year
Annual	12 months (1 year)	1
Semi-annual	6 months	2
Quarterly	3 months	4
Monthly	1 month	12

The relationship between the periodic rate of interest and the nominal annual rate of interest can be stated in the form of a formula.

$$i = \frac{j}{m}$$ ——————————————————— **Formula 9.2**

where i = periodic rate of interest
j = nominal annual rate of interest
m = number of compounding (conversion) periods per year

EXAMPLE 9.1A Determine the periodic rate of interest i for

(i) 9% p.a. compounded annually;

(ii) 7% p.a. compounded semi-annually;

(iii) 12% p.a. compounded quarterly;

(iv) 10.5% p.a. compounded monthly.

Solution

	(i)	(ii)	(iii)	(iv)
The nominal annual rate j	9%	7%	12%	10.5%
The compounding (conversion) frequency	annual	semi-annual	quarterly	monthly
The length of the compounding (conversion) period	12 months	6 months	3 months	1 month
The number of compounding (conversion) periods per year m	1	2	4	12
The periodic rate of interest $i = \dfrac{j}{m}$	$\dfrac{9\%}{1}$	$\dfrac{7\%}{2}$	$\dfrac{12\%}{4}$	$\dfrac{10.5\%}{12}$
	= 9.0%	= 3.5%	= 3.0%	= 0.875%

E. Determining the number of compounding (conversion) periods in the term of an investment or loan

To find the number of compounding (conversion) periods in the term of an investment or a loan, multiply the number of years in the term by the number of compounding periods per year.

EXAMPLE 9.1B Determine the number of compounding periods when

(i) compounding annually for 14 years;

(ii) compounding semi-annually for 15 years;

(iii) compounding quarterly for 12.5 years;

(iv) compounding monthly for 10.75 years;

(v) compounding quarterly for 30 months;

(vi) compounding semi-annually for 42 months.

Solution

	Term (in years)	Compounding Frequency	Number of Compounding Periods per Year, m	Number of Compounding Periods in Term, n
(i)	14	annual	1	$14(1) = 14$
(ii)	15	semi-annual	2	$15(2) = 30$
(iii)	12.5	quarterly	4	$12.5(4) = 50$
(iv)	10.75	monthly	12	$10.75(12) = 129$
(v)	$\frac{30}{12} = 2.5$	quarterly	4	$2.5(4) = 10$
(vi)	$\frac{42}{12} = 3.5$	semi-annual	2	$3.5(2) = 7$

F. Setting up the compounding factor $(1 + i)^n$

The *compounding (accumulation) factor* $(1 + i)^n$ can be set up by first determining i and n and then substituting i and n in the general form of the factor, $(1 + i)^n$.

EXAMPLE 9.1C　Set up the compounding factor $(1 + i)^n$ for

(i) 9% p.a. compounded annually for 14 years;

(ii) 7% p.a. compounded semi-annually for 15 years;

(iii) 12% p.a. compounded quarterly for 12.5 years;

(iv) 10.5% p.a. compounded monthly for 10.75 years;

(v) 8% p.a. compounded quarterly for 30 months;

(vi) 9.5% p.a. compounded semi-annually for 42 months.

Solution

	i	m	n	$(1 + i)^n$
(i)	$9\% = 0.09$	1	$14(1) = 14$	$(1 + 0.09)^{14} = 1.09^{14}$
(ii)	$3.5\% = 0.035$	2	$15(2) = 30$	$(1 + 0.035)^{30} = 1.035^{30}$
(iii)	$3.0\% = 0.03$	4	$12.5(4) = 50$	$(1 + 0.03)^{50} = 1.03^{50}$
(iv)	$0.875\% = 0.00875$	12	$10.75(12) = 129$	$(1 + 0.00875)^{129} = 1.00875^{129}$
(v)	$2\% = 0.02$	4	$2.5(4) = 10$	$(1 + 0.02)^{10} = 1.02^{10}$
(vi)	$4.75\% = 0.0475$	2	$3.5(2) = 7$	$(1 + 0.0475)^7 = 1.0475^7$

G. Computing the numerical value of the compounding factor $(1 + i)^n$

The numerical value of the compounding factor can now be computed using an electronic calculator. For calculators equipped with the exponential function feature Y^x , the numerical value of the compounding factor can be computed directly.

STEP 1   Enter the numerical value of $(1 + i)$ in the keyboard.

STEP 2   Press the function key Y^x .

STEP 3   Enter the numerical value of n in the keyboard.

STEP 4   Press $=$.

STEP 5   Read the answer in the display.

The numerical value of the compounding factors in Example 9.1C are obtained as follows.

	(i)	(ii)	(iii)	(iv)	(v)	(vi)
Step 1 Enter	1.09	1.035	1.03	1.00875	1.02	1.0475
Step 2 Press	Y^x	Y^x	Y^x	Y^x	Y^x	Y^x
Step 3 Enter	14	30	50	129	10	7
Step 4 Press	$=$	$=$	$=$	$=$	$=$	$=$
Step 5 Read	3.341727	2.8067937	4.383906	3.0766469	1.2189944	1.3838156

Note: Do not be concerned if your calculator shows a difference in the last decimal. There is no error. It reflects the precision of the calculator.

With the increasing availability of inexpensive electronic calculators, the two traditional methods of determining the compounding factor $(1 + i)^n$ are rapidly falling into disuse. The use of logarithms for this purpose has virtually disappeared and the use of tables is diminishing. Neither method is used in this text.

Exercise 9.1

A. Determine m, i, and n for each of the following.

1. 12% compounded annually for 5 years

2. 7.4% compounded semi-annually for 8 years

3. 5.5% compounded quarterly for 9 years

4. 7% compounded monthly for 4 years

5. 11.5% compounded semi-annually for 13.5 years

6. 11.5% compounded quarterly for five and three-quarter years

7. 8% compounded monthly for 12.5 years

8. 10.75% compounded quarterly for three years, nine months

9. 12.25% compounded semi-annually for 54 months

10. 8.1% compounded monthly for 15.5 years

DID YOU KNOW?

A loonie invested for 100 years at 2% p.a. compounded annually accumulates to about $7.24. If the 2% p.a. is compounded daily, the result is about $7.39.

A loonie invested for 100 years at 10% p.a. compounded annually accumulates to about $13 780.61. If the 10% p.a. is compounded daily, the result is about $21 996.26.

A loonie invested for 100 years at 20% p.a. compounded annually accumulates to about $82 817 974.00. If the 20% p.a. is compounded daily, the result is about $482 510 000.00.

The rate of compound interest and the compounding frequency make all the difference!

B. Set up and compute the compounding factor $(1 + i)^n$ for each of the questions in part A.

C. Answer each of the following questions.

1. For a sum of money invested at 10% compounded quarterly for 12 years, state
   (a) the number of compounding periods;
   (b) the periodic rate of interest;
   (c) the compounding factor $(1 + i)^n$;
   (d) the numerical value of the compounding factor.

2. For each of the following periodic rates of interest, determine the nominal annual compounding rate.
   (a) $i = 2\%$; compounding is quarterly
   (b) $i = 0.75\%$; compounding is monthly
   (c) $i = 5.5\%$; compounding is semi-annual
   (d) $i = 9.75\%$; compounding is annual

9.2   USING THE FORMULA FOR THE FUTURE VALUE OF A COMPOUND AMOUNT $S = P(1 + i)^n$

A. Finding the future value (maturity value) of an investment

EXAMPLE 9.2A   Find the amount to which $6000.00 will grow if invested at 10% per annum compounded quarterly for 5 years.

Solution   The original principal P = 6000.00;
the nominal annual rate $j = 10\%$;
the number of compounding periods per year $m = 4$;
the quarterly rate of interest $i = \dfrac{10\%}{4} = 2.5\% = 0.025$;
the number of compounding periods (quarters) $n = (5)(4) = 20$.

$S = P(1 + i)^n$ ———————————————— using Formula 9.1A

$= 6000.00(1 + 0.025)^{20}$ ———————— substituting for P, i, n

$= 6000.00(1.025)^{20}$ ———————————— exponential form of factor

$= 6000.00(1.6386164)$ ——————— using a calculator

$= \$9831.70$

EXAMPLE 9.2B

What is the future value after 78 months of $2500 invested at 11.25% p.a. compounded semi-annually?

Solution

The original principal P = 2500.00;

the nominal annual rate $j = 11.25$;

the number of compounding periods per year $m = 2$;

the semi-annual rate of interest $i = \dfrac{11.25\%}{2} = 5.625\% = 0.05625$;

the number of compounding periods (each period is six months)

$n = \left(\dfrac{78}{12}\right)(2) = (6.5)(2) = 13.$

$S = P(1 + i)^n$

$= 2500.00(1 + 0.05625)^{13}$

$= 2500.00(1.05625)^{13}$

$= 2500.00(2.0368891)$

$= \$5092.22$

EXAMPLE 9.2C

Accumulate a deposit of $1750.00 made into a Registered Retirement Savings Plan from March 1, 1982, to December 1, 2000, at 11.5% p.a. compounded quarterly.

Solution

The original principal P = 1750.00; $j = 11.5\%$; $m = 4$;

the quarterly rate of interest $i = \dfrac{11.5\%}{4} = 2.875\% = 0.02875$;

the time period from March 1, 1982, to December 1, 2000, contains 18 years and 9 months, or 18.75 years: $n = (18.75)(4) = 75.$

$S = P(1 + i)^n$

$= 1750.00(1 + 0.02875)^{75}$

$= 1750.00(1.02875)^{75}$

$= 1750.00(8.3798958)$

$= \$14\,664.82$

B. Using preprogrammed financial calculators

Compound interest calculations, which can become complex, are performed frequently and repeatedly. Doing the calculations algebraically can be time consuming, labourious, and subject to mechanical errors. Preprogrammed financial calculators are now available at reasonable cost. They save time and, assuming there are no input errors, eliminate mechanical errors.

Different models of financial calculators may vary slightly in their operation and labelling of the function keys. Refer to your instruction booklet for your particular model.

Five function keys correspond to the five variables used in compound interest calculations. They are shown in Table 9.3.

TABLE 9.3 **Financial Calculator Function Keys that Correspond to Variables Used in Compound Interest Calculations**

Variable	Algebraic Symbol	Function Key
The number of compounding periods	n	N
The periodic rate of interest	i	%i
The periodic annuity payment	R	PMT
The present value or principal	P	PV
The future value or maturity value	S	FV

The function keys are used to first enter the numerical values of the known variables and then to execute the calculation and to retrieve the answer at the same time.

Most preprogrammed financial calculators operate in more than one mode. To use the preprogrammed feature, most calculators must be in the financial mode, identified by the letters FIN appearing in the display.

Follow the steps below to compute the future value of a sum of money using the formula $S = P(1 + i)^n$ and a financial calculator.

STEP 1   Set the calculator to the financial mode. FIN must appear in the display.

STEP 2   Always enter zero followed by the function key labelled $\boxed{PMT}$. We do this because the periodic payment R is not one of the variables we need for compound interest calculations.

STEP 3   Enter the numerical values of the known variables n, i, and P, each followed by the function keys labelled $\boxed{N}$, $\boxed{\%i}$, and $\boxed{PV}$, respectively.

STEP 4   Press the compute key $\boxed{CPT}$ followed by the function key $\boxed{FV}$ to compute the answer and display the answer. (Note that some models of financial calculators, such as the Texas Instruments BA-II, do not have a $\boxed{CPT}$. Press the key labelled $\boxed{2nd}$ instead.)

To solve Example 9.2A in which P = 6000, i = 2.5%, and n = 20, use the following procedure.

Display

Key in	Press	shows	
0	PMT	0	—— this step ensures that the calculator performs a compound interest calculation
6000	PV	6000	—— this enters the present value (principal) P
2.5	%i	2.5	—— this enters the interest rate i
20	N	20	—— this enters the number of compounding periods n
	CPT FV	9831.6986	—— this retrieves and displays the unknown future value S

Note: If your calculator does not have a CPT key, press 2nd FV .
The future value is $9831.70.

C. Applications involving changes in interest rate or principal

EXAMPLE 9.2D A deposit of $2000.00 earns interest at 6% p.a. compounded monthly for four years. At that time, the interest rate changes to 7% p.a. compounded quarterly. What is the value of the deposit three years after the change in the rate of interest?

Solution The data given can be represented on a time diagram as shown in Figure 9.1.

FIGURE 9.1 Graphic Representation of Data

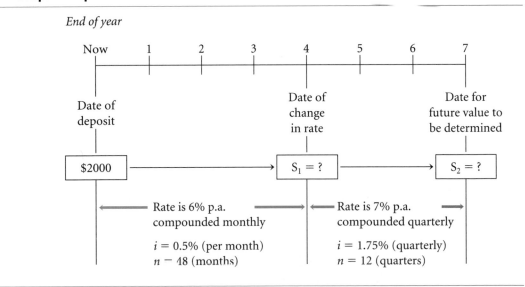

STEP 1   Determine the accumulated value of the original deposit at the time the interest rate changes, that is, after 4 years.

P = 2000.00; $i = 0.5\% = 0.005$; $n = 48$

$S_1 = 2000.00(1 + 0.005)^{48} = 2000.00(1.2704892) = \$2540.98$

STEP 2   Use the accumulated value after four years as new principal and calculate its accumulated value three years later using the new rate of interest.

P = 2540.98; $i = 1.75\% = 0.0175$; $n = 12$

$S_2 = 2540.98(1 + 0.0175)^{12} = 2540.98(1.2314393) = \$3129.06$

Solution by preprogrammed calculator

STEP 1

Key in	Press	Display shows
0	PMT	0
2000	PV	2000
0.5	%i	0.5
48	N	48
	CPT	←———— (if no CPT , press 2nd)
	FV	2540.9783 ———— answer to Step 1 (S_1 = 2540.9783)

Do *not* clear your display. Proceed to Step 2.

STEP 2

Key in	Press	Display shows
	PV	2540.9783 ———— this step enters the new principal
1.75	%i	1.75
12	N	12
	CPT	
	FV	3129.0606 ———— final answer (S_2 = $3129.06)

EXAMPLE 9.2E   A debt of $500 accumulates interest at 12% p.a. compounded quarterly from April 1, 1998, to July 1, 1999, and 9% p.a. compounded monthly thereafter. Determine the accumulated value of the debt on December 1, 2000.

Solution

STEP 1   Determine the accumulated value of the debt on July 1, 1999.

P = 500.00; $i = 3\% = 0.03$;

the period April 1, 1998, to July 1, 1999, contains 15 months: $n = 5$

$S_1 = 500.00(1.03)^5 = 500.00(1.1592741) = \$579.64$

STEP 2   Use the result of Step 1 as new principal and find its accumulated value on December 1, 2000.

$P = 579.64$; $i = 0.75\% = 0.0075$;

the period July 1, 1999, to December 1, 2000, contains 17 months: $n = 17$

$S_2 = 579.64(1.0075)^{17} = 579.64(1.1354446) = \$658.15$

Programmed solution

STEP 1

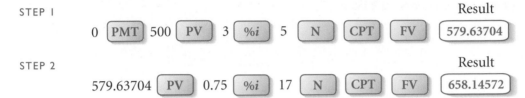

	Result

0 [PMT] 500 [PV] 3 [%i] 5 [N] [CPT] [FV] [579.63704]

STEP 2

	Result

579.63704 [PV] 0.75 [%i] 17 [N] [CPT] [FV] [658.14572]

EXAMPLE 9.2F   Jay opened a Registered Retirement Savings Plan account with his credit union on February 1, 1994, with a deposit of \$2000.00. He added \$1900.00 on February 1, 1995, and another \$1700.00 on February 1, 1998. What will his account amount to on August 1, 2004, if the plan earns a fixed rate of interest of 11% p.a. compounded semi-annually?

Solution

FIGURE 9.2   Graphic Representation of Data

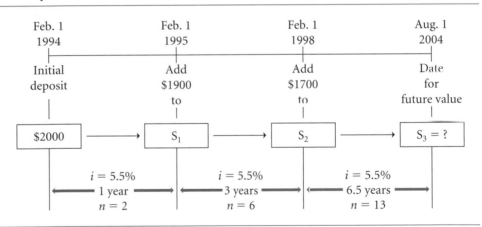

STEP 1   Determine the future value, S_1, of the initial deposit on February 1, 1995.

$P = 2000.00$; $i = 5.5\% = 0.055$;

the period February 1, 1994, to February 1, 1995, contains 1 year: $n = 2$

$S_1 = 2000.00(1.055)^2 = 2000.00(1.113025) = \$2226.05$

STEP 2   Add the deposit of \$1900.00 to the amount of \$2226.05 to obtain the new principal as of February 1, 1995, and determine its future value, S_2, on February 1, 1998.

$P = 2226.05 + 1900.00 = 4126.05$; $i = 0.055$;

the period February 1, 1995, to February 1, 1998, contains 3 years: $n = 6$

$S_2 = 4126.05(1.055)^6 = 4126.05(1.3788428) = \$5689.17$

STEP 3   Add the deposit of $1700.00 to the amount of $5689.17 to obtain the new principal as of February 1, 1998, and determine its future value, S_3, on August 1, 2004.

$P = 5689.17 + 1700.00 = 7389.17; \quad i = 0.055;$

the period February 1, 1998, to August 1, 2004, contains 6.5 years: $n = 13$

$S_3 = 7389.17(1.055)^{13} = 7389.17(2.0057739) = \$14\ 821.00$

Programmed solution

STEP 1

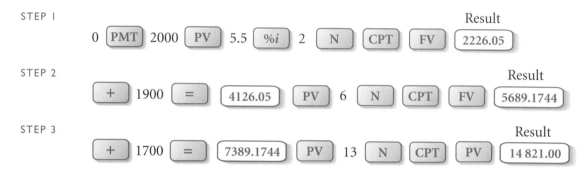

$$0 \boxed{\text{PMT}} \ 2000 \boxed{\text{PV}} \ 5.5 \boxed{\%i} \ 2 \boxed{\text{N}} \boxed{\text{CPT}} \boxed{\text{FV}} \quad \text{Result} \quad \boxed{2226.05}$$

STEP 2

$$\boxed{+} \ 1900 \boxed{=} \boxed{4126.05} \boxed{\text{PV}} \ 6 \boxed{\text{N}} \boxed{\text{CPT}} \boxed{\text{FV}} \quad \text{Result} \quad \boxed{5689.1744}$$

STEP 3

$$\boxed{+} \ 1700 \boxed{=} \boxed{7389.1744} \boxed{\text{PV}} \ 13 \boxed{\text{N}} \boxed{\text{CPT}} \boxed{\text{PV}} \quad \text{Result} \quad \boxed{14\ 821.00}$$

Note: There is no need to key in the rate in Steps 2 and 3—it is already programmed from Step 1.

EXAMPLE 9.2G   A demand loan of $10 000.00 is repaid by payments of $5000.00 in one year, $6000.00 in four years, and a final payment in six years. Interest on the loan is 10% p.a. compounded quarterly during the first year, 8% p.a. compounded semi-annually for the next three years, and 7.5% p.a. compounded annually for the remaining years. Determine the final payment.

Solution

FIGURE 9.3   **Graphic Representation of Data**

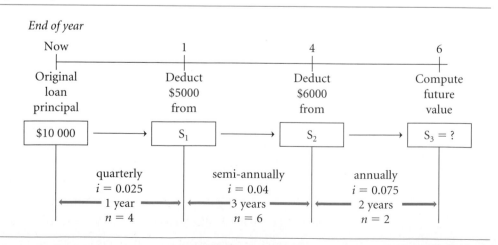

STEP 1   Determine the accumulated value of the debt at the time of the first payment.

$P = 10\,000.00;\quad i = 2.5\% = 0.025;\quad n = 4$

$S_1 = 10\,000.00(1.025)^4 = 10\,000.00(1.10381289) = \$11\,038.13$

STEP 2   Subtract the payment of $5000.00 from the accumulated value of $11 038.13 to obtain the debt balance. Now determine its accumulated value at the time of the second payment three years later.

$P = 11\,038.13 - 5000.00 = 6038.13;\quad i = 4\% = 0.04;\quad n = 6$

$S_2 = 6038.13(1.04)^6 = 6038.13(1.265319) = \$7640.16$

STEP 3   Subtract the payment of $6000.00 from the accumulated value of $7640.16 to obtain the debt balance. Now determine its accumulated value two years later.

$P = 7640.16 - 6000.00 = 1640.16;\quad i = 7.5\% = 0.075;\quad n = 2$

$S_3 = 1640.16(1.075)^2 = 1640.16(1.155625) = \$1895.41$

The final payment after six years is $1895.41.

Programmed solution

STEP 1

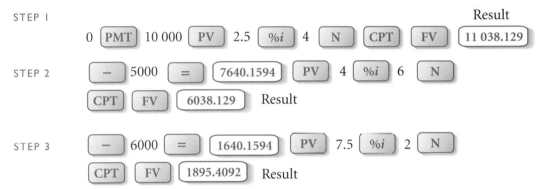

STEP 2

STEP 3

Exercise 9.2

A. Find the future value for each of the ten investments in the table below.

	Principal	Nominal Rate	Frequency of Conversion	Time
1.	$ 400.00	7.5%	annually	8 years
2.	1000.00	12.5%	semi-annually	12 years
3.	1250.00	6.5%	quarterly	9 years
4.	500.00	12%	monthly	3 years
5.	1700.00	8%	quarterly	14.75 years
6.	840.00	5.5%	semi-annually	8.5 years
7.	2500.00	8%	monthly	12.25 years
8.	150.00	10.8%	quarterly	27 months
9.	480.00	9.4%	semi-annually	42 months
10.	1400.00	4.8%	monthly	18.75 years

B. Answer each of the following questions.

1. What is the maturity value of a five-year term deposit of $5000.00 at 12.5% compounded semi-annually? How much interest did the deposit earn?

2. How much will a registered retirement savings deposit of $1500.00 be worth in 15 years at 8% compounded quarterly? How much of the amount is interest?

3. You made a registered retirement savings plan deposit of $1000.00 on December 1, 1992, at a fixed rate of 11% compounded monthly. If you withdraw the deposit on August 1, 1999, how much will you receive?

4. Roy's parents made a trust deposit of $500.00 on October 31, 1982, to be withdrawn on Roy's eighteenth birthday on July 31, 2000. To what will the deposit amount on that date at 13% compounded quarterly?

5. What is the accumulated value of $100.00 invested for eight years at 9% p.a. compounded
   (a) annually?   (b) semi-annually?   (c) quarterly?   (d) monthly?

6. To what future value will a principal of $500.00 amount in five years at 7.5% p.a. compounded
   (a) annually?   (b) semi-annually?   (c) quarterly?   (d) monthly?

7. What is the future value of and the amount of compound interest for $100.00 invested at 8% compounded quarterly for
   (a) five years?   (b) 10 years?   (c) 20 years?

8. Find the future value of and the compound interest on $500.00 invested at 12% compounded monthly for
   (a) 3.5 years;   (b) 6 years;   (c) 11.5 years.

9. The Canadian consumer price index was approximately 120 at the beginning of 1990. If inflation continues at an average annual rate of 3%, what will the index be at the beginning of 2000?

10. Peel Credit Union expects an average annual growth rate of 20% for the next five years. If the assets of the credit union currently amount to $2.5 million, what will the forecasted assets be in five years?

11. A local bank offers $5000.00 five-year certificates at 6.75% compounded semi-annually. Your credit union makes the same type of deposit available at 6.5% compounded monthly.
    (a) Which investment gives more interest over the five years?
    (b) What is the difference in the amount of interest?

12. The Continental Bank advertises capital savings at 7.25% compounded semi-annually while National Trust offers premium savings at 7% compounded monthly. Suppose you have $1000.00 to invest for two years.
    (a) Which deposit will earn more interest?
    (b) What is the difference in the amount of interest?

C. Answer each of the following questions.

1. A deposit of $2000.00 earns interest at 7% p.a. compounded quarterly. After two and a half years, the interest rate is changed to 6.75% compounded monthly. How much is the account worth after six years?

2. An investment of $2500.00 earns interest at 9% p.a. compounded monthly for three years. At that time the interest rate is changed to 9% compounded quarterly. How much will the accumulated value be one and a half years after the change?

3. A debt of $800.00 accumulates interest at 10% compounded semi-annually from February 1, 1996, to August 1, 1998, and 11% compounded quarterly thereafter. Determine the accumulated value of the debt on November 1, 2001.

4. Accumulate $1300.00 at 8.5% p.a. compounded monthly from March 1, 1995, to July 1, 1997, and thereafter at 8% p.a. compounded quarterly. What is the amount on April 1, 2000?

5. Pat opened an RRSP deposit account on December 1, 1998, with a deposit of $1000.00. He added $1000.00 on July 1, 1999, and $1000.00 on November 1, 2000. How much is in his account on January 1, 2002, if the deposit earns 12% p.a. compounded monthly?

6. Terri started an RRSP on March 1, 1996, with a deposit of $2000.00. She added $1800.00 on December 1, 1998, and $1700.00 on September 1, 2000. What is the accumulated value of her account on December 1, 2003, if interest is 11.5% compounded quarterly?

7. A debt of $4000.00 is repaid by payments of $1500.00 in nine months, $2000.00 in 18 months, and a final payment in 27 months. If interest was 10% compounded quarterly, what was the amount of the final payment?

8. Sheridan Service has a line of credit loan with the Bank of Nova Scotia. The initial loan balance was $6000.00. Payments of $2000.00 and $3000.00 were made after four months and nine months respectively. At the end of one year, Sheridan Service borrowed an additional $4000.00. Six months later, the line of credit loan was converted into a collateral mortgage loan. What was the amount of the mortgage if the line of credit interest was 9% compounded monthly?

9. A demand loan of $3000.00 is repaid by payments of $1500.00 after two years, $1500.00 after four years, and a final payment after seven years. Interest is 9% compounded quarterly for the first year, 10% compounded semi-annually for the next three years, and 10% compounded monthly thereafter. What is the size of the final payment?

10. A variable rate demand loan showed an initial balance of $12 000.00, payments of $5000.00 after eighteen months, $4000.00 after thirty months, and a final payment after five years. Interest was 11% compounded semi-annually for the first two years and 12% compounded monthly for the remaining time. How much was the size of the final payment?

9.3 PRESENT VALUE AND COMPOUND DISCOUNT

A. The present value concept and related terms

EXAMPLE 9.3A

Find the principal that will amount in six years to $17 715.61 at 10% p.a. compounded annually.

Solution

The problem may be graphically represented as shown in Figure 9.4.

FIGURE 9.4   Graphic Representation of Data

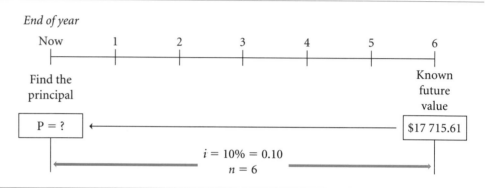

This problem is the inverse of the problem used to illustrate the meaning of compound interest. Instead of knowing the value of the principal and finding its future value, we know that the future value is $17 715.61. What we want to determine is the value of the principal.

To solve the problem, we use the future value formula $S = P(1 + i)^n$ and substitute the known values.

$$S = 17\,715.61; \quad i = 10\% = 0.10; \quad n = 6$$

$17\,715.61 = P(1.10)^6$ ————————— by substituting in $S = P(1 + i)^n$
$17\,715.61 = P(1.771561)$ ————————— computing $(1.10)^6$

$$P = \frac{17\,715.61}{1.771561}$$ ————————— solve for P by dividing both sides by 1.771561

$$P = \$10\,000.00$$

The principal that will grow to $17 715.61 in six years at 10% p.a. compounded annually is $10 000.00.

This principal is called the **present value** or **discounted value** or **proceeds** of the known future amount.

The difference between the known future amount of $17 715.61 and the computed present value (principal) of $10 000.00 is the **compound discount** and represents the compound interest accumulating on the computed present value.

The process of computing the present value or discounted value or proceeds is called **discounting**.

B. The present value formula

The present value of an amount at a given time at compound interest is defined as the principal that will grow to the given amount if compounded at a given periodic rate of interest over a given number of conversion periods.

Since the problem of finding the present value is equivalent to finding the principal when the future value, the periodic rate of interest, and the number of conversion periods are given, the formula for the future value formula, $S = P(1 + i)^n$, applies.

However, because the problem of finding the present value of an amount is frequently encountered in financial analysis, it is useful to solve the future value formula for P to obtain the present value formula.

$$S = P(1 + i)^n$$ ————————— start with the future value formula, Formula 9.1A

$$\frac{S}{(1 + i)^n} = \frac{P(1 + i)^n}{(1 + i)^n}$$ ————————— divide both sides by the compounding factor $(1 + i)^n$

$$\frac{S}{(1 + i)^n} = P$$ ————————— reduce the fraction $\frac{(1 + i)^n}{(1 + i)^n}$ to 1

The present value formula for compound interest is:

$$\boxed{P = \frac{S}{(1 + i)^n}}$$ ————————— **Formula 9.1B**

EXAMPLE 9.3B   Find the present value of $11 593.11 due in nine years at 12% p.a. compounded quarterly.

Solution $S = 11\ 593.11; \quad i = 3\% = 0.03; \quad n = 36$

$$P = \frac{S}{(1 + i)^n}$$ ————————— using the present value formula

$$= \frac{11\ 593.11}{(1 + 0.03)^{36}}$$ ————————— by substitution

$$= \frac{11\ 593.11}{2.8982783}$$

$$= \$4000.00$$

Note: The division of 11 593.11 by 2.8982783, like any division, may be changed to a multiplication by using the reciprocal of the divisor.

$$\frac{11\ 593.11}{2.8982783}$$ ————————— the division to be changed into a multiplication

$$= 11\ 593.11\left(\frac{1}{2.8982783}\right)$$ ————————— the reciprocal of the divisor 2.8982783 is found by dividing 1 by 2.8982783

$$= 11\ 593.11(0.3450324)$$ ————————— computed value of the reciprocal

$$= \$4000.00$$

For calculators equipped with the reciprocal function key $\boxed{\frac{1}{x}}$, converting the division into a multiplication is easily accomplished by first computing the compounding factor and then using the $\boxed{\frac{1}{x}}$ key to obtain the reciprocal.

EXAMPLE 9.3C

What principal will amount to $5000.00 seven years from today if interest is 9% p.a. compounded monthly?

Solution

Finding the principal that amounts to a future sum of money is equivalent to finding the present value.

$$S = 5000.00; \quad i = 0.75\% = 0.0075; \quad n = 84$$

$$P = \frac{5000.00}{(1.0075)^{84}} \quad\text{------------- using Formula 9.1B}$$

$$= \frac{5000.00}{1.8732019} \quad\text{------------- computing the factor } (1.0075)^{84}$$

$$= 5000.00(0.5338453) \quad\text{------------- using the reciprocal function key}$$

$$= \$2669.23$$

Using the reciprocal of the divisor to change division into multiplication is reflected in the practice of stating the present value formula with a *negative* exponent.

$$\frac{1}{a^n} = a^{-n} \quad\text{------------- negative exponent rule}$$

$$\frac{1}{(1+i)^n} = (1+i)^{-n}$$

$$\frac{S}{(1+i)^n} = S(1+i)^{-n}$$

Formula 9.1B, the present value formula, can be restated in multiplication form using a negative exponent.

$$\boxed{P = S(1+i)^{-n}} \quad\text{------------- \textbf{Formula 9.1C}}$$

The factor $(1+i)^{-n}$ is called the **discount factor** and is the reciprocal of the compounding factor $(1+i)^n$.

C. Using preprogrammed financial calculators to find present value

As explained in Section 9.2B, preprogrammed calculators provide quick solutions to compound interest calculations. Three of the four variables are entered and the value of the fourth variable is retrieved.

To solve Example 9.3C, in which S = 5000, i = 0.75%, n = 84, and P is to be determined, use the following procedure.

	Press	*Display shows*	
0	PMT	0	—— this step ensures that the calculator performs a compound interest calculation
5000	FV	5000	—— this enters the future value amount S
0.75	%i	0.75	—— this enters the conversion rate i
84	N	84	—— this enters the number of compounding periods n
	CPT PV	2669.2264	—— this retrieves the unknown principal (present value) P

(If there is no CPT key, press 2nd PV .)

The principal is $2669.23.

Exercise 9.3

A. Find the present value of each of the following amounts.

	Amount	Nominal Rate	Frequency of Conversion	Time
1.	$1000.00	8%	quarterly	7 years
2.	1500.00	6.5%	semi-annually	10 years
3.	600.00	8%	monthly	6 years
4.	350.00	7.5%	annually	8 years
5.	1200.00	9%	monthly	12 years
6.	3000.00	12.25%	semi-annually	5 years, 6 months
7.	900.00	6.4%	quarterly	9 years, 3 months
8.	500.00	8.4%	monthly	15 years

B. Answer each of the following questions.

1. Find the present value and the compound discount of $1600.00 due four and a half years from now if money is worth 10.5% compounded semi-annually.

2. Find the present value and the compound discount of $2500.00 due in six years, three months, if interest is 6% compounded quarterly.

3. Find the principal that will amount to $1250.00 in five years at 10% p.a. compounded quarterly.

4. What sum of money will grow to $2000.00 in seven years at 9% compounded monthly?

5. A debt of $5000.00 is due November 1, 2004. What is the value of the obligation on February 1, 1998, if money is worth 7% compounded quarterly?

6. How much would you have to deposit in an account today to have $3000.00 in a five-year term deposit at maturity if interest is 7.75% compounded annually?

9.4 DISCOUNTING PROMISSORY NOTES AT COMPOUND INTEREST

A. Discounting long-term promissory notes

Long-term promissory notes (written for a term longer than one year) are usually subject to compound interest. As with short-term promissory notes, long-term promissory notes are negotiable and can be bought and sold (*discounted*) at any time before maturity.

The principles involved in discounting long-term promissory notes are similar to those used in discounting short-term promissory notes by the simple discount method except that no requirement exists to add three days of grace in determining the legal due date of a long-term promissory note.

The discounted value (or proceeds) of a long-term promissory note is the present value at the date of discount of the maturity value of the note. It is found using the present value formula $P = \dfrac{S}{(1 + i)^n}$ or $P = S(1 + i)^{-n}$.

For non-interest-bearing notes, the maturity value is the face value. However, for interest-bearing promissory notes, the maturity value must be determined first by using the future value formula $S = P(1 + i)^n$.

B. Discounting non-interest-bearing promissory notes

Since the face value of a non-interest-bearing note is also its maturity value, the proceeds of a non-interest-bearing note are the present value of its face value at the date of discount.

EXAMPLE 9.4A   Determine the proceeds of a non-interest-bearing note for $1500.00 discounted two and a quarter years before its due date at 9% p.a. compounded monthly.

Solution   The maturity value S = 1500.00;

the rate of discount $i = \left(\dfrac{9}{12}\right)\% = 0.75\% = 0.0075$;

the number of conversion periods $n = (2.25)(12) = 27$.

$$P = S(1 + i)^{-n} \qquad\qquad\qquad\qquad\text{using Formula 9.1C}$$
$$= 1500.00(1 + 0.0075)^{-27}$$
$$= 1500.00\left(\frac{1}{1.2235352}\right)$$
$$= 1500.00(0.8173038)$$
$$= \$1225.96$$

Programmed solution

0 `PMT` 1500 `FV` 0.75 `%i` 27 `N` `CPT` `PV` 1225.9557

C. Discounting interest-bearing promissory notes

The proceeds of an interest-bearing note are equal to the present value at the date of discount of the value of the note at maturity. Therefore, the maturity value of an interest-bearing promissory note must be determined before finding the discounted value.

EXAMPLE 9.4B

Determine the proceeds of a promissory note for $3600.00 with interest at 10% p.a. compounded quarterly, issued September 1, 1998, due on June 1, 2004, and discounted on December 1, 2000, at 12% p.a. compounded semi-annually.

Solution

STEP 1

Find the maturity value of the note using Formula 9.1A, $S = P(1 + i)^n$.

$P = 3600.00$; the interest rate $i = 2.5\% = 0.025$; the interest period, September 1, 1998, to June 1, 2004, contains 5 years and 9 months: $n = (5\tfrac{9}{12})(4) = 23$.

$$S = 3600.00(1 + 0.025)^{23}$$
$$= 3600.00(1.7646107)$$
$$= \$6352.60$$

STEP 2

Find the present value at the date of discount of the maturity value found in Step 1 using $P = S(1 + i)^{-n}$.

$S = 6352.60$; the rate of discount, $i = 6\% = 0.06$;

the discount period, December 1, 2000, to June 1, 2004, contains 3 years and 6 months: $n = (3\tfrac{6}{12})(2) = 7$.
$$P = 6352.60(1 + 0.06)^{-7}$$
$$= 6352.60(0.6650571)$$
$$= \$4224.84$$

The proceeds of the note on December 1, 2000, are $4224.84. The method and the data are represented graphically in Figure 9.5.

FIGURE 9.5 **Graphic Representation of Method and Data**

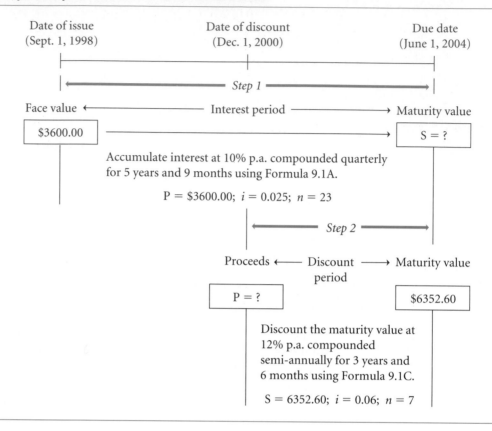

Programmed solution

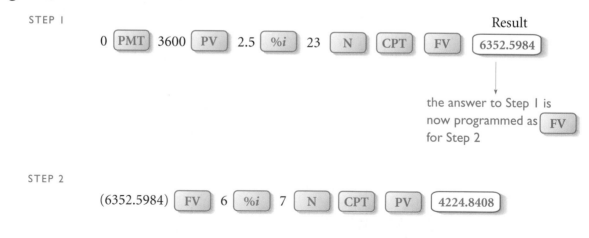

Exercise 9.4

A. Find the proceeds and the compound discount for each of the six long-term promissory notes shown in the table on the next page. Note that the first two are non-interest-bearing promissory notes.

	Face Value	Date of Issue	Term	Int. Rate	Frequency of Conversion	Date of Discount	Discount Rate	Frequency of Conversion
1.	$2000.00	1996-06-30	5 years	—	—	1998-12-31	12%	semi-annually
2.	700.00	1994-04-01	10 years	—	—	1999-07-01	10%	quarterly
3.	1500.00	1995-05-31	8 years	10.5%	annually	2000-05-31	11%	semi-annually
4.	4000.00	1997-09-30	4 years	11%	semi-annually	1999-03-31	9%	quarterly
5.	800.00	1996-02-01	7 yr., 9 mo.	12%	quarterly	2001-11-01	10%	monthly
6.	2200.00	1994-10-31	8.25 years	12%	monthly	1997-01-31	10%	quarterly

B. Find the proceeds of each of the following promissory notes.

1. A non-interest-bearing promissory note for $6000.00, discounted 54 months before its due date at 11% compounded quarterly.

2. A $4200.00, non-interest-bearing note due August 1, 2003, discounted on March 1, 1999, at 7.5% compounded monthly.

3. A promissory note with a maturity value of $1800.00 due on September 30, 2002, discounted at 8.5% compounded semi-annually on March 31, 1999.

4. A fifteen-year promissory note discounted after six years at 9% compounded quarterly has a maturity value of $7500.00.

5. A five-year promissory note for $3000.00 with interest at 8% compounded semi-annually, discounted 21 months before maturity at 9% compounded quarterly.

6. A $5000.00, seven-year note bearing interest at 8.0% compounded quarterly, discounted two and a half years after the date of issue at 6.0% compounded monthly.

7. A six-year, $900.00 note bearing interest at 10% compounded quarterly, issued June 1, 1994, discounted on December 1, 1999, to yield 12.5% compounded semi-annually.

8. A ten-year promissory note dated April 1, 1996, with a face value of $1300.00 bearing interest at 7% compounded semi-annually, discounted seven years later when money was worth 9% compounded quarterly.

BUSINESS MATH NEWS BOX

STARTING EARLY—THE POWER OF COMPOUND GROWTH

One of the most costly mistakes Canadians make with their Registered Retirement Savings Plans (RRSPs) is not starting them early enough. According to a recent Angus Reid survey, only about 22% of eligible Canadians make their first RRSP contribution between the ages of 25 and 29. Fully 40% don't make that first contribution until they're between 30 and 44.

The longer you wait, the more you miss out on one of the key benefits of your registered plan: the incredible power of long-term tax-deferred compound growth.

The more years you have to invest, and the higher your investment return, the more dramatic this growth potential will be (see table).

Watch Your Savings Grow

This table illustrates the effect of compound growth on a single investment of $1,000, assuming that you cash it in at age 60*. The higher the rate of return, and the longer you invest, the more powerful the effect.

Rate of return	Years Invested		
	20	25	30
6%	$3 207	$ 4 292	$ 5 743
8%	$4 661	$ 6 848	$10 063
10%	$6 727	$10 835	$17 449

*The effect of taxation is not taken into account in these examples.

QUESTIONS

1. What principal is used to calculate the figures in the table?

2. Suppose you were 25 years old when you made your first $1000 RRSP contribution. What would the value of your investment be when you reach age 60, given each of the following rates of return?
   (a) 6%   (b) 8%   (c) 10%

3. Compare the values of the investment you calculated in question 2 with the values of the investment made at age 30 given in the table. For each interest rate, what is the difference in the values of the investment at age 60?

4. Suppose you were 30 years old when you made your first $1000 RRSP contribution. Suppose your investment would earn 6% for the first ten years and 8% for the next twenty years. What would the value of your contribution be when you turned 60?

9.5 EQUIVALENT VALUES

A. Equations of value

As discussed in Chapter 7, sums of money have different values at different times. Because of their time value, sums of money coming due at different times are not directly comparable. To make such sums of money comparable, a specific time, the **comparison date** or **focal date**, must be chosen. Allowance must be made for interest from the due dates of the sums of money to the selected focal date; that is, the dated values of the sums of money must be determined.

When compounding, any time may be chosen as the focal date. The selection of the focal date does not affect the answers; it only determines which formula has to be used. For compound interest, equations of value can be set up using the future value formula $S = P(1 + i)^n$ or the present value formula $P = S(1 + i)^{-n}$.

As with simple interest, the appropriate formula depends on the position of the due dates relative to the focal date:

(a) If the due date falls *before* the focal date, use the *future value* formula (see Figure 9.6).

(b) If the due date falls *after* the focal date, use the *present value* formula (see Figure 9.7).

B. Finding the equivalent single payment

Equivalent values are the dated values of an original sum of money.

EXAMPLE 9.5A $4000.00 is payable three years from now. If money is worth 9% p.a. compounded semi-annually, determine the equivalent value

(i) seven years from now;   (ii) now.

Solution   (i) Using "seven years from now" as the focal date, the method and the data can be represented graphically as shown in Figure 9.6.

FIGURE 9.6   **Graphic Representation of Method and Data**

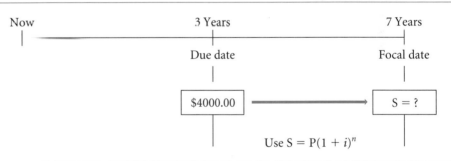

Since the due date falls *before* the focal date, use the future value formula.

$$P = 4000.00; \quad i = \frac{9\%}{2} = 0.045; \quad n = 4(2) = 8$$

$$S = 4000.00(1 + 0.045)^8 = 4000.00(1.4221006) = \$5688.40$$

The equivalent value of the $4000.00 seven years from now is $5688.40.

(ii) Using "now" as the focal date, the method and the data can be represented graphically as shown in Figure 9.7.

FIGURE 9.7 **Graphic Representation of Method and Data**

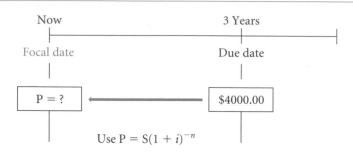

Since the due date falls *after* the focal date, use the present value formula.

$$S = 4000.00; \quad i = \frac{9\%}{2} = 0.045; \quad n = 3(2) = 6$$

$$P = 4000.00(1 + 0.045)^{-6} = 4000.00(0.7678957) = \$3071.58$$

The equivalent value of the $4000.00 now is $3071.58.

Programmed solution

(i) 0 | PMT | 4000 | PV | 4.5 | %i | 8 | N | CPT | FV | 5688.4025

(ii) 0 | PMT | 4000 | FV | 4.5 | %i | 6 | N | CPT | PV | 3071.583

EXAMPLE 9.5B Joanna plans to pay off a debt by payments of $1600.00 one year from now, $1800.00 eighteen months from now, and $2000.00 thirty months from now. Determine the single payment now that would settle the debt if money is worth 8% p.a. compounded quarterly.

Solution While any date may be selected as the focal date, a logical choice for the focal date is the time designated "now", since the single payment "now" is wanted. As is shown in Figure 9.8, the due dates of the three payments are *after* the focal date. Therefore, the present value formula $P = S(1 + i)^{-n}$ is appropriate for finding the equivalent values of the three payments.

The equivalents of the three payments at the selected focal date are

$$P_1 = 1600.00(1 + 0.02)^{-4} = 1600.00(0.9238454) = \$1478.15$$

$$P_2 = 1800.00(1 + 0.02)^{-6} = 1800.00(0.8879714) = \$1598.35$$

$$P_3 = 2000.00(1 + 0.02)^{-10} = 2000.00(0.8203483) = \$1640.70$$

The equivalent single payment to settle the debt now is $4717.20.

FIGURE 9.8   Graphic Representation of Method and Data

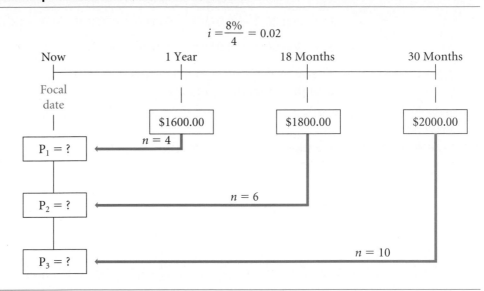

Programmed solution

P_1 0 [PMT] 1600 [FV] 2 [%i] 4 [N] [CPT] [PV] [1478.1527]

P_2 0 [PMT] 1800 [FV] 2 [%i] 6 [N] [CPT] [PV] [1598.3485]

P_3 0 [PMT] 2000 [FV] 2 [%i] 10 [N] [CPT] [PV] [1640.6966]

1478.1527 + 1598.3485 + 1640.6966 = 4717.1978 = 4717.20

EXAMPLE 9.5C

Debt payments of $400.00 due five months ago, $600.00 due today, and $800 due in nine months are to be combined into one payment due three months from today at 12% p.a. compounded monthly.

Solution

The logical choice for the focal date is "3 months from now," the date when the equivalent single payment is to be made.

As shown in Figure 9.9, the first two payments are due *before* the focal date; the future value formula $S = P(1 + i)^n$ should be used. However, the third payment is due *after* the focal date which means that, for it, the present value formula $P = S(1 + i)^{-n}$ applies.

The equivalent values (designated E_1, E_2, E_3) of the debt payments at the selected focal date are

$$E_1 = 400.00(1 + 0.01)^8 = 400.00(1.0828567) = \$ \; 433.14$$

$$E_2 = 600.00(1 + 0.01)^3 = 600.00(1.030301) = \$ \; 618.18$$

$$E_3 = 800.00(1 + 0.01)^{-6} = 800.00(0.9420452) = \underline{\$ \; 753.64}$$

The equivalent single payment to settle the debt three months from now is $\underline{\$1804.96}$

FIGURE 9.9 **Graphic Representation of Method and Data**

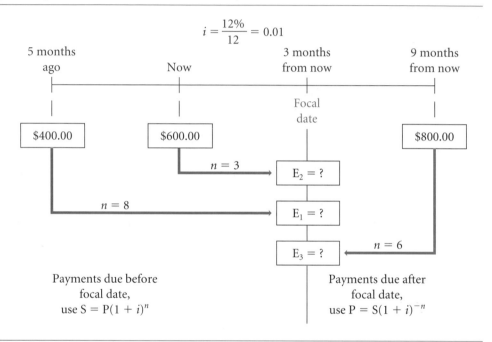

$$i = \frac{12\%}{12} = 0.01$$

Programmed solution

E_1 0 [PMT] 400 [PV] 1 [%i] 8 [N] [CPT] [FV]   433.14268

E_2 0 [PMT] 600 [PV] 1 [%i] 3 [N] [CPT] [FV]   618.1806

E_3 0 [PMT] 800 [FV] 1 [%i] 6 [N] [CPT] [PV]   753.63619

$433.14268 + 618.1806 + 753.63619 = 1804.9595 = 1804.96$

EXAMPLE 9.5D   Payments of $500.00 are due at the end of each of the next five years. Determine the equivalent single payment five years from now (just after the last payment is due) if money is worth 10% p.a. compounded annually.

Solution   Select as the focal date "five years from now."

Let the equivalent single payment be represented by E and the dated values of the first four payments be represented by E_1, E_2, E_3, E_4 as indicated in Figure 9.10. Then the following equation of values can be set up.

$$
\begin{aligned}
E &= 500.00 + E_4 + E_3 + E_2 + E_1 \\
&= 500.00 + 500.00(1.1) + 500.00(1.1)^2 + 500.00(1.1)^3 + 500.00(1.1)^4 \\
&= 500.00[1 + (1.1) + (1.1)^2 + (1.1)^3 + (1.1)^4] \\
&= 500.00(1 + 1.1 + 1.21 + 1.331 + 1.4641) \\
&= 500.00(6.1051) \\
&= 3052.55
\end{aligned}
$$

The equivalent single payment after five years is $3052.55.

FIGURE 9.10   Graphic Representation of Method and Data

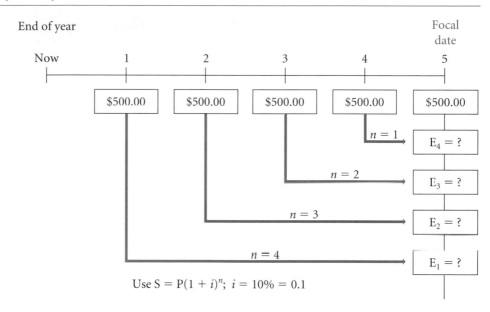

Use $S = P(1 + i)^n$; $i = 10\% = 0.1$

EXAMPLE 9.5E   Payments of $200.00 are due at the end of each of the next five quarters. Determine the equivalent single payment that will settle the debt now if interest is 9% p.a. compounded quarterly.

Solution   Select as the focal date "now."

Let the equivalent single payment be represented by E and the dated values of the five payments by E_1, E_2, E_3, E_4, E_5 respectively as shown in Figure 9.11. Then the following equation of values can be set up.

$$E = E_1 + E_2 + E_3 + E_4 + E_5$$
$$= 200.00(1.0225)^{-1} + 200.00(1.0225)^{-2} + 200.00(1.0225)^{-3}$$
$$+ 200.00(1.0225)^{-4} + 200.00(1.0225)^{-5}$$
$$= 200.00[(1.0225)^{-1} + (1.0225)^{-2} + (1.0225)^{-3} + (1.0225)^{-4} + (1.0225)^{-5}]$$
$$= 200.00(0.9779951 + 0.9564744 + 0.9354273 + 0.9148433 + 0.8947123)$$
$$= 200.00(4.6794524)$$
$$= 935.89$$

The equivalent single payment now is $935.89.

FIGURE 9.11 **Graphic Representation of Method and Data**

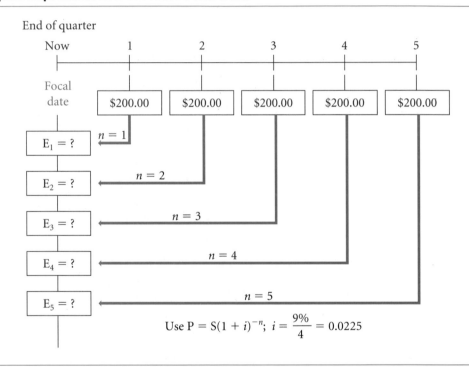

C. Finding the value of two or more equivalent payments

When two or more equivalent payments are needed, an equation of values matching the dated values of the original debt payments against the dated values of the proposed replacement payments on a selected focal date should be set up. This procedure is similar to the one used for simple interest in Chapter 7.

EXAMPLE 9.5F

Debt payments of $1000.00 due today and $2000.00 due one year from now are to be settled by a payment of $1500.00 three months from now and a final payment eighteen months from now. Determine the size of the final payment if interest is 10% p.a. compounded quarterly.

Solution

Let the size of the final payment be $x. The logical focal date is the date of the final payment.

FIGURE 9.12   Graphic Representation of Method and Data

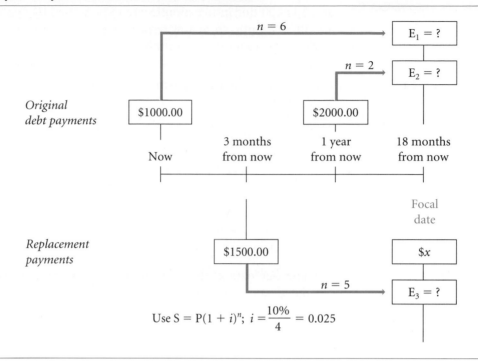

$$\text{Use } S = P(1 + i)^n; \ i = \frac{10\%}{4} = 0.025$$

As shown in Figure 9.12, the two original debt payments and the first replacement payment are due before the selected focal date. The amount formula $S = P(1 + i)^n$ applies. Because the final payment is dated on the focal date, its dated value is x.

The equivalent values of the original debt payments at the selected focal date, designated E_1 and E_2, are matched against the equivalent values of the replacement payments, designated E_3 and x, giving rise to the equation of values.

$$E_1 + E_2 = x + E_3$$
$$1000.00(1.025)^6 + 2000.00(1.025)^2 = x + 1500.00(1.025)^5$$
$$1000.00(1.1596934) + 2000.00(1.050625) = x + 1500.00(1.1314082)$$
$$1159.69 + 2101.25 = x + 1697.11$$
$$x = 1563.83$$

The final payment is $1563.83.

Programmed solution

E_1 0 [PMT] 1000 [PV] 2.5 [%i] 6 [N] [CPT] [FV] (1159.6934)

E_2 0 [PMT] 2000 [PV] 2.5 [%i] 2 [N] [CPT] [FV] (2101.25)

E_3 0 [PMT] 1500 [PV] 2.5 [%i] 5 [N] [CPT] [FV] (1697.1123)

$$1159.6934 + 2101.25 = x + 1697.1123$$
$$x = 1563.83$$

EXAMPLE 9.5G   Debt payments of $750.00 due seven months ago, $600.00 due two months ago, and $900.00 due in five months are to be settled by two equal payments due now and three months from now respectively. Determine the size of the equal payments at 9% p.a. compounded monthly.

Solution   Let the size of the equal payments be represented by $x and choose "now" as the focal date.

$$i = \frac{9\%}{12} = 0.0075$$

First, consider the dated values of the original debt payments at the chosen focal date.

The due dates of the debt payments of $750.00 and $600.00 are seven months and two months respectively before the focal date. Their dated values at the focal date are $750.00(1.0075)^7$ and $600.00(1.0075)^2$ respectively.

The due date of the $900.00 payment is five months after the focal date. Its dated value is $900.00(1.0075)^{-5}$.

Second, consider the dated values of the replacement payments at the selected focal date.

The first replacement payment due at the focal date is $x. The second replacement payment is due three months after the focal date. Its dated value is $x(1.0075)^{-3}$.

Now equate the dated values of the replacement payments with the dated values of the original debt payments to set up the equation of values.

$$x + x(1.0075)^{-3} = 750.00(1.0075)^7 + 600.00(1.0075)^2 + 900.00(1.0075)^{-5}$$
$$x + 0.9778333x = 750.00(1.0536961) + 600.00(1.0150562) + 900.00(0.9633292)$$
$$1.9778333x = 790.27 + 609.03 + 867.00$$
$$1.9778333x = 2266.30$$
$$x = \frac{2266.30}{1.9778333}$$
$$x = 1145.85$$

The size of the two equal payments is $1145.85.

Programmed solution

$$x + x(1.0075)^{-3}$$

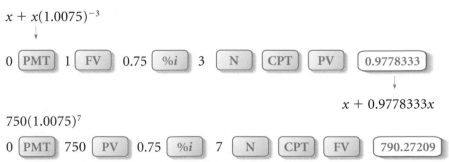

$600(1.0075)^2$

0 [PMT] 600 [PV] 0.75 [%i] 2 [N] [CPT] [FV] [609.03375]

$900(1.0075)^{-5}$

0 [PMT] 900 [FV] 0.75 [%i] 5 [N] [CPT] [PV] [866.99629]

$x + 0.9778333x = 790.27209 + 609.03375 + 866.99628$
$\qquad 1.9778333x = 2266.3021$
$\qquad\qquad x = 1145.85$

Note: In $x(1.0075)^{-3}$, [FV] is not known. To obtain the factor $(1.0075)^{-3}$, use [FV] $= 1$.

EXAMPLE 9.5H

Two debts, one of $4000 due in three months with interest at 9% compounded quarterly and the other of $3000 due in eighteen months with interest at 8.5% compounded semi-annually, are to be discharged by making two equal payments. What is the size of the equal payments if the first is due one year from now, the second two years from now, and money is now worth 10% compounded monthly?

Solution

Let the size of the equal payments be represented by $x and choose "one year from now" as the focal date.

Since the two debts are interest-bearing, first determine the maturity value of the two debts.

The maturity value of $4000 due in three months at 9% compounded quarterly $= 4000(1.0225)^1 = \$4090.00$

The maturity value of $3000 due in eighteen months at 8.5% compounded semi-annually $= 3000(1.0425)^3$
$\qquad\qquad\qquad = 3000(1.1329955) = \$3398.99$

Now determine the dated values of the two maturity values at the selected focal date subject to 10% compounded monthly.

The first debt matures nine months before the selected focal date. Its dated value $= 4090.00(1.008\dot{3})^9 = 4090.00(1.0775489) = \$4407.18$

The second debt matures six months after the selected focal date. Its dated value $= 3398.99(1.008\dot{3})^{-6} = 3398.99(0.9514267) = \$3233.89$

The dated values of the two replacement payments at the selected focal date are $x and $x(1.008\dot{3})^{-12}$. Therefore, the equation of values is

$x + x(1.008\dot{3})^{-12} = 4407.18 + 3233.89$
$x + 0.9052124x = 7641.07$
$$x = \frac{7641.07}{1.9052124}$$
$x = 4010.61$

The size of the two equal payments is $4010.61.

Programmed solution

Maturity value of $4000

0 $\boxed{\text{PMT}}$ 4000 $\boxed{\text{PV}}$ 2.25 $\boxed{\%i}$ 1 $\boxed{\text{N}}$ $\boxed{\text{CPT}}$ $\boxed{\text{FV}}$ $\boxed{\text{4090}}$

Maturity value of $3000

0 $\boxed{\text{PMT}}$ 3000 $\boxed{\text{PV}}$ 4.25 $\boxed{\%i}$ 3 $\boxed{\text{N}}$ $\boxed{\text{CPT}}$ $\boxed{\text{FV}}$ $\boxed{\text{3398.9865}}$

$x + x(1.00\dot{8}\dot{3})^{-12}$

$\downarrow$

0 $\boxed{\text{PMT}}$ 1 $\boxed{\text{FV}}$ 0.8333333 $\boxed{\%i}$ 12 $\boxed{\text{N}}$ $\boxed{\text{CPT}}$ $\boxed{\text{PV}}$ $\boxed{\text{0.9052124}}$

$\downarrow$

this gives $x + 0.9052124x$

$4090.00(1.00\dot{8}\dot{3})^9$

0 $\boxed{\text{PMT}}$ 4090 $\boxed{\text{PV}}$ 0.8333333 $\boxed{\%i}$ 9 $\boxed{\text{N}}$ $\boxed{\text{CPT}}$ $\boxed{\text{FV}}$ $\boxed{\text{4407.1763}}$

$3398.99(1.00\dot{8}\dot{3})^{-6}$

0 $\boxed{\text{PMT}}$ 3398.99 $\boxed{\text{FV}}$ 0.8333333 $\boxed{\%i}$ 6 $\boxed{\text{N}}$ $\boxed{\text{CPT}}$ $\boxed{\text{PV}}$ $\boxed{\text{3233.8893}}$

$$x + 0.9052124x = 4407.1763 + 3233.8893$$
$$1.9052124x = 7641.0656$$
$$x = 4010.61$$

EXAMPLE 9.5I

What is the size of the equal payments that must be made at the end of each of the next five years to settle a debt of $5000.00 due in five years if money is worth 9% p.a. compounded annually?

Solution

Select as the focal date "five years from now." Let the equal payments be represented by x and let the dated values of the first four payments be represented by $E_1, E_2, E_3,$ and E_4 respectively as shown in Figure 9.13.

Then the equation of values may be set up.

$$5000.00 = x + E_4 + E_3 + E_2 + E_1$$
$$5000.00 = x + x(1.09) + x(1.09)^2 + x(1.09)^3 + x(1.09)^4$$
$$5000.00 = x[1 + (1.09) + (1.09)^2 + (1.09)^3 + (1.09)^4]$$

$$5000.00 = x(1 + 1.09 + 1.1881 + 1.295029 + 1.4115816)$$

$$5000.00 = 5.9847106x$$
$$x = 835.46$$

The size of the equal payments is $835.46.

EXAMPLE 9.5J

What is the size of the equal payments that must be made at the end of each of the next five quarters to settle a debt of $3000.00 due now if money is worth 12% p.a. compounded quarterly?

Solution

Select as the focal date "now." Let the size of the equal payments be represented by x and let the dated values of the five payments be represented by $E_1, E_2, E_3, E_4,$ and E_5 respectively as shown in Figure 9.14.

FIGURE 9.13   Graphic Representation of Method and Data

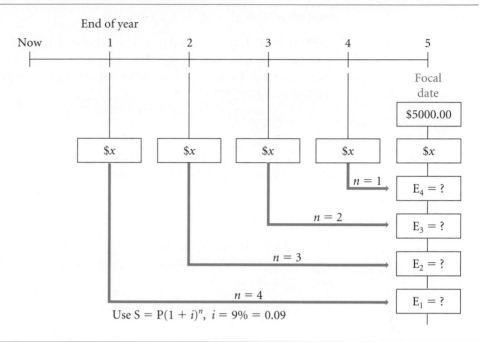

FIGURE 9.14   Graphic Representation of Method and Data

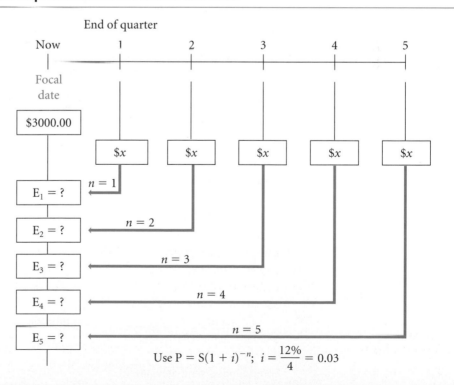

Then the equation of values may be set up.

$3000.00 = E_1 + E_2 + E_3 + E_4 + E_5$

$3000.00 = x(1.03)^{-1} + x(1.03)^{-2} + x(1.03)^{-3} + x(1.03)^{-4} + x(1.03)^{-5}$
$3000.00 = x[(1.03)^{-1} + (1.03)^{-2} + (1.03)^{-3} + (1.03)^{-4} + (1.03)^{-5}]$
$3000.00 = x(0.9708737 + 0.9425959 + 0.9151417 + 0.8884871 + 0.8626088)$
$3000.00 = 4.5797073x$

$$x = \frac{3000.00}{4.5797073}$$

$$x = 655.06$$

The size of the equal payments is $655.06.

Exercise 9.5

A. Find the equivalent single payment on the given focal date for each of the following ten loan situations.

Original Payments	Int. Rate	Frequency of Conversion	Focal Date
1. $5000.00 due in 2 years	12%	monthly	5 years from now
2. $1600.00 due in 18 months	8%	quarterly	42 months from now
3. $3400.00 due in 4 years	10%	semi-annually	1 year from now
4. $2700.00 due in 60 months	7%	quarterly	6 months from now
5. $800.00 due in 6 months and $700.00 due in 15 months	9.5%	monthly	2 years from now
6. $1000.00 due in 9 months and $1200.00 due in 18 months	8.8%	quarterly	3 years from now
7. $400.00 due in 3 years and $600.00 due in 5 years	11%	semi-annually	now
8. $2000.00 due in 20 months and $1500.00 due in 40 months	10.5%	monthly	9 months from now
9. $800.00 due today and $1400.00 due in 3 years with interest at 12% compounded annually	11.75%	quarterly	1 year from now
10. $500.00 due in 6 months with interest at 12% compounded quarterly and $800.00 due in 18 months with interest at 10% compounded semi-annually	9%	monthly	9 months from now

B. Find the equivalent replacement payments for each of the following.

	Original Payments	Int. Rate	Frequency of Conversion	Replacement Payments	Focal Date
1.	$2000.00 due now and $2000.00 due in 4 years	10.5%	annually	$2000.00 due in 2 years, a second payment due in 7 years	7 years from now
2.	$1500.00 due in 6 months and $1900.00 due in 21 months	7%	quarterly	$2000.000 due in 3 years, the remainder due in 45 months	45 months from now
3.	$800.00 due 2 years ago and $1000.00 due in 5 years	12%	semi-annually	2 equal payments; first payment due in 4 years, second payment due in 8 years	4 years from now
4.	$3000.00 due 1 year ago and $2500.00 due in 4 years	6.9%	monthly	2 equal payments; first due now, second payment due in 6 years	now
5.	$900.00 due in 3 months and $800.00 due in 30 months with interest at 10% compounded quarterly	9%	monthly	2 equal payments; first due today, second due in 3 years	today
6.	$1400.00 due today and $1600.00 due in 5 years with interest at 11.5% compounded annually	11%	quarterly	2 equal payments; first due in 18 months, second due in 4 years	18 months from now

C. Solve each of the following problems.

1. A loan of $4000.00 is due in five years. If money is worth 12% compounded annually, find the equivalent payment that would settle the debt
   (a) now;   (b) in 2 years;   (c) in 5 years;   (d) in 10 years.

2. A debt payment of $5500 is due in 27 months. If money is worth 11.5% p.a. compounded quarterly, what is the equivalent payment
   (a) now?   (b) 15 months from now?
   (c) 27 months from now?   (d) 36 months from now?

3. A debt can be paid by payments of $2000.00 today, $2000.00 in three years, and $2000.00 in six years. What single payment would settle the debt four years from now if money is worth 10% compounded semi-annually?

4. Loans of $600.00, $800.00, and $1200.00 are due in one year, three years, and six years respectively. What is the equivalent single sum of money due two and a half years from now if interest is 12% compounded monthly?

5. Debt payments of $400.00 due today and $700.00 due in eight months with interest at 12% compounded monthly are to be settled by a payment of $500.00 six months from now and a final payment in fifteen months. Determine the size of the final payment if money is worth 6% compounded monthly.

6. Payments of $1200.00 due one year ago and $1000.00 due six months ago are to be replaced by a payment of $800.00 now, a second payment of $1000.00 nine months from now, and a final payment eighteen months from now. What is the size of the final payment if interest is 10.8% compounded quarterly?

7. An obligation of $8000.00 due one year ago is to be settled by four equal payments due at the beginning of each of the next four years respectively. What is the size of the equal payments if interest is 8% compounded semi-annually?

8. A loan of $3000.00 made today is to be repaid in three equal instalments due in one year, three years, and five years respectively. What is the size of the equal instalments if money is worth 12% compounded monthly?

9. Payments of $500.00 each are due at the end of each of the next five years. If money is worth 11% compounded annually, what is the single equivalent payment
   (a) five years from now?   (b) now?

10. Rework Problem 9 with payments due at the beginning of each of the next five years. (You can obtain the solution directly from your solution to Problem 9.)

11. What is the size of the equal payments that must be made at the end of each of the next four years to settle a debt of $3000.00 subject to interest at 10% p.a. compounded annually
    (a) due four years from now?   (b) due now?

12. Rework Problem 11 with payments made at the beginning of each of the next four years. (You can obtain the solution directly from your solution to Problem 11.)

REVIEW EXERCISE

1. What is the accumulated value of $500.00 in fifteen years at 6% compounded
   (a) annually?   (b) quarterly?   (c) monthly?

2. What is the amount of $10 000.00 at 10.5% compounded monthly

   (a) in four years?   (b) in eight and one-half years?
   (c) in twenty years?

3. Landmark Trust offers five-year investment certificates at 7.5% compounded semi-annually.

   (a) What is the value of a $2000 certificate at maturity?
   (b) How much of the maturity value is interest?

4. Western Savings offers three-year term deposits at 9.25% compounded annually while your credit union offers such deposits at 9.0% compounded quarterly. If you have $5000 to invest, what is the maturity value of your deposit

   (a) at Western Savings?   (b) at your credit union?

5. Find the future value and the compound interest of

   (a) $1800.00 invested at 8% compounded quarterly for 15.5 years;
   (b) $1250.00 invested at 6.5% compounded monthly for 15 years.

6. Find the present value and the compound discount of

   (a) $3600.00 due in 9 years if interest is 8% compounded semi-annually;
   (b) $9000.00 due in 5 years if money is worth 6.8% compounded quarterly.

7. The Peel Company borrowed $20 000.00 at 10% compounded semi-annually and made payments toward the loan of $8000.00 after two years and $10 000.00 after three and a half years. How much is required to pay off the loan one year after the second payment?

8. Ted deposited $1750.00 in an RRSP on March 1, 1990, at 10% compounded quarterly. Subsequently the interest rate was changed to 12% compounded monthly on September 1, 1992, and to 11% compounded semi-annually on June 1, 1994. What was the value of the RRSP deposit on December 1, 2000, if no further changes in interest were made?

9. A non-interest-bearing note for $1500.00 is due on June 30, 2004. The note is discounted at 10% compounded quarterly on September 30, 1998. What are the proceeds of the note?

10. An investment of $2500 is accumulated at 5% compounded quarterly for two and one-half years. At that time the interest rate is changed to 6% compounded monthly. How much is the investment worth two years after the change in interest rate?

11. To ensure that funds are available to repay the principal at maturity, a borrower deposits $2000 each year for three years. If interest is 6% compounded

quarterly, how much will the borrower have on deposit four years after the first deposit was made?

12. Cindy started a registered retirement savings plan on February 1, 1989, with a deposit of $2500. She added $2000 on February 1, 1990, and $1500 on February 1, 1991. What is the accumulated value of her RRSP account on August 1, 1999, if interest is 10% compounded quarterly?

13. A demand loan of $8000 is repaid by payments of $3000 after fifteen months, $4000 after thirty months, and a final payment after four years. If interest was 8% for the first two years and 9% for the remaining time, and compounding is quarterly, what is the size of the final payment?

14. Find the present value and the compound discount of $4000 due in seven years and six months if interest is 8.8% compounded quarterly.

15. Find the principal that will accumulate to $6000 in fifteen years at 5% compounded monthly.

16. Find the proceeds of a non-interest-bearing promissory note for $75 000 discounted 42 months before maturity at 11.5% compounded semi-annually.

17. A ten-year promissory note for $1750.00 dated May 1, 1992, bearing interest at 11% compounded semi-annually is discounted on August 1, 1998, to yield 12% compounded quarterly. Determine the proceeds of the note.

18. A seven-year, $10 000 promissory note bearing interest at 12% compounded quarterly is discounted four years after the date of issue at 10% compounded semi-annually. What are the proceeds of the note?

19. A $40 000, 15-year promissory note dated June 1, 1995, bearing interest at 12% compounded semi-annually is discounted on September 1, 1999, at 11% compounded quarterly. What are the proceeds of the note?

20. A sum of money has a value of $3000 eighteen months from now. If money is worth 6% compounded monthly, what is its equivalent value

    (a) now?   (b) one year from now?   (c) three years from now?

21. Payments of $1000, $1200, and $1500 are due in six months, eighteen months, and thirty months from now respectively. What is the equivalent single payment two years from now if money is worth 9.6% compounded quarterly?

22. An obligation of $10 000 is due one year from now with interest at 10% compounded semi-annually. The obligation is to be settled by a payment of $6000 in six months and a final payment in fifteen months. What is the size of the second payment if interest is now 12% compounded monthly?

23. Waldon Toys owes $3000 due in two years with interest at 11% compounded semi-annually and $2500 due in fifteen months at 9% compounded quarterly. If the company wants to discharge these debts by making two equal payments, the first one now and the second eighteen months from now, what is the size of the two payments if money is now worth 8.4% compounded monthly?

24. Debt payments of $400.00 due today, $500.00 due in eighteen months, and $900.00 due in three years are to be combined into a single payment due two years from now. What is the size of the single payment if interest is 8% p.a. compounded quarterly?

25. Debt payments of $2600.00 due one year ago and $2400.00 due two years from now are to be replaced by two equal payments due one year from now and four years from now respectively. What is the size of the equal payments if money is worth 9.6% p.a. compounded semi-annually?

26. A loan of $7000.00 taken out two years ago is to be repaid by three equal instalments due now, two years from now, and three years from now respectively. What is the size of the equal instalments if interest on the debt is 12% p.a. compounded monthly?

SELF-TEST

1. What sum of money invested at 12% compounded quarterly will grow to $3300 in 11 years?

2. Find the compound interest earned by $1300 invested at 7.5% compounded monthly for seven years.

3. Determine the compounding factor for a sum of money invested for 14.5 years at 7% compounded semi-annually.

4. Five years after Anne deposited $3600 in a savings account that earned interest at 4.8% compounded monthly, the rate of interest was changed to 6% compounded semi-annually. How much was in the account twelve years after the deposit was made?

5. A debt can be repaid by payments of $4000 today, $4000 in five years, and $3000 in six years. What single payment would settle the debt one year from now if money is worth 7% compounded semi-annually?

6. A $10 200 debt will accumulate for five years at 11.6% compounded semi-annually. For how much will the debt sell three years after it was incurred if the buyer of the debt charges 10% compounded quarterly?

7. What is the present value of $5900 payable in 15 years if the current interest rate is 7.5% compounded semi-annually?

8. Determine the compound discount on $8800 due in 7.5 years if interest is 9.6% compounded monthly.

9. Two debt payments, the first for $800 due today and the second for $600 due in nine months with interest at 10.5% compounded monthly, are to be settled by a payment of $800 six months from now and a final payment in 24 months. Determine the size of the final payment if money is now worth 9.5% compounded quarterly.

10. A note dated July 1, 1994, promises to pay $8000 with interest at 12.5% compounded quarterly on January 1, 2003. Find the proceeds from the sale of the note on July 1, 1998, if money is then worth 8% compounded semi-annually.

11. Adam borrowed $5000 at 10% compounded semi-annually. He repaid $2000 after two years and $2500 after three years. How much will he owe after five years?

12. A debt of $7000 due today is to be settled by three equal payments due three months from now, 15 months from now, and 27 months from now respectively. What is the size of the equal payments at 11% compounded quarterly?

CHALLENGE PROBLEMS

1. Jean-Guy Renoir wanted to leave some money to his grandchildren in his will. He decided that they should each receive the same amount of money when they each turn 21. When he died, his grandchildren were 19, 16, and 13 respectively. How much will they each receive when they turn 21 if Jean-Guy left a lump sum of $50 000 to be shared among them equally? Assume the interest rate will remain at 7.75% p.a. compounded semi-annually from the time of Jean-Guy's death until the youngest grandchild turns 21.

2. Miranda has $1000 to invest. She has narrowed her options to two four-year certificates, A and B. Certificate A pays interest at 8% p.a. compounded semi-annually the first year, 8% p.a. compounded quarterly the second year, 8% p.a. compounded monthly the third year, and 8% p.a. compounded daily the fourth year. Certificate B pays 8% p.a. compounded daily the first year, 8% p.a. compounded monthly the second year, 8% p.a. compounded quarterly the third year, and 8% p.a. compounded semi-annually the fourth year.

   (a) What is the value of each certificate at the end of the four years?

   (b) How do the values of certificates A and B compare with the value of a third certificate that pays interest at 7% compounded daily for the full four-year term?

CASE STUDY 9.1   WHAT'S IN YOUR BEST INTEREST?

Marika was standing in line at the bank one day and noticed the list of interest rates paid by the bank on each type of savings account. She discovered that the bank offered four different savings accounts. The Daily Interest Savings Account had an interest rate of 3.50%. The Monthly Interest Savings Account had an interest rate of 3.60%. The Investment Savings Account had an interest rate of 4.05%. The Basic Savings Account had an interest rate of 4.00%.

When Marika reached the teller, she asked him to describe the features of each account and to explain how interest was calculated on each account. In response, the teller explained that all accounts involve compound interest, but the calculation for each is different. Compound interest on the Daily Interest Savings Account is calculated on the minimum balance in the account each day and is paid monthly. Compound interest on the Monthly Interest Savings Account is calculated on the minimum balance in the account during the month and is paid monthly. Compound interest on the Investment Savings Account is calculated on the minimum balance in the account during the month, but only when the balance remains above $5000.00 for the whole month. If the balance in the account drops below $5000.00 at any time during the month, no interest is paid that month. Compound interest on the Basic Savings Account is calculated on the minimum balance in the account during the six-month periods ending April 30 and October 31, and is paid on April 30 and October 31.

The teller told Marika that many customers were switching their accounts from the Basic Savings Account (which used to be the only savings account banks offered) to savings accounts that paid interest more often. He advised that each account had its benefits depending on the number of transactions made through the account each month or each year. Marika finished her banking and took a brochure that summarized these accounts so that she could consider the options.

QUESTIONS

1. Suppose Marika had a $3000.00 income tax refund that she wanted to put into a savings account. She planned to leave the money in the account for one year. Assume that the bank's interest rates will stay the same during the year.
   (a) For each of the bank's four savings accounts, how much interest would Marika earn in one year's time?
   (b) Which savings account would pay the most interest?

2. Suppose Marika had $6000.000 to put into a savings account.
   (a) For each of the Bank's four savings accounts, how much interest would Marika earn in one year's time if she left the money in the account for one year? Assume that the bank's interest rates will stay the same during the year.
   (b) Which savings account would pay the most interest?
   (c) Suppose Marika knew she would have to withdraw $2000.00 after ten months. Which savings account would pay the most interest?

3. Suppose Marika had $6000.00 to put into a savings account. She planned to leave the money in the account for one year, then withdraw $2000.00. She would then leave the remaining balance in the account for one more year. Which savings account would pay the most interest? Assume that the bank's interest rates will stay the same over the next two years.

4. For the savings accounts at your bank, credit union, or trust company, find the features and interest rates offered for each. If you had $3000.00 to deposit for one year, which account would you choose?

CASE STUDY 9.2   PLANNING AHEAD

Brunner Company, a successful Canadian manufacturer, has been growing steadily. The past year was unusually profitable, so management has decided to set aside $2 000 000 to expand the company's factory over the next five years.

Management has developed two different plans for expanding over the next five years, Plan A and Plan B. Plan A would require equal amounts of $550 000 one year from now, two years from now, four years from now, and five years from now. Plan B would require $200 000 now, $500 000 one year from now, $800 000 three years from now, and $850 000 five years from now.

The company has decided to fund the expansion with only the $2 000 000 and any interest it can earn on it. Before deciding which plan to use, the company asked its treasurer to predict the rates of interest it can earn on the $2 000 000. The treasurer expects that Brunner Company can invest the $2 000 000 and earn interest at a rate of 5.0% p.a. compounded semi-annually during Year 1, 6.0% p.a. compounded semi-annually during Years 2 and 3, 6.5% p.a. compounded semi-annually during Year 4, and 6.75% p.a. compounded semi-annually during Year 5. The company can withdraw part of the money from this investment at any time without penalty.

QUESTIONS

1. (a) Could Brunner Company meet the cash requirement of Plan A by investing the $2 000 000 as described above? (Use "now" as the focal date.)
   (b) What is the exact difference between the cash required and the cash available from the investment?

2. (a) Could Brunner Company meet the cash requirements of Plan B by investing the $2 000 000 as described above? (Use "now" as the focal date.)
   (b) What is the difference between the cash required and the cash available from the investment?

3. (a) Suppose Plan A was changed so that it required equal amounts of $550 000 now, one year from now, two years from now, and four years from now. Could Brunner Company meet the cash requirements of the new Plan A by investing the $2 000 000 as described above?(Use "now" as the focal date.)

(b) What is the difference between the cash required and the cash available from the investment?

4. Suppose the treasurer found another way to invest the $2 000 000 that earned interest at a rate of 5.8% compounded quarterly for the next five years.
   (a) Could the company meet the cash requirements of the original Plan A with this new investment? (Show all your calculations.)
   (b) Could the company meet the cash requirements of Plan B with this new investment? (Show all your calculations.)
   (c) If the company could meet the cash requirements of both plans, which plan would the treasurer recommend? In other words, which plan would have the lower present value?

SUMMARY OF FORMULAE

Formula 9.1A
$$S = P(1 + i)^n$$
Finding the future value (or maturity value) when the original principal, the rate of interest, and the time period are known

Formula 9.1B
$$P = \frac{S}{(1 + i)^n}$$
Finding the present value (or principal or proceeds or discounted value) when the future value, the rate of interest, and the time period are known

Formula 9.1C
$$P = S(1 + i)^{-n}$$
Finding the present value by means of the discount factor (the reciprocal of the compounding factor)

Formula 9.2
$$i = \frac{j}{m}$$
Finding the periodic rate of interest

GLOSSARY

Accumulation factor   see *Compounding factor*

Comparison date   see *Focal date*

Compound discount   the difference between a given future amount and its present value (or proceeds or discounted value) at a specified time

Compound interest   a procedure for computing interest whereby interest earned during an interest period is added onto the principal at the end of the interest period

Compounding factor   the factor $(1 + i)^n$ found in compound interest formulae

Compounding frequency   the number of times interest is compounded during a given time period (usually one year)

Compounding period   the time between two successive interest dates

Conversion frequency   see *Compounding frequency*

Conversion period   see *Compounding period*

Discount factor   the factor $(1 + i)^{-n}$; the reciprocal of the compounding factor

Discounted value   see *Present value*

Discounting   the process of computing the present value (or proceeds or discounted value) of a future sum of money

Equivalent values   the dated values of an original sum of money

Focal date   a specific date chosen to compare the time values of one or more dated sums of money

Future value   the sum of money to which a principal will grow at compound interest in a specific number of compounding or conversion periods at a specified periodic rate of interest

Maturity value   see *Future value*

Nominal rate of interest   the stated rate at which the compounding is done one or more times per year; usually stated as an annual rate

Present value   the principal at any time that will grow at compound interest to a given future value over a given number of compounding periods at a given rate of interest

Proceeds   see *Present value*

10

Compound Interest— Further Topics

Introduction

In the previous chapter, we considered future value and present value when using compound interest. In this chapter, we will look at other aspects of compound interest, including computations with fractional conversion periods, finding interest rates, finding the number of conversion periods, computing equated dates and equivalent rates, and using continuous compounding.

For the calculations in this and the following chapters, we will start to use the power function and the natural logarithm function on our electronic calculators. We can save time on our calculations by using the memory of the calculator when working with these functions. The number of digits retained in memory is almost always greater than the number of digits displayed. Thus, we might get slightly different results if we use the memory rather than rekey the displayed digits. However, we can ignore such differences because they are insignificant. For the worked examples in this text, we have used the memory whenever it was convenient to do so.

OBJECTIVES

Upon completing this chapter, you will be able to do the following with compound interest by using an electronic calculator (equipped with the universal power function, the natural logarithm function, and the antilogarithm function):

1. Find the future value when n is a fractional value.
2. Find discounted values for fractional compounding periods.
3. Discount promissory notes involving fractional compounding periods.
4. Compute periodic, nominal, and effective rates of interest and determine the number of conversion periods.
5. Find equated dates and equivalent rates.
6. Solve problems involving continuous compounding.

10.1 FINDING THE FUTURE VALUE WHEN n IS A FRACTIONAL VALUE

A. Two methods for solving the problem

The value of n in the compounding factor $(1 + i)^n$ is not restricted to integral values; n may take any *fractional* value. The future value can be determined by means of the formula $S = P(1 + i)^n$ whether the time period contains an integral number of conversion periods or not.

Using the formula with n as a fractional value is the theoretically correct method to give the exact accumulated value. Historically, however, the computation when using a fractional n was laborious and required the use of logarithms. To avoid using logarithms, in practice an *approximation* method using simple interest for the fractional conversion period was used.

With the advent of electronic calculators equipped with an exponential function, the problem of computing with fractional values of n no longer exists. In fact, using the exact method with an electronic calculator is more direct than the approximation method. Only the exact method is used in this text.

B. Examples using the exact method

Use Formula 9.1A, $S = P(1 + i)^n$, where n is a fractional value representing the entire time period.

EXAMPLE 10.1A   Find the accumulated value of $1000.00 invested for two years and nine months at 10% p.a. compounded annually using the exact method.

Solution   The entire time period is 2 years and 9 months; the number of whole conversion periods is 2; the fractional conversion period is 9/12 of a year.

$P = 1000.00$; $i = 10\% = 0.10$; $n = 2\frac{9}{12} = 2.75$

$$S = 1000.00(1.10)^{2.75} = 1000.00(1.2996604) = \$1299.66$$

Programmed solution

0 [PMT] 1000 [PV] 10 [%i] 2.75 [N] [CPT] [FV] [1299.6604]

EXAMPLE 10.1B Determine the compound amount of $400.00 invested at 12% p.a. compounded quarterly for three years and five months using the exact method.

Solution $P = 400.00;$ $i = 3.0\% = 0.03;$

$$n = \left(3\tfrac{5}{12}\right)(4) = \left(\frac{41}{12}\right)(4) = \frac{41}{3} = 13\tfrac{2}{3} = 13.666667$$

$$S = 400.00(1.03)^{13.666667} = 400.00(1.4977595) = \$599.10$$

Programmed solution

0 [PMT] 400 [PV] 3.0 [%i] 13.666667 [N] [CPT] [FV] [599.10379]

EXAMPLE 10.1C Find the maturity value of a promissory note for $2000.00 dated February 1, 1994, and due on October 1, 2000, if interest is 11% p.a. compounded semi-annually.

Solution $P = 2000.00;$ $i = 5.5\% = 0.055$

The time period February 1, 1994, to October 1, 2000, contains 6 years and 8 months: $n = \left(6\tfrac{8}{12}\right)(2) = \left(\frac{80}{12}\right)(2) = 13.3333333.$

$$S = 2000.00(1.055)^{13.3333333} = 2000.00(2.0418921) = \$4083.78$$

Programmed solution

0 [PMT] 2000 [PV] 5.5 [%i] 13.3333333 [N] [CPT] [FV] [4083.7843]

EXAMPLE 10.1D A debt of $3500.00 dated August 31, 1998, is payable together with interest at 9% p.a. compounded quarterly on June 30, 2001. Determine the amount to be paid.

Solution $P = 3500.00;$ $i = 2.25\% = 0.0225;$ the time period August 31, 1998, to June 30, 2001, contains 2 years and 10 months; the number of quarters $n = 11.333333.$

$$S = 3500.00(1.0225)^{11.333333}$$
$$= 3500.00(1.2868194)$$
$$= \$4503.87$$

Programmed solution

0 [PMT] 3500 [PV] 2.25 [%i] 11.333333 [N] [CPT] [FV] [4503.8679]

Exercise 10.1

A. 1. Find the accumulated value of each of the following four investments.

	Principal	Rate	Frequency of Conversion	Time
(a)	$2500.00	7%	annually	7 years, 6 months
(b)	400.00	9%	quarterly	3 years, 8 months
(c)	1300.00	12%	semi-annually	9 years, 3 months
(d)	4500.00	10%	monthly	7.5 months

2. Find the compound interest for each of the following four investments.

	Principal	Rate	Frequency of Conversion	Time
(a)	$ 600.00	12.5%	annually	4 years, 7 months
(b)	1400.00	11.5%	semi-annually	15 years, 2 months
(c)	950.00	8.0%	quarterly	9 years, 10 months
(d)	3000.00	10.5%	annually	50 months

B. Solve each of the following problems.

1. A demand loan for $5000.00 with interest at 9.75% compounded semi-annually is repaid after five years, ten months. What is the amount of interest paid?

2. Suppose $4000.00 is invested for four years, eight months at 8.5% compounded annually. What is the compounded amount?

3. Determine the maturity value of a $600.00 promissory note dated August 1, 1996, and due on June 1, 2001, if interest is 11% p.a. compounded semi-annually.

4. Find the maturity value of a promissory note for $3200.00 dated March 31, 1995, and due on August 31, 2001, if interest is 7% compounded quarterly.

5. A debt of $8000.00 is payable in seven years and five months. Determine the accumulated value of the debt at 10.8% p.a. compounded annually.

6. A $6000.00 investment matures in three years, eleven months. Find the maturity value if interest is 9% p.a. compounded quarterly.

10.2 DISCOUNTED VALUE FOR A FRACTIONAL COMPOUNDING PERIOD

A. Exact method for solving the problem

Using fractional values of *n* when finding the future value is relevant to finding the present value or discounted value of a future sum of money for a fractional time period. Only the exact method is used in this text.

Use Formula 9.1A, $S = P(1 + i)^n$, or Formula 9.1B, $P = \dfrac{S}{(1 + i)^n}$, or Formula 9.1C, $P = S(1 + i)^{-n}$ where n is a fractional value representing the *entire* time period, S is a known value, and P is to be determined.

B. Examples

EXAMPLE 10.2A Find the present value of $2000.00 due in three years and eight months if money is worth 8% p.a. compounded quarterly.

Solution $S = 2000.00;\quad i = \dfrac{8\%}{4} = 2\% = 0.02;\quad n = \left(3\tfrac{8}{12}\right)(4) = 14\tfrac{2}{3} = 14.666667$

$P = \dfrac{S}{(1 + i)^n}$ ——————————————— using Formula 9.1B

$\quad = \dfrac{2000.00}{(1 + 0.02)^{14.666667}}$ ———————— use as many decimals as are available in your calculator

$\quad = 2000.00(0.7479355)$ ——————— multiply by the reciprocal

$\quad = \$1495.87$

Programmed solution

0 [PMT] 2000 [FV] 2 [%i] 14.666667 [N] [CPT] [PV] 1495.8710

EXAMPLE 10.2B Determine the principal that will accumulate to $2837.18 from September 1, 1996, to April 1, 2000, at 10% p.a. compounded semi-annually.

Solution   Finding the principal that will grow to the given amount of $2837.18 is equivalent to finding the present value or discounted value of this amount.

The time period September 1, 1996, to April 1, 2000, contains three years and seven months; that is, it consists of seven whole conversion periods of six months each and a fractional conversion period of one month.

Use $P = \dfrac{S}{(1 + i)^n}$.

$S = 2837.18;\quad i = 5\% = 0.05;\quad n = \left(3\tfrac{7}{12}\right)(2) = 7\tfrac{1}{6} = 7.1666667$

$P = \dfrac{2837.18}{(1.05)^{7.1666667}}$

$\quad = \dfrac{2837.18}{1.4185892}$

$\quad = 2837.18(0.7049257)$

$\quad = \$2000.00$

Programmed solution

0 [PMT] 2837.18 [FV] 5 [%i] 7.1666667 [N] [CPT] [PV] 2000.0012

Exercise 10.2

A. 1. Find the present value of each of the following.

	Amount	Rate	Frequency of Conversion	Time Due
(a)	$1500.00	10.5%	annually	in 15 years, 9 months
(b)	900.00	11.5%	semi-annually	in 8 years, 10 months
(c)	6400.00	7%	quarterly	in 5 years, 7 months
(d)	7200.00	6%	monthly	in 21.5 months

2. Find the compound discount for each of the following.

	Amount	Rate	Frequency of Conversion	Time Due
(a)	$7500.00	12%	quarterly	in 4 years, 5 months
(b)	4800.00	10.5%	semi-annually	in 9 years, 9 months
(c)	870.00	9%	monthly	in 45.5 months
(d)	1250.00	5.5%	annually	in 12 years, 4 months

B. Solve each of the following problems.

1. What is the principal that will grow to $3000.00 in eight years, eight months at 9% compounded semi-annually?

2. Find the sum of money that accumulates to $1600.00 at 11% compounded quarterly in six years, four months.

3. Determine the proceeds of an investment with a maturity value of $10 000.00 if discounted at 9% compounded monthly 22.5 months before the date of maturity.

4. Compute the discounted value of $7000.00 due in three years, five months if money is worth 8% compounded quarterly.

5. Find the discounted value of $3800.00 due in six years, eight months if interest is 7.5% compounded annually.

6. Calculate the proceeds of $5500.00 due in seven years, eight months discounted at 11.5% compounded semi-annually.

10.3 DISCOUNTING PROMISSORY NOTES INVOLVING FRACTIONAL CONVERSION PERIODS

A. Non-interest-bearing notes

EXAMPLE 10.3A   A four-year, non-interest-bearing promissory note for $6000.00 dated August 31, 1996, was discounted on October 31, 1997, at 11% p.a. compounded quarterly. Determine the proceeds of the note.

Solution   The due date of the note is August 31, 2000; the discount period October 31, 1997, to August 31, 2000, contains 2 years and 10 months.

$$S = 6000.00; \quad i = 2.75\% = 0.0275; \quad n = \left(2\tfrac{10}{12}\right)(4) = 11\tfrac{1}{3} = 11.333333$$

$$\begin{aligned} P &= S(1 + i)^{-n} \\ &= 6000.00(1 + 0.0275)^{-11.333333} \\ &= 6000.00(0.7353136) \\ &= \$4411.88 \end{aligned}$$

Programmed solution

0 [PMT] 6000 [FV] 2.75 [%i] 11.333333 [N] [CPT] [PV] [4411.8815]

EXAMPLE 10.3B   You signed a promissory note at the Continental Bank for $3000.00 due in 27 months. If the bank charges interest at 12% p.a. compounded semi-annually, determine the proceeds of the note.

Solution   The amount shown on the note is the sum of money due in 27 months, that is, the maturity value of the note.

$$S = 3000.00; \quad i = 6\% = 0.06; \quad n = \left(\frac{27}{12}\right)(2) = 4.5$$

$$\begin{aligned} P &= S(1 + i)^{-n} \\ &= 3000.00(1 + 0.06)^{-4.5} \\ &= 3000.00(0.7693494) \\ &= \$2308.05 \end{aligned}$$

Programmed solution

0 [PMT] 3000 [FV] 6 [%i] 4.5 [N] [CPT] [PV] [2308.0481]

B. Interest-bearing notes

EXAMPLE 10.3C   A five-year note for $8000.00 bearing interest at 12% p.a. compounded monthly is discounted two years and five months before the due date at 14% p.a. compounded semi-annually. Determine the proceeds of the note.

Solution

STEP 1   Find the maturity value using $S = P(1 + i)^n$.

$$P = 8000.00; \quad i = 1\% = 0.01; \quad n = 60$$

$$S = 8000.00(1.01)^{60}$$
$$= 8000.00(1.8166967)$$
$$= \$14\,533.57$$

STEP 2   Find the present value of the maturity value found in Step 1 using $P = S(1 + i)^{-n}$.

$$S = 14\,533.57; \quad i = 7\% = 0.07; \quad n = \left(\frac{29}{12}\right)(2) = 4.8333333$$

$$P = 14\,533.57(1.07)^{-4.8333333}$$
$$= 14\,533.57(0.7210716)$$
$$= \$10\,479.75$$

Programmed solution

STEP 1   0 [PMT] 8000 [PV] 1 [%i] 60 [N] [CPT] [FV] [14 533.574]

STEP 2   (14 533.574) [FV] 7 [%i] 4.8333333 [N] [CPT] [PV] [10 479.747]

Exercise 10.3

A. Find the proceeds of each of the following eight promissory notes.

	Face Value	Date of Issue	Term	Interest Rate	Freq. of Conversion	Date of Discount	Disc. Rate	Freq. of Conversion
1	$5000	1994-04-01	10 years	—	—	1999-08-01	10%	annually
2	900	1995-08-31	8 years	—	—	2000-06-30	12%	quarterly
3	3200	1996-03-31	6 years	—	—	1999-10-31	8%	quarterly
4	1450	1993-10-01	9 years	—	—	1998-12-01	6%	semi-annually
5	780	1997-09-30	10 years	8%	annually	2001-04-30	10%	quarterly
6	2100	1991-02-01	12 years	6%	monthly	1998-07-01	7%	semi-annually
7	1850	1999-11-01	5 years	10%	quarterly	2001-10-01	12%	semi-annually
8	3400	1995-01-31	7 years	9%	monthly	1999-12-31	7.5%	quarterly

B. Solve each of the following problems.

1. A four-year non-interest-bearing promissory note for $3750.00 is discounted thirty-two months after the date of issue at 11.5% compounded semi-annually. Find the proceeds of the note.

2. A seven-year non-interest-bearing note for $5200.00 is discounted three years, eight months before its due date at 9% compounded quarterly. Find the proceeds of the note.

3. A non-interest-bearing eight-year note for $4500.00 issued August 1, 1994, is discounted April 1, 1998, at 12.5% compounded annually. Find the compound discount.

4. A $2800.00 promissory note issued without interest for five years on September 30, 1997, is discounted on July 31, 2000, at 8% compounded quarterly. Find the compound discount.

5. A six-year note for $1750.00 issued on December 1, 1996, with interest at 6.5% compounded annually is discounted on March 1, 1999, at 7% compounded semi-annually. What are the proceeds of the note?

6. A ten-year note for $1200.00 bearing interest at 6% compounded monthly is discounted at 8% compounded quarterly three years and ten months after the date of issue. Find the proceeds of the note.

7. Four years, seven months before its due date, a seven-year note for $2650.00 bearing interest at 12% compounded quarterly is discounted at 8% compounded semi-annually. Find the compound discount.

8. On April 15, 1996, a ten-year note dated June 15, 1991, is discounted at 10% compounded quarterly. If the face value of the note is $4000.00 and interest is 8% compounded quarterly, find the compound discount.

10.4 FINDING i AND n

A. Finding the periodic rate and the nominal annual rate of interest

If the original principal P, the future value S, and the number of conversion periods n are known, the periodic rate of interest (conversion rate) i can be determined by substituting in Formula 9.1A, $S = P(1 + i)^n$ and solving for i. The nominal annual rate of interest j can then be found by multiplying i by the number of conversion periods per year m.

EXAMPLE 10.4A What is the annual compounding rate if $200 accumulates to $495.19 in eight years?

Solution $P = 200.00; \quad S = 495.19; \quad m = 1; \quad n = 8$

$$495.19 = 200.00(1 + i)^8 \quad\text{——————} \quad i \text{ is an } \textit{annual} \text{ rate}$$
$$(1 + i)^8 = 2.47595$$
$$[(1 + i)^8]^{\frac{1}{8}} = 2.47595^{0.125} \quad\text{——————} \quad \text{raise each side to the power } \tfrac{1}{8}$$
$$1 + i = 2.47595^{0.125}$$
$$1 + i = 1.1199993$$
$$i = 0.1199993$$
$$= 11.99993\% \quad\text{——————} \quad \text{the desired annual rate}$$

The annual compounding rate is 12.0%.

Programmed solution

You can use preprogrammed financial calculators to find i by the same procedure used previously to determine S or P. That is, select the compound interest mode, enter the given variables S, P, and n, and retrieve the fourth variable i.

0 PMT 200 PV 495.19 FV 8 N CPT %i 11.999925

(annual)

Note: As we emphasized in Chapter 2, it is important to know how to rearrange the terms of an equation. For instance, another way to solve Example 10.4A is first to rearrange Formula 9.1A to solve for i:

$$S = P(1 + i)^n$$

$$(1 + i)^n = \frac{S}{P}$$

$$1 + i = \left(\frac{S}{P}\right)^{\frac{1}{n}}$$

$$i = \left(\frac{S}{P}\right)^{\frac{1}{n}} - 1$$

Recall that i is the periodic rate of interest. If interest is calculated m times per year, then the nominal annual rate of interest $j = m(i)$.

Remember, you do not have to memorize this equation if you understand the principles of formula rearrangement.

EXAMPLE 10.4B

Find the nominal annual rate of interest compounded quarterly if $1200.00 accumulates to $2000.00 in five years.

Solution

$P = 1200.00;$ $S = 2064.51;$ $n = 20;$ $m = 4$

$2064.51 = 1200.00(1 + i)^{20}$ —— i is a *quarterly* rate
$(1 + i)^{20} = 1.720425$
$1 + i = 1.720425^{0.05}$ ———— raise both sides to the power $\frac{1}{20}$, that is, 0.05
$1 + i = 1.0274999$
$i = 0.0274999$
$= 2.74999\%$

The quarterly compounding rate is 2.75%.

Programmed solution

0 PMT 1200 PV 2064.51 FV 20 N CPT %i 2.7499898

Since 2.75% is a quarterly rate, the nominal annual rate of interest is $(2.75\%)(4) = 11.00\%$.

EXAMPLE 10.4C

At what nominal rate of interest compounded quarterly will money double in four years?

Solution   While neither P nor S are given, any sum of money may be used as principal. For this calculation, a convenient value for the principal is $1.00.

$$P = 1; \quad S = 2; \quad n = 16; \quad m = 4$$

$$2 = 1(1 + i)^{16} \quad\text{——} \quad i \text{ is a } quarterly \text{ rate}$$
$$(1 + i)^{16} = 2$$
$$1 + i = 2^{\frac{1}{16}}$$
$$1 + i = 2^{0.0625}$$
$$1 + i = 1.0442738$$
$$i = 0.0442738$$
$$= 4.42738\%$$

Programmed solution

0 [PMT] 1 [PV] 2 [FV] 16 [N] [CPT] [%i] [4.4273781]

(quarterly)

The nominal annual rate is 4(4.4273781%) = 17.71% (approximately).

EXAMPLE 10.4D   Suppose $1000.00 earns interest of $93.81 in one year.

(i) What is the annual rate of interest?

(ii) What is the nominal annual rate of interest compounded monthly?

Solution   (i) $P = 1000.00; \quad I = 93.81; \quad S = P + I = 1093.81; \quad n = 1$

$$1093.81 = 1000.00(1 + i)^1 \quad\text{——} \quad i \text{ is an } annual \text{ rate } (m = 1)$$
$$1 + i = 1.09381$$
$$i = 0.09381$$
$$= 9.381\%$$

Programmed solution

0 [PMT] 1000 [PV] 1093.81 [FV] 1 [N] [CPT] [%i] [9.381000]

The annual rate of interest is about 9.381%.

(ii) $1093.81 = 1000.00(1 + i)^{12} \quad\text{————} \quad i \text{ is a } monthly \text{ rate } (m = 12)$
$$(1 + i)^{12} = 1.09381$$
$$1 + i = 1.09381^{\frac{1}{12}}$$
$$1 + i = 1.09381^{0.0833333}$$
$$1 + i = 1.007500$$
$$i = 1.007500$$
$$= 0.75\%$$

Programmed solution

$$0 \boxed{\text{PMT}} \quad 1000 \boxed{\text{PV}} \quad 1093.81 \boxed{\text{FV}} \quad 12 \boxed{\text{N}} \quad \boxed{\text{CPT}} \quad \boxed{\%i} \quad \boxed{0.7500238}$$

The nominal annual rate of interest compounded monthly is
$(0.75\%)(12) = 9.0\%$.

B. Effective rate of interest

In Example 10.4D, compounding at an annual rate of interest of 9.381% has the same effect as compounding at 9.0% p.a. compounded monthly since, in both cases, the interest amounts to $93.81.

The annual rate of 9.381% is called the **effective rate of interest**. This rate is defined as the rate of interest compounded annually that yields the same amount of interest as a nominal annual rate of interest compounded a number of times per year other than one.

A formula for finding the effective rate of interest can be obtained as follows:

> Let the nominal annual rate of interest be compounded m times per year and let the interest rate per conversion period be i.
> Then the accumulated amount after one year is $S_1 = P(1 + i)^m$.
> Let the corresponding effective annual rate of interest be f.
> Then the accumulated amount after one year is $S_1 = P(1 + f)^1$.

$$P(1 + f)^1 = P(1 + i)^m \quad \text{------------ the amounts are equal by definition}$$
$$1 + f = (1 + i)^m \quad \text{------------ divide both sides by P}$$

$$\boxed{f = (1 + i)^m - 1} \quad \text{------------ Formula 10.1}$$

EXAMPLE 10.4E Determine the effective rate of interest corresponding to 9% p.a. compounded

  (i) monthly;

 (ii) quarterly;

(iii) semi-annually;

(iv) annually;

 (v) daily.

Solution

(i) $i = \left(\dfrac{9\%}{12}\right) = 0.0075; \ m = 12$

$f = (1 + i)^m - 1 \quad \text{------------ using Formula 10.1}$
$\quad = (1 + 0.0075)^{12} - 1$
$\quad = 1.0938069 - 1$
$\quad = 0.0938069$
$\quad = 9.381\%$

(ii) $i = \left(\dfrac{9\%}{4}\right) = 0.0225; \quad m = 4$

$f = (1.0225)^4 - 1$
$= 1.0930833 - 1$
$= 0.0930833$
$= 9.308\%$

(iii) $i = \left(\dfrac{9\%}{2}\right) = 0.045; \quad m = 2$

$f = (1.045)^2 - 1$
$= 1.092025 - 1$
$= 9.2025\%$

(iv) $i = 9\% = 0.09; \quad m = 1$

$f = (1.09)^1 - 1$
$= 9.000\%$

(v) $i = \left(\dfrac{9\%}{365}\right) = 0.0002466; \quad m = 365$

$f = (1.0002466)^{365} - 1$
$= 1.0941720 - 1$
$= 9.417\%$

Summary of Results

For a nominal annual rate of 9% p.a., effective rates are

when compounding annually ($m = 1$)	$f = 9.000\%$
when compounding semi-annually ($m = 2$)	$f = 9.2025\%$
when compounding quarterly ($m = 4$)	$f = 9.308\%$
when compounding monthly ($m = 12$)	$f = 9.381\%$
when compounding daily ($m = 365$)	$f = 9.417\%$

Interpretation of Results

(a) The nominal annual rate is the effective rate of interest if the number of conversion periods per year is 1, that is, if compounding annually.
(b) For a given nominal annual rate, the effective rate of interest increases as the number of conversion periods per year increases.

EXAMPLE 10.4F   You have money to invest in interest-earning deposits. You have determined that suitable deposits are available at your bank paying 6.5% p.a. compounded semi-annually, at a local trust company paying 6.625% p.a., and at your credit union paying 6.45% p.a. compounded monthly. What institution offers the best rate of interest?

Solution   Since the methods of conversion differ, the interest rates are not directly comparable. To make the rates comparable, determine the effective rates of interest corresponding to the nominal annual rates.

For the bank

$$i = \left(\frac{6.5\%}{2}\right) = 0.0325; \quad m = 2$$

$$f = (1 + 0.0325)^2 - 1 = 1.0660563 - 1 = 0.0660563 = 6.606\%$$

For the trust company

$$i = 6.625 = 0.0625; \quad m = 1$$

$$f = i = 6.625\%$$

For the credit union

$$i = \left(\frac{6.45\%}{12}\right) = 0.005375; \quad m = 12$$

$$f = (1.005375)^{12} - 1 = 1.0664414 - 1 = 0.0664414 = 6.644\%$$

While the nominal rate offered by the credit union is lowest, the corresponding effective rate of interest is highest due to the higher frequency of conversion. The rate offered by the credit union is best.

C. Finding the number of conversion periods

If the principal P, the future value S, and the periodic rate of interest i are known, the number of conversion periods n can be determined by substituting the known values in $S = P(1 + i)^n$ and solving for n.

EXAMPLE 10.4G   In how many years will $2000.00 grow to $3277.24 at 10% compounded quarterly?

Solution $P = 2000.00; \quad S = 3277.24; \quad i = 2.5\% = 0.025$

$3277.24 = 2000.00(1.025)^n$ ———————— substituting in Formula 9.1A

$(1.025)^n = 1.63862$

$n \ln 1.025 = \ln 1.63862$ ———————— solve for n using the natural logarithm

$0.0246926n = 0.4938544$ ———————— obtain the numerical values using the $\boxed{\ln x}$ key

$$n = \frac{0.4938544}{0.0246926}$$

$$= 20.000087$$

$$= 20 \text{ (quarters)}$$

$$\text{Number of years} = \frac{20}{4} = 5$$

Programmed solution

You can use preprogrammed financial calculators to find n by the same procedure previously used to find S, P, or i.

0 $\boxed{\text{PMT}}$ 2000 $\boxed{\text{PV}}$ 3277.24 $\boxed{\text{FV}}$ 2.5 $\boxed{\%i}$ $\boxed{\text{CPT}}$ $\boxed{\text{N}}$ $\boxed{20}$

At 10% compounded quarterly, $2000.00 will grow to $3277.24 in five years.

Note: Another way to solve Example 10.4G is first to rearrange Formula 9.1A to solve for *n*:

$$S = P(1 + i)^n$$

$$(1 + i)^n = \frac{S}{P}$$

$$n \ln(1 + i) = \ln\left(\frac{S}{P}\right)$$

$$n = \frac{\ln\left(\dfrac{S}{P}\right)}{\ln(1 + i)}$$

Recall that the total number of conversion periods is *n*. To convert to years if compounding semi-annually, divide *n* by 2; if compounding quarterly, divide by 4; if compounding monthly, divide by 12; and if compounding daily, divide by 365.

Remember, you do not have to memorize this equation if you understand the principles of formula rearrangement.

EXAMPLE 10.4H   How long does it take for money to double

(i) at 10% p.a.?

(ii) at 12% p.a. compounded monthly?

(iii) at 16% p.a. compounded semi-annually?

(iv) at 20% p.a. compounded quarterly?

Solution   While neither P nor S is given, any sum of money may be used as principal. For this calculation, a convenient value for the principal is $1.00.

$$P = 1.00; \quad S = 2.00$$

(i) At 10% p.a., $i = 10\% = 0.10$
$$2 = 1(1 + 0.10)^n$$
$$1.10^n = 2$$
$$n \ln 1.10 = \ln 2$$
$$0.0953102n = 0.6931472$$
$$n = 7.2725409 \text{ (years)}$$

Programmed solution

0 [PMT] 1 [PV] 2 [FV] 10 [%i] [CPT] [N] [7.273]

(years)

At 10% p.a., money doubles in approximately 7 years and 3 months.

(ii) At 12% p.a. compounded monthly, $i = 1\% = 0.01$
$$2 = 1(1.01)^n$$
$$1.01^n = 2$$
$$n \ln 1.01 = \ln 2$$
$$0.0099503n = 0.6931472$$
$$n = 69.660717 \text{ (months)}$$

Programmed solution

(months)

At 12% p.a. compounded monthly, money doubles in approximately 5 years and 10 months.

(iii) At 16% p.a. compounded semi-annually, $i = 8\% = 0.08$

$$1.08^n = 2$$
$$n \ln 1.08 = \ln 2$$
$$0.0769610n = 0.6931472$$
$$n = 9.0064683 \text{ (half-year periods)}$$

Programmed solution

(half-year periods)

At 16% p.a. compounded semi-annually, money doubles in approximately 4.5 years.

(iv) At 20% p.a. compounded quarterly, $i = 5\% = 0.05$

$$1.05^n = 2$$
$$n \ln 1.05 = \ln 2$$
$$0.0487902n = 0.6931472$$
$$n = 14.206699 \text{ (quarters)}$$

Programmed solution

0 [PMT] 1 [PV] 2 [FV] 5 [%i] [CPT] [N] [14.21]

(quarters)

At 20% p.a. compounded quarterly, money doubles in approximately 3 years and 6 months.

DID YOU KNOW?

The Rule of 70

Did you know that there is a quick way to estimate the number of conversion periods needed to double an amount of money? It is known as the *Rule of 70*. According to this rule, the number of conversion periods required to double money is 70 divided by the periodic rate of interest *i*.

Suppose we want to estimate how long it will take to double money if the interest rate is 10% compounded semi-annually. Applying the Rule of 70, we find it will take about 7 years (i.e., 70/5 half-year conversion periods). By comparison, if we calculate the time using the standard formulae, we get a result of about 7.103 years (i.e., about 14.207 half-year conversion periods).

EXAMPLE 10.4I   How long will it take for money to triple at 6% compounded monthly?

Solution   Let P = 1;   then S = 3; $i = 0.5\%$

$$3 = 1(1.005)^n$$
$$1.005^n = 3$$
$$n \ln 1.005 = \ln 3$$
$$0.0049875n = 1.0986123$$
$$n = 220.271 \text{ (months)}$$

Programmed solution

At 6% compounded monthly, money triples in approximately 18 years and 4 months.

Exercise 10.4

A.   Compute the rate of interest or the number of interest periods as indicated.

  1. Compute the effective rate of interest for each of the following.
     (a) 9.5% compounded semi-annually
     (b) 10.5% compounded quarterly
     (c) 5.0% compounded monthly
     (d) 7.2% compounded monthly
     (e) 11.6% compounded quarterly
     (f) 8.2% compounded semi-annually

  2. Find the nominal annual rate of interest for each of the following six investments.

	Principal	Future Value	Time Due	Frequency of Conversion
(a)	$1400.00	$3192.98	7 years	annually
(b)	2350.00	3850.00	5 years	quarterly
(c)	690.00	1225.00	6 years	monthly
(d)	1240.00	4720.80	12 years	semi-annually
(e)	3160.00	5000.00	4 years, 9 months	quarterly
(f)	785.00	1200.00	3 years, 8 months	monthly

3. Determine the number of compounding periods for each of the following six investments.

	Principal	Future Value	Interest Rate	Frequency of Conversion
(a)	$2600.00	$6437.50	7%	annually
(b)	1240.00	2837.00	12%	quarterly
(c)	560.00	1350.00	9%	monthly
(d)	3480.00	4762.60	8%	semi-annually
(e)	950.00	1900.00	7.5%	quarterly
(f)	1300.00	3900.00	6%	semi-annually

B. Solve each of the following.

1. What is the nominal rate of interest compounded quarterly at which $420.00 will accumulate to $1000.00 in nine years and six months?

2. A principal of $1250.00 compounded monthly amounts to $2800.00 in 7.25 years. What is the nominal annual rate of interest?

3. At what nominal rate of interest will money double itself in
   (a) six years, nine months if compounded quarterly?
   (b) nine years, two months if compounded monthly?

4. What is the nominal rate of interest at which money will triple itself in
   (a) twelve years if compounded annually?
   (b) seven years and six months if compounded semi-annually?

5. What is the effective rate of interest if $100.00 grows to $150.00 in six years compounded quarterly?

6. If $1100.00 accumulates to $1850.00 in four years, six months compounded semi-annually, what is the effective rate of interest?

7. Find the nominal annual rate of interest compounded quarterly that is equal to an effective rate of 9.25%.

8. If the effective rate of interest on an investment is 6.4%, what is the nominal rate of interest compounded monthly?

9. How long will it take $400.00 to accumulate to $760.00 at 7% p.a. compounded semi-annually?

10. In how many days will $540.00 grow to $600.00 at 13.5% p.a. compounded monthly?

11. In how many years will money quadruple at 8% compounded quarterly?

12. In how many months will money triple at 9% compounded semi-annually?

13. If an investment of $800.00 earned interest of $320.00 at 12% compounded monthly, for how many years was the money invested?

14. A loan of $2000.00 was repaid together with interest of $1164.00. If interest was 14% compounded quarterly, for how many months was the loan taken out?

15. If you borrowed $1000.00 on May 1, 2000, at 10% compounded semi-annually and interest on the loan amounts to $157.63, on what date is the loan due?

16. A promissory note for $600.00 dated May 15, 1998, requires an interest payment of $150.00 at maturity. If interest is at 9% compounded monthly, determine the due date of the note.

17. A non-interest-bearing promissory note for $1500.00 was discounted at 13% p.a. compounded quarterly. If the proceeds of the note were $1199.11, how many months before the due date was the note discounted?

18. A five-year, $1000.00 note bearing interest at 9% compounded annually was discounted at 12% compounded semi-annually yielding proceeds of $1416.56. How many months before the due date was the discount date?

BUSINESS MATH NEWS BOX

MAKE THE SMART MOVE IN A GIC

Move your RRSP to a CIBC RRSP GIC and get an exceptional rate.

"Earn double CIBC's best GIC rates on 10% of RRSP funds when you transfer $10,000 or more from an RRSP held at another financial institution to a CIBC RRSP GIC.

"For example, if you transfer $10,000 to a CIBC RRSP GIC, you'd receive our best rate on $9,000 . . . and double that rate on $1,000!"

In this advertisement, CIBC offers five RRSP Guaranteed Investment Certificate (GIC) terms. You can invest in the RRSP GIC for one year, two years, three years, four years, or five years, at the rates shown in the chart. Interest is compounded annually, but paid to you at the end of the GIC term.

New CIBC Double Rate RRSP GIC					
	1 Year	2 Year	3 Year	4 Year	5 Year
$9,000 CIBC RRSP GIC at CIBC's best rate	2.5%	3.5%	4.0%	4.5%	5.0%
$1,000 CIBC RRSP GIC at the Double Rate	5.0%	7.0%	8.0%	9.0%	10.0%

These rates are current as at January 13, 1997. Interest rates are subject to change without notice. Interest is calculated annually and paid at maturity.

QUESTIONS

1. Suppose you have $10 000.00 in an RRSP held at another financial institution. You are considering a transfer of this money to a CIBC RRSP GIC to take advantage of the interest rates shown in the chart. What is the effective rate of interest you would earn on the $10 000.00 for each of the five terms using the interest rates shown in the chart?

2. Suppose another financial institution offered a five-year RRSP GIC with interest at 5.3% compounded quarterly, paid to you at the end of the term. Is this investment better than the five-year CIBC RRSP GIC described above? Assume an investment of $10 000.00 to make your comparison. What is the difference in interest earned on this $10 000.00 investment?

10.5 SPECIAL PROBLEMS—EQUATED DATE, EQUIVALENT RATES, CONTINUOUS COMPOUNDING

A. Equated date

Chapter 9, Section 9.5, considered the concept of *equivalence* of values when using the compound interest method. In solving problems of equivalence, the unknown value was always the size of a payment at the selected focal date. While this type is the most frequently arising problem, occasionally the value to be found is the focal date or the interest rate.

The **equated date** is the date on which a single sum of money is equal to the sum of two or more dated sums of money. To find an equated date, an equation of values can be set up by the same technique, used in Section 9.5. However, solving the equation for n requires the same technique as used in Section 10.4C. Since this method involves the use of logarithms, you can solve the problem using an electronic calculator as long as the calculator is equipped with the natural logarithm function ($\boxed{\ln x}$ key).

EXAMPLE 10.5A A financial obligation requires the payment of $2000.00 in six months, $3000.00 in fifteen months, and $5000.00 in 24 months. When can the obligation be discharged by the single payment equal to the sum of the required payments if money is worth 9% p.a. compounded monthly?

Solution The single payment equal to the sum of the required payments is $2000.00 plus $3000.00 plus $5000.00, or $10 000.00. Select as the focal date "now." Let the number of compounding periods from the focal date to the equated date be represented by n. Since the compounding is done monthly, n will be a number of months and $i = \frac{9\%}{12} = 0.75\% = 0.0075$. The method and data are shown graphically in Figure 10.1.

Let E_1, E_2, and E_3 represent the equivalent values of the original payments at the focal date as shown in Figure 10.1.

Let E_4 represent the equivalent value of the single payment of $10 000.00 at the focal date.

The equation of values can now be set up.

$$E_4 = E_1 + E_2 + E_3$$

$$10\ 000.00(1.0075)^{-n} = 2000.00(1.0075)^{-6} + 3000.00(1.0075)^{-15}$$
$$+ 5000.00(1.0075)^{-24}$$

$$10\ 000.00(1.0075)^{-n} = 2000.00(0.956158) + 3000.00(0.8939725)$$
$$+ 5000.00(0.8358314)$$

$$10\ 000.00(1.0075)^{-n} = 1912.32 + 2681.92 + 4179.16$$

$$10\ 000.00(1.0075)^{-n} = 8773.40$$

$$(1.0075)^{-n} = \frac{8773.40}{10\ 000.00}$$

$$(1.0075)^{-n} = 0.87734$$

$$-n(\ln 1.0075) = \ln 0.87734$$

$$-n(0.007472) = -0.1308607$$

$$n = \frac{0.1308607}{0.007472}$$

$$n = 17.513477$$

FIGURE 10.1   Graphic Representation of Method and Data

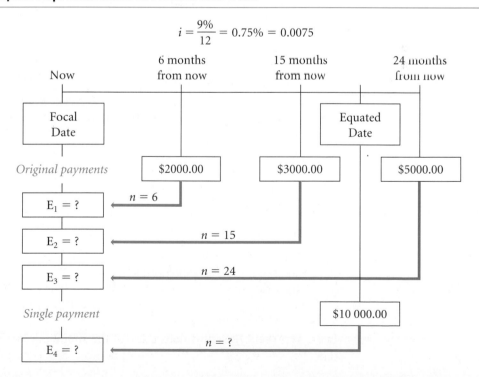

$$i = \frac{9\%}{12} = 0.75\% = 0.0075$$

Programmed solution

First simplify the equation $E_4 = E_1 + E_2 + E_3$.

$$10\ 000(1.0075)^{-n} = 2000.00(1.0075)^{-6} + 3000(1.0075)^{-15} + 5000(1.0075)^{-24}$$

$2000(1.0075)^{-6}$

0 PMT 2000 FV 0.75 %i 6 N CPT PV 1912.316

$3000(1.0075)^{-15}$

0 PMT 3000 FV 0.75 %i 15 N CPT PV 2681.9176

$5000(1.0075)^{-24}$

0 PMT 5000 FV 0.75 %i 24 N CPT PV 4179.1571

$$10\ 000(1.0075)^{-n} = 1912.32 + 2681.92 + 4179.16$$
$$10\ 000(1.0075)^{-n} = 8773.40$$

Now solve the simplified equation

$$10\ 000(1.0075)^{-n} = 8773.40$$

in which S = 10 000; P = 8773.40; $i = 0.75\%$

0 PMT 10 000 FV 8773.40 PV 0.75 %i CPT N 17.51

The equated date is about 17.5 months from now.

While the definition of equated date requires that the single sum of money be equal to the sum of the dated sums of money considered, the method used in solving the problem can be applied to problems in which the single sum of money does not equal the sum of the dated sums of money considered.

EXAMPLE 10.5B A loan is to be repaid by three equal payments of $1500.00 due now, two years from now, and four years from now respectively. When can the obligation be paid off by a single payment of $5010.00 if interest is 10% compounded annually?

Solution Select as the focal date "now." Let the number of compounding periods from the focal date to the equated date be represented by n. Since the compounding is done annually, n will be a number of years and $i = 10\% = 0.10$.

Let E_1, E_2, and E_3 represent the equivalent values of the original payments at the focal date.

$$
\begin{aligned}
E_1 &= 1500.00 &&= 1500.00\\
E_2 &= 1500.00(1.10)^{-2} = 1500.00(0.8264463) &&= 1239.67\\
E_3 &= 1500.00(1.10)^{-4} = 1500.00(0.6830135) &&= \underline{1024.52}\\
&& E_1 + E_2 + E_3 &= 3764.19
\end{aligned}
$$

Let E_4 represent the equivalent value of the single payment of $5010.00 at the focal date.

$$E_4 = 5010.00(1.10)^{-n}$$
$$E_4 = E_1 + E_2 + E_3$$
$$5010.00(1.10)^{-n} = 3764.19$$
$$(1.10)^{-n} = 0.7513353$$
$$-n(\ln 1.10) = \ln 0.7513353$$
$$-0.0953102n = -0.2859033$$
$$n = 3$$

Programmed solution

$$E_4 = E_1 + E_2 + E_3$$

$$5010.00(1.10)^{-n} = 1500.00 + 1500(1.10)^{-2} + 1500(1.10)^{-4}$$

$$1500(1.10)^{-2}$$

0 [PMT] 1500 [FV] 10 [%i] 2 [N] [CPT] [PV] [1239.6694]

$$1500(1.10)^{-4}$$

0 [PMT] 1500 [FV] 10 [%i] 4 [N] [CPT] [PV] [1024.5202]

$$5010.00(1.10)^{-n} = 1500.00 + 1239.67 + 1024.52$$
$$5010.00(1.10)^{-n} = 3764.19$$

0 [PMT] 5010 [FV] 3764.19 [PV] 10 [%i] [CPT] [N] [3]

The single payment should be made three years from now.

EXAMPLE 10.5C   A loan of $2000.00 taken out today is to be repaid by a payment of $1200.00 in six months and a final payment of $1000.00. If interest is 12% compounded monthly, when should the final payment be made?

Solution   Let the focal point be "now"; $i = \dfrac{12\%}{12} = 1.0\% = 0.01$.

$$2000.00 = 1200.00(1.01)^{-6} + 1000.00(1.01)^{-n}$$
$$2000.00 = 1200.00(0.9420452) + 1000.00(1.01)^{-n}$$
$$2000.00 = 1130.45 + 1000.00(1.01)^{-n}$$
$$869.55 = 1000.00(1.01)^{-n}$$
$$(1.01)^{-n} = 0.86955$$
$$-n(\ln 1.01) = \ln 0.86955$$
$$-0.0099503n = -0.1397794$$
$$n = 14.0457 \text{ (months)}$$

Programmed solution
$$2000.00 = 1200.00(1.01)^{-6} + 1000(1.01)^{-n}$$
$$1200.00(1.01)^{-6}$$

0 [PMT] 1200 [FV] 1 [%i] 6 [N] [CPT] [PV] [1130.4543]

$$2000.00 = 1130.4543 + 1000(1.01)^{-n}$$
$$869.5457 = 1000(1.01)^{-n}$$

$$869.5457 \boxed{\text{PV}} \quad 1000 \boxed{\text{FV}} \quad 1 \boxed{\%i} \quad \boxed{\text{CPT}} \quad \boxed{\text{PV}} \quad \boxed{14.05}$$
(months)

$$n = 427 \; days \quad \underline{\hspace{6cm}} \left(\frac{14.047757}{12}\right)(365)$$

The final payment should be made in 427 days.

B. Equivalent rates

Interest rates that increase a given principal to the same future value over the same period of time are called **equivalent rates**.

EXAMPLE 10.5D Find the future value after one year of $100.00 accumulated at

(i) 12.55% compounded annually;

(ii) 12.18% compounded semi-annually;

(iii) 12.00% compounded quarterly;

(iv) 11.88% compounded monthly.

	(i)	**(ii)**	**(iii)**	**(iv)**
Principal	100.00	100.00	100.00	100.00
Nominal rate	12.55%	12.18%	12.00%	11.88%
i	0.1255	0.0609	0.03	0.0099
n	1	2	4	12
future value	$100.00(1.1255)^1$ $= 100.00(1.1255)$ $= \$112.55$	$100.00(1.0609)^2$ $= 100.00(1.1255088)$ $= \$112.55$	$100.00(1.03)^4$ $= 100.00(1.1255088)$ $= \$112.55$	$100.00(1.0099)^{12}$ $= 100.00(1.1254870)$ $= \$112.55$

Solution

Note: The four different nominal annual rates produce the same future value of $112.55 for the same principal of $100.00 over the same time period of one year. By definition, the four nominal rates are equivalent rates.

To find equivalent rates, we need to equate the accumulated values of $1 for the rates under consideration based on a selected time period, usually one year.

EXAMPLE 10.5E Find the nominal annual rate compounded semi-annually that is equivalent to an effective annual rate of 12%.

Solution   Let the semi-annual rate of interest be represented by i.
For P = 1, $n = 2$, the accumulated value $S_1 = (1 + i)^2$.
For the given effective rate, the accumulated value $S_2 = (1 + 0.12)^1$.
By definition, to be equivalent, $S_1 = S_2$.

$$(1 + i)^2 = 1.12$$
$$1 + i = 1.12^{0.5}$$
$$1 + i = 1.0583005$$
$$i = 0.0583005 \text{ ———————— semi-annual rate}$$

Programmed solution

$$1 \qquad (1 + i)^2 = \qquad 1.12$$
$$\downarrow \qquad\qquad\qquad\qquad \downarrow$$
$$P \qquad\qquad\qquad\qquad S$$

0 [PMT] 1 [PV] 1.12 [FV] 2 [N] [CPT] [%i] 5.8300523

(semi-annually)

The nominal annual rate is $2(0.0583005) = 0.1166010 = 11.66\%$.

EXAMPLE 10.5F   What nominal rate compounded quarterly is equivalent to 11.4% p.a. compounded monthly?

Solution   Let the quarterly rate be i; P = 1; $n = 4$.
The accumulated value of $1 after one year $S_1 = (1 + i)^4$.

For the given rate $i = \dfrac{11.4\%}{12} = 0.95\% = 0.0095$; $n = 12$.

The accumulated value of $1 after one year $S_2 = (1.0095)^{12}$.
To be equivalent, $S_1 = S_2$.

$$(1 + i)^4 = (1.0095)^{12}$$
$$1 + i = (1.0095)^3$$
$$1 + i = 1.0287716$$
$$i = 0.0287716 \text{ ———————— quarterly rate}$$

Programmed solution
$$(1 + i)^4 = (1.0095)^{12}$$
$$(1.0095)^{12}$$

0 [PMT] 1 [PV] 0.95 [%i] 12 [N] [CPT] [FV] 1.1201492

$$1(1 + i)^4 = 1.1201492$$

0 [PMT] 1 [PV] 1.1201492 [FV] 4 [N] [CPT] [%i] 2.8771602

(quarterly)

The nominal annual rate is $4(0.0287716) = 0.1150864 = 11.51\%$.

EXAMPLE 10.5G   Peel Credit Union offers premium savings deposits at 8% interest paid semi-annually. The Board of Directors wants to change to monthly payment of interest. What nominal rate should the board set to maintain the same effective rate?

Solution

Let the monthly rate be i; $n = 12$; $P = 1$.
The accumulated value of \$1 after one year $S_1 = (1 + i)^{12}$.
For the existing rate, $n = 2$, $i = 0.04$.
The accumulated value of \$1 in one year $S_2 = (1.04)^2$.
To yield the same effective rate, the two rates must be equivalent.

$$(1 + i)^{12} = (1.04)^2$$
$$1 + i = (1.04)^{\frac{1}{6}}$$
$$1 + i = 1.0065582$$
$$i = 0.0065582 \quad\text{———— monthly rate}$$

Programmed solution

$$(1 + i)^{12} = (1.04)^2$$

$$(1.04)^2$$

0 PMT 1 PV 4 %i 2 N CPT FV 1.0816

$$1(1 + i)^{12} = 1.0816$$

0 PMT 1 PV 1.0816 FV 12 N CPT %i 0.6558196

(monthly)

The nominal rate is $12(0.0065582) = 0.0786984 = 7.87\%$.

Note: The effective annual rate of interest using Formula 10.1, $f = (1 + i)^m - 1$, for the existing rate is

$$f = (1 + 0.04)^2 - 1 = 1.0816 - 1 = 0.0816 = 8.16\%$$

and for the new nominal rate compounded monthly is

$$f = (1 + 0.0065582)^{12} - 1 = 1.0816 - 1 = 0.0816 = 8.16\%$$

C. Continuous compounding

Compounding is not restricted to the commonly used annual, semi-annual, quarterly, and monthly intervals. Rather, it can be done at any time interval. Daily compounding has become quite feasible with the widespread installation of computers in financial institutions. Shorter and shorter time intervals can be used until the limiting case, known as **continuous compounding**, is reached.

Formulae for continuous compounding have been developed and are listed below (Formulae 10.2A, 10.2B, and 10.3). You can solve problems involving continuous compounding using an electronic calculator equipped with an antilog function (e^x key). This function is normally available on calculators equipped with a ln x key.

Caution: The programming feature *cannot* be used for continuous compounding.

(a) *Finding the compound amount*

$$S = Pe^{nj} \quad\text{———— Formula 10.2A}$$

COMPOUND INTEREST—FURTHER TOPICS

e = the universal constant 2.7182818 (approximately);
n = the number of years for compounding;
j = the nominal annual rate of interest.

(b) *Finding the present value*

$$\boxed{P = Se^{-nj}}$$ ——————————————— **Formula 10.2B**

(c) *Finding the effective rate of interest*

$$\boxed{f = e^j - 1}$$ ——————————————— **Formula 10.3**

EXAMPLE 10.5H To how much will $100.00 grow at 10% compounded continuously in

(i) one year?

(ii) two years?

(iii) eight years?

Solution

(i) $P = 100.00$; $n = 1$; $j = 10\% = 0.10$

$S = 100.00[e^{1(0.10)}]$ ——————————— substituting in Formula 10.2A

$= 100.00(e^{0.10})$

$= 100.00(1.1051709)$ ——————————— enter 0.10 in calculator and use the

$= \$110.52$ $\boxed{e^x}$ key

(ii) $P = 100.00$; $n = 2$; $j = 10\% = 0.10$

$S = 100.00[e^{2(0.10)}] = 100.00(e^{0.20}) = 100.00(1.2214028) = \$122.14$

(iii) $P = 100.00$; $n = 8$; $j = 10\% = 0.10$

$S = 100.00[e^{8(0.10)}] = 100.00(e^{0.80}) = 100.00(2.2255409) = \$222.55$

EXAMPLE 10.5I What is the present value of $1000.00 at 12% compounded continuously due in

(i) 2.5 years?

(ii) 5 years, 9 months?

(iii) 12 years, 8 months?

Solution

(i) $S = 1000.00$; $n = 2.5$; $j = 12\% = 0.12$

$P = 1000.00[e^{-2.5(0.12)}]$ ——————————— substituting in Formula 10.2B

$= 1000.00(e^{-0.30})$

$= 1000.00(0.7408182)$

$= \$740.82$

(ii) $S = 1000.00; \quad n = 5.75; \quad j = 12\% = 0.12$

$$P = 1000.00[e^{-5.75(0.12)}]$$
$$= 1000.00(e^{-0.69})$$
$$= 1000.00(0.5015761)$$
$$= \$501.58$$

(iii) $S = 1000.00; \quad n = 12.666667; \quad j = 12\% = 0.12$

$$P = 1000.00[e^{-12.666667(0.12)}]$$
$$= 1000.00(e^{-1.52})$$
$$= 1000.00(0.2187119)$$
$$= \$218.71$$

EXAMPLE 10.5J

Find the effective rate of interest for each of the following nominal rates compounded continuously:

(i) 10%

(ii) 15%

Solution

(i) $f = e^j - 1$ ———————————————— substituting in Formula 10.3
$$= e^{0.10} - 1$$
$$= 1.1051709 - 1$$
$$= 0.1051709$$

$$= 10.517\%$$

(ii) $f = e^{0.15} - 1$
$$= 1.1618342 - 1$$
$$= 0.1618342$$

$$= 16.18\%$$

EXAMPLE 10.5K

How long will it take money to double if compounded continuously at

(i) 10%?

(ii) 18%?

Solution

$P = 1.00; S = 2.00$

$$2.00 = 1.00(e^{nj})$$ ———————————— substituting in Formula 10.2A
$$e^{nj} = 2$$
$$nj(\ln e) = \ln 2$$ ———————————— using the natural logarithm

$$nj = \frac{\ln 2}{\ln e}$$

$$nj = \ln 2$$ ———————————— $\ln e = 1$

$$n = \frac{\ln 2}{j}$$ ———————————— a general solution for doubling money

(i) $j = 10\% = 0.10$

$$n = \frac{\ln 2}{0.10}$$
$$= \frac{0.6931472}{0.10}$$
$$= 6.9314718 \text{ (years)}$$
$$= 83 \text{ months}$$

(ii) $j = 18\% = 0.18$

$$n = \frac{\ln 2}{0.18}$$
$$= \frac{0.6931472}{0.18}$$
$$= 3.8508177 \text{ (years)}$$
$$= 46 \text{ months}$$

Note: The Rule of 70 referred to in the Did You Know? section, used to estimate the number of conversion periods required to double money, originates from the general solution for doubling money when compounding continuously. Since $\ln 2 = 0.69314718$ or approximately 0.70, an estimate of n is given by $n = {}^{0.70}\!/_j$. To convert the interest to percent form, multiply 0.70 by 100—the Rule of 70. Similar rules could have been established for tripling, quadrupling, etc.

To triple money, $n = \frac{\ln 3}{j} = \frac{1.0986123}{j}$ or approximately $\frac{110}{\text{rate of interest}}$ (this is the Rule of 110). For $j = 10\%$, money triples in about $\frac{110}{10} = 11$ compounding periods.

To quadruple money, $n = \frac{\ln 4}{j} = \frac{1.3862944}{j}$ or approximately $\frac{139}{\text{rate of interest}}$.

For $j = 10\%$, money quadruples in about $\frac{139}{10} = 14$ periods.

EXAMPLE 10.5L   What is the nominal rate compounded continuously that is equivalent to 12% compounded quarterly?

Solution   Let the nominal rate compounded continuously be represented by j.
For P $= 1$ and $n = 1$, the accumulated value in one year $S_1 = e^j$.
For 12% compounded quarterly, the accumulated value in one year $S_2 = (1.03)^4$.
To be equivalent, $S_1 = S_2$.

$$e^j = (1.03)^4$$
$$e^j = 1.1255088$$
$$j(\ln e) = \ln 1.1255088$$
$$j = 0.1182352 \quad\text{———}\quad \ln e = 1$$
$$j = 11.82\%$$

Exercise 10.5

A. Answer each of the following.

1. Find the equated date at which the original payments are equivalent to the single payment for each of the following four sets of payments.

Original Payments	Interest Rate	Frequency of Conversion	Single Payment
(a) $400 due in 9 months and $700 due in 21 months	12%	quarterly	$1256.86
(b) $1200 due today and $2000 due in 5 years	8%	semi-annually	$3808.70
(c) $1000 due 8 months ago, $1200 due in 6 months, and $1500 due in 16 months	9%	monthly	$3600.00
(d) $600 due in 2 years, $800 due in 3.5 years, and $900 due in 5 years	10%	quarterly	$1800.00

2. Find the nominal annual rate of interest equivalent to each of the following.
   (a) 12.5% compounded semi-annually
   (b) 6% compounded monthly
   (c) 7.2% compounded quarterly
   (d) 10.2% compounded monthly

3. Find the accumulated value of each of the following sums of money compounded continuously.
   (a) $400.00 at 7% for six years
   (b) $2700.00 at 11.5% for 12 years
   (c) $1800.00 at 5.5% for four years, seven months
   (d) $3700.00 at 10.4% for three years, ten months

4. Find the present value of each of the following amounts if interest is compounded continuously.
   (a) $6000.00 due in 18 years at 7.75%
   (b) $3400.00 due in nine years, six months at 9.8%
   (c) $4500.00 due in two years, five months at 6.25%
   (d) $1000.00 due in one year, nine months at $12\frac{3}{8}$%

5. Find the effective rate of each of the following nominal rates compounded continuously.
   (a) 11.5%
   (b) 7.3%

B. Solve each of the following problems.

1. A contract requires payments of $4000.00 today, $5000.00 in three years, and $6000.00 in five years. When can the contract be fulfilled by a single payment equal to the sum of the required payments if money is worth 9% p.a. compounded monthly?

2. A financial obligation requires the payment of $500.00 in nine months, $700.00 in fifteen months, and $600.00 in 27 months. When can the obligation be discharged by a single payment of $1600.00 if interest is 10% compounded quarterly?

3. When Brenda bought Sheridan Service from Ken, she agreed to make three payments of $6000.00 each in one year, three years, and five years respectively. Because of initial cash flow difficulties, Brenda offered to pay $8000.00 in two years and a second payment of $10 000.00 at a later date. When should she make the second payment if interest is 9.75% compounded semi-annually?

4. Leo sold a property and is to receive $3000.00 in six months, $4000.00 in 24 months, and $5000.00 in 36 months. The deal was renegotiated after nine months at which time Leo received a payment of $7000.00; he was to receive a further payment of $6000.00 later. When should Leo receive the second payment if money is worth 11% compounded quarterly?

5. The Central Bank pays 7.5% compounded semi-annually on certain types of deposits. If interest is compounded monthly, what nominal rate of interest will maintain the same effective rate of interest?

6. The treasurer of Sheridan Credit Union proposes changing the method of compounding interest on premium savings accounts to daily compounding. If the current rate is 6% compounded quarterly, what nominal rate should the treasurer suggest to the Board of Directors to maintain the same effective rate of interest?

7. You have invested $1000.00 for five years at 8% compounded quarterly. How much more interest would you earn if interest were compounded continuously?

8. A private lender requires interest of 9.5% compounded continuously. A local bank charges 9.6% compounded monthly. How much more is the private lender's interest on a loan of $8000.00 taken out for eight years?

9. What single payment made today would pay off two debt payments of $1600.00 each, due in 15 months and 30 months respectively, if interest is 8% compounded continuously?

10. A contract offers $4000.00 in three years, $7000.00 in six years, and $9000.00 in eight years. What single sum of money paid today would satisfy the contract if money is worth 11.75% compounded continuously?

11. What nominal rate of interest compounded quarterly is equivalent to 5% compounded continuously?

12. Compute the nominal rate of interest compounded monthly that is equivalent to 12.5% compounded continuously.

13. How long will it take money to double if compounded continuously at
    (a) 6%?
    (b) 11.4%?

14. What length of time will it take money
    (a) to triple at 9% compounded continuously?
    (b) to quadruple at 10.4% compounded continuously?

15. What nominal rate compounded continuously is equivalent to 7% compounded quarterly?

16. Find the nominal rate compounded continuously that is equivalent to 6.6% compounded monthly.

REVIEW EXERCISE

1. If $6000.00 is invested for six years and seven months at 6% compounded semi-annually, what is the interest that the investment earns?

2. Determine the sum of money that will grow to $14 000 in four years, eight months at 5% compounded quarterly.

3. Compute the maturity value of a $5000 promissory note dated November 15, 1990, and due on June 15, 2000, if interest is 8% compounded quarterly.

4. Determine the proceeds of $9000 three years and ten months before the due date if interest is 7% compounded semi-annually.

5. A fifteen-year promissory note for $16 500 bearing interest at 15% compounded monthly is discounted at 9% compounded semi-annually three years and four months after the date of issue. Compute the proceeds of the note.

6. An eight-year promissory note for $20 000 dated May 2, 1998, bearing interest at 10% compounded quarterly, is discounted on September 2, 2000, at 9.5% compounded semi-annually. Determine the proceeds of the note.

7. An investment of $2000.00 is made for three years, four months at 12.5% compounded semi-annually. What is the amount of interest?

8. Determine the discounted value now of $5200.00 due in forty months at 6.5% compounded quarterly.

9. Compute the proceeds of a non-interest-bearing promissory note for $1600.00 two years and eight months before the due date if money is worth 9.5% compounded annually.

10. At what nominal rate of interest compounded monthly will $400.00 earn $300.00 interest in four years?

11. What nominal rate of interest compounded monthly is equivalent to an effective rate of 6.2%?

12. Find the equated date at which two payments of $500.00 due six months ago and $600.00 due today could be settled by a payment of $1300.00 if interest is 9% compounded monthly.

13. Find the accumulated value of $700.00 at 8.5% compounded continuously for seven years.

14. Find the principal that will grow to $1450.00 at 11% compounded continuously in six years and nine months.

15. In what period of time will money triple at 10% compounded semi-annually?

16. Find the effective rate equivalent to 6.75% compounded continuously.

17. Find the future value of

   (a) $3500 compounded continuously for six years at 7%;

   (b) $8400 compounded continuously for three years, eight months at 8%.

18. Find the present value of

   (a) $10 000 due in ten years if interest is 4% compounded continuously;

   (b) $7000 due in four years, four months if interest is 5.5% compounded continuously.

19. Find the nominal annual rate of interest correct to two decimals

   (a) at which $2500 will grow to $7000 in eight years compounded quarterly;

   (b) at which money will double in five years compounded semi-annually;

   (c) if the effective annual rate of interest is 9.2% and compounding is done monthly;

   (d) which is equivalent to 8% compounded quarterly;

   (e) which is equivalent to 8% compounded continuously.

20. Compute the effective annual rate of interest correct to two decimals

    (a) for 10.5% compounded monthly;

    (b) at which $2000 will grow to $4800 in seven years compounded quarterly;

    (c) for 9% compounded continuously.

21. (a) What is the nominal annual rate of interest compounded monthly that is equivalent to 8.5% compounded quarterly?

    (b) What is the nominal annual rate of interest compounded quarterly that is equivalent to an effective annual rate of 12%?

22. (a) How many years will it take for $7500 to accumulate to $17 664.48 at 11% compounded semi-annually?

    (b) Over what period of time will money triple at 9% compounded quarterly?

    (c) How long will it take for a loan of $10 000 to amount to $13 684 at 10.5% compounded monthly?

    (d) In how many years will money double if compounded continuously at 9%?

23. A financial obligation requires the payment of $2000 now, $2500 in six months, and $4000 in one year. When will a single payment of $9000 discharge the obligation if interest is 6% compounded monthly?

24. Gitu owes two debt payments—a payment of $5000 due in six months and a payment of $6000 due in fifteen months. If Gitu makes a payment of $5000 now, when should he make a second payment of $6000 if money is worth 11% compounded semi-annually?

25. Payment of a debt of $10 000 incurred on December 1, 1997, with interest at 9.5% compounded semi-annually is due on December 1, 2000. If a payment of $7500 is made on December 1, 1999, on what date should a second payment of $7500 be made if money is worth 12% compounded quarterly?

26. Debts of $700 due in six months, $500 due in fifteen months, and $900 due in two years are to be settled by a single payment one year from now. What is the size of that single payment if interest is 10.5% compounded continuously?

27. Three years and five months after its date of issue, a six-year promissory note for $3300.00 bearing interest at 12% compounded monthly is discounted at 11% compounded semi-annually. Find the proceeds of the note.

28. A seven-year, $1500.00 promissory note with interest at 10.5% compounded semi-annually was discounted at 12% compounded quarterly yielding proceeds of $2150.00. How many months before the due date was the discount date?

29. A contract requires payments of $2000.00 in one year and $4000.00 in five years. The contract was renegotiated and met by a payment of $3000.00 in two years and a final payment of $4500.00. If interest was 7.5% compounded continuously, when was the second payment made?

30. What is the nominal rate compounded continuously which is equivalent to 7% compounded semi-annually?

SELF-TEST

1. A ten-year, $9200 promissory note with interest at 12% compounded monthly is discounted at 10% compounded semi-annually yielding proceeds of $18 191.35. How many months before the due date was the date of discount?

2. Determine the maturity value of $1400 due in 71 months compounding annually at 7.75%.

3. Determine the effective annual rate of interest equivalent to 15% compounded monthly.

4. What is the nominal rate of interest compounded continuously that is equivalent to 13% compounded quarterly?

5. How many months from now can a payment of $1000 due twelve months ago and a payment of $400 due six months from now be settled by a payment of $1746.56 if interest is 10.2% compounded monthly?

6. At what nominal rate of interest compounded semi-annually will $6900 earn $6400 interest in five years?

7. In how many years will money double at 7.2% compounded quarterly?

8. What is the nominal rate of interest compounded semi-annually that is equivalent to an effective rate of 10.25%?

9. Seven years and two months after its date of issue, an eleven-year promissory note for $8200 bearing interest at 13.5% compounded monthly is discounted at 10.5% compounded semi-annually. Find the proceeds of the note.

10. Find the accumulated value of $5100 invested at 8.9% compounded continuously for ten years and six months.

11. Compute the proceeds of a non-interest-bearing note for $1100 three years and seven months before the due date if money is worth 11% p.a. compounded annually.

12. Find the principal that will grow to $7400 at 5% compounded continuously in ten years and eight months.

CHALLENGE PROBLEMS

1. Olga deposited $800 in an investment certificate paying 9% compounded semi-annually. On the same day, her sister Ursula deposited $600 in an account paying 7% compounded semi-annually. To the nearest day, when will the future value of Olga's investment be equal to twice the future value of Ursula's investment?

2. A financial institution is advertising a new three-year investment certificate. The interest rate is 7.5% compounded quarterly the first year, 6.5% compounded monthly the second year, and 6% compounded daily the third year. What rate of interest compounded continuously for three years would a competing institution have to offer to match the interest produced by this investment certificate?

CASE STUDY 10.1 CHOOSING A CREDIT CARD

Win Leung received an advertisement in the mail from a large credit card company describing the features of its new credit card. This new credit card has no annual fee and a Preferred Customer Interest Rate. If Win applies for this credit card before the end of the year, he will receive the Introductory Interest Rate of 9.9% for the first six months if he pays the minimum monthly payments on time. He will then receive the Preferred Customer Interest Rate of 13.95% if he pays the minimum monthly payments on time. The advertisement emphasized that the Standard Interest Rate on their card is 17.95%, so Win can save 4% with this new promotion.

Additional information was given in small print at the end of the advertisement:

• Current equivalent annual rates: 9.9% Introductory Interest Rate; 13.95% Preferred Customer Interest Rate; 17.95% Standard Interest Rate. For example, interest on a $1000 average daily balance for 30 days will be $1000 × 1/365 × applicable annual rate × 30. The Standard Interest Rate always applies to cash advances and also applies when you do not qualify for the Preferred Customer Interest Rate or the Introductory Interest Rate.

- You will not be assessed interest only if you pay your monthly statement *in full* by the payment due date *and* no cash advances have been taken by you during the billing period. If your new balance is not paid in full, interest will be charged: (1) on your outstanding balance from the statement closing date; and (2) on future purchases from the day the purchases are posted to your account. On cash advance transactions, interest is always charged from the date you take the cash advance.

QUESTIONS

1. Using the formula given in the advertisement's small print, calculate the interest charge for a $1000 average daily balance for 30 days using each of the three interest rates. Are these simple interest or compound interest calculations?

2. Win chose this credit card and received the Introductory Interest Rate for the first six months and the Preferred Customer Interest Rate for the next six months because he made the minimum monthly payments on time. Under these circumstances, what is the effective annual rate of interest over the twelve-month period?

3. The Introductory Interest Rate fell to 8.9% and the Preferred Customer Interest Rate increased to 14.25%. Because Win made the minimum monthly payments on time, he received the Introductory Interest Rate for the first six months and the Preferred Customer Interest Rate for the next six months. Under these circumstances, what is the effective annual rate of interest over the twelve-month period?

4. Win has been using the new credit card for more than one year.
   (a) Suppose Win makes the minimum monthly payments on time so that he receives the Preferred Customer Interest Rate of 13.95%. What is the effective annual rate of interest if the 13.95% is compounded monthly for one year?
   (b) Suppose Win does not make the minimum monthly payments on time, so he must pay the Standard Interest Rate of 17.25%. What is the effective annual rate of interest if the 17.25% is compounded monthly for one year?

5. What is the effective annual rate of interest if
   (a) Win makes the minimum monthly payments and the Preferred Customer Interest Rate increases to 14.95%?
   (b) Win does not make the minimum monthly payments and the Standard Interest Rate increases to 18.95%?

6. If you have a credit card, how do the rates and conditions of your credit card compare with the card described in the advertisement?

CASE STUDY 10.2 COMPARING CAR LOANS

After reading some car guides and receiving advice from family and friends, Naina has chosen the new car she wants to buy. She now wants to research her financing options to choose the best way to pay for the car.

Naina knows that with taxes, licence, and delivery fees, her car will cost $17 000.00. She has saved $5000.00 toward the purchase price but must borrow the rest. She has narrowed her financing choices to three options: dealer financing, credit union financing, and bank financing.

(i) The car dealer has offered 48-month financing at 5.9% compounded monthly.

(ii) The credit union has offered 36-month financing at 5.95% compounded quarterly. It has also offered 48-month financing at 6.0% compounded quarterly.

(iii) The bank has offered 36-month financing at 6.0% compounded semi-annually. It has also offered 48-month financing at 6.10% compounded semi-annually.

Naina wants to choose the financing option that offers the best interest rate. However, she also wants to explore the financing options that allow her to pay off her car loan more quickly.

QUESTIONS

1. Naina wants to compare the 48-month car loan options offered by the car dealer, the credit union, and the bank.

   (a) What is the effective annual rate of interest for each 48-month option?
   (b) How much interest will Naina save by choosing the best option compared with the worst option?

2. Suppose Naina wants to try to pay off her car loan within three years.

   (a) What is the effective annual rate of interest for both of the 36-month options?
   (b) How much interest will Naina save by choosing the better option?

3. If you wanted to get a car loan today, what are the rates of interest for 36-month and 48-month terms? Are car dealers currently offering better interest rates than the banks?

SUMMARY OF FORMULAE

Formula 9.1A

$S = P(1 + i)^n$ — Finding the future value of a sum of money when n is a fractional value using the exact method

Formula 9.1B

$P = \dfrac{S}{(1 + i)^n}$ — Finding the present value (discounted value or proceeds) when n is a fractional value using the exact method

Formula 10.1

$f = (1 + i)^m - 1$ — Finding the effective rate of interest f for a nominal annual rate compounded m times per year

Formula 10.2A

$S = Pe^{nj}$ — Finding the future value when using continuous compounding

Formula 10.2B

$P = Se^{-nj}$ — Finding the present value when using continuous compounding

Formula 10.3

$f = e^j - 1$ — Finding the effective rate of interest for a nominal rate compounded continuously

GLOSSARY

Continuous compounding the limiting case in compounding with regard to the length of the conversion period

Effective rate of interest the annual rate of interest that yields the same amount of interest per year as a nominal rate compounded a number of times per year

Equated date the date on which a single sum of money is equal to the sum of two or more dated sums of money

Equivalent rates interest rates that accumulate a given principal to the same future value over the same period of time

11

Ordinary Annuities— Future Value and Present Value

In the previous four chapters, we saw that there were many personal and business situations when we use simple and compound interest. There are also many other situations where we pay or receive regular, equal amounts of money. Many people make regular, equal payments for rent, insurance, car loans, student loans, and mortgages. And many people receive regular, equal amounts of money, such as wages, salaries, and pensions. Whether we realize it or not, these are all examples of *annuities*. All of the examples above are based on the same principles. Annuity formulae and calculations enable us to answer questions such as "How much money will I have at retirement if I invest $4000 per year now?" and "Where should I buy my big-screen TV if I don't have to pay for one full year?"

Introduction

An annuity is a series of payments, usually of equal size, made at periodic time intervals. The word *annuity* implies yearly payments but the term applies to all periodic payment plans, the most frequent of which require annual, semi-annual, quarterly, or monthly payments. As we mentioned above, practical applications of annuities are widely encountered in the finances of businesses and individuals alike. Various types of annuities are identified based on the term of an annuity, the date of payment, and the length of the conversion period. In this chapter, we will deal with the future value and present value of ordinary annuities.

OBJECTIVES

Upon completing this chapter, you will be able to do the following:

1. **Distinguish between types of annuities based on term, payment date, and conversion period.**
2. **Compute the future value (or accumulated value) of ordinary simple annuities.**
3. **Compute the present value (or discounted value) of ordinary simple annuities.**

4. Compute the future value (or accumulated value) of ordinary general annuities.
5. Compute the present value (or discounted value) of ordinary general annuities.

11.1 INTRODUCTION TO ANNUITIES

A. Basic concepts

An **annuity** is a series of payments, usually of equal size, made at periodic intervals. The length of time between the successive payments is called the **payment interval** or **payment period**. The length of time from the beginning of the first payment interval to the end of the last payment interval is called the **term of the annuity**. The size of each of the regular payments is the **periodic rent** and the sum of the periodic payments in one year is the **annual rent**.

B. Types of annuities

Several time variables affect annuities, and annuities are classified according to the time variable considered. Depending on whether the term of the annuity is fixed or indefinite, annuities are classified as **annuities certain** or **contingent annuities**.

Typical examples of annuities certain (annuities for which the term is fixed, that is, for which both the beginning date and the ending date are known) include rental payments for real estate, lease payments on equipment, instalment payments on loans, mortgage payments, and interest payments on bonds and debentures.

Examples of contingent annuities (annuities for which the beginning date or the ending date or both are uncertain) are life insurance premiums and pension payments or payments from an RRSP converted into a life annuity. The ending date is unknown for these annuities since they terminate with the death of the recipient. Some contingent annuities are the result of clauses in wills, where the beginning date of periodic payments to a beneficiary is unknown, or of payments from a trust fund for the remaining life of a surviving spouse since neither the beginning date nor the ending date is known.

A special type of annuity is the **perpetuity**, an annuity for which the payments continue forever. Perpetuities result when the size of the period rent is equal to or less than the periodic interest earned by a fund, such as a scholarship fund or an endowment fund to a university.

Variations in the date of payment are another way to classify annuities certain. If payments are made at the end of each payment period, we are dealing with an **ordinary annuity**. If, on the other hand, payments are made at the beginning of each payment period, we are dealing with an **annuity due**.

Typical examples of ordinary annuities are instalment payments on loans, mortgage payments, and interest payments on bonds and debentures. Rent payments on real estate and lease payments on equipment rentals are examples of annuities due.

Deferring the first payment for a specified period of time gives rise to a **deferred annuity**. This type may be either an ordinary annuity or an annuity due depending on whether the future payments are at the beginning or at the end of each payment interval.

A third time variable used to classify annuities is the length of the conversion period relative to the payment period. We distinguish between **simple annuities** and **general annuities** depending on whether or not the conversion period coincides with the payment interval.

An example of a simple annuity is the monthly payments on a loan for which the interest is compounded monthly, since the interest period coincides with the payment period. However, a typical mortgage on homes is compounded semi-annually but repaid by monthly payments. It is an example of a general annuity since the conversion period is different from the payment period.

EXAMPLE 11.1A   Classify each of the following annuities by

(i) term;   (ii) date of payment;   (iii) conversion period.

(a) Deposits of $150.00 earning interest at 12% compounded quarterly are made at the beginning of each quarter for four years.

Solution

(i) annuity certain (the term is fixed: four years)

(ii) annuity due (payments are made at the beginning of each quarter)

(iii) simple annuity (the quarterly conversion period equals the quarterly payment period)

(b) Payments of $200.00 are made at the end of each month for five years. Interest is 9% compounded semi-annually.

Solution

(i) annuity certain (the term is fixed: five years)

(ii) ordinary annuity (payments are made at the end of each month)

(iii) general annuity (semi-annual conversion period does not match the monthly payment period)

(c) A fund of $10 000.00 is deposited in a trust account earning interest compounded annually. Starting five years from the date of deposit, the interest earned for the year is to be paid out as a scholarship.

Solution

(i) perpetuity (the payments can go on forever)

(ii) deferred annuity (the first payment is deferred for 5 years)

(iii) simple annuity (the annual conversion period equals the annual interest period) (**d**) In his will, Dr. C. directed that part of his estate be invested in a trust fund earning interest compounded quarterly. His surviving wife was to be paid, for the remainder of her life, $2000.00 at the end of every three months starting three months after his death.

Solution

(i)   contingent annuity (both the starting date and the ending date are uncertain)

(ii) ordinary annuity (payments at the end of every three months)

(iii) simple annuity (the quarterly conversion period equals the quarterly payment period)

Exercise 11.1

A. Classify each of the following by (a) term; (b) date of payment; (c) conversion period.

1. Payments of $50.00 are made at the beginning of each month for five years at 12% compounded semi-annually.

2. Deposits of $500.00 are made at the end of each quarter for nine years earning interest at 7% compounded quarterly.

3. A fund with an initial deposit of $50 000.00 is set up to provide annual scholarships to eligible business students in an amount not exceeding the annual interest earned by the fund. Scholarship payments are to begin three years from the date of deposit. Interest earned by the fund is compounded semi-annually.

4. The Saskatoon Board of Education introduced a long-term disability plan for its employees. The plan provides for monthly payments equal to 90% of regular salary starting one month after the beginning of the disability. Assume that the plan is subject to monthly compounding.

5. Gary invested $10 000.00 in an account paying interest compounded monthly with the provision that equal monthly payments be made to him from the account for fifteen years at the beginning of each month starting ten years from the date of deposit.

6. Ms. Baka set up a trust fund earning interest compounded semi-annually to provide equal monthly support payments for her surviving husband starting one month after her death.

11.2 FUTURE VALUE OF AN ORDINARY SIMPLE ANNUITY

A. Future value of a series of payments—basic computation

EXAMPLE 11.2A Find the future value of deposits of $2000.00, $4000.00, $5000.00, $1000.00, and $3000.00 made at the end of each of five consecutive years respectively at 12% compounded annually, just after the last deposit was made.

Solution   The series of deposits can be represented on a time graph as shown:

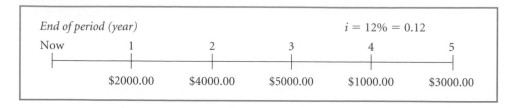

To find the future value of the series of deposits, we need to determine the combined value of the five deposits, including interest, at the focal point *five years from now*. This can be done using Formula 9.1A, $S = P(1 + i)^n$. A graphic representation of the method and data is shown in Figure 11.1 below.

FIGURE 11.1   Graphic Representation of Method and Data

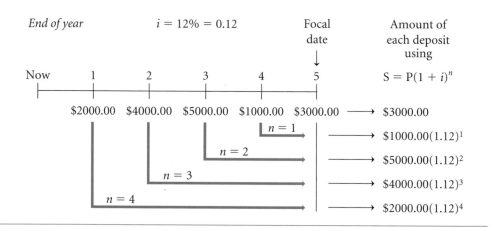

Explanations regarding the amount of each deposit:
The deposit of $3000.00 has just been made and has a value of $3000.00 at the focal date. The deposit of $1000.00 has been in for one year ($n = 1$) and has earned interest for one year at the focal date. Similarly, the deposit of $5000.00 has been in for two years ($n = 2$), the deposit of $4000.00 for three years ($n = 3$), and the deposit of $2000.00 for four years ($n = 4$).

The problem can now be solved by computing the future value of the individual deposits and adding.

Deposit 5	3000.00	= $ 3 000.00
Deposit 4	$1000.00(1.12)^1 = 1000.00(1.12)$	= 1 120.00
Deposit 3	$5000.00(1.12)^2 = 5000.00(1.2544)$	= 6 272.00
Deposit 2	$4000.00(1.12)^3 = 4000.00(1.4049280)$	= 5 619.71
Deposit 1	$2000.00(1.12)^4 = 2000.00(1.5735194)$	= 3 147.04
	TOTAL	$19 158.75

EXAMPLE 11.2B Find the future value of five deposits of $3000.00 each made at the end of each of five consecutive years respectively at 12% compounded annually, just after the last deposit has been made.

Solution This example is basically the same as Example 11.2A except that all deposits are equal in size. The problem can be solved in the same way.

FIGURE 11.2   **Graphic Representation of Method and Data**

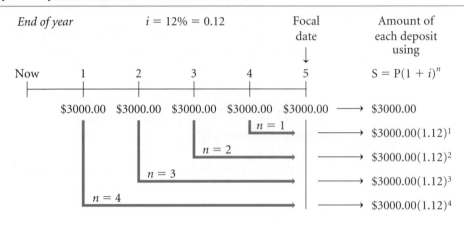

While the approach to solving the problem is fundamentally the same as in Example 11.2A, the fact that the deposits are *equal in size* permits a useful mathematical simplification. The equal deposit of $3000.00 can be taken out as a common factor and the individual compounding factors can be added. This method avoids computing the amount of each individual deposit. In other words, it avoids computing separately $3000.00(1)$, $3000.00(1.12)^1$, $3000.00(1.12)^2$, and so on.

Deposit 5	$3000.00(1)$	$=$	(1)	$=$	$(1.0$
Deposit 4	$3000.00(1.12)^1$	$=$	$(1.12)^1$	$=$	$(1.12$
Deposit 3	$3000.00(1.12)^2$	$= 3000.00(1.12)^2$	$= 3000.00($	1.2544
Deposit 2	$3000.00(1.12)^3$	$=$	$(1.12)^3$	$=$	$(1.404928$
Deposit 1	$3000.00(1.12)^4$	$=$	$(1.12)^4$	$=$	(1.5735194)

$$= 3000.00(6.3528474)$$
$$= \$19\ 058.54$$

Since the deposits in Example 11.2B are equal in size and are made at the end of each period and the payment interval is the same as the compounding period (one year), the problem is an ordinary simple annuity.

B. Formula for finding the future value of an ordinary simple annuity

Because annuities are geometric progressions, the following formula has been developed for finding the accumulated value of this type of series of payments.

$$S_n = R\left[\frac{(1 + i)^n - 1}{i}\right] \quad \text{—— Formula 11.1 ——} \quad \text{future value of an ordinary simple annuity}$$

where S_n = the future value (accumulated value) of an ordinary simple annuity;
R = the size of the periodic payment (rent);
i = the interest rate per conversion period;
n = the number of periodic payments (which for simple annuities is also the number of conversion periods).

The factor $\dfrac{(1 + i)^n - 1}{i}$ is called the **compounding** or **accumulation factor for annuities** or the **accumulated value of one dollar per period.**

EXAMPLE 11.2C Find the accumulated value of quarterly payments of $50.00 made at the end of each quarter for ten years just after the last payment has been made if interest is 8% compounded quarterly.

Solution Since the payments are of equal size made at the end of each quarter and compounding is quarterly, the problem is an ordinary simple annuity.

$$R = 50.00; \quad i = \frac{8\%}{4} = 2\% = 0.02; \quad n = 10(4) = 40$$

$$S_n = 50.00\left[\frac{(1 + 0.02)^{40} - 1}{0.02}\right] \quad \text{—— substituting in Formula 11.1}$$

$$= 50.00\left(\frac{2.2080397 - 1}{0.02}\right)$$

$$= 50.00\left(\frac{1.2080397}{0.02}\right)$$

$$= 50.00(60.401985)$$

$$= \$3020.10$$

EXAMPLE 11.2D You deposit $10.00 at the end of each month for five years in an account paying 6% compounded monthly.

(i) What will be the balance in your account at the end of the five-year term?

(ii) How much of the balance will you have contributed?

(iii) How much is interest?

Solution (i) $R = 10.00; \quad i = 0.5\% = 0.005; \quad n = 60$

$$S_n = 10.00\left[\frac{(1 + i)^n - 1}{i}\right]$$

$$= 10.00\left(\frac{1.005^{60} - 1}{0.005}\right)$$

$$= 10.00\left[\frac{(1.3488501 - 1)}{0.005}\right]$$

$$= 10.00(69.770027)$$
$$= \$697.70$$

(ii) Your contribution is \$10.00 per month for 60 months, or 10.00(60) = \$600.00.

(iii) Since your contribution is \$600.00, the interest earned is 697.70 − 600.00 = \$97.70.

C. Using preprogrammed financial calculators

You can use preprogrammed financial calculators efficiently to solve annuity problems by selecting the financial mode, entering the given values, and retrieving the answer.

The five variables used in ordinary simple annuity calculations are S_n, A_n, R, i, n. They are programmed into the calculator and are used by pressing keys as follows. Make sure the calculator is set in the financial mode.

Key	Press to enter or retrieve
FV	the future value or accumulated value S_n
PV	the present value A_n
PMT	the periodic payment or rent R
%i	the periodic rate (conversion rate) i
N	the number of periodic payments n

To begin an ordinary simple annuity calculation, enter the given values in any order. The value of the unknown variable is then retrieved by pressing CPT (in some models 2nd) followed by the key representing the unknown variable.

When performing an annuity calculation, only one of the present value A_n or the present value S_n is involved. To avoid incorrect answers, the present value PV should be set to zero when determining the future value FV and vice versa.

To solve Example 11.2D, in which R = 10.00, i = 0.5%, and n = 60, use the following procedure.

Key in	Press	Display shows	
0	PV	0	——— a precaution to avoid incorrect answers
10	PMT	10	——— this enters the periodic payment R
0.5	%i	0.5	——— this enters the conversion rate i
60	N	60	——— this enters the number of payments n
CPT	FV	697.70030	——— this retrieves the wanted amount S_n

The future value is about \$697.70.

Note: Your calculator may display a negative sign in front of your answer. Your calculator's instruction booklet should explain the reason for the negative sign. For the problems in this chapter, you can ignore the negative sign.

D. Applications

EXAMPLE 11.2E

Jim West set up a savings plan with City Trust of Victoria whereby he deposits $300.00 at the end of each quarter for eight years. The amount in his account at that time will become a term deposit withdrawable after a further five years. Interest throughout the total time period is 11% compounded quarterly.

(i) How much will be in Jim's account just after he makes his last deposit?

(ii) What will be the balance of his account when he can withdraw the deposit?

(iii) How much of the total at the time of withdrawal did Jim contribute?

(iv) How much is the interest earned?

Solution

As Figure 11.3 shows, problems of this type may be solved in stages. The first stage involves finding the future value of an *ordinary annuity*. This amount becomes the principal for the second stage, which involves finding the future value of a *single sum of money* invested for five years.

FIGURE II.3   **Graphic Representation of Method and Data**

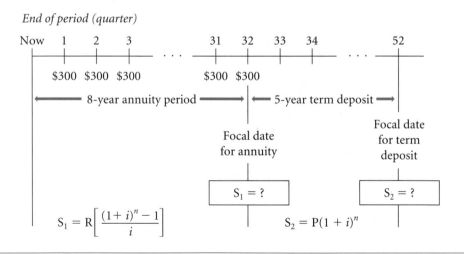

(i) $R = 300.00;$ $i = \dfrac{11\%}{4} = 2.75\% = 0.0275;$ $n = 8(4) = 32$

$$S_1 = 300.00\left[\frac{(1.0275^{32} - 1)}{0.0275}\right] \text{———— Formula II.I}$$

$$= 300.00\left[\frac{(2.3824214 - 1)}{0.0275}\right]$$

$$= 300.00(50.269869)$$

$$= \$15\,080.96$$

(ii) $P = S_1 = 15\,080.96;$ $i = 0.0275;$ $n = 5(4) = 20$

$S_2 = 15\,080.96(1.0275)^{20}$ ———— **Formula 9.1A**
$= 15\,080.96(1.7204284)$
$= \$25\,945.71$

(iii) Jim's contribution $= 32(300.00) = \$9600.00.$

(iv) The amount of interest earned $= 25\,945.71 - 9600.00 = \$16\,345.71.$

Programmed solution for parts (i) and (ii)

(i) 0 $\boxed{\text{PV}}$ 300 $\boxed{\text{PMT}}$ 2.75 $\boxed{\%i}$ 32 $\boxed{\text{N}}$ $\boxed{\text{CPT}}$ $\boxed{\text{FV}}$ $\boxed{15\,080.96}$

(ii) 15 080.96 $\boxed{\text{PV}}$ 0 $\boxed{\text{PMT}}$ 2.75 $\boxed{\%i}$ 20 $\boxed{\text{N}}$ $\boxed{\text{CPT}}$ $\boxed{\text{FV}}$ $\boxed{25\,945.71}$

EXAMPLE 11.2F   The Gordons saved for the purchase of their dream home by making deposits of $1000.00 per year for ten consecutive years in an account with Cooperative Trust in Saskatoon. The account earned interest at 5.75% compounded annually. At the end of the ten-year contribution period, the deposit was left for a further six years earning interest at 5.5% compounded semi-annually.

(i) What down payment were the Gordons able to make on their house?

(ii) How much of the down payment was interest?

Solution   (i) First, find the amount in the account at the end of the term of the ordinary annuity formed by the yearly deposits.

$R = 1000.00;$ $i = 5.75\% = 0.0575;$ $n = 10$

$S_1 = 1000.00\left[\dfrac{(1.0575^{10} - 1)}{0.0575}\right]$

$= 1000.00\left[\dfrac{(1.7490562 - 1)}{0.0575}\right]$

$= 1000.00(13.027064)$

$= \$13\,027.06$

Second, compute the accumulated value of S_1 in six years.

$P = S_1 = 13\,027.06;$ $i = \dfrac{5.5\%}{2} = 2.75\% = 0.0275;$ $n = 12$

$S_2 = 13\,027.06(1.0275)^{12}$
$= 13\,027.06(1.3847838)$
$= \$18\,039.66$

The Gordons made a down payment of $18 039.66.

(ii) Since the Gordons contributed $(1000.00)(10) = \$10\,000.00$, the amount of interest in the down payment is $8039.66.

Programmed solution for part (i)

EXAMPLE 11.2G   Marise has contributed $1500.00 per year for the last twelve years into an RRSP deposit account with her caisse populaire in Quebec City. Interest earned by these deposits was 9.5% compounded annually for the first eight years and 10.5% compounded annually for the last four years. Five years after the last deposit, she converted her RRSP into a Registered Retirement Income Fund (RRIF). How much was the beginning balance in the RRIF if interest for those five years remained at 10.5%?

Solution   As Figure 11.4 shows, the problem may be divided into two simple annuities. The first simple annuity covers the deposits for the first eight years; the second simple annuity covers the next four payments.

The focal date for the first annuity is at the end of year 8 (Focal date 1).

The accumulated value (future value) of this simple annuity is computed using Formula 11.1.

FIGURE 11.4   Graphic Representation of Method and Data

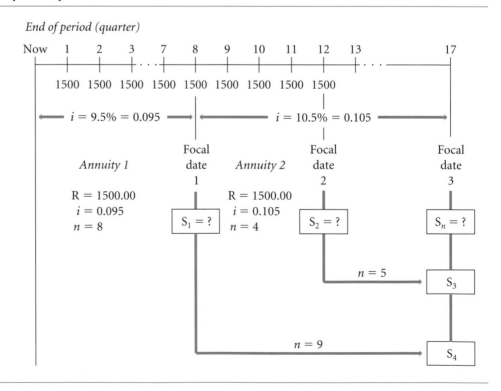

$$S_1 = 1500.00\left[\frac{(1.095^8 - 1)}{0.095}\right]$$
$$= 1500.00\left[\frac{(2.0668690 - 1)}{0.095}\right]$$
$$= 1500.00(11.230200)$$
$$= \$16\ 845.30$$

S_1 then accumulates for nine years (to the end of Year 17) at 10.5% to obtain S_4 at the focal date for the beginning balance in the RRIF (Focal date 3).

$$S_4 = 16\ 845.30(1.105)^9$$
$$= 16\ 845.30(2.4561818)$$
$$= \$41\ 375.12$$

The focal date for the second simple annuity is at the end of Year 12 (Focal date 2).

$$S_2 = 1500.00\left[\frac{(1.105^4 - 1)}{0.105}\right]$$
$$= 1500.00\left[\frac{(1.4909021 - 1)}{0.105}\right]$$
$$= 1500.00(4.6752576)$$
$$= \$7012.89$$

S_2 then accumulates for five years (to the end of Year 17) to obtain S_3 at Focal date 3.

$$S_3 = 7012.89(1.105)^5$$
$$= 7012.89(1.6474468)$$
$$= \$11\ 553.36$$

The beginning balance S_n in the RRIF is then obtained by adding S_3 and S_4.

$$S_n = 11\ 553.36 + 41\ 375.12$$
$$= \$52\ 928.48$$

Programmed solution

S_1

| 0 | PV | 1500 | PMT | 9.5 | %i | 8 | N | CPT | FV | 16 845.30 |

S_4

| 16 845.30 | PV | 0 | PMT | 10.5 | %i | 9 | N | CPT | FV | 41 375.12 |

S_2

| 0 | PV | 1500 | PMT | 10.5 | %i | 4 | N | CPT | FV | 7 012.889 |

S_3

| 7012.89 | PV | 0 | PMT | 10.5 | %i | 5 | N | CPT | FV | 11 553.357 |

$S_n = S_3 + S_4 = 11\ 553.36 + 41\ 375.12 = 52\ 928.48$

Exercise 11.2

A. Find the future value of the ordinary simple annuity for each of the following six series of payments.

	Periodic Payment	Payment Interval	Term	Interest Rate	Conversion Period
1.	$1500.00	1 quarter	$7\frac{1}{2}$ years	5%	quarterly
2.	$20.00	1 month	6.75 years	12%	monthly
3.	$700.00	6 months	20 years	7%	semi-annually
4.	$10.00	1 month	15 years	9%	monthly
5.	$320.00	3 months	8 years, 9 months	10.4%	quarterly
6.	$2000.00	$\frac{1}{2}$ year	11 years, 6 months	8.8%	semi-annually

B. Answer each of the following questions.

1. Find the accumulated value of payments of $200.00 made at the end of every three months for twelve years if money is worth 5% compounded quarterly.

2. To what will deposits of $60.00 made at the end of each month amount to after six years if interest is 10.8% compounded monthly?

3. How much interest is included in the future value of an ordinary simple annuity of $1500.00 paid every six months at 7% compounded semi-annually if the term of the annuity is fifteen years?

4. Jane Alleyre made ordinary annuity payments of $15.00 per month for sixteen years earning 9% compounded monthly. How much interest is included in the future value of the annuity?

5. Saving for his retirement 25 years from now, Jimmy Olsen set up a savings plan whereby he will deposit $25.00 at the end of each month for the next 15 years. Interest is 12% compounded monthly.
   a) How much money will be in Mr. Olsen's account on the date of his retirement?
   b) How much will Mr. Olsen contribute?
   c) How much is interest?

6. Mr. and Mrs. Wolf have each contributed $1000.00 per year for the last ten years into RRSP accounts earning 6% compounded annually. Suppose they leave their accumulated contributions for another five years in the RRSP at the same rate of interest.
   a) How much will Mr. and Mrs. Wolf have in total in their RRSP accounts?
   b) How much did the Wolfs contribute?
   c) How much will be interest?

7. Ms. Pitt has made quarterly payments of $1375.00 at the end of each quarter into an RRSP for the last seven years earning interest at 7% compounded quarterly. If she leaves the accumulated money in the RRSP for another three years at 8% compounded semi-annually, how much will she

be able to transfer at the end of the three years into a Registered Retirement Income Fund?

8. For the last six years Joe Borelli has made deposits of $300.00 at the end of every six months earning interest at 5% compounded semi-annually. If he leaves the accumulated balance for another ten years at 6% compounded quarterly, what will the balance be in Joe's account?

11.3 PRESENT VALUE OF AN ORDINARY SIMPLE ANNUITY

A. Present value of series of payments—Basic computation

EXAMPLE 11.3A   Find the single sum of money whose value now is equivalent to payments of $2000.00, $4000.00, $5000.00, $1000.00, and $3000.00 made at the end of each of five consecutive years respectively at 12% compounded annually.

Solution   The series of payments can be represented on a time graph.

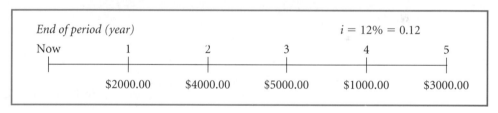

To find the present value of the series of payments, we need to determine the *combined* present value of the five payments at the focal point "now." This can be done using Formula 9.1C, $P = S(1 + i)^{-n}$. A graphic representation of the method and data is shown in Figure 11.5.

FIGURE 11.5   **Graphic Representation of Method and Data**

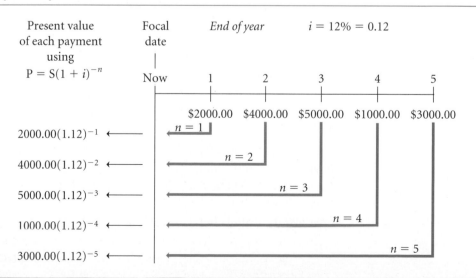

The solution to the problem can be completed by computing the present value of the individual payments and adding.

Payment 1 $2000.00(1.12)^{-1} = 2000.00(0.8928571) = \$\ \ 1\ 785.71$
Payment 2 $4000.00(1.12)^{-2} = 4000.00(0.7971939) = \ \ \ \ 3\ 188.78$
Payment 3 $5000.00(1.12)^{-3} = 5000.00(0.7117802) = \ \ \ \ 3\ 558.90$
Payment 4 $1000.00(1.12)^{-4} = 1000.00(0.6355181) = \ \ \ \ \ \ \ 635.52$
Payment 5 $3000.00(1.12)^{-5} = 3000.00(0.5674269) = \ \ \ \ 1\ 702.28$

TOTAL $\underline{\underline{\$10\ 871.19}}$

EXAMPLE 11.3B Find the present value of five payments of $3000.00 made at the end of each of five consecutive years respectively if money is worth 12% compounded annually.

Solution This example is basically the same as Example 11.3A except that all payments are equal in size.

FIGURE 11.6 **Graphic Representation of Method and Data**

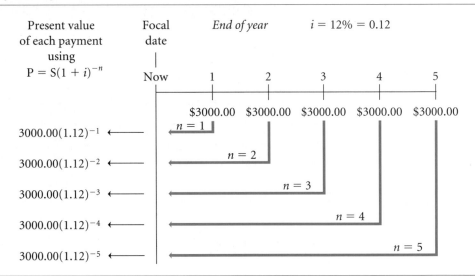

While the approach to solving the problem is fundamentally the same as in Example 11.3A, the fact that the payments are equal in size permits the same mathematical simplification used for Example 11.2B. The equal payment of $3000.00 can be taken out as a common factor and the individual discount factors can be added.

Payment 1 $3000.00(1.12)^{-1} = \ \ \ \ \ \ \ \ \ \ \ \ \ \ (1.12)^{-1} = \ \ \ \ \ \ \ \ \ \ (0.8928571)$
Payment 2 $3000.00(1.12)^{-2} = \ \ \ \ \ \ \ \ \ \ \ \ \ \ (1.12)^{-2} = \ \ \ \ \ \ \ \ \ \ (0.7971939)$
Payment 3 $3000.00(1.12)^{-3} = 3000.00(1.12)^{-3} = 3000.00(0.7117802)$
Payment 4 $3000.00(1.12)^{-4} = \ \ \ \ \ \ \ \ \ \ \ \ \ \ (1.12)^{-4} = \ \ \ \ \ \ \ \ \ \ (0.6355181)$
Payment 5 $3000.00(1.12)^{-5} = \ \ \ \ \ \ \ \ \ \ \ \ \ \ (1.12)^{-5} = \ \ \ \ \ \ \underline{(0.5674269)}$

$= 3000.00(3.6047762)$
$= \$10\ 814.33$

Since the payments in Example 11.3B are equal in size and are made at the end of each period, and the payment period is the same as the compounding period (one year), the problem is an ordinary simple annuity. Finding the sum of the present values of the individual payments at the beginning of the term of an annuity is defined as finding the **present value of an annuity**. It is useful to carry the mathematical simplification beyond simply taking out the common factor 3000.00.

B. Formula for finding the present value of an ordinary simple annuity

Because annuities are geometric progressions, the following formula for finding the present value of an ordinary simple annuity has been developed.

$$A_n = R\left[\frac{1 - (1 + i)^{-n}}{i}\right]$$ ——— **Formula 11.2** ——— Present value of an ordinary simple annuity

where A_n = the present value (discounted value) of an ordinary simple annuity;
R = the size of the periodic payment (rent);
i = the interest rate per conversion period;
n = the number of periodic payments (which for simple annuities equals the number of conversion periods).

The factor $\dfrac{1 - (1 + i)^{-n}}{i}$ is called the **present value factor** or **discount factor for annuities** or the **discounted value of one dollar per period**.

EXAMPLE 11.3C Find the present value at the beginning of the first payment period of payments of $50.00 made at the end of each quarter for ten years, if interest is 8% compounded quarterly.

Solution Because the payments are of equal size made at the end of each quarter and compounding is quarterly, the problem is an ordinary simple annuity. Since the focal date is the beginning of the term of the annuity, the formula for finding the present value of an ordinary simple annuity applies.

$$R = 50.00; \quad i = \frac{8\%}{4} = 0.02; \quad n = 10(4) = 40$$

$$A_n = 50.00\left[\frac{1 - (1 + 0.02)^{-40}}{0.02}\right]$$ ——————— substituting in Formula 11.2

$$= 50.00\left(\frac{1 - 0.4528904}{0.02}\right)$$

$$= 50.00\left(\frac{0.5471096}{0.02}\right)$$

$$= 50.00(27.355480)$$

$$= \$1367.77$$

EXAMPLE 11.3D Suppose you want to withdraw $100.00 at the end of each month for five years from an account paying 12% compounded monthly.

(i) How much must you have on deposit at the beginning of the month in which the first withdrawal is made?

(ii) How much will you receive in total?

(iii) How much of what you will receive is interest?

Solution

(i) $R = 100.00; \quad i = 1\% = 0.01; \quad n = 60$

$$A_n = 100.00\left[\frac{1 - (1 + i)^{-n}}{i}\right]$$

$$= 100.00\left[\frac{(1 - 1.01^{-60})}{0.01}\right]$$

$$= 100.00\left[\frac{(1 - 0.5504496)}{0.01}\right]$$

$$= 100.00\left(\frac{0.4495504}{0.01}\right)$$

$$= 100.00(44.95504)$$

$$= \$4495.50$$

(ii) Total receipts will be $100.00 per month for 60 months or $6000.00.

(iii) Since the initial balance must be $4495.50, the interest received will be $6000.00 − 4495.50 = \$1504.50$.

C. Present value using preprogrammed financial calculators

To find the present value of the ordinary simple annuity in Example 11.3D in which $R = 100.00, \quad i = 1\%, \quad$ and $\quad n = 60$, proceed as follows.

Key in	Press	Display shows	
0	FV	0	a precaution
100	PMT	100	
1	%i	1	
60	N	60	
CPT	PV	4495.5039	pressing the PV key retrieves the unknown present value A_n

You must have about $4495.50 on deposit.

D. Applications

EXAMPLE 11.3E   Mr. and Mrs. Hong bought a vacation property for $3000.00 down and $1000.00 every half-year for twelve years. If interest is 7% compounded semi-annually, what was the cash value of the property?

Solution   The cash value is the price of the property at the date of purchase and represents the dated value of all payments at that date.

$$\text{CASH VALUE} = \text{DOWN PAYMENT} + \begin{array}{c}\text{PRESENT VALUE OF}\\ \text{THE PERIODIC PAYMENTS}\end{array}$$

Since the first half-yearly payment is due at the end of the first six-month period and compounding is semi-annual, the present value of the periodic payments is the present value of an ordinary simple annuity.

$$R = 1000.00; \quad i = \frac{7\%}{2} = 3.5\% = 0.035; \quad n = 12(2) = 24$$

$$
\begin{aligned}
A_n &= 1000.00\left[\frac{(1 - 1.035^{-24})}{0.035}\right] \\
&= 1000.00\left[\frac{(1 - 0.4379571)}{0.035}\right] \\
&= 1000.00\left(\frac{0.5620429}{0.035}\right) \\
&= 1000.00(16.058369) \\
&= \$16\,058.37
\end{aligned}
$$

Programmed solution

$$0 \;\boxed{\text{FV}}\; 1000 \;\boxed{\text{PMT}}\; 3.5 \;\boxed{\%i}\; 24 \;\boxed{\text{N}}\; \boxed{\text{CPT}}\; \boxed{\text{PV}}\; \boxed{16\,058.368}$$

The cash value = 3000.00 + 16 058.37 = $19 058.37.

EXAMPLE 11.3F   Armand Rice expects to retire in seven years and would like to receive $500.00 per month for ten years starting at the end of the first month after his retirement. To achieve this goal, he deposited part of the proceeds of $50 000.00 from the sale of a property into a fund earning 10.5% compounded monthly.

   (i) How much must be in the fund at the date of his retirement?

  (ii) How much of the proceeds did he deposit in the fund?

 (iii) How much does he expect to receive from the fund?

 (iv) How much of what he will receive is interest?

Solution   As Figure 11.7 shows, problems of this type should be solved in stages. The first stage involves finding the present value of an annuity. This sum of money becomes the future amount for the second stage, which involves finding the present value of that future amount at the date of deposit.

FIGURE 11.7 Graphic Representation of Method and Data

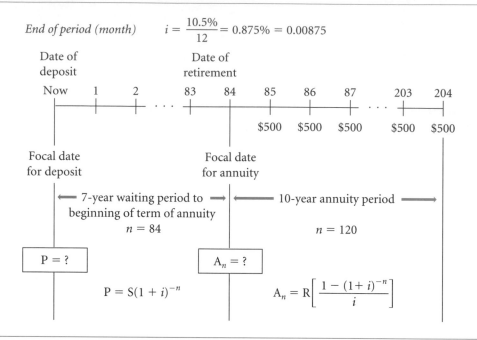

(i) $R = 500.00$; $i = 0.00875$; $n = 120$

$$A_n = 500.00\left[\frac{(1 - 1.00875^{-120})}{0.00875}\right]$$
$$= 500.00\left[\frac{(1 - 0.3515396)}{0.00875}\right]$$
$$= 500.00(74.109758)$$
$$= \$37\,054.88$$

(ii) $S = A_n = 37\,054.88$; $i = 0.00875$; $n = 84$

$$P = 37\,054.88(1.00875)^{-84}$$
$$= 37\,054.88(0.4810409)$$
$$= \$17\,824.91$$

(iii) He expects to receive $500.00(120) = \$60\,000.00$.

(iv) Interest received will be $60\,000.00 - 17\,824.91 = \$42\,175.09$.

Programmed solution for parts (i) and (ii)

(i)

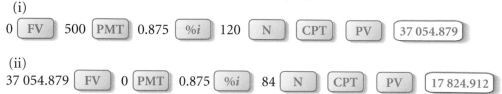

(ii)
37 054.879 FV   0 PMT   0.875 %i   84 N   CPT   PV   17 824.912

EXAMPLE 11.3G Sheila Davidson borrowed money from her credit union and agreed to repay the loan in blended monthly payments of $161.75 over a four-year period. Interest on the loan was 9% compounded monthly.

(i) How much did she borrow?

(ii) If she missed the first eleven payments, how much would she have to pay at the end of the first year to bring her payments up to date?

(iii) If the credit union demanded payment in full after one year, how much money would Sheila Davidson need?

(iv) If the loan is paid off after one year, what would have been its total cost?

(v) How much of the total loan cost is additional interest paid on the missed payments?

Solution

(i) The amount borrowed is the present value (or discounted value) of the 48 payments as the time diagram shows.

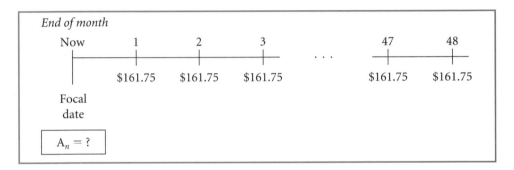

$$R = 161.75; \quad i = \frac{9\%}{12} = 0.75\% = 0.0075; \quad n = 4(12) = 48$$

$$A_n = 161.75\left[\frac{(1 - 1.0075^{-48})}{0.0075}\right] \quad\text{——— using Formula 11.2}$$

$$= 161.75\left[\frac{(1 - 0.6986141)}{0.0075}\right]$$

$$= 161.75(40.184782)$$

$$= 6499.89$$

Programmed solution

(ii) As the diagram below shows, Sheila Davidson must pay the accumulated value of the first twelve payments to bring her payments up to date after one year.

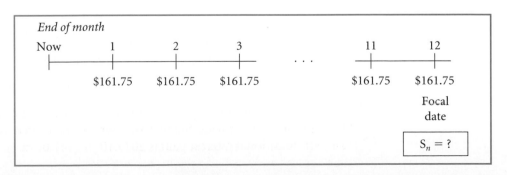

$$R = 161.75; \quad i = 0.0075; \quad n = 12$$

$$S_n = 161.75\left[\frac{(1.0075^{12} - 1)}{0.0075}\right] \qquad \text{using Formula 11.1}$$

$$= 161.75\left[\frac{(1.0938069 - 1)}{0.0075}\right]$$

$$= 161.75(12.507587)$$

$$= \$2023.10$$

Programmed solution

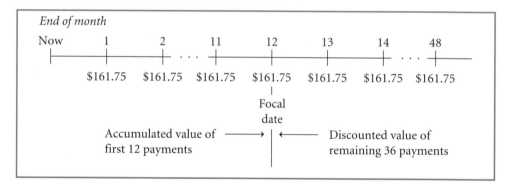

0 [PV] 161.75 [PMT] 0.75 [%i] 12 [N] [CPT] [FV]   2023.1019

(iii) The sum of money required to pay off the loan in full is the sum of the accumulated values of the first twelve payments plus the discounted values of the remaining 36 payments.

End of month

Now | 1 | 2 | 11 | 12 | 13 | 14 | 48

$161.75 $161.75 $161.75 $161.75 $161.75 $161.75 $161.75

Focal date

Accumulated value of first 12 payments ⟶ | ⟵ Discounted value of remaining 36 payments

The accumulated value of the first 12 payments, as computed in part (ii) above, is $2023.10. The discounted value of the remaining payments is found using Formula 11.2.

$$R = 161.75; \quad i = 0.0075; \quad n = 36$$

$$A_n = 161.75\left[\frac{(1 - 1.0075^{-36})}{0.0075}\right]$$

$$= 161.75\left[\frac{(1 - 0.7641490)}{0.0075}\right]$$

$$= 161.75(31.446800)$$

$$= \$5086.52$$

Programmed solution

0 [FV] 161.75 [PMT] 0.75 [%i] 36 [N] [CPT] [PV]   5086.5205

The amount of money needed is 5086.52 + 2023.10 = $7109.62.

(iv) The total cost of the loan if paid off after one year is 7109.62 − 6499.89 = $609.73.

(v) To bring the payments up to date, $2023.10 is needed. Since the normal amount paid during the first year would have been 161.75(12) = $1941.00, the additional interest paid is 2023.10 − 1941.00 = $82.10.

Exercise 11.3

A. Determine the present value of the ordinary simple annuity for each of the following series of payments.

	Periodic Payment	Payment Interval	Term	Interest Rate	Compounding Period
1.	$1600.00	6 months	$3\frac{1}{2}$ years	8.5%	semi-annually
2.	$700.00	1 quarter	4 years, 9 months	15%	quarterly
3.	$4000.00	1 year	12 years	12.5%	annually
4.	$45.00	1 month	18 years	6.6%	monthly
5.	$250.00	3 months	14 years, 3 months	4.4%	quarterly
6.	$80.00	1 month	9.25 years	7.2%	monthly

B. Answer each of the following questions.

1. Find the present value of payments of $375.00 made at the end of every six months for fifteen years if money is worth 7% compounded semi-annually.

2. What is the discounted value of deposits of $60.00 made at the end of each month for nine years if interest is 4.5% compounded monthly?

3. You want to receive $600.00 at the end of every three months for five years. Interest is 7.6% compounded quarterly.
   a) How much would you have to deposit at the beginning of the five-year period?
   b) How much of what you receive is interest?

4. An instalment contract for the purchase of a car requires payments of $270.60 at the end of each month for the next three years. Suppose interest is 13.8% p.a. compounded monthly.
   a) What is the amount financed?
   b) How much is the interest cost?

5. For home entertainment equipment, Ted paid $400.00 down and signed an instalment contract that required payments of $69.33 at the end of each month for three years. Suppose interest is 10.8% compounded monthly.
   a) What was the cash price of the equipment?
   b) How much was the cost of financing?

6. Elynor bought a vacation property for $2500.00 down and quarterly mortgage payments of $550.41 at the end of each quarter for five years. Interest is 8% compounded quarterly.
   a) What was the purchase price of the property?
   b) How much interest will Elynor pay?

7. Ed intends to retire in eight years. To supplement his pension he would like to receive $450.00 every three months for fifteen years. If he is to receive the first payment three months after his retirement and interest is

5% p.a. compounded quarterly, how much must he invest today to achieve his goal?

8. Planning for their son's college education, Vivien and Adrian Marsh opened an account paying 6.3% compounded monthly. If ordinary annuity payments of $200.00 per month are to be paid out of the account for three years starting seven years from now, how much did the Marshes deposit?

9. Kimiko signed a mortgage requiring payments of $234.60 at the end of every month for six years at 12% compounded monthly.
   a) How much was the original mortgage balance?
   b) If Kimiko missed the first five payments, how much would she have to pay after six months to bring the mortgage payments up to date?
   c) How much would Kimiko have to pay after six months to pay off the mortgage?
   d) If the mortgage were paid off after six months, what would the total interest cost be?
   e) How much of the total interest cost is additional interest because of the missed payments?

10. Field Construction agreed to lease payments of $642.79 on construction equipment to be made at the end of each month for three years. Financing is at 18% compounded monthy.
   a) What is the value of the original lease contract?
   b) If, due to delays, the first eight payments were deferred, how much money would be needed after nine months to bring the lease payments up to date?
   c) How much money would be required to pay off the lease after nine months?
   d) If the lease were paid off after nine months, what would the total interest be?
   e) How much of the total interest would be due to deferring the first eight payments?

11.4 FUTURE VALUE OF AN ORDINARY GENERAL ANNUITY

A. Basic concepts and computation

Sections 11.2 and 11.3 considered ordinary simple annuities in detail. Simple annuities are a special case in which the payment interval and the interest conversion period are the same length. However, interest is often compounded more or less frequently than payments are made. In Canada, for example, residential mortgages are usually compounded semi-annually while payments are made monthly.

Annuities in which the length of the interest conversion period is different from the length of the payment interval are called *general annuities*.

The basic method of solving problems involving interest uses equivalent sets of financial obligations at a selected focal date. Thus, when dealing with any kind of annuity, including general annuities, the essential tool is an equation of value. This basic approach is used to make the basic computations and develop useful formulae.

EXAMPLE 11.4A   What is the accumulated value of $100.00 deposited at the end of every six months for three years if interest is 12% compounded annually?

Solution   Since the payments are made semi-annually while the compounding is done annually, this annuity is classified as a general annuity. Furthermore, since the payments are at the end of each payment interval, the annuity is an ordinary general annuity. While the difference in the length of the payment period compared to the length of the compounding period introduces a mathematical complication, the basic approach to finding the amount of the ordinary general annuity is the same as is used in finding the amount of an ordinary simple annuity.

The basic solution and data for the problem are graphically shown in Figure 11.8. Since deposits are made at the end of every six months for three years, there are six deposits of $100.00 at the times indicated. Because interest is compounded annually, $i = 12\% = 0.12$ and there are three conversion periods.

FIGURE 11.8   **Graphic Representation of Method and Data**

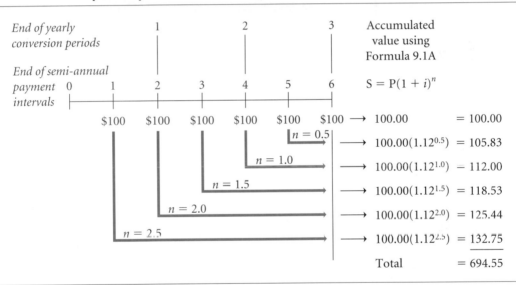

The focal point is at the end of Year 3. The last deposit is made at the focal date and has a value of $100.00 on that date. The fifth deposit is made after 2.5 years and, in terms of conversion periods, has accumulated for a half conversion period ($n = 0.5$); its accumulated value is $100.00(1.12^{0.5}) = \$105.83$ at the focal date. The fourth deposit is made after two years and has accumulated for one conversion period ($n = 1.0$); its accumulated value at the focal date is $100.00(1.12^{1.0}) = \$112.00$. Similarly, the accumulated value of the third deposit is $100.00(1.12^{1.5}) = \$118.53$, while the accumulated value of the second deposit is $100.00(1.12^{2.0}) = \$125.44$. Finally, the accumulated value of the first deposit is $100.00(1.12^{2.5}) = \$132.75$. The total accumulated value after three years is $694.55.

EXAMPLE 11.4B   What is the accumulated value of deposits of $100.00 made at the end of each year for four years if interest is 12% compounded quarterly?

Solution   Since the deposits are made at the end of every year for four years, there are four payments of $100.00 at the times shown in Figure 11.9. Since interest is compounded quarterly, $i = \frac{12\%}{4} = 3\%$ and there are $4(4) = 16$ conversion periods.

FIGURE 11.9   Graphic Representation of Method and Data

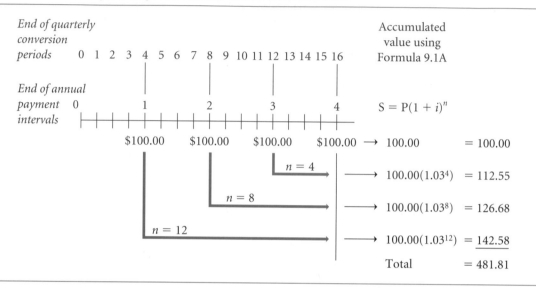

The focal point is the end of Year 4. The last payment is made at the focal point and has a value of $100.00 at that date. The third payment is made after three years and, in terms of conversion periods, has accumulated for four conversion periods ($n = 4$); its accumulated value is $100.00(1.03^4) = \$112.55$. The second deposit has accumulated for 8 conversion periods ($n = 8$); its accumulated value is $100.00(1.03^8) = \$126.68$. The first deposit has accumulated for 12 conversion periods ($n = 12$); its accumulated value is $100.00(1.03^{12}) = \$142.58$. The total accumulated value of the deposits after four years is $481.81.

B. Relationship between payment interval and interest conversion period

Examples 11.4A and 11.4B illustrate the two possible cases of ordinary general annuities.

CASE 1   The interest conversion period is *longer* than the payment period; each payment interval contains only a fraction of one conversion period.

CASE 2   The interest conversion period is *shorter* than the payment period; each payment period contains more than one conversion period.

The number of interest conversion periods per payment interval, designated by the letter c, can be determined from the following ratio.

$$c = \frac{\text{THE NUMBER OF INTEREST CONVERSION PERIODS PER YEAR}}{\text{THE NUMBER OF PAYMENT PERIODS PER YEAR}}$$

In dealing with general annuities it is important to understand clearly the relationship between the *payment interval* and the number of *interest conversion periods* per payment interval.

For Case 1 (see Example 11.4A), c has a fractional value less than 1.

For Case 2 (see Example 11.4B), c has a value greater than 1.

The following table provides a sampling of possible combinations of payment intervals and interest conversion periods you might encounter when dealing with general annuities. One of the most important is the monthly payment interval combined with semi-annual compounding since this combination is usually encountered with residential mortgages in Canada.

TABLE 11.1   Some Possible Combinations of Payment Intervals and Interest Conversion Periods

Payment Interval	Interest Conversion Period	Number of Interest Conversion Periods per Payment Interval
semi-annually	monthly	$c = \dfrac{12}{2} = 6$
quarterly	monthly	$c = \dfrac{12}{4} = 3$
annually	quarterly	$c = \dfrac{4}{1} = 4$
semi-annually	annually	$c = \dfrac{1}{2} = 0.5$
quarterly	annually	$c = \dfrac{1}{4} = 0.25$
monthly	semi-annually	$c = \dfrac{2}{12} = \dfrac{1}{6}$
monthly	quarterly	$c = \dfrac{4}{12} = \dfrac{1}{3}$
monthly	annually	$c = \dfrac{1}{12}$

C. Computing the equivalent effective rate of interest per payment period

When using an electronic calculator equipped with a universal power key, the given periodic rate of interest i can be easily converted into the equivalent effective rate of interest per payment period.

Represent the equivalent effective rate of interest per payment period by f.

$$1 + f = (1 + i)^c$$

Formula 10.1 except that m is replaced by c

EXAMPLE 11.4C   Jean receives annuity payments at the end of every six months. If she deposits these payments in an account earning interest at 9% compounded monthly, what is the equivalent semi-annual rate of interest?

Solution   Since the payments are made at the end of every six months while interest is compounded monthly,

$$c = \frac{\text{THE NUMBER OF INTEREST CONVERSION PERIODS PER YEAR}}{\text{THE NUMBER OF PAYMENT PERIODS PER YEAR}} = \frac{12}{2} = 6$$

$$i = \frac{9\%}{12} = 0.75\% = 0.0075$$

$1 + f = 1.0075^6$
$1 + f = 1.0458522$
$\quad f = 0.0458522 = 4.58522\%$

The equivalent semi-annual rate of interest is 4.58522%.

EXAMPLE 11.4D Peel Credit Union pays 6% compounded quarterly on its Premium Savings Accounts. If Roland Catchpole deposits $25.00 in his account at the end of every month, what is the equivalent monthly rate of interest?

Solution Since the payments are made at the end of every month while interest is compounded quarterly,

$$c = \frac{4}{12} = \frac{1}{3}; \quad i = \frac{6\%}{4} = 1.5\% = 0.015$$

$1 + f = 1.015^{\frac{1}{3}}$
$1 + f = 1.0049752$
$\quad f = 0.0049752 = 0.49752\%$

The equivalent monthly rate of interest is 0.49752%.

D. Future value of an ordinary general annuity using the equivalent effective rate of interest per payment period

Determining the equivalent rate per payment period f allows us to convert the ordinary general annuity problem into an ordinary simple annuity problem. Consistent with the symbols previously used for developing formulae for ordinary simple annuities, we will use the following notation:

S_{nc} = the future value (or accumulated value) of an ordinary general annuity;
R = the size of the periodic payment;
n = the number of periodic payments;
c = the number of interest conversion periods per payment interval;
i = the interest rate per interest conversion period;
f = the effective rate of interest per payment period.

Substituting f for i in Formula 11.1, we obtain

$$S_{nc} = R\left[\frac{(1 + f)^n - 1}{f}\right] \text{ where } f = (1 + i)^c - 1 \qquad \text{Formula 11.3}$$

EXAMPLE 11.4E Determine the accumulated value after ten years of payments of $2000.00 made at the end of each year if interest is 6% compounded monthly.

Solution This problem is an ordinary general annuity.

$$R = 2000.00; \quad n = 10; \quad c = 12; \quad i = \frac{6\%}{12} = 0.5\% = 0.005$$

The equivalent effective annual rate

$$f = 1.005^{12} - 1 = 1.0616778 - 1 = 0.0616778 = 6.16778\%$$

The given ordinary general annuity can be converted into an ordinary simple annuity.

$$R = 2000.00; \quad n = 10; \quad f = 0.0616778$$

$$S_{nc} = 2000.00\left(\frac{1.0616778^{10} - 1}{0.0616778}\right) \quad\text{——————— substituting in Formula 11.3}$$

$$= 2000.00(13.285113)$$
$$= \$26\ 570.23$$

The accumulated value after ten years is about $26 570.23.

EXAMPLE 11.4F Creditview Farms set aside $1250.00 at the end of each month for the purchase of a combine. How much money will be available after five years if interest is 6.0% compounded semi-annually?

Solution This problem involves an ordinary general annuity.

$$R = 1250.00; \quad n = 5(12) = 60; \quad c = \frac{2}{12} = \frac{1}{6}; \quad i = \frac{6.0\%}{2} = 3.0\% = 0.03$$

The equivalent effective monthly rate of interest

$$f = 1.03^{\frac{1}{6}} - 1 = 1.0049386 - 1 = 0.0049386 = 0.49386\%$$

$$S_{nc} = 1250.00\left(\frac{1.0049386^{60} - 1}{0.0049386}\right) \quad\text{——————— substituting in Formula 11.3}$$

$$= 1250.00(69.638419)$$
$$= \$87\ 048.02$$

After five years, the amount available is $87 048.02.

E. Using preprogrammed calculators to find the future value of an ordinary general annuity

The use of f rather than i as the rate of interest is the only difference in the programmed solution for the general annuity compared to the programmed solution for a simple annuity.

EXAMPLE 11.4G Find the future value of $2500.00 deposited at the end of every six months for ten years if interest is 10% compounded quarterly.

Solution $R = 2500.00;$ $n = 2(10) = 20;$ $c = \dfrac{4}{2} = 2;$ $i = \dfrac{10\%}{4} = 2.5\% = 0.025$

STEP 1   Convert i into the equivalent effective rate of interest.
$f = 1.025^2 - 1 = 1.050625 - 1 = 0.050625 = 5.0625\%$

STEP 2   Using f as the interest rate per payment period, determine the amount of the ordinary annuity.

Key in	Press	Display shows	
5.0625	%i	5.0625	
0	PV	0	
2500	PMT	2500	
20	N	20	—— the number of payments
CPT	FV	83 213.027	

The amount on deposit after ten years will be about $83 213.03.

EXAMPLE 11.4H   Determine the accumulated value of payments of $1250.00 made at the end of each quarter for eight years if interest is 12.5% compounded annually.

Solution $R = 1250.00;$ $n = 8(4) = 32;$ $c = \dfrac{1}{4} = 0.25;$ $i = 12.5\% = 0.125$

$f = 1.125^{0.25} - 1 = 1.0298836 - 1 = 0.0298836 = 2.9883570\%$

Key in	Press	Display shows
2.988357	%i	2.988357
0	PV	0
1250	PMT	1250
32	N	32
CPT	FV	65 495.201

The accumulated value of the payments is $65 495.20.

Exercise 11.4

A. Find the future value of each of the following eight ordinary annuities.

	Periodic Payment	Payment Interval	Term	Interest Rate	Conversion Period
1.	$2500.00	6 months	7 years	8%	quarterly
2.	$900.00	3 months	5 years	12%	monthly
3.	$72.00	1 month	15 years	3%	semi-annually
4.	$225.00	3 months	10 years	5%	annually
5.	$1750.00	6 months	12 years	7%	semi-annually
6.	$680.00	1 month	3 years	9%	monthly
7.	$7500.00	1 year	4 years	6%	quarterly
8.	$143.00	1 month	9 years	4%	quarterly

B. Answer each of the following questions.

1. Find the future value of payments of $425.00 made at the end of every three months for nine years if interest is 9% compounded monthly.

2. What is the accumulated value of deposits of $1500.00 made at the end of every six months for six years if interest is 12% compounded quarterly?

3. How much will deposits of $15.00 made at the end of each month amount to after ten years if interest is 5% compounded quarterly?

4. What is the future value of payments of $250.00 made at the end of every three months in fifteen years if interest is 7.5% compounded annually?

5. Mr. Tomas has contributed $1000.00 at the end of each year into an RRSP paying 6% compounded quarterly.
   a) How much will Mr. Tomas have in the RRSP after ten years?
   b) After ten years, how much of the amount is interest?

6. Alexa Sanchez saves $5.00 at the end of each month and deposits the money in an account, paying 4% compounded quarterly.
   a) How much will she accumulate in 25 years?
   b) How much of the accumulated amount is interest?

7. Edwin Ng has made deposits of $500.00 into his savings account at the end of every three months for ten years. If interest is 4.5% compounded semi-annually and if he leaves the accumulated balance for another five years, what will be the balance in his account then?

8. Mrs. Cook has made deposits of $950.00 at the end of every six months for fifteen years. If interest is 3% compounded monthly, how much will Mrs. Cook have accumulated ten years after the last deposit?

B U S I N E S S   M A T H   N E W S   B O X

ON THE MONEY with Gordon Pape

Start the savings habit

PAPE'S TIP: *If you're having trouble saving, start small and build from there.*

Everyone knows it's a good idea to save money. The problem is how to do it when the family budget is already stretched to the limit. Even if the extra cash amounts to only a few dollars a week, get started. Then keep adding to your savings at every opportunity.

Extra money

Whenever you receive some additional cash, earmark a portion for savings. Aim for 50% of the amount you receive. That way, you can save and spend at the same time. Possible sources of extra money:
- Income tax refund.
- Salary increase.
- Increase in take-home pay (Canada Pension Plan is paid off, a tax cut is introduced, etc).
- Bonus or unusually high commission.
- Financial gift.

What to do with it

As your savings build, use the money in the most effective ways. Good choices include:
- Paying off credit cards and other consumer debt.
- Maximizing registered retirement savings plan contributions.
- Paying down the mortgage.
- Setting up an education fund for the children.
- Creating an investment portfolio.

How it grows

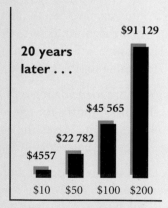

20 years later . . .

$4557 — $10
$22 782 — $50
$45 565 — $100
$91 129 — $200

Savings per month

How your savings will grow over 20 years, assuming an average annual return of 6% (taxes not taken into account).

QUESTIONS

1. The diagram in the article shows how savings will grow over twenty years at an average annual rate of return of 6%. What compounding period do the numbers in the diagram represent most closely: annual, semi-annual, or quarterly? Use the $10 savings per month to calculate your answer.

2. To what amount would your savings grow if you invested $10.00 per month at 6% compounded daily for twenty years? How does your answer compare with the $10.00-per-month amount shown in the diagram?

3. For each of the four levels of savings in the diagram, find the amount of money that represents contributions and interest on the contributions for 20 years.

4. To what amount will your savings grow over twenty years if you invested $200.00 per month and earned interest of 7% compounded semi-annually? How does this amount compare with the $200.00-per-month investment shown in the diagram?

SOURCE: Adapted from "On the Money" with Gordon Pape. © 1997 ArtPress International, reproduced with permission.

11.5 PRESENT VALUE OF AN ORDINARY GENERAL ANNUITY

A. Present value of an ordinary general annuity using the equivalent effective rate of interest per payment period

As with the future value of an ordinary general annuity, we can convert the given periodic rate of interest i into the equivalent effective rate of interest per payment period.

$$f = (1 + i)^c - 1$$

The use of f converts the ordinary general annuity problem into an ordinary simple annuity problem.

Substituting f for i in Formula 11.2, we obtain

$$A_{nc} = R\left[\frac{1 - (1 + f)^{-n}}{f}\right]$$ ——————— Formula 11.4

EXAMPLE 11.5A   A loan is repaid by making payments of $2000.00 at the end of every six months for twelve years. If interest on the loan is 8% compounded quarterly, what was the principal of the loan?

Solution $R = 2000.00; \quad n = 12(2) = 24; \quad c - \dfrac{4}{2} = 2; \quad i - \dfrac{8\%}{4} = 2\% = 0.02$

The equivalent effective semi-annual rate of interest

$$f = 1.02^2 - 1 = 1.0404 - 1 = 0.0404 = 4.04\%$$

$$A_{nc} = 2000.00\left(\frac{1 - 1.0404^{-24}}{0.0404}\right) \qquad\text{——— substituting in Formula 11.4}$$
$$= 2000.00(15.184713)$$
$$= \$30\,369.43$$

The loan principal was $30 369.43.

EXAMPLE 11.5B A second mortgage requires payments of $370.00 at the end of each month for 15 years. If interest is 11% compounded semi-annually, what was the amount borrowed?

Solution $R = 370.00; \quad n = 15(12) = 180; \quad c = \dfrac{2}{12} = \dfrac{1}{6}; \quad i = \dfrac{11\%}{2} = 5.5\% = 0.055$

The equivalent effective monthly rate of interest

$$f = 1.055^{\frac{1}{6}} - 1 = 1.0089634 - 1 = 0.0089634 = 0.89634\%$$

$$A_{nc} = 370.00\left(\frac{1 - 1.0089634^{-180}}{0.0089634}\right) \qquad\text{——— substituting in Formula 11.4}$$
$$= 370.00(89.180057)$$
$$= \$32\,996.62$$

The amount borrowed was $32 996.62.

B. Using preprogrammed calculators to find the present value of an ordinary general annuity

STEP 1 Convert i into the equivalent effective rate of interest as shown in Section 11.4C.

STEP 2 Using f as the interest rate per payment period, determine the present value of the ordinary annuity.

EXAMPLE 11.5C A contract is fulfilled by making payments of $8500.00 at the end of every year for fifteen years. If interest is 7% compounded quarterly, what is the cash price of the contract?

Solution $R = 8500.00; \quad n = 15; \quad c = 4; \quad i = \dfrac{7\%}{4} = 1.75\%$

STEP 1 $f = 1.0175^4 - 1 = 1.071859 - 1 = 0.071859 = 7.1859\%$

STEP 2 7.1859 %i 0 FV 8500 PMT 15 N CPT PV 76 516.394

The cash price of the contract is $76 516.39.

EXAMPLE 11.5D A 25-year mortgage on a house requires payments of $619.94 at the end of each month. If interest is 9.5% compounded semi-annually, what was the mortgage principal?

Solution $R = 619.94; \quad n = 25(12) = 300; \quad c = \dfrac{2}{12} = \dfrac{1}{6}; \quad i = \dfrac{9.5\%}{2} = 4.75\%$

$f = 1.0475^{\frac{1}{6}} - 1 = 1.0077644 - 1 = 0.0077644 = 0.77644\%$

0.77644 [%i] 0 [FV] 619.94 [PMT] 300 [N] [CPT] [PV] [71 999.895]

The mortgage principal was $72 000.

Exercise 11.5

A. Find the present value of the following eight ordinary annuities.

	Periodic Payment	Payment Interval	Term	Interest Rate	Conversion Period
1.	$1400.00	3 months	12 years	6%	monthly
2.	$6000.00	1 year	9 years	10%	quarterly
3.	$3000.00	3 months	4 years	6%	annually
4.	$200.00	1 month	2 years	12%	semi-annually
5.	$95.00	1 month	5 years	4.5%	monthly
6.	$975.00	6 months	8 years	8%	semi-annually
7.	$1890.00	6 months	15 years	7%	quarterly
8.	$155.00	1 month	10 years	8%	quarterly

B. Answer each of the following questions.

1. Find the present value of payments of $250.00 made at the end of every three months for twelve years if money is worth 12% compounded monthly.

2. What is the discounted value of $1560.00 paid at the end of each year for nine years if interest is 6% compounded quarterly?

3. What cash payment is equivalent to making payments of $825.00 at the end of every three months for 16 years if interest is 7% compounded semi-annually?

4. What is the principal from which $175.00 can be withdrawn at the end of each month for twenty years if interest is 5% compounded quarterly?

5. A property was purchased for $5000.00 down and payments of $2500.00 at the end of every six months for six years. Interest is 12% compounded monthly.
   a) What was the purchase price of the property?
   b) How much is the cost of financing?

6. A car was purchased for $1500.00 down and payments of $265.00 at the end of each month for four years. Interest is 9% compounded monthly.
   a) What was the purchase price of the car?
   b) How much will be the amount of interest paid?

7. Payments of $715.59 are made at the end of each month to repay a 25-year mortgage. If interest is 10% compounded semi-annually, what is the original mortgage principal?

8. A 15-year mortgage is amortized by making payments of $1031.61 at the end of every three months. If interest is 8.25% compounded annually, what was the original mortgage balance?

9. Cedomir Dale expects to retire in seven years. He bought a retirement annuity paying $1200.00 every three months for twenty years. If the first payment is due three months after his retirement and interest is 12% compounded monthly, how much did Mr. Dale invest?

10. For her daughter's university education, Georgina Harcourt has invested an inheritance in a fund paying 11% compounded quarterly. If ordinary annuity payments of $450.00 per month are to be made out of the fund for four years and the annuity begins twelve years from now, how much was the inheritance?

REVIEW EXERCISE

1. Payments of $360.00 are made into a fund at the end of every three months for twelve years. The fund earns interest at 7% compounded quarterly.

   a) What will the balance in the fund be after twelve years?

   b) How much of the balance is deposits?

   c) How much of the balance is interest?

2. A trust fund is set up to make payments of $950.00 at the end of each month for seven and a half years. Interest on the fund is 7.8% compounded monthly.

   a) How much money must be deposited into the fund?

   b) How much will be paid out of the fund?

   c) How much interest is earned by the fund?

3. How much interest is included in the accumulated value of $75.90 paid at the end of each month for four years if interest is 9% compounded monthly?

4. If a loan was repaid by quarterly payments of $320.00 in five years at 8% compounded quarterly, how much money had been borrowed?

5. Payments of $375.00 made every three months are accumulated at 12% compounded monthly. What is their future value after eight years if the payments are made at the end of every three months?

6. What is the accumulated value after twelve years of monthly deposits of $145.00 earning interest at 5% compounded semi-annually if the deposits are made at the end of each month?

7. What single cash payment is equivalent to payments of $3500.00 every six months at 7% compounded quarterly if the payments are made at the end of every six months for fifteen years?

8. What is the principal invested at 6.5% compounded semi-annually from which monthly withdrawals of $240.00 can be made at the end of each month for 25 years?

9. If you contribute $1500.00 into an RRSP every six months for twelve years and interest on the deposits is 8% compounded semi-annually, how much would the balance in the RRSP be seven years after the last contribution?

10. Doris purchased a piano with $300.00 down and monthly payments of $124.00 for two and a half years at 9% compounded monthly. What was the purchase price of the piano?

11. Contributions of $500.00 are made at the end of every three months into an RRSP. What is the accumulated balance after twenty years if interest is 6% compounded semi-annually?

12. A 25-year mortgage is amortized by payments of $761.50 made at the end of each month. If interest is 9.5% compounded semi-annually, what is the mortgage principal?

13. Glenn has made contributions of $250.00 every three months into an RRSP for ten years. Interest for the first four years was 10% compounded quarterly. Since then the interest rate has been 11% compounded quarterly. How much will Glenn have in his RRSP three years after the last contribution?

14. Avi expects to retire in twelve years. Beginning one month after his retirement he would like to receive $500.00 per month for twenty years. How much must he deposit into a fund today to be able to do so if the rate of interest on the deposit is 6% compounded monthly?

15. A contract is signed requiring payments of $750.00 at the end of every three months for eight years.

    a) How much is the cash value of the contract if money is worth 9% compounded quarterly?

    b) If the first three payments are missed, how much would have to be paid after one year to bring the contract up to date?

    c) If, because of the missed payments, the contract has to be paid off at the end of one year, how much money is needed?

    d) How much of the total interest paid is due to the missed payments?

SELF-TEST

1. You won $100 000 in a lottery and you want to set some of that sum aside for ten years. After ten years, you would like to receive $2400 at the end of every three months for eight years. How much of your winnings must you set aside if interest is 10.5% compounded quarterly?

2. A debt can be repaid by payments of $2000 today, $4000 in five years, and $3000 in eight years. What single payment would settle the debt three years from today if money is worth 9% compounded quarterly?

3. Monthly deposits of $480.00 were made at the end of each month for eight years. If interest is 9.5% compounded semi-annually, what amount can be withdrawn five years after the last deposit?

4. A loan was repaid in five years by quarterly payments of $1200.00 at 9.5% compounded semi-annually. How much interest was paid?

5. Wen borrowed $7500 at 10.5% compounded quarterly. He repaid $4500 after two years and $3500 after five years. How much will Wen owe at the end of nine years?

6. A loan was repaid in seven years by monthly payments of $450. If interest was 12% compounded monthly, how much interest was paid?

7. Ms. Simms made quarterly deposits of $540 into a savings account. For the first five years interest was 5% compounded quarterly. Since then the rate of interest has been 5.5% compounded quarterly. How much is the account balance after thirteen years?

8. How much interest is included in the accumulated value of $3200 paid at the end of every six months for four years if the interest rate is 10.5% compounded semi-annually?

CHALLENGE PROBLEMS

1. After winning some money at a casino, Tony is considering purchasing an annuity that promises to pay him $300 at the end of each month for 12 months, then $350 at the end of each month for 24 months, and then $375 at the end of each month for 36 months. If the first payment is due at the end of the first month and interest is 7.5% compounded annually over the life of the annuity, find Tony's purchase price.

2. On March 1, 1997, Yves decided to save for a new truck. He deposited $500.00 at the end of every three months in a bank account earning interest at 5% compounded quarterly. He made his first deposit on June 1, 1997. On June 1, 1999, Yves decided that he needed the money to go to college, so on September 1, 1999, he stopped making deposits and started withdrawing $300.00. He with-

drew this amount at the end of each quarter until December 1, 2000. How much is left in his account after the last withdrawal if his bank account interest rate changed to 6.5% compounded quarterly on March 1, 2000?

CASE STUDY 11.1 SAVING FOR RETIREMENT

Melina Tuncali is an engineer at a plastics company. When she approached age 50, she realized that the company pension plan would not pay her enough pension to allow her to travel when she retired. To provide more money for her retirement, she decided to deposit money into an investment that guaranteed an interest rate of 6% compounded quarterly for up to twenty years. As a result, she invested $1000.00 at the end of each quarter, with the end of the first quarter being her fiftieth birthday.

A few months before she turned 60, Melina was approached by an investment counsellor who suggested moving the money into a fund that guaranteed an interest rate of 8% compounded monthly for up to ten years. The higher interest rate appealed to her, so instead of investing $1000.00 in the old investment, she celebrated her sixtieth birthday by transferring all the money from the old investment into the new fund. Also, since the interest in the new fund was compounded monthly, she decided to make monthly deposits instead of quarterly deposits. She began to make $350.00 deposits each month, beginning exactly one month after her sixtieth birthday. Melina plans to retire when she turns 65.

QUESTIONS

1. a) How much money did Melina have in her original investment when she turned 60?

    b) How much of this amount was interest?

2. a) How much money will be in the new fund when she turns 65?

    b) How much of this amount will be interest?

3. Suppose Melina had not switched investment plans at age 60. Suppose she had continued investing $1000.00 at the end of each quarter and earned 6% interest compounded quarterly. How much money would have been in the investment when she turned 65?

4. Suppose Melina had decided to keep the original investment but had stopped making payments to it at age 60. The investment would continue to earn 6% interest compounded quarterly. Then suppose, one month after she turned 60, she began making monthly deposits of $350.00 to the new fund that paid 8% interest compounded monthly. How much money would Melina have had when she turned 65?

CASE STUDY 11.2 GETTING THE PICTURE

Suzanne had a summer job working in the business office of Blast-It TV and Stereo, a local chain of home electronics stores. When Petr Jacobssen, the owner of the chain, heard she had completed one year of business courses, he asked Suzanne to calculate the profitability of two new large-screen TVs. He plans to offer a special payment plan for the two new models to attract customers to his stores. He wants to promote heavily the more profitable TV.

When Petr gave Suzanne the information about the two TVs, he told her to ignore all taxes when making her calculations. The cost of TV A to the company is $1720.00 and the cost of TV B to the company is $1680.00, after all trade discounts have been taken. The company plans to sell TV A for a $300.00 down payment and $210.00 per month for twelve months, beginning one month from the date of the purchase. The company plans to sell TV B for a $100.00 down payment and $160.00 per month for eighteen months, beginning one month from the date of purchase. The monthly payments for both TVs reflect an interest rate of 13.5% compounded monthly.

Petr wants Suzanne to calculate the profit of TV A and TV B as a percent of the TV's cost to the company. To calculate profit, Petr deducts overhead (which he calculates as 15% of cost) and the cost of the item from the selling price of the item. When he sells items that are paid for at a later time, he calculates the selling price as the *cash value* of the item. (Remember that cash value equals the down payment plus the present value of the periodic payments.)

Suzanne realized that she could calculate the profitability of each TV by using her knowledge of ordinary annuities. She went to work on her assignment to provide Petr with the information he requested.

QUESTIONS

1. a) What is the cash value of TV A? Round your answer to the nearest dollar.

   b) What is the cash value of TV B? Round your answer to the nearest dollar.

2. a) Given Petr's system of calculations, how much overhead should be assigned to TV A?

   b) How much overhead should be assigned to TV B?

3. a) According to Petr's system of calculations, what is the profit of TV A as a percent of its cost?

   b) What is the profit of TV B as a percent of its cost?

   c) Which TV should Suzanne recommend be more heavily promoted?

4. Three months later, due to Blast-It's successful sales of TV A and TV B, the suppliers of each model gave the company new volume discounts. For TV A, Blast-It received a discount of 8% off its current cost. For TV B, the company received a discount of 5% off its current cost. The special payment plans for TV A and TV B will stay the same. Under these new conditions, which TV should Suzanne recommend be more heavily promoted?

SUMMARY OF FORMULAE

Formula 9.1A

$S = P(1 + i)^n$

Finding the future value of a compound amount (maturity value) when the original principal, the rate of interest, and the time period are known

Formula 9.1C

$P = S(1 + i)^{-n}$

Finding the present value by means of the discount factor (the reciprocal of the compounding factor)

Formula 10.1

$f = (1 + i)^m - 1$

Finding the effective rate of interest f for a nominal annual rate compounded m times per year

Formula 11.1

$S_n = R\left[\dfrac{(1 + i)^n - 1}{i}\right]$

Finding the future value (accumulated value) of an ordinary simple annuity

Formula 11.2

$A_n = R\left[\dfrac{1 - (1 + i)^{-n}}{i}\right]$

Finding the present value (discounted value) of an ordinary simple annuity

Formula 11.3

$S_{nc} = R\left[\dfrac{(1 + f)^n - 1}{f}\right]$

where $f = (1 + i)^c - 1$

Finding the future value of an ordinary general annuity using the equivalent effective rate of interest per payment period

Formula 11.4

$A_{nc} = R\left[\dfrac{1 - (1 + f)^{-n}}{f}\right]$

where $f = (1 + i)^c - 1$

Finding the present value of an ordinary general annuity using the equivalent effective rate of interest per payment period

GLOSSARY

Accumulated value of one dollar per period   see *Accumulation factor for annuities*

Accumulation factor for annuities   the factor $\dfrac{(1 + i)^n - 1}{i}$

Annual rent   the sum of the periodic payments in one year

Annuity   a series of payments, usually equal in size, made at equal periodic time intervals

Annuity certain   an annuity for which the term is fixed

Annuity due   an annuity in which the periodic payments are made at the beginning of each payment interval

Compounding factor for annuities   see *Accumulation factor for annuities*

Contingent annuity   an annuity in which the term is uncertain; that is, either the beginning date of the term or the ending date of the term or both are unknown

Deferred annuity   an annuity in which the first payment is delayed for a number of payment periods

Discount factor of annuities   see *Present value factor for annuities*

Discounted value of one dollar per period   see *Present value factor for annuities*

Future value of an annuity   the sum of the accumulated values of the periodic payments at the end of the term of the annuity

General annuity   an annuity in which the conversion (or compounding) period is different from the payment interval

Ordinary annuity   an annuity in which the payments are made at the end of each payment interval

Payment interval   the length of time between successive payments

Payment period   see *Payment interval*

Periodic rent   the size of the regular periodic payment

Perpetuity   an annuity for which the payments continue forever

Present value factor for annuities   the factor $\dfrac{1 - (1 + i)^{-n}}{i}$

Present value of an annuity   the sum of the present values (or discounted values) of the periodic payments at the beginning of the term of the annuity

Simple annuity   an annuity in which the conversion period is the same as the payment interval

Term of annuity   the length of time from the beginning of the first payment interval to the end of the last payment interval

12 Other Annuities—Future Value and Present Value

The rent you pay on an apartment or a house consists of a series of regular, equal payments due at the *beginning* of each month. This series of payments represents a type of annuity called an *annuity due*. Its payment schedule differs from that of an *ordinary annuity* (which we discussed in Chapter 11), where payments are due at the *end* of each month.

Sometimes, a series of regular, equal payments does not begin until some future time. Such schemes are known as *deferred annuities*. For example, if you won a large amount of money today and you wanted a series of regular, equal payments to begin five years from today, you would set up a deferred annuity. Both ordinary annuities and annuities due can be deferred.

Introduction

In the previous chapter, we considered ordinary annuities, in which the payments are made at the end of each payment period.

In this chapter we will consider other annuities resulting from variations in the payment dates. These include *annuities due* (in which payments are made in advance), *deferred annuities* (in which the first payment is made after the end of the first payment interval), and *perpetuities* (in which payments continue indefinitely).

OBJECTIVES

Upon completing this chapter, you will be able to do the following:

1. Determine the future value and present value of simple annuities due.
2. Determine the future value and present value of general annuities due.
3. Determine the future value and present value of ordinary deferred annuities and deferred annuities due.
4. Determine the present value of ordinary perpetuities, perpetuities due, and deferred perpetuities.

12.1 SIMPLE ANNUITIES DUE—FUTURE VALUE AND PRESENT VALUE

A. Future value of a simple annuity due

By definition, an **annuity due** is an annuity in which the periodic payments are made at the beginning of each payment interval.

Finding the future value of such an annuity is similar to finding the future value of an ordinary annuity. In fact, the future value of an annuity due is closely related to the future value of an ordinary annuity. This same close relationship also holds for the present value.

EXAMPLE 12.1A Find the accumulated value (future value) at the end date of the last payment period of deposits of $3000.00 each made at the beginning of five consecutive years respectively at 12% compounded annually.

Solution As for any problem involving a series of payments, the method of solution and the data can be shown on a time diagram.

FIGURE 12.1   Graphic Representation of Method and Data

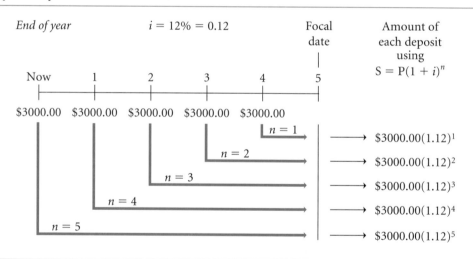

As shown in the diagram, the first deposit is located at the beginning of Year 1, which is the same as "now"; the second deposit is located at the beginning of Year 2, which is the same as the end of Year 1; the third at the beginning of Year 3; the fourth at the beginning of Year 4; and the fifth and last deposit at the beginning of Year 5, which is also the beginning of the last payment period. The focal date, however, is located at the *end* of the last payment period.

The accumulated values of the individual deposits are obtained by using Formula 9.1A, $S = P(1 + i)^n$. Finding the combined total of the five accumulated values is made easier by taking out the common factors 3000.00 and 1.12 as shown below.

Deposit 5	$3000.00(1.12)^1 =$	(1.0)	(1.0)
Deposit 4	$3000.00(1.12)^2 =$	(1.12)	(1.12)
Deposit 3	$3000.00(1.12)^3 = 3000.00(1.12)(1.12)^2 =$	$3000.00(1.12)(1.2544)$	
Deposit 2	$3000.00(1.12)^4 =$	$(1.12)^3$	(1.404928)
Deposit 1	$3000.00(1.12)^5 =$	$(1.12)^4$	(1.5735194)

$$= 3000.00(1.12)(6.3528474)$$
$$= 19\ 058.54(1.12)$$
$$= \$21\ 345.56$$

Note: This example is the same as Example 11.2B except that the deposits are made at the beginning of each payment period rather than at the end. The answer to Example 11.2B was \$19 058.54. We could have obtained the answer to Example 12.1A simply by multiplying \$19 058.54 by 1.12. It appears that the future value of the annuity due can be obtained by multiplying the future value of the ordinary annuity by the factor $(1 + i)$.

The general notation for simple annuities due is the same as for ordinary simple annuities except that the accumulated value (future value) of the annuity due is represented by the symbol $S_n(\text{due})$.

The formula for the future value of a simple annuity due is:

$$S_n(\text{due}) = R(1 + i)\left[\frac{(1 + i)^n - 1}{i}\right] \quad \text{—— Formula 12.1}$$

Note: Formula 12.1, the future value of a simple annuity due, differs from Formula 11.1, the future value of an ordinary simple annuity, only by the factor $(1 + i)$.

$$\begin{array}{c}\text{FUTURE VALUE OF} \\ \text{A SIMPLE ANNUITY DUE}\end{array} - (1 + i) \times \begin{array}{c}\text{FUTURE VALUE OF THE} \\ \text{ORDINARY SIMPLE ANNUITY}\end{array}$$

The relationship between an annuity due and the corresponding ordinary annuity is graphically illustrated in the comparison of the line diagrams.

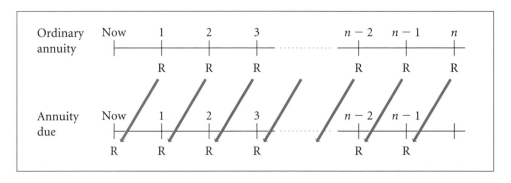

The two line graphs show the shift of the payments by one period. In an annuity due, every payment earns interest for one more period than in an ordinary annuity and this explains the factor $(1 + i)$.

EXAMPLE 12.1B   Find the accumulated value at the end of the last payment period of quarterly payments of $50.00 made at the beginning of each quarter for ten years if interest is 6% compounded quarterly.

Solution   Since the payments are of equal size made at the beginning of each period, the payment series is an annuity due and since the focal date is the end of the last payment period, the future value of the annuity due is to be found.

$$R = 50.00; \quad i = \frac{6\%}{4} = 0.015; \quad n = 10(4) = 40$$

$$S_n(\text{due}) = 50.00(1.015)\left(\frac{1.015^{40} - 1}{0.015}\right) \qquad \text{—— substituting in Formula 12.1}$$
$$= 50.00(1.015)(54.2678939)$$
$$= 2713.39(1.015)$$
$$= \$2754.10$$

EXAMPLE 12.1C   You deposit $10.00 at the beginning of each month for five years in an account paying 12% compounded monthly.

   (i)   What will the balance in your account be at the end of five years?

   (ii) How much of the balance will you have contributed?

   (iii) How much of the balance will be interest?

Solution   (i) $R = 10.00; \quad i = \dfrac{12\%}{12} = 1\% = 0.01; \quad n = 5(12) = 60$

$$S_n(\text{due}) = 10.00(1.01)\left(\frac{1.01^{60} - 1}{0.01}\right)$$
$$= 10.00(1.01)(81.66967)$$
$$= 816.6967(1.01)$$
$$= 824.86$$

   (ii) Your contribution is $(10.00)(60) = \$600.00$.

   (iii) The interest earned $= 824.86 - 600.00 = \$224.86$.

B. Present value of a simple annuity due

EXAMPLE 12.1D   Find the present value of five payments of $3000.00 each made at the beginning of each of five consecutive years respectively if money is worth 12% compounded annually.

Solution   As Figure 12.2 shows, the present value of the individual payments is obtained using Formula 9.1C, $P = S(1 + i)^{-n}$. The sum of the individual present values is easier to find when the common factor 3000.00 is taken out.

FIGURE 12.2   **Graphic Representation of Method and Data**

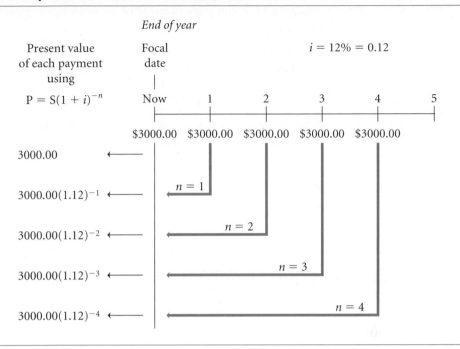

Payment 1	3000.00		(1)		(1.0000000)
Payment 1	3000.00		(1)		(1.0000000)
Payment 2	$3000.00(1.12)^{-1}$		$(1.12)^{-1}$		(0.8928571)
Payment 3	$3000.00(1.12)^{-2} =$	$3000.00(1.12)^{-2} =$		$3000.00(0.7971939)$	
Payment 4	$3000.00(1.12)^{-3}$		$(1.12)^{-3}$		(0.7117802)
Payment 5	$3000.00(1.12)^{-4}$		$(1.12)^{-4}$		(0.6355181)

$$= 3000.00(4.0373493)$$
$$= \$12\ 112.05$$

Example 12.1D is the same as Example 11.3B, except that the payments are made at the beginning of each payment period. The answer to Example 11.3B was $10 814.33. If this amount is multiplied by 1.12, the result is $12 112.05, the answer to Example 12.1D.

This result implies that we could have obtained the present value of the annuity due in Example 12.1D by multiplying the present value of the ordinary annuity in Example 11.3B by the factor 1.12, which is the factor $(1 + i)$.

The present value of an annuity due is represented by the symbol A_n (due). The formula for the present value of a simple annuity due is:

$$A_n(\text{due}) = R(1 + i)\left[\frac{1 - (1 + i)^{-n}}{i}\right]$$ ——— **Formula 12.2**

Note: Formula 12.2, the present value of a simple annuity due, differs from Formula 11.2, the present value of an ordinary simple annuity, only by the factor $(1 + i)$.

$$\begin{matrix} \text{PRESENT VALUE} \\ \text{OF A SIMPLE ANNUITY DUE} \end{matrix} = (1 + i) \times \begin{matrix} \text{PRESENT VALUE OF THE} \\ \text{ORDINARY SIMPLE ANNUITY} \end{matrix}$$

EXAMPLE 12.1E Find the present value of payments of \$50.00 made at the beginning of each quarter for ten years if interest is 6% compounded quarterly.

Solution

$R = 50.00;\quad i = \dfrac{6\%}{4} = 1.5\% = 0.015;\quad n = 10(4) = 40$

$A_n(\text{due}) = 50.00(1.015)\left[\dfrac{1 - (1.015)^{-40}}{(0.015)}\right]$ ——— substituting in Formula 12.2

$\quad = 50.00(1.015)(29.9158452)$

$\quad = 1495.79(1.015)$

$\quad = \$1518.23$

EXAMPLE 12.1F What is the cash value of a three-year lease of office facilities renting for \$536.50 payable at the beginning of each month if money is worth 9% compounded monthly?

Solution Since the payments are at the beginning of each payment period, the problem involves an annuity due, and since we want the cash value, the present value of the annuity due is required.

$R = 536.50;\quad i = \dfrac{9\%}{12} = 0.75\% = 0.0075;\quad n = 3(12) = 36$

$A_n(\text{due}) = 536.50(1.0075)\left[\dfrac{1 - (1.0075)^{-36}}{0.0075}\right]$

$\quad = 536.50(31.446805)(1.0075)$

$\quad = 16\ 871.21(1.0075)$

$\quad = \$16\ 997.74$

The cash value of the lease is \$16 997.74.

C. Using preprogrammed financial calculators

You can easily determine the future value $S_n(\text{due})$ or the present value $A_n(\text{due})$ using a preprogrammed financial calculator. Find the corresponding value for an ordinary simple annuity and multiply by $(1 + i)$ or, if a DUE key is available, by pressing DUE instead of CPT (or 2nd) when retrieving the answer. If DUE is a secondary function, press 2nd followed by the primary function key. If your calculator displays a negative result, ignore the negative sign.

EXAMPLE 12.1G Payments of $425 are to be made at the beginning of each quarter for 10 years. If money is worth 6% compounded quarterly, determine

  (i) the accumulated value of the payments;

  (ii) the present value of the payments.

Solution   (i) $R = 425$; $i = 1.5\%$; $n = 40$

Key in	Press	Display shows
0	PV	0
425	PMT	425
1.5	%i	1.5
40	N	40
DUE (or 2nd CPT)	FV	23 409.813 — this retrieves the future value of an annuity due

The accumulated value of the annuity due is $23 409.81.

(ii)

Key in	Press	Display shows
0	FV	0
425	PMT	425
1.5	%i	1.5
40	N	40
DUE (or 2nd CPT)	PV	12 904.948 — this retrieves the present value of an annuity due

The present value of the annuity due is $12 904.95.

EXAMPLE 12.1H Frank deposited monthly rent receipts of $250.00 due at the beginning of each month in a savings account paying 10.5% compounded monthly for four years. Frank made no further deposits after four years but left the money in the account.

  (i) What will the balance be twelve full years after he made the first deposit?

  (ii) How much of the total will be due to rent?

  (iii) How much will be interest?

Solution   (i) First determine the balance at the end of four years. This problem involves finding the future value of a simple annuity due.

$$R = 250.00; \quad i = \frac{10.5\%}{12} = 0.875\%; \quad n = 48$$

$$S_n(\text{due}) = 250.00(1.00875)\left(\frac{1.00875^{48} - 1}{0.00875}\right)$$
$$= 250.00(1.00875)(59.335279)$$
$$= 14\,833.82(1.00875)$$
$$= \$14\,963.62$$

Now accumulate $14 963.62 for another eight years.

$$P = 14\,963.62; \quad i = 0.00875; \quad n = 8(12) = 96$$

$$S = 14\,963.62(1.00875)^{96} \quad\text{—————————— substituting in Formula 9.1A}$$
$$= 14\,963.62(2.3079191)$$
$$= \$34\,534.82$$

Programmed solution

0 [PV] 250 [PMT] 0.875 [%i] 48 [N] [DUE] (or [2nd] [CPT])

[FV] [14 963.616]

14 963.616 [PV] 0 [PMT] 0.875 [%i] 96 [N] [CPT]

[FV] [34 534.815]

The balance in the account after 12 years is $34 534.82.

(ii) The rent receipts in the total are 250.00(48) = $12 000.00.

(iii) Interest in the balance is 34 534.82 − 12 000.00 = $22 534.82.

EXAMPLE 12.1I Mei Willis would like to receive annuity payments of $2000.00 at the beginning of each quarter for seven years. The annuity is to start five years from now and interest is 5% compounded quarterly.

(i) How much must Mei invest today?

(ii) How much will Mei receive from the annuity?

(iii) How much of what she receives will be interest?

Solution (i) First, find the present value of the annuity due (the focal point is five years from now).

$$R = 2000.00; \quad i = \frac{5\%}{4} = 1.25\% = 0.0125; \quad n = 7(4) = 28$$

$$A_n(\text{due}) = 2000.00(1.0125)\left[\frac{1 - 1.0125^{-28}}{0.0125}\right]$$
$$= 2000.00(23.502517)(1.0125)$$
$$= 47\,005.035(1.0125)$$
$$= \$47\,592.60$$

Second, determine the present value of $47 592.60 (the focal point is "now").

$$S = 47\,592.60; \quad i = 1.25\%; \quad n = 5(4) = 20$$

$$P = 47\,592.60(1.0125)^{-20}$$
$$= 47\,592.60(0.7800085)$$
$$= \$37\,122.63$$

Programmed solution

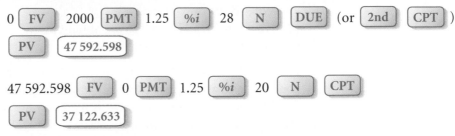

Mei will have to invest $37 122.63.

(ii) Mei will receive 28(2000.00) = $56 000.00.

(iii) Interest will be 56 000.00 − 37 122.63 = $18 877.37.

Exercise 12.1

A. Find the future value and the present value of each of the following six annuities due.

	Periodic Payment	Payment Interval	Term	Interest Rate	Conversion Period
1.	$3000.00	3 months	8 years	8%	quarterly
2.	$750.00	1 month	5 years	12%	monthly
3.	$2000.00	6 months	12 years	5.6%	semi-annually
4.	$450.00	3 months	15 years	4.4%	quarterly
5.	$65.00	1 month	20 years	9%	monthly
6.	$160.00	1 month	15 years	6%	monthly

B. Answer each of the following questions.

1. Find the amount of an annuity due of $300.00 payable at the beginning of every month for seven years at 12% compounded monthly.

2. Determine the accumulated value after twelve years of deposits of $360.00 made at the beginning of every three months and earning interest at 7% compounded quarterly.

3. Find the present value of payments of $2500.00 made at the beginning of every six months for ten years if money is worth 9.5% compounded semi-annually.

4. What is the discounted value of deposits of $240.00 made at the beginning of every three months for seven years if money is worth 8.8% compounded quarterly?

5. A washer-dryer combination can be purchased from a department store by making monthly credit card payments of $52.50 for two and a half years. The first payment is due on the date of sale and interest is 21% compounded monthly.

    a) What is the purchase price?
    b) How much will be paid in instalments?
    c) How much is the cost of financing?

6. Diane Wallace bought a living-room suite on credit, signing an instalment contract with a finance company that requires monthly payments of $62.25 for three years. The first payment is made on the date of signing and interest is 24% compounded monthly.

    a) What was the cash price?
    b) How much will Diane pay in total?
    c) How much of what she pays will be interest?

7. Until he retires sixteen years from now, Mr. Lait plans to deposit $300.00 at the beginning of every three months in an account paying interest at 5% compounded quarterly.

    a) What will be the balance in his account when he retires?
    b) How much of the balance will be interest?

8. Joanna contributes $750.00 at the beginning of every six months into an RRSP paying interest at 8% compounded semi-annually.

    a) How much will her RRSP deposits amount to in twenty years?
    b) How much of the amount will be interest?

9. The monthly premium on a three-year insurance policy is $64.00 payable in advance. What is the cash value of the policy if money is worth 4.8% compounded monthly?

10. The monthly rent payment on office space is $535.00 payable in advance. What yearly payment in advance would satisfy the lease if interest is 6.6% compounded monthly?

12.2 GENERAL ANNUITIES DUE–FUTURE VALUE AND PRESENT VALUE

A. Future value of a general annuity due

As with a simple annuity due, the future value of a **general annuity due** is greater than the future value of the corresponding ordinary general annuity by the interest on it for one payment period.

Since the interest on a general annuity for one payment period is $(1 + i)^c$, or $(1 + f)$,

$$\text{PRESENT VALUE OF A GENERAL ANNUITY DUE} = (1 + f) \times \text{PRESENT VALUE OF THE CORRESPONDING ORDINARY GENERAL ANNUITY}$$

Thus, the formula for the future value of a general annuity due can be derived directly from Formula 11.3:

$$S_{nc}(\text{due}) = R(1 + f)\left[\frac{(1 + f)^n - 1}{f}\right]$$
$$\text{where } f = (1 + i)^c - 1$$

————— **Formula 12.3**

EXAMPLE 12.2A   What is the accumulated value after five years of payments of $20 000 made at the beginning of each year if interest is 7% compounded quarterly?

Solution $R = 20\ 000.00; \quad n = 5; \quad c = 4; \quad i = \dfrac{7\%}{4} = 1.75\% = 0.0175$

The equivalent effective annual rate of interest

$f = 1.0175^4 - 1 = 1.0718590 - 1 = 0.0718590 = 7.18590\%$

$S_{nc}(\text{due}) = 20\ 000.00(1.0718590)\left(\dfrac{1.0718590^5 - 1}{0.0718590}\right)$ — substituting in Formula 12.3

$\qquad = 20\ 000.00(1.0718590)(5.7721095)$
$\qquad = 20\ 000.00(6.1868875)$
$\qquad = \$123\ 737.75$

Programmed solution

7.18590 [%i] 0 [PV] 20 000 [PMT] 5 [N] [DUE] (or [2nd] [CPT])
[FV] [123 737.75]

The accumulated value after five years is $123 737.75.

B. Present value of a general annuity due

For a general annuity due, the present value is greater than the present value of the corresponding ordinary general annuity by the interest on it for one payment period.

$$\text{THE PRESENT VALUE OF A GENERAL ANNUITY DUE} = (1 + f) \times \text{THE PRESENT VALUE OF THE CORRESPONDING ORDINARY GENERAL ANNUITY}$$

Thus, the formula for the present value of a general annuity due can be derived directly from Formula 11.4. Using the equivalent effective rate of interest per payment period,

$$A_{nc}(\text{due}) = R(1 + f)\left[\frac{1 - (1 + f)^{-n}}{f}\right]$$
where $f = (1 + i)^c - 1$

— Formula 12.4

EXAMPLE 12.2B A three-year lease requires payments of $1600.00 at the beginning of every three months. If money is worth 9.0% compounded monthly, what is the cash value of the lease?

Solution $R = 1600.00; \quad n = 3(4) = 12; \quad c = \dfrac{12}{4} = 3; \quad i = \dfrac{9.0\%}{12} = 0.75\% = 0.0075$

The equivalent effective quarterly rate of interest

$f = 1.0075^3 - 1 = 1.00226692 - 1 = 0.0226692 = 2.26692\%$

$$A_{nc}(\text{due}) = 1600.00(1.0226692)\left(\frac{1 - 1.0226692^{-12}}{0.0226692}\right) \quad\text{— substituting in}$$
Formula 12.4

$\qquad = 1600.00(1.0226692)(10.4040412)$

$\qquad = 1600.00(10.639892)$

$\qquad = \$17\,023.83$

Programmed solution

2.26692 %i 0 FV 1600 PMT 12 N DUE (or 2nd CPT)

PV 17 023.828

The cash value of the lease is $17 023.83.

Exercise 12.2

A. For each of the following four annuities due, determine the unknown value represented by the question mark.

Future Value $S_{nc}(\text{due})$	Present Value $A_{nc}(\text{due})$	Periodic Payment R	Payment Interval	Term	Nominal Rate of Interest	Conversion Period
1. ?		$1500.00	6 months	10 years	13%	quarterly
2. ?		$175.00	1 month	7 years	7%	semi-annually
3.	?	$650.00	3 months	6 years	12%	monthly
4.	?	$93.00	1 month	4 years	4%	quarterly

B. Answer each of the following questions.

1. Bomac Steel sets aside $5000.00 at the beginning of every six months in a fund to replace erecting equipment. If interest is 6% compounded quarterly, how much will be in the fund after five years?

2. Jamie Dean contributes $125.00 at the beginning of each month into an RRSP paying interest at 6.5% compounded semi-annually. What will be the accumulated balance in the RRSP at the end of 25 years?

3. What is the cash value of a lease requiring payments of $750.00 at the beginning of each month for three years if interest is 8% compounded quarterly?

4. Gerald Carter and Marysia Wokawski bought a property by making semi-annual payments of $2500.00 for seven years. If the first payment is due on the date of purchase and interest is 9% compounded quarterly, what is the purchase price of the property?

QUESTIONS

1. **a)** Using the numbers given in the table, calculate (to two decimal places) the percent of the $500.00 investment income that the investor receives after taxes if the investment income is
   i) interest;
   ii) capital gains;
   iii) dividends.
   b) How much do the percents you calculated above differ from the rates stated in the text of the article?

2. Suppose you had to make a choice. You could receive $1500.00 in dividends every six months for five years, starting today. Or, you could receive $1500.00 in interest every six months for five years, starting today. Assume that income tax is deducted before you receive your investment income. Assume the tax rates you have calculated from the table will be the same for five years and money will be worth 5% compounded semi-annually for the next five years. Using five years from now as the focal date, how much more after-tax investment income would you have if you chose the dividends?

3. Suppose you had a different choice. You could receive $1500.00 in capital gains every six months for five years, starting today. Or, you could receive the interest income described in Question 2. How much more after-tax investment income would you have if you chose the capital gains rather than the interest income? (Use the same assumptions as in Question 2.)

12.3 DEFERRED ANNUITIES

A. Basic concepts and computation of the future value of an ordinary deferred annuity

A **deferred annuity** is one in which the first payment is made at a time *later* than the end of the first payment interval. The time period from the time referred to as "now" to the starting point of the term of the annuity is called the **period of deferment**. The number of compounding periods in the period of deferment is designated by the letter symbol d. The future value of a deferred ordinary simple annuity (designated by the symbol $S_n(\text{defer})$) is the accumulated value of the periodic payments at the end of the term of the annuity.

EXAMPLE 12.3A Payments of $500.00 are due at the end of each year for ten years. If the annuity is deferred for four years and interest is 12% compounded annually, determine the future value of the deferred annuity.

Solution

FIGURE 12.3   Graphic Representation of Method and Data

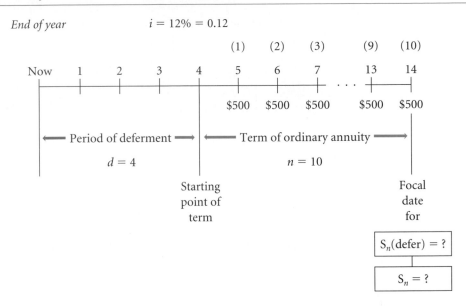

$$R = 500.00; \quad i = 12\% = 0.12; \quad n = 10; \quad d = 4$$

$$S_n(\text{defer}) = S_n = 500.00\left(\frac{1.12^{10} - 1}{0.12}\right) \quad\text{——— using Formula 11.1}$$
$$= 500.00(17.548735)$$
$$= \$8774.37$$

Note: The period of deferment does *not* affect the solution to the problem of finding the future value of a deferred annuity: $S_n(\text{defer}) = S_n$. Therefore, the problem of finding the future value of a deferred annuity is identical to the problem of finding the future value of an annuity. No further consideration is given in this text to the problem of finding the future value of a deferred annuity.

B. Present value of an ordinary deferred annuity

The **present value of a deferred annuity** is the discounted value of the periodic payment at the beginning of the period of deferment.

The present value of a deferred simple annuity is designated by the symbol $A_n(\text{defer})$.

The present value of a deferred general annuity is designated by the symbol $A_{nc}(\text{defer})$.

EXAMPLE 12.3B   Payments of $500.00 are due at the end of each year for ten years. If the annuity is deferred for four years and interest is 12% compounded annually, determine the present value of the deferred annuity.

Solution

FIGURE 12.4 **Graphic Representation of Method and Data**

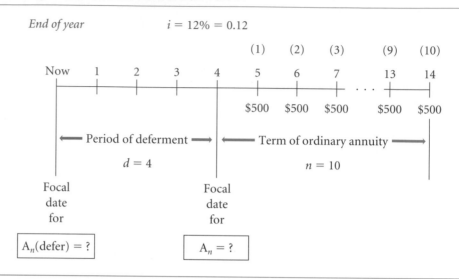

The problem of finding the present value of a deferred annuity can be divided into two smaller problems. We have used this approach in solving Example 11.3F in Chapter 11 and Example 12.1I in this chapter. We use it again in this problem to find the present value of the deferred annuity.

First, find the present value of the ordinary annuity (focal date at the beginning of the term of the annuity).

$$A_n = 500.00\left(\frac{1 - 1.12^{-10}}{0.12}\right) \quad\text{——— using Formula 11.2}$$
$$= 500.00(5.6502230)$$
$$= \$2825.11$$

Second, find the present value of A_n at the focal date "now."

$$A_n(\text{defer}) = P = 2825.11(1.12^{-4}) \quad\text{——— using Formula 9.1C}$$
$$= 2825.11(0.6355181)$$
$$= \$1795.41$$

Programmed solution

0 [FV] 500 [PMT] 12 [%i] 10 [N] [CPT] [PV] ⟨2825.1115⟩

0 [PMT] 2825.11 [FV] 12 [%i] 4 [N] [CPT] [PV] ⟨1795.4094⟩

Alternatively, you can find the present value of the deferred annuity by assuming that periodic payments were made during the period of deferment. This assumption shifts the beginning date of the term of the annuity to the focal date "now," as Figure 12.5 shows. To obtain the present value of the deferred annuity, deduct the present value of the annuity representing the assumed payments from the present value of the annuity representing all payments.

FIGURE 12.5   Graphic Representation of Method and Data

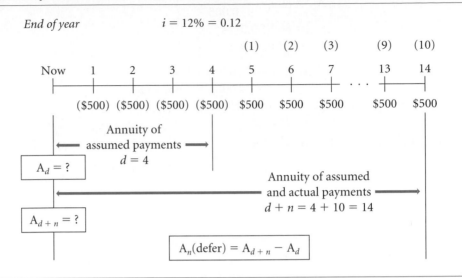

$$A_{d+n} = 500.00\left(\frac{1 - 1.12^{-14}}{0.12}\right) \text{────── using Formula 11.2}$$

$$= 500.00(6.6281682)$$

$$= \$3314.08$$

$$A_d = 500.00\left(\frac{1 - 1.12^{-4}}{0.12}\right) \text{──────using Formula 11.2}$$

$$= 500.00(3.0373493)$$

$$= \$1518.67$$

$$A_n(\text{defer}) = 3314.08 - 1518.67 = \$1795.41$$

Programmed alternative solution

0 FV   500 PMT   12 %i   14 N   CPT   PV   3314.0841

0 FV   500 PMT   12 %i   4 N   CPT   PV   1518.6747

3314.0841 − 1518.6747 = 1795.4094, that is $1795.41

EXAMPLE 12.3C   Mr. Peric wants to receive payments of $800.00 at the end of each month for ten years after his retirement. If he retires in seven years, how much must Mr. Peric invest now if interest on the investments is 6% compounded monthly?

Solution   The monthly payments after retirement form an ordinary annuity.

$$R = 800.00; \quad i = \frac{6\%}{12} = 0.5\% = 0.005; \quad n = 10(12) = 120$$

The period of deferment is 7 years, so $d = 7(12) = 84$.
The amount to be invested now is the present value of the deferred annuity.

$$A_n = 800\left(\frac{1 - 1.005^{-120}}{0.005}\right)$$
$$= 800(90.073453)$$
$$= 72\,058.76$$

$$A_n(\text{defer}) = 72\,058.76(1.005)^{-84}$$
$$= 72\,058.76(0.6577348)$$
$$= 47\,395.55$$

Programmed solution

0 [FV] 800 [PMT] 0.5 [%i] 120 [N] [CPT] [PV] [72 058.76]

72 058.76 [FV] 0 [PMT] 0.5 [%i] 84 [N] [CPT] [PV] [47 395.554]

Mr. Peric must invest $47 395.55.

EXAMPLE 12.3D Payments of $1000.00 are due at the end of each year for five years. If the payments are deferred for three years and interest is 10% compounded quarterly, what is the present value of the deferred payments?

Solution

STEP 1   Find the present value of the ordinary general annuity.

$$R = 1000.00; \quad n = 5; \quad c = 4; \quad i = \frac{10\%}{4} = 2.5\% = 0.025$$

The equivalent effective annual rate of interest

$$f = 1.025^4 - 1 = 1.1038129 - 1 = 0.1038129 = 10.38129\%$$

$$A_{nc} = 1000.00\left(\frac{1 - 1.1038129^{-5}}{0.1038129}\right) \qquad \text{— substituting in Formula 11.4}$$
$$= 1000.00(3.7541489)$$
$$= \$3754.15$$

Programmed solution

10.38129 [%i] 0 [FV] 1000 [PMT] 5 [N] [CPT] [PV] [3754.1489]

STEP 2   Find the present value of A_{nc} at the beginning of the period of deferment.

$S = 3754.15$ is the present value of the general annuity A_{nc};
$d = 3$ is the number of deferred payment intervals;
$f = 10.38129\%$ is the equivalent effective rate of interest per payment interval.

$$A_{nc}(\text{defer}) = P = 3754.15(1.1038129^{-3}) \qquad \text{— substituting in Formula 9.2C}$$
$$= 3754.15(0.7435559)$$
$$= \$2791.42$$

Programmed solution

$$10.38129 \boxed{\%i} \ 3754.15 \boxed{FV} \ 0 \boxed{PMT} \ 3 \boxed{N} \boxed{CPT} \boxed{PV} \boxed{2791.4203}$$

The present value of the deferred payments is $2791.42.

Alternative

Assume that periodic payments have been made during the period of deferment. Then the number of actual payments is $n = 5$ and the number of assumed payments is $d = 3$.

STEP 1   Find the present value of the annuity in which the number of payments is $d + n = 3 + 5 = 8$.

$$A_{(d + n)c} = 1000.00\left(\frac{1 - 1.1038129^{-8}}{0.1038129}\right)$$
$$= 1000.00(5.2616725)$$
$$= \$5261.67$$

Programmed solution

$$10.38129 \boxed{\%i} \ 0 \boxed{FV} \ 1000 \boxed{PMT} \ 8 \boxed{N} \boxed{CPT} \boxed{PV} \boxed{5261.6725}$$

STEP 2   Find the present value of the annuity consisting of the assumed payments $d = 3$.

$$A_{dc} = 1000.00\left(\frac{1 - 1.1038129^{-3}}{0.1038129}\right)$$
$$= 1000.00(2.4702531)$$
$$= \$2470.25$$

Programmed solution

$$10.38129 \boxed{\%i} \ 0 \boxed{FV} \ 1000 \boxed{PMT} \ 3 \boxed{N} \boxed{CPT} \boxed{PV} \boxed{2470.2531}$$

The first three values need not be programmed (since they are already programmed from Step 1.)

STEP 3   Find the present value of the deferred general annuity by finding the difference.

$$A_{nc}(\text{defer}) = A_{(d + n)c} - A_{dc} = 5261.67 - 2470.25 = \$2791.42.$$

C. Present value of a deferred annuity due

You can find the present value of a deferred annuity due by the approach used in Examples 12.3B and 12.3C except that Formula 12.2 or Formula 12.4 is used in Step 1.

EXAMPLE 12.3E $2000.00 is to be withdrawn from a fund at the beginning of every three months for twelve years starting ten years from now. If interest is 10% compounded quarterly, what must be the balance in the fund today to permit the withdrawals?

Solution   The withdrawals form an annuity due.

$$R = 2000.00; \quad i = \frac{10\%}{4} = 2.5\% = 0.025; \quad n = 12(4) = 48$$

The period of deferment is 10 years, so $d = (10)(4) = 40$.

$$A_n(\text{due}) = 2000.00(1.025)\left[\frac{1 - (1.025)^{-48}}{0.025}\right]$$
$$= 2000(1.025)(27.773154)$$
$$= 56\,934.97$$

$$A_n(\text{defer}) = 56\,934.97(1.025)^{-40}$$
$$= 56\,934.97(0.3724306)$$
$$= 21\,204.33$$

Programmed solution

0 [FV] 2000 [PMT] 2.5 [%i] 48 [N] [DUE] (or [2nd] [CPT])

[PV] [56 934.965]

56 934.965 [FV] 0 [PMT] 2.5 [%i] 40 [N] [CPT] [PV] [21 204.325]

The balance in the fund today must be $21 204.33.

EXAMPLE 12.3F   Tom Casey wants to withdraw $925.00 at the beginning of each quarter for twelve years. If the withdrawals are to begin ten years from now and interest is 4.5% compounded monthly, how much must Tom deposit today to be able to make the withdrawals?

Solution $R = 925.00; \quad n = 12(4) = 48; \quad d = 10(4) = 40; \quad c = \frac{12}{4} = 3;$

$$i = \frac{4.5\%}{12} = 0.375\% = 0.00375$$

The equivalent effective quarterly rate of interest

$$f = 1.00375^3 - 1 = 1.0112922 - 1 = 0.0112922 = 1.12922\%$$

STEP 1   Find the present value of the general annuity due.

$$A_{nc}(\text{due}) = 925.00(1.0112922)\left(\frac{1 - 1.0112922^{-48}}{0.0112922}\right) \quad \text{— substituting in Formula 12.4}$$

$$= 925.00(1.0112922)(36.898193)$$
$$= \$34\,516.24$$

Programmed solution

1.12922 [%i] 0 [FV] 925 [PMT] 48 [N] [DUE] (or [2nd] [CPT])

[PV] [34 516.24]

STEP 2   Find the present value of A_{nc}(due) at the beginning of the period of deferment.

$S = 34\ 516.24$ is the present value of the general annuity A_{nc}(due)
$d = 40$ is the number of deferred payment intervals;
$f = 1.12922\%$ is the equivalent effective rate of interest per payment interval

A_{nc}(defer) $= P = 34\ 516.24(1.0112922)^{-40}$ ——— substituting in Formula 9.2C
$\qquad\qquad\quad = 34\ 516.24(0.6381661)$
$\qquad\qquad\quad = 22\ 027.09$

Programmed solution

1.12922 $\boxed{\%i}$ $34\ 516.24$ $\boxed{FV}$ 0 $\boxed{PMT}$ 40 $\boxed{N}$ $\boxed{CPT}$ $\boxed{PV}$ $\boxed{22\ 027.093}$

Tom must deposit \$22 027.09 to make the withdrawals.

Exercise 12.3

A. Find the present value of each of the following ten deferred annuities.

	Periodic Payment	Made At:	Payment Period	Period of Deferment	Term	Interest Rate	Conversion Period
1.	$850.00	beginning	1 year	3 years	10 years	7.5%	annually
2.	$45.00	end	1 month	5 years	7 years	12%	monthly
3.	$125.00	end	6 months	8 years	15 years	7%	semi-annually
4.	$720.00	beginning	3 months	6 years	12 years	4%	quarterly
5.	$85.00	beginning	1 month	20 years	15 years	6%	monthly
6.	$225.00	end	1 month	12 years	20 years	10.5%	monthly
7.	$720.00	end	3 months	4 years	10 years	12%	monthly
8.	$145.00	beginning	6 months	3 years	5 years	8%	quarterly
9.	$225.00	beginning	3 months	6 years	8 years	9%	annually
10.	$1500.00	end	1 month	2 years	3 years	5%	semi-annually

B. Answer each of the following questions.

1. Calvin Jones bought his neighbour's farm for \$10 000 down and payments of \$5000.00 at the end of every three months for ten years. If the payments are deferred for two years and interest is 8% compounded quarterly, what was the purchase price of the farm?

2. Denise Kadawalski intends to retire in twelve years and would like to receive \$2400.00 every six months for fifteen years starting on the date of her retirement. How much must Denise deposit in an account today if interest is 6.5% compounded semi-annually?

3. Mrs. Bell expects to retire in seven years and would like to receive \$800.00 at the end of each month for ten years following the date of her retirement. How much must Mrs. Bell deposit today in an account paying 7.5% compounded semi-annually to receive the monthly payments?

4. The sale of a property provides for payments of $2000.00 due at the beginning of every three months for five years. If the payments are deferred for two years and interest is 9% compounded monthly, what is the cash value of the property?

5. Arlene and Mario Dumont want to set up a fund to finance their daughter's university education. They want to be able to withdraw $400.00 from the fund at the beginning of each month for four years. Their daughter enters university in seven and a half years and interest is 12% compounded monthly.

   a) How much must the Dumonts deposit in the fund today?
   b) What will be the amount of the total withdrawals?
   c) How much of the amount withdrawn will be interest?

6. The Omega Venture Group needs to borrow to finance a project. Repayment of the loan involves payments of $8500.00 at the end of every three months for eight years. No payments are to be made during the development period of three years. Interest is 9% compounded quarterly.

   a) How much should the Group borrow?
   b) What amount will be repaid?
   c) How much of that amount will be interest?

7. What sum of money invested now will provide payments of $1200.00 at the end of every three months for six years if the payments are deferred for nine years and interest is 10% compounded quarterly?

8. An investment in a lease offers returns of $2500 per month due at the beginning of each month for five years. What investment is justified if the returns are deferred for two years and the interest required is 12% compounded monthly?

12.4 PERPETUITIES

A. Basic concepts

A **perpetuity** is an annuity in which the periodic payments begin on a fixed date and continue indefinitely. Interest payments on permanently invested sums of money are prime examples of perpetuities. Dividends on preferred shares fall into this category assuming that the issuing corporation has a indefinite life. Scholarships paid perpetually from an endowment fit the definition of perpetuity.

As there is no end to the term, it is *not* possible to determine the future value of a perpetuity. However, the present value of a perpetuity *is* a definite value and this section deals with the present value of simple perpetuities.

B. Present value of ordinary perpetuities

The following symbols are commonly used when dealing with perpetuities:

A = the present value of the perpetuity;
R = the periodic rent (or perpetuity payment);
i = the rate of interest per conversion period.

FIGURE 12.6 **Graphic Representation of an Ordinary Perpetuity**

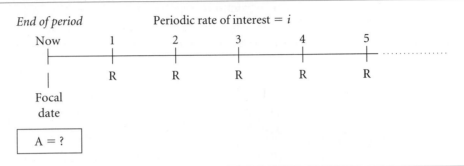

The **perpetuity payment** R is the interest earned by the present value of the perpetuity in one interest period.

R = iA

Thus, the formula for finding the present value of an ordinary simple perpetuity is:

$$A - \frac{R}{i}$$ ———————————————— Formula 12.5

For an ordinary general perpetuity, the payment R is the interest earned by the present value of the perpetuity in one payment interval. That is,

R = fA

Thus, the formula for finding the present value of an ordinary general perpetuity is:

$$A = \frac{R}{f}$$
$$\text{where } f = (1 + i)^c - 1$$ ———————————————— Formula 12.6

where

f = the effective rate of interest per payment interval equivalent to i;
c = the number of conversion periods per payment period.

EXAMPLE 12.4A   What sum of money invested today at 10% compounded annually will provide a scholarship of $1500.00 at the end of every year?

Solution $R = 1500.00; \quad i = 10\% = 0.10$

$$A = \frac{1500.00}{0.10} = \$15\ 000.00 \quad\text{——— substituting in Formula 12.5}$$

EXAMPLE 12.4B   The maintenance cost for Northern Railroad of a crossing with a provincial highway is $2000.00 at the end of each month. Proposed construction of an overpass would eliminate the monthly maintenance cost. If money is worth 12% compounded monthly, how much should Northern be willing to contribute toward the cost of construction?

Solution   The monthly maintenance expense payments form an *ordinary simple perpetuity*.

$$R = 2000.00; \quad i = \frac{12\%}{12} = 0.01$$

$$A = \frac{2000.00}{0.01} = \$200\ 000.00$$

Northern should be willing to contribute $200 000.00 toward construction.

EXAMPLE 12.4C   What sum of money invested today at 8% compounded quarterly will provide a scholarship of $2500.00 at the end of each year?

Solution   Since the payments are to continue indefinitely, the payments form a perpetuity. Furthermore, since the payments are made at the end of each payment interval and the interest conversion period is not the same length as the payment interval, the problem involves an *ordinary general perpetuity*.

$$R = 2500.00; \quad c = 4; \quad i = \frac{8\%}{4} = 2\% = 0.02$$

The equivalent effective annual rate of interest

$$f = 1.02^4 - 1 = 1.0824322 - 1 = 0.0824322 = 8.24322\%$$

$$A = \frac{2500.00}{0.0824322} = \$30\ 327.95 \quad\text{——— substituting in Formula 12.6}$$

The required sum of money is $30 327.95.

EXAMPLE 12.4D   A will gives an endowment of $50 000.00 to a college with the provision that a scholarship be paid at the end of each year. If the money is invested at 11% compounded annually, how much is the annual scholarship?

Solution $A = 50\ 000.00; \quad i = 11\% = 0.11$

By rearranging the terms of Formula 12.5, we get the equation $R = Ai$.

$$R = 50\ 000.00(0.11) = \$5500.00$$

EXAMPLE 12.4E   The alumni of Peel College collected $32 000.00 to provide a fund for bursaries. If the money is invested at 7% compounded annually, what is the size of the bursary that can be paid every six months?

Solution $A = 32\ 000.00; \quad c = \dfrac{1}{2}; \quad i = 7\% = 0.07$

The equivalent effective semi-annual rate of interest

$f = 1.07^{0.5} - 1 = 1.0344080 - 1 = 0.0344080 = 3.44080\%$

By rearranging the terms of Formula 12.6, we get the equation $R = fA$.

$R = fA = 0.0344080(32\ 000.00) = \$1101.06$

The size of the bursary is $1101.06.

C. Present value of perpetuities due

A perpetuity due differs from an ordinary perpetuity only in that the first payment is made at the focal date. Therefore, a simple perpetuity due may be treated as consisting of an immediate payment R followed by an ordinary perpetuity. The formula for finding the present value of a simple perpetuity due is:

$$A(due) = R + \frac{R}{i}$$ ———————— **Formula 12.7**

As in the case of the simple perpetuity due, the general perpetuity due can be treated as consisting of an immediate payment R followed by an ordinary general perpetuity. Using the symbol $A(due)$ for the present value, the formula for finding the present value of a general perpetuity due is:

$$A(due) = R + \frac{R}{f}$$
$$\text{where } f = (1 + i)^c - 1$$ ———————— **Formula 12.8**

EXAMPLE 12.4F   A tract of land is leased in perpetuity at $1250.00 due at the beginning of each month. If money is worth 7.5% compounded monthly, what is the present value of the lease?

Solution $R = 1250.00; \quad i = \dfrac{7.5\%}{12} = 0.625\% = 0.00625$

$A = 1250.00 + \dfrac{1250.00}{0.00625}$ ———————— substituting in Formula 12.7

$= 1250.00 + 200\ 000.00$

$= \$201\ 250.00$

EXAMPLE 12.4G   What is the present value of perpetuity payments of $750.00 made at the beginning of each month if interest is 8.5% compounded semi-annually?

Solution $R = 750.00; \quad c = \dfrac{2}{12} = \dfrac{1}{6}; \quad i = \dfrac{8.5\%}{2} = 4.25\% = 0.0425$

The equivalent effective monthly rate of interest

$f = 1.0425^{\frac{1}{6}} - 1 = 1.0069611 - 1 = 0.0069611 = 0.69611\%$

$A(\text{due}) = 750.00 + \dfrac{750.00}{0.0069611} = \$108\ 491.59$ ——— substituting in Formula 12.8

The present value of the perpetuity is $108 491.59.

EXAMPLE 12.4H   How much money must be invested today in a fund earning 11.5% compounded annually to pay annual scholarships of $2000.00 starting

(i) one year from now?

(ii) immediately?

(iii) four years from now?

Solution $R = 2000.00; \quad i = 11.5\% = 0.115$

(i) The annual scholarship payments form an ordinary perpetuity.

$A = \dfrac{2000.00}{0.115} = \$17\ 391.30$

The required sum of money is $17 391.30.

(ii) The annual scholarship payments form a perpetuity due.

$A = 2000.00 + \dfrac{2000.00}{0.115}$
$= 2000.00 + 17\ 391.30$
$= \$19\ 391.30$

The required sum of money is $19 391.30.

(iii) The annual scholarship payments form an ordinary perpetuity deferred for three years.

$A(\text{defer}) = A(1.115^{-3})$
$= 17\ 391.30(0.7213988)$
$= \$12\ 546.06$

The required sum of money is $12 546.06.

EXAMPLE 12.4I   What sum of money invested today in a fund earning 12% compounded monthly will provide perpetuity payments of $395.00 every three months starting

(i) immediately?

(ii) three months from now?

(iii) one year from now?

Solution

$$R = 395.00; \quad c = \frac{12}{4} = 3; \quad i = \frac{12\%}{12} = 1\% = 0.01$$

The equivalent effective quarterly rate of interest

$$f = 1.01^3 - 1 = 1.030301 - 1 = 0.030301 = 3.0301\%$$

(i) Because the perpetuity payments are at the beginning of each payment interval, they form a *perpetuity due*.

$$A(\text{due}) = 395.00 + \frac{395.00}{0.030301} = 395.00 + 13\,035.87 = \$13\,430.87$$

The required sum of money is $13 430.87.

(ii) Since the first payment is three months from now, the perpetuity payments form an *ordinary perpetuity*.

$$A = \frac{395.00}{0.030301} = \$13\,035.87$$

The required sum of money is $13 035.87.

(iii) If you consider that the payments are deferred for one year, they form a *deferred perpetuity due*.

$$A(\text{defer}) = A(\text{due}) \times (1.01)^{-12}$$
$$= 13\,430.87(0.8874492)$$
$$= \$11\,919.22$$

The required sum of money is $11 919.22.

Exercise 12.4

A. Find the present value of each of the following eight perpetuities.

	Perpetuity Payment	Made At:	Payment Interval	Interest Rate	Conversion Period
1.	$1250.00	end	3 months	6.8%	quarterly
2.	$985.00	beginning	6 months	11.5%	semi-annually
3.	$125.00	beginning	1 month	12.6%	monthly
4.	$3420.00	end	1 year	8.3%	annually
5.	$5600.00	end	6 months	12%	monthly
6.	$2150.00	beginning	3 months	9%	monthly
7.	$725.00	beginning	1 month	10%	quarterly
8.	$380.00	end	3 months	8%	semi-annually

B. Answer each of the following questions.

1. Alain Rich wants to set up a scholarship fund for his alma mater. The annual scholarship payment is to be $2500.00 with the first such payment due four years after his deposit into the fund. If the fund pays 7.25% compounded annually, how much must Mr. Rich deposit?

2. A rental property provides a monthly income of $1150.00 due at the beginning of every month. What is the cash value of the property if money is worth 6.6% compounded monthly?

3. The Xorex company pays a dividend of $4.25 every three months per preferred share. What is the expected market price per share if money is worth 8% compounded semi-annually?

4. Transcontinental Pipelines is considering a technical process that is expected to reduce annual maintenance costs by $85 000.00. What is the maximum amount of money that could be invested in the process to be economically feasible if interest is 7% compounded quarterly?

5. A rental property provides a net income of $4200.00 at the beginning of every three months. What is the cash value of the property if money is worth 9% compounded monthly?

6. Municipal Hydro offers to acquire a right-of-way from a property owner who receives annual lease payments of $2225.00 due in advance. What is a fair offer if money is worth 11.5% compounded quarterly?

7. The faculty of Central College collected $1400.00 for the purpose of setting up a memorial fund from which an annual award is to be made to a qualifying student. If the money is invested at 7% compounded annually and the first annual award payment is to be made five years after the money was deposited, what is the size of the annual award payment?

8. Barbara Katzman bought an income property for $28 000.00 three years ago. She has held the property for the three years without renting it. If she rents the property out now, what should be the size of the monthly rent payment due in advance be if money is worth 6% compounded monthly?

9. What is the size of the scholarship that can be paid at the end of every six months from a fund of $25 000.00 if interest is 11% compounded quarterly?

10. What monthly lease payment due in advance should be charged for a tract of land valued at $35 000 if the agreed interest is 8.5% compounded semi-annually?

REVIEW EXERCISE

1. Find the future value and the present value of semi-annual payments of $540.00 for seven and a half years if interest is 9.0% compounded semi-annually and the payments are made

   a) at the end of every six months;

   b) at the beginning of every six months.

2. Determine the future value and the present value of monthly payments of $50.00 each for eight years at 6% compounded monthly if

   a) the payments form an annuity due;

   b) the payments form an ordinary annuity.

3. Payments of $375.00 made every three months are accumulated at 12% compounded monthly. What is their amount after eight years if the payments are made

   a) at the end of every three months?

   b) at the beginning of every three months?

4. What is the accumulated value after twelve years of monthly deposits of $145.00 earning interest at 5% compounded semi-annually if the deposits are made

   a) at the end of each month?

   b) at the beginning of each month?

5. A collateral mortgage can be discharged by making payments of $368.00 at the end of each month for fifteen years. If interest is 10.5% compounded monthly, what was the original principal borrowed?

6. Robert Deed deposited $100.00 in a trust account on the day of his son's birth and every three months thereafter. If interest paid is 7% compounded quarterly, what will the balance in the trust account be before the deposit is made on the son's twenty-first birthday?

7. What single cash payment made now is equivalent to payments of $3500.00 every six months at 8% compounded quarterly if the payments are made

   a) at the end of every six months for fifteen years?

   b) at the beginning of every six months for ten years?

   c) at the end of every six months for eight years but deferred for four years?

d) at the beginning of every six months for nine years but deferred for three years?

e) at the end of every six months in perpetuity?

f) at the beginning of every six months in perpetuity?

8. What is the principal invested at 12.5% compounded semi-annually from which monthly withdrawals of $240.00 can be made

a) at the end of each month for 25 years?

b) at the beginning of each month for 15 years?

c) at the end of each month for 20 years but deferred for 10 years?

d) at the beginning of each month for 15 years but deferred for 12 years?

e) at the end of each month in perpetuity?

f) at the beginning of each month in perpetuity?

9. If you save $25.00 at the beginning of each month and interest is 4% compounded quarterly, how much will you accumulate in thirty years?

10. A property was purchased for quarterly payments of $1350.00 for ten years. If the first payment was made on the date of purchase and interest is 5.5% compounded annually, what was the purchase price of the property?

11. Mr. Maxwell intends to retire in ten years and wishes to receive $4800.00 every three months for twenty years starting on the date of his retirement. How much must he deposit now to receive the quarterly payments from an account paying 6% compounded quarterly?

12. Tomac Swim Club bought electronic timing equipment on a contract requiring monthly payments of $725.00 for three years beginning eighteen months after the date of purchase. What was the cash value of the equipment if interest is 7.5% compounded monthly?

13. What sum of money invested today in a retirement fund will permit withdrawals of $800.00 at the end of each month for twenty years if interest is 12% compounded semi-annually and the payments are deferred for fifteen years?

14. A lease requires semi-annual payments of $6000.00 for five years. If the first payment is due in four years and interest is 9% compounded monthly, what is the cash value of the lease?

15. An income property is estimated to net $1750.00 per month continually. If money is worth 6.6% compounded monthly, what is the cash price of the property?

16. Western Pipelines pays $8000.00 at the beginning of each year for using a tract of land. What should the company offer the property owner as a purchase price if interest is 9.5% compounded annually?

17. The semi-annual dividend per preferred share issued by InterCity Trust is $7.50. If comparable investments yield 14% compounded quarterly, what should be the selling price of these shares?

18. A fund to provide an annual scholarship of $4000.00 is to be set up. If the first payment is due in three years and interest is 11% compounded quarterly, what sum of money must be deposited in the scholarship fund today?

19. Home entertainment equipment can be purchased by making monthly payments of $82.00 for three and a half years. The first payment is due at the time of purchase and the financing cost is 16.5% compounded monthly.

    a) What is the purchase price?

    b) How much will be paid in instalments?

    c) How much is the cost of financing?

20. Jim Wong makes deposits of $225.00 at the beginning of every three months. Interest earned by the deposits is 3% compounded quarterly.

    a) What will the balance in Jim's account be after eight years?

    b) How much of the balance will Jim have contributed?

    c) How much of the balance is interest?

SELF-TEST

1. Payments of $1080.00 are made into a fund at the beginning of every three months for eleven years. If the fund earns interest at 9.5% compounded quarterly, how much will the balance in the fund be after eleven years?

2. What sum of money must be deposited in a trust fund to provide a scholarship of $960.00 payable at the end of each month if interest is 7.5% compounded monthly?

3. Find the present value of payments of $960.00 made at the beginning of every month for seven years if money is worth 6% compounded monthly.

4. Sally Smedley and Roberto Jones bought their neighbour's farm for $30 000.00 down and payments of $6000.00 at the end of every six months for six years. What is the purchase price of the farm if the semi-annual payments are deferred for four years and interest is 8.5% compounded semi-annually?

5. A bank pays a quarterly dividend of $0.75 per share. If comparable investments yield 13.5% compounded monthly, what is the sales value of the shares?

6. A lease requires monthly payments of $950.00 due in advance. If interest is 12% compounded quarterly and the term of the lease is five years, what is the cash value of the lease?

7. Western Pipelines pays $480.00 at the beginning of every half-year for using a tract of land. What should the company offer the property owner as a purchase price if interest is 11% compounded semi-annually?

8. Ken acquired his sister's share of their business by agreeing to make payments of $4000.00 at the end of each year for twelve years. If the payments are deferred for three years and money is worth 5% compounded quarterly, what is the cash value of the sister's share of the business?

9. Mr. Smart wants to set up an annual scholarship of $3000.00. If the first payment is to be made in five years and interest is 7.0% compounded annually, how much must Mr. Smart pay into the scholarship fund?

10. Carla plans to invest in a property that after three years will yield $1200.00 at the end of each month indefinitely. How much should Carla be willing to pay if an alternative investment yields 18% compounded monthly?

CHALLENGE PROBLEMS

1. Herman has agreed to repay a debt by using the following repayment schedule. Starting today, he will make $100.00 payments at the beginning of each month for the next two and a half years. He will then pay nothing for the next two years. Finally, after four and a half years, he will make $200.00 payments at the beginning of each month for one year, which will pay off his debt completely. For the first four and a half years, the interest on the debt is 9% compounded monthly. For the final year, the interest is lowered to 8.5% compounded monthly. Find the size of Herman's debt. Round your answer to the nearest dollar.

2. Garfield Mahoney made deposits of $300 into an account paying 6.5% compounded quarterly at the beginning of each month. He made the first deposit on September 1, 1998. In February 1999 he ran into financial difficulties and missed the March-to-June deposits. He started making the deposits again on July 1, 1999 and made his last deposit on September 1, 2000. How much is in Garfield's account on October 1, 2000?

CASE STUDY 12.1 FROM CASINO TO COLLEGE

Hermia and Chan Chen have three young daughters. Their daughters are Su, who turned ten years old in April, Joy, who turned seven in January, and Wei, who turned four in March. In May, the Chens visited a charity casino, and Lady Luck was with them. They won a jackpot of $50 000.00. They decided to invest a large part of their winnings that year in order to create future education funds for their three daughters.

Since it will be a number of years before the girls are ready for college or university, Hermia and Chan had to make some assumptions regarding the girls' futures. They have assumed that each daughter will take a three-year course and that the costs of education will continue to increase. Based on these assumptions, Hermia and Chan decided to provide each daughter with a monthly allowance that would cover tuition and some living expenses. Because they were uncertain about the girls' finding summer jobs in the future, Hermia and Chan decided their daughters would receive the allowance for twelve months of the year. Su will receive an allowance of $1000.00 at the beginning of each month, starting September 1 of the year she turns eighteen. Because of the increasing costs of education, Joy will receive an allowance that is 6% more than Su's allowance. She will receive it at the beginning of each month, starting September 1 of the year she turns eighteen. Wei will receive an allowance that is 6% more than Joy's at the beginning of each month, starting September 1 of the year she turns eighteen.

The week after winning the money at the casino, Hermia and Chan visited their local bank manager to set up the investment that would pay the girls the allowances when they were ready for college or university. The bank manager suggested an investment paying interest of 7.5% compounded monthly from now until the three girls had each completed their three years of education. Hermia and Chan thought this sounded reasonable. So on June 1, a week after talking with the bank manager, they deposited the sum of money necessary to finance their daughters' post-secondary educations.

QUESTIONS

1. How much money must Hermia and Chan invest on June 1 to provide the desired allowance to Su?

2. a) How much allowance will Joy receive each month for tuition and living expenses?

   b) How much money must Hermia and Chan invest on June 1 to provide the desired allowance to Joy?

3. a) How much allowance will Wei receive each month for tuition and living expenses?

   b) How much money must Hermia and Chan invest on June 1 to provide the desired allowance to Wei?

4. After making their investment on June 1, how much of their winnings do Hermia and Chan have left to spend on themselves?

CASE STUDY 12.2 | SETTING UP SCHOLARSHIPS

Recently, Northern University launched a drive to raise money for three new scholarships. Members of the university's Scholarship Committee convinced three organizations in the community to create and fund a scholarship. The organizations were: Fund Friends, Help-All, and the City Service Club. These organizations were all convinced that the best way to fund the scholarships was to make one large donation to the university. The donation would be invested so that it would continue to grow over time, and regular, annual scholarships would be paid out indefinitely.

The Fund Friends organization agreed to donate a sum of money on September 1 that would allow its scholarship to be awarded immediately on September 1. It wants to award one scholarship of $1500.00 per year. It has agreed to let the university choose a worthy local student to receive its scholarship each year.

The Help-All organization would like to earn some interest on its September 1 donation before awarding its first scholarship on December 1, three months later. Help-All has agreed to award one scholarship of $1200.00 per year. It will choose the winner from all applications received.

The City Service Club has agreed to award one scholarship of $750.00 per year. The Club will make its donation on September 1 but it wants to award its first scholarship on September 1 next year. This will give club members time to develop the criteria for choosing its bursary recipients.

QUESTIONS

1. What sum of money must the Fund Friends organization invest today if its scholarship is expected to earn 8% compounded semi-annually?

2. What sum of money must the Help-All organization invest today if its scholarship fund is expected to earn 8.2% compounded quarterly?

3. What sum of money must the City Service Club invest today if its bursary fund is expected to earn 7.80% compounded monthly?

SUMMARY OF FORMULAE

Formula 9.1A

$S = P(1 + i)^n$ Finding the future value (maturity value) when the original principal, the rate of interest, and the time period are known

Formula 9.1C

$P = S(1 + i)^{-n}$ Finding the present value by means of the discount factor (the reciprocal of the compounding factor) when the compound amount, the rate of interest, and the time period are known

Formula 11.4

$$A_{nc} = R\left[\frac{1 - (1 + f)^{-n}}{f}\right]$$

where $f = (1 + i)^c - 1$

Finding the present value of an ordinary general annuity using the equivalent effective rate of interest per payment period

Formula 12.1

$$S_n(\text{due}) = R(1 + i)\left[\frac{(1 + i)^n - 1}{i}\right]$$

Finding the future value of an annuity due

Formula 12.2

$$A_n(\text{due}) = R(1 + i)\left[\frac{1 - (1 + i)^{-n}}{i}\right]$$

Finding the present value of an annuity due

Formula 12.3

$$S_{nc}(\text{due}) = R(1 + f)\left[\frac{(1 + f)^n - 1}{f}\right]$$

where $f = (1 + i)^c - 1$

Finding the future value of a general annuity due using the equivalent effective rate of interest per payment period

Formula 12.4

$$A_{nc}(\text{due}) = R(1 + f)\left[\frac{1 - (1 + f)^{-n}}{f}\right]$$

where $f = (1 + i)^c - 1$

Finding the present value of a general annuity due using the equivalent effective rate of interest per payment period

Formula 12.5

$$A = \frac{R}{i}$$

Finding the present value of an ordinary simple perpetuity

Formula 12.6

$$A = \frac{R}{f}$$

where $f = (1 + i)^c - 1$

Finding the present value of an ordinary general perpetuity

Formula 12.7

$$A(\text{due}) = R + \frac{R}{i}$$

Finding the present value of a simple perpetuity due

Formula 12.8

$$A(\text{due}) = R + \frac{R}{f}$$

where $f = (1 + i)^c - 1$

Finding the present value of a general perpetuity due

GLOSSARY

Annuity due   an annuity in which the periodic payments are made at the beginning of each payment interval

Deferred annuity   an annuity in which the first payment is made at a time later than the end of the first payment interval

General annuity due   a general annuity in which the payments are made at the beginning of each payment period

Period of deferment   the period from the time referred to as "now" to the starting point of the term of the annuity

Perpetuity   an annuity in which the periodic payments begin at a fixed date and continue indefinitely

Perpetuity payment   the perpetual periodic payment that equals the interest earned by the present value of these payments in one interest period

Present value of a deferred annuity   the discounted value of the periodic payments at the beginning of the period of deferment

13

Annuities—Finding R, *n*, or *i*

Understanding other aspects of annuities is vital in our day-to-day budgeting. For example, we often need to know things like the amount of money we have to pay each month for the new car we want to buy, the number of years we must make the monthly payments, and the rate of interest we are paying. If we know how to calculate R, *i*, and *n*, we can make informed decisions about different payment options. When considering buying a car, should we use the car dealer's low financing rate? Or would it be cheaper to borrow the money from the bank and pay cash for the car? When considering joining a fitness club, which payment option should we choose? And how much interest would we really be paying with each payment option?

Introduction

To answer other important questions about annuities, we do not need to introduce any new formulae. We can use the formulae we already know, rearranging them when appropriate.

In Chapters 11 and 12, we calculated the present value and future value of all types of annuities: ordinary simple annuities, ordinary general annuities, simple annuities due, general annuities due, ordinary deferred annuities, and deferred annuities due. We also calculated the present value of ordinary perpetuities, perpetuities due, and deferred perpetuities.

In this chapter, we will use the formulae from Chapters 11 and 12 to find the periodic payment R, the term *n*, and the periodic rate of interest *i* for all types of annuities.

OBJECTIVES

Upon completing this chapter, you will be able to do the following:

1. Calculate the periodic payment **R** of annuities when the future value is known or when the present value is known.
2. Calculate the periodic payment **R** of deferred annuities.
3. Calculate the term *n* of annuities when the future value is known or when the present value is known.
4. Calculate the term *n* of deferred annuities.
5. Calculate the periodic rate of interest *i* for simple annuities and general annuities using preprogrammed financial calculators.

13.1 FINDING THE PERIODIC PAYMENT R

A. Finding the periodic payment R when the future value of an annuity is known

If the future value of an annuity S_n, S_{nc}, S_n(due), or S_{nc}(due), the number of conversion periods n, and the conversion rate i are known, you can find the periodic payment R by substituting the given values in the appropriate future value formula.

For ordinary simple annuities, use Formula 11.1.

$$S_n = R\left[\frac{(1 + i)^n - 1}{i}\right]$$ ———————— **Formula 11.1**

For ordinary general annuities, use Formula 11.3.

$$S_{nc} = R\left[\frac{(1 + f)^n - 1}{f}\right]$$
$$\text{where } f = (1 + i)^c - 1$$ ———————— **Formula 11.3**

For simple annuities due, use Formula 12.1.

$$S_n(\text{due}) = R(1 + i)\left[\frac{(1 + i)^n - 1}{i}\right]$$ ——— **Formula 12.1**

For general annuities due, use Formula 12.3.

$$S_{nc}(\text{due}) = R(1 + f)\left[\frac{(1 + f)^n - 1}{f}\right]$$
$$\text{where } f = (1 + i)^c - 1$$ ——— **Formula 12.3**

When using a preprogrammed financial calculator, you can find R by entering the three known values (future value, n, and i) and pressing $\boxed{\text{CPT}}$ $\boxed{\text{PMT}}$.

EXAMPLE 13.1A What deposit made at the end of each quarter will accumulate to $10 000.00 in four years at 4% compounded quarterly?

Solution

$$S_n = 10\ 000.00; \quad i = \frac{4\%}{4} = 1.0\% = 0.01; \quad n = 16$$

$$10\ 000.00 = R\left(\frac{1.01^{16} - 1}{0.01}\right)$$ ———————— substituting in Formula 11.1

$$10\ 000.00 = R\left(\frac{1.1725786 - 1}{0.01}\right)$$

$$10\ 000.00 = R(17.25786)$$

$$R = \frac{10\ 000.00}{17.25786}$$

$$R = \$579.45$$

As we have emphasized throughout this book, beginning in Chapter 2, understanding how to rearrange terms in a formula is a very important skill. By knowing how to do this, you avoid having to memorize equivalent forms of the same formula.

When using a scientific calculator, you can find R by first rearranging the terms of the future value formulae as shown below. Then substitute the three known values (future value, *n*, and *i*) into the rearranged formula and use the calculator to solve for R.

$$S_n = R\left[\frac{(1 + i)^n - 1}{i}\right] \quad \text{———— Formula 11.1}$$

$$R = \frac{S_n}{\left[\dfrac{(1 + i)^n - 1}{i}\right]} \quad \text{———— divide both sides by } \left[\dfrac{(1 + i)^n - 1}{i}\right]$$

$$R = \frac{S_n i}{(1 + i)^n - 1} \quad \text{———— dividing by a fraction is the same as inverting the fraction and multiplying}$$

$$S_n = 10\ 000.00; \quad i = 0.01; \quad n - 16$$

$$R = \frac{10\ 000.00(0.01)}{1.01^{16} - 1} \quad \text{———— substituting in rearranged Formula 11.1}$$

$$R = \$579.45$$

EXAMPLE 13.1B If you want to have \$5000.00 on deposit in your bank account in three years, how much must you deposit at the end of each month if interest is 4.5% compounded monthly?

Solution $S_n = 5000.00; \quad i = 0.375\% ; \quad n = 36$

0 | PV | 5000 | FV | 0.375 | %i | 36 | N | CPT | PMT | 129.98463

(Ignore any negative signs.)

The monthly deposit required is \$129.98.

EXAMPLE 13.1C   What sum of money must be deposited at the end of every three months into an account paying 10% compounded monthly to accumulate to $25 000.00 in ten years?

Solution $S_{nc} = 25\,000.00; \quad n = 10(4) = 40; \quad c = \dfrac{12}{4} = 3; \quad i = \dfrac{10\%}{12} = \dfrac{5}{6}\% = 0.0083333$

The equivalent effective quarterly rate of interest

$f = 1.0083333^3 - 1 = 1.0252088 - 1 = 0.0252088 = 2.52088\%$

$25\,000.00 = R\left(\dfrac{1.0252088^{40} - 1}{0.0252088}\right)$ ———— substituting in Formula 11.3

$25\,000.00 = R(67.715625)$

$R = \dfrac{25\,000.00}{67.715625}$

$R = \$369.19$

When the terms of Formula 11.3 are rearranged, the formula becomes

$R = \dfrac{S_{nc}f}{(1 + f)^n - 1}$

$R = \dfrac{25\,000.00(0.0252088)}{1.0252088^{40} - 1}$ ———— substituting in rearranged Formula 11.3

$R = \$369.19$

With a preprogrammed calculator, the procedure, after finding f, is

2.52088 | %i | 0 | PV | 25 000 | FV | 40 | N | CPT | PMT | 369.19101

The required quarterly deposit is $369.19.

EXAMPLE 13.1D   What semi-annual payment must be made into a fund at the beginning of every six months to accumulate to $9600.00 in ten years at 11% compounded semi-annually?

Solution $S_n(\text{due}) = 9600.00; \quad i = \dfrac{11\%}{2} = 5.5\% = 0.055; \quad n = 10(2) = 20$

$9600.00 = R(1.055)\left(\dfrac{1.055^{20} - 1}{0.055}\right)$ ———— substituting in Formula 12.1

$9600.00 = R(1.055)(34.868318)$
$9600.00 = R(36.786075)$

$R = \dfrac{9600.00}{36.786075}$

$R = \$260.97$

Programmed solution

Ignore a negative sign in the answer if one appears.

0 [PV] 9600 [FV] 5.5 [%i] 20 [N] [DUE] (or [2nd] [CPT])

[PMT] [260.96831]

The semi-annual payment is $260.97.

EXAMPLE 13.1E   What deposit made at the beginning of each month will accumulate to $18 000.00 at 5% compounded quarterly at the end of eight years?

Solution $S_{nc}(\text{due}) = 18\,000.00; \quad n = 8(12) = 96; \quad c = \dfrac{4}{12} = \dfrac{1}{3}$

$i = \dfrac{5\%}{4} = 1.25\% = 0.0125$

The equivalent effective monthly rate of interest

$f = 1.0125^{\frac{1}{3}} - 1 = 1.0041494 - 1 = 0.0041494 = 0.41494\%$

$18\,000.00 = R(1.0041494)\left(\dfrac{1.0041494^{96} - 1}{0.0041494}\right)$ ——— substituting in Formula 12.3

$18\,000.00 = R(1.0041494)(117.6381049)$
$18\,000.00 = R(118.1262324)$

$R = \dfrac{18\,000.00}{118.1262324}$

$R = \$152.38$

Programmed solution

0.41494 [%i] 0 [PV] 18 000 [FV] 96 [N] (or [2nd] [CPT])

[PMT] [152.37956]

The monthly deposit is $152.38.

B. Finding the periodic payment R when the present value of an annuity is known

If the present value of an annuity A_n, A_{nc}, $A_n(\text{due})$, or $A_{nc}(\text{due})$, the number of conversion periods n, and the conversion rate i are known, you can find the periodic payment R by substituting the given values in the appropriate present value formula. For ordinary simple annuities, use Formula 11.2.

$$A_n = R\left[\frac{1 - (1 + i)^{-n}}{i}\right]$$ ——— **Formula 11.2**

For ordinary general annuities, use Formula 11.4.

$$A_{nc} = R\left[\frac{1 - (1 + f)^{-n}}{f}\right]$$

where $f = (1 + i)^c - 1$

———— **Formula 11.4**

For simple annuities due, use Formula 12.2.

$$A_n(\text{due}) = R(1 + i)\left[\frac{1 - (1 + i)^{-n}}{i}\right]$$

———— **Formula 12.2**

For general annuities due, use Formula 12.4.

$$A_{nc}(\text{due}) = R(1 + f)\left[\frac{1 - (1 + f)^{-n}}{f}\right]$$

where $f = (1 + i)^c - 1$

———— **Formula 12.4**

When using a scientific calculator, you can find R by first rearranging the terms of the present value formulae above. Then substitute the three known values (present value, n, and i) into the rearranged formula and solve for R.

When using a preprogrammed financial calculator, you can find R by entering the three known values (present value, n, and i) and pressing $\boxed{\text{CPT}}$ $\boxed{\text{PMT}}$.

EXAMPLE 13.1F

What semi-annual payment is required to pay off a loan of $8000.00 in ten years if interest is 10% compounded semi-annually?

Solution

$A_n = 8000.00$; $\quad i = \dfrac{10\%}{2} = 5\% = 0.05$; $\quad n = 10(2) = 20$

$8000.00 = R\left(\dfrac{1 - 1.05^{-20}}{0.05}\right)$ ———————— substituting in Formula 11.2

$8000.00 = R\left(\dfrac{1 - 0.3768895}{0.05}\right)$

$8000.00 = R(12.462210)$

$R = \dfrac{8000.00}{12.462210}$

$R = \$641.94$

Alternatively, you can first rearrange the terms of Formula 11.2 to solve for R.

$A_n = R\left[\dfrac{1 - (1 + i)^{-n}}{i}\right]$ ———————— Formula 11.2

$$R = \dfrac{A_n}{\left[\dfrac{1 - (1 + i)^{-n}}{i}\right]}$$ divide both sides by $\left[\dfrac{1 - (1 + i)^{-n}}{i}\right]$

$$R = \dfrac{A_n i}{1 - (1 + i)^{-n}}$$ dividing by a fraction is the same as inverting the fraction and multiplying

$A_n = 8000.00; \quad i = 0.05; \quad n = 20$

$$R = \dfrac{8000.00(0.05)}{1 - 1.05^{-20}}$$

$R = \$641.94$

EXAMPLE 13.1G Derek bought a new car valued at $9500.00. He paid $2000.00 down and financed the remainder over five years at 9% compounded monthly. How much must Derek pay each month?

Solution $A_n = 9500.00 - 2000.00 = 7500.00; \quad i = \dfrac{9\%}{12} = 0.75\%; \quad n = 60$

0 FV 7500 PV 0.75 %i 60 N CPT PMT 155.68767

Derek's monthly payment is $155.69.

EXAMPLE 13.1H Mr. and Mrs. White applied to their credit union for a first mortgage of $60 000.00 to buy a house. The mortgage is to be amortized over 25 years and interest on the mortgage is 8.5% compounded semi-annually. What is the size of the monthly payment if payments are made at the end of each month?

Solution $A_{nc} = 60\ 000.00; \quad n = 25(12) = 300; \quad c = \dfrac{2}{12} = \dfrac{1}{6};$

$i = \dfrac{8.5\%}{2} = 4.25\% = 0.0425$

The equivalent effective monthly rate of interest

$f = 1.0425^{\frac{1}{6}} - 1 = 1.0069611 - 1 = 0.0069611 = 0.69611\%$

$60\ 000.00 = R\left(\dfrac{1 - 1.0069611^{-300}}{0.0069611}\right)$ ———— substituting in Formula 11.4

$60\ 000.00 = R(125.72819)$

$R = \dfrac{60\ 000.00}{125.72819}$

$R = \$477.22$

Programmed solution

0.69611 $\boxed{\%i}$ 0 $\boxed{\text{FV}}$ 60 000 $\boxed{\text{PV}}$ 300 $\boxed{\text{N}}$ $\boxed{\text{CPT}}$ $\boxed{\text{PMT}}$ $\boxed{477.21994}$

The monthly payment is $477.22.

EXAMPLE 13.1I What monthly payment must be made at the beginning of each month on a five-year lease valued at $100 000.00 if interest is 10% compounded semi-annually?

Solution $A_{nc}(\text{due}) = 100\,000.00; \quad n = 5(12) = 60; \quad c = \dfrac{2}{12} = \dfrac{1}{6};$

$i = \dfrac{10\%}{2} = 5\% = 0.05$

The equivalent effective monthly rate of interest

$f = 1.05^{\frac{1}{6}} - 1 = 1.0081648 - 1 = 0.0081648 = 0.81648\%$

$100\,000.00 = R(1.0081648)\left(\dfrac{1 - 1.0081648^{-60}}{0.0081648}\right)$ —— substituting in Formula 12.4

$100\,000.00 = R(1.0081648)(47.286531)$
$100\,000.00 = R(47.672616)$

$R = \dfrac{100\,000.00}{47.672616}$

$R = \$2097.64$

Programmed solution

0.81648 $\boxed{\%i}$ 0 $\boxed{\text{FV}}$ 100 000 $\boxed{\text{PV}}$ 60 $\boxed{\text{N}}$ (or $\boxed{\text{2nd}}$ $\boxed{\text{CPT}}$)

$\boxed{\text{PMT}}$ $\boxed{2097.6404}$

The monthly payment is $2097.64.

EXAMPLE 13.1J What monthly rent payment at the beginning of each month for four years is required to fulfill a lease contract worth $7000.00 if money is worth 12% compounded monthly?

Solution $A_{n}(\text{due}) = 7000.00; \quad i = \dfrac{12\%}{12} = 1.0\% = 0.01; \quad n = 4(12) = 48$

$7000.00 = R(1.01)\left(\dfrac{1 - 1.01^{-48}}{0.01}\right)$ ———— substituting in Formula 12.2

$7000.00 = R(1.01)(37.973960)$
$7000.00 = R(38.353699)$

$R = \dfrac{7000.00}{38.353699}$

$R = \$182.51$

Programmed solution

0 [FV] 7000 [PV] 1 [%i] 48 [N] [DUE] (or [2nd] [CPT])

[PMT] [182.51173]

The monthly rent payment due at the beginning of each month is $182.51.

C. Finding the periodic payment R for deferred annuities

You can find the periodic payment R for deferred annuities by first determining the future value of the known present value at the end of the period of deferment. Then substitute in the appropriate annuity formula.

EXAMPLE 13.1K Find the size of the payment required at the end of every three months to repay a five-year loan of $25 000.00 if the payments are deferred for two years and interest is 6% compounded quarterly.

Solution The payments form a deferred ordinary annuity.

$$A_n(\text{defer}) = 25\ 000.00; \quad i = \frac{6\%}{4} = 1.5\% = 0.015; \quad n = 5(4) = 20; \quad d = 2(4) = 8$$

Value of $25 000.00 at the end of the period of deferment,

$$S = 25\ 000.00(1.015)^8 \quad\text{——————— using Formula 9.1A}$$
$$= 25\ 000.00(1.1264926)$$
$$= 28\ 162.32$$

$$28\ 162.32 = R\left(\frac{1 - 1.015^{-20}}{0.015}\right) \quad\text{——————— substituting in Formula 11.2}$$

$$28\ 162.32 - 17.168639R$$

$$R = \frac{28\ 162.32}{17.168639}$$

$$R = 1640.34$$

Programmed solution

0 [PMT] 25 000 [PV] 1.5 [%i] 8 [N] [CPT] [FV] [28 162.315]

0 [FV] 28 162.315 [PV] 1.5 [%i] 20 [N] [CPT] [PMT] [1640.3348]

The size of the required payment is $1640.33.

EXAMPLE 13.1L A contract that has a cash value of $36 000.00 requires payments at the end of every three months for six years. If the payments are deferred for three years and interest is 9% compounded semi-annually, what is the size of the quarterly payments?

Solution

$A_{nc}(\text{defer}) = 36\,000.00;\quad n = 6(4) = 24;\quad d = 3(4) = 12;$

$c = \dfrac{2}{4} = 0.5;\quad i = \dfrac{9\%}{2} = 4.5\% = 0.045$

The equivalent effective quarterly rate of interest

$f = 1.045^{0.5} - 1 = 1.0222524 - 1 = 0.0222524 = 2.22524\%$

First determine the accumulated value of the deposit at the end of the period of deferment.

$S = 36\,000.00(1.0222524)^{12}$ ————— substituting in Formula 9.1A
$= 36\,000.00(1.3022599)$
$= 46\,881.36$

Programmed solution

2.22524 [%i] 0 [PMT] 36 000 [PV] 12 [N] [CPT] [FV] [46 881.356]

Now determine the periodic payment for the ordinary general annuity whose present value is $46 881.36.

$46\,881.36 = R\left(\dfrac{1 - 1.0222524^{-24}}{0.0222524}\right)$ ————— substituting in Formula 11.4

$46\,881.36 = R(18.440075)$

$R = \dfrac{46\,881.36}{18.440075}$

$R = \$2542.36$

Programmed solution

46 881.36 [PV] 0 [FV] 2.22524 [%i] 24 [N] [CPT] [PMT] [2542.3627]

The required quarterly payment is $2542.36.

EXAMPLE 13.1M What payment can be made at the beginning of each month for six years if $5000.00 is invested today at 12% compounded monthly and the payments are deferred for ten years?

Solution

The payments form a deferred annuity due.

$A_n(\text{defer}) = 5000.00;\quad i = \dfrac{12\%}{12} = 1\% = 0.01;\quad n = 6(12) = 72;$
$d = 10(12) = 120$

Value of the $5000 at the end of the period of deferment,

$S = 5000.00(1.01)^{120}$
$= 5000.00(3.3003869)$
$= 16\,501.94$

$$16\,501.94 = R(1.01)\left(\frac{1 - 1.01^{-72}}{0.01}\right) \quad\text{——— substituting in Formula 12.2}$$

$$16\,501.94 = R(1.01)(51.150392)$$
$$16\,501.94 = 51.661896R$$

$$R = \frac{16\,501.94}{51.661896}$$

$$R = 319.42$$

Programmed solution

0 [PMT] 5000 [PV] 1 [%i] 120 [N] [CPT] [FV] [16 501.935]

0 [FV] 16 501.94 [PV] 1 [%i] 72 [N] [DUE] (or [2nd] [CPT])

[PMT] [319.42188]

The monthly payment is $319.42.

EXAMPLE 13.1N   A lease contract that has a cash value of $64 000.00 requires payments at the beginning of each month for seven years. If the payments are deferred for two years and interest is 8% compounded quarterly, what is the size of the monthly payment?

Solution $A_{nc}(\text{defer}) = 64\,000.00; \quad n = 7(12) = 84; \quad d = 2(12) = 24;$

$$c = \frac{4}{12} = \frac{1}{3}; \quad i = \frac{8\%}{4} = 2\% = 0.02$$

The equivalent effective monthly rate of interest

$$f = 1.02^{\frac{1}{3}} - 1 = 1.0066227 - 1 = 0.66227\%$$

First determine the accumulated value of the cash value at the end of the period of deferment.
$$S = 64\,000.00(1.0066227)^{24}$$
$$= 64\,000.00(1.1716591)$$
$$= 74986.18$$

Programmed solution

0.66227 [%i] 0 [PMT] 64 000 [PV] 24 [N] [CPT] [FV] [74 986.183]

Now determine the periodic payment for the general annuity due whose present value is $74 986.18.

$$74\,986.18 = R(1.0066227)\left(\frac{1 - 1.0066227^{-84}}{0.0066227}\right)$$

$$74\,986.18 = R(1.0066227)(64.267594)$$
$$74\,986.18 = R(64.693219)$$
$$R = 1159.10$$

Programmed solution

74 986.18 [PV] 0 [FV] 0.66227 [%i] 84 [N] [DUE] (or [2nd] [CPT])

[PMT] [1159.1042]

The monthly payment is $1159.10.

D. Applications

EXAMPLE 13.1O Cecile Tremblay, age 37, expects to retire at age 62. To plan for her retirement, she intends to deposit $1500.00 at the end of each of the next 25 years in a registered retirement savings plan. After her last contribution, she intends to convert the existing balance into a registered retirement income fund from which she expects to make 20 equal annual withdrawals. If she makes the first withdrawal one year after her last contribution and interest is 10.5% compounded annually, how much is the size of the annual withdrawal?

Solution

As the time diagram below shows, the problem can be broken into two steps.

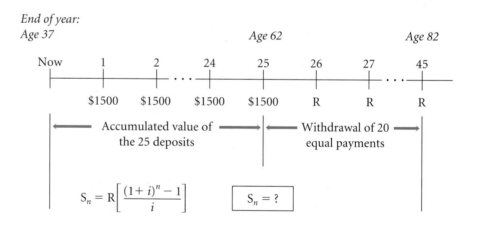

STEP I Compute the *accumulated* value S_n of the 25 annual deposits of $1500.00 into the RRSP.

$R = 1500.00;$ $i = 10.5\% = 0.105;$ $n = 25$

$$S_n = 1500.00\left(\frac{1.105^{25} - 1}{0.105}\right) \text{——————— substituting in Formula 11.1}$$

$= 1500.00(106.05219)$

$= \$159\ 078.28$

STEP 2   Compute the annual payment that can be withdrawn from the RRIF that has an initial balance of $159 078.28.

$$A_n = 159\ 078.28; \quad i = 0.105; \quad n = 20$$

$$159\ 078.28 = R\left(\frac{1 - 1.105^{-20}}{0.105}\right) \quad\text{——— using Formula 11.2}$$

$$159\ 078.28 = R(8.2309089)$$
$$R = 19\ 326.94$$

Programmed Solution

STEP 1   0 [PV] 1500 [PMT] 10.5 [%i] 25 [N] [CPT] [FV] [159 078.28]

STEP 2   0 [FV] 159 078.28 [PV] 10.5 [%i] 20 [N] [CPT] [PMT] [19 326.94]

The sum of money that Cecile can withdraw each year is $19 326.94.

EXAMPLE 13.1P   How much will you have to deposit into an account at the beginning of every three months for twelve years if you want to have a balance of $100 000.00 twenty years from now and interest is 8% compounded quarterly?

Solution   First, find the balance that you must have in the account at the end of the term of the annuity (after 12 years).

$$S = 100\ 000.00; \quad i = \frac{8\%}{4} = 2\% = 0.02; \quad n = 8(4) = 32$$

$$P = 100\ 000.00(1.02)^{-32}$$
$$= 100\ 000.00(0.5306333)$$
$$= \$53\ 063.33$$

Next, find the quarterly payment needed at the beginning of each quarter to accumulate to $53 063.33.

$$S_n(\text{due}) = 53\ 063.33; \quad i = 0.02; \quad n = 12(4) = 48$$

$$53\ 063.33 = R(1.02)\left(\frac{1.02^{48} - 1}{0.02}\right)$$

$$53\ 063.33 = R(1.02)(79.3535193)$$
$$53\ 063.33 = R(80.94058968)$$

$$R = \frac{53\ 063.33}{80.94058968}$$

$$R = 53\ 063.33(0.01235474)$$
$$R = \$655.58$$

Programmed solution

0 [PMT] 100 000 [FV] 2 [%i] 32 [N] [CPT] [PV] [53 063.331]

0 [PV] 53 063.331 [FV] 2 [%i] 48 [N] [DUE] (or [2nd] [CPT])
[PMT] [655.58371]

The quarterly deposit at the beginning of each payment period is $655.58.

EXAMPLE 13.1Q   What payment can be received at the beginning of each month for fifteen years if $10 000.00 is deposited in a fund ten years before the first payment is made and interest is 12% compounded monthly?

Solution   First, find the accumulated value of the initial deposit at the beginning of the term of the annuity due ten years after the deposit.

$$P = 10\ 000.00; \quad i = \frac{12\%}{12} = 1\% = 0.01; \quad n = 10(12) = 120$$

$$S = 10\ 000(1.01)^{120}$$
$$= 10\ 000.00(3.3003869)$$
$$= \$33\ 003.87$$

Now determine the monthly withdrawal that can be made at the beginning of each month from the initial balance of $33 003.87.

$$A_n(\text{due}) = 33\ 003.87; \quad i = 1\%; \quad n = 15(12) = 180$$

$$33\ 003.87 = R(1.01)\left[\frac{1 - (1.01)^{-180}}{0.01}\right]$$

$$33\ 003.87 = R(1.01)(83.321664)$$

$$R = \frac{33\ 003.87}{84.154881}$$

$$R = 33\ 003.87(0.0118829)$$
$$R = \$392.18$$

Programmed solution

0 [PMT] 10 000 [PV] 1 [%i] 120 [N] [CPT] [FV] [33 003.869]

0 [FV] 33 003.869 [PV] 1 [%i] 180 [N] [DUE] (or [2nd] [CPT])
[PMT] [392.18009]

A payment of $392.18 can be made at the beginning of each month.

Exercise 13.1

A. For each of the following ten ordinary annuities, determine the size of the periodic rent.

	Future Value	Present Value	Payment Period	Term of Annuity	Interest Rate	Conversion Period
1.	$15 000.00		6 months	7 years, 6 months	5.5%	semi-annually
2.	$6000.00		1 quarter	9 years, 9 months	13%	quarterly
3.		$12 000.00	12 months	15 years	4.5%	annually
4.		$7000.00	6 months	12.5 years	7.5%	semi-annually
5.	$8000.00		3 months	6 years	6.8%	quarterly
6.		$20 000.00	1 month	20 years	12%	monthly
7.	$45 000.00		3 months	10 years	9%	monthly
8.		$35 000.00	1 year	15 years	20%	quarterly
9.		$20 000.00	1 month	8 years	7%	semi-annually
10.	$16 500.00		3 months	15 years	16%	annually

B. Find the periodic payment for each of the following eight annuities due.

	Future Value	Present Value	Payment Period	Term	Interest Rate	Conversion Period
1.	$20 000.00		3 months	15 years	6%	quarterly
2.		$12 000.00	1 year	8 years	7%	annually
3.		$18 500.00	6 months	12 years	3%	semi-annually
4.	$9400.00		1 month	5 years	12%	monthly
5.	$16 500.00		1 year	10 years	14%	quarterly
6.	$9200.00		3 months	5 years	5%	semi-annually
7.		$10 000.00	3 months	3 years	6%	monthly
8.		$24 300.00	1 month	20 years	9%	semi-annually

C. For each of the following four deferred annuities, find the periodic payment.

	Present Value	Made At:	Payment Interval	Period of Deferment	Term	Int. Rate	Compounding Period
1.	$7 200.00	beginning	3 months	3 years	5 years	9%	quarterly
2.	$14 500.00	end	6 months	7 years	10 years	7%	semi-annually
3.	$9 000.00	end	1 month	3 years	7 years	5%	quarterly
4.	$12 650.00	beginning	6 months	2 years	4 years	6%	quarterly

D. Answer each of the following questions.

1. What deposit made at the end of each quarter for 15 years will accumulate to $20 000.00 at 6% compounded quarterly?

2. What payment is required at the end of each month for five years to repay a loan of $8000.00 at 8.4% compounded monthly?

3. A contract can be fulfilled by making an immediate payment of $7500.00 or equal payments at the end of every six months for ten years. What is the size of the semi-annual payments at 9.6% compounded semi-annually?

4. What payment made at the end of each month for eighteen years will amount to $16 000.00 at 9.6% compounded monthly?

5. What payment is required at the end of each month for fifteen years to amortize a $32 000.00 mortgage if interest is 9.5% compounded semi-annually?

6. How much must be deposited at the end of each quarter for ten years to accumulate to $12 000.00 at 6% compounded monthly?

7. What payment made at the end of every three months for twenty years will accumulate to $20 000.00 at 7% compounded semi-annually?

8. Deragh bought a car priced at $9300.00 for 15% down and equal monthly payments for four years. If interest is 8% compounded semi-annually, what is the size of the monthly payment?

9. Elspeth McNab bought a boat valued at $12 500.00 on the instalment plan requiring equal monthly payments for four years. If the first payment is due on the date of purchase and interest is 7.5% compounded monthly, what is the size of the monthly payment?

10. How much does a depositor have to save at the beginning of every three months for nine years to accumulate $35 000.00 if interest is 8% compounded quarterly?

11. How much would you have to pay into an account at the beginning of every six months to accumulate $10 000.00 in eight years if interest is 7% compounded quarterly?

12. Peel Credit Union entered a lease contract valued at $5400.00. The contract provides for payments at the beginning of each month for three years. If interest is 11% compounded quarterly, what is the size of the monthly payment?

13. A deposit of $20 000.00 is made for a twenty-year term. After the term expires, equal withdrawals are to be made for twelve years at the end of every six months. What is the size of the semi-annual withdrawal if interest is 10% compounded semi-annually?

14. Payments on a seven-year lease valued at $12 200.00 are to be made at the beginning of each month during the last five years of the lease. If interest is 9% compounded monthly, what is the size of the monthly payments?

15. Dr. Young bought $18 000.00 worth of equipment from Medical Supply Company. The purchase agreement requires equal payments every six months for eight years. If the first payment is due two years after the date of purchase and interest is 7% compounded quarterly, what is the size of the payments?

16. Ed Ainsley borrowed $10 000.00 from his uncle to finance his post-graduate studies. The loan agreement calls for equal payments at the end of each month for ten years. The payments are deferred for four years and interest is 8% compounded semi-annually. What is the size of the monthly payments?

17. Olivia bought a car priced at $10 600.00 for 10% down and the balance in equal monthly payments over four years at 7.2% compounded monthly. How much does Olivia have to pay each month?

18. The Watsons bought a rental property valued at $50 000.00 by paying 20% down and mortgaging the balance over 25 years through equal quarterly payments at 10% compounded quarterly. What was the size of the quarterly payments?

19. George plans to deposit $1200.00 at the end of every six months for fifteen years into an RRSP account. After the last deposit, he intends to convert the existing balance into an RRIF and withdraw equal amounts at the end of every six months for twenty years. If interest is expected to be 7.5% compounded semi-annually, how much will George be able to collect every six months?

20. Starting three months after her grandson Robin's birth, Mrs. Devine made deposits of $60.00 into a trust fund every three months until Robin was twenty-one years old. The trust fund provides for equal withdrawals at the end of each quarter for four years beginning three months after the last deposit. If interest is 10% compounded quarterly, how much will Robin receive every three months?

21. On the day of his daughter's birth, Mr. Dodd deposited $2000.00 in a trust fund with his credit union at 5% compounded quarterly. Following her eighteenth birthday, the daughter is to receive equal payments at the end of each month for four years while she is at college. If interest is to be 6.0% compounded monthly after the daughter's eighteenth birthday, how much will she receive every month?

22. Equal payments are to be made at the end of each month for fifteen years with interest at 9% compounded monthly. After the last payment, the fund is to be invested for seven years at 10% compounded quarterly and have a maturity value of $20 000.00. What is the size of the monthly payment?

23. Julia deposited $1500.00 in an RRSP at the beginning of every six months for twenty years. The money earned interest at 11% compounded semi-annually. After twenty years, she converted the RRSP into an RRIF from which she wants to withdraw equal amounts at the beginning of each month for fifteen years. If interest on the RRIF is 12% compounded monthly, how much does she receive each month?

24. Mr. Clark wants to receive payments of $900.00 at the beginning of every three months for twenty years starting on the date of his retirement. If he retires in twenty-five years, how much must he deposit in an account at the beginning of every three months if interest on the account is 10% compounded quarterly?

25. To finance the development of a new product, a company borrowed $50 000.00 at 7% compounded quarterly. If the loan is to be repaid in equal quarterly payments over seven years and the first payment is due three years after the date of the loan, what is the size of the quarterly payment?

26. Mr. Talbot received a retirement gratuity of $18 000.00, which he deposited in an RRSP. He intends to leave the money for fourteen years, then transfer the balance into an RRIF and make equal withdrawals at the end of every six months for twenty years. If interest is 10.5% compounded semi-annually, what will be the size of each withdrawal?

13.2 FINDING THE TERM n OF AN ANNUITY

A. Finding the term n when the future value of an annuity is known

If the future value of an annuity S_n, S_{nc}, S_n (due), or S_{nc} (due), the periodic payment R, and the conversion rate i are known, you can find the term of the annuity n by substituting the given values in the appropriate future value formula.

For ordinary simple annuities, use Formula 11.1.

$$S_n = R\left[\frac{(1 + i)^n - 1}{i}\right]$$ —————— Formula 11.1

For ordinary general annuities, use Formula 11.3.

$$S_{nc} = R\left[\frac{(1 + f)^n - 1}{f}\right]$$
$$\text{where } f = (1 + i)^c - 1$$ —————— Formula 11.3

For simple annuities due, use Formula 12.1.

$$S_n(\text{due}) = R(1 + i)\left[\frac{(1 + i)^n - 1}{i}\right]$$ — Formula 12.1

For general annuities due, use Formula 12.3.

$$S_{nc}(\text{due}) = R(1 + f)\left[\frac{(1 + f)^n - 1}{f}\right]$$

where $f = (1 + i)^c - 1$

——— **Formula 12.3**

When using a scientific calculator, you can find *n* by first rearranging the terms of the future value formulae above. Then substitute the three known values (future value, R, and *i*) into the rearranged formula and solve for *n*.

When using a preprogrammed financial calculator, you can find *n* by entering the three known values (future value, R, and *i*) and pressing [CPT] [N].

EXAMPLE 13.2A   How long will it take for $200.00 deposited at the end of each quarter to amount to $6885.29 at 12% compounded quarterly?

Solution

$S_n = 6885.29; \quad i = \dfrac{12\%}{4} = 3\% = 0.03; \quad R = 200.00$

$6885.29 = 200.00\left(\dfrac{1.03^n - 1}{0.03}\right)$ ——————— substituting in Formula 11.1

$34.42645 = \dfrac{1.03^n - 1}{0.03}$ ——————— divide both sides by 200.00

$1.0327935 = 1.03^n - 1$ ——————— multiply both sides by 0.03
$1.03^n = 2.0327935$ ——————— add 1 to both sides
$n \ln 1.03 = \ln 2.0327935$ ——————— solve for *n* using natural logarithms
$0.0295588n = 0.709411$

$n = \dfrac{0.709411}{0.0295588}$

$n = 24 \text{ (quarters)}$

It will take six years for $200.00 per quarter to grow to $6885.29.

Alternatively, you can first rearrange the terms of Formula 11.1 to solve for *n*.

$S_n = R\left[\dfrac{(1 + i)^n - 1}{i}\right]$ ——————— Formula 11.1

$\dfrac{S_n}{R} = \dfrac{(1 + i)^n - 1}{i}$ ——————— divide both sides by R

$(1 + i)^n = \left(\dfrac{S_n i}{R}\right) + 1$ ——————— multiply both sides by *i* and add 1 to both sides

$n \ln(1 + i) = \ln[(S_n i/R) + 1]$ ——————— solve for *n* using natural logarithms

$n = \dfrac{\ln[(S_n i/R) + 1]}{\ln(1 + i)}$ ——————— divide both sides by $\ln(1 + i)$

$$S_n = 6885.29; \quad i = 0.03; \quad R = 200.00$$

$$n = \frac{\ln[(6885.29 \times 0.03/200.00) + 1]}{\ln 1.03}$$

$$n = \frac{0.709411}{0.0295588}$$

$$n = 24 \text{ (quarters)}$$

EXAMPLE 13.2B In how many months will your bank account grow to $3000.00 if you deposit $150.00 at the end of each month and the account earns 9% compounded monthly?

Solution $S_n = 3000.00; \quad R = 150.00; \quad i = \dfrac{9\%}{12} = 0.75\%$

0 [PV] 3000 [FV] 150 [PMT] 0.75 [%i] [CPT] [N] [18.7]
            (or −150)   ↑
                                                            months

It will take about 19 months to accumulate $3000.00.

Interpretation of result
When S_n, R, and i are known, it is unlikely that n will be a whole number. The fractional time period of 0.7 month indicates that the accumulated value of 18 deposits of $150.00 will be less than $3000.00, while the accumulated value of 19 deposits will be more than $3000.00. This point can be verified by computing S_{18} and S_{19}.

$$S_{18} = 150.00\left(\frac{1.0075^{18} - 1}{0.0075}\right) = 150.00(19.194717) = \$2879.21$$

$$S_{19} = 150.00\left(\frac{1.0075^{19} - 1}{0.0075}\right) = 150.00(20.338677) = \$3050.80$$

The definition of an annuity does not provide for making payments at unequal time intervals. The appropriate answer to problems in which n is a fractional value is a whole number. The usual approach is to round upwards so that in this case $n = 19$.

Rounding upwards implies that the deposit made at the end of the nineteenth month is smaller than the usual deposit of $150.00. The method of computing the size of the final deposit or payment when the term of the annuity is a fractional value rounded upwards is considered in Chapter 14.

EXAMPLE 13.2C What period of time is required for $125.00 deposited at the end of each month at 11% compounded quarterly to grow to $15 000.00?

Solution $S_{nc} = 15\ 000.00; \quad R = 125.00; \quad c = \dfrac{4}{12} = \dfrac{1}{3};$

$i = \dfrac{11\%}{4} = 2.75\% = 0.0275$

The equivalent effective monthly rate of interest

$f = 1.0275^{\frac{1}{3}} - 1 = 1.0090839 - 1 = 0.0090839 = 0.90839\%$

$15\ 000.00 = 125.00\left(\dfrac{1.0090839^{n} - 1}{0.0090839}\right)$ ——— using Formula 11.3

$120.00 = \dfrac{(1.0090839^{n} - 1)}{0.0090839}$

$1.0900678 = 1.0090839^{n} - 1$

$1.0090839^{n} = 2.0900678$

$n \ln 1.0090839 = \ln 2.0900678$

$n(0.0090429) = 0.7371965$

$n = \dfrac{0.7371965}{0.0090429}$

$n = 81.522227$

$n = 82$ months approximately

With a preprogrammed calculator, the procedure, after finding f, is

0.90839 [%i] 0 [PV] 15 000 [FV] 125 [PMT] [CPT] [N] [81.52]
(or −125)

It will take about 6 years and 10 months to accumulate $15 000.00.

EXAMPLE 13.2D   Over what length of time will $75.00 deposited at the beginning of each month grow to $6500.00 at 12% compounded monthly?

Solution $S_{n}(\text{due}) = 6500.00; \quad R = 75.00; \quad i = \dfrac{12\%}{12} = 1\% = 0.01$

$6500.00 = 75.00(1.01)\left(\dfrac{1.01^{n} - 1}{0.01}\right)$ ——— substituting in Formula 12.1

$6500.00 = 7575.00(1.01^{n} - 1)$

$\dfrac{6500.00}{7575.00} = 1.01^{n} - 1$

$0.8580858 + 1 = 1.01^{n}$

$n \ln(1.01) = \ln 1.8580858$

$n(0.0099503) = 0.6195468$

$n = \dfrac{0.6195468}{0.0099503}$

$n = 62.263942$

As discussed in Example 13.2B, n should be rounded upwards.

$n = 63$ (months)

It will take 5 years and 3 months to accumulate $6500.00.

EXAMPLE 13.2E   Sheridan Credit Union intends to accumulate a building fund of $150 000.00 by depositing $4125.00 at the beginning of every three months at 7% compounded quarterly. How long will it take for the fund to reach the desired amount?

Solution $S_n(\text{due}) = 150\ 000.00;\quad R = 4125.00;\quad i = \dfrac{7\%}{4} = 1.75\%$

Programmed solution

0 PV 150 000 FV 4125 PMT 1.75 %i DUE (or 2nd CPT)

N 28   (or −4125)

$n = 28$ quarters (approximately)

It will take seven years to build up the fund.

EXAMPLE 13.2F   Ted Davis wants to accumulate $140 000.00 in an RRSP by making annual contributions of $5500.00 at the beginning of each year. If interest on the RRSP is 11% compounded quarterly, for how long will Ted have to make contributions?

Solution $S_{nc}(\text{due}) = 140\ 000.00;\quad R = 5500.00;\quad c = 4;$

$i = \dfrac{11\%}{4} = 2.75\% = 0.0275$

The equivalent effective annual rate of interest

$f = 1.0275^4 - 1 = 1.1146213 - 1 = 0.1146213 = 11.46213\%$

$140\ 000.00 = 5500.00(1.1146213)\left(\dfrac{1.1146213^n - 1}{0.1146213}\right)$ —— using Formula 12.3

$140\ 000.00 = 53\ 484.101(1.1146213^n - 1)$

$2.6176003 = 1.1146213^n - 1$

$1.1146213^n = 3.6176003$

$n \ln 1.1146213 = \ln 3.6176003$

$n(0.1085147) = 1.2858109$

$n = \dfrac{1.2858109}{0.1085147}$

$n = 11.849186$

$n = 12$ years (approximately)

Programmed solution

11.46213 [%i] 0 [PV] 5500 [PMT] 140 000 [FV] [DUE]
                     (or −5500)

(or [2nd] [CPT]) [N] [11.85]

Ted will have to contribute for about 12 years.

B. Finding the term *n* when the present value of an annuity is known

If the present value A_n, A_{nc}, A_n(due), or A_{nc} (due), the periodic payment R, and the conversion rate *i* are known, you can find the term of the annuity *n* by substituting the given values in the appropriate present value formula.

For ordinary simple annuities, use Formula 11.2.

$$A_n = R\left[\frac{1 - (1 + i)^{-n}}{i}\right] \qquad\text{——— Formula 11.2}$$

For ordinary general annuities, use Formula 11.4.

$$A_{nc} = R\left[\frac{1 - (1 + f)^{-n}}{f}\right]$$
$$\text{where } f = (1 + i)^c - 1 \qquad\text{——— Formula 11.4}$$

For simple annuities due, use Formula 12.2.

$$A_n(\text{due}) = R(1 + i)\left[\frac{1 - (1 + i)^{-n}}{i}\right] \qquad\text{——— Formula 12.2}$$

For general annuities due, use Formula 12.4.

$$A_{nc}(\text{due}) = R(1 + f)\left[\frac{1 - (1 + f)^{-n}}{f}\right]$$
$$\text{where } f = (1 + i)^c - 1 \qquad\text{——— Formula 12.4}$$

When using a scientific calculator, you can find *n* by first rearranging the terms of the present value formulae above. Then substitute the three known values (present value, R, and *i*) into the rearranged formula and solve for *n*.

When using a preprogrammed financial calculator, you can find *n* by entering the three known values (present value, R, and *i*) and pressing [CPT] [N].

EXAMPLE 13.2G How many quarterly payments of $600.00 are required to repay a loan of $5400.00 at % compounded quarterly?

$$A_n = 5400.00; \quad R = 600.00; \quad i = \frac{6\%}{4} = 1.5\% = 0.015$$

$$5400.00 = 600.00\left(\frac{1 - 1.015^{-n}}{0.015}\right) \quad \text{—— substituting in Formula 11.2}$$

$$9.00 = \frac{1 - 1.015^{-n}}{0.015} \quad \text{—— divide both sides by 600.00}$$

$$0.135 = 1 - 1.015^{-n} \quad \text{—— multiply both sides by 0.015}$$

$$1.015^{-n} = 0.865$$

$$-n \ln 1.015 = \ln 0.865 \quad \text{—— solve for } n \text{ using natural logarithms}$$

$$-0.0148886n = -0.1450258$$

$$n = \frac{0.1450258}{0.0148886}$$

$$n = 9.7407259$$

$$n = 10 \text{ quarters}$$

10 quarterly payments are required to repay the loan.

Alternatively, you can first rearrange the terms of Formula 11.2 to solve for n.

$$A_n = R\left[\frac{1 - (1 + i)^{-n}}{i}\right] \quad \text{— Formula 11.2}$$

$$\frac{A_n}{R} = \frac{1 - (1 + i)^{-n}}{i} \quad \text{—— divide both sides by R}$$

$$\left(\frac{A_n i}{R}\right) - 1 = -(1 + i)^{-n} \quad \text{—— multiply both sides by } i \text{ and subtract 1 from both sides}$$

$$(1 + i)^{-n} = 1 - \left(\frac{A_n i}{R}\right) \quad \text{—— multiply both sides by } -1$$

$$-n \ln(1 + i) = \ln\left[1 - \left(\frac{A_n i}{R}\right)\right] \quad \text{—— solve for } n \text{ using natural logarithms}$$

$$n = \frac{\ln\left[1 - \left(\frac{A_n i}{R}\right)\right]}{-\ln(1 + i)} \quad \text{—— divide both sides by } -\ln(1 + i)$$

$$A_n = 5400.00; \quad R = 600.00; \quad i = 0.015$$

$$n = \frac{\ln\left[1 - \dfrac{(5400.00)(0.015)}{600.00}\right]}{-\ln(1.015)} \qquad\text{— substituting in rearranged Formula 11.2}$$

$$n = \frac{-0.1450258}{-0.0148886}$$

$$n = 9.7407177$$
$$n = 10 \text{ quarters}$$

EXAMPLE 13.2H On his retirement, Art received a gratuity of $8000.00 from his employer. Taking advantage of the existing tax legislation, he invested the money in an income averaging annuity that provides for semi-annual payments of $1200.00 at the end of every six months. If interest is 11.5% compounded semi-annually, how long will the annuity exist?

Solution $A_n = 8000.00; \quad R = 1200.00; \quad i = \dfrac{11.5\%}{2} = 5.75\%$

0 [FV] 8000 [PV] 1200 [PMT] 5.75 [%i] [CPT] [N] [8.647]

half-year periods

The annuity will be in existence for four and a half years. Art will receive eight payments of $1200.00 and a final payment that will be less than $1200.00.

EXAMPLE 13.2I A business valued at $96 000.00 is bought for a down payment of 25% and payments of $4000.00 at the end of every three months. If interest is 9% compounded monthly, for how long will payments have to be made?

Solution $A_{nc} = 96\,000.00(0.75) = 72\,000.00; \quad R = 4000.00;$

$$c = \frac{12}{4} = 3; \quad i = \frac{9\%}{12} = 0.75\% = 0.0075$$

The equivalent effective quarterly rate of interest

$$f = 1.0075^3 - 1 = 1.0226692 - 1 = 0.0226692 = 2.26692\%$$

$$72\,000.00 = 4000.00\left(\frac{1 - 1.0226692^{-n}}{0.0226692}\right) \qquad\text{— using Formula 11.4}$$

$$0.4080456 = 1 - 1.0226692^{-n}$$
$$1.0226692^{-n} = 0.5919544$$
$$-n \ln 1.0226692 = \ln 0.5919544$$
$$-n(0.0224161) = -0.5243257$$
$$n = 23.390585 \text{ (quarters)}$$

Programmed solution

2.26692 $\boxed{\%i}$ 0 $\boxed{\text{FV}}$ 72 000 $\boxed{\text{PV}}$ 4000 $\boxed{\text{PMT}}$ $\boxed{\text{CPT}}$ $\boxed{\text{N}}$ $\boxed{23.39}$

Payments will have to be made for 6 years.

EXAMPLE 13.2J For how long can you withdraw $480.00 at the beginning of every three months from a fund of $9000.00 if interest is 10% compounded quarterly?

Solution $A_n(\text{due}) = 9000.00; \quad R = 480.00; \quad i = \dfrac{10\%}{4} = 2.5\% = 0.025$

$$9000.00 = 480.00(1.025)\left(\frac{1 - 1.025^{-n}}{0.025}\right) \quad\text{—— substituting in Formula 12.2}$$

$$9000.00 = 19\,680.00(1 - 1.025^{-n})$$

$$\frac{9000.00}{19\,680.00} = 1 - 1.025^{-n}$$

$$0.4573171 = 1 - 1.025^{-n}$$
$$1.025^{-n} = 1 - 0.4573171$$
$$1.025^{-n} = 0.5426829$$
$$-n \ln 1.025 = \ln 0.5426829$$
$$-n(0.0246926) = -0.6112301$$

$$n = \frac{0.6112301}{0.0246926}$$

$$n = 24.753561$$
$$n = 25 \text{ (quarters)}$$

Withdrawals of $480.00 can be made for 6 years and 3 months. (The last withdrawal will be less than $480.00.)

EXAMPLE 13.2K A lease contract valued at $7800.00 is to be fulfilled by rental payments of $180.00 due at the beginning of each month. If money is worth 9% compounded monthly, what should the term of the lease be?

Solution $A_n(\text{due}) = 7800.00; \quad R = 180.00; \quad i = \dfrac{9\%}{12} = 0.75\%$

Programmed solution

0 $\boxed{\text{FV}}$ 7800 $\boxed{\text{PV}}$ 180 $\boxed{\text{PMT}}$ 0.75 $\boxed{\%i}$ $\boxed{\text{DUE}}$ (or $\boxed{\text{2nd}}$ $\boxed{\text{CPT}}$)

$\boxed{\text{N}}$ $\boxed{52.12}$

$n = 53$ months (approximately)

The term of the lease should be 4 years and 5 months.

EXAMPLE 13.2L   Ted Davis, having reached his goal of a $140 000.00 balance in his RRSP, immediately converts it into an RRIF and withdraws from it $1650.00 at the beginning of each month. If interest continues at 11% compounded quarterly, for how long can he make withdrawals?

Solution $A_{nc}(\text{due}) = 140\ 000.00; \quad R = 1650.00; \quad c = \dfrac{4}{12} = \dfrac{1}{3};$

$i = \dfrac{11\%}{4} = 2.75\% = 0.0275$

The equivalent effective monthly rate of interest

$f = 1.0275^{\frac{1}{3}} - 1 = 1.0090839 - 1 = 0.0090839 = 0.90839\%$

$$140\ 000.00 = 1650.00(1.0090839)\left(\dfrac{1 - 1.0090839^{-n}}{0.0090839}\right) \quad \text{— using Formula 12.4}$$

$$140\ 000.00 = 183\ 290.04(1 - 1.0090839^{-n})$$
$$0.7638167 = 1 - 1.0090839^{-n}$$
$$1.0090839^{-n} = 0.2361833$$
$$-n \ln 1.0090839 = \ln 0.2361833$$
$$-n(0.0090429) = -1.4431471$$
$$n = 159.58897$$
$$n = 160 \text{ months (approximately)}$$

Programmed solution

0.90839 $\boxed{\%i}$ 0 $\boxed{\text{FV}}$ 140 000 $\boxed{\text{PV}}$ 1650 $\boxed{\text{PMT}}$ $\boxed{\text{DUE}}$ (or $\boxed{\text{2nd}}$ $\boxed{\text{CPT}}$)

$\boxed{\text{N}}$ $\boxed{159.6}$

Ted will be able to make withdrawals for 13 years and 4 months.

C. Finding the term *n* of a deferred annuity

You can find the term for deferred ordinary annuities by the same approach used to determine the periodic payment R.

EXAMPLE 13.2M   For how long can you pay $500.00 at the end of each month out of a fund of $10 000.00, deposited today at 10.5% compounded monthly, if the payments are deferred for nine years?

Solution   The payments form a deferred ordinary annuity.

$A_n(\text{defer}) = 10\ 000.00; \quad R = 500.00; \quad i = \dfrac{10.5\%}{12} = 0.875\% - 0.00875;$

$d = 9(12) = 108$

The value of the $10\ 000 at the end of the period of deferment,

$$S = 10\ 000.00(1.00875)^{108}$$
$$= 10\ 000.00(2.5622598)$$
$$= 25\ 622.60$$

$$25\ 622.60 = 500.00\left(\frac{1 - 1.00875^{-n}}{0.00875}\right)$$

$$25\ 622.60 = 57\ 142.857(1 - 1.00875^{-n})$$

$$\frac{25\ 622.60}{57\ 142.857} = 1 - 1.00875^{-n}$$

$$0.4483955 = 1 - 1.00875^{-n}$$
$$1.00875^{-n} = 0.5516045$$
$$-n \ln 1.00875 = \ln 0.5516045$$
$$-n(0.0087119) = -0.5949239$$

$$n = \frac{0.5949239}{0.0087119}$$

$$n = 68.288334$$
$$n = 69 \text{ (months)}$$

Programmed solution

0 [PMT] 10 000 [PV] 0.875 [%i] 108 [N] [CPT] [FV] [25 622.598]

0 [FV] 25 622.60 [PV] 0.875 [%i] 500 [PMT] [CPT] [N] [68.29]

Payments can be made for 5 years and 9 months.

EXAMPLE 13.2N A scholarship of $3000.00 per year is to be paid at the beginning of each year from a scholarship fund of $15 000.00 invested at 11% compounded annually. How long will the scholarship be paid if payments are deferred for five years?

Solution The annual payments form a deferred annuity due.

$$A_n(\text{defer}) = 15\ 000.00; \quad R = 3000.00; \quad i = 11\% = 0.11; \quad d = 5$$

The value of the $15 000.00 at the end of the period of deferment,

$$S = 15\ 000.00(1.11)^5$$
$$= 15\ 000.00(1.6850582)$$
$$= 25\ 275.87$$

$$25\ 275.87 = 3000.00(1.11)\left(\frac{1 - 1.11^{-n}}{0.11}\right)$$

$$25\ 275.87 = 30\ 272.727(1 - 1.11^{-n})$$
$$0.8349387 = 1 - 1.11^{-n}$$
$$1.11^{-n} = 0.1650613$$

$$-n \ln 1.11 = \ln 0.1650613$$
$$-0.10436n = -1.8014385$$

$$n = \frac{1.8014385}{0.10436}$$

$$n = 17.261769$$
$$n = 18 \text{ years (approximately)}$$

Programmed solution

0 [PMT] 15 000 [PV] 11 [%i] 5 [N] [CPT] [FV] [25 275.872]

0 [FV] 25 275.87 [PV] 11 [%i] 3000 [PMT] [DUE] (or [2nd] [CPT])

[N] [17.26]

The scholarship fund will provide 17 payments of $3000 and a final payment of less than $3000.00.

EXAMPLE 13.20   Mr. Kovacs deposited a retirement gratuity of $21 500.00 in an income averaging annuity paying $375.00 at the end of each month. If payments are deferred for nine months and interest is 12% compounded quarterly, for what period of time will Mr. Kovacs receive annuity payments?

Solution $A_{nc}(\text{defer}) = 21\,500.00; \quad R = 375.00; \quad d = 9; \quad c = \frac{4}{12} = \frac{1}{3};$

$i = \dfrac{12\%}{4} = 3\% = 0.03$

The equivalent effective monthly rate of interest

$f = 1.03^{\frac{1}{3}} - 1 = 1.0099016 - 1 = 0.0099016 = 0.99016\%.$

First find the accumulated value at the end of the period of deferment.

$S = 21\,500.00(1.0099016)^9$
$\quad = 21\,500.00(1.092727)$
$\quad = 23\,493.63$

Programmed solution

0.99016 [%i] 0 [PMT] 21 500 [PV] 9 [N] [CPT] [FV] [23 493.623]

Then find the number of payments for an ordinary annuity with a present value of $23 493.63.

$$23\,493.63 = 375.00\left(\frac{1 - 1.0099016^{-n}}{0.0099016}\right)$$

$$23\,493.63 = 37\,872.667(1 - 1.0099016^{-n})$$
$$0.6203321 = 1 - 1.0099016^{-n}$$

$$1.0099016^{-n} = 0.3796679$$
$$-n \ln 1.0099016 = \ln 0.3796679$$
$$-n(0.0098529) = -0.9684583$$

$$n = \frac{0.9684583}{0.0098529}$$

$$n = 98.291701$$
$$n = 99 \text{ months}$$

Programmed solution

23 493.63 [PV] 0 [FV] 0.99016 [%i] 375 [PMT] [CPT] [N] [98.29]

Mr. Kovacs will receive payments for 8 years and 3 months.

EXAMPLE 13.2P By age 65, Janice Berstein had accumulated $120 000.00 in an RRSP by making yearly contributions over a period of years. At age 69, she converted the existing balance into an RRIF from which she started to withdraw $2000.00 per month. If the first withdrawal was on the date of conversion and interest on the account is 11% compounded quarterly, for how long will Janice Berstein receive annuity payments?

Solution $A_{nc}(\text{defer}) = 120\ 000.00; \quad R = 2000.00; \quad d = 4(12) = 48;$

$$c = \frac{4}{12} = \frac{1}{3}; \quad i = \frac{11\%}{4} = 2.75\% = 0.0275$$

The equivalent effective monthly rate of interest

$$f = 1.0275^{\frac{1}{3}} - 1 = 1.0090839 - 1 = 0.0090839 = 0.90839\%$$

Since payments are at the beginning of each month, the problem involves a deferred general annuity due.

First find the accumulated value at the end of the period of deferment.

$$S = 120\ 000.00(1.0090839)^{48}$$
$$= 120\ 000.00(1.5435095)$$
$$= 185\ 221.14$$

Programmed solution

0.90839 [%i] 0 [PMT] 120 000 [PV] 48 [N] [CPT] [FV] [185 221.14]

Then find the number of payments for an annuity due with a present value of $185 221.14.

$$185\ 221.14 = 2000.00(1.0090839)\left(\frac{1 - 1.0090839^{-n}}{0.0090839}\right)$$

$$185\ 221.14 = 222\ 169.75(1 - 1.0090839^{-n})$$
$$0.8336920 = 1 - 1.0090839^{-n}$$
$$1.0090839^{-n} = 0.1663080$$

$$-n \ln 1.0090839 = \ln 0.1663080$$
$$-n(0.0090429) = -1.7939138$$
$$n = 198.37815$$
$$n = 199 \text{ months}$$

Programmed solution

185 221.13 $\boxed{PV}$ 0 $\boxed{FV}$ 0.90839 $\boxed{\%i}$ 2000 $\boxed{PMT}$ $\boxed{DUE}$

(or $\boxed{2nd}$ $\boxed{CPT}$) $\boxed{N}$ $\boxed{198.4}$

Janice Berstein will receive payments for 16 years and 7 months.

Exercise 13.2

A. Find the term of each of the following ten ordinary annuities. (State your answer in years and months.)

	Future Value	Present Value	Periodic Rent	Payment Interval	Interest Rate	Compounding Period
1.	$20 000.00		$800.00	1 year	7.5%	annually
2.	$17 000.00		$35.00	1 month	12%	monthly
3.		$14 500.00	$190.00	1 month	15%	monthly
4.		$5000.00	$300.00	3 months	4%	quarterly
5.	$3600.00		$175.00	6 months	7.4%	semi-annually
6.		$9500.00	$740.00	1 quarter	5.2%	quarterly
7.		$21 400.00	$1660.00	6 months	4.5%	monthly
8.	$13 600.00		$140.00	6 months	8%	quarterly
9.	$7200.00		$90.00	1 month	13%	semi-annually
10.		$11 700.00	$315.00	3 months	11%	annually

B. Find the length of the term for each of the following eight annuities due.

	Future Value	Present Value	Periodic Payment	Payment Period	Interest Rate	Conversion Period
1.	$5300.00		$35.00	1 month	6%	monthly
2.		$8400.00	$440.00	3 months	7%	quarterly
3.		$6450.00	$1120.00	1 year	10%	annually
4.	$15 400.00		$396.00	6 months	5%	semi-annually
5.	$32 000.00		$450.00	6 months	7.5%	monthly
6.	$7500.00		$150.00	3 months	11%	annually
7.		$12 500.00	$860.00	3 months	9%	monthly
8.		$45 000.00	$540.00	1 month	14%	semi-annually

C. For each of the following four deferred annuities, find the term.

	Present Value	Periodic Payment	Made At:	Payment Interval	Period of Deferment	Int. Rate	Comp. Period
1.	$21 000.00	$3485.00	beginning	3 months	8 years	10%	quarterly
2.	$8800.00	$325.00	end	1 month	3 years	6%	monthly
3.	$22 750.00	$385.00	end	1 month	1 year	13%	semi-annually
4.	$3740.00	$1100.00	beginning	1 year	10 years	8%	monthly

D. Answer each of the following questions.

1. How long would it take you to save $4500.00 by making deposits of $50.00 at the end of every month into a savings account earning 6% compounded monthly?

2. In what period of time could you pay back a loan of $3600.00 by making monthly payments of $96.00 if interest is 10.5% compounded monthly?

3. How long will it take to save $15 000.00 by making deposits of $90.00 at the end of every month into an account earning interest at 10% compounded quarterly?

4. For how long will Jack have to make payments of $350.00 at the end of every three months to repay a loan of $6000.00 if interest is 9% compounded monthly?

5. Quarterly payments of $1445.00 are to be made at the beginning of every three months on a lease valued at $25 000.00. What should the term of the lease be if money is worth 8% compounded quarterly?

6. Tom is saving $600.00 at the beginning of each month. How soon can he retire if he wants to have a retirement fund of $120 000.00 and interest is 12% compounded monthly?

7. Sarah Ling has saved $85 000.00. If she decides to withdraw $3000.00 at the beginning of every three months and interest is 11.5% compounded annually, for how long can she make withdrawals?

8. For how long must contributions of $1600.00 be made at the beginning of each year to accumulate to $96 000.00 at 10% compounded quarterly?

9. A deposit of $4000.00 is made today for a five-year period. For how long can $500.00 be withdrawn from the account at the end of every three months starting three months after the end of the five-year term if interest is 11% compounded quarterly?

10. Suppose $646.56 is deposited at the end of every six months into an account earning 6.5% compounded semi-annually. If the balance in the account four years after the last deposit is to be $20 000.00, how many deposits are needed?

11. If you save $75.00 at the beginning of every month for ten years, for how long can you withdraw $260.00 at the beginning of each month starting ten years from now, assuming that interest is 12% compounded monthly?

12. Ali deposits $450.00 at the beginning of every three months. He wants to build up his account so that he can withdraw $1000.00 every three months starting three months after the last deposit. If he wants to make the withdrawals for fifteen years and interest is 10% compounded quarterly, for how long must Ali make the quarterly deposits?

13. For how long can $1000.00 be withdrawn at the end of each month from an account containing $16 000.00, if the withdrawals are deferred for six years and interest is 12% compounded monthly?

14. Mrs. Woo paid $24 000.00 into a retirement fund paying interest at 11% compounded semi-annually. If she retires in seventeen years, for how long can Mrs. Woo withdraw $10 000.00 from the fund every six months? Assume that the first withdrawal is on the date of retirement.

15. Greg borrowed $6500.00 at 8.4% compounded monthly to help finance his education. He contracted to repay the loan in monthly payments of $300.00 each. If the payments are due at the end of each month and the payments are deferred for four years, for how long will Greg have to make monthly payments?

16. A lease valued at $32 000.00 requires payments of $4000.00 every three months. If the first payment is due three years after the lease was signed and interest is 12% compounded quarterly, what is the term of the lease?

17. A mortgage of $18 600.00 is to be repaid by making payments of $260.00 at the end of each month. If interest is 8% compounded semi-annually, what is the term of the mortgage?

18. Mr. Deneau accumulated $100 000.00 in an RRSP. He converted the RRSP into an RRIF and started to withdraw $4500.00 at the end of every three months from the fund. If interest is 12% compounded monthly, for how long can Mr. Deneau make withdrawals?

19. A property development agreement valued at $45 000.00 requires annual lease payments of $15 000.00. The first payment is due five years after the date of the agreement and interest is 11% compounded semi-annually. For how long will payments be made?

20. A retirement gratuity of $23 600.00 is invested in an annuity deferred for twelve years. The annuity provides payments of $4000.00 due at the beginning of every six months. If interest is 10% compounded annually, for how long will annuity payments be made?

13.3 FINDING THE RATE OF INTEREST *i* USING PREPROGRAMMED FINANCIAL CALCULATORS

A. Finding the rate of interest for simple annuities

Preprogrammed financial calculators are especially helpful when solving for the conversion rate *i*. Determining *i* without a financial calculator is extremely time consuming. However, it *can* be done by hand, as illustrated in Appendix III.

When the future value or present value, the periodic payment R, and the term *n* of an annuity are known, the periodic rate of interest *i* can be found by entering the three known values into a preprogammed financial calculator. For ordinary simple annuities, retrieve the answer by pressing [CPT] [%*i*]. For simple annuities due retrieve the answer by pressing [DUE] [%*i*]. You can then obtain the nominal annual rate of interest by multiplying *i* by the number of compounding periods per year *m*.

EXAMPLE 13.3A Compute the nominal rate of interest at which $100.00 deposited at the end of each month for ten years will amount to $15 000.00.

Solution $S_n = 15\,000.00$;   R = 100.00; $n = 120$; $m = 12$

0 [PV] 15 000 [FV] 100 [PMT] 120 [N] [CPT] [%*i*] [0.3625048]
                    (or −100)
                                                                    ↑
                                                        allow several seconds
                                                         for the computation

The monthly conversion rate is 0.3625048%. The nominal rate of interest is (12)(0.3625048%) = 4.35% approximately.

EXAMPLE 13.3B A loan of $6000.00 is paid off over five years by monthly payments of $120.23. What is the nominal rate of interest on the loan?

Solution $A_n = 6000.00$;   R = 120.23; $n = 60$; $m = 12$

0 [FV] 6000 [PV] 120.23 [PMT] 60 [N] [CPT] [%*i*] [0.6250674]
                                                                    ↑
                                                        allow several seconds
                                                         for the computation

The monthly compounding rate is 0.6250674%. The nominal rate of interest is (12)(0.6250674%) = 7.5% approximately.

EXAMPLE 13.3C Compute the nominal rate of interest at which $100.00 deposited at the beginning of each month for ten years will amount to $15 000.00.

Solution $S_n(\text{due}) = 15\,000;\quad R = 100.00;\quad n = 120;\quad m = 12$

0 PV   15 000 FV   100 PMT   120 N   DUE   (or 2nd   CPT)
(or −100)

%i   0.3569002

↑
allow several seconds
for the computation

The monthly conversion rate is 0.3569002.
The nominal rate of interest is (12)(0.3569002%) = 4.28% approximately.

EXAMPLE 13.3D A lease agreement valued at $7500.00 requires payment of $450.00 at the beginning of every quarter for five years. What is the nominal rate of interest charged?

Solution $A_n(\text{due}) = 7500.00;\quad R = 450.00;\quad n = 20;\quad m = 4$

0 FV   7500 PV   450.00 PMT   20 N   DUE   (or 2nd   CPT)

%i   2.0081616

↑
allow several seconds
for the computation

The quarterly compounding rate is 2.0081616%.
The nominal rate of interest is (4)(2.0081616%) = 8.03% approximately.

QUESTIONS

1. What is the nominal rate of interest you pay if you purchase the Multimedia Desktop Computer using the monthly payment option?

2. What is the nominal rate of interest you pay if you purchase the Laptop Computer using the monthly payment option?

3. What is the nominal rate of interest you pay if you purchase the Colour Laser Printer using the monthly payment option?

B. Finding the rate of interest for general annuities

When the future value or present value, the periodic payment R, and the term n of a general annuity are known, you must first find the effective interest rate per payment period f. This is done by entering the three known values into a preprogrammed financial calculator. For ordinary general annuities, retrieve the value of f by pressing $\boxed{\text{CPT}}$ $\boxed{\%i}$. For general annuities due, retrieve the value of f by pressing $\boxed{\text{DUE}}$ $\boxed{\%i}$.

You can then find the interest rate per conversion period i by using the relationship $1 + f = (1 + i)^c$. Finally, you can obtain the nominal annual rate of interest by multiplying i by the number of compounding periods per year.

EXAMPLE 13.3E

Irina deposited $150.00 in a savings account at the end of each month for 52 months. If the accumulated value of the deposits was $10 000.00 and interest is compounded semi-annually, what was the nominal rate of interest?

Solution

$S_{nc} = 10\ 000.00; \quad R = 150.00; \quad n = 52; \quad c = \dfrac{2}{12} = \dfrac{1}{6}; \quad m = 2$

First, find the effective monthly rate of interest.

$0 \boxed{\text{PV}}$ $10\ 000 \boxed{\text{FV}}$ $150 \boxed{\text{PMT}}$ $52 \boxed{\text{N}}$ $\boxed{\text{CPT}}$ $\boxed{\%i}$ $\boxed{0.940152}$
(or -150)

The effective monthly rate f is 0.940152%.

Second, convert the effective monthly rate f into a semi-annual compounding rate.

$(1 + i)^{\frac{1}{6}} = 1 + 0.00940152$
$1 + i = 1.00940152^6$
$1 + i = 1.0577516$
$i = 0.0577516$

The semi-annual compounding rate is 5.77516%; the nominal rate of interest is $2(5.77516\%) = 11.55\%$ approximately.

EXAMPLE 13.3F   Compute the nominal rate of interest compounded monthly at which $500.00 deposited at the beginning of every three months for ten years will amount to $30 000.00.

Solution $S_{nc}(\text{due}) = 30\ 000.00; \quad R = 500.00; \quad n = 40; \quad c = \dfrac{12}{4} = 3; \quad m = 12$

0 [PV]   30 000 [FV]   500 [PMT]   40 [N]   [DUE]   [%i]   [1.882838]
　　(or −30 000)

↑ the quarterly rate *f*

Converting the quarterly rate into a monthly rate,

$(1 + i)^3 = 1.0188282$

$1 + i = 1.0188282^{\frac{1}{3}}$

$1 + i = 1.0062371$

$i = 0.0062371$

The monthly compounding rate is 0.62371%; the nominal rate is 12(0.62371%) = 7.48% approximately.

C. Finding the conversion rate *i* for deferred annuities

You can determine the periodic rate of interest for deferred annuities by trial and error using the method explained in Appendix III.

Exercise 13.3

A. Compute the nominal rate of interest for each of the following eight simple annuities.

	Future Value	Present Value	Periodic Rent	Made At	Payment Interval	Term	Compounding Period
1.	$9000.00		$143.54	End	3 months	8 years	quarterly
2.	$4800.00		$49.00	End	1 month	5 years	monthly
3.		$7400.00	$119.06	End	1 month	7 years	monthly
4.		$5540.00	$800.00	End	6 months	5 years	semi-annually
5.	$70 000.00		$367.00	Start	1 year	25 years	annually
6.		$42 000.00	$528.00	Start	1 month	10 years	monthly
7.		$28 700.00	$2015.00	Start	6 months	15 years	semi-annually
8.	$36 000.00		$235.00	Start	3 months	12 years	quarterly

B. For each of the following eight general annuities, determine the nominal annual rate of interest.

	Future Value	Present Value	Periodic Payment	Made At	Payment Interval	Term	Conversion Period
1.	$39 200.00		$1100.00	End	1 year	12 years	monthly
2.		$9600.00	$1220.00	End	6 months	5 years	monthly
3.		$62 400.00	$5200.00	End	6 months	25 years	annually
4.	$55 500.00		$75.00	End	1 month	20 years	semi-annually
5.	$6400.00		$200.00	Start	6 months	9 years	monthly
6.	$25 000.00		$790.00	Start	1 year	15 years	quarterly
7.		$7500.00	$420.00	Start	3 months	5 years	monthly
8.		$60 000.00	$725.00	Start	1 month	25 years	semi-annually

C. Answer each of the following questions.

1. Compute the nominal rate of interest at which $350.00 paid at the end of every three months for six years accumulates to $12 239.76.

2. What is the nominal rate of interest if a four-year loan of $6000.00 is repaid by monthly payments of $171.58?

3. Rene contributed $250.00 every three months into an RRSP for ten years. What nominal rate of interest did the RRSP earn if the balance in Rene's account just after he made his last contribution was $19 955.40?

4. Rita converted an RRSP balance of $199 875.67 into an RRIF that will pay her $1800.00 at the end of every month for nine years. What is the nominal rate of interest?

5. A car valued at $11 400.00 can be bought for 10% down and monthly payments of $318.56 for three and a half years. What is the effective cost of financing?

6. A property worth $40 000.00 can be purchased for 20% down and quarterly mortgage payments of $1100.00 for 25 years. What effective rate of interest is charged?

7. What nominal rate of interest was paid if contributions of $250.00 made into an RRSP at the beginning of every three months amounted to $14 559.00 after ten years?

8. A vacation property valued at $25 000.00 was bought for fifteen payments of $2750.00 due at the beginning of every six months. What nominal rate of interest was charged?

9. What is the effective rate of interest on a lease contract valued at $13 500.00 if payments of $1500.00 are made at the beginning of every six months for seven years?

10. An insurance policy provides a benefit of $250 000.00 twenty years from now. Alternatively, the policy pays $4220.00 at the beginning of each year for twenty years. What is the effective rate of interest paid?

11. Compute the rate of interest compounded monthly at which $400.00 paid at the end of every three months for eight years accumulates to $20 000.00.

12. What is the rate of interest compounded quarterly if a loan of $21 500.00 is repaid in seven years by payments of $2500.00 made at the end of every six months?

13. A mortgage of $27 500.00 is repaid by making payments of $280.00 at the end of each month for fifteen years. What is the rate of interest compounded semi-annually?

14. A property worth $35 000.00 is purchased for 10% down and semi-annual payments of $2750.00 for twelve years. What is the effective rate of interest if interest is compounded quarterly?

15. What is the rate of interest compounded annually on a lease valued at $21 600.00 if payments of $730.00 are made at the beginning of each month for three years?

16. An insurance policy provides for a lump sum benefit of $50 000.00 fifteen years from now. Alternatively, payments of $1700.00 may be received at the beginning of each of the next fifteen years. What is the effective rate of interest if interest is compounded quarterly?

REVIEW EXERCISE

1. Suppose you would like to have $10 000.00 in your savings account and interest is 8% compounded quarterly. How much must you deposit every three months for five years if the deposits are made

   a) at the end of each quarter?

   b) at the beginning of each quarter?

2. Equal sums of money are withdrawn monthly from a fund of $20 000.00 for fifteen years. If interest is 9% compounded monthly, what is the size of each withdrawal

   a) if the withdrawal is made at the beginning of each month?

   b) if the withdrawal is made at the end of each month?

3. How much must be deposited into an account to accumulate to $32 000.00 at 7% compounded semi-annually

   a) at the beginning of each month for twenty years?

   b) at the end of each year for fifteen years?

4. What sum of money can be withdrawn from a fund of $16 750.00 invested at 16.5% compounded semi-annually

   a) at the end of every three months for twelve years?

   b) at the beginning of each year for twenty years?

c) at the end of each month for fifteen years but deferred for ten years?

d) at the beginning of every three months for 12 years but deferred for 20 years?

e) at the end of each month in perpetuity?

f) at the beginning of each year in perpetuity?

5. How long will it take to build up a fund of $10 000.00 by saving $300.00 every six months at 10.5% compounded semi-annually?

6. What is the term of a mortgage of $35 000.00 repaid by monthly payments of $475.00 if interest is 7.5% compounded monthly?

7. How long will it take to accumulate $18 000.00 at 6% compounded monthly if $125.00 is deposited in an account at the beginning of every month?

8. A contract valued at $11 500.00 requires payment of $1450.00 at the beginning of every six months. If interest is 10.5% compounded semi-annually, what is the term of the contract?

9. In what period of time will payments of $450.00 accumulate to $20 000.00 at 6% compounded monthly if made

a) at the end of every three months?

b) at the beginning of every six months?

10. What nominal rate of interest is paid on quarterly RRSP contributions of $750.00 made for fifteen years if the balance just after the last contribution is $106 000.00?

11. What nominal rate of interest was charged on a loan of $5600.00 repaid in monthly instalments of $148.90 in four and a half years?

12. At what nominal rate of interest compounded semi-annually will $1200.00 deposited at the beginning of every six months accumulate to $40 000.00 in nine years?

13. What is the effective rate of interest charged on a four-year lease valued at $9600.00 if payments of $300.00 are made at the beginning of each month for the four years?

14. Frank invested a retirement gratuity of $15 000.00 in an income averaging annuity paying 12% compounded monthly. He withdraws the money in equal monthly amounts over five years. If the first withdrawal is made nine months after the deposit, what is the size of each withdrawal?

15. The amount of $10 000.00 is put into a five-year term deposit paying 7.5% compounded semi-annually. After five years the deposit is converted into an

ordinary annuity of equal semi-annual payments of $2000.00 each. If interest remains the same, what is the term of the annuity?

16. A debt of $20 000.00 is repaid by making payments of $3500.00. If interest is 9% compounded monthly, for how long will payments have to be made

    a) at the end of every six months?

    b) at the beginning of each year?

    c) at the end of every three months with payments deferred for five years?

    d) at the beginning of every six months with payments deferred for three years?

17. What is the rate of interest compounded quarterly at which payments of $400.00 made at the beginning of every six months accumulate to $8400.00 in eight years?

18. A $60 000.00 mortgage with a 25-year term is repaid by making monthly payments of $480.00. What is the rate of interest compounded semi-annually on the mortgage?

19. For how long must $1000.00 be deposited at the beginning of every year to accumulate to $180 000.00 twelve years after the end of the year in which the last deposit was made if interest is 7.5% compounded annually?

20. Alicia Sidlo invested a retirement gratuity of $12 500.00 in an RRSP paying 10.5% compounded semi-annually for ten years. At the end of ten years, she rolled the RRSP balance over into an RRIF paying $500.00 at the beginning of each month starting with the date of rollover. If interest on the RRIF is 10.5% compounded monthly, for how long will Alicia receive monthly payments?

21. Mirielle has deposited $125.00 at the end of each month for 15 years at 7.5% compounded monthly. After her last deposit she converted the balance into an ordinary annuity paying $1200.00 every three months for twelve years. If interest on the annuity is compounded quarterly, what is the effective rate of interest paid by the annuity?

22. Anne received $45 000.00 from her mother's estate. She wants to set aside part of her inheritance for her retirement nine years from now. At that time she would like to receive a pension supplement of $600.00 at the end of each month for 25 years. If the first payment is due one month after her retirement and interest is 10% compounded monthly, how much must Anne set aside?

23. Ty received a separation payment of $5000.00 at age 35. He invested that sum of money at 11.5% compounded semi-annually until he was 65. At that time he converted the existing balance into an ordinary annuity paying $8000.00 every three months with interest at 11% compounded quarterly. For how long will the annuity run?

24. Mrs. Bean contributes $450.00 at the beginning of every three months to an RRSP. Interest on the account is 6% compounded quarterly.

   a) What will the balance in the account be after seven years?

   b) How much of the balance will be interest?

   c) If Mrs. Bean converts the balance after seven years into an RRIF paying 5% compounded quarterly and makes equal quarterly withdrawals for twelve years starting three months after the conversion into the RRIF, what is the size of the quarterly withdrawal?

   d) What is the combined interest earned by the RRSP and the RRIF?

25. Art will receive monthly payments of $850.00 from a trust account starting on the date of his retirement and continuing for twenty years. Interest is 10.5% compounded monthly.

   a) What is the balance in the trust account on the date of Art's retirement?

   b) How much interest will be included in the payments Art receives?

   c) If Art made equal monthly deposits at the beginning of each month for fifteen years before his retirement, how much did he deposit each month?

   d) How much interest will Art receive in total?

26. How much must be contributed into an RRSP at the end of each year for 25 years to accumulate to $100 000.00 if interest is 8% compounded quarterly?

27. Kelly Associates are the makers of a ten-year $75 000.00 promissory note bearing interest at 16% compounded semi-annually. To pay off the note on its due date, the company is making payments at the beginning of every three months into a fund paying 13.5% compounded monthly. What is the size of the monthly payments?

28. A debt of $40 000.00 is to be repaid in instalments due at the end of each month for seven years. If the payments are deferred for three years and interest is 7% compounded quarterly, what is the size of the monthly payments?

29. Redden Ogilvie bought his parents' farm for $200 000.00. The transfer agreement requires Redden to make quarterly payments for twenty years. If the first payment is due in five years and the rate of interest is 10% compounded annually, what is the size of the quarterly payments?

30. Sally contributed $500.00 every six months for fourteen years into an RRSP earning interest at 6.5% compounded semi-annually. Seven years after the last contribution, Sally converted the RRSP into an RRIF that is to pay her equal quarterly amounts for sixteen years. If the first payment is due three months after the conversion into the RRIF and interest on the RRIF is 7% compounded quarterly, how much will Sally receive every three months?

31. Wendy deposited $500.00 into an RRSP every three months for 25 years. Upon her retirement she converted the RRSP balance into an RRIF that is to pay her equal quarterly amounts for twenty years. If the first payment is due three months after her retirement and interest is 9% compounded quarterly, how much will Wendy receive every three months?

32. Kelly Farms bought a tractor priced at $10 500.00 on February 1. Kelly agreed to make monthly payments of $475.00 beginning December 1 of the same year. For how long will Kelly Farms have to make these payments if interest is 10.5% compounded monthly?

33. Okanagan Vineyards borrowed $75 000.00 on a five-year promissory note. It agreed to make payments of $6000.00 every three months starting on the date of maturity. If interest is 14% compounded quarterly, for how long will the company have to make the payments?

34. Preferred shares of Western Oil paying a quarterly dividend are to be offered at $55.65 per share. If money is worth 9% compounded semi-annually, what is the minimum quarterly dividend to make investment in such shares economically feasible?

35. A church congregation has raised $37 625.00 for future outreach work. If the money is invested in a fund paying 7% compounded quarterly, what annual payment can be made from the fund to its mission if the first payment is to be made four years from the date of investment in the fund?

36. For how long must $75.00 be deposited at the end of each month to accumulate to $8500.00 at 6% compounded quarterly?

37. Over what period of time will RRSP contributions of $1350.00 made at the beginning of each year amount to $125 000.00 if interest is 7% compounded quarterly?

38. A $60 000.00 mortgage is amortized by making monthly payments of $618.19. If interest is 12.5% compounded semi-annually, what is the term of the mortgage?

39. A lease contract valued at $50 000.00 requires semi-annual payments of $5200.00. If the first payment is due at the date of signing the contract and interest is 9% compounded monthly, what is the term of the lease?

40. A contract is signed requiring payments of $750.00 at the end of every three months for eight years.

    a) How much is the cash value of the contract if money is worth 10.5% compounded quarterly?

    b) If the first three payments are missed, how much would have to be paid after one year to bring the contract up to date?

c) If, because of the missed payments, the contract has to be paid out at the end of one year, how much money is needed?

d) How much of the total interest paid is due to the missed payments?

41. Aaron deposited $900.00 every six months for twenty years into a fund paying 5.5% compounded semi-annually. Five years after the last deposit he converted the existing balance in the fund into an ordinary annuity paying him equal monthly payments for fifteen years. If interest on the annuity is 6% compounded monthly, what is the size of the monthly payment he will receive?

42. $8000.00 was invested at a fixed rate of 12.5% compounded semi-annually for seven years. After seven years, the fund was converted into an ordinary annuity paying $750.00 per month. If interest on the annuity was 12% compounded monthly, what was the term of the annuity?

43. A savings plan requiring quarterly deposits of $400.00 for twenty years provides for a lump sum payment of $92 000.00 just after the last deposit has been made.

a) What is the effective rate of interest on the savings plan?

b) If, instead of the lump sum, monthly ordinary annuity payments of $1350.00 may be accepted at the same nominal rate of interest (correct to two decimals) but compounded monthly, what is the term of the annuity?

44. Mrs. Ball deposits $550.00 at the beginning of every three months. Starting three months after the last deposit, she intends to withdraw $3500.00 every three months for fourteen years. If interest is 8% compounded quarterly, for how long must Mrs. Ball make deposits?

45. Terry saves $50.00 at the beginning of each month for sixteen years. Beginning one month after his last deposit, he intends to withdraw $375.00 per month. If interest is 6% compounded monthly, for how long can Terry make withdrawals?

46. An annuity provides payments of $3600.00 at the end of every three months. The annuity is bought for $33 500.00 and payments are deferred for twelve years. If interest is 12% compounded monthly, for how long will payments be received?

47. A retirement gratuity of $25 000.00 is invested in an income averaging annuity paying $1400.00 every three months. If the interest is 11.5% compounded semi-annually and the first payment is due in one year, for how long will payments be received?

SELF-TEST

1. A sum of money is deposited at the end of every month for ten years at 7.5% compounded monthly. After the last deposit, interest for the account is to be 6% compounded quarterly and the account is to be paid out by quarterly payments of $4800.00 over six years. What is the size of the monthly deposit?

2. Compute the nominal annual rate of interest on a loan of $48 000.00 repaid in semi-annual instalments of $4000.00 in ten years.

3. A loan of $14 400.00 is to be repaid in quarterly payments of $600.00. How many payments are required to repay the loan at 10.5% compounded quarterly?

4. A mortgage of $95 000.00 is to be amortized by monthly payments over twenty-five years. If the payments are made at the end of each month and interest is 8.5% compounded semi-annually, what is the size of the monthly payments?

5. Sara Eng wants to withdraw $3000.00 at the beginning of every three months for thirty years starting at the date of her retirement. If she retires in twenty years and interest is 10% compounded quarterly, how much must Ms. Eng deposit into an account every month for the next twenty years starting now?

6. What is the nominal annual rate of interest charged on a lease valued at $3840.00 if payments of $240.00 are made at the beginning of every three months for six years?

7. The amount of $57 426.00 is invested at 12% compounded monthly for six years. After the initial six-year period, the balance in the fund is converted into an annuity due paying $5600.00 every three months. If interest on the annuity is 10.5% compounded quarterly, what is the term of the annuity in months?

8. The amount of $46 200.00 is invested at 9.5% compounded quarterly for four years. After four years the balance in the fund is converted into an annuity. If interest on the annuity is 6.5% compounded semi-annually and payments are made at the end of every six months for seven years, what is the size of the payments?

9. An obligation of $5000.00 due in four years is to be settled by four equal payments due today, fifteen months from now, twenty-seven months from now, and thirty-six months from now respectively. What is the size of the equal payments at 9.5% compounded quarterly?

10. Tim bought a boat valued at $10 104.00 on the instalment plan. He made equal semi-annual payments for five years. If the first payment is due on the date of purchase and interest is 10.5% compounded semi-annually, what is the size of the semi-annual payments?

11. Deposits of $1200.00 made at the beginning of every three months amount to $40 000.00 after six years. What is the effective annual rate of interest earned by the deposits if interest is compounded quarterly?

12. A $45 000.00 mortgage is repaid in twenty years by making monthly payments of $486.44. What is the nominal annual rate of interest compounded semi-annually?

13. For how long would you have to deposit $491.00 at the end of every three months to accumulate $20 000.00 at 6.0% compounded monthly?

14. What is the size of semi-annual deposits that will accumulate to $67 200.00 after eight years at 6.5% compounded semi-annually?

15. Sue contributed $800.00 every three months for five years into an RRSP earning 7.5% compounded quarterly. Six years after the last contribution, she converted the RRSP into an annuity that is to pay her monthly for thirty years. If the first payment is due one month after the conversion into the annuity and interest on the annuity is 5.4% compounded monthly, how much will Sue receive every month?

16. Eden would like to receive $3000.00 at the end of every six months for seven years after her retirement. If she retires ten years from now and interest is 6.5% compounded semi-annually, how much must she deposit into an account every six months starting now?

17. J.J. deposited $1680.00 at the beginning of every six months for eight years into a fund paying 5.5% compounded semi-annually. Fifteen years after the first deposit, he converted the existing balance into an annuity paying him equal monthly payments for twenty years. If the payments are made at the end of each month and interest is 6% compounded monthly, what is the size of the monthly payments?

CHALLENGE PROBLEMS

1. A regular deposit of $100.00 is made at the beginning of each year for twenty years. Simple interest is calculated at i% per year for the twenty years. At the end of the twenty-year period, the total interest in the account is $840.00. Suppose that interest of i% compounded annually had been paid instead. How much interest would have been in the account at the end of the twenty years?

2. A loan of $5600.00 is to be repaid at 9% compounded annually by making ten payments at the end of each quarter. Each of the last six payments is two times the amount of each of the first four payments. What is the size of each payment?

CASE STUDY 13.1 CASH-BACK OPTIONS

Hari Puri wants to buy a new car. He has noticed that a number of car manu-facturers are offering special deals to sell off this year's cars before next year's new models arrive. Hari's local car dealer is advertising 3.7% financing for a full 48 months (i.e., 3.7% compounded monthly) or up to $1750.00 cash back on selected vehicles.

The car that Hari wants to buy costs $18 550.00 including taxes and delivery charges. This car qualifies for $1400.00 cash back if Hari pays cash for the car. Hari has a steady job and a good credit rating, so he is confident that his bank would arrange a car loan for the full price of any car he chooses. Alternatively, Hari could take the dealer financing offered at 3.7% for 48 months.

To compare these two financing options, Hari wants to see which option requires the lower monthly payment. He knows he can use annuity formulae to calculate the monthly payments.

QUESTIONS

1. Suppose Hari buys the car on July 1. What monthly payment must Hari make if he chooses the dealer's 3.7% financing option and pays off the loan over 48 months? (Assume he makes each monthly payment at the end of the month and his first payment is due on July 31.)

2. Suppose the bank offers Hari a 48-month loan with the interest compounded monthly and the payments due at the end of each month. If Hari accepts the bank loan, he can get $1400.00 cash back on this car.

    Hari works out a method to calculate the bank rate of interest required to make bank financing the same cost as dealer financing. First, calculate the monthly rate of interest that would make the monthly bank payments equal to the monthly dealer payments. Then, calculate the effective rate of interest represented by the monthly compounded rate. If the financing from the bank is at a lower rate of interest compounded monthly, choose the bank financing. The reason is that the monthly payments for the bank's financing would be lower than the monthly payments for the dealer's 3.7% financing.

    a) How much money would Hari have to borrow from the bank to pay cash for this car?

    b) Using the method above, calculate the effective annual rate of interest and the nominal annual rate of interest required to make the monthly payments for bank financing exactly the same as for dealer financing.

3. Suppose Hari decides to explore the costs of financing a more expensive car. The more expensive car costs $26 590.00 in total and qualifies for 3.7% dealer financing for 48 months or $1750.00 cash back. What is the highest effective annual rate of interest at which Hari should borrow from the bank instead of using the dealer's 3.7% financing?

CASE STUDY 13.2 FITNESS FINANCES

Jocelyn is planning to open Fitness Fundamentals, a new health and fitness club. She must decide what to charge for each type of membership and what payment options to offer.

Jocelyn plans to offer two types of memberships. The General membership allows members to use all facilities, and it provides a simple locker room. The Health Club membership allows members to use all facilities, and it provides towels, shower supplies, and a sauna. When members pay for their annual membership when they join, the fee is $450.00 for the General membership and $750.00 for the Health Club membership.

QUESTIONS

1. Jocelyn wants to offer members the option of paying their annual membership fees in twelve equal monthly instalments. The first instalment would be due on the day of joining.

   a) To the nearest dollar how much should Jocelyn charge General members monthly if she wants to make interest of 15% compounded monthly?

   b) To the nearest dollar how much should she charge Health Club members monthly if she wants to make interest of 20% compounded monthly?

2. Jocelyn knows that many of the Health Club members will be executives whose companies will pay for their memberships. Many companies prefer to make quarterly payments for annual memberships. For this reason, Jocelyn decides to offer a quarterly payment option. The first instalment would be due on the day of joining. To the nearest dollar how much should Jocelyn charge Health Club members quarterly if she wants to make interest of 20% compounded monthly?

3. As an opening special, Jocelyn wants to offer all members who join during the opening week three free months of membership. To calculate the nominal rate of interest she would earn on these opening special memberships, Jocelyn will add the payments made for the year for a membership, then spread the total payments equally over fifteen months as if the payment period were fifteen months. (For example, if the total monthly payments were 12 × $X, under this scheme Jocelyn would calculate the new monthly payments as 12 × $X/15.) She would then calculate the nominal rate of interest earned on these new monthly payments over the fifteen-month membership period.

   a) What is the nominal rate of interest earned on the opening special for the General membership with the monthly payment option?

   b) What is the nominal rate of interest earned on the opening special for the Health Club membership with the monthly payment option?

   c) What is the nominal rate of interest earned on the opening special for the Health Club membership with the quarterly payment option?

SUMMARY OF FORMULAE

No new formulae were introduced in this chapter. However, some of the formulae introduced in Chapters 11 and 12 have been used and are listed below.

Formula 11.1

$$S_n = R\left[\frac{(1 + i)^n - 1}{i}\right]$$

Formula 11.2

$$A_n = R\left[\frac{1 - (1 + i)^{-n}}{i}\right]$$

Formula 11.3

$$S_{nc} = R\left[\frac{(1 + f)^n - 1}{f}\right]$$

where $f = (1 + i)^c - 1$

Formula 11.4

$$A_{nc} = R\left[\frac{1 - (1 + f)^{-n}}{f}\right]$$

where $f = (1 + i)^c - 1$

Formula 12.1

$$S_n(\text{due}) = R(1 + i)\left[\frac{(1 + i)^n - 1}{i}\right]$$

Formula 12.2

$$A_n(\text{due}) = R(1 + i)\left[\frac{1 - (1 + i)^{-n}}{i}\right]$$

Formula 12.3

$$S_{nc}(\text{due}) = R(1 + f)\left[\frac{(1 + f)^n - 1}{f}\right]$$

where $f = (1 + i)^c - 1$

Formula 12.4

$$A_{nc}(\text{due}) = R(1 + f)\left[\frac{1 - (1 + f)^{-n}}{f}\right]$$

where $f - (1 + i)^c - 1$

14 Amortization of Loans, Including Residential Mortgages

When budgeting for the future, businesses often consider arranging various loans. If you know the interest rate, you might want to calculate what the loan will cost over various time periods. You can do this by using the formulae for annuities that you are already very familiar with. By knowing what the size of your equal loan payments would be, you can make an informed decision about what loans to arrange.

One of the largest loans most of us will ever have is a mortgage on a house or a condominium. Given the monthly payments, we can calculate the amount of each payment that goes toward principal and the amount that goes toward interest. This information can help us decide what we can afford to buy and how quickly we can pay off the mortgage.

Introduction

Amortization refers to the repayment of interest-bearing debts by a series of payments, usually equal in size, made at equal intervals of time. The periodic payments, when equal in size, form an annuity whose present value is equivalent to the original loan principal. Mortgages and many consumer loans are repaid by this method. An amortization schedule shows the allocation of each payment to first cover the interest due and then reduce the principal.

OBJECTIVES

Upon completing this chapter, you will be able to do the following:

1. Perform computations associated with amortization of debts involving simple annuities, including the size of the periodic payments, outstanding balance, interest due, and principal repaid, and construct complete or partial amortization schedules.
2. Perform computations as in Objective 1 associated with the amortization of debts when the payments form general annuities, and construct complete or partial amortization schedules.
3. Find the size of the final payment when all payments except the final payment are equal in size.
4. Compute the effective interest rate for fixed-rate residential mortgages.

5. Compute the periodic payments for fixed-rate mortgages and for demand mortgages.
6. Distinguish between regular mortgage payments and rounded mortgage payments.
7. Create statements for various types of residential mortgages.

14.1 AMORTIZATION INVOLVING SIMPLE ANNUITIES

A. Finding the periodic payment

What is **amortization**? An interest-bearing debt is *amortized* if both principal and interest are repaid by a series of equal payments made at equal intervals of time.

The basic problem in amortizing a debt is finding the size of the periodic payment. If the payment interval and the interest conversion period are equal in length, the problem involves finding the periodic payment for a simple annuity. Since debts are generally repaid by making payments at the end of the payment interval, the method and formula for ordinary simple annuities apply.

$$A_n = R\left[\frac{1 - (1 + i)^{-n}}{i}\right]$$ —————— Formula 11.2

EXAMPLE 14.1A   A debt of $5000.00 with interest at 12% compounded annually is to be repaid by equal payments at the end of each year for six years. What is the size of the annual payments?

Solution

FIGURE 14.1   **Graphic Representation of Method of Solution and Data**

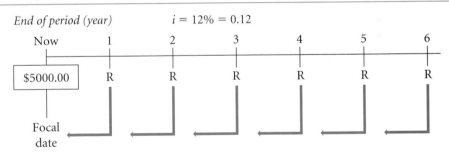

As Figure 14.1 shows, the equal annual payments (designated by R) form an ordinary simple annuity in which

$A_n = 5000.000$; $n = 6$; $i = 12\% = 0.12$

Using "now" as the focal date, you can find the value of the annual payment R using Formula 11.2.

$$5000.00 = R\left(\frac{1 - 1.12^{-6}}{0.12}\right)$$ —————— using Formula 11.2

$$5000.00 = R\,(4.1114073)$$
$$R = \$1216.13$$

Programmed solution

$$0 \boxed{\text{FV}} \quad 5000 \boxed{\text{PV}} \quad 12 \boxed{\%i} \quad 6 \boxed{\text{N}} \quad \boxed{\text{CPT}} \boxed{\text{PMT}} \boxed{1216.1286}$$

The annual payment is $1216.13.

EXAMPLE 14.1B   A loan of $8000.00 made at 6% compounded monthly is amortized over five years by making equal monthly payments.

(i) What is the size of the monthly payment?

(ii) What is the total amount paid to amortize the loan?

(iii) What is the cost of financing?

Solution   (i) $A_n = 8000.00; \quad n = 5(12) = 60; \quad i = \dfrac{6\%}{12} = 0.5\%$

$$8000.00 = R\left(\frac{1 - 1.005^{-60}}{0.005}\right) \qquad \text{using Formula 11.2}$$

$$8000.00 = R(51.7255607)$$
$$R = \$154.66$$

Programmed solution

$$0 \boxed{\text{FV}} \quad 8000 \boxed{\text{PV}} \quad 0.5 \boxed{\%i} \quad 60 \boxed{\text{N}} \quad \boxed{\text{CPT}} \boxed{\text{PMT}} \boxed{154.66242}$$

The monthly payment is $154.66.

(ii) The total amount paid is 60(154.66) = $9279.60.

(iii) The cost of financing is 9279.60 − 8000.00 = $1279.60.

B. Amortization schedules

As previously discussed in Section 8.8, **amortization schedules** show in detail how a debt is repaid. Such schedules normally show the payment number (or payment date), the amount paid, the interest paid, the principal repaid, and the outstanding debt balance.

1. Amortization Schedule When All Payments Are Equal (Blended Payments)

When all payments are equal, you must first determine the size of the periodic payment as shown in Examples 14.1A and 14.1B.

EXAMPLE 14.1C   A debt of $5000.00 is amortized by making equal payments at the end of every three months for two years. If interest is 8% compounded quarterly, construct an amortization schedule.

Solution

STEP I   Determine the size of the quarterly payments.

$$A_n = 5000.00; \quad n = 4(2) = 8; \quad i = \frac{8\%}{4} = 2.0\%$$

$$5000.00 = R\left(\frac{1 - 1.02^{-8}}{0.02}\right)$$

$$5000.00 = R(7.3254813)$$
$$R = \$682.55$$

Programmed solution

$$0 \boxed{\text{FV}} \ 5000 \boxed{\text{PV}} \ 2.0 \boxed{\%i} \ 8 \boxed{\text{N}} \ \boxed{\text{CPT}} \ \boxed{\text{PMT}} \ \boxed{682.54901}$$

STEP 2   Construct the amortization schedule as shown below.

Payment Number	Amount Paid	Interest Paid $i = 0.02$	Principal Repaid	Outstanding Principal Balance
0				5000.00
1	682.55	100.00	582.55	4417.45
2	682.55	88.35	594.20	3823.25
3	682.55	76.47	606.08	3217.17
4	682.55	64.34	618.21	2598.96
5	682.55	51.98	630.57	1968.39
6	682.55	39.37	643.18	1325.21
7	682.55	26.50	656.05	669.16
8	682.54	13.38	669.16	0.00
TOTAL	5460.39	460.39	5000.00	

Explanations regarding the construction of the amortization schedule

1. Payment number 0 is used to introduce the initial balance of the loan.
2. The interest included in the first payment is $0.02 \times 5000.00 = \$100.00$. Since the amount paid is \$682.55, the amount available for repayment of principal is $682.55 - 100.00 = \$582.55$. The outstanding principal balance after the first payment is $5000.00 - 582.55 = \$4417.45$.
3. The interest included in the second payment is $0.02 \times 4417.45 = \$88.35$. Since the amount paid is \$682.55, the amount available for repayment of principal is $682.55 - 88.35 = \$594.20$. The outstanding principal is $4417.45 - 594.20 = \$3823.25$.
4. Computation of interest, principal repaid, and outstanding balance for payments 3 to 7 are made in a similar manner.
5. The last payment of \$682.54 is slightly different from the other payments as a result of rounding in the amount paid or the interest paid. To allow for such rounding

errors, the last payment is computed by adding the interest due in the last payment (0.02 × 669.16 = $13.38) to the outstanding balance: 669.16 + 13.38 = $682.54.

6. The three totals provide useful information and can be used as a check on the accuracy of the schedule.

   (a) The total principal repaid must equal the original outstanding balance;

   (b) the total amount paid is the periodic payment times the number of such payments plus/minus any adjustment in the last payment, 682.55 × 8 − 0.01 = 5460.40 − 0.01 = $5460.39.

   (c) the total interest paid is the difference between the amount paid and the original principal, 5460.39 − 5000.00 = $460.39.

2. Amortization Schedule When All Payments Except the Final Payment Are Equal

When the size of the periodic payment is determined by agreement, usually because it is a convenient round figure rather than a computed blended payment, the size of the final payment will probably be different from the preceding agreed-upon payments. This final payment is obtained in the amortization schedule by adding the interest due on the outstanding balance to the outstanding balance.

This type of loan repayment schedule has been illustrated and explained in Section 8.8. The following example is included for review.

EXAMPLE 14.1D Sheridan Service borrowed $15 000.00 from Peel Community Credit Union at 10% compounded quarterly. The loan agreement requires payment of $2500.00 at the end of every three months. Construct an amortization schedule.

Solution $i = \dfrac{10\%}{4} = 2.5\% = 0.025$

Payment Number	Amount Paid	Interest Paid $i = 0.025$	Principal Repaid	Outstanding Principal Balance
0				15 000.00
1	2 500.00	375.00	2 125.00	12 875.00
2	2 500.00	321.88	2 178.12	10 696.88
3	2 500.00	267.42	2 232.58	8 464.30
4	2 500.00	211.61	2 288.39	6 175.91
5	2 500.00	154.40	2 345.60	3 830.31
6	2 500.00	95.76	2 404.24	1 426.07
7	1 461.72	35.65	1 426.07	0.00
TOTAL	16 461.72	1461.72	15 000.00	

Note: After payment number 6, the outstanding principal is less than the agreed-upon payment. When this happens, the final payment will be the outstanding balance plus the interest due on the outstanding balance.

1426.07 + 1426.07 × 0.025 = 1426.07 + 35.65 = $1461.72

C. Finding the outstanding principal balance

For various reasons, such as early partial repayment or early full repayment or refinancing, either the borrower or the lender needs to know the outstanding balance at a certain time. This can be done by checking the amortization schedule, if available, or by direct mathematical computation. This computation is also useful for checking the accuracy of the schedule as it is developed.

1. Finding the Outstanding Principal When All Payments Are Equal

EXAMPLE 14.1E For Example 14.1C, compute the outstanding balance just after the third payment has been made.

Solution The loan history showing the quarterly payments of $682.55 can be represented on a time diagram as shown in Figure 14.2.

FIGURE 14.2 Graphic Representation of Loan Payments

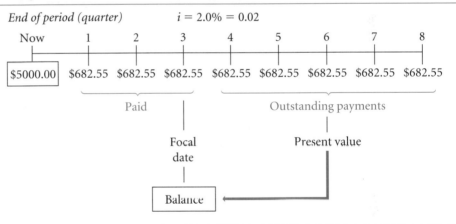

In the same way in which the original loan balance of $5000.00 equals the present value of the number of payments that are necessary to amortize the loan, the outstanding balance at the end of any payment interval just after a payment has been made is the present value of the outstanding payments.

$$\text{OUTSTANDING BALANCE} = \text{PRESENT VALUE OF THE OUTSTANDING PAYMENTS}$$

To answer this problem, use Formula 11.2. Since three of the eight payments have been made, five payments remain outstanding.

$$R = 682.55; \quad n = 5; \quad i = 2.0\% = 0.02$$

$$A_3 = 682.55\left(\frac{1 - 1.02^{-5}}{0.02}\right) \qquad \text{using Formula 11.2}$$

$$= 682.55(4.7134595)$$

$$= \$3217.17$$

Programmed solution

$$0 \;\boxed{\text{FV}}\; 682.55 \;\boxed{\text{PMT}}\; 2.0 \;\boxed{\%i}\; 5 \;\boxed{\text{N}}\; \boxed{\text{CPT}}\; \boxed{\text{PV}}\; \boxed{3217.1717}$$

The outstanding balance after the third payment is $3217.17.

Note: Any difference in the amortization schedule is due to rounding.

EXAMPLE 14.1F You borrow $7500.00 from a finance company at 13.5% compounded monthly. If the loan is amortized over five years, what is the loan balance after two years?

Solution First determine the size of the monthly payment.

$$A_n = 7500.00; \quad n = 5(12) = 60; \quad i = \frac{13.5\%}{12} = 1.125\% = 0.01125$$

$$7500.00 = R\left(\frac{1 - 1.01125^{-60}}{0.01125}\right)$$

$$7500.00 = R(43.459657)$$

$$R = \$172.57$$

Programmed solution

$$0 \;\boxed{\text{FV}}\; 7500 \;\boxed{\text{PV}}\; 1.125 \;\boxed{\%i}\; 60 \;\boxed{\text{N}}\; \boxed{\text{CPT}}\; \boxed{\text{PMT}}\; \boxed{172.57384}$$

Now determine the balance after two years.

After two years, 24 of the 60 payments have been made; 36 payments remain outstanding.

$$R = 172.57; \quad n = 36; \quad i = 1.125\%$$

$$A_{24} = 172.57\left(\frac{1 - 1.01125^{-36}}{0.01125}\right)$$

$$= 172.57(29.467851)$$

$$= \$5085.27$$

Programmed solution

$$172.57 \;\boxed{\text{PMT}}\; 0 \;\boxed{\text{FV}}\; 1.125 \;\boxed{\%i}\; 36 \;\boxed{\text{N}}\; \boxed{\text{CPT}}\; \boxed{\text{PV}}\; \boxed{5085.2671}$$

The outstanding balance after two years is $5085.27.

The method used in Examples 14.1E and 14.1F is called the **prospective method** of finding the outstanding balance because it considers the future prospects of the debt—the payments that remain outstanding.

Alternatively, the outstanding balance can be found by the **retrospective method**, which considers the payments that have been made. This method finds the outstanding balance by deducting the accumulated value of the payments that have been made from the accumulated value of the original debt.

$$\text{OUTSTANDING BALANCE} = \begin{array}{l} \text{ACCUMULATED VALUE OF THE ORIGINAL DEBT} - \\ \text{ACCUMULATED VALUE OF THE PAYMENTS MADE} \end{array}$$

For Example 14.1E
The accumulated value of the original debt at the end of three payment intervals

$$S = 5000.00(1.02^3) \hspace{2cm} \text{using Formula 9.1A}$$
$$= \$5000.00(1.061208)$$
$$= \$5306.04$$

The accumulated value of the payments made

$$S_3 = 682.55\left(\frac{1.02^3 - 1}{0.02}\right)$$
$$= 682.55(3.0604000)$$
$$= \$2088.88$$

Programmed solution

$$0 \boxed{PMT} \; 5000 \boxed{PV} \; 2 \boxed{\%i} \; 3 \boxed{N} \; \boxed{CPT} \; \boxed{FV} \quad \boxed{5306.04}$$

$$0 \boxed{PV} \; 682.55 \boxed{PMT} \; 2 \boxed{\%i} \; 3 \boxed{N} \; \boxed{CPT} \; \boxed{FV} \quad \boxed{2088.876}$$

The outstanding balance is $5306.04 - 2088.88 = \$3217.16$.

For Example 14.1F
The accumulated value of the debt after two years (24 payments)

$$S = 7500.00(1.01125^{24})$$
$$= 7500.00(1.3079912)$$
$$= \$9809.93$$

The accumulated value of the 24 payments made

$$S_{24} = 172.57\left(\frac{1.01125^{24} - 1}{0.01125}\right)$$
$$= 172.57(27.376998)$$
$$= \$4724.45$$

Programmed solution

$$0 \boxed{PMT} \; 7500 \boxed{PV} \; 1.125 \boxed{\%i} \; 24 \boxed{N} \; \boxed{CPT} \; \boxed{FV} \quad \boxed{9809.9342}$$

$$0 \boxed{PV} \; 172.57 \boxed{PMT} \; 1.125 \boxed{\%i} \; 24 \boxed{N} \; \boxed{CPT} \; \boxed{FV} \quad \boxed{4724.4485}$$

The outstanding balance is $9809.93 - 4724.45 = \$5085.48$.

Note: The difference in the two methods—$5085.48 versus $5085.27—is due to rounding in the payment.

Because the prospective method is more direct, it is preferred when finding the outstanding balance of loans repaid by instalments that are all equal.

2. Finding the Outstanding Balance When All Payments Except the Final Payment Are Equal

When the last payment is different from the other payments, the retrospective method for finding the outstanding balance is preferable.

EXAMPLE 14.1G For Example 14.1D, compute the outstanding balance after four payments.

Solution The accumulated value of the original debt after four payments

$$S = 15\,000.00(1.025^4)$$
$$= 15\,000.00(1.1038129)$$
$$= \$16\,557.19$$

The accumulated value of the four payments

$$S_4 = 2500.00\left(\frac{1.025^4 - 1}{0.025}\right)$$
$$= 2500.00(4.1525156)$$
$$= \$10\,381.29$$

Programmed solution

0 PMT $15\,000$ PV 2.5 %i 4 N CPT FV $\boxed{16\,557.193}$

0 PV 2500 PMT 2.5 %i 4 N CPT FV $\boxed{10\,381.289}$

The outstanding balance is $16\,557.19 - 10\,381.29 = \$6175.90$.

EXAMPLE 14.1H A debt of $25\,000.00 with interest at 14% compounded semi-annually is amortized by making payments of $2000.00 at the end of every six months. Determine the outstanding balance after five years.

Solution $A_n = P = 25\,000.00; \quad i = \dfrac{14\%}{2} = 7\% = 0.07$

The accumulated value of the original principal after five years

$$S = 25\,000.00(1.07^{10})$$
$$= 25\,000.00(1.9671514)$$
$$= \$49\,178.78$$

The accumulated value of the first ten payments

$$S_{10} = 2000.00\left(\frac{1.07^{10} - 1}{0.07}\right)$$
$$= 2000.00(13.816448)$$
$$= \$27\,632.90$$

Programmed solution

0 [PMT] 25 000 [PV] 7 [%i] 10 [N] [CPT] [FV] [49 178.784]

0 [PV] 2000 [PMT] 7 [%i] 10 [N] [CPT] [FV] [27 632.896]

The outstanding balance after five years is 49 178.78 − 27 632.90 = $21 545.88.

D. Finding the interest paid and the principal repaid; constructing partial amortization schedules

Apart from computing the outstanding balance at any one time, all the other information contained in an amortization schedule, such as interest paid and principal repaid, can also be computed.

EXAMPLE 14.1I For Example 14.1C, compute

(i) the interest paid by the fifth payment;

(ii) the principal repaid by the fifth payment.

Solution (i) The interest due for any given payment period is based on the outstanding balance at the beginning of the period. This balance is the same as the outstanding balance at the end of the previous payment period.

To find the interest paid by the fifth payment, we need to know the outstanding balance after the fourth payment.

$$A_4 = 682.55\left(\frac{1 - 1.02^{-4}}{0.02}\right)$$
$$= 682.55(3.8077287)$$
$$= \$2598.97$$

Programmed solution

0 [FV] 682.55 [PMT] 2 [%i] 4 [N] [CPT] [PV] [2598.9652]

Interest for Payment Period 5 is 2598.97(0.02) = $51.98.

(ii) Principal repaid = Amount paid − Interest paid
= 682.55 − 51.98
= $630.57

EXAMPLE 14.1J Jackie Kim borrowed $6000.00 from her trust company at 9% compounded monthly. The loan is amortized over five years.

(i) What is the interest included in the 20th payment?

(ii) What is the principal repaid by the 36th payment?

(iii) Construct a partial amortization schedule showing the details of the first three payments, the 20th payment, the 36th payment, and the last three payments, and determine the totals of amount paid, interest paid, and principal repaid.

Solution $A_n = 6000.00;$ $n = 5(12) = 60;$ $i = \dfrac{9\%}{12} = 0.75\% = 0.0075$

$$6000.00 = R\left(\frac{1 - 1.0075^{-60}}{0.0075}\right)$$
$$6000.00 = R(48.173374)$$
$$R = \$124.55$$

Programmed solution

0 [FV] 6000 [PV] 0.75 [%i] 60 [N] [CPT] [PMT] ⟨ 124.55014 ⟩

(i) The outstanding balance after the 19th payment,

$$A_{19} = 124.55\left(\frac{1 - 1.0075^{-41}}{0.0075}\right)$$

$$= 124.55(35.183064)$$
$$= \$4382.05$$

Programmed solution

0 [FV] 124.55 [PMT] 0.75 [%i] 41 [N] [CPT] [PV] ⟨ 4382.0506 ⟩

The interest paid by the 20th payment is $4382.05(0.0075) = \$32.86$.

(ii) The outstanding balance after the 35th payment,

$$A_{35} = 124.55\left(\frac{1 - 1.0075^{-25}}{0.0075}\right)$$

$$= 124.55(22.718755)$$
$$= \$2829.62$$

Programmed solution

0 [FV] 124.55 [PMT] 0.75 [%i] 25 [N] [CPT] [PV] ⟨ 2829.6208 ⟩

The interest included in Payment 36 is $2829.62(0.0075) = \$21.22$.
The principal repaid by Payment 36 is $124.55 - 21.22 = \$103.33$.

(iii) We can develop the first three payments of the amortization schedule in the usual way. To show the details of the 20th payment, we need to know the outstanding balance after 19 payments (computed in part (i)). For the 36th payment, we need to know the outstanding balance after 35 payments (computed in part (ii)). Since there are 60 payments, the last three payments are Payments 58, 59, and 60. To show the details of these payments, we must determine the outstanding balance after Payment 57.

$$A_{57} = 124.55\left(\frac{1 - 1.0075^{-3}}{0.0075}\right)$$
$$= 124.55(2.9555562)$$
$$= \$368.11$$

Programmed solution

0 [FV] 124.55 [PMT] 0.75 [%i] 3 [N] [CPT] [PV] [368.11449]

Partial amortization schedule

Payment Number	Amount Paid	Interest Paid $i = 0.0075$	Principal Repaid	Outstanding Principal Balance
0				6000.00
1	124.55	45.00	79.55	5920.45
2	124.55	44.40	80.15	5840.30
3	124.55	43.80	80.75	5759.55
•	•	•	•	•
•	•	•	•	•
19	•	•	•	4382.05
20	124.55	32.87	91.68	4290.37
•	•	•	•	•
•	•	•	•	•
35	•	•	•	2829.62
36	124.55	21.22	103.33	2726.29
•	•	•	•	•
•	•	•	•	•
57	•	•	•	368.11
58	124.55	2.76	121.79	246.32
59	124.55	1.85	122.70	123.62
60	124.55	0.93	123.62	0.00
TOTAL	7473.00	1473.00	6000.00	

Note: The total principal repaid must be $6000.00; the total amount paid is $124.55(60) = \$7473.00$; the total interest paid is $7473.00 - 6000.00 = \$1473.00$.

EXAMPLE 14.1K The Erin Construction Company borrowed $75 000.00 at 14% compounded quarterly to buy construction equipment. Payments of $3500.00 are to be made at the end of every three months.

(i) Determine the principal repaid in the 16th payment.

(ii) Construct a partial amortization schedule showing the details of the first three payments, the 16th payment, the last three payments, and the totals.

Solution   (i) Since the quarterly payments are not computed blended payments, the last payment will probably be different from the preceding equal payments. Use the retrospective method for finding the outstanding balance.

$$P = 75\,000.00; \quad R = 3500.00; \quad i = \frac{14\%}{4} = 3.5\% = 0.035$$

The accumulated value of the original principal after the 15th payment,

$$\begin{aligned} S &= 75\,000.00(1.035^{15}) \\ &= 75\,000.00(1.6753488) \\ &= \$125\,651.16 \end{aligned}$$

Programmed solution

0 PMT 75 000 PV 3.5 %i 15 N CPT FV 125 651.16

The accumulated value of the first 15 payments,

$$S_{15} = 3500.00\left(\frac{1.035^{15} - 1}{0.035}\right)$$

$$S_{15} = 3500.00(19.295681)$$
$$S_{15} = \$67\,534.88$$

Programmed solution

0 PV 3500 PMT 3.5 %i 15 N CPT FV 67 534.883

The outstanding principal after the 15th payment
$$= 125\,651.16 - 67\,534.88$$
$$= \$58\,116.28$$

The interest included in the 16th payment is $58\,116.28(0.035) = \$2034.07$. The principal repaid by the 16th payment is $3500.00 - 2034.07 = \$1465.93$.

(ii) To show details of the last three payments, we need to know the number of payments required to amortize the loan principal.

$$A_n = 75\,000.00; \quad R = 3500.00; \quad i = 3.5\%$$

$$75\,000.00 = 3500.00\left(\frac{1 - 1.035^{-n}}{0.035}\right)$$

$$\begin{aligned} 0.75 &= 1 - 1.035^{-n} \\ 1.035^{-n} &= 0.25 \\ -n\ln 1.035 &= \ln 0.25 \\ -n(0.0344014) &= -1.3862944 \\ n &= 40.297584 \end{aligned}$$

Programmed solution

0 FV 75 000 PV 3500 PMT 3.5 %i CPT N 40.3

41 payments (40 payments of $3500.00 each plus a final payment) are required. This means the amortization schedule should show details of Payments 39, 40, and 41. To do so, we need to know the outstanding balance after 38 payments. The accumulated value of the original loan principal after 38 payments

$$S = 75\,000.00(1.035^{38})$$
$$= 75\,000.00(3.6960113)$$
$$= \$277\,200.85$$

Programmed solution

0 $\boxed{\text{PMT}}$ 75 000 $\boxed{\text{PV}}$ 3.5 $\boxed{\%i}$ 38 $\boxed{\text{N}}$ $\boxed{\text{CPT}}$ $\boxed{\text{FV}}$ $\boxed{277\,200.85}$

The accumulated value of the first 38 payments

$$S_{38} = 3500.00\left(\frac{1.035^{38} - 1}{0.035}\right)$$
$$= 3500.00(77.028895)$$
$$= \$269\,601.13$$

Programmed solution

0 $\boxed{\text{PV}}$ 3500 $\boxed{\text{PMT}}$ 3.5 $\boxed{\%i}$ 38 $\boxed{\text{N}}$ $\boxed{\text{CPT}}$ $\boxed{\text{FV}}$ $\boxed{269\,601.13}$

The outstanding balance after the 38th payment

$$= 277\,200.85 - 269\,601.13$$
$$= \$7599.72$$

Partial amortization schedule

Payment Number	Amount Paid	Interest Paid $i = 0.035$	Principal Repaid	Outstanding Principal Balance
0				75 000.00
1	3 500.00	2 625.00	875.00	74 125.00
2	3 500.00	2 594.38	905.62	73 219.38
3	3 500.00	2 562.68	937.32	72 282.06
•	•	•	•	•
•	•	•	•	•
•	•	•	•	•
15	•	•	•	58 116.28
16	3 500.00	2 034.07	1 465.93	56 650.35
•	•	•	•	•
•	•	•	•	•
•	•	•	•	•
38	•	•	•	7 599.72
39	3 500.00	265.99	3 234.01	4 365.71
40	3 500.00	152.80	3 347.20	1 018.51
41	1 054.16	35.65	1 018.51	0.00
TOTAL	141 054.16	66 054.16	75 000.00	

E. Computer application—Amortization schedule

As previously discussed in Section 8.8, spreadsheet programs like EXCEL and Lotus 1-2-3 make creating amortization schedules much easier. Once you create an amortization schedule in a spreadsheet, you can change the details of the loan and see immediately the effect of the change on the amortization schedule, without inputting all the formulae again. The procedures that follow are general instructions for creating the amortization schedule for Example 14.1C in a spreadsheet. The formulae in the spreadsheet diagram were created using EXCEL. Many other spreadsheet programs work in a similar way. Modify the procedures below if your spreadsheet program requires different instructions.

STEP 1   To create the amortization schedule for Example 14.1C in a spreadsheet, open a new spreadsheet file. Enter the labels, formulae, and numbers shown in the diagram below. To display the labels in row 1, you can widen the columns (as shown below) or shorten the labels. (In EXCEL, you can widen columns by going to the Format menu, choosing Column, then choosing Width. Type numbers until you get the column width you want. You can also widen columns by placing the cursor between columns until the cursor changes to double-pointed arrow. Drag the side of the column until you get the column width you want.)

To reduce inputting time and avoid inputting errors, copy as many formulae and numbers as possible within the spreadsheet. (To copy and paste formulae and numbers in EXCEL, click on the cell you want to copy. Go to the Edit menu and choose Copy. Then highlight the cell or cells you want to copy into. Go to the Edit menu and choose Paste. You can also copy formulae into the cells below a particular cell. Highlight the particular cell and all the cells below it that you want to fill. Go to the Edit menu, choose Fill, then choose Down.) The numbers and formulae in cells B3, C3, D3, and E3 can be copied into many of the cells that appear below these cells. Notice that the formulae in cells B3 and C3 include F2 and F4 respectively. In EXCEL, the $ symbols are required for *absolute cell references*. This is to make sure that when you copy the formulae in cells B3 and C3, the new formulae you create will always link to cells F2 and F4.

FIGURE 14.3

	A	B	C	D	E	F
					Workbook 1	
		A	B	C	D	E	F
1	Payment Number	Amount Paid	Interest Paid	Principal Repaid	Outstanding Principal Balance	
2	0				5000.00	682.55
3	1	= F2	= F4*E2	= B3−C3	= E2−D3	
4	2	= F2	= F4*E3	= B4−C4	= E3−D4	= 0.08/4
5	3	= F2	= F4*E4	= B5−C5	= E4−D5	
6	4	= F2	= F4*E5	= B6−C6	= E5−D6	
7	5	= F2	= F4*E6	= B7−C7	= E6−D7	
8	6	= F2	= F4*E7	= B8−C8	= E7−D8	
9	7	= F2	= F4*E8	= B9−C9	= E8−D9	
10	8	= C10+D10	= F4*E9	= E9	= E9−D10	
11	Totals	= SUM(B3:B10)	= SUM(C3:C10)	= SUM(D3:D10)		

STEP 2　To make the spreadsheet easier to read, format the numbers to two decimal places. (In EXCEL, change the format by highlighting cells B3 to E11. Go to the Format menu, choose Cells, then choose **0.00** from the Number section.)

STEP 3　Notice the formulae that are entered in cells B10, C10, and D10. They calculate the principal and interest required to pay off the outstanding loan balance. For an explanation of these amounts, refer to explanatory note 5 on page 579.

STEP 4　Notice the formulae that are entered in cells B11, C11, and D11. The sum in cell B11 must equal the total of all the payments made (seven payments of $682.55 each plus the final payment of $682.54). The sum in cell C11 is the total interest paid, and must be the difference between cells B11 (total payments made) and D11 (the principal). The sum in cell D11 is the total principal repaid and must equal the loan amount of $5000.00 entered in cell E2.

　　　Now that you have created the amortization schedule in a spreadsheet, you can change aspects of the loan and create a new amortization schedule quickly. After determining the size of the new payment, enter the new payment amount in cell F2. If the interest rate has changed, revise the formula in cell F4. If the term of the loan has changed, increase or decrease the number of rows in the spreadsheet as required.

Exercise 14.1

A. For each of the following six debts amortized by equal payments made at the end of each payment interval, compute (a) the size of the periodic payments; (b) the outstanding principal at the time indicated; (c) the interest paid; and (d) the principal repaid by the payment following the time indicated for finding the outstanding principal.

	Debt Principal	Repayment Period	Payment Interval	Interest Rate	Conversion Period	Outstanding Principal Required After:
1.	$12 000.00	8 years	3 months	12%	quarterly	20th payment
2.	$8000.00	5 years	1 month	15%	monthly	30th payment
3.	$15 000.00	10 years	6 months	8%	semi-annually	15th payment
4.	$9600.00	7 years	3 months	6%	quarterly	12th payment
5.	$5500.00	4 years	1 month	9%	monthly	14th payment
6.	$24 000.00	12 years	6 months	7%	semi-annually	8th payment

B. For each of the following four debts repaid by periodic payments as shown, compute (a) the number of payments required to amortize the debts; (b) the outstanding principal at the time indicated.

	Debt Principal	Debt Payment	Payment Interval	Interest Rate	Conversion Period	Outstanding Principal Required After:
1.	$12 000.00	$750.00	3 months	8%	quarterly	16th payment
2.	$7800.00	$175.00	1 month	12%	monthly	24th payment
3.	$21 000.00	$2000.00	6 months	9%	semi-annually	10th payment
4.	$15 000.00	$800.00	3 months	6%	quarterly	12th payment

C. Answer each of the following questions.

1. Mr. and Mrs. Good purchased a ski chalet for $36 000.00. They paid $4000.00 down and agreed to make equal payments at the end of every three months for fifteen years. Interest is 8% compounded quarterly.

   a) What size payment are the Goods making every three months?
   b) How much will they owe after ten years?
   c) How much will they have paid in total after fifteen years?
   d) How much interest will they pay in total?

2. A contractor's price for a new building was $96 000.00. Slade Inc., the buyers of the building, paid $12 000.00 down and financed the balance by making equal payments at the end of every six months for twelve years. Interest is 12% compounded semi-annually.

   a) What is the size of the semi-annual payment?
   b) How much will Slade Inc. owe after eight years?
   c) What is the total cost of the building for Slade Inc.?
   d) What is the total interest included in the payments?

3. A loan of $10 000.00 with interest at 10% compounded annually is to be amortized by equal payments at the end of each year for seven years. Find the size of the annual payments and construct an amortization schedule showing the total paid and the cost of financing.

4. A loan of $8000.00 is repaid by equal payments made at the end of every three months for two years. If interest is 14% compounded quarterly, find the size of the quarterly payments and construct an amortization schedule showing the total paid and the total cost of the loan.

5. Hansco borrowed $9200.00 paying interest at 13% compounded annually. If the loan is repaid by payments of $2000.00 made at the end of each year, construct an amortization schedule showing the total paid and the total interest paid.

6. Pinto Bros. are repaying a loan of $14 500.00 by making payments of $2600.00 at the end of every six months. If interest is 7% compounded semi-annually, construct an amortization schedule showing the total paid and the total cost of the loan.

7. For question 3, calculate the interest included in the fourth payment. Verify your answer by checking the amortization schedule.

8. For question 4, calculate the principal repaid by the fifth payment. Verify your answer by checking the amortization schedule.

9. For question 5, calculate the principal repaid by the fourth payment. Verify your answer by checking the amortization schedule.

10. For question 6, calculate the interest included in the fifth payment. Verify your answer by checking the amortization schedule.

11. Apex Corporation borrowed $85 000.00 at 8% compounded quarterly for eight years to buy a warehouse. Equal payments are made at the end of every three months.

    a) Determine the size of the quarterly payments.
    b) Compute the interest included in the 16th payment.
    c) Determine the principal repaid by the 20th payment.
    d) Construct a partial amortization schedule showing details of the first three payments, the last three payments, and totals.

12. Mr. Brabham borrowed $7500.00 at 15% compounded monthly. He agreed to repay the loan in equal monthly payments over five years.

    a) What is the size of the monthly payment?
    b) How much of the 25th payment is interest?
    c) What is the principal repaid by the 40th payment?
    d) Prepare a partial amortization schedule showing details of the first three payments, the last three payments, and totals.

13. Thornhill Equipment Co. borrowed $24 000.00 at 11% compounded semi-annually. It is to repay the loan by payments of $2500.00 at the end of every six months.

    a) How many payments are required to repay the loan?
    b) How much of the sixth payment is interest?
    c) How much of the principal will be repaid by the tenth payment?
    d) Construct a partial amortization schedule showing details of the first three payments, the last three payments, and totals.

14. Locust Inc. owes $16 000.00 to be repaid by monthly payments of $475.00. Interest is 6% compounded monthly.

    a) How many payments will Locust Inc. have to make?
    b) How much interest is included in the 18th payment?
    c) How much of the principal will be repaid by the 30th payment?
    d) Construct a partial amortization schedule showing details of the first three payments, the last three payments, and totals.

14.2 AMORTIZATION INVOLVING GENERAL ANNUITIES

A. Finding the periodic payment and constructing amortization schedules

If the length of the payment interval is different from the length of the interest conversion period, the equal debt payments form a general annuity. The amortization of such debts involves the same principles and methods discussed in Section 14.1 except that general annuity formulae are applicable. Provided that the payments are made at the end of the payment intervals, use Formula 11.4.

$$A_{nc} = R\left[\frac{1 - (1 + f)^{-n}}{f}\right]$$

where $f = (1 + i)^c - 1$

———— Formula 11.4

EXAMPLE 14.2A A debt of $30 000.00 with interest at 12% compounded quarterly is to be repaid by equal payments at the end of each year for seven years.

(i) Compute the size of the yearly payments.

(ii) Construct an amortization schedule.

Solution

(i) $A_{nc} = 30\,000.00$; $n = 7$; $c = 4$; $i = \dfrac{12\%}{4} = 3\% = 0.03$

$f = 1.03^4 - 1 = 1.1255088 - 1 = 0.1255088 = 12.55088\%$

$30\,000.00 = R\left(\dfrac{1 - 1.1255088^{-7}}{0.1255088}\right)$

$30\,000.00 = R(4.4851295)$

$R = \$6688.77$

Programmed solution

0 [FV] 30 000 [PV] 12.55088 [%i] 7 [N] [CPT] [PMT] [6688.7701]

(ii) *Amortization schedule*

Payment Number	Amount Paid	Interest Paid $i = 0.1255088$	Principal Repaid	Outstanding Principal Balance
0				30 000.00
1	6688.77	3765.26	2923.51	27 076.49
2	6688.77	3398.34	3290.43	23 786.06
3	6688.77	2985.36	3703.41	20 082.65
4	6688.77	2520.55	4168.22	15 914.43
5	6688.77	1997.40	4691.37	11 223.06
6	6688.77	1408.59	5280.18	5942.88
7	6688.76	745.88	5942.88	0.00
TOTAL	46 821.38	16 821.38	30 000.00	

B. Finding the outstanding principal

1. Finding the Outstanding Principal When All Payments Are Equal

When all payments are equal, the prospective method used in Section 14.1 is the more direct method.

EXAMPLE 14.2B For Example 14.2A, compute the outstanding balance after three payments.

Solution The outstanding balance after three payments is the present value of the remaining four payments.

$R = 6688.77; \quad n = 4; \quad c = 4; \quad i = 3\%; \quad f = 12.55088\%$

$$A_{nc} = 6688.77\left(\frac{1 - 1.1255088^{-4}}{0.1255088}\right)$$

$$= 6688.77(3.0024432)$$

$$= \$20\,082.65$$

Programmed solution

0 [FV] 6688.77 [PMT] 12.55088 [%i] 4 [N] [CPT] [PV] [20 082.652]

The outstanding balance after three payments is $20 082.65.

EXAMPLE 14.2C A $25 000.00 mortgage amortized by monthly payments over twenty years is renewable after five years.

(i) If interest is 8.5% compounded semi-annually, what is the outstanding balance at the end of the five-year term?

(ii) If the mortgage is renewed for a further three-year term at 8% compounded semi-annually, what is the size of the new monthly payment?

(iii) What is the payout figure at the end of the three-year term?

Solution

(i) $A_{nc} = 25\,000.00; \quad n = 20(12) = 240; \quad c = \dfrac{2}{12} = \dfrac{1}{6};$

$i = \dfrac{8.5\%}{2} = 4.25\% = 0.0425;$

$f = 1.0425^{\frac{1}{6}} - 1 = 1.0069611 - 1 = 0.0069611 = 0.69611\%$

$25\,000.00 = R\left(\dfrac{1 - 1.0069611^{-240}}{0.0069611}\right)$

$25\,000.00 = R(116.47382)$

$R = \$214.64$

The number of outstanding payments after five years is $15(12) = 180$.

$$A_{nc} = 214.64\left(\frac{1 - 1.0069611^{-180}}{0.0069611}\right)$$

$$= 214.64(102.44217)$$

$$= \$21\,988.19$$

Programmed solution

0 | FV | $25\,000$ | PV | 0.69611 | %i | 240 | N | CPT | PMT | 214.64052

0 | FV | 214.64 | PMT | 0.69611 | %i | 180 | N | CPT | PV | $21\,988.187$

The outstanding balance after five years is $\$21\,988.19$.

(ii) After the five-year term is up, the outstanding balance of $\$21\,988.19$ is to be amortized over the remaining 15 years.

$$A_{nc} = 21\,988.19; \quad n = 15(12) = 180; \quad c = \frac{1}{6};$$

$$i = \frac{8\%}{2} = 4\% = 0.04;$$

$$f = 1.04^{\frac{1}{6}} - 1 = 1.0065582 - 1 = 0.0065582 = 0.65582\%$$

$$21\,988.19 = R\left(\frac{1 - 1.0065582^{-180}}{0.0065582}\right)$$

$$21\,988.19 = R(105.46819)$$
$$R = \$208.48$$

Programmed solution

0 | FV | $21\,988.19$ | PV | 0.65582 | %i | 180 | N | CPT | PMT | 208.48172

The monthly payment for the three-year term will be $\$208.48$.

(iii) At the end of the three-year term, the number of outstanding payments is 144.

$$A_{nc} = 208.48\left(\frac{1 - 1.0065582^{-144}}{0.0065582}\right)$$

$$= 208.48(92.99483)$$
$$= \$19\,387.56$$

Programmed solution

0 | FV | 208.48 | PMT | 0.65582 | %i | 144 | N | CPT | PV | $19\,387.562$

The outstanding balance at the end of the three-year term will be $\$19\,387.56$.

2. **Finding the Outstanding Balance When All Payments Except the Final Payment Are Equal**

When the final payment is different from the preceding payments, use the retrospective method for finding the outstanding balance. Since this method requires finding the future value of an ordinary general annuity, Formula 11.3 applies.

$$S_{nc} = R\left[\frac{(1+f)^n - 1}{f}\right]$$

where $f = (1 + i)^c - 1$

————— **Formula 11.3**

EXAMPLE 14.2D A loan of $12 000.00 with interest at 12% compounded monthly and amortized by payments of $700.00 at the end of every three months is repaid in full after three years. What is the payout figure just after the last regular payment?

Solution Accumulate the value of the original principal after three years.

$$P = 12\,000.00; \quad n = 3(12) = 36; \quad i = \frac{12\%}{12} = 1\% = 0.01$$

$$S = 12\,000.00(1.01^{36})$$
$$= 12\,000.00(1.4307688)$$
$$= \$17\,169.23$$

Programmed solution

0 [PMT] 12 000 [PV] 1 [%i] 36 [N] [CPT] [FV] [17 169.225]

Accumulate the value of the twelve payments made.

$$R = 700.00; \quad n = 3(4) = 12; \quad c = \frac{12}{4} = 3; \quad i = 1\%$$

$$f = 1.01^3 - 1 = 1.030301 - 1 = 0.030301 = 3.0301\%$$

$$S_{nc} = 700.00\left(\frac{1.030301^{12} - 1}{0.030301}\right)$$
$$= 700.00(14.216322)$$
$$= \$9951.43$$

Programmed solution

0 [PV] 700 [PMT] 3.0301 [%i] 12 [N] [CPT] [FV] [9951.4257]

The outstanding balance after three years is $17\,169.23 - 9951.43 = \$7217.80$. The payout figure after three years is $7217.80.

C. Finding the interest paid and the principal repaid; constructing partial amortization schedules

EXAMPLE 14.2E Mr. and Mrs. Poh took out a $40 000.00, 25-year mortgage renewable after five years. The mortgage bears interest at 9.5% compounded semi-annually and is amortized by equal monthly payments.

(i) What is the interest included in the 13th payment?

(ii) How much of the principal is repaid by the 13th payment?

(iii) What is the total interest cost during the first year?

(iv) What is the total interest cost during the fifth year?

(v) What will be the total interest paid by the Pohs during the initial five-year term?

Solution (i) First find the size of the monthly payment.

$$A_{nc} = 40\ 000.00; \quad n = 300; \quad c = \frac{1}{6}; \quad i = 4.75\%$$

$$f = 1.0475^{\frac{1}{6}} - 1 = 1.0077644 - 1 = 0.0077644 = 0.77644\%$$

$$40\ 000.00 = R\left(\frac{1 - 1.0077644^{-300}}{0.0077644}\right)$$

$$40\ 000.00 = R(116.14003)$$

$$R = \$344.41$$

Programmed solution

0 [FV] 40 000 [PV] 0.77644 [%i] 300 [N] [CPT] [PMT] [344.41161]

Now find the outstanding balance after one year.

$R = 344.41; \quad f = 0.77644\%$

The number of outstanding payments after one year $n = 288$.

$$A_{nc} = R\left(\frac{1 - 1.0077644^{-288}}{0.0077644}\right)$$

$$= 344.41(114.90953)$$

$$= \$39\ 575.99$$

Programmed solution

0 [FV] 344.41 [PMT] 0.77644 [%i] 288 [N] [CPT] [PV] [39 575.992]

The interest in the 13th payment is $39\ 575.99(0.0077644) = \$307.28$.

(ii) The principal repaid in the 13th payment is 344.41 − 307.28 = $37.13.

(iii) The total amount paid during the first year is 344.41(12) = $4132.92
The total principal repaid is 40 000.00 − 39 575.99   = 424.01

The total cost of interest for the first year   = $3708.91

(iv) After four years, $n = 300 - 48 = 252$.

$$A_{nc} = 344.41\left(\frac{1 - 1.0077644^{-252}}{0.0077644}\right)$$
$$= 344.41(110.45204)$$
$$= \$38\,040.79$$

Programmed solution

0 [FV] 344.41 [PMT] 0.77644 [%i] 252 [N] [CPT] [PV] [38 040.787]

After five years, $n = 300 - 60 = 240$.

$$A_{nc} = 344.41\left(\frac{1 - 1.0077644^{-240}}{0.0077644}\right)$$

$$= 344.41(108.66827)$$
$$= \$37\,426.44$$

Programmed solution

0 [FV] 344.41 [PMT] 0.77644 [%i] 240 [N] [CPT] [PV] [37 426.438]

The total amount paid during the fifth year is 344.41(12)   = $4132.92
The total principal repaid in Year 5 is 38 040.79 − 37 426.44 = 614.35
The total cost of interest in Year 5   = $3518.57

(v) The total amount paid during the first five years is 344.41(60) = $20 664.60
The total principal repaid is 40 000.00 − 37 426.44   = 2573.56
The total cost of interest for the first five years   = $18 091.04

EXAMPLE 14.2F Confederated Venture Company financed a project by borrowing $120 000.00 at 7% compounded annually and is repaying the loan at the rate of $7000.00 due at the end of every three months.

(i) Compute the interest paid and the principal repaid by the tenth payment.

(ii) Construct a partial amortization schedule showing the first three payments, the tenth payment, the last three payments, and the totals.

Solution   (i) Accumulate the value of the original loan after nine payments.

$$P = 120\,000.00; \quad n = 9; \quad c = \frac{1}{4} = 0.25; \quad i = 7\% = 0.07;$$
$$f = 1.07^{0.25} - 1 = 1.0170585 - 1 = 0.0170585 = 1.70585\%$$

$$S = 120\,000.00(1.0170585^9)$$
$$= 120\,000.00(1.16443)$$
$$= \$139\,731.61$$

Programmed solution

0 [PMT] 120 000 [PV] 1.70585 [%i] 9 [N] [CPT] [FV] [139 731.61]

Accumulate the value of the first nine payments.

$$R = 7000.00; \quad n = 9$$

$$S_{nc} = 7000.00\left(\frac{1.0170585^9 - 1}{0.0170585}\right)$$

$$= 7000.00(9.6391856)$$
$$= \$67\,474.30$$

Programmed solution

0 [PV] 7000 [PMT] 1.70585 [%i] 9 [N] [CPT] [FV] [67 474.298]

The outstanding balance after nine payments is $139\,731.61 - 67\,474.30 = \$72\,257.31$.

The interest included in the tenth payment is $72\,257.31(0.0170585) = \$1232.60$.

The principal repaid by the tenth payment is $7000.00 - 1232.60 = \$5767.40$.

(ii) To show the details of the last three payments, we need to know the number of payments required to amortize the loan.

$$A_{nc} = 120\,000.00; \quad R = 7000.00; \quad f = 1.70585\%$$

$$120\,000.00 = 7000.00\left(\frac{1 - 1.0170585^{-n}}{0.0170585}\right)$$

$$0.2924314 = 1 - 1.0170585^{-n}$$
$$1.0170585^{-n} = 0.7075686$$
$$-n\ln 1.0170585 = \ln 0.7075686$$
$$-n(0.0169146) = -0.3459207$$
$$n = 20.451013$$

Programmed solution

0 [FV] 120 000 [PV] 7000 [PMT] 1.70585 [%i] [CPT] [N] [20.45]

21 payments (20 payments of $7000.00 plus a final payment) are required. This means the amortization schedule needs to show details of Payments 19, 20, and 21. To do so, we need to know the outstanding balance after 18 payments. Accumulate the value of the original principal after 18 payments.

$$S = 120\,000.00(1.0170585^{18})$$
$$= 120\,000.00(1.3558973)$$
$$= \$162\,707.68$$

Programmed solution

0 [PMT] 120 000 [PV] 1.70585 [%i] 18 [N] [CPT] [FV] [162 707.68]

Accumulate the value of the first 18 payments.

$$S_{nc} = 7000.00\left(\frac{1.0170585^{18} - 1}{0.0170585}\right)$$

$$= 7000.00(20.863343)$$
$$= \$146\,043.40$$

Programmed solution

0 [PV] 7000 [PMT] 1.70585 [%i] 18 [N] [CPT] [FV] [146 043.40]

The outstanding balance after 18 payments is $162\,707.68 - 146\,043.40 = \$16\,664.28$.

Partial amortization schedule

Payment Number	Amount Paid	Interest Paid $f = 0.0170585$	Principal Repaid	Outstanding Principal Balance
0				120 000.00
1	7 000.00	2047.02	4952.98	115 047.02
2	7 000.00	1962.53	5037.47	110 009.55
3	7 000.00	1876.60	5123.40	104 886.15
•	•	•	•	•
•	•	•	•	•
9	•	•	•	72 257.31
10	7 000.00	1232.60	5767.40	66 489.91
•	•	•	•	•
•	•	•	•	•
•	•	•	•	•
18	•	•	•	16 664.28
19	7 000.00	284.27	6715.73	9 948.55
20	7 000.00	169.71	6830.29	3 118.26
21	3 171.45	53.19	3118.26	0.00
TOTAL	143 171.45	23 171.45	120 000.00	

D. Computer application—Amortization schedule

As shown in Section 14.1E, amortization schedules can be created using spreadsheet programs like EXCEL or Lotus 1-2-3. Refer to Section 14.1E for instructions for creating amortization schedules in spreadsheets. Using those instructions and the formulae shown in Figure 14.4 below, you can create the amortization schedule for the debt in Example 14.2A.

FIGURE 14.4

	A	B	C	D	E	F
1	Payment Number	Amount Paid	Interest Paid	Principal Repaid	Outstanding Principal Balance	
2	0				30000.00	6688.77
3	1	= F2	= F4*E2	= B3−C3	= E2−D3	
4	2	= F2	= F4*E3	= B4−C4	= E3−D4	0.1255088
5	3	= F2	= F4*E4	= B5−C5	= E4−D5	
6	4	= F2	= F4*E5	= B6−C6	= E5−D6	
7	5	= F2	= F4*E6	= B7−C7	= E6−D7	
8	6	= F2	= F4*E7	= B8−C8	= E7−D8	
9	7	= C9+D9	= F4*E8	= E8	= E8−D9	
10	Totals	= SUM(B3:B9)	= SUM(C3:C9)	= SUM(D3:D9)		

Workbook 1

Exercise 14.2

A. For each of the following six debts amortized by equal payments made at the end of each payment interval, compute: (a) the size of the periodic payments; (b) the outstanding principal at the time indicated; (c) the interest paid; and (d) the principal repaid by the payment following the time indicated for finding the outstanding principal.

	Debt Principal	Repayment Period	Payment Interval	Interest Rate	Conversion Period	Outstanding Principal Required After:
1.	$36 000.00	20 years	6 months	8%	quarterly	25th payment
2.	$15 000.00	10 years	3 months	12%	monthly	15th payment
3.	$8500.00	5 years	1 month	6%	semi-annually	30th payment
4.	$9600.00	7 years	3 months	9%	semi-annually	10th payment
5.	$45 000.00	15 years	6 months	9%	monthly	12th payment
6.	$60 000.00	25 years	1 month	14%	semi-annually	120th payment

B. For each of the following four debts repaid by periodic payments as indicated, compute: (a) the number of payments required to amortize the debts; (b) the outstanding principal at the time indicated.

	Debt Principal	Repayment Period	Payment Interval	Interest Rate	Conversion Period	Outstanding Principal Required After:
1.	$6000.00	$400.00	3 months	6%	monthly	10th payment
2.	$8400.00	$1200.00	6 months	10%	quarterly	5th payment
3.	$23 500.00	$1800.00	3 months	7%	annually	14th payment
4.	$18 200.00	$430.00	1 month	8%	semi-annually	48th payment

C. Answer each of the following questions.

1. A $36 000.00 mortgage amortized by monthly payments over 25 years is renewable after three years.

   a) If interest is 7% compounded semi-annually, what is the size of each monthly payment?
   b) What is the mortgage balance at the end of the three-year term?
   c) How much interest will have been paid during the first three years?
   d) If the mortgage is renewed for a further three-year term at 9% compounded semi-annually, what will be the size of the monthly payments for the renewal period?

2. Fink and Associates bought a property valued at $80 000.00 for $15 000.00 down and a mortgage amortized over fifteen years. The firm makes equal payments due at the end of every three months. Interest on the mortgage is 6.5% compounded annually and the mortgage is renewable after five years.

   a) What is the size of each quarterly payment?
   b) What is the outstanding principal at the end of the five year term?
   c) What is the cost of the mortgage for the first five years?
   d) If the mortgage is renewed for a further five years at 9% compounded semi-annually, what will be the size of each quarterly payment?

3. A loan of $10 000.00 with interest at 10% compounded quarterly is repaid by payments of $950.00 made at the end of every six months.

   a) How many payments will be required to amortize the loan?
   b) If the loan is repaid in full after six years, what is the payout figure?
   c) If paid out, what is the total cost of the loan?

4. The owner of the Blue Goose Motel borrowed $12 500.00 at 12% compounded semi-annually and agreed to repay the loan by making payments of $700.00 at the end of every three months.

   a) How many payments will be needed to repay the loan?
   b) How much will be owed at the end of five years?
   c) How much of the payments made at the end of five years will be interest?

5. A loan of $16 000.00 with interest at 9% compounded quarterly is repaid in seven years by equal payments made at the end of each year. Find the size of the annual payments and construct an amortization schedule showing the total paid and the total interest.

6. A debt of $12 500.00 with interest at 7% compounded semi-annually is repaid by payments of $1900.00 made at the end of every three months. Construct an amortization schedule showing the total paid and the total cost of the debt.

7. For Question 5, calculate the interest included in the fifth payment. Verify your answer by checking the amortization schedule.

8. For Question 6, compute the principal repaid by the sixth payment. Verify your answer by checking the amortization schedule.

9. A $40 000.00 mortgage amortized by monthly payments over 25 years is renewable after five years.

   a) If interest is 8.5% compounded semi-annually, what is the size of each monthly payment?
   b) Find the total interest paid during the first year.
   c) Compute the interest included in the 48th payment.
   d) If the mortgage is renewed after five years at 10.5% compounded semi-annually, what is the size of the monthly payment for the renewal period?
   e) Construct a partial amortization schedule showing details of the first three payments for each of the two five-year terms.

10. A debt of $32 000.00 is repaid by payments of $2950.00 made at the end of every six months. Interest is 12% compounded quarterly.

   a) What is the number of payments needed to retire the debt?
   b) What is the cost of the debt for the first five years?
   c) What is the interest paid by the tenth payment?
   d) Construct a partial amortization schedule showing details of the first three payments, the last three payments, and totals.

14.3 FINDING THE SIZE OF THE FINAL PAYMENT

A. Three methods for computing the final payment

When all payments except the final payment are equal, three methods are available to compute the size of the final payment.

METHOD 1 Compute the value of the term n and determine the present value of the outstanding fractional payment. If the final payment is made at the end of the payment interval, add interest for one payment interval to the present value.

METHOD 2 Use the retrospective method to compute the outstanding principal after the last of the equal payments. If the final payment is made at the end of the payment interval, add to the outstanding principal the interest for one payment interval.

METHOD 3   Assume all payments to be equal, compute the overpayment, and subtract the overpayment from the size of the equal payments. This method must not be used when the payments are made at the beginning of the payment interval.

EXAMPLE 14.3A   For Example 14.1D, compute the size of the final payment using each of the three methods. Compare the results with the size of the payment shown in the amortization schedule.

Solution

METHOD 1 $A_n = 15\,000.00; \quad R = 2500.00; \quad i = 2.5\%$

$$15\,000.00 = 2500.00\left(\frac{1 - 1.025^{-n}}{0.025}\right)$$

$$6.00 = \frac{1 - 1.025^{-n}}{0.025}$$

$$0.15 = 1 - 1.025^{-n}$$
$$1.025^{-n} = 0.85$$
$$-n \ln 1.025 = \ln 0.85$$
$$-n(0.0246926) = -0.1625189$$
$$n = 6.5816844$$

Programmed solution

$$0 \;\boxed{\text{FV}}\; 15\,000 \;\boxed{\text{PV}}\; 2500 \;\boxed{\text{PMT}}\; 2.5 \;\boxed{\%i}\; \boxed{\text{CPT}}\; \boxed{\text{N}}\; \boxed{6.582}$$

$R = 2500.00; \quad i = 2.5\%; \quad n = 0.5816844$

$$A_n = 2500.00\left(\frac{1 - 1.025^{-0.5816844}}{0.025}\right)$$

$$= 2500.00(0.5704258)$$
$$= \$1426.06$$

Programmed solution

$$0 \;\boxed{\text{FV}}\; 2500 \;\boxed{\text{PMT}}\; 2.5 \;\boxed{\%i}\; 0.5816844 \;\boxed{\text{N}}\; \boxed{\text{CPT}}\; \boxed{\text{PV}}\; \boxed{1426.0647}$$

Interest for one interval is $1426.06(0.025) = \$35.65$.
Final payment is $1426.06 + 35.65 = \$1461.71$.

METHOD 2   Compute the value of n as done in Method 1.
Since $n = 6.5816844$, the number of equal payments is 6.
The accumulated value of the original principal after six payments

$$S = 15\,000.00(1.025^6)$$
$$= 15\,000.00(1.1596934)$$
$$= \$17\,395.40$$

Programmed solution

0 PMT 15 000 PV 2.5 %i 6 N CPT FV 17 395.401

The accumulated value of the first six payments

$$S_6 = 2500.00\left(\frac{1.025^6 - 1}{0.025}\right)$$

$$= 2500.00(6.3877366)$$
$$= \$15\,969.34$$

Programmed solution

0 PV 2500 PMT 2.5 %i 6 N CPT FV 15 969.342

The outstanding balance after six payments is $17\,395.40 - 15\,969.34 = \$1426.06$.
The final payment = outstanding balance + interest for one period
$\quad\quad\quad\quad\quad\quad\quad\quad$ = the accumulated value of $1426.06 for one year
$\quad\quad\quad\quad\quad\quad\quad\quad$ = 1426.06(1.025)
$\quad\quad\quad\quad\quad\quad\quad\quad$ = \$1461.71

METHOD 3 Compute the value of n as done in Method 1.
Since $n = 6.5816844$, the number of assumed full payments is 7.
The accumulated value of the original principal after seven payments

$$S = 15\,000.00(1.025^7)$$
$$= 15\,000.00(1.1886857)$$
$$= \$17\,830.29$$

Programmed solution

0 PMT 15 000 PV 2.5 %i 7 N CPT FV 17 830.286

The accumulated value of seven payments

$$S_7 = 2500.00\left(\frac{1.025^7 - 1}{0.025}\right)$$

$$= 2500.00(7.5474302)$$
$$= \$18\,868.58$$

Programmed solution

0 PV 2500 PMT 2.5 %i 7 N CPT FV 18 868.575

Since the accumulated value of seven payments is greater than the accumulated value of the original principal, there is an overpayment.

$18\,868.58 - 17\,830.29 = \$1038.29$

The size of the final payment is 2500.00 − 1038.29 = $1461.71.

Note:

1. For all three methods, you must determine the term n using the methods shown in Chapter 13.
2. When using a scientific calculator, Method 1 is preferable because it is the most direct method. It is the method used in Subsection B below.

B. Applications

EXAMPLE 14.3B   On his retirement, Art received a gratuity of $8000.00 from his employer. Taking advantage of the existing tax legislation, he invested his money in an income averaging annuity that provides for semi-annual payments of $1200.00 at the end of every six months. If interest is 11.5% compounded semi-annually, determine the size of the final payment (see Chapter 13, Example 13.2H).

Solution $A_n = 8000.00;\quad R = 1200.00;\quad i = \dfrac{11.5\%}{2} = 5.75\%$

$$8000.00 = 1200.00\left(\frac{1 - 1.0575^{-n}}{0.0575}\right)$$

$$0.3833333 = 1 - 1.0575^{-n}$$
$$1.0575^{-n} = 0.616667$$
$$-n \ln 1.0575 = \ln 0.616667$$
$$-n(0.0559076) = -0.4834266$$
$$n = 8.6468812 \text{ (half-year periods)}$$

The annuity will be in existence for four and a half years. Art will receive eight payments of $1200.00 and a final payment that will be less than $1200.00.

$$R = 1200.00;\quad i = 5.75\%;\quad n = 0.6468812$$

$$A_n = 1200.00\left(\frac{1 - 1.0575^{-0.6468812}}{0.0575}\right)$$

$$= 1200.00(0.6177293)$$
$$= \$741.28$$

Programmed solution

0 [FV] 8000 [PV] 1200 [PMT] 5.75 [%i] [CPT] [N] 8.6468812

0 [FV] 1200 [PMT] 5.75 [%i] 0.6468812 [N] [CPT] [PV] 741.29626

Final payment including the interest for one payment interval is 741.28(1.0575) = $783.90.

EXAMPLE 14.3C A lease contract valued at \$7800.00 is to be fulfilled by rental payments of \$180.00 due at the beginning of each month. If money is worth 9% compounded monthly, determine the size of the final lease payment (see Chapter 13, Example 13.2K).

Solution

$$A_n(\text{due}) = 7800.00; \quad R = 180.00; \quad i = \frac{9\%}{12} = 0.75\%$$

$n = 52.123\,125$ (see solution to Example 13.2K)

Present value of the final payment

$$R = 180.00; \quad i = 0.75\%; \quad n = 0.123125$$

$$A_n(\text{due}) = 180.00(1.0075)\left(\frac{1 - 1.0075^{-0.123125}}{0.0075}\right) \quad\text{------- Formula 12.2}$$

$$= 180.00(1.0075)(0.1226092)$$
$$= 180.00(0.1235287)$$
$$= \$22.24$$

Programmed solution

0 [FV] 180 [PMT] 0.75 [%i] 7800 [PV] [DUE] (or [2nd] [CPT])
[N] [52.123125]

0 [FV] 180 [PMT] 0.75 [%i] 0.123125 [N] [DUE] (or [2nd] [CPT])
[PV] [22.24]

Since the payment is made at the beginning of the last payment interval, no interest is added. The final payment is \$22.24.

EXAMPLE 14.3D Payments of \$500.00 deferred for nine years are received at the end of each month from a fund of \$10 000.00 deposited at 10.5% compounded monthly. Determine the size of the final payment (see Chapter 13, Example 13.2M).

Solution

$$A_n(\text{defer}) = 10\,000.00; \quad R = 500.00; \quad d = 9(12) = 108;$$

$$i = \frac{10.5\%}{12} = 0.875\%$$

$n = 68.288334$ (see solution to Example 13.2M)

Present value of the final payment:

$$R = 500.00; \quad i = 0.875\%; \quad n = 0.288334$$

$$A_n = 500.00\left(\frac{1 - 1.00875^{-0.288334}}{0.00875}\right)$$

$$= 500.00(0.2867195)$$
$$= \$143.36$$

Programmed solution

0 | FV | 500 | PMT | 0.875 | %i | 0.288334 | N | CPT | PV | 143.35979

The size of the final payment is 143.36(1.00875) = $144.61.

EXAMPLE 14.3E   A business valued at $96 000.00 is bought for a down payment of 25% and payments of $4000.00 at the end of every three months. If interest is 9% compounded monthly, what is the size of the final payment? (See Chapter 13, Example 13.2I.)

Solution $A_{nc} = 96\,000.00(0.75) = 72\,000.00;\quad R = 4000.00;\quad c = \dfrac{12}{4} = 3;$

$i = \dfrac{9\%}{12} = 0.75\% = 0.0075;\quad f = 1.0075^3 - 1 = 2.26692\%;$

$n = 23.390584$ (see solution to Example 13.2I)

Present value of the final payment:

$R = 4000.00;\quad f = 2.26692\%;\quad n = 0.390584$

$$A_n = 4000.00\left(\dfrac{1 - 1.0226692^{-0.390584}}{0.0226692}\right)$$

$$= 4000.00(0.3845368)$$
$$= \$1538.15$$

Programmed solution

0 | FV | 4000 | PMT | 2.26692 | %i | 0.390584 | N | CPT | PV | 1538.1474

The final payment is 1538.15(1.0226692) = $1573.02.

EXAMPLE 14.3F   Ted Davis, having reached his goal of a $140 000.00 balance in his RRSP, converts it into an RRIF and withdraws from it $1650.00 at the beginning of each month. If interest is 11% compounded quarterly, what is the size of the final withdrawal? (See Chapter 13, Example 13.2L.)

Solution $A_{nc}(\text{due}) = 140\,000.00;\quad R = 1650.00;\quad c = \dfrac{4}{12} = \dfrac{1}{3};$

$i = \dfrac{11\%}{4} = 2.75\% = 0.0275;$

$f = 1.0275^{\frac{1}{3}} - 1 = 1.0090839 - 1 = 0.90839\%$
$n = 159.58897$ (see solution to Example 13.2L)

Present value of final payment:

$R = 1650.00;$ $f = 0.90839\%;$ $n = 0.58897$

$$A_n = 1650.00(1.0090839)\left(\frac{1 - 1.0090839^{-0.58897}}{0.0090839}\right)$$

$$= 1650.00(1.0090839)(0.5847524)$$
$$= 1650.00(0.5900642)$$
$$= \$973.61$$

Programmed solution

0 PV 1650 PMT 0.90839 %i 0.58897 N DUE PV 973.60606

Since the payment is at the beginning of the last payment interval, its size is $973.61.

Exercise 14.3

A. For each of the following eight loans, compute the size of the final payment.

	Principal	Periodic Payment	Payment Interval	Payment Made At:	Interest Rate	Conversion Period
1.	$17 500.00	$1100.00	3 months	end	14%	quarterly
2.	$35 000.00	$925.00	1 month	end	12%	monthly
3.	$7800.00	$775.00	6 months	beginning	7%	semi-annually
4.	$9300.00	$580.00	3 months	beginning	7%	quarterly
5.	$15 400.00	$1600.00	6 months	end	8%	quarterly
6.	$29 500.00	$1650.00	3 months	end	9%	monthly
7.	$17 300.00	$425.00	1 month	beginning	6%	quarterly
8.	$10 500.00	$900.00	3 months	beginning	11%	semi-annually

B. Answer each of the following questions.

1. A loan of $7200.00 is repaid by payments of $360.00 at the end of every three months. Interest is 11% compounded quarterly.

   a) How many payments are required to repay the debt?
   b) What is the size of the final payment?

2. Seanna O'Brien receives pension payments of $3200.00 at the end of every six months from a retirement fund of $50 000.00. The fund earns 12% compounded semi-annually.

   a) How many payments will Seanna receive?
   b) What is the size of the final pension payment?

3. Payments of $1200.00 are made out of a fund of $25 000.00 at the end of every three months. If interest is 12% compounded monthly, what is the size of the final payment?

4. A debt of $30 000.00 is repaid in monthly instalments of $550.00. If interest is 8% compounded quarterly, what is the size of the final payment?

5. A lease valued at $20 000.00 requires payments of $1000.00 every three months due in advance. If money is worth 7% compounded quarterly, what is the size of the final lease payment?

6. Eduardo Martinez has saved $125 000.00. If he withdraws $1250.00 at the beginning of every month and interest is 10.5% compounded monthly, what is the size of the last withdrawal?

7. Equipment priced at $42 000.00 was purchased on a contract requiring payments of $5000.00 at the beginning of every six months. If interest is 9% compounded quarterly, what is the size of the final payment?

8. Noreen Leung has agreed to purchase her partner's share in the business by making payments of $1100.00 every three months. The agreed transfer value is $16 500.00 and interest is 10% compounded annually. If the first payment is due at the date of the agreement, what is the size of the final payment?

9. David Jones has paid $16 000.00 for a retirement annuity from which he will receive $1375.00 at the end of every three months. The payments are deferred for ten years and interest is 10% compounded quarterly.

   a) How many payments will David receive?
   b) What is the size of the final payment?
   c) How much will David receive in total?
   d) How much of what he receives will be interest?

10. A contract valued at $27 500.00 requires payments of $6000.00 every six months. The first payment is due in four years and interest is 11% compounded semi-annually.

    a) How many payments are required?
    b) What is the size of the last payment?
    c) How much will be paid in total?
    d) How much of what is paid is interest?

14.4 RESIDENTIAL MORTGAGES IN CANADA

A. Basic concepts and definitions

A **residential mortgage** is a claim to a residential property given by a borrower to a lender as security for the repayment of a loan. It is often the largest amount of money ever borrowed by an individual. The borrower is called the *mortgagor*; the lender is called the *mortgagee*. The *mortgage contract* spells out the obligations of the borrower and the rights of the lender, including the lender's rights in case of default in payment by the borrower. If the borrower is unable to make the mortgage payments, the lender ultimately has the right to dispose of the property under *power of sale* provisions.

To secure legal claim against a residential property, the lender must register the mortgage against the property at the provincial government's land titles office. A **first mortgage** is the first legal claim against a residential property if the mortgage payments cannot be made and the property must be sold. **Equity** in a property is the difference between the property's market value and the total debts, or mortgages, registered against the property. It is possible to have a **second mortgage** on a residential property that is backed by equity in the property, even if there is a first mortgage already registered against the property. If the borrower defaults on the mortgage payments and the property must be sold, the first mortgagee gets paid before the second mortgagee. For this reason, second mortgages are considered riskier investments than first mortgages. They command higher interest rates than first mortgages to compensate for this risk. Home improvement loans and home equity loans are often secured by second mortgages. It is even possible to obtain *third mortgages* against residential properties. Third mortgagees rank behind first and second mortgages. Thus, they command much higher interest rates.

Financial institutions offer two types of mortgages—fixed-rate mortgages and demand (or variable-rate) mortgages. A **fixed-rate mortgage** is a mortgage for which the rate of interest is fixed for a specific period of time. A **demand** (or **variable-rate**) **mortgage** is a mortgage for which the rate of interest changes as money market conditions change. The interest rate change is usually related to the change in a bank's prime lending rate. Both types of mortgages are usually repaid by equal payments that blend principal and interest. Payments are often required to be made monthly, but some lenders are more flexible and allow semi-monthly, bi-weekly, and even weekly payments.

For all types of mortgages, the amortization period is a part of the mortgage agreement. The amortization period is used to calculate the amount of the blended payments. The most common amortization period is 25 years for fixed-rate mortgages and 20 years for demand mortgages. Shorter amortization periods may be used at the discretion of the lender or the borrower.

The *term* of the mortgage specifies the period of time for which the interest rate is fixed. By definition, only fixed-rate mortgages have terms. The term ranges from six months to five years. Longer terms, such as seven and ten years, are becoming more frequently available.

For fixed-rate mortgages, Canadian law dictates that interest must be calculated semi-annually or annually, not in advance. In this context, "not in advance" means that interest is calculated at the end of each six-month or twelve-month period, not at the beginning. It is Canadian practice to calculate fixed-rate mortgage interest semi-annually, not in advance.

Fixed-rate mortgages can be either open or closed. Closed mortgages restrict the borrower's ability to increase payments, make lump-sum payments, change the term of the mortgage, or transfer the mortgage to another lender without penalty. Most closed mortgages contain some prepayment privileges. For example, some mortgages allow a lump-sum payment each year of up to 10% or 15% of the original mortgage principal, usually on the anniversary date of the mortgage. Some lenders permit increases in the periodic payments up to 10% or 15% once each calendar year. Changes in the term or transfers are usually subject to prohibitive penalties.

Open mortgages allow prepayment or repayment of the mortgage at any time without penalty. They are available from most lenders for terms of up to two years. However, interest rates on open mortgages are significantly higher than interest rates on closed mortgages. For a six-month term, the usual charge (i.e., the premium) for an open mortgage is an interest rate at least 0.5% (i.e., 50 basis points) higher than for a closed mortgage. For one-year and two-year terms, the interest rate is usually at least 1.0% (i.e., 100 basis points) higher.

As we stated above, a demand (or variable-rate) mortgage is a mortgage for which the rate of interest changes over time. Interest is calculated on a daily basis. Therefore, demand mortgages are not subject to the legal restriction of compounding semi-annually, not in advance. Demand mortgages also do not have a fixed term, because the interest rate may fluctuate.

B. CMHC mortgages

Fixed-rate mortgages and demand mortgages are usually available from financial institutions for up to 75% of the value of a property (calculated as the lesser of the purchase price and the appraised value of a property). This means the borrower needs to have at least a 25% down payment for the purchase of a residential property or at least 25% equity in a property. To borrow beyond the 75% level, the mortgage must be insured by the Canada Mortgage and Housing Corporation (CMHC).

Canada Mortgage and Housing Corporation (**CMHC**) is the corporation of the federal government that administers the National Housing Act (NHA) and provides mortgage insurance to lenders. CMHC acts as the insurer for the lender in the event that the borrower defaults on the mortgage payments. If the mortgage is insured by CMHC, regular home buyers can borrow up to 90% of the purchase price of a residential property and first-time buyers can borrow up to 95% of the purchase price. The borrower must pay to CMHC a fixed administration fee as well as an insurance premium. The borrower can pay these fees separately or have them added to the mortgage balance.

Effective March 31, 1997, all CMHC borrowers must meet the following conditions:

- The maximum **Gross Debt Service** (**GDS**) **ratio**, including heating costs, is 32%. (Recall from Chapter 1 that the GDS ratio is the percent of your gross annual income required to cover housing costs such as mortgage payments, property taxes, and heating costs.)
- The maximum **Total Debt Service** (**TDS**) **ratio** is 40%. (Recall from Chapter 1 that the TDS ratio is the percent of your gross annual income required to cover housing costs *and* all other debts and obligations, such as a car loan.)
- The maximum amortization period is 25 years.
- Borrowers are required to demonstrate, at the time of their application, their ability to cover closing costs equal to at least 1.5% of the purchase price.
- If a borrower is using a financial gift to pay a part of the down payment, the borrower must be in possession of the funds 30 days before making an offer to purchase.

The CMHC lending program distinguishes between *first-time home buyers* and *regular home buyers*. A *first-time home buyer* is defined by CMHC to be anyone buying or building a home in Canada as a principal residence who has not owned a principal residence in Canada during the last five years. If there is more than one buyer involved, only one must satisfy the five-year requirement. (CMHC will consider justifiable exceptions to the five-year condition under certain hardship situations.) Different mortgage terms and conditions apply to the regular and first-time home buyers, as shown in the following table.

	First-Time Home Buyers	**Regular Home Buyers**
Minimum Down Payment	5% of purchase price	10% of purchase price
Maximum Mortgage Loan	95% of purchase price subject to maximum house price based on location. Maximum house price ranges from $125 000 for most places in Canada to $250 000 for greater Toronto and Vancouver.	90% of the first $180 000 plus 80% of the balance of the purchase price
Minimum Term	3 years based on five-year interest rate	6 months

EXAMPLE 14.4A A regular home buyer wants to purchase a $240 000.00 home with a CMHC-approved mortgage. According to the CMHC terms and conditions, calculate

(i) the maximum loan amount

(ii) the minimum down payment requirement

(iii) the minimum equity requirement

Solution

(i) The maximum loan amount is calculated as:

First $180 000.00 of the $240 000.000 purchase price at 90%	$162 000.00
Remaining $60 000.00 of purchase price at 80%	$ 48 000.00
	$210 000.00

The maximum mortgage loan is $210 000.00.

(ii) The minimum down payment = purchase price − maximum loan
$$= 240\,000.00 - 210\,000.00$$
$$= \$30\,000.00$$
The minimum down payment required is $30 000.00.

(iii) The minimum equity requirement = 10% of purchase price
$$= 0.10 \times 240\,000.00$$
$$= \$24\,000.00$$

The minimum equity required is $24 000.00.

The difference between the minimum down payment and the minimum equity is $30 000.00 − 24 000.00 = $6000.00. This difference may be borrowed from other sources.

C. Computing the effective rate of interest for fixed-rate mortgages

DID YOU KNOW?

When the bank's loan officer is determining how expensive a house you can afford to buy, one rule of thumb used is the calculation of two and a half times your gross family income. The chart below will give you an idea of what you can afford and the size of your 5% down payment. In order to qualify for a 5% down payment, your mortgage must be insured by Canada Mortgage and Housing Corporation (CMHC), and you must be a first-time purchaser of a principal residence.

On a Family Income Of:	You Could Afford a House Up To:	And Your 5% Down Payment Would Be:
$50 000	$125 000	$6 250
55 000	137 500	6 875
60 000	150 000	7 500
65 000	162 500	8 125
70 000	175 000	8 750
75 000	187 500	9 375
80 000	200 000	10 000
85 000	212 500	10 625
90 000	225 000	11 250
95 000	237 500	11 875
100 000	250 000	12 500

SOURCE: Canada Mortgage and Housing Corporation (CMHC).

For residential mortgages, Canadian legislation requires the rate of interest charged by the lender to be calculated annually or semi-annually, not in advance. The fixed rates advertised, posted, or quoted by lenders are usually nominal annual rates. To meet the legislated requirements, the applicable nominal annual rate of interest must be converted into the equivalent effective rate of interest per payment period.

This is done as explained in Section 11.3A by using Formula 11.3.

$$1 + f = (1 + i)^c$$

where f = the effective rate of interest per payment period

i = the rate per conversion period

$$c = \frac{\text{THE NUMBER OF INTEREST CONVERSION PERIODS PER YEAR}}{\text{THE NUMBER OF PAYMENT PERIODS PER YEAR}}$$

The prevailing practice is semi-annual compounding and monthly payment for most mortgages. For most mortgages (with semi-annual compounding and monthly payment),

$$c = \frac{2 \text{ (compounding periods per year)}}{12 \text{ (payments per year)}} = \frac{1}{6}$$

EXAMPLE 14.4B   Suppose a financial institution posted the interest rates for closed mortgages shown below. The interest is compounded semi-annually and the mortgages require monthly payments.

Term	Interest Rate
6 months	5.25%
1 year	5.50%
2 years	6.50%
3 years	7.00%
4 years	7.25%
5 years	7.50%

Compute the effective rate of interest per payment period for each term.

Solution

$$c = \frac{1}{6}; \quad 1 + f = (1 + i)^{\frac{1}{6}}$$

For the six-month term, $i = \dfrac{5.25\%}{2} = 2.625\% = 0.02625$

$$1 + f = (1 + 0.02625)^{\frac{1}{6}}$$
$$1 + f = 1.0043279$$
$$f = 1.0043279 - 1$$
$$f = 0.0043279, \text{ or } 0.43279\%$$

For the one-year term, $i = 2.75\% = 0.0275$

$$f = (1.0275^{\frac{1}{6}}) - 1 = 0.0045317 = 0.45317\%$$

You can obtain the effective rates using a preprogrammed financial calculator by using the function keys as follows:

0 [PMT] 1 [PV] 0.1666667 [N] (enter applicable interest rate) [%i] [CPT]

[FV] | Display Shows $(1 + f)$ |

For the two-year term,

0 [PMT] 1 [PV] 0.1666667 [N] 3.25 [%i] [CPT] [FV] [1.0053447]

$f = 0.53447\%$
(Note that if you perform these calculations in succession, you do not have to key in PMT, PV, and N each time.)

For the three-year term,

0 [PMT] 1 [PV] 0.1666667 [N] 3.5 [%i] [CPT] [FV] [1.0057500]

$f = 0.57500\%$

For the four-year term,

0 [PMT] 1 [PV] 0.1666667 [N] 3.625 [%i] [CPT] [FV] [1.0059524]

$f = 0.59524\%$

For the five-year term,

0 [PMT] 1 [PV] 0.1666667 [N] 3.75 [%i] [CPT] [FV] [1.0061545]

$f = 0.61545\%$

D. Computing mortgage payments and balances

Blended residential mortgage payments are ordinary general annuities. Therefore, Formula 11.4 applies.

$$A_{nc} = R\left[\frac{1 - (1 + f)^{-n}}{f}\right], \text{ where } 1 + f = (1 + i)^c$$

The periodic payment R is calculated using the method shown in Section 13.1.

EXAMPLE 14.4C A mortgage for $120\,000.00$ is amortized over 25 years. Interest is 7.5% p.a., compounded semi-annually, for a five-year term and payments are monthly.

(i) Compute the monthly payment.

(ii) Compute the balance at the end of the five-year term.

(iii) Compute the monthly payment if the mortgage is renewed for a four-year term at 7.0% compounded semi-annually.

Solution

(i) When computing the monthly payment, n is the total number of payments in the amortization period. The term for which the rate of interest is fixed (in this case, five years) does not enter the calculation.

$$A_{nc} - 120\,000.00; \quad n = 12(25) = 300; \quad i = \frac{7.5\%}{2} = 3.75\%; \quad c = \frac{1}{6}$$

We must first compute the effective monthly rate of interest.

$$1 + f = (1.0375)^{\frac{1}{6}}$$
$$f = 1.0061545 - 1 = 0.0061545 = 0.061545\%$$

$$120\,000.00 = R\left(\frac{1 - 1.0061545^{-300}}{0.0061545}\right) \quad \text{— using Formula 11.4}$$

$$120\,000.00 = R(136.695485)$$
$$R = \$877.86$$

Programmed solution

0 [PMT] 1 [PV] 3.75 [%i] 0.166667 [N] [CPT] [FV] [1.0061545]

$f = 0.61545\%$

0 [FV] 120 000 [PV] 0.61545 [%i] 300 [N] [CPT] [PMT] [877.86368]

The monthly payment for the original five-year term is $877.86.

(ii) The balance at the end of the five-year term is the present value of the out-standing payments. After five years, 60 of the required 300 payments have been made; 240 payments remain outstanding.

$R = 877.86; \quad n = 240; \quad f = 0.61545\%$

$$A_{nc} = 877.86\left(\frac{1 - 1.0061545^{-240}}{0.0061545}\right) \quad \text{——— using Formula 11.4}$$

$$= 877.86(125.219078)$$
$$= \$109\,924.82$$

Programmed solution

0 [FV] 877.86 [PMT] 240 [N] 0.61545 [%i] [CPT] [PV] [109 924.82]

The mortgage balance at the end of the first five-year term is $109 924.82.

(iii) For the renewed term, the starting principal is the balance at the end of the five-year term. The amortization period is the number of years remaining after the initial term. We must recalculate f for the new interest rate.

$A_{nc} = 109\,924.82; \quad n = 12(20) = 240; \quad i = 3.5\%$

$$1 + f = (1.035)^{\frac{1}{6}}$$
$$f = 1.0057500 - 1 = 0.0057500 = 0.57500\%$$
$$109\,924.82 = R\left(\frac{1 - 1.0057500^{-240}}{0.0057500}\right)$$
$$109\,924.82 = R(129.987397)$$
$$R = 845.66$$

Programmed solution

0 [PMT] 1 [PV] 3.5 [%i] 0.1666667 [N] [CPT] [FV] [1.0057500]

$f = 0.57500\%$

0 [FV] 109 924.82 [PV] 0.57500 [%i] 240 [N] [CPT] [PMT] [845.66022]

The monthly payment for the renewed four-year term is $845.66.

E. Rounded payments

Mortgage payments are sometimes rounded up to an exact dollar value (such as to the next dollar, the next five dollars, or the next ten dollars). The payment of $877.86 might be rounded up to $878 or $880 or even $900. Rounded payments up to a higher value will result in a lower balance at the end of the term. In the final renewal term, rounding will affect the size of the final payment.

EXAMPLE 14.4D   A mortgage balance of $17 322.35 is renewed for the remaining amortization period of three years at 8% compounded semi-annually.

(i) Compute the size of the monthly payments.

(ii) Determine the size of the last payment if the payments computed in part (a) have been rounded up to the next ten dollars.

Solution

(i) $A_{nc} = 17\,322.35$; $n = 12(3) = 36$; $i = 4\%$; $c = \dfrac{1}{6}$

$1 + f = (1.04)^{\frac{1}{6}}$
$\quad f = 1.0065582 - 1 = 0.65582\%$

$17\,322.35 = R\left(\dfrac{1 - 1.0065582^{-36}}{0.0065582}\right)$

$17\,322.35 = R(31.973035)$
$\qquad\quad R = \$541.78$

Programmed solution

0 [PMT] 1 [PV] 4 [%i] 0.1666667 [N] [CPT] [FV] [1.0065582]

$f = 0.65582\%$

0 [FV] 17 322.35 [PV] 0.65582 [%i] 36 [N] [CPT] [PMT] [541.77997]

The monthly payment is $541.78.

(ii) If payments are rounded to $550.00, the last payment will be less than $550.00. To calculate the size of the last payment we need to determine the number of payments of $550.00 that are required to amortize the loan balance.

$A_{nc} = 17\,322.35$; $R = 550.00$; $f = 0.65582\%$

$17\,322.35 = 550.00\left(\dfrac{1 - 1.0065582^{-n}}{0.0065582}\right)$

$0.2065517 = 1 - 1.0065582^{-n}$
$1.0065582^{-n} = 0.7934483$
$-n(\ln 1.0065582) = \ln 0.7934483$
$-n(0.0065368) = -0.2313669$
$n = 35.394582$

Programmed solution

0 $\boxed{FV}$ $17\,322.35$ $\boxed{PV}$ 0.65582 $\boxed{\%i}$ 550 $\boxed{PMT}$ $\boxed{CPT}$ $\boxed{N}$ $\boxed{35.394582}$

There will be 35 payments of $550.00 and a final payment smaller than $550.00. We need to determine the balance after the 35th payment.

$R = 550.00; \quad n = 0.394582; \quad f = 0.65582\%$

$$A_{nc} = 550.00 \left(\frac{1 - 1.0065582^{-0.394582}}{0.0065582} \right)$$

$$= 550.00(0.3927850)$$
$$= \$216.03$$

Programmed solution

0 $\boxed{FV}$ 550.00 $\boxed{PMT}$ 0.65582 $\boxed{\%i}$ 0.394582 $\boxed{N}$ $\boxed{CPT}$ $\boxed{PV}$ $\boxed{216.03284}$

The final payment includes interest on the balance of $216.03.

$$\text{Final payment} = \$216.03(1.0065582) = \$217.45$$

BUSINESS MATH NEWS BOX

THE RATE GAME HAS ITS PRICE

They may be hard on the stomach as financial markets gyrate, but the one-year mortgage is often easier on the wallet over the long run, a Bank of Montreal study has found.

Many borrowers choose to pay higher rates on a five-year mortgage—even though that may cost them thousands of dollars more in payments over the longer term—in order to know they will not face unknown fluctuations in their payments, said Tim O'Neill, chief economist at Bank of Montreal.

The study looks at the cost of that "peace of mind" so that consumers can weigh it against other options, he said.

The premium paid for the stability of five-year rates was as much as $28 200 in one of three scenarios studied by the bank. It was $11 000 in another instance and was a negligible amount in a third case, according to the bank's study.

The study examined three interest rate environments since the early 1980s. In each case, the borrower financed 75% of the current average house price.

When interest rates were high in September 1981, a borrower financing a $106 800 house at a one-year rate of 21.25% and renewing annually as rates fell would have saved $28 200, rather than taking a five-year fixed rate at 21.75%. As the term rolled over, the rates moved to 17.2%, 10.94%, 12.94%, and 10% in subsequent years. The principal and interest paid were $55 700 at short-term rates, compared with $83 900 for the five-year loan.

In January 1987, when rates had bottomed out and a fast-growing economy was causing rates to rise, many borrowers considered it a good time to lock in at a longer term rate. In this case, someone who chose the five-year rate of 10.75% to purchase a $122 700 house did benefit over those taking short-term loans, but the gain was trivial, the bank said. The principal and interest cost over five years would have been $52 216, while one-year terms would amount to $52 321. The one-year rate was 9.5% in the first year, followed by 10.25%, 12.13%, 12.65%, and 12.2% for the renewals.

In May 1992, when rates were volatile, the savings gained by opting for a short-term mortgage was $11 000 for a $142 000 house. The one-year rate was 8.5% at that time, and 7.25%, 7.95%, 8.6%, and 6.5% for each renewal.

QUESTIONS

1. Refer to the article for the data for the five-year period beginning September 1981.
   a) If an average house in September 1981 cost $106 800, what was the amount of the purchase price that was financed by a mortgage?
   b) Calculate the total principal and interest that would be paid over five years using the five-year fixed rate of interest. How close is your answer to the total of $83 900 given in the article? (Although it is not stated, the article assumes the mortgage is amortized over 25 years, interest is calculated semi-annually not in advance, and mortgage payments are made monthly.)
   c) To check the reasonableness of the total principal and interest amount of $55 700 given in the article, first calculate the average interest rate in effect over the five-year period. Then, using the assumptions from part (b), calculate the total principal and interest that would be paid over a five-year term using the average interest rate you just calculated. How different is your calculation from the $55 700 figure given in the article?

2. In May 1992, the five-year rate was 10.16%. For the five year term, the one-year was 8.5% in the first year, followed by 7.25%, 7.85%, 8.6% and 6.5%. Using the same method described in Question 1, how different is your answer from the $11 000 figure given in the article?

SOURCE: Adapted from Marian Stinson, "The Rate Game Has Its Price," *The Globe and Mail Report on Business*, April 22, 1997, p. B1. Reprinted with permission from *The Globe and Mail*.

F. Mortgage statement

Currently, when financial institutions record monthly mortgage payments, they calculate interest for the exact number of days that have elapsed since the last payment. This is done by multiplying the effective monthly rate of interest by 12 to convert it into a simple annual rate of interest. The annual rate is then multiplied by the number of days expressed as a fraction of 365.

For example, $f = 0.65582\%$ becomes the simple annual interest rate $12(0.65582\%) = 7.86984\%$.

This approach takes into account that the number of days elapsed between payments fluctuates depending on the number of days in a particular month. It also allows for fluctuations in receiving payments, and permits semi-monthly, bi-weekly, or weekly payments for mortgages requiring contractual monthly payments.

EXAMPLE 14.4E

A credit union member made the contractual mortgage payment of $725.00 on May 31, leaving a mortgage loan balance of $75 411.79. The effective monthly fixed rate was 0.53447%. The member made the contractual payments on June 28, July 31, August 30, September 30, October 29, November 28, and December 30. The credit union agreed to convert the fixed-rate mortgage to a demand mortgage on October 29 at 5.25% compounded annually. This rate was changed to 4.75% on December 2. Determine the mortgage balance on December 30.

Solution

The monthly effective rate $f = 0.53447\%$ is equivalent to the simple annual rate $12(0.53447\%) = 6.41364\%$.

Payment Date	Number of Days	Amount Paid	Interest Paid	Principal	Balance Repaid
May 31	rate is 6.41364%				75 411.79
Jun 28	28	725.00	371.03	353.97	75 057.82
Jul 31	33	725.00	435.23	289.77	74 768.05
Aug 30	30	725.00	394.14	330.86	74 437.19
Sept 30	31	725.00	405.47	319.53	74 117.66
Oct 29	29	725.00	377.69	347.31	73 770.35
Oct 29	rate becomes 5.25%				
Nov 28	30	725.00	318.32	406.68	73 363.67
Dec 02	rate becomes 4.75%				
Dec 30	32	725.00	309.54[*]	415.46	72 948.21

[*]Note: Interest calculation for December is

4 days at 5.25% on $73 363.67	$ 42.21
28 days at 4.75% on $73 363.67	267.33
Total	$309.54

EXAMPLE 14.4F

A mortgage of $55 000.00 closed on April 12, amortized over 15 years at 8.50% compounded semi-annually for a 5-year term. It requires contractual monthly payments rounded up to the nearest $10. The lender agreed to accept bi-weekly payments of half the contractual monthly amount starting April 24. The mortgagor's second June payment was three days late.

(i) Determine the size of the contractual monthly payment.

(ii) Produce a mortgage statement to June 30.

(iii) Compute the accrued interest on June 30.

Solution

(i) $A_{nc} = 55\,000.00;\quad n = 12(15) = 180;\quad i = 4.25;\quad c = \dfrac{1}{6}$

$f = (1.0425)^{\frac{1}{6}} - 1 = 1.0069611 - 1 = 0.0069611\%$

$55\,000.00 = R\left(\dfrac{1 - 1.0069611^{-180}}{0.0069611}\right)$

$55\,000.00 = R(102.44)$
$\qquad\quad R = 536.89$

The contractual monthly payment is $540.00.

(ii) The bi-weekly payment is $270.00.
The annual rate of interest $= 12(0.69611) = 8.35332\%$.

Payment Date	Number of Days	Amount Paid	Interest Paid	Principal	Balance Repaid
April 12					55 000.00
April 24	12	270.00	151.05	118.95	54 881.05
May 8	14	270.00	175.84	94.16	54 786.89
May 22	14	270.00	175.54	94.46	54 692.43
June 5	14	270.00	175.24	94.76	54 597.67
June 22	17	270.00	212.42	57.58	54 540.09

The mortgage balance on June 30 is $54 540.09.

(iii) On June 30 interest has accrued for 8 days.
The amount of accrued interest

$= 54\,540.09(0.0835332)\left(\dfrac{8}{365}\right) = \$99.86.$

Exercise 14.4

A. Answer each of the following questions.

1. A $90 000.00 mortgage is to be amortized by making monthly payments for 25 years. Interest is 8.5% compounded semi-annually for a five-year term.

a) Compute the size of the monthly payment.

b) Determine the balance at the end of the five-year term.

c) If the mortgage is renewed for a three-year term at 7% compounded semi-annually, what is the size of the monthly payment for the renewal term?

2. A demand (variable rate) mortgage of $150 000.00 is amortized over 20 years by equal monthly payments. After 18 months the original interest rate of 6% p.a. was raised to 6.6% p.a. Two years after the mortgage was taken out, it was renewed at the request of the mortgagor at a fixed rate of 7.5% for a four-year term.

a) Calculate the mortgage balance after 18 months.

b) Compute the size of the new monthly payment at the 6.6% rate of interest.

c) Determine the mortgage balance at the end of the four-year term.

3. A $40 000.00 mortgage is to be repaid over a ten-year period by monthly payments rounded up to the next higher $50.00. Interest is 9% compounded semi-annually.

a) Determine the number of rounded payments required to repay the mortgage.

b) Determine the size of the last payment.

c) Calculate the amount of interest saved by rounding the payments up to the next higher $50.

4. A mortgage balance of $23 960.70 is to be repaid over a seven-year term by equal monthly payments at 11% compounded semi-annually. At the request of the mortgagor, the monthly payments were set at $440.00.

a) How many payments will the mortgagor have to make?

b) What is the size of last payment?

c) Determine the difference between the total actual amount paid and the total amount required to amortize the mortgage by the contractual monthly payments.

5. A mortgage of $80 000.00 is amortized over 15 years by monthly payments of $826.58. What is the nominal annual rate of interest compounded semi-annually?

6. At what nominal annual rate of interest will a $195 000.00 demand (variable-rate) mortgage be amortized by monthly payments of $1606.87 over 20 years?

7. Interest for the initial four-year term of a $105 000.00 mortgage is 7.25% compounded semi-annually. The mortgage is to be repaid by equal monthly payments over 20 years. The mortgage contract permits lump-sum payments at each anniversary date up to 10% of the original principal.

a) What is the balance at the end of the four-year term if a lump-sum payment of $7000.00 is made at the end of the third year?

b) How many more payments will be required after the four-year term if there is no change in the interest rate?

c) What is the difference in the cost of the mortgage if no lump-sum payment is made?

8. The Berezins agreed to monthly payments rounded up to the nearest $100.00 on a mortgage of $36 000.00 amortized over ten years. Interest for the first five years was 8.75% compounded semi-annually. After 30 months, as permitted by the mortgage agreement, the Berezins increased the rounded monthly payment by 10%.

a) Determine the mortgage balance at the end of the five-year term.

b) If the interest rate remains unchanged over the remaining term, how many more of the increased payments will amortize the mortgage balance?

c) How much did the Berezins save by exercising the increase-in-payment option?

9. A $40 000.00 mortgage taken out on June 1 is to be repaid by monthly payments rounded up to the nearest $10.00. The payments are due on the first day of each month starting July 1. The amortization period is 12 years and interest is 5.5% compounded semi-annually for a six-month term. Construct an amortization schedule for the six-month term.

10. For Question 9, produce the mortgage statement for the six-month term. Assume all payments have been made on time. Compare the balance to the balance in Question 9 and explain why there may be a difference.

11. For the mortgage in Question 9, develop a mortgage statement for the six-month term if semi-monthly payments equal to one-half of the monthly payment are made on the first day and the 16th day of each month. The first payment is due June 16. Compare the balance to the balances in Question 9 and Question 10. Explain why there are differences.

12. For the mortgage in Question 9, develop a mortgage statement for the six-month term if bi-weekly payments equal to one-half of the rounded monthly payments are made starting June 16. Compare the balance to the balances in Questions 9, 10, and 11. Explain why it differs significantly from the other three balances.

REVIEW EXERCISE

1. Sylvie Cardinal bought a business for $45 000.00. She made a down payment of $10 000.00 and agreed to repay the balance by equal payments at the end of every three months for eight years. Interest is 8% compounded quarterly.

a) What is the size of the quarterly payments?

b) What will be the total cost of financing?

c) How much will Sylvie owe after five years?

d) How much interest will be included in the 20th payment?

e) How much of the principal will be repaid by the 24th payment?

f) Construct a partial amortization schedule showing details of the first three payments, Payments 10, 11, 12, the last three payments, and totals.

2. Angelo Lemay borrowed $8000.00 from his credit union. He agreed to repay the loan by making equal monthly payments for five years. Interest is 9% compounded monthly.

   a) What is the size of the monthly payments?

   b) How much will the loan cost him?

   c) How much will Angelo owe after eighteen months?

   d) How much interest will he pay in his 36th payment?

   e) How much of the principal will be repaid by the 48th payment?

   f) Prepare a partial amortization schedule showing details of the first three payments, Payments 24, 25, 26, the last three payments, and totals.

3. Comfort Swim Limited borrowed $40 000.00 for replacement of equipment. The debt is repaid in instalments of $2000.00 made at the end of every three months.

   a) If interest is 7% compounded quarterly, how many payments are needed?

   b) How much will Comfort Swim owe after two years?

   c) How much of the 12th payment is interest?

   d) How much of the principal will be repaid by the 20th payment?

   e) Construct a partial amortization schedule showing details of the first three payments, the last three payments, and totals.

4. A $48 000.00 mortgage amortized by monthly payments over 35 years is renewable after five years. Interest is 9% compounded semi-annually.

   a) What is the size of the monthly payments?

   b) How much interest is paid during the first year?

   c) How much of the principal is repaid during the first five-year term?

   d) If the mortgage is renewed for a further five-year term at 8% compounded semi-annually, what will be the size of the monthly payments?

   e) Construct a partial amortization schedule showing details of the first three payments for each of the two five-year terms, the last three payments for the second five-year term, and totals at the end of the second five-year term.

5. Pelican Recreational Services owes $27 500.00 secured by a collateral mortgage. The mortgage is amortized over fifteen years by equal payments made at the end of every three months and is renewable after three years.

a)   If interest is 7% compounded annually, what is the size of the payments?

b)   How much of the principal is repaid by the fourth payment?

c)   What is the balance at the end of the three-year term?

d)   If the mortgage is renewed for a further four years but amortized over eight years and interest is 7.5% compounded semi-annually, what is the size of the quarterly payments for the renewal period?

e)   Construct a partial amortization schedule showing details of the first three payments for each of the two terms, the last three payments in the four-year term, and totals at the end of the four-year term.

6. A debt of $17 500.00 is repaid by payments of $2850.00 made at the end of each year. Interest is 14% compounded semi-annually.

a)   How many payments are needed to repay the debt?

b)   What is the cost of the debt for the first three years?

c)   What is the principal repaid in the seventh year?

d)   Construct an amortization schedule showing details of the first three payments, the last three payments, and totals.

7. A debt of $25 000.00 is repaid by payments of $3500.00 made at the end of every six months. Interest is 11% compounded semi-annually.

a)   How many payments are needed to repay the debt?

b)   What is the size of the final payment?

8. Jane Evans receives payments of $900.00 at the beginning of each month from a pension fund of $72 500.00. Interest earned by the fund is 12% compounded monthly.

a)   What is the number of payments Jane will receive?

b)   What is the size of the final payment?

9. A lease agreement valued at $33 000.00 requires payment of $4300.00 every three months in advance. The payments are deferred for three years and money is worth 10% compounded quarterly.

a)   How many lease payments are to be made under the contract?

b)   What is the size of the final lease payment?

10. A contract worth $52 000.00 provides benefits of $20 000.00 at the end of each year. The benefits are deferred for ten years and interest is 11% compounded quarterly.

a)   How many payments are to be made under the contract?

b)   What is the size of the last benefit payment?

11. A mortgage for $135 000.00 is amortized over 25 years. Interest is 8.7% p.a., compounded semi-annually, for a five-year term and payments are monthly.

    a) Compute the monthly payment.

    b) Compute the balance at the end of the five-year term.

    c) Compute the monthly payment if the mortgage is renewed for a three-year term at 7.8% compounded semi-annually.

12. A $180 000.00 mortgage is to be amortized by making monthly payments for 25 years. Interest is 7.9% compounded semi-annually for a four-year term.

    a) Compute the size of the monthly payment.

    b) Determine the balance at the end of the four-year term.

    c) If the mortgage is renewed for a five-year term at 8.8% compounded semi-annually, what is the size of the monthly payment for the renewal term?

13. An $80 000.00 mortgage is to be repaid over a 10-year period by monthly payments rounded up to the next higher $50.00. Interest is 8.5% compounded semi-annually.

    a) What is the number of rounded payments required to repay the mortgage?

    b) What is the size of the last payment?

    c) How much interest was saved by rounding the payments up to the next higher $50.00?

14. A $160 000.00 mortgage is to be repaid over a 20-year period by monthly payments rounded up to the next higher $100.00. Interest is 9.2% compounded semi-annually.

    a) Determine the number of rounded payments required to repay the mortgage.

    b) Determine the size of the last payment.

    c) Calculate the amount of interest saved by rounding the payments up to the next higher $100.00.

15. A debt of $6500.00 is repaid in equal monthly instalments over four years. Interest is 9% compounded monthly.

    a) What is the size of the monthly payments?

    b) What will be the total cost of borrowing?

    c) What is the outstanding balance after one year?

    d) How much of the 30th payment is interest?

    e) Construct a partial amortization schedule showing details of the first three payments, the last three payments, and totals.

16. Milton Investments borrowed $32 000.00 at 11% compounded semi-annually. The loan is repaid by payments of $4500.00 due at the end of every six months.

    a) How many payments are needed?

    b) How much of the principal will be repaid by the fifth payment?

    c) Prepare a partial amortization schedule showing the details of the last three payments and totals.

17. A mortgage of $95 000.00 is amortized over 25 years by monthly payments of $748.06. What is the nominal rate of interest compounded semi-annually?

18. At what nominal annual rate of interest will a $135 000.00 mortgage be amortized by monthly payments of $1370.69 over 15 years?

19. A $28 000.00 mortgage is amortized by quarterly payments over twenty years. The mortgage is renewable after three years and interest is 6% compounded semi-annually.

    a) What is the size of the quarterly payments?

    b) How much interest will be paid during the first year?

    c) What is the balance at the end of the three-year term?

    d) If the mortgage is renewed for another three years at 7% compounded annually, what will be the size of the quarterly payments for the renewal period?

20. The Superior Tool Company is repaying a debt of $16 000.00 by payments of $1000.00 made at the end of every three months. Interest is 7.5% compounded monthly.

    a) How many payments are needed to repay the debt?

    b) What is the size of the final payment?

SELF-TEST

1. A $9000.00 loan is repaid by equal monthly payments over five years. What is the outstanding balance after two years if interest is 12% compounded monthly?

2. A loan of $15 000.00 is repaid by quarterly payments of $700.00 each at 18% compounded quarterly. What is the principal repaid by the twenty-fifth payment?

3. A $50 000.00 mortgage is amortized by monthly payments over twenty years. If interest is 9% compounded semi-annually, how much interest will be paid during the first three years?

4. A debt of $24 000.00 is repaid by quarterly payments of $1100.00. If interest is 6% compounded quarterly, what is the size of the final payment?

5. A $190 000.00 mortgage is to be amortized by making monthly payments for 20 years. Interest is 6.5% compounded semi-annually for a three-year term.

   a) Compute the size of the monthly payment.

   b) Determine the balance at the end of the three-year term.

   c) If the mortgage is renewed for a five-year term at 7.25% compounded semi-annually, what is the size of the monthly payment for the renewal term?

6. A $140 000.00 mortgage is to repaid over a 15-year period by monthly payments rounded up to the next higher $50.00. Interest is 8.25% compounded semi-annually.

   a) Determine the number of rounded payments required to repay the mortgage.

   b) Determine the size of the last payment.

   c) Calculate the amount of interest saved by rounding the payments up to the next higher $50.00.

7. A mortgage of $145 000 is amortized over 25 years by monthly payments of $1297.00. What is the nominal annual rate of interest compounded semi-annually?

8. A loan of $12 000.00 is amortized over ten years by equal monthly payments at 15% compounded monthly. Construct an amortization schedule showing details of the first three payments, the fortieth payment, the last three payments, and totals.

CHALLENGE PROBLEMS

1. A debt is amortized by monthly payments of $250.00. Interest is 8% compounded monthly. If the outstanding balance is $3225.68 just after a particular payment (say, the xth payment), what was the balance just after the previous payment (i.e., the $(x - 1)$th payment)

2. Captain Sinclair has been posted to Cold Lake, Alberta. He prefers to purchase a condo rather than live on the base. He knows that in four years he will be posted overseas. The condo he wishes to purchase will require a mortgage of $130 000, and he has narrowed his choices to two lenders. Trust Company A is offering a five-year mortgage at 6.75% compounded semi-annually. This mortgage can be paid off at any time but there is a penalty clause in the agreement requiring two months' interest on the

remaining principal. Trust Company B is offering a five-year mortgage for 7% compounded semi-annually. It can be paid off at any time without penalty. Both mortgages are amortized over 25 years and require monthly payments. Captain Sinclair will have to sell his condo in four years and pay off the mortgage at that time before moving overseas. Given that he expects to earn 3% compounded annually on his money over the next five years, which mortgage offer is cheaper? By how much is it cheaper?

CASE STUDY 14.1 MORTGAGE MANEUVERS

Orest and Hetty Frankowski purchased their first home, a four-year-old bungalow. The previous owner of this house had had a five-year mortgage on which he paid 13% interest. Since the interest rates had fallen, the previous owner was glad to sell the house and pay off his mortgage. When Orest and Hetty bought the house, the interest rate on a mortgage with a five-year term was $9\frac{3}{4}$%, which was much better than the previous owner's mortgage rate. Since the interest rates seemed reasonable and the process of negotiating a mortgage was new to them, Orest and Hetty decided that they didn't want to worry about refinancing in the short term. Therefore, they arranged a mortgage with their bank for $100 000.00 amortized over 25 years. The interest rate was $9\frac{3}{4}$% compounded semi-annually for a five-year term, and payments were made monthly.

After three years, interest rates had dropped even further. Interest on mortgages with a five-year term was 7% compounded semi-annually. Orest and Hetty decided to see whether they could change their mortgage so that they could pay the new lower interest rates. They met with their bank's loans officer, who informed them that there is a penalty for renegotiating a mortgage early, before the end of their five-year term. According to their mortgage contract, the penalty for renegotiating the mortgage before the end of the five-year term is the *greater* of:

A. Three month's interest at the original rate of interest. (Banks generally calculate this as one month's interest on the mortgage principal remaining to be paid, multiplied by three.)

B. The interest differential over the remainder of the original term. (Banks generally calculate this as the difference between the interest the bank would have earned over the remainder of the original term at the original [higher] mortgage rate and at the renegotiated [lower] mortgage rate.)

The loans officer also explained that there are two options for paying the penalty amount: (1) you can pay the full amount of the penalty at the beginning of the new mortgage period; (2) the penalty amount can be added to the principal when the mortgage is renegotiated, allowing the penalty to be paid off over the term of the new mortgage.

Orest and Hetty agreed to look at their options before giving the loans officer their final answer.

QUESTIONS

1. Suppose there was no penalty for refinancing the mortgage after three years. How much would Orest and Hetty save per month by refinancing their mortgage for a five-year term at the new rate?

2. Suppose Orest and Hetty decide to refinance their mortgage for a five-year term at the new interest rate.
   a) What is the amount of penalty A?
   b) What is the amount of penalty B?
   c) What penalty would Orest and Hetty have to pay in this situation?

3. If they pay the full amount of the penalty at the beginning of the new five-year term, what will Orest and Hetty's new monthly payment be?

4. If the penalty amount is added to the principal when the mortgage is renegotiated, what will the new monthly payment be?

CASE STUDY 14.2 STEERING THE BUSINESS

On February 1, 1997, Sandra and her friend Francisco arranged a loan to purchase two used black limousines for $35 000.00 and $50 000.00 respectively, and launched their new business, Classy Limousine Services. The loan was for two years at 9.5% compounded semi-annually. Payments were made quarterly beginning on May 1, 1997.

Business was brisk, especially for weddings. To meet the demand, the partners bought a new white stretch limousine on April 1, 1998, for $110 000.00. They arranged a three-year loan for this amount at 8.8% interest compounded monthly. Payments were made monthly beginning on May 1, 1998.

On August 1, 1998, the partners were given an opportunity to buy a black super-stretch limousine for $140 000.00. They arranged a three-year loan for this amount at 7.8% interest compounded monthly. The monthly payments began on September 1, 1998.

Business continued to increase. Sandra and Francisco discussed the need for a new parking garage and office space they could own instead of rent. When an industrial warehouse large enough to house their expanding fleet became available, they decided to purchase it. The $280 000.00 mortgage had an interest rate of 8.9% compounded semi-annually for a five-year term. It was amortized over 20 years, and the monthly mortgage payments began on March 1, 1999.

Concerned about their cash flows, Sandra and Francisco decided to make no more large purchases for the next year.

QUESTIONS

1. What is the size of the quarterly payments for the original loan obtained on February 1, 1997?

2. What is the size of the monthly payments for the loan on the white stretch limousine?

3. What is the size of the monthly payments for the loan on the black super-stretch limousine?

4. **a)** What is the size of the monthly payments required for the mortgage on the warehouse?

   b) What principal will remain to be paid at the end of the mortgage's five-year term?

5. On each of the following dates, what is the total of all the loan payments that must be paid?
   a) May 1, 1998
   b) November 1, 1998
   c) July 1, 1999

SUMMARY OF FORMULAE

No new formulae were introduced in this chapter. However, some of the formulae introduced in Chapters 9 to 12 have been used and are listed below.

Formula 9.1A
$$S = P(1 + i)^n$$

Formula 11.1
$$S_n = R\left[\frac{(1 + i)^n - 1}{i}\right]$$

Formula 11.2
$$A_n = R\left[\frac{1 - (1 + i)^{-n}}{i}\right]$$

Formula 11.3
$$S_{nc} = R\left[\frac{(1 + f)^n - 1}{f}\right] \text{ where } f = (1 + i)^c - 1$$

Formula 11.4
$$A_{nc} = R\left[\frac{1 - (1 + f)^{-n}}{f}\right] \text{ where } f = (1 + i)^c - 1$$

Formula 12.2
$$A_n(\text{due}) = R(1 + i)\left[\frac{1 - (1 + i)^{-n}}{i}\right]$$

GLOSSARY

Amortization repayment of both interest and principal of interest-bearing debts by a series of equal payments made at equal intervals of time

Amortization schedule a schedule showing in detail how a debt is repaid

Canada Mortgage and Housing Corporation (CMHC) the corporation of the federal government that administers the National Housing Act (NHA) and provides mortgage insurance to lenders

Demand mortgage a mortgage for which the rate of interest changes as money market conditions change

Equity the difference between the price for which a property could be sold and the total debts registered against the property

First mortgage the first legal claim registered against a property; in the event of default by the borrower, first mortgagees are paid before all other claimants

Fixed-rate mortgage a mortgage for which the rate of interest is fixed for a specific period of time; it can be open or closed

Gross Debt Service (GDS) ratio the percent of gross annual income required to cover such housing costs as mortgage payments, property taxes, and heating costs

Prospective method a method for finding the outstanding debt balance that considers the payments that remain outstanding

Residential mortgage a claim to a residential property given by a borrower to a lender as security for the repayment of a loan

Retrospective method a method of finding the outstanding balance of a debt that considers the payments that have been made

Second mortgage the second legal claim registered against a property; in the event of default by the borrower, second-mortgage holders are paid only after first-mortgage holders have been paid

Total Debt Service (TDS) ratio the percent of gross annual income required to cover such housing costs as mortgage payments, property taxes, and heat, and all other debts and obligations

Variable-rate mortgage see *Demand mortgage*

15 Bond Valuation and Sinking Funds

$\mathbf{M}$any financial planners recommend bonds as a part of a balanced investment portfolio. Historically, bonds represent a less risky investment than stocks. Companies and governments issue bonds to raise large sums of money. To have the funds to pay for the bonds when they mature, companies often create a *sinking fund* by making regular equal investments from the outset of the bond issue. Both individuals and companies use annuity formulae to decide about possible investments in bonds and sinking funds.

Introduction

Bonds are contracts used to borrow sizeable sums of money, usually from a large group of investors. The indenture, or contract, for most bonds provides for the repayment of the principal at a specified future date plus periodic payment of interest at a specified percent of the face value. Bonds are negotiable; that is, they can be freely bought and sold. The mathematical issues arising from the trading of bonds are the topic of this chapter.

OBJECTIVES

Upon completing this chapter, you will be able to do the following:

1. Determine the purchase price of bonds, redeemable at par or otherwise, bought on or between interest dates.
2. Calculate the premium or discount on the purchase of a bond.
3. Construct bond schedules showing the amortization of premiums or accumulation of discounts.
4. Calculate the yield rate for bonds bought on the market by the method of averages and, more accurately, by trial and error.
5. Make sinking fund computations when payments form simple annuities, including the size of the periodic payments, accumulated balance, interest earned, and increase in the fund.
6. Construct complete or partial sinking fund schedules.

15.1 PURCHASE PRICE OF BONDS

A. Basic concepts and terminology

Corporations and governments use bonds to borrow money, usually from a large group of lenders (investors). To deal with the expected large number of investors, the borrower prints up written contracts, called bonds or **debentures**, in advance. The printed bonds specify the terms of the contract including

(a) the **face value** (or **par value** or **denomination**), which is the amount owed to the holder of the bond, usually a multiple of $100 such as $100, $1000, $5000, $10 000, $25 000, $100 000;

(b) the **bond rate** (or **coupon rate** or **nominal rate**), which is the rate of interest paid, usually semi-annually, based on the face value of the bond;

(c) the **redemption date** (or **maturity date** or **due date**), which is the date on which the principal of the bond is to be repaid;

(d) the **redemption price**, which is the money paid by the issuer to the bond-holder at the date of surrender of the bonds.

Most bonds are **redeemable at par**; that is, they are redeemable at their *face* value. However, some bonds have a redemption feature either to make the bonds more attractive to the investor or because they are callable, that is, because they can be redeemed *before* maturity. In either case, the bonds will be **redeemed at a premium**, that is, at a price *greater* than their face price. The redemption price in such cases is stated as a percent of the face values. For example, the redemption price of a $5000 bond redeemable at 104 is 104% of $5000, or $5200.

Investors in bonds expect to receive periodic interest payments during the term of the bond from the date of issue to the date of maturity and they expect to receive the principal at the date of maturity.

To facilitate the payment of interest, most bonds have dated interest **coupons** attached that can be cashed on or after the stated interest payment date at any bank. For example, a twenty-year, $1000.00 bond bearing interest at 10% payable semi-annually will have attached to it at the date of issue forty coupons of $50.00 each. Each coupon represents the semi-annual interest due on each of the forty interest payment dates.

The issuer may or may not offer security such as real estate, plant, or equipment as a guarantee for the repayment of the principal. Bonds for which no security is offered are called **debentures**.

Bonds are marketable and may be freely bought and sold. When investors acquire bonds, they buy two promises:

1. A promise to be paid the redemption price of the bond at maturity.
2. A promise to be paid the periodic interest payments according to the rate of interest stated on the bond.

Two basic problems arise for investors when buying bonds:

1. What should be the purchase price of a bond to provide the investor with a given rate of return?
2. What is the rate of interest which a bond will yield if bought at a given price?

In this section we will deal with the first of these two problems.

B. Purchase price of a bond bought on an interest date

EXAMPLE 15.1A   A $1000 bond bearing interest at 10% payable semi-annually is due in four years. If money is worth 12% compounded semi-annually, what is the value of the bond if purchased today?

Solution   The buyer of the bond acquires two promises:

1. A promise of $1000.00 four years from now.
2. A promise of $50.00 interest due at the end of every six months (the annual interest is 10% of 1000.00 = $100.00, half of which is paid after the first six months, the other half at the end of the year).

The two promises can be represented on a time graph as Figure 15.1 shows.

FIGURE 15.1   **Graphic Representation of Method and Data**

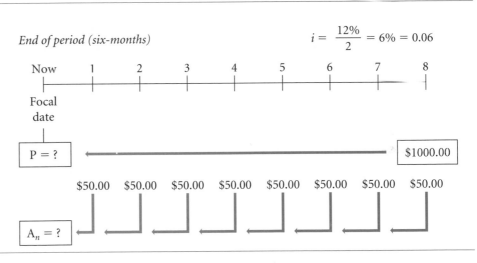

The focal date for evaluating the two promises is "now" and the rate of interest to be used for the valuation is 12% compounded semi-annually.

The value at the focal date of the redemption price of $1000.00 is its present value.

$$S = 1000.00; \quad n = 4(2) = 8; \quad i = \frac{12\%}{2} = 6\% = 0.06$$

$P = 1000.00(1.06)^{-8}$ ———————————— **using Formula 9.1C**
$P = 1000.00(0.6274124)$
$P = \$627.41$

Programmed solution

0 [PMT] 1000 [FV] 6 [%i] 8 [N] [CPT] [PV] [627.41237]

The value "now" of the semi-annual interest payments is the present value of an ordinary annuity.

$$R = \frac{10\% \text{ of } 1000.00}{2} = 50.00; \quad n = 8; \quad i = 6\%$$

$$A_n = 50.00\left(\frac{1 - 1.06^{-8}}{0.06}\right) \quad\text{——— using Formula 11.2}$$

$$= 50.00(6.2097938)$$
$$= \$310.49$$

Programmed solution

0 [FV] 50 [PMT] 6 [%i] 8 [N] [CPT] [PV] [310.48969]

The purchase price of the bond is the sum of the present values of the two promises

$$= P + A_n$$
$$= 627.41 + 310.49 = \$937.90$$

THE PURCHASE PRICE OF A BOND BOUGHT ON AN INTEREST PAYMENT DATE	=	THE PRESENT VALUE OF THE REDEMPTION PRICE	+	THE PRESENT VALUE OF THE INTEREST PAYMENTS

The two steps involved in using the above relationship can be combined.

$$\text{PURCHASE PRICE} = P + A_n$$
$$= S(1 + i)^{-n} + R\left[\frac{1 - (1 + i)^{-n}}{i}\right] \quad\text{——— Formula 15.1}$$

where S = the redemption price of the bond;
  R = the periodic interest payment (coupon);
  n = the number of outstanding interest payments (or compounding periods);
  i = the yield rate per payment interval.

Note: It is important to recognize that two rates of interest are used in determining the purchase price:

1. the bond rate, which determines the size of the periodic interest payments (coupons);
2. the **yield rate**, which is used to determine the present values of the two promises.

EXAMPLE 15.1B A $5000 bond bearing interest at 10.5% payable semi-annually is redeemable at par in ten years. If it is bought to yield 9% compounded semi-annually, what is the purchase price of the bond?

Solution

The redemption price S = 5000.00;

the coupon $R = \dfrac{5000.00(0.105)}{2} = 262.50$;

$n = 10(2) = 20$; $\quad i = \dfrac{9\%}{2} = 4.5\% = 0.045$

$$\text{Purchase price} = \begin{array}{c}\text{PRESENT VALUE OF THE}\\ \text{REDEMPTION PRICE}\end{array} + \begin{array}{c}\text{PRESENT VALUE}\\ \text{OF THE COUPONS}\end{array}$$

$$= \text{P} \qquad\qquad + \text{A}_n$$

$$= 5000.00(1.045^{-20}) \quad + 262.50\left(\dfrac{1 - 1.045^{-20}}{0.045}\right)$$

$$= 5000.00(0.4146429) \;+ 262.50(13.007936)$$

$$= 2073.21 + 3414.58$$

$$= \$5487.79$$

Programmed solution

0 [PMT] 5000 [FV] 4.5 [%i] 20 [N] [CPT] [PV] [2073.2143]

0 [FV] 262.50 [PMT] 4.5 [%i] 20 [N] [CPT] [PV] [3414.5833]

(These keystrokes can be eliminated since they are still programmed in the calculator from the previous step)

The purchase price is 2073.21 + 3414.58 = \$5487.79.

EXAMPLE 15.1C A bond with a par value of \$10 000 is redeemable at 106 in 25 years. The coupon rate is 8% payable semi-annually. What is the purchase price of the bond to yield 10% compounded semi-annually?

Solution

The redemption price S = 10 000.00(1.06) = 10 600.00;

the coupon $R = \dfrac{10\,000.00(0.08)}{2} = 400.00$;

$n = 25(2) = 50$; $\quad i = \dfrac{10\%}{2} = 5\% = 0.05$

Purchase price = P + A$_n$

$$= 10\,600.00(1.05^{-50}) + 400.00\left(\dfrac{1 - 1.05^{-50}}{0.05}\right)$$

$$= 10\,600.00(0.0872037) + 400.00(18.255925)$$

$$= 924.36 + 7302.37$$

$$= \$8226.73$$

Programmed solution

0 [PMT] 10 600 [FV] 5 [%i] 50 [N] [CPT] [PV] [924.35951]

0 [FV] 400 [PMT] 5 [%i] 50 [N] [CPT] [PV] [7302.3702]

The purchase price is 924.36 + 7302.37 = $8226.73

EXAMPLE 15.1D A $25 000 bond bearing interest at 11% payable quarterly is redeemable at 107 in twelve years. Find the purchase price of the bond to yield 10% compounded quarterly.

Solution The redemption price S = 25 000.00(1.07) = 26 750.00;

the coupon $R = \dfrac{25\,000.00(0.11)}{4} = 687.50$;

$n = 12(4) = 48;\quad i = \dfrac{10\%}{4} = 2.5\% = 0.025$

Purchase price $= 26\,750.00(1.025^{-48}) + 687.50\left(\dfrac{1 - 1.025^{-48}}{0.025}\right)$

$= 26\,750.00(0.3056712) + 687.50(27.773154)$
$= 8176.70 + 19\,094.04$
$= \$27\,270.74$

Programmed solution

0 [PMT] 26 750 [FV] 2.5 [%i] 48 [N] [CPT] [PV] [8176.7035]

0 [FV] 687.50 [PMT] 2.5 [%i] 48 [N] [CPT] [PV] [19 094.043]

The purchase price is 8176.70 + 19 094.04 = 27 270.74.

In the preceding problems, the bond interest payment period and the yield rate conversion period were equal in length. This permitted the use of simple annuity formulae. However, when the bond interest payment period and the yield rate conversion period are not equal in length, general annuity formulae must be used.

EXAMPLE 15.1E A municipality issues ten-year bonds in the amount of $1 000 000. Interest on the bonds is 10% payable annually. What is the issue price of the bonds if the bonds are sold to yield 11% compounded quarterly?

Solution The redemption price of the bonds S = 1 000 000.00;

the annual interest payment R = 1 000 000.00(0.10) = $100 000.00.

Since the interest payment period (annual) is not equal in length to the yield rate conversion period (quarterly), the interest payments form an ordinary general annuity.

$$n = 10; \quad c = \frac{4}{1} = 4; \quad i = \frac{11\%}{4} = 2.75\% = 0.0275;$$

$$f = 1.0275^4 - 1 = 1.1146213 - 1 = 0.1146213 = 11.46213\%$$

The present value of the redemption price

$$P = 1\,000\,000.00(1.1146213^{-10})$$
$$= 1\,000\,000.00(0.3378521)$$
$$= \$337\,852.10$$

The present value of the annual interest payments

$$A_{nc} = 100\,000.00\left[\frac{(1 - 1.1146213^{-10})}{0.1146213}\right] \quad \text{—— using Formula 11.4}$$

$$= 100\,000.00(5.7768312)$$
$$= \$577\,683.12$$

Programmed solution

$$\boxed{0}\,\boxed{\text{PMT}}\,1\,000\,000\,\boxed{\text{FV}}\,11.46213\,\boxed{\%i}\,10\,\boxed{\text{N}}\,\boxed{\text{CPT}}\,\boxed{\text{PV}}\,\boxed{337\,852.10}$$

$$\boxed{0}\,\boxed{\text{FV}}\,100\,000\,\boxed{\text{PMT}}\,11.46213\,\boxed{\%i}\,10\,\boxed{\text{N}}\,\boxed{\text{CPT}}\,\boxed{\text{PV}}\,\boxed{557\,683.12}$$

The issue price is $337\,852.10 + 577\,683.12 = \$915\,535.22$.

We can modify Formula 15.1 to allow for the general annuity case by using Formula 11.4.

$$\text{PURCHASE PRICE} = P + A_{nc} = S(1 + f)^{-n} + R\left[\frac{1 - (1 + f)^{-n}}{f}\right]$$

$$\text{where } f = (1 + i)^c - 1 \quad \text{—— Formula 15.2}$$

EXAMPLE 15.1F A $100\,000 bond redeemable at 103 bearing interest at 11.5% payable semi-annually is bought eight years before maturity to yield 10% compounded quarterly. What is the purchase price of the bond?

Solution The redemption price $S = 100\,000.00(1.03) = \$103\,000.00$;

the size of the semi-annual coupon $R = 100\,000.00\left(\frac{0.115}{2}\right) = \$5750.00$

$$n = 8(2) = 16; \quad c = \frac{4}{2} = 2; \quad i = \frac{10\%}{4} = 2.5\% = 0.025;$$

$$f = 1.025^2 - 1 = 1.050625 - 1 = 0.050625 = 5.0625\%$$

The purchase price of the bond using Formula 15.2

$$= 103\,000.00(1.050625^{-16}) + 5750.00\left(\frac{1 - 1.050625^{-16}}{0.050625}\right)$$

$$= 103\,000.00(0.4537706) + 5750.00(10.789717)$$
$$= 46\,738.37 + 62\,040.87$$
$$= \$108\,779.24$$

Programmed solution

0 [PMT] 103 000 [FV] 5.0625 [%i] 16 [N] [CPT] [PV] [46 738.367]

0 [FV] 5750 [PMT] 5.0625 [%i] 16 [N] [CPT] [PV] [62 040.875]

The purchase price is 46 738.37 + 62 040.87 = \$108 779.24.

C. Purchase price of bonds between interest dates

The trading of bonds is, of course, not restricted to interest dates. In practice, most bonds are bought and sold between interest dates.

In such cases, we can compute the price of the bond on the date of purchase by first finding the purchase price on the interest date immediately preceding the date of purchase. The resulting value can then be accumulated using the future value formula for simple interest at the nominal yield rate for the number of days elapsed between the interest payment date and the purchase date.

EXAMPLE 15.1G   A bond with a face value of $1000 bearing interest at 10% payable semi-annually matures on August 1, 2000. What is the purchase price of the bond on April 18, 1998, to yield 9% compounded semi-annually?

Solution

STEP 1   Find the purchase price on the preceding interest date.

The redemption price S = $1000.00;

the semi-annual coupon R $= 1000.00\left(\dfrac{0.10}{2}\right) = \$50.00.$

Since the maturity date is August 1, the semi-annual interest dates are February 1 and August 1. The interest date preceding the date of purchase is February 1, 1998. The time period from February 1, 1998, to the date of maturity is 2.5 years.

$$n = 2.5(2) = 5; \quad i = \dfrac{9\%}{2} = 4.5\% = 0.045$$

The purchase price of the bond on February 1, 1998

$$= 1000.00(1.045^{-5}) + 50.00\left(\dfrac{1 - 1.045^{-5}}{0.045}\right)$$

$$= 1000.00(0.802451) + 50.00(4.3899767)$$
$$= 802.45 + 219.50$$
$$= \$1021.95$$

Programmed solution

0 [PMT]   1000 [FV]   4.5 [%i]   5 [N]   [CPT]   [PV]   [802.45105]

0 [FV]   50 [PMT]   4.5 [%i]   5 [N]   [CPT]   [PV]   [219.49884]

The purchase price is 802.45 + 219.50 = $1021.95.

STEP 2   Accumulate the purchase price on February 1, 1998, to the purchase date at simple interest.

The number of days from February 1, 1998, to April 18, 1998, is 76; the number of days in the interest interval February 1, 1998, to August 1, 1998, is 181.

$$P = 1021.95; \quad r = i = 0.045; \quad t = \dfrac{76}{181}$$

$$S = 1021.95\left[1 + 0.045\left(\dfrac{76}{181}\right)\right] = 1021.95(1.018895) = \$1041.26.$$

The purchase price of the bond on April 18, 1998, is $1041.26.

D. Flat price and quoted price

In Example 15.1G, the total purchase price of $1041.26 is called the **flat price**. This price includes interest that has accrued from February 1, 1998, to April 18, 1998, but will not be paid until August 1, 1998.

The actual accrued interest is $1000.00(0.05)\left(\dfrac{76}{181}\right) = \$20.99$.

As far as the seller of the bond is concerned, the net price of the bond is $1041.26 - 20.99 = \$1020.27$. This price is called the **quoted price** or **market price.**

QUOTED PRICE $=$ FLAT PRICE $-$ ACCRUED INTEREST

FLAT PRICE $=$ QUOTED PRICE $+$ ACCRUED INTEREST

In a stable market, the flat price of bonds increases as the accrued interest increases and drops suddenly by the amount of the interest paid on the interest date. To avoid this fluctuation in price, which is entirely due to the accrued interest, bonds are offered for sale at the quoted price. The accrued interest is added to obtain the total price or flat price.

EXAMPLE 15.1H   A $5000 bond redeemable at par in seven years and four months bearing interest at 10.5% payable semi-annually is bought to yield 11.5% compounded semi-annually. Determine

  (i) the purchase price (flat price);

 (ii) the accrued interest;

(iii) the market price (quoted price).

Solution   (i) The redemption price S $= \$5000.00$;

the semi-annual coupon R $= 5000.00\left(\dfrac{0.105}{2}\right) = \$262.50$.

The interest date preceding the purchase date is 7.5 years before maturity.

$n = 7.5(2) = 15; \quad i = \dfrac{11.5\%}{2} = 5.75\% = 0.0575$

The purchase price on the interest date preceding the date of purchase

$= 5000.00(1.0575^{-15}) + 262.50\left(\dfrac{1 - 1.0575^{-15}}{0.0575}\right)$

$= 5000.00(0.4323091) + 262.50(9.8728855)$
$= 2161.55 + 2591.63$
$= \$4753.18$

Programmed solution

0 | PMT | 5000 | FV | 5.75 | %i | 15 | N | | CPT | | PV | | 2161.5454 |

0 | FV | 262.50 | PMT | 5.75 | %i | 15 | N | | CPT | | PV | | 2591.6325 |

The purchase price is $2161.55 + 2591.63 = \$4753.18$.

The accumulated value two months later

$$P = 4753.18; \quad r = i = 0.0575; \quad t = \frac{2}{6};$$

$$S = 4753.18\left[1 + 0.0575\left(\frac{2}{6}\right)\right]$$

$$= 4753.18(1.0191667)$$
$$= \$4844.28$$

The purchase price (flat price) is $\$4844.28$.

(ii) The accrued interest is $5000.00(0.0525)\left(\dfrac{2}{6}\right) = \$87.50$.

(iii) The quoted price (market price) is $4844.28 - 87.50 = \$4756.78$.

EXAMPLE 15.1I A $\$10\,000$, 11% bond redeemable at 108 matures on May 1, 2010. Interest is payable semi-annually. The bond is purchased on March 21, 1998, to yield 10% compounded semi-annually.

(i) What is the purchase price of the bond?

(ii) What is the accrued interest?

(iii) What is the quoted price?

Solution (i) The redemption price $S = 10\,000.00(1.08) = \$10\,800.00$;

the semi-annual coupon $R = 10\,000.00\left(\dfrac{0.11}{2}\right) = \$550.00$.

The interest dates on the bond are May 1 and November 1.
The interest date preceding the date of purchase is November 1, 1997.
The time period November 1, 1997, to May 1, 2010, is 12.5 years.

$$n = 12.5(2) = 25; \quad i = \frac{10\%}{2} = 5\% = 0.05$$

The purchase price on November 1, 1997,

$$= 10\,800.00(1.05^{-25}) + 550.00\left(\frac{1 - 1.05^{-25}}{0.05}\right)$$

$$= 10\,800.00(0.2953028) + 550.00(14.093945)$$
$$= 3189.27 + 7751.67$$
$$= \$10\,940.94$$

Programmed solution

0 [PMT] 10 800 [FV] 5 [%i] 25 [N] [CPT] [PV] [3189.27]

0 [FV] 550 [PMT] 5 [%i] 25 [N] [CPT] [PV] [7751.6695]

The purchase price is 3189.27 + 7751.67 = $10 940.94.

The time period November 1, 1997, to March 21, 1998, contains 140 days; the number of days in the interest payment interval November 1, 1997, to May 1, 1998, is 181.

$$P = 10\,940.94; \quad r = i = 0.05; \quad t = \frac{140}{181}$$

The accumulated value on March 21, 1998,

$$= 10\,940.94\left[1 + 0.05\left(\frac{140}{181}\right)\right] = 10\,940.94(1.0386740) = \$11\,364.07$$

(ii) The actual accrued interest is $10\,000.00(0.055)\left(\dfrac{140}{181}\right) = \$425.41$.

(iii) The quoted price is $11\,364.07 - 425.41 = \$10\,938.66$.

EXERCISE 15.1

A. Determine the purchase price at the indicated time before redemption of each of the twelve bonds shown in the table below.

	Par Value	Redeemed At:	Bond Rate Payable Semi-annually	Time Before Redemption	Yield Rate	Conversion Period
1.	$100 000	par	15.5%	5.5 years	13.5%	semi-annually
2.	$5000	par	10%	12 years	12%	semi-annually
3.	$25 000	103	16%	7 years	14%	semi-annually
4.	$1000	110	8.5%	12.5 years	13.5%	semi-annually
5.	$50 000	par	14%	10 years	13%	annually
6.	$20 000	par	10.5%	6.5 years	13%	quarterly
7.	$8000	104	11.5%	18.5 years	9%	monthly
8.	$3000	107	10%	20 years	12%	quarterly
9.	$15 000	par	9.5%	6 yr., 4 mo.	15%	semi-annually
10.	$5000	par	11%	12 yr., 9 mo.	12%	semi-annually
11.	$10 000	108	12%	9 yr., 5 mo.	14%	semi-annually
12.	$2000	105	7.5%	5 yr., 10 mo.	9.5%	semi-annually

B. Answer each of the following questions.

1. A $500 bond is redeemable at par on March 1, 2006. Interest is 11% payable semi-annually. Find the purchase price of the bond on September 1, 2000, to yield 16.5% compounded semi-annually.

2. A $25 000, 13% bond redeemable at par is purchased twelve years before maturity to yield 16% compounded semi-annually. If the bond interest is payable semi-annually, what is the purchase price of the bond?

3. A $1000, 11.5% bond redeemable at 104 is purchased 8.5 years before maturity to yield 13% compounded semi-annually. If the bond interest is payable semi-annually, what is the purchase price of the bond?

4. A $100 000 bond is redeemable at 108 in fifteen years. If interest on the bond is 15.5% payable semi-annually, what is the purchase price to yield 14% compounded semi-annually?

5. A 25-year bond issue of $5 000 000 redeemable at par and bearing interest at 7.25% payable annually is sold to yield 8.5% compounded semi-annually. What is the issue price of the bonds?

6. A $100 000 bond bearing interest at 16% payable semi-annually is bought eight years before maturity to yield 14.5% compounded annually. If the bond is redeemable at par, what is the purchase price?

7. Bonds with a par value of $40 000 redeemable at 103 in 7.5 years bearing interest at 13% payable quarterly are sold to yield 14% compounded semi-annually. Determine the purchase price of the bonds.

8. Six $1000 bonds with 11.5% coupons payable semi-annually are bought to yield 18% compounded monthly. If the bonds are redeemable at 109 in eight years, what is the purchase price?

9. A $25 000, 10% bond redeemable at par on December 1, 2011, is purchased on September 25, 2000, to yield 14.5% compounded semi-annually. Bond interest is payable semi-annually.

   a) What is the flat price of the bond?
   b) What is the accrued interest?
   c) What is the quoted price?

10. A $100 000 bond redeemable at par on October 1, 2021, is purchased on January 15, 2000. Interest is 13% payable semi-annually and the yield is 11.5% compounded semi-annually.

    a) What is the purchase price of the bond?
    b) How much interest has accrued?
    c) What is the market price?

11. A $5000, 15% bond redeemable at 104 matures on August 1, 2008. If the coupons are payable semi-annually, what is the quoted price on May 10, 1999, to yield 13.5% compounded semi-annually?

12. Bonds in denominations of $1000 redeemable at 107 are offered for sale. If the bonds mature in six years and ten months and the coupon rate is 9.5% payable quarterly, what is the market price of the bonds to yield 12% compounded quarterly?

15.2 PREMIUM AND DISCOUNT

A. Basic concepts—bond rate versus yield (or market) rate

Comparing the redemption values with the purchase prices obtained in Examples 15.1A to 15.1I (see Table 15.1 below) shows that the purchase price is sometimes less than and sometimes more than the redemption value.

TABLE 15.1   Comparison of Redemption Values with Purchase Prices for Examples 15.1A to 15.1I

Example	Redemption Value S	Purchase (Flat) Price PP	Comparison of S and PP	Premium or Discount	Amount of Premium or Discount	Bond Rate b	Yield Rate i	b Versus i
15.1A	$1000.00	$937.90	S > PP	discount	$62.10	5%	6%	$b < i$
15.1B	$5000.00	$5487.79	PP > S	premium	$487.79	5.25%	4.5%	$b > i$
15.1C	$10 600.00	$8226.73	S > PP	discount	$2373.27	4%	5%	$b < i$
15.1D	$26 750.00	$27 270.74	PP > S	premium	$520.74	2.75%	2.5%	$b > i$
15.1E	$1 000 000.00	$915 535.22	S > PP	discount	$84 464.78	10%	11.46%	$b < i$
15.1F	$103 000.00	$108 779.24	PP > S	premium	$5779.24	5.75%	5.06%	$b > i$
15.1G	$1000.00	$1041.26	PP > S	premium	$41.26	5%	4.5%	$b > i$
15.1H	$5000.00	$4844.28	S > PP	discount	$155.72	5.25%	5.75%	$b < i$
15.1I	$10 800.00	$11 364.07	PP > S	premium	$564.07	5.5%	5%	$b > i$

If the purchase price of a bond is greater than the redemption price, the bond is said to be bought at a premium and the difference between the purchase price and the redemption price is called the **premium**.

PREMIUM = PURCHASE PRICE − REDEMPTION PRICE
where purchase price > redemption price

If the purchase price of a bond is less than the redemption price, the bond is said to be bought at a discount and the difference between the redemption price and the purchase price is called the **discount**.

DISCOUNT = REDEMPTION PRICE − PURCHASE PRICE
where redemption price > purchase price

An examination of the size of the bond rate b relative to the size of the market rate i shows that this relationship determines whether there is a premium or discount.

The bond rate (or coupon rate) stated on the bond is the percent of the *face* value of the bond that will be paid at the end of each interest period to the bondholder. This rate is established at the time of issue of the bonds and remains the same throughout the term of the bond.

On the other hand, the rate at which lenders are willing to provide money fluctuates in response to economic conditions. The combination of factors at work in the capital market at any given time in conjunction with the perceived risk associated with a particular bond determines the yield rate (or market rate) for a bond and thus the price at which a bond will be bought or sold.

The bond rate and the market rate are usually *not* equal. However, if the two rates happen to be equal, then bonds that are redeemable at par will sell at their face value. If the bond rate is *less* than the market rate, the bond will sell at a price less than the face value, that is, at a *discount*. If the bond rate is *greater* than the market rate, the bond will sell at a price above its face value, that is, at a *premium*.

Conversely, if a bond is redeemable at par (that is, at 100), purchasers will realize the bond rate if they pay 100. They will realize less than the bond rate if they buy at a premium and more than the bond rate if they buy at a discount.

At any time, one of three possible situations exists for any given bond:

(1) Bond rate = Market rate $(b = i)$ The bond sells at *par*.

(2) Bond rate < Market rate $(b < i)$ The bond sells at a *discount*.

(3) Bond rate > Market rate $(b > i)$ The bond sells at a *premium*.

EXAMPLE 15.2A A $10 000 bond is redeemable at par and bears interest at 10% compounded semi-annually.

(i) What is the purchase price ten years before maturity if the market rate compounded semi-annually is

(a) 10%; (b) 12%; (c) 8%?

(ii) What is the purchase price five years before maturity if the market rate compounded semi-annually is

(a) 10%; (b) 12%; (c) 8%?

Solution (i) $S = 10\,000.00$; $R = 10\,000.00(0.05) = 500.00$; $n = 10(2) = 20$; $b = 5\%$

(a) $i = \dfrac{10\%}{2} = 5\% = 0.05$; $(b = i)$

$$\text{Purchase price} = 10\,000.00(1.05^{-20}) + 500.00\left(\frac{1 - 1.05^{-20}}{0.05}\right)$$

$$= 10\,000.00(0.3768895) + 500.00(12.46221)$$
$$= 3768.90 + 6231.11$$
$$= \$10\,000.01$$

Programmed solution

0 [PMT] 10 000 [FV] 5 [%i] 20 [N] [CPT] [PV] 3768.8948

0 [FV] 500 [PMT] 5 [%i] 20 [N] [CPT] [PV] 6231.1052

The purchase price is $3768.90 + 6231.11 = \$10\,000.01$.

The bond sells at par.

(b) $i = \dfrac{12\%}{2} = 6\% = 0.06;\quad (b < i)$

$\text{Purchase price} = 10\,000.00(1.06^{-20}) + 500.00\left(\dfrac{1 - 1.06^{-20}}{0.06}\right)$

$= 10\,000.00(0.3118047) + 500.00(11.469921)$
$= 3118.05 + 5734.96$
$= \$8853.01$

Programmed solution

0 PMT 10 000 FV 6 %i 20 N CPT PV 3118.0473

0 FV 500 PMT 6 %i 20 N CPT PV 5734.9606

The purchase price is is $3118.05 + 5734.96 = \$8853.01$.

The bond sells below par.

The discount is $10\,000.00 - 8853.01 = \$1146.99$.

(c) $i = \dfrac{8\%}{2} = 4\% = 0.04;\quad (b > i)$

$\text{Purchase price} = 10\,000.00(1.04^{-20}) + 500.00\left(\dfrac{1 - 1.04^{-20}}{0.04}\right)$

$= 10\,000.00(0.4563869) + 500.00(13.590326)$
$= 4563.87 + 6795.16$
$= \$11\,359.03$

Programmed solution

0 PMT 10 000 FV 4 %i 20 N CPT PV 4563.8695

0 FV 500 PMT 4 %i 20 N CPT PV 6795.1631

The purchase price is $4563.87 + 6795.16 = \$11\,359.03$.

The bond sells above par.

The premium is $11\,359.03 - 10\,000.00 = \$1359.03$.

(ii) $S = 10\,000.00;\quad R = 500.00;\quad n = 5(2) = 10;\quad b = 5\%$

(a) $i = 5\%$; (see part (b)) $(b = i)$

$\text{Purchase price} = 10\,000.00(1.05^{-10}) + 500.00\left(\dfrac{1 - 1.05^{-10}}{0.05}\right)$

$= 6139.13 + 3860.87$
$= \$10\,000.00$

Programmed solution

0 [PMT] 10 000 [FV] 5 [%i] 10 [N] [CPT] [PV] [6139.1326]

0 [FV] 500 [PMT] 5 [%i] 10 [N] [CPT] [PV] [3860.8674]

The purchase price is 6139.13 + 3860.87 = $10 000.00.

The bond sells at par.

(b) $i = 6\%$; $(b < i)$

Purchase price = $10\,000.00(1.06^{-10}) + 500.00\left(\dfrac{1 - 1.06^{-10}}{0.06}\right)$

$= 5583.95 + 3680.04$
$= \$9263.99$

Programmed solution

0 [PMT] 10 000 [FV] 6 [%i] 10 [N] [CPT] [PV] [5583.9478]

0 [FV] 500 [PMT] 6 [%i] 10 [N] [CPT] [PV] [3680.0435]

The purchase price is 5583.95 + 3680.04 = $9263.99.

The bond sells below par.

The discount is 10 000.00 − 9263.99 = $736.01. It is smaller than in part (i) because the time to maturity is shorter.

(c) $i = 4\%$; $(b > i)$

Purchase price = $10\,000.00(1.04^{-10}) + 500.00\left(\dfrac{1 - 1.04^{-10}}{0.04}\right)$

$= 6755.64 + 4055.45$
$= \$10\,811.09$

Programmed solution

0 [PMT] 10 000 [FV] 4 [%i] 10 [N] [CPT] [PV] [6755.6417]

0 [FV] 500 [PMT] 4 [%i] 10 [N] [CPT] [PV] [4055.4479]

The purchase price is 6755.64 + 4055.45 = $10 811.09.

The bond sells above par.

The premium is 10 811.09 − 10 000.00 = $811.09. It is smaller than in part (i) because the time to maturity is shorter.

B. Direct method of computing the premium or discount—alternate method for finding the purchase price

EXAMPLE 15.2B   A $5000, 12% bond with semi-annual coupons is bought six years before maturity to yield 10% compounded semi-annually. Determine the premium.

Solution

$$S = 5000.00; \quad b = \frac{12\%}{2} = 6\% = 0.06; \quad R = 5000.00(0.06) = 300.00;$$

$$i = \frac{10\%}{2} = 5\% = 0.05; \quad n = 6(2) = 12$$

Since $b > i$, the bond will sell at a premium.

$$\text{Purchase price} = 5000.00(1.05^{-12}) + 300.00\left(\frac{1 - 1.05^{-12}}{0.05}\right)$$

$$= 5000.00(0.5568374) + 300.00(8.8632516)$$
$$= 2784.19 + 2658.97$$
$$= \$5443.16$$

Programmed solution

| 0 | PMT | 5000 | FV | 5 | %i | 12 | N | CPT | PV | 2784.1871 |

| 0 | FV | 300 | PMT | 5 | %i | 12 | N | CPT | PV | 2658.9755 |

The purchase price is $2784.19 + 2658.97 = \$5443.16$.

The premium is $5443.16 - 5000.00 = \$443.16$.

While you can always determine the premium by the basic method using Formula 15.1, it is more convenient to determine the premium directly by considering the relationship between the bond rate b and the yield rate i.

As previously discussed, a premium results when $b > i$. When this is the case, the premium is paid because the periodic interest payments received exceed the periodic interest required according to the yield rate.

In Example 15.2B
The semi-annual interest payment $5000.00(0.06) = \$300.00$

The required semi-annual interest based
on the yield rate $5000.00(0.05) = \underline{\$250.00}$

The excess of the actual interest received
over the required interest to make the yield rate $= \underline{\underline{\$\ \ 50.00}}$

This excess is received at the end of every payment interval; thus it forms an ordinary annuity whose present value can be computed at the yield rate i.

R (the excess interest) $= 50.00; \quad i = 5\%; \quad n = 12$

$$A_n = 50.00\left(\frac{1 - 1.05^{-12}}{0.05}\right)$$

$$= 50.00(8.8632516)$$
$$= \$443.16$$

Programmed solution

0 [FV] 50 [PMT] 5 [%i] 12 [N] [CPT] [PV] [443.16258]

The premium is $443.16.

The purchase price is $5000.00 + 443.16 = \$5443.16$.

The premium is the present value of the ordinary annuity formed by the excess of the actual bond interest over the required interest based on the yield rate. We can obtain the purchase price by adding the premium to the redemption price.

$$\text{PREMIUM} = (\text{PERIODIC BOND INTEREST} - \text{REQUIRED INTEREST})\left[\frac{1 - (1 + i)^{-n}}{i}\right]$$

$$= (\text{FACE VALUE} \times b - \text{REDEMPTION PRICE} \times i)\left[\frac{1 - (1 + i)^{-n}}{i}\right]$$

EXAMPLE 15.2C   A $5000, 12% bond with semi-annual coupons is bought six years before maturity to yield 14% compounded semi-annually. Determine the discount.

Solution $S = 5000.00; \quad b = \dfrac{12\%}{2} = 6\% = 0.06; \quad R = 5000.00(0.06) = 300.00;$

$i = \dfrac{14\%}{2} = 7\% = 0.07; \quad n = 6(2) = 12$

Since $b < i$, the bond will sell at a discount.

$\text{Purchase price} = 5000.00(1.07^{-12}) + 300.00\left(\dfrac{1 - 1.07^{-12}}{0.07}\right)$

$$= 5000.00(0.444012) + 300.00(7.9426863)$$
$$= 2220.06 + 2382.81$$
$$= \$4602.87$$

Programmed solution

0 [PMT] 5000 [FV] 7 [%i] 12 [N] [CPT] [PV] [2220.0598]

0 [FV] 300 [PMT] 7 [%i] 12 [N] [CPT] [PV] [2382.8059]

The purchase price is $2220.06 + 2382.81 = \$4602.87$.

The discount is $5000.00 - 4602.87 = \$397.13$.

As in the case of a premium, while you can always determine the discount by the basic method using Formula 15.1, it is more convenient to determine the discount directly.

When $b < i$, a discount results. The discount on a bond is received because the periodic interest payments are less than the periodic interest required to earn the yield rate.

In Example 15.2C

The semi-annual interest payment	$5000.00(0.06) = \$300.00$
The required semi-annual interest based on the yield rate	$5000.00(0.07) = \$350.00$
The shortage of the actual interest receivables compared to the required interest based on the yield rate	$= \underline{\$\ \ 50.00}$

This shortage occurs at the end of every interest payment interval; it forms an ordinary annuity whose present value can be computed at the yield rate i.

$$R = 50.00; \quad i = 7\%; \quad n = 12$$

$$A_n = 50.00\left(\frac{1 - 1.07^{-12}}{0.07}\right)$$

$$= 50.00(7.9426863)$$
$$= \$397.13$$

Programmed solution

$$\boxed{0}\ \boxed{\text{FV}}\ \boxed{50}\ \boxed{\text{PMT}}\ \boxed{7}\ \boxed{\%i}\ \boxed{12}\ \boxed{\text{N}}\ \boxed{\text{CPT}}\ \boxed{\text{PV}}\ \boxed{397.13431}$$

The discount is $397.13.

The purchase price is $5000.00 - 397.13 = \$4602.87$.

The discount is the present value of the ordinary annuity formed by the shortage of the actual bond interest received as compared to the required interest based on the yield rate. We can obtain the purchase price by subtracting the discount from the redemption price.

$$\text{DISCOUNT} = (\text{REQUIRED INTEREST} - \text{PERIODIC BOND INTEREST})\left[\frac{1 - (1 + i)^{-n}}{i}\right]$$

$$= -(\text{PERIODIC BOND INTEREST} - \text{REQUIRED INTEREST})\left[\frac{1 - (1 + i)^{-n}}{i}\right]$$

$$= -(\text{FACE VALUE} \times b - \text{REDEMPTION PRICE} \times i)\left[\frac{1 - (1 + i)^{-n}}{i}\right]$$

Since in both cases the difference between the periodic bond interest and the required interest is involved, the premium or discount on the purchase of a bond can be obtained using the same relationship.

$$\begin{array}{l} \text{PREMIUM} \\ \text{or} \\ \text{DISCOUNT} \end{array} = (b \times \text{FACE VALUE} - i \times \text{REDEMPTION PRICE})\left[\frac{1 - (1 + i)^{-n}}{i}\right] \qquad \text{Formula } 15.3$$

EXAMPLE 15.2D A $1000, 11.5% bond with semi-annual coupons redeemable at par in fifteen years is bought to yield 10% compounded semi-annually. Determine

(i) the premium or discount;

(ii) the purchase price.

Solution

(i) $S = 1000.00; \quad b = \dfrac{11.5\%}{2} = 5.75\% = 0.0575;$

$R = 1000.00(0.0575) = 57.50;$

$i = \dfrac{10\%}{2} = 5\% = 0.05; \quad n = 15(2) = 30$

Since $b > i$, the bond will sell at a premium.

The required interest based on the yield rate is $1000.00(0.05) = 50.00$; the excess interest is $57.50 - 50.00 = 7.50$.

The premium is $7.50\left(\dfrac{1 - 1.05^{-30}}{0.05}\right) = 7.50(15.372451) = \$115.29.$

Programmed solution

0 $\boxed{\text{FV}}$ 7.50 $\boxed{\text{PMT}}$ 5 $\boxed{\%i}$ 30 $\boxed{\text{N}}$ $\boxed{\text{CPT}}$ $\boxed{\text{PV}}$ $\boxed{115.29338}$

(ii) The purchase price is $1000.00 + 115.29 = \$1115.29.$

EXAMPLE 15.2E A $50 000, 10% bond with quarterly coupons redeemable at par in ten years is purchased to yield 11% compounded quarterly.

(i) What is the premium or discount?

(ii) What is the purchase price?

Solution

(i) $S = 50\,000.00; \quad b = \dfrac{10\%}{4} = 2.5\% = 0.025;$

$n = 10(4) = 40; \quad i = \dfrac{11\%}{4} = 2.75\% = 0.0275$

Since $b < i$, the bond will sell at a discount.

$\text{Discount} = (0.025 \times 50\,000.00 - 0.0275 \times 50\,000.00)\left(\dfrac{1 - 1.0275^{-40}}{0.0275}\right)$ — using **Formula 15.3**

$= (1250.00 - 1375.00)(24.078101)$

$= -(125.00)(24.078101)$

$= -\$3009.76$ ———————— the negative sign indicates a discount

Programmed solution

First compute PMT $= (0.025 \times 50\,000 - 0.0275 \times 50\,000) = -125.00$

0 [FV] 125 [PMT] 2.75 [%i] 40 [N] [CPT] [PV] [3009.7626]

(ii) The purchase price is $50\,000.00 - 3009.76 = \$46\,990.24$.

EXAMPLE 15.2F Bonds with a face value of \$15 000 redeemable at 108 with interest at 9% payable semi-annually are bought twelve years before maturity to yield 11% compounded semi-annually.

(i) What is the premium or discount?

(ii) What is the purchase price?

Solution (i) $S = 15\,000.00(1.08) = 16\,200.00; \quad b = \dfrac{9\%}{2} = 4.5\% = 0.045;$

$n = 12(2) = 24; \quad i = \dfrac{11\%}{2} = 5.5\% = 0.055$

Since $b < i$ and the redemption price is greater than par, the bond will sell at a discount.

$$\text{Discount} = (0.045 \times 15\,000.00 - 0.055 \times 16\,200.00)\left(\dfrac{1 - 1.055^{-24}}{0.055}\right)$$

$$= (675.00 - 891.00)(13.151699)$$
$$= (-216.00)(13.151699)$$
$$= -\$2840.77$$

Programmed solution

$\text{PMT} = (0.045 \times 15\,000 - 0.055 \times 16\,200) = -216.00$

0 [FV] 216 [PMT] 5.5 [%i] 24 [N] [CPT] [PV] [2840.767]

(ii) The purchase price is $16\,200.00 - 2840.77 = \$13\,359.23$.

EXAMPLE 15.2G A \$10 000, 13% bond with quarterly coupons redeemable at 106 in seven years is purchased to yield 11% compounded quarterly.

(i) What is the premium or discount?

(ii) What is the purchase price?

Solution (i) $S = 10\,000.00(1.06) = 10\,600.00; \quad b = \dfrac{13\%}{4} = 3.25\% = 0.0325;$

$n = 7(4) = 28; \quad i = \dfrac{11\%}{4} = 2.75\% = 0.0275$

Since $b > i$, the bond is expected to sell at a premium.

$$\text{Premium} = (0.0325 \times 10\,000.00 - 0.0275 \times 10\,600.00)\left(\frac{1 - 1.0275^{-28}}{0.0275}\right)$$

$$= (325.00 - 291.50)(19.350826)$$
$$= (33.50)(19.350826)$$
$$= \$648.25$$

Programmed solution

$$\text{PMT} = (0.0325 \times 10\,000 - 0.0275 \times 10\,600 \times 0.0275) = 33.50$$

0 [FV] 33.50 [PMT] 2.75 [%i] 28 [N] [CPT] [PV] [648.25268]

(ii) The purchase price is $10\,600.00 + 648.25 = \$11\,248.25$.

EXAMPLE 15.2H A \$1000, 11.5% bond redeemable at 110 with interest payable annually is bought nine years before maturity to yield 11% compounded annually. Determine

(i) the premium or discount;

(ii) the purchase price.

Solution

(i) $S = 1000.00(1.10) = 1100.00;$ $b = 11.5\% = 0.115;$

$n = 9;$ $i = 11\% = 0.11$

Since $b > i$, the bond is expected to be sold at a premium. While this is always true for bonds redeemable at par, it does not necessarily follow for bonds redeemable above par.

In this particular case:

the actual bond interest per year $1000.00(0.115) = \$115.00$
the interest required to make the yield rate $1100.00(0.11)$ $= \$121.00$

Because of the redemption premium, the required interest exceeds the actual interest: the bond will, in fact, sell at a discount. This conclusion is borne out when using Formula 15.3.

$$\text{Premium/Discount} = (0.115 \times 1000.00 - 0.11 \times 1100.00)\left(\frac{1 - 1.11^{-9}}{0.11}\right)$$

$$= (115.00 - 121.00)(5.5370475)$$
$$= (-6.00)(5.5370475)$$
$$= -\$33.22$$

Programmed solution

$$\text{PMT} = (0.115 \times 1000 - 0.11 \times 1100) = -6.00$$

0 [FV] 6 [PMT] 11 [%i] 9 [N] [CPT] [PV] [33.222285]

(ii) Since the answer (PMT) is negative, the bond sells at a discount of \$33.22. The purchase price is $1100.00 - 33.22 = \$1066.78$.

EXAMPLE 15.2I A $25 000 bond, redeemable at 104 on July 1, 2006, with 11% coupons payable quarterly, is bought on May 20, 1997, to yield 10% compounded quarterly. What is

  (i) the premium or discount?

  (ii) the purchase price?

  (iii) the quoted price?

Solution $S = 25\,000.00(1.04) = 26\,000.00; \quad b = \dfrac{11\%}{4} = 2.75\% = 0.0275;$

$i = \dfrac{10\%}{4} = 2.5\% = 0.025$

The interest payment dates are October 1, January 1, April 1, and July 1. The interest payment date preceding the date of purchase is April 1, 1997. The time period April 1, 1997, to July 1, 2006, contains 9 years and 3 months; $n = 9.25(4) = 37$.

The premium on April 1, 1997,

$$= (25\,000.00 \times 0.0275 - 26\,000.00 \times 0.025)\left(\frac{1 - 1.025^{-37}}{0.025}\right)$$

$$= (687.50 - 650.00)(23.957318)$$
$$= (37.50)(23.957318)$$
$$= \$898.40$$

Programmed solution

$$PMT = (25\,000 \times 0.0275 - 26\,000 \times 0.025) = 37.50$$

0 | FV | 37.50 | PMT | 2.5 | %i | 37 | N | CPT | PV | 898.39942

The purchase price on April 1, 1997, is $26\,000.00 + 898.40 = \$26\,898.40$.

The time period April 1 to May 20 contains 49 days; the number of days in the interest payment interval April 1 to July 1 is 91.

$P = 26\,898.40; \quad r = i = 0.025; \quad t = \dfrac{49}{91}$

The accumulated value on May 20, 1997,

$$= 26\,898.40\left[1 + 0.025\left(\frac{49}{91}\right)\right]$$

$$= 26\,898.40(1.0134615)$$
$$= \$27\,260.49$$

The accrued interest to May 20 is $25\,000.00(0.0275)\left(\dfrac{49}{91}\right) = \$370.19$.

The quoted price is $27\,260.49 - 370.19 = \$26\,890.30$.

Thus, on May 20, 1997,

  (i) the premium is $26\,890.30 - 26\,000.00 = \$890.30$;

  (ii) the purchase price is $27\,260.49$;

  (iii) the quoted price is $26\,890.30$.

EXAMPLE 15.2J A $2 000 000.00 issue of twenty-year municipal bonds redeemable at 104 is offered for sale to yield 11% compounded quarterly. If the bond interest is 12% payable annually, what is the issue price of the bonds?

Solution $S = 2\,000\,000.00(1.04) = 2\,080\,000.00; \quad n = 20; \quad c = 4;$

$b = 12\% = 0.12; \quad i = \dfrac{11\%}{4} = 2.75\% = 0.0275;$

$f = 1.0275^4 - 1 = 1.1146213 - 1 = 0.1146213 = 11.46213\%$

Since $b > f$, the issue is expected to sell at a premium.

$\text{Premium} = (0.12 \times 2\,000\,000.00 - 0.1146213 \times 2\,080\,000.00)\left(\dfrac{1 - 1.1146213^{-20}}{0.1146213}\right)$

$= (240\,000.00 - 238\,412.30)(7.7284570)$
$= (1587.70)(7.7284570)$
$= \$12\,270.47$

Programmed solution

$\text{PMT} = (0.12 \times 2\,000\,000 - 0.1146213 \times 2\,080\,000) = 1587.70$

0 **FV** 1587.70 **PMT** 11.46213 **%i** 20 **N** **CPT** **PV** $12\,270.615$

The issue price is $2\,080\,000.00 + 12\,270.62 = \$2\,092\,270.62.$

Exercise 15.2

A. For each of the eight bonds in the table below, use Formula 15.3 to determine
  a) the premium or discount;
  b) the purchase price.

	Par Value	Redeemed At:	Bond Rate Payable Semi-annually	Time Before Redemption	Yield Rate Compounded Semi-annually
1.	$25 000	par	12%	10 years	15%
2.	$5000	par	16.5%	8 years	14%
3.	$10 000	104	9%	15 years	11%
4.	$3000	107	13.5%	9 years	10.5%
5.	$60 000	108	7%	7 years	9.5%
6.	$7000	110	9%	5 years	8.5%
7.	$1000	105	13%	6 years, 10 months	17%
8.	$50 000	108	12%	4 years, 5 months	11.5%

B. Answer each of the following questions.

1. A $100 000, 11% bond redeemable at par with quarterly coupons is purchased to yield 16.5% compounded quarterly. Find the premium or discount and the purchase price if the bond is purchased

   a) fifteen years before maturity; b) five years before maturity.

2. A $25 000, 9% bond redeemable at par with interest payable annually is bought six years before maturity. Determine the premium or discount and the purchase price if the bond is purchased to yield

   a) 13.5% compounded annually; b) 6% compounded annually.

3. A $5000, 14.5% bond redeemable at 104 with semi-annual coupons is purchased to yield 13% compounded semi-annually. What is the premium or discount and the purchase price if the bond is bought

   a) ten years before maturity? b) six years before maturity?

4. A $1000, 14% bond redeemable at 108 in seven years bears coupons payable annually. Compute the premium or discount and the purchase price if the yield, compounded annually, is

   a) 12.5%; b) 13.5%; c) 15.5%.

5. Twelve $1000 bonds redeemable at par bearing interest at 10% payable semi-annually and maturing on September 1, 2006, are bought on June 18, 2001, to yield 17.5% compounded semi-annually. Determine

   a) the premium or discount on the preceding interest payment date;
   b) the purchase price;
   c) the quoted price.

6. Bonds with a face value of $30 000 redeemable at 107 on June 1, 2007, are offered for sale to yield 15.5% compounded quarterly. If interest is 17% payable quarterly and the bonds are bought on January 24, 1998, what is

   a) the premium or discount on the interest payment date preceding the date of sale?
   b) the purchase price?
   c) the quoted price?

7. A $5 000 000 issue of ten-year bonds redeemable at par offers 14% coupons payable semi-annually. What is the issue price of the bonds to yield 15% compounded monthly?

8. Twenty $5000 bonds redeemable at 110 bearing 12% coupons payable quarterly are sold eight years before maturity to yield 11.5% compounded annually. What is the purchase price of the bonds?

BUSINESS MATH NEWS BOX

TRANSFER TO CANADA RRSP BONDS.
It's in your best interest.

While another RRSP deadline has come and gone, you have until April 1997 to take advantage of this 100% guaranteed investment from the Government of Canada, by transferring your RRSP money to Canada RRSP Bonds.

Take a look at all they have to offer. A combination of the security you need to invest in your future with the flexibility to withdraw or transfer once annually without penalty, all at a rate of interest that is absolutely guaranteed over the next ten years.

Year 1:	2.75%
Year 2:	4.00%
Year 3:	5.00%
Year 4:	6.00%
Year 5:	6.25%
Year 6:	6.50%
Year 7:	6.75%
Year 8:	7.00%
Year 9:	7.50%
Year 10:	8.50%

(6.01% guaranteed annual compound rate if held for the full ten-year term.)

QUESTIONS

1. a) Calculate the future value of $1.00 if it is invested in the Canada RRSP Bond for 10 years. (Use the Year 1 to Year 10 rates and compound. Give your answer to seven decimal places.)

   b) Verify that the annual compound rate for the ten-year term is 6.01% by calculating the future value of $1.00 invested at this rate for ten years. (Give your answer to seven decimal places.) How close is 6.01% to your answer in part (a)?

2. Suppose you want to add an investment to your RRSP, and you plan to keep the investment in your RRSP for ten years. As an alternative to the Canada RRSP Bond above, you are considering purchasing a $5000 bond bearing interest at 7.2% payable annually and redeemable at par in ten years. What should you pay for this bond if you want to match the 6.01% annual compound rate of the Canada RRSP Bond? (Give your answer to two decimal places.)

3. Suppose you are considering another bond having a par value of $5000 that is redeemable at 103 in ten years. Its coupon rate is 6.8% payable semi-annually. What should you pay for this bond if you want to match the 6.01% annual compounded rate of the Canada RRSP Bond? (Give your answer to two decimal places.)

15.3 BOND SCHEDULES

A. Amortization of premium

If a bond is bought at more than the redemption price, the resulting premium is not recovered when the bond is redeemed at maturity and becomes a capital *loss*. To avoid the capital loss at maturity, the premium is written down gradually over the period from the date of purchase to the maturity date. The writing down of the premium gradually reduces the bond's book value until it equals the redemption price at the date of maturity.

The process of writing down the premium is called **amortization of the premium**. The most direct method of amortizing a premium assigns the difference between the interest received (coupon) and the interest required according to the yield rate to write down the premium. The details of writing down the premium are often shown in a tabulation referred to as a *schedule of amortization of premium*.

EXAMPLE 15.3A   A $1000, 12% bond redeemable at par matures in three years. The coupons are payable semi-annually and the bond is bought to yield 10% compounded semi-annually.

(i) Compute the purchase price.

(ii) Construct a schedule of amortization of premium.

Solution   (i) S = 1000.00; $n = 3(2) = 6$;

$$b = \frac{12\%}{2} = 6\% = 0.06; \quad i = \frac{10\%}{2} = 5\% = 0.05$$

Since $b > i$, the bond sells at a premium.

$$\text{Premium} = (0.06 \times 1000.00 - 0.05 \times 1000.00)\left(\frac{1 - 1.05^{-6}}{0.05}\right)$$

$$= (60.00 - 50.00)(5.075692)$$
$$= (10.00)(5.075692)$$
$$= \$50.76$$

Programmed solution

$$\text{PMT} = (0.06 \times 1000.00 - 0.05 \times 1000.00) = 10.00$$

0 FV 10 PMT 5 %i 6 N CPT PV 50.75692

The purchase price is 1000.00 + 50.76 = $1050.76.

(ii) *Schedule of amortization of premium*

End of Interest Payment Interval	Bond Interest Received (Coupon) $b = 6\%$	Interest on Book Value at Yield Rate $i = 5\%$	Amount of Premium Amortized	Book Value of Bond	Remaining Premium
0				1050.76	50.76
1	60.00	52.54	7.46	1043.30	43.30
2	60.00	52.17	7.83	1035.47	35.47
3	60.00	51.77	8.23	1027.24	27.24
4	60.00	51.36	8.64	1018.60	18.60
5	60.00	50.93	9.07	1009.53	9.53
6	60.00	50.47	9.53	1000.00	0.00
TOTAL	360.00	309.24	50.76		

Explanations of schedule

1. The original book value shown is the purchase price of $1050.76.

2. At the end of the first interest payment interval, the interest received (coupon) is $1000.00(0.06) = \$60.00$; the interest required according to the yield rate is $1050.76(0.05) = \$52.54$; the difference $60.00 - 52.54 = 7.46$ is used to write down the premium to $43.30 and reduces the book value from $1050.76 to $1043.30.

3. The coupon at the end of the second interest payment interval is again $60.00. The interest required according to the yield rate is $1043.30(0.05) = \$52.17$; the difference $60.00 - 52.17 = 7.83$ reduces the premium to $35.47 and the book value of the bond to $1035.47.

4. Continue in a similar manner until the maturity date when the redemption price is reached. If a rounding error becomes apparent at the end of the final interest payment interval, adjust the final interest on the book value at the yield rate to make the premium zero and to obtain the exact redemption price as the book value.

5. The totals provide useful accounting information showing the total interest received ($360.00) and the net income realized ($309.24).

EXAMPLE 15.3B A $25 000, 12.5% bond redeemable at 106 with coupons payable annually matures in seven years. The bond is bought to yield 11% compounded annually.

(i) Compute the premium and the purchase price.

(ii) Construct a schedule of amortization of premium.

Solution

(i) $S = 25\,000.00(1.06) = 26\,500.00; \quad n = 7;$

$b = 12.5\% = 0.125; \quad i = 11\% = 0.11$

Since $b > i$, the bond is expected to sell at a premium.

$$\text{Premium} = (0.125 \times 25\,000.00 - 0.11 \times 26\,500.00)\left(\frac{1 - 1.11^{-7}}{0.11}\right)$$

$$= (3125.00 - 2915.00)(4.7121963)$$
$$= (210.00)(4.7121963)$$
$$= \$989.56$$

Programmed solution

$$\text{PMT} = (0.125 \times 25\,000 - 0.11 \times 26\,500) = 210$$

0 | FV | 210 | PMT | 11 | %i | 7 | N | CPT | PV | 989.56121

The purchase price is $26\,500.00 + 989.56 = \$27\,489.56$.

(ii) *Schedule of amortization of premium*

End of Interest Payment Interval	Coupon $b = 12.5\%$	Interest on Book Value at Yield Rate $i = 11\%$	Amount of Premium Amortized	Book Value of Bond	Remaining Premium
0				27 489.56	989.56
1	3 125.00	3 023.85	101.15	27 388.41	888.41
2	3 125.00	3 012.73	112.27	27 276.14	776.14
3	3 125.00	3 000.38	124.62	27 151.52	651.52
4	3 125.00	2 986.67	138.33	27 013.19	513.19
5	3 125.00	2 971.45	153.55	26 859.64	359.64
6	3 125.00	2 954.56	170.44	26 689.20	189.20
7	3 125.00	2 935.80	189.20	26 500.00	0.00
TOTAL	21 875.00	20 885.44	989.56		

B. Accumulation of discount

If a bond is bought at less than the redemption price, there will be a gain at the time of redemption equal to the amount of discount. It is generally accepted accounting practice that this gain does not accrue in total to the accounting period in which the bond is redeemed. Instead, some of the gain accrues to each of the accounting periods from the date of purchase to the date of redemption.

To adhere to this practice, the discount is decreased gradually so that the book value of the bond increases gradually until, at the date of redemption, the discount is reduced to zero while the book value equals the redemption price. The process of reducing the discount so as to increase the book value is called **accumulation of discount**.

In the case of discount, the interest required according to the yield rate is greater than the actual interest received (the coupon). Similar to amortization of a premium, the most direct method of accumulating a discount assigns the difference between the interest required by the yield rate and the coupon to reduce the discount. The details of decreasing the discount while increasing the book value of a bond are often shown in a tabulation called a *schedule of accumulation of discount.*

EXAMPLE 15.3C A $10 000 bond, redeemable at par in four years with 11.5% coupons payable semi-annually, is bought to yield 13% compounded semi-annually.

(i) Determine the discount and the purchase price.

(ii) Construct a schedule of accumulation of discount.

Solution

(i) $S = 10\,000.00$; $n = 4(2) = 8$;

$$b = \frac{11.5\%}{2} = 5.75\% = 0.0575; \quad i = \frac{13\%}{2} = 6.5\% = 0.065$$

Since $b < i$, the bond sells at a discount.

$$\text{Discount} = (0.0575 \times 10\,000.00 - 0.065 \times 10\,000.00)\left(\frac{1 - 1.065^{-8}}{0.065}\right)$$

$$= (575.00 - 650.00)(6.088751)$$
$$= (-75.00)(6.088751)$$
$$= -\$456.66$$

Programmed solution

$$\text{PMT} = (0.0575 \times 10\,000 - 0.065 \times 10\,000) = -75.00$$

0 ⌈FV⌉ 75 ⌈PMT⌉ 6.5 ⌈%i⌉ 8 ⌈N⌉ ⌈CPT⌉ ⌈PV⌉ ⌈456.65632⌉

The purchase price is $10\,000.00 - 456.66 = \$9543.34$.

(ii) *Schedule of accumulation of discount*

End of Interest Payment Interval	Coupon $b = 5.75\%$	Interest on Book Value at Yield Rate $i = 6.5\%$	Amount of Discount Accumulated	Book Value of Bond	Remaining Discount
0				9 543.34	456.66
1	575.00	620.32	45.32	9 588.66	411.34
2	575.00	623.26	48.26	9 636.92	363.08
3	575.00	626.40	51.40	9 688.32	311.68
4	575.00	629.74	54.74	9 743.06	256.94
5	575.00	633.30	58.30	9 801.36	198.64
6	575.00	637.09	62.09	9 863.45	136.55
7	575.00	641.12	66.12	9 929.57	70.43
8	575.00	645.43	70.43	10 000.00	0.00
TOTAL	4 600.00	5056.66	456.66		

Explanations of schedule

1. The original book value shown is the purchase price of $9543.34.

2. At the end of the first interest payment interval, the coupon is 10 000.00(0.0575) = $575.00; the interest required according to the yield rate is 9543.34(0.065) = $620.32; the difference used to reduce the discount and to increase the book value is 620.32 − 575.00 = $45.32; the book value is 9543.34 + 48.32 = $9588.66, and the remaining discount is 456.66 − 48.32 = $411.34.

3. The coupon at the end of the second interest payment interval is again $575.00; the interest required on the book value is 9588.66(0.065) = $623.26; the difference is 623.26 − 575.00 = $48.26; the book value is 9588.66 + 48.26 = $9636.92; and the remaining discount is 411.34 − 48.26 = $363.08.

4. Continue in a similar manner until the maturity date when the redemption price is reached. If a rounding error becomes apparent at the end of the final interest payment interval, adjust the final interest on the book value at the yield rate to make the remaining discount equal to zero and obtain the exact redemption price as the book value.

5. The totals provide useful accounting information showing the total interest received ($4600.00) and the net income realized ($5056.66).

EXAMPLE 15.3D A $5000, 10% bond redeemable at 102 on April 1, 2000, with coupons payable quarterly is bought on October 1, 1998, to yield 13% compounded quarterly.

(i) Compute the discount and the purchase price.

(ii) Construct a schedule showing the accumulation of the discount.

Solution

(i) $S = 5000.00(1.02) = 5100.00;$

the time period October 1, 1998, to April 1, 2000, contains 18 months.

$$n = \frac{18}{3} = 6 \text{ (quarters)};$$

$$b = \frac{10\%}{4} = 2.5\% = 0.025; \quad i = \frac{13\%}{4} = 3.25\% = 0.0325$$

Since $b < i$, the bond sells at a discount.

$$\text{Discount} = (0.025 \times 5000.00 - 0.0325 \times 5100.00)\left(\frac{1 - 1.0325^{-6}}{0.0325}\right)$$

$$= (125.00 - 165.75)(5.3725899)$$
$$= (-40.75)(5.3725899)$$
$$= -\$218.93$$

Programmed solution

$$\text{PMT} = (0.025 \times 5000 - 0.0325 \times 5100) = -40.75$$

0 [FV] 40.75 [PMT] 3.25 [%i] 6 [N] [CPT] [PV] [218.93304]

The purchase price is 5100.00 − 218.93 = $4881.07.

(ii) *Schedule of accumulation of discount*

End of Interest Payment Interval	Coupon $b = 2.5\%$	Interest on Book Value at Yield Rate $i = 3.25\%$	Amount of Discount Accumulated	Book Value of Bond	Remaining Discount
Oct. 1, 1998				4881.07	218.93
Jan. 1, 1999	125.00	158.63	33.63	4914.70	185.30
Apr. 1, 1999	125.00	159.73	34.73	4949.43	150.57
July 1, 1999	125.00	160.86	35.86	4985.29	114.71
Oct. 1, 1999	125.00	162.02	37.02	5022.31	77.69
Jan. 1, 2000	125.00	163.23	38.23	5060.54	39.46
Apr. 1, 2000	125.00	164.46	39.46	5100.00	0.00
TOTAL	750.00	968.93	218.93		

C. Book value of a bond—finding the gain or loss on the sale of a bond

EXAMPLE 15.3E   A $10 000, 12% bond redeemable at par with semi-annual coupons was purchased fifteen years before maturity to yield 10% compounded semi-annually. The bond was sold three years later at $101\frac{1}{4}$. Find the gain or loss on the sale of the bond.

Solution   The market quotation of $101\frac{1}{4}$ indicates that the bond was sold at 101.25% of its face value. The proceeds from the sale of the bond are $10\,000.00(1.0125) = \$10\,125.00$. To find the gain or loss on the sale of the bond, we need to know the book value of the bond at the date of sale. This we can do by determining the original purchase price, constructing a bond schedule, and reading the book value at the time of sale from the schedule.

$$S = 10\,000.00; \quad n = 15(2) = 30$$

$$b = \frac{12\%}{2} = 6\% = 0.06; \quad i = \frac{10\%}{2} = 5\% = 0.05$$

Since $b > i$, the bond was bought at a premium.

$$\text{Premium} = (0.06 \times 10\,000.00 - 0.05 \times 10\,000.00)\left(\frac{1 - 1.05^{-30}}{0.05}\right)$$

$$= (600.00 - 500.00)(15.372451)$$
$$= (100.00)(15.372451)$$
$$= \$1537.25$$

Programmed solution

$$\text{PMT} = (0.06 \times 10\,000 - 0.05 \times 10\,000) = 100.00$$

0 [FV]   100 [PMT]   5 [%i]   30 [N]   [CPT]   [PV]   [1537.2451]

The purchase price is $10\,000.00 + 1537.25 = \$11\,537.25$.

Schedule of amortization of premium

End of Interest Payment Interval	Coupon $b = 6\%$	Interest on Book Value at Yield Rate $i = 5\%$	Amount of Premium Amortized	Book Value of Bond	Remaining Premium
0				11 537.25	1 537.25
1	600.00	576.86	23.14	11 514.11	1 514.11
2	600.00	575.71	24.29	11 489.82	1 489.82
3	600.00	574.49	25.51	11 464.31	1 464.31
4	600.00	573.22	26.78	11 437.53	1 437.53
5	600.00	571.88	28.12	11 409.41	1 409.41
6	600.00	570.47	29.53	11 379.88	1 379.88
	etc.				

The book value after three years (six semi-annual periods) is $11 379.88. Since the book value is greater than the proceeds, the loss on the sale of the bond is $11 379.88 - 10 125.00 = \$1254.88$.

We can solve this problem more quickly by computing the book value directly. The book value of a bond at a given time is the purchase price of the bond on that date. We can determine the book value of a bond without constructing a bond schedule by using Formula 15.1 or 15.3. This approach can also be used to verify book values in a bond schedule.

$S = 10\ 000.00; \quad n = (15 - 3)(2) = 24; \quad b = 6\%; \quad i = 5\%$

$$\text{Premium} = (0.06 \times 10\ 000.00 - 0.05 \times 10\ 000.00)\left(\frac{1 - 1.05^{-24}}{0.05}\right)$$

$$= (100.00)(13.798642)$$
$$= \$1379.86$$

Programmed solution

$\text{PMT} = (0.06 \times 10\ 000 - 0.05 \times 10\ 000) = 100.00$

0 [FV] 100 [PMT] 5 [%i] 24 [N] [CPT] [PV] 1379.8642

The purchase price is $10\ 000.00 + 1379.86 = \$11\ 379.86$.

The loss on the sale is $11\ 379.86 - 10\ 125.00 = \$1254.86$. (The difference in the loss is due to rounding.)

EXAMPLE 15.3F A $5000, 11% bond redeemable at 106 with semi-annual coupons was purchased twelve years before maturity to yield 10.5% compounded semi-annually. The bond is sold five years later at $98\frac{7}{8}$. Find the gain or loss on the sale of the bond.

Solution

Proceeds from the sale of the bond are 5000.00(0.98875) = $4943.75.

$$S = 5000.00(1.06) = 5300.00; \quad n = (12 - 5)(2) = 14;$$

$$b = \frac{11\%}{2} = 5.5\% = 0.055; \quad i = \frac{10.5\%}{2} = 5.25\% = 0.0525$$

$$\text{Premium/Discount} = (0.055 \times 5000.00 - 0.0525 \times 5300.00)\left(\frac{1 - 1.0525^{-14}}{0.0525}\right)$$

$$= (275.00 - 278.25)(9.7423008)$$
$$= (-3.25)(9.7423008)$$
$$= -\$31.66 \quad\underline{\hspace{3cm}} \text{ discount}$$

Programmed solution

$$\text{PMT} = (0.055 \times 5000 - 0.0525 \times 5300) = -3.25$$

0 | FV | 3.25 | PMT | 5.25 | %i | 14 | N | CPT | PV | 31.662478

The purchase price or book value is 5300.00 − 31.66 = $5268.34.
The loss on the sale is 5268.34 − 4943.75 = $324.59.

EXAMPLE 15.3G A $1000, 10% bond with quarterly coupons redeemable at 104 on May 1, 2008, was purchased on August 1, 1998, to yield 12% compounded quarterly. If the bond is sold at $95\frac{1}{2}$ on December 11, 2001, what is the gain or loss on the sale of the bond?

Solution

The interest payment dates are August 1, November 1, February 1, and May 1. The interest date preceding the date of sale is November 1, 2001.

The proceeds from the sale of the bond on December 11, 2001,

$$= 1000.00(0.955) + \text{accrued interest from November 1 to December 11}$$

$$= 955.00 + 1000.00(0.025)\left(\frac{40}{92}\right)$$

$$= 955.00 + 10.87$$
$$= \$965.87$$

$$S = 1000.00(1.04) = 1040.00;$$

$$b = \frac{10\%}{4} = 2.5\% = 0.025; \quad i = \frac{12\%}{4} = 3\% = 0.03$$

The time interval November 1, 2001, to May 1, 2008, contains six years and six months: $n = 6.5(4) = 26$.

Since $b < i$, the bond will sell at a discount.

$$\text{Discount} = (0.025 \times 1000.00 - 0.03 \times 1040.00)\left(\frac{1 - 1.03^{-26}}{0.03}\right)$$

$$= (25.00 - 31.20)(17.876842)$$
$$= (-6.20)(17.876842)$$
$$= -\$110.84$$

Programmed solution

$$\text{PMT} = (0.025 \times 1000 - 0.03 \times 1040) = -6.20$$

0 [FV] 6.20 [PMT] 3 [%i] 26 [N] [CPT] [PV] [110.83642]

The purchase price on November 1, 2001, is $1040.00 - 110.84 = \$929.16$.

The accumulated value on December 11, 2001,

$$= 929.16 \left[1 + 0.03 \left(\frac{40}{92} \right) \right]$$

$$= 929.16(1.0130435)$$
$$= \$941.28$$

The gain from the sale of the bond is $965.87 - 941.28 = \$24.59$.

Exercise 15.3

A. For each of the following bonds, compute the premium or discount and the purchase price, and construct the appropriate bond schedule.

1. A $5000, 9% bond redeemable at par in three-and-a-half years with semi-annual coupons is purchased to yield 16.5% compounded semi-annually.

2. A $25 000 bond with interest at 12.5% payable quarterly redeemable at par is bought two years before maturity to yield 11% compounded quarterly.

3. A $1000, 12% bond with semi-annual coupons redeemable at 103 on September 1, 2002, is bought on March 1, 1999, to yield 10% compounded semi-annually.

4. A $10 000, 14.75% bond with annual coupons redeemable at 110 in seven years is bought to yield 14.25% compounded annually.

B. Find the gain or loss on the sale of each of the following bonds without constructing a bond schedule.

1. A $25 000, 10.5% bond redeemable at par with semi-annual coupons bought ten years before maturity to yield 12% compounded semi-annually is sold four years before maturity at $99\frac{1}{4}$.

2. Four $5000, 14.5% bonds with interest payable semi-annually redeemable at par were bought twenty years before maturity to yield 13.5% compounded semi-annually. The bonds were sold three years later at $103\frac{5}{8}$.

3. Seven $1000, 9.25% bonds with annual coupons redeemable at 107 were bought nine years before maturity to yield 13.25% compounded annually. The bonds are sold three years before maturity at $94\frac{1}{2}$.

4. A $100 000, 13% bond with semi-annual coupons redeemable at 102 was purchased eleven-and-a-half years before maturity to yield 12% compounded semi-annually. The bond was sold five years later at $99\frac{1}{8}$.

5. A $5000 bond with 15% interest payable semi-annually redeemable at par on June 1, 2012, was bought on December 1, 1998, to yield 16% compounded semi-annually. The bond was sold on September 22, 2002, at $101\frac{3}{8}$.

6. Three $10 000, 10.5% bonds with quarterly coupons redeemable at 109 on August 1, 2006, were bought on May 1, 1992, to yield 12% compounded quarterly. The bonds were sold on January 16, 2000, at $93\frac{1}{2}$.

15.4 FINDING THE YIELD RATE

A. Quoted price of a bond–buying bonds on the market

Bonds are usually bought or sold through a bond exchange where agents trade bonds on behalf of their clients. To allow for the different denominations, bonds are offered at a quoted price stated as a percent of their face value.

It is understood that, if the bond is bought between interest dates, such a quoted price does not include any accrued interest. As explained in Section 15.1, the seller of a bond is entitled to the interest earned by the bond to the date of sale and the interest is added to the quoted price to obtain the purchase price (flat price).

EXAMPLE 15.4A A $5000, 12% bond with semi-annual coupons payable April 1 and October 1 is purchased on August 25 at $104\frac{3}{4}$. What is the purchase price of the bond?

Solution The quoted price is 5000.00(1.0475) = $5237.50.

The time period April 1 to August 25 contains 146 days; the number of days in the interest payment interval April 1 to October 1 is 183.

$$P = 5000.00; \quad r = i = \frac{12\%}{2} = 6\% = 0.06; \quad t = \frac{146}{183}$$

The accrued interest is $5000.00(0.06)\frac{146}{183} = \$239.34$.

The purchase price (flat price) is 5237.50 + 239.34 = $5476.84.

B. Finding the yield rate–the average investment method

When bonds are bought on the market, the yield rate is not directly available; it needs to be determined. The simplest method in use is the so-called **method of averages,** which gives a reasonable approximation of the yield rate as the ratio of the average income per interest payment interval to the average book value.

$$\text{APPROXIMATE VALUE OF } i = \frac{\text{AVERAGE INCOME PER INTEREST PAYMENT INTERVAL}}{\text{AVERAGE BOOK VALUE}}$$

where

$$\text{AVERAGE BOOK VALUE} = \frac{1}{2}(\text{QUOTED PRICE} + \text{REDEMPTION PRICE})$$

and

$$\begin{array}{l} \text{AVERAGE INCOME} \\ \text{PER INTEREST} \\ \text{PAYMENT INTERVAL} \end{array} = \frac{\text{TOTAL INTEREST PAYMENTS} \begin{array}{l} - \text{ PREMIUM} \\ + \text{ DISCOUNT} \end{array}}{\text{NUMBER OF INTEREST PAYMENT INTERVALS}}$$

EXAMPLE 15.4B A $25 000, 11.5% bond with semi-annual coupons redeemable at par in ten years is purchased at $103\frac{1}{2}$. What is the approximate yield rate?

Solution The quoted price (initial book value) is $25\,000.00(1.035) = \$25\,875.00$; the redemption price is $25\,000.00.

The average book value is $\frac{1}{2}(25\,875.00 + 25\,000.00) = \$25\,437.50$.

The semi-annual interest payment is $25\,000.00\left(\frac{0.115}{2}\right) = \$1437.50$;

the number of interest payments to maturity is $10(2) = 20$;
the total interest payments are $20(1437.50) = \$28\,750.00$;
the premium is $25\,875.00 - 25\,000.00 = \$875.00$.

$$\text{Average income per interest payment interval} = \frac{(28\,750.00 - 875.00)}{20}$$

$$= \$1393.75$$

$$\text{Approximate value of } i = \frac{1393.75}{25437.50} = 0.0547912 = 5.48\%$$

The yield rate is $2(5.48) = 10.96\%$.

EXAMPLE 15.4C Eight $1000, 10% bonds with semi-annual coupons redeemable at 105 in seventeen years are purchased at $97\frac{3}{8}$. What is the approximate yield rate?

Solution The quoted price is $8000.00(0.97375) = \$7790.00$;
the redemption price is $8000.00(1.05) = \$8400.00$;

the average book value is $\frac{(7790.00 + 8400.00)}{2} = \$8095.00$.

The semi-annual interest payment is $8000.00\left(\frac{0.10}{2}\right) = \$400.00$;

the number of interest payments to maturity is $17(2) = 34$;
the total interest payments are $34(400.00) = \$13\,600.00$;
the bond discount is $8400.00 - 7790.00 = \$610.00$.

$$\text{Average income per interest payment interval} = \frac{(13\,600.00 + 610.00)}{34}$$

$$= \$417.94$$

The approximate value of i is $\frac{417.94}{8095.00} = 0.0516295 = 5.16\%$.

The approximate yield rate is $2(5.16\%) = 10.32\%$.

EXAMPLE 15.4D A $5000, 10% bond with semi-annual coupons redeemable at par on July 15, 2012, is quoted on December 2, 2000, at $103\frac{3}{4}$. What is the approximate yield rate?

Solution

To find the approximate yield rate for a bond purchased between interest dates, assume that the price was quoted on the nearest interest date. Since the interest dates are January 15 and July 15, the nearest interest date is January 15, 2001, which is 11.5 years before maturity.

The quoted price is $5000.00(1.0375) = \$5187.50$;

the redemption price is 5000.00;

the average book value is $\dfrac{(5187.50 + 5000.00)}{2} = \$5093.75$.

The semi-annual interest is $5000.00\left(\dfrac{0.10}{2}\right) = \$250.00$;

the number of interest payments to maturity is $11.5(2) = 23$;
the total interest payments are $23(250.00) = \$5750.00$;
the premium is $5187.50 - 5000.00 = \$187.50$.

The average income per interest payment interval $= \dfrac{(5750.00 - 187.50)}{23}$

$$= \$241.85$$

The approximate value of i is $\dfrac{241.85}{5093.75} = 0.047479 = 4.75\%$.

The approximate yield rate is $2(4.75\%) = 9.50\%$.

C. Finding the accurate yield rate by trial and error

A method of trial and error similar to the one used to find the nominal rate of interest may be used to obtain as precise an approximation to the yield rate as desired. The method is illustrated in Appendix III.

Exercise 15.4

Use the method of averages to find the approximate yield rate for each of the six bonds shown in the table below.

	Face Value	Bond Rate Payable Semi-annually	Time Before Redemption	Redeemed At:	Market Quotation
1.	$10 000	12%	15 years	par	$101\frac{3}{8}$
2.	$5 000	10.5%	7 years	par	$94\frac{3}{4}$
3.	$25 000	11.5%	10 years	104	$97\frac{1}{8}$
4.	$1 000	15.5%	8 years	109	101
5.	$50 000	13%	5 years, 4 months	par	$98\frac{7}{8}$
6.	$20 000	17%	9 years, 8 months	106	$109\frac{1}{4}$

15.5 SINKING FUNDS

A. Finding the size of the periodic payment

Sinking funds are interest-bearing funds into which payments are made at periodic intervals to provide a desired sum of money at a specified future time. Such funds usually involve large sums of money used by both the private and the public sector to repay loans, redeem bonds, finance future capital acquisitions, provide for the replacement of depreciable plant and equipment, and recover investments in depletable natural resources.

The basic problem in dealing with sinking funds is to determine the *size of the periodic payments* that will accumulate to a known future amount. These payments form an annuity in which the accumulated value is known.

Depending on whether the periodic payments are made at the end or at the beginning of each payment period, the annuity formed is an ordinary annuity or an annuity due. Depending on whether or not the payment interval is equal in length to the interest conversion period, the annuity formed is a simple annuity or a general annuity. However, since sinking funds are normally set up so that the payment interval and the interest conversion period are equal in length, only the simple annuity cases are considered in this text.

(a) For sinking funds with payments at the end of each payment interval,

$$S_n = R\left[\frac{(1 + i)^n - 1}{i}\right]$$

(b) For sinking funds with payments at the beginning of each payment interval,

$$S_n(\text{due}) = R(1 + i)\left[\frac{(1 + i)^n - 1}{i}\right]$$

EXAMPLE 15.5A Western Oil plans to create a sinking fund of $20 000.00 by making equal deposits at the end of every six months for four years. Interest is 12% compounded semi-annually.

(i) What is the size of the semi-annual deposit into the fund?

(ii) What is the total amount deposited into the fund?

(iii) How much of the fund will be interest?

Solution

(i) $S_n = 20\,000.00$; $n = 4(2) = 8$; $i = \dfrac{12\%}{2} = 6\%$

$$20\,000.00 = R\left(\frac{1.06^8 - 1}{0.06}\right)$$

$$20\,000.00 = R(9.8974679)$$
$$R = \$2020.72$$

Programmed solution

$$0 \boxed{\text{PV}} \quad 20\,000 \boxed{\text{FV}} \quad 6 \boxed{\%i} \quad 8 \boxed{\text{N}} \quad \boxed{\text{CPT}} \boxed{\text{PMT}} \boxed{2020.7189}$$

The size of the semi-annual payment is $2020.72.

(ii) The total deposited into the sinking fund is 8(2020.72) = $16 165.76.

(iii) The amount of interest in the fund is 20 000.00 − 16 165.76 = $3834.24.

EXAMPLE 15.5B Ace Machinery wants to provide for replacement of equipment seven years from now estimated to cost $60 000.00. To do so, the company set up a sinking fund into which it will pay equal sums of money at the beginning of each of the next seven years. Interest paid by the fund is 11.5% compounded annually.

(i) What is the size of annual payment into the fund?

(ii) What is the total paid into the fund by Ace Machinery?

(iii) How much of the fund will be interest?

Solution

(i) $S_n(\text{due}) = 60\,000.00$; $n = 7$; $i = 11.5\%$

$$60\,000.00 = R(1.115)\left(\frac{1.115^7 - 1}{0.115}\right)$$

$$60\,000.00 = R(1.115)(9.9349216)$$
$$60\,000.00 = R(11.077438)$$
$$R = \$5416.42$$

Programmed solution

$$0 \boxed{\text{PV}} \quad 60\,000 \boxed{\text{FV}} \quad 11.5 \boxed{\%i} \quad 7 \boxed{\text{N}} \quad \boxed{\text{DUE}} \boxed{\text{PMT}} \boxed{5416.4151}$$

The size of the annual payment is $5416.42.

(ii) The total paid into the fund by Ace Machinery will be
7(5416.42) = $37 914.94.

(iii) The interest earned by the fund will be 60 000.00 − 37 914.94 = $22 085.06.

B. Constructing sinking fund schedules

The details of a sinking fund can be presented in the form of a schedule. Sinking fund schedules normally show the payment number (or payment date), the periodic payment into the fund, the interest earned by the fund, the increase in the fund, and the accumulated balance.

EXAMPLE 15.5C Construct a sinking fund schedule for Example 15.5A.

Solution

$R = 2020.72$; $n = 8$; $i = 6\% = 0.06$

Sinking fund schedule

Payment Interval Number	Periodic Payment	Interest for Payment Interval $i = 0.06$	Increase in Fund	Balance in Fund at End of Payment Interval
0				0.00
1	2 020.72	0.00	2 020.72	2 020.72
2	2 020.72	121.24	2 141.96	4 162.68
3	2 020.72	249.76	2 270.48	6 433.16
4	2 020.72	385.99	2 406.71	8 839.87
5	2 020.72	530.39	2 551.11	11 390.98
6	2 020.72	683.46	2 704.18	14 095.16
7	2 020.72	845.71	2 866.43	16 961.59
8	2 020.72	1017.70	3 038.42	20 000.01
TOTAL	16 165.76	3834.25	20 000.01	

Explanations regarding the construction of the sinking fund schedule
1. The payment number 0 is used to introduce the beginning balance.
2. The first deposit is made at the end of the first payment interval. The interest earned by the fund during the first payment interval is $0, the increase in the fund is $2020.72, and the balance is $2020.72.
3. The second deposit is added at the end of the second payment interval. The interest for the interval is $0.06(2020.72) = \$121.24$. The increase in the fund is $2020.72 + 121.24 = \$2141.96$ and the new balance in the fund is $2020.72 + 2141.96 = \$4162.68$.
4. The third deposit is made at the end of the third payment interval. The interest for the interval is $0.06(4162.68) = \$249.76$, the increase in the fund is $2020.72 + 249.76 = \$2270.48$, and the new balance in the fund is $2270.48 + 4162.68 = \$6433.16$.
5. Calculations for the remaining payment intervals are made in a similar manner.
6. The final balance in the sinking fund will probably be slightly different from the expected value. This difference is a result of rounding. The balance may be left as shown ($20 000.01) or the exact balance of $20 000.00 may be obtained by adjusting the last payment to $2020.71.
7. The three totals shown are useful and should be obtained for each schedule. The total increase in the fund must be the same as the final balance. The total periodic payments are $8(2020.72) = 16 165.76$. The total interest is the difference: $20 000.01 - 16 165.76 = \$3834.25$.

EXAMPLE 15.5D Construct a sinking fund schedule for Example 15.5B (an annuity due with payments at the beginning of each payment interval).

Solution R = 5416.42 (made at the beginning); $n = 7$; $i = 11.5\% = 0.115$

Sinking fund schedule

Payment Interval Number	Periodic Payment	Interest for Payment Interval $i = 0.115$	Increase in Fund	Balance in Fund at End of Payment Interval
0				0.00
1	5416.42	622.89	6039.31	6039.31
2	5416.42	1317.41	6733.83	12773.14
3	5416.42	2091.80	7508.22	20281.36
4	5416.42	2955.24	8371.66	28653.02
5	5416.42	3917.99	9334.41	37987.43
6	5416.42	4991.44	10407.86	48395.29
7	5416.42	6188.35	11604.77	60000.06
TOTAL	37914.94	22085.12	60000.06	

Explanations regarding the construction of the sinking fund schedule
1. The starting balance is $0.00.
2. The first deposit is made at the beginning of the first payment interval and the interest earned by the fund during the first payment interval is 0.115(5416.42) = $622.89. The increase in the fund is 5416.42 + 622.89 = $6039.31 and the balance is $6039.31.
3. The second deposit is made at the beginning of the second payment interval, the interest earned is 0.115(6039.31 + 5416.42) = $1317.41, the increase is 5416.42 + 1317.41 = $6733.83, and the balance is 6039.31 + 6733.83 = $12 773.14.
4. The third deposit is made at the beginning of the third payment interval, the interest earned is 0.115(12 773.14 + 5416.42) = $2091.80, the increase is 5416.42 + 2091.80 = $7508.22, and the balance is 12 773.14 + 7508.22 = $20 281.36.
5. Calculations for the remaining payment intervals are made in a similar manner. Be careful to add the deposit to the previous balance when computing the interest earned.
6. The final balance of $60 000.06 is slightly different from the expected balance of $60 000.00 due to rounding. The exact balance may be obtained by adjusting the last payment to $5416.36.
7. The total increase in the fund must equal the final balance of $60 000.06. The total periodic payments are 7(5416.42) = $37 914.94. The total interest is 60 000.06 − 37 914.94 = $22 085.12.

C. Finding the accumulated balance and interest earned or increase in a sinking fund for a payment interval; constructing partial sinking fund schedules

EXAMPLE 15.5E For Examples 15.5A and 15.5B, compute

    (i) the accumulated value in the fund at the end of the third payment interval;

   (ii) the interest earned by the fund in the fifth payment interval;

  (iii) the increase in the fund in the fifth interval.

Solution

(i) The balance in a sinking fund at any time is the accumulated value of the payments made into the fund.

For Example 15.5A (when payments are made at the end of each payment interval)

$$R = 2020.72; \quad n = 3; \quad i = 6\%$$

$$S_n = 2020.72\left(\frac{1.06^3 - 1}{0.06}\right)$$

$$= 2020.72(3.1836000)$$
$$= \$6433.16 \quad \text{———— see Sinking Fund Schedule,}$$
$$\text{Example 15.5C}$$

Programmed solution

0 [PV] 2020.72 [PMT] 6 [%i] 3 [N] [CPT] [FV] [6433.1641]

For Example 15.5B (when payments are made at the beginning of each payment interval)

$$R = 5416.42; \quad n = 3; \quad i = 11.5\%$$

$$S_n(\text{due}) = 5416.42(1.115)\left(\frac{1.115^3 - 1}{0.115}\right)$$

$$= 5416.42(1.115)(3.3582250)$$
$$= \$20\,281.36 \quad \text{———— see Sinking Fund Schedule,}$$
$$\text{Example 15.5D}$$

Programmed solution

0 [PV] 5416.42 [PMT] 11.5 [%i] 3 [N] [DUE] [FV] [20 281.356]

(ii) The interest earned during any given payment interval is based on the balance in the fund at the beginning of the interval. This figure is the same as the balance at the end of the previous payment interval.

For Example 15.5A
The balance at the end of the fourth payment interval

$$S_4 = 2020.72\left(\frac{1.06^4 - 1}{0.06}\right)$$

$$= 2020.72(4.3746160)$$
$$= \$8839.87$$

Programmed solution

0 [PV] 2020.72 [PMT] 6 [%i] 4 [N] [CPT] [FV] [8839.874]

The interest earned by the fund in the fifth payment interval is
$0.06(8839.87) = \$530.39$.

For Example 15.5B
The balance in the fund at the end of the fourth payment interval

$$S_4 = 5416.42(1.115)\left(\frac{1.115^4 - 1}{0.115}\right)$$

$$= 5416.42(1.115)(4.7444209)$$
$$= \$28\,653.02$$

Programmed solution

0 [PV] 5416.42 [PMT] 11.5 [%i] 4 [N] [DUE] [FV] [28 653.02]

The interest earned by the fund in the fifth payment interval is
$0.115(28\,653.02 + 5416.42) = 0.115(34\,069.44) = \$3917.99$.

(iii) The increase in the sinking fund in any given payment interval is the interest earned by the fund during the payment interval plus the periodic payment.

For Example 15.5A
The increase in the fund during the fifth payment interval is
$530.39 + 2020.72 = \$2551.11$.

For Example 15.5B
The increase in the fund during the fifth payment interval is
$3917.99 + 5416.42 = \$9334.41$.

EXAMPLE 15.5F The Board of Directors of Peel Credit Union decided to establish a building fund of $130 000.00 by making equal deposits into a sinking fund at the end of every three months for seven years. Interest is 12% compounded quarterly.

(i) Compute the increase in the fund during the twelfth payment interval.

(ii) Construct a partial sinking fund schedule showing details of the first three deposits, the twelfth deposit, the last three deposits, and totals.

Solution   Size of the quarterly deposit:

$$S_n = 130\,000.00; \quad n = 7(4) = 28; \quad i = \frac{12\%}{4} = 3\%$$

$$130\,000.00 = R\left(\frac{1.03^{28} - 1}{0.03}\right)$$

$$130\,000.00 = R(42.930922)$$
$$R = 3028.12$$

Programmed solution

0 | PV | 130 000 | FV | 3 | %i | 28 | N | | CPT | | PMT | | 3028.1204 |

(i) Balance in the fund at the end of the eleventh payment interval

$$S_n = 3028.12\left(\frac{1.03^{11} - 1}{0.03}\right)$$

$$= 3028.12(12.807796)$$
$$= \$38\,783.54$$

Programmed solution

0 | PV | 3028.12 | PMT | 3 | %i | 11 | N | | CPT | | FV | | 38 783.542 |

The interest earned by the fund during the twelfth payment interval is $0.03(38\,783.54) = \$1163.51$.

The increase in the fund during the twelfth payment interval is $1163.51 + 3028.12 = \$4191.63$.

(ii) The last three payments are Payments 26, 27, and 28. To show details of these, we must know the accumulated value after 25 payment intervals.

$$S_{25} = 3028.12\left(\frac{1.03^{25} - 1}{0.03}\right) = 3028.12(36.459264) = \$110\,403.03$$

Programmed solution

0 | PV | 3028.12 | PMT | 3 | %i | 25 | N | | CPT | | FV | | 110 403.03 |

Partial sinking fund schedule

Payment Interval Number	Periodic Payment Made at End	Interest for Payment Interval $i = 0.03$	Increase in Fund	Balance in Fund at End of Payment Interval
0				0.00
1	3 028.12	0.00	3 028.12	3 028.12
2	3 028.12	90.84	3 118.96	6 147.08
3	3 028.12	184.41	3 212.53	9 359.61
•	•	•	•	•
•	•	•	•	•
11	•	•	•	38 783.54
12	3 028.12	1 163.51	4 191.63	42 975.17
•	•	•	•	•
•	•	•	•	•
25	•	•	•	110 403.03
26	3 028.12	3 312.09	6 340.21	116 743.24
27	3 028.12	3 502.30	6 530.42	123 273.66
28	3 028.12	3 698.21	6 726.33	129 999.99
TOTAL	84 787.36	45 212.63	129 999.99	

EXAMPLE 15.5G Laurin and Company want to build up a fund of $75 000.00 by making payments of $2000.00 at the beginning of every six months into a sinking fund earning 11% compounded semi-annually. Construct a partial sinking fund schedule showing details of the first three payments, the last three payments, and totals.

Solution To show details of the last three payments, we need to know the number of payments.

$$S_n(\text{due}) = 75\,000.00; \ R = 2000.00; \ i = \frac{11\%}{2} = 5.5\%$$

$$75\,000.00 = 2000.00(1.055)\left(\frac{1.055^n - 1}{0.055}\right)$$

$$1.055^n = 2.9549763$$
$$n \ln 1.055 = \ln 2.9549763$$
$$n(0.0535408) = 1.0834906$$
$$n = 20.236741$$

Programmed solution

0 [PV] 75 000 [FV] 2000 [PMT] 5.5 [%i] [DUE] [N] [20.236741]
(or −2000)

Twenty-one payments are needed. The last three payments are Payments 19, 20, and 21. The balance in the fund at the end of the 18th payment interval

$$S_{18}(\text{due}) = 2000.00(1.055)\left(\frac{1.055^{18} - 1}{0.055}\right)$$

$$= 2000.00(1.055)(29.481205)$$
$$= \$62\,205.34$$

Programmed solution

0 [PV] 2000 [PMT] 5.5 [%i] 18 [N] [DUE] [FV] [62 205.342]

Partial sinking fund schedule

Payment Interval Number	Periodic Payment Made at Beginning	Interest for Payment Interval $i = 0.055$	Increase in Fund	Balance in Fund at End of Payment Interval
0				0.00
1	2 000.00	110.00	2 110.00	2 110.00
2	2 000.00	226.05	2 226.05	4 336.05
3	2 000.00	348.48	23 348.48	6 684.53
•	•	•	•	•
•	•	•	•	•
18	•	•	•	62 205.34
19	2 000.00	3 531.29	5 531.29	67 736.63
20	2 000.00	3 835.51	5 835.51	73 572.14
21	1 427.86	0.00	1 427.86	75 000.00
TOTAL	41 427.86	33 572.14	75 000.00	

Note: The desired balance in the sinking fund will be reached at the beginning of the 21st payment interval by depositing $1427.86.

D. Computer application—Sinking fund schedule

Spreadsheet programs like EXCEL and Lotus 1-2-3 make creating sinking fund schedules much easier. Once you create a sinking fund schedule in a spreadsheet, you can change details of the sinking fund and see immediately the effect of the change on the sinking fund schedule, without inputting all the formulae again. The procedures that follow are general instructions for creating the sinking fund schedule for Example 15.5C in a spreadsheet. The formulae in the spreadsheet diagram were created using EXCEL. Many other spreadsheet programs work in a similar way. Modify the procedures below if your spreadsheet program requires different instructions.

STEP 1   To create the sinking fund schedule for Example 15.5C (Figure 15.2) in a spreadsheet, open a new spreadsheet file. Enter the labels, formulae, and numbers shown in the diagram below. To display the labels in row 1, you can widen the columns (as shown below) or shorten the labels. (In EXCEL, you can widen the columns by going to the Format menu, choosing Column, then choosing Width. Type numbers until you get the column width you want. You can also widen columns by placing the cursor between columns until the cursor changes to a double-pointed arrow. Drag the side column until you get the column width you want.)

To reduce inputting time and avoid inputting errors, copy as many formulae and numbers as possible within the spreadsheet. (To copy and paste formulae and numbers in EXCEL, click on the cell you want to copy. Go to the Edit menu and choose Copy. Then highlight the cell or cells you want to copy into. Go to the Edit menu and choose Paste. You can also copy formulae into the cells below a particular cell. Highlight the particular cell and all the cells below it that you want to fill. Go to the Edit menu, choose Fill, then choose Down.) The numbers and formulae in cells B3, C3, and E3 can be copied into many of the cells that appear below these cells. Notice that the formulae in cells B3 and C3 include F2 and F4 respectively. In EXCEL, the $ symbols are required for *absolute cell references*. This is to make sure that when you copy the formulae in cells B3 and C3, the new formulae you create will always link to cells F2 and F4.

FIGURE 15.2

	A	B	C	D	E	F
					Workbook 1	
1	Payment Interval	Periodic Payment	Interest	Increase in Fund	Balance at End	
2	0				0	2020.72
3	1	= F2	= F4*E2	= B3+C3	= E2+D3	
4	2	= F2	= F4*E3	= B4+C4	= E3+D4	= 0.06
5	3	= F2	= F4*E4	= B5+C5	= E4+D5	
6	4	= F2	= F4*E5	= B6+C6	= E5+D6	
7	5	= F2	= F4*E6	= B7+C7	= E6+D7	
8	6	= F2	= F4*E7	= B8+C8	= E7+D8	
9	7	= F2	= F4*E8	= B9+C9	= E8+D9	
10	8	= F2	= F4*E9	= B10+C10	= E9+D10	
11	Totals	= SUM(B3:B10)	= SUM(C3:C10)	= SUM(D3:D10)		

STEP 2   To make the spreadsheet easier to read, format the numbers to two decimal places. (In EXCEL, change the format by highlighting cells B3 to F9. Go to the Format menu, choose Cells, then choose 0.00 from the Number section.)

STEP 3   Notice the formulae that are entered in cells B11, C11, and D11. They total the values in columns B, C, and D respectively. For an explanation of these amounts, refer to explanatory notes 6 and 7 on page 676.

STEP 4   Notice the formulae entered in cells B11, C11 and D11. The sum in cell B11 must equal the total of all the sinking fund payments made (eight payments of $2020.72 each). The sum in cell C11 is the total interest paid, and must be the difference between cells B11 (total payments made) and D11 (the sinking fund balance required).

Now that you have created the sinking fund schedule in a spreadsheet, you can change aspects of the sinking fund and create a new sinking fund schedule quickly. For any sinking fund deposit made at the end of the first payment interval, determine the size of the sinking fund payment. Enter this amount in cell F2. If the interest rate has changed, enter the new rate in cell F4. If the number of payment intervals changes, increase or decrease the number of rows in the spreadsheet as required.

For sinking fund deposits made at the beginning of the first payment interval, interest is earned during the first payment interval. This must be reflected in your spreadsheet by altering the formulae in column C, the interest calculation column.

Figure 15.3 below shows the sinking fund schedule for Example 15.5D, which requires sinking fund payments at the beginning of each payment interval. Notice that the formulae in column C add the amount of the sinking fund payments from column B to the previous period's balance before calculating the interest for the period. For a further explanation of this sinking fund schedule, see the explanatory notes on page 677.

FIGURE 15.3

	A	B	C	D	E	F
			Workbook 1			
1	Payment Interval	Periodic Payment	Interest	Increase in Fund	Balance at End	
2	0				0	5416.42
3	1	= F2	= F4(E2+B3)	= B3+C3	= E2+D3	
4	2	= F2	= F4(E3+B4)	= B4+C4	= E3+D4	= 0.115
5	3	= F2	= F4(E4+B5)	= B5+C5	= E4+D5	
6	4	= F2	= F4(E5+B6)	= B6+C6	= E5+D6	
7	5	= F2	= F4(E6+B7)	= B7+C7	= E6+D7	
8	6	= F2	= F4(E7+B8)	= B8+C8	= E7+D8	
9	7	= F2	= F4(E8+B9)	= B9+C9	= E8 D9	
10	Totals	= SUM(B3:B9)	= SUM(C3:C9)	= SUM(D3:D9)		

E. Debt retirement by the sinking fund method

When a sinking fund is created to retire a debt, the debt principal is repaid in total at the due date from the proceeds of the sinking fund while interest on the principal is paid periodically. The payments into the sinking fund are usually made at the same time as the interest payments are made. The sum of the two payments (debt interest payment plus payment into the sinking fund) is called the **periodic cost of the debt**. The difference between the debt principal and the sinking fund balance at any point is called the **book value of the debt**.

EXAMPLE 15.5H   The City Board of Education borrowed $750 000.00 for twenty years at 13% compounded annually to finance construction of Hillview Elementary School. The board created a sinking fund to repay the debt at the end of twenty years. Equal payments are made into the sinking fund at the end of each year and interest earned by the fund is 10.5% compounded annually. Rounding all computations to the nearest dollar,

(i)   determine the annual cost of the debt;

(ii)   compute the book value of the debt at the end of ten years;

(iii)   construct a partial sinking fund schedule showing the book value of the debt, the three first payments, the three last payments, and the totals.

Solution   (i)   The annual interest cost on the principal:

$P = 750\,000;\ i = 13\% = 0.13;$
$I = 750\,000(0.13) = \$97\,500$

The annual payment into the sinking fund:

$S_n = 750\,000;\quad n = 20;\quad i = 10.5\%$

$$750\,000 = R\left(\frac{1.105^{20} - 1}{0.105}\right)$$

$750\,000 = R(60.630808)$
$R = \$12\,370$

Programmed solution

$0\ \boxed{PV}\ \ 750\,000\ \boxed{FV}\ \ 10.5\ \boxed{\%i}\ \ 20\ \boxed{N}\ \ \boxed{CPT}\ \ \boxed{PMT}\ \ \boxed{12\,369.949}$

The annual cost of the debt is $97\,500 + 12\,370 = \$109\,870$.

(ii)   The balance in the sinking fund after the tenth payment

$$S_{10} = 12\,370\left(\frac{1.105^{10} - 1}{0.105}\right)$$

$= 12\,370(16.324579)$
$= \$201\,935$

Programmed solution

$0\ \boxed{PV}\ \ 12\,370\ \boxed{PMT}\ \ 10.5\ \boxed{\%i}\ \ 10\ \boxed{N}\ \ \boxed{CPT}\ \ \boxed{FV}\ \ \boxed{201\,935.05}$

The book value of the debt at the end of the tenth year is
$750\,000 - 201\,935 = \$548\,065$.

(iii) The last three payments are Payments 18, 19, and 20. The balance in the sinking fund at the end of Year 17

$$S_{17} = 12\,370\left(\frac{1.105^{17} - 1}{0.105}\right) = 12\,370(42.47213) = \$525\,380$$

Programmed solution

0 [PV] 12 370 [PMT] 10.5 [%i] 17 [N] [CPT] [FV] [525 380.24]

Partial sinking fund schedule

Payment Interval Number	Periodic Payment Made at End	Interest for Payment Interval $i = 0.105$	Increase in Fund	Balance in Fund at End of Payment Interval	Book Value of Debt
0				0	750 000
1	12 370	0	12 370	12 370	737 630
2	12 370	1 299	13 669	26 039	723 961
3	12 370	2 734	15 104	41 143	708 857
•	•	•	•	•	•
•	•	•	•	•	•
17	•	•	•	525 380	224 620
18	12 370	55 165	67 535	592 915	157 085
19	12 370	62 256	74 626	667 541	82 459
20	12 367	70 092	82 459	750 000	0
TOTAL	247 397	502 603	750 000		

Note: The last payment has been adjusted to create a fund of exactly $750 000.

Exercise 15.5

A. For each of the six sinking funds listed in the table below, compute (a) the size of the periodic payment; (b) the accumulated balance at the time indicated.

	Amount of Sinking Fund	Payment Interval	Payments Made At:	Term	Interest Rate	Conversion Period	Accumulated Balance Required After:
1.	$15 000.00	6 months	end	10 years	6%	semi-annually	10th payment
2.	$9600.00	1 month	end	8 years	12%	monthly	36th payment
3.	$8400.00	1 month	beginning	15 years	9%	monthly	96th payment
4.	$21 000.00	3 months	beginning	20 years	8%	quarterly	28th payment
5.	$45 000.00	3 months	end	12 years	10%	quarterly	16th payment
6.	$72 000.00	6 months	beginning	15 years	13%	semi-annually	20th payment

B. Each of the six debts listed in the table below is retired by the sinking fund method. Interest payments on the debt are made at the end of each payment interval and the payments into the sinking fund are made at the same time. Determine

a) the size of the periodic interest expense of the debt;

b) the size of the periodic payment into the sinking fund;

c) the periodic cost of the debt;

d) the book value of the debt at the time indicated.

	Debt Principal	Term of Debt	Payment Interval	Interest Rate On Debt	On Fund	Conversion Period	Book Value Required After:
1.	$20 000.00	10 years	3 months	14%	12%	quarterly	6 years
2.	$14 500.00	8 years	6 months	15%	12.5%	semi-annually	5 years
3.	$10 000.00	5 years	1 month	7.5%	6.0%	monthly	4 years
4.	$40 000.00	15 years	3 months	8.0%	7.0%	quarterly	10 years
5.	$95 000.00	20 years	6 months	9.0%	7.0%	semi-annually	15 years
6.	$80 000.00	12 years	1 month	15%	13.5%	monthly	8 years

C. Answer each of the following questions.

1. Hein Engineering expects to expand its plant facilities in six years at an estimated cost of $75 000.00. To provide for the expansion, a sinking fund has been established into which equal payments are made at the end of every three months. Interest is 5% compounded quarterly.

a) What is the size of the quarterly payments?

b) How much of the maturity value will be payments?

c) How much interest will the fund contain?

2. To redeem a $100 000.00 promissory note due in ten years, Cobblestone Enterprises has set up a sinking fund earning 7.5% compounded semi-annually. Equal deposits are made at the beginning of every six months.

a) What is the size of the semi-annual deposits?

b) How much of the maturity value of the fund is deposits?

c) How much is interest?

3. Equal deposits are made into a sinking fund at the end of each year for seven years. Interest is 5.5% compounded annually and the maturity value of the fund is $20 000.00. Find the size of the annual deposits and construct a sinking fund schedule showing totals.

4. A sinking fund amounting to $15 000.00 is to be created by making payments at the beginning of every six months for four years. Interest earned by the fund is 12.5% compounded semi-annually. Determine the size of the semi-annual payments and prepare a sinking fund schedule showing totals.

5. For Question 3, calculate the increase in the fund for the fourth year. Verify your answer by checking the sinking fund schedule.

6. For Question 4, compute the interest earned during the fifth payment interval. Verify your answer by checking the sinking fund schedule.

7. Kirk, Klein & Co. requires $100 000.00 fifteen years from now to retire a debt. A sinking fund is established into which equal payments are made at the end of every month. Interest is 7.5% compounded monthly.

   a) What is the size of the monthly payment?

   b) What is the balance in the sinking fund after five years?

   c) How much interest will be earned by the fund in the 100th payment interval?

   d) By how much will the fund increase during the 150th payment interval?

   e) Construct a partial sinking fund schedule showing details of the first three payments, the last three payments, and totals.

8. The Town of Keewatin issued debentures worth $120 000.00 maturing in ten years to finance construction of water and sewer facilities. To redeem the debentures, the town council decided to make equal deposits into a sinking fund at the beginning of every three months. Interest earned by the sinking fund is 6% compounded quarterly.

   a) What is the size of the quarterly payment into the sinking fund?

   b) What is the balance in the fund after six years?

   c) How much interest is earned by the fund in the 28th payment interval?

   d) By how much will the fund increase in the 33rd payment interval?

   e) Prepare a partial sinking fund schedule showing details of the first three payments, the last three payments, and totals.

9. The Township of Jeffrey Melnick borrowed $300 000.00 for road improvements. The debt agreement requires that the township pay the interest on the loan at the end of each year and make equal deposits at the time of the interest payments into a sinking fund until the loan is retired in twenty years. Interest on the loan is 8.25% compounded annually and interest earned by the sinking fund is 5.5% compounded annually. (Round all answers to the nearest dollar.)

   a) What is the annual interest expense?

   b) What is the size of the annual deposit into the sinking fund?

c) What is the total annual cost of the debt?

d) How much is the increase in the sinking fund in the tenth year?

e) What is the book value of the debt after fifteen years?

f) Construct a partial sinking fund schedule showing details, including the book value of the debt, for the first three years, the last three years, and totals.

10. Sheridan Credit Union borrowed $225 000.00 at 13% compounded semi-annually from League Central to build an office complex. The loan agreement requires payment of interest at the end of every six months. In addition, the credit union is to make equal payments into a sinking fund so that the principal can be retired in total after fifteen years. Interest earned by the fund is 11% compounded semi-annually. (Round all answers to the nearest dollar.)

a) What is the semi-annual interest payment on the debt?

b) What is the size of the semi-annual deposits into the sinking fund?

c) What is the total annual cost of the debt?

d) What is the interest earned by the fund in the 20th payment interval?

e) What is the book value of the debt after twelve years?

f) Prepare a partial sinking fund schedule showing details, including the book value of the debt, for the first three years, the last three years, and totals.

REVIEW EXERCISE

1. A $5000, 11.5% bond with interest payable semi-annually is redeemable at par in twelve years. What is the purchase price to yield

   a) 10.5% compounded semi-annually? **b)** 13% compounded semi-annually?

2. A $10 000, 6% bond with semi-annual coupons is redeemable at 108. What is the purchase price to yield 7.5% compounded semi-annually

   a) nine years before maturity?   **b)** fifteen years before maturity?

3. A $25 000, 13% bond with interest payable quarterly is redeemable at 104 in six years. What is the purchase price to yield 14.25% compounded annually?

4. A $1000, 9.5% bond with semi-annual coupons redeemable at par on March 1, 2004, was purchased on September 19, 1995, to yield 15% compounded semi-annually. What was the purchase price?

5. Four $5000, 13% bonds with semi-annual coupons are bought seven years before maturity to yield 12% compounded semi annually. Find the premium or discount and the purchase price if the bonds are redeemable

   a) at par;   **b)** at 107.

6. Nine $1000, 14% bonds with interest payable semi-annually and redeemable at par are purchased ten years before maturity. Find the premium or discount and the purchase price if the bonds are bought to yield

   a) 10%; **b)** 14%; **c)** 16%.

7. A $100 000, 15% bond with interest payable semi-annually redeemable at par on July 15, 2007, was purchased on April 18, 1996, to yield 17% compounded semi-annually. Determine

   a) the premium or discount;

   b) the purchase price;

   c) the quoted price.

8. Four $10 000 bonds bearing interest at 16% payable quarterly and redeemable at 106 on September 1, 2008, were purchased on January 23, 1996, to yield 15% compounded quarterly. Determine

   a) the premium or discount;

   b) the purchase price;

   c) the quoted price.

9. A $5000, 8% bond with semi-annual coupons redeemable at 108 in ten years is purchased to yield 10% compounded semi-annually. What is the purchase price?

10. A $1000 bond bearing interest at 16% payable semi-annually redeemable at par on February 1, 2002, was purchased on October 12, 1995, to yield 15% compounded semi-annually. Determine the purchase price.

11. A $25 000, 13% bond with semi-annual coupons redeemable at 107 on June 15, 2008, was purchased on May 9, 1997, to yield 14.5% compounded semi-annually. Determine

    a) the premium or discount;

    b) the purchase price;

    c) the quoted price.

12. A $50 000, 11% bond with semi-annual coupons redeemable at par on April 15, 2003, was purchased on June 25, 1996, at $92\frac{3}{8}$. What was the approximate yield rate?

13. A $1000, 14.5% bond with interest payable annually is purchased six years before maturity to yield 16.5% compounded annually. Compute the premium or discount and the purchase price and construct the appropriate bond schedule.

14. A $5000, 12.25% bond with interest payable annually redeemable at par in seven years is purchased to yield 13.5% compounded annually. Find the premium or discount and the purchase price and construct the appropriate bond schedule.

15. A $20 000, 15.5% bond with semi-annual coupons redeemable at 105 in three years is purchased to yield 14% compounded semi-annually. Find the premium or discount and purchase price and construct the appropriate bond schedule.

16. Three $25 000, 11% bonds with semi-annual coupons redeemable at par were bought eight years before maturity to yield 12% compounded semi-annually. Determine the gain or loss if the bonds are sold at $89\frac{3}{8}$ five years later.

17. A $10 000 bond with 13% interest payable quarterly redeemable at 106 on November 15, 2006, was bought on July 2, 1990, to yield 17% compounded quarterly. If the bond was sold at $92\frac{3}{4}$ on September 10, 1996, what was the gain or loss on the sale?

18. A $25 000, 9.5% bond with semi-annual coupons redeemable at par is bought sixteen years before maturity at $78\frac{1}{4}$. What was the approximate yield rate?

19. A $10 000, 15% bond with quarterly coupons redeemable at 102 on October 15, 2003, was purchased on May 5, 1991, at $98\frac{3}{4}$. What is the approximate yield rate?

20. What is the approximate yield realized if the bond in Question 19 was sold on August 7, 1996, at 92?

21. A 14.5% annuity bond of $50 000 with interest payable quarterly is to be redeemable at par in twelve years.

    a) What is the purchase price to yield 16% compounded quarterly?

    b) What is the book value after nine years?

    c) What is the gain or loss if the bond is sold nine years after the date of purchase at $99\frac{5}{8}$?

22. A $100 000, 10.75% bond with interest payable annually is redeemable at 103 in eight years. What is the purchase price to yield 12% compounded quarterly?

23. A $5000, 14.5% bond with semi-annual coupons redeemable at par on August 1, 2004, was purchased on March 5, 1993, at $95\frac{1}{2}$. What was the approximate yield rate?

24. A $25 000, 18% bond with semi-annual coupons, redeemable at 104 in fifteen years, is purchased to yield 16% compounded semi-annually. Determine the gain or loss if the bond is sold three years later at $107\frac{1}{4}$.

25. To provide for the purchase of heavy construction equipment estimated to cost $110 000.00, Valmar Construction is paying equal sums of money at the end of every six months for five years into a sinking fund earning 7.5% compounded semi-annually.

    a) What is the size of the semi-annual payment into the sinking fund?

    b) Compute the balance in the fund after the third payment.

    c) Compute the amount of interest earned during the sixth payment interval.

    d) Construct a sinking fund schedule showing totals. Check your answers to parts (b) and (c) with the values in the schedule.

26. Alpha Corporation is depositing equal sums of money at the beginning of every three months into a sinking fund to redeem a $65 000.00 promissory note due eight years from now. Interest earned by the fund is 12% compounded quarterly.

a) Determine the size of the quarterly payments into the sinking fund.

b) Compute the balance in the fund after three years.

c) Compute the increase in the fund during the 24th payment interval.

d) Construct a partial sinking fund schedule showing details of the first three deposits, the last three deposits, and totals.

27. The municipality of Kirkfield borrowed $100 000.00 to build a recreation centre. The debt principal is to be repaid in eight years and interest at 13.75% compounded annually is to be paid annually. To provide for the retirement of the debt, the municipal council set up a sinking fund into which equal payments are made at the time of the annual interest payments. Interest earned by the fund is 11.5% compounded annually.

a) What is the annual interest payment?

b) What is the size of the annual payment into the sinking fund?

c) What is the total annual cost of the debt?

d) Compute the book value of the debt after three years.

e) Compute the interest earned by the fund in Year 6.

f) Construct a sinking fund schedule showing the book value of the debt and totals. Verify your computations in parts (d) and (e) against the schedule.

28. The Harrow Board of Education financed the acquisition of a building site through a $300 000.00 long-term promissory note due in fifteen years. Interest on the promissory note is 9.25% compounded semi-annually and is payable at the end of every six months. To provide for the redemption of the note, the board agreed to make equal payments at the end of every six months into a sinking fund paying 8% compounded semi-annually. (Round all answers to the nearest dollar.)

a) What is the semi-annual interest payment?

b) What is the size of the semi-annual payment into the sinking fund?

c) What is the annual cost of the debt?

d) Compute the book value of the debt after five years.

e) Compute the increase in the sinking fund in the 20th payment interval.

f) Construct a partial sinking fund schedule showing details, including the book value of the debt, for the first three years, the last three years, and totals.

29. Northern Flying Service is preparing to buy an aircraft estimated to cost $60 000.00 by making equal payments at the end of every three months into a sinking fund for five years. Interest earned by the fund is 8% compounded quarterly.

    a) What is the size of the quarterly payment into the sinking fund?

    b) How much of the maturity value of the fund will be interest?

    c) What is the accumulated value of the fund after two years?

    d) How much interest will the fund earn in the 15th payment interval?

30. A sinking fund of $10 000.00 is to be created by equal annual payments at the beginning of each year for seven years. Interest earned by the fund is 7.5% compounded annually.

    a) Compute the annual deposit into the fund.

    b) Construct a sinking fund schedule showing totals.

31. Joe Ngosa bought a retirement fund for $15 000.00. Beginning twenty-five years from the date of purchase, he will receive payments of $17 500.00 at the beginning of every six months. Interest earned by the fund is 12% compounded semi-annually.

    a) How many payments will Joe receive?

    b) What is the size of the last payment?

32. The town of Kildare bought firefighting equipment for $96 000.00. The financing agreement provides for annual interest payments and equal payments into a sinking fund for ten years. After ten years the proceeds of the sinking fund will be used to retire the principal. Interest on the debt is 14.5% compounded annually and interest earned by the sinking fund is 13% compounded annually.

    a) What is the annual interest payment?

    b) What is the size of the annual payment into the sinking fund?

    c) What is the total annual cost of the debt?

    d) What is the book value of the debt after four years?

    e) Construct a partial sinking fund schedule showing details, including the book value of the debt, for the last three years and totals.

SELF-TEST

1. A $10 000, 10% bond with quarterly coupons redeemable at par in fifteen years is purchased to yield 11% compounded quarterly. Determine the purchase price of the bond.

2. What is the purchase price of a $1000, 13.5% bond with semi-annual coupons redeemable at 108 in ten years if the bond is bought to yield 12% compounded semi-annually?

3. A $5000, 8% bond with semi-annual coupons redeemable at 104 is bought six years before maturity to yield 6.5% compounded semi-annually. Determine the premium or discount.

4. A $20 000, 16% bond with semi-annual coupons redeemable at par March 1, 2003, was purchased on November 15, 1996, to yield 15% compounded semi-annually. What was the purchase price of the bond?

5. A $5000, 13% bond with semi-annual coupons redeemable at 102 on December 15, 2006, was purchased on November 9, 1995, to yield 14.5% compounded semi-annually. Determine the quoted price.

6. A $5000, 11.5% bond with semi-annual coupons redeemable at 105 is bought four years before maturity to yield 13% compounded semi-annually. Construct a bond schedule.

7. A $100 000, 13% bond with semi-annual interest payments redeemable at par on July 15, 2003, is bought on September 10, 1996, at $102\frac{5}{8}$. What was the approximate yield rate?

8. A $25 000, 14% bond with semi-annual coupons redeemable at 106 in twenty years is purchased to yield 16% compounded semi-annually. Determine the gain or loss if the bond is sold seven years after the date of purchase at $98\frac{1}{4}$.

9. A $10 000, 12% bond with semi-annual coupons redeemable at par on December 1, 2007, was purchased on July 20, 1996, at $93\frac{7}{8}$. Compute the approximate yield rate.

10. Cottingham Pies made semi-annual payments into a sinking fund for ten years. If the fund had a balance of $100 000.00 after ten years and interest is 11% compounded semi-annually, what was the accumulated balance in the fund after seven years?

11. A fund of $165 000.00 is to be accumulated in six years by making equal payments at the beginning of each month. If interest is 13.5% compounded monthly, how much interest is earned by the fund in the twentieth payment interval?

12. Gillian Armes invested $10 000.00 in an income fund at 13% compounded semi-annually for twenty years. After twenty years, she is to receive semi-annual payments of $10 000.00 at the end of every six-month period until the fund is exhausted. What is the size of the final payment?

13. A company financed a plant expansion of $750 000.00 at 14% compounded annually. The financing agreement requires annual payments of interest and the funding of the debt through equal annual payments for fifteen years into a sinking fund earning 12% compounded annually. What is the book value of the debt after five years?

14. Annual sinking fund payments made at the beginning of every year for six years earning 11.5% compounded annually amount to $25 000.00 at the end of six years. Construct a sinking fund schedule showing totals.

CHALLENGE PROBLEMS

1. A $2000 bond with annual coupons is redeemable at par in five years. If the first coupon is $400, and subsequent annual coupons are worth 75% of the previous year's coupon, find the purchase price of the bond that would yield an interest rate of 10% compounded annually.

2. An issue of bonds, redeemable at par in *n* years, is to bear coupons at 9% compounded semi-annually. An investor offers to buy the entire issue at a premium of 15%. At the same time, the investor advises that if the coupon rate were raised to 10% compounded semi-annually, he would offer to buy the whole issue at a premium of 25%. At what yield rate compounded semi-annually are these two offers equivalent?

CASE STUDY 15.1 INVESTING IN BONDS

Recently Ruja attended a personal financial planning seminar. The speaker mentioned that bonds should be a part of everyone's balanced investment portfolio, even if they are only a small part. Ruja's RRSP contains mutual funds and a Guaranteed Investment Certificate (GIC), but no bonds. She has decided to invest up to $4500.00 of her RRSP funds in bonds and has narrowed her choices to three.

Bond A is a $1000, 6.8% bond with semi-annual coupons redeemable in five years. Ruja can purchase up to four of these bonds at 104.25.

Bond B is a $1000, 7.1% bond with semi-annual coupons redeemable in four years. She can purchase up to four of these bonds at 103.10.

Bond C is a $1000, 6.2% bond with semi-annual coupons redeemable in seven years. Ruja can purchase up to four of these bonds at 101.85.

QUESTIONS

1. Suppose Ruja wants to invest in only one bond. Use the average investment method to answer the following questions.

   a) What is the approximate yield rate of Bond A?

   b) What is the approximate yield rate of Bond B?

   c) What is the approximate yield rate of Bond C?

   d) Assume Ruja is willing to hold the bond she chooses until it matures. Which bond has the highest yield?

2. Suppose Ruja decides to buy two $1000 denominations of Bond A. Bond A's semi-annual coupons are payable on January 1 and July 1. Suppose Ruja purchases these bonds on February 27.

   a) What is the accrued interest on these two bonds up to the date of Ruja's purchase?

   b) What is Ruja's purchase price (or flat price) for these two bonds?

3. Suppose Ruja decides to buy two $1000 denominations of Bond B on February 27. Bond B's semi-annual coupons are payable on February 1 and August 1.

   a) What is the accrued interest on these two bonds up to the date of Ruja's purchase?

   b) What is Ruja's purchase price (or flat price) for these two bonds?

CASE STUDY 15.2 THE BUSINESS OF BONDS

Beaucage Development Company is developing a new process to manufacture compact discs. The development costs were higher than expected, so Beaucage required an immediate cash inflow of $4 800 000.00. To raise this money, the company decided to issue bonds. Since Beaucage had no expertise in issuing and selling bonds, the company decided to work with an investment dealer. The investment dealer bought the company's entire bond issue at a discount, then sold the bonds to the public at face value or the current market value. To ensure it would raise the $4 800 000.00 it required, Beaucage issued 5000 bonds with a face value of $1000 each on January 20, 1998. Interest is paid semi-annually on July 20 and January 20, beginning July 20, 1998. The bonds pay interest at 7.5% compounded semi-annually.

Beaucage directors realize that when the bonds mature on January 20, 2018, there must be $5 000 000.00 available to repay the bondholders. To have enough money on hand to meet this obligation, the directors set up a sinking fund using a specially designated savings account. The company earns interest of 5.5% compounded semi-annually on this sinking fund account. The directors began making semi-annual payments to the sinking fund on July 20, 1998.

Beaucage Development Company issued the bonds, sold them all to the investment dealer, and used the money raised to continue its research and development.

QUESTIONS

1. How much would an investor have to pay for one of these bonds to earn 8% compounded semi-annually?

2. a) What is the size of the sinking fund payment?

b) What will be the total amount deposited into the sinking fund account?

c) How much of the sinking fund will be interest?

3. Suppose Beaucage discovers on January 20, 2008, that it can earn 8% interest compounded semi-annually on its sinking fund account.

a) What is the balance in the sinking fund after the January 20, 2008, sinking fund payment?

b) What is the new sinking fund payment if the fund begins to earn 8% on January 21, 2008?

c) What will be the total amount deposited into the sinking fund account over the life of the bonds?

d) How much of the sinking fund will then be interest?

e) How does the amount of sinking fund interest calculated in part (d) compare to the amount of interest calculated in Question 2(c)?

SUMMARY OF FORMULAE

Formula 9.1C

$$P = S(1 + i)^{-n}$$

Finding the present value by means of the discount factor (the reciprocal of the compounding factor)

Formula 11.2

$$A_n = R\left[\frac{1 - (1 + i)^{-n}}{i}\right]$$

Finding the present value of an ordinary simple annuity

Formula 11.4

$$A_{nc} = R\left[\frac{1 - (1 + f)^{-n}}{f}\right]$$

where $f = (1 + i)^c - 1$

Preferred formula for finding the present value using the equivalent effective rate of interest per payment period

Formula 15.1

$$PP = S(1 + i)^{-n} + R\left[\frac{1 - (1 + i)^{-n}}{i}\right]$$

Basic formula for finding the purchase price of a bond when the interest payment interval and the yield rate conversion period are equal

Formula 15.2

$$PP = S(1 + f)^{-n} + R\left[\frac{1 - (1 + f)^{-n}}{f}\right]$$

where $f = (1 + i)^c - 1$

Basic formula for finding the purchase price of a bond when the interest payment interval and the yield rate conversion period are different

Formula 15.3

PREMIUM or DISCOUNT

$= (b \times \text{FACE VALUE} - i \times$

$\text{REDEMPTION PRICE})\left[\dfrac{1 - (1 + i)^{-n}}{i}\right]$

Direct formula for finding the premium or discount of a bond (a negative answer indicates a discount)

GLOSSARY

Accumulation of discount   the process of reducing a bond discount

Amortization of premium   the process of writing down a bond premium

Bond rate   the rate of interest paid by a bond, stated as a percent of the face value

Book value of a debt   the difference at any time between the debt principal and the associated sinking fund balance

Coupon   a voucher attached to a bond to facilitate the collection of interest by the bondholder

Coupon rate   see *Bond rate*

Debentures   bonds for which no security is offered

Denomination   see *Face value*

Discount   the difference between the purchase price of a bond and its redemption price when the purchase price is less than the redemption price

Due date   see *Redemption date*

Face value   amount owed by the issuer of the bond to the bondholder

Flat price   total purchase price of a bond (including any accrued interest)

Market price   see *Quoted price*

Maturity date   see *Redemption date*

Method of averages   a method for finding the approximate yield rate

Nominal rate   see *Bond rate*

Par value   see *Face value*

Periodic cost of a debt   the sum of the interest paid and the payment into the sinking fund when a debt is retired by the sinking fund method

Premium   the difference between the purchase price of a bond and its redemption price when the purchase price is greater than the redemption price

Quoted price   the net price of a bond (without accrued interest) at which a bond is offered for sale

Redeemable at a premium   bonds whose redemption price is greater than the face value

Redeemable at par   bonds that are redeemed at their face value

Redemption date   date at which the bond principal is repaid

Redemption price   the amount that the issuer of the bond pays to the bondholder upon surrender of the bond on or after the date of maturity

Sinking fund   a fund into which payments are made to provide a specific sum of money at a future time; usually set up for the purpose of meeting some future obligation

Yield rate   the rate of interest that an investor earns on his or her investment in a bond

16 Investment Decision Applications

> Individuals and companies often have to choose among different investment opportunities. Whether it is deciding between buying and leasing a car or deciding how to increase plant capacity, understanding the time value of money is critical. When comparing different ways of achieving the same goal, we should always examine cash flows at the same point in time. Only then can we know whether it is cheaper to buy or lease that car, and whether it is cheaper to expand the plant in one or two stages.

Introduction

When making investment decisions, all decision makers must consider the comparative effects of alternative courses of action on the cash flows of a business or of an individual. Since cash flow analysis needs to take into account the time value of money (interest), present-value concepts are useful.

When only cash inflows are considered, the value of the discounted cash flows is helpful in guiding management toward a rational decision. If outlays as well as inflows are considered, the net present value concept is applicable in evaluating projects.

While the net present value method indicates whether or not a project will yield a specified rate of return, knowing the actual rate of return provides useful information to the decision maker. The rate of return may be computed using the net present value concept.

OBJECTIVES

Upon completing this chapter, you will be able to do the following:

1. Determine the discounted value of cash flows and choose between alternative investments on the basis of the discounted cash-flow criterion.
2. Determine the net present value of a capital investment project and infer from the net present value whether a project is feasible or not.
3. Compute the rate of return on investment.

16.1 DISCOUNTED CASH FLOW

A. Evaluation of capital expenditures—basic concepts

Capital investment projects are projects involving cash outlays that are expected to generate a continuous flow of future benefits. Benefits may be non-monetary but the methods of analysis considered in this chapter will deal only with investment projects generating an inflow of monetary benefits.

While capital expenditures normally result in the acquisition of assets, the primary purpose of capital expenditures is the acquisition of a future stream of benefits in the form of an inflow of cash. In considering investments involving the acquisition of assets and in making decisions about replacing assets or whether to buy or lease, the decision maker needs to analyze the effects of alternative courses of action on the future cash flow.

While factors other than financial concerns often enter into the decision-making process, the analysis techniques considered here are concerned only with the amount and the timing of cash receipts and cash payments under the assumption that the amount and timing of the cash flow is certain.

From the mathematical point of view, the major issue in evaluating capital expenditure projects is the time value of money. This value prevents direct comparison of cash received and cash payments made at different times. The concept of present value, as introduced in Chapter 9 and used in the following chapters, provides the vehicle for making sums of money received or paid at different times comparable at a chosen time.

B. Discounted cash flow

Discounted cash flow is the present value of all cash payments. When using the discounting technique to evaluate alternatives, two fundamental principles serve as decision criteria.

1. The *bird-in-the-hand principle*—Given that all other factors are equal, earlier benefits are preferable to later benefits.
2. The *the-bigger-the-better principle*—Given that all other factors are equal, bigger benefits are preferable to smaller benefits.

EXAMPLE 16.1A   Suppose you are offered a choice of receiving $1000.00 today or receiving $1000.00 three years from now. What is the preferred choice?

Solution   Accepting the bird-in-the-hand principle, you should prefer to receive $1000.00 today rather than three years from now. The rationale is that $1000.00 can be invested to earn interest and will accumulate in three years to a sum of money greater than $1000.00. Stated another way, the present value of $1000.00 to be received in three years is less than $1000.00 today.

EXAMPLE 16.1B   Consider a choice of $2000.00 today or $3221.00 five years from now. Which alternative is preferable?

Solution   No definite answer is possible without considering interest. A rational choice must consider the time value of money; that is, we need to know the rate of interest. Once a rate of interest is established, we can make the proper choice by considering the present value of the two sums of money and applying the the-bigger-the-better principle.

If you choose "now" as the focal date, three outcomes are possible.

1. The present value of $3221.00 is greater than $2000.00. In this case, the preferred choice is $3221.00 five years from now.

2. The present value of $3221.00 is less than $2000.00. In this case, the preferred choice is $2000.00 now.

3. The present value of $3221.00 equals $2000.00. In this case, either choice is equally acceptable.

   (a) *Suppose the rate of interest is 8%.*
   $S = 3221.00; \quad i = 8\% = 0.08; \quad n = 5$
   $P = 3221.00(1.08^{-5}) = 3221.00(0.6805832) = \$2192.16$
   Since at 8% the discounted value of $3221.00 is greater than $2000.00, the preferred choice at 8% is $3221.00 five years from now.

   (b) *Suppose the rate of interest is 12%.*
   $S = 3221.00; \quad i = 12\% = 0.12; \quad n = 5$
   $P = 3221.00(1.12^{-5}) = 3221.00(0.5674269) = \$1827.68$
   Since at 12% the discounted value is less than $2000.00, the preferred choice is $2000.00 now.

   (c) *Suppose the rate of interest is 10%.*
   $S = 3221.00; \quad i = 10\% = 0.10; \quad n = 5$
   $P = 3221.00(1.10^{-5}) = 3221.00(0.6209213) = \$1999.99$
   Since at 10% the discounted value is equal to $2000.00, the two choices are equally acceptable.

Programmed solution

(a) 0 [PMT] 3221 [FV] 8 [%i] 5 [N] [CPT] [PV] [2192.1585]

(b) 0 [PMT] 3221 [FV] 12 [%i] 5 [N] [CPT] [PV] [1827.6819]

(c) 0 [PMT] 3221 [FV] 10 [%i] 5 [N] [CPT] [PV] [1999.9876]

EXAMPLE 16.1C   Two investments are available. Alternative A yields a return of $6000 in two years and $10 000 in five years. Alternative B yields a return of $7000 now and $7000 in seven years. Which alternative is preferable if money is worth

(i) 11%?   (ii) 15%?

Solution   To determine which alternative is preferable, we need to compute the present value of each alternative and choose the alternative with the higher present value. Let the focal point be "now."

(i) For $i = 11\%$

Alternative A

The present value of Alternative A is the sum of the present values of $6000 in two years and $10 000 in five years.

Present value of $6000 in two years		
$= 6000(1.11^{-2}) = 6000(0.8116224)$	=	$ 4 870
Present value of $10 000 in five years		
$= 10\,000(1.11^{-5}) = 10\,000(0.5934513)$	=	5 935
The present value of Alternative A	=	$10 805

Alternative B

The present value of Alternative B is the sum of the present values of $7000 now and $7000 in seven years.

Present value of $7000 now	=	$ 7 000
Present value of $7000 in seven years		
$= 7000(1.11^{-7}) = 7000(0.4816584)$	=	3 372
The present value of Alternative B	=	$10 372

Programmed solution

Alternative A

0 [PMT] 6000 [FV] 11 [%i] 2 [N] [CPT] [PV] [4869.7346]

0 [PMT] 10 000 [FV] 11 [%i] 5 [N] [CPT] [PV] [5934.5133]

$4870 + 5935 = $10 805.

Alternative B

0 [PMT] 7000 [FV] 11 [%i] 7 [N] [CPT] [PV] [3371.6089]

$3372 + 7000 = $10 372.

Since at 11% the present value of Alternative A is greater than the present value of Alternative B, Alternative A is preferable.

(ii) For $i = 15\%$

Alternative A

Present value of $6000 in two years		
$= 6000(1.15^{-2}) = 6000(0.7561437)$	=	$ 4 537
Present value of $10 000 in five years		
$= 10\,000(1.15^{-5}) = 10\,000(0.4971767)$	=	$ 4 972
The present value of Alternative A	=	$ 9 509

Alternative B

Present value of $7000 now	=	$ 7000
Present value of $7000 in seven years		
$= 7000(1.15^{-7}) = 7000(0.3759370)$	=	$ 2 632
The present value of Alternative B	=	$ 9 632

Programmed solution

Alternative A

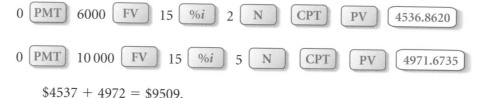

0 PMT 6000 FV 15 %i 2 N CPT PV 4536.8620

0 PMT 10 000 FV 15 %i 5 N CPT PV 4971.6735

$4537 + 4972 = \$9509.$

Alternative B

0 PMT 7000 FV 15 %i 7 N CPT PV 2631.5593

$2632 + 7000 = \$9632.$

Since at 15% the present value of Alternative B is greater than the present value of Alternative A, Alternative B is preferable.

Note: Applying present value techniques to capital investment problems usually involves estimates. For this reason, dollar amounts in the preceding example and all following examples are rounded to the nearest dollar. We suggest that you do the same when working on problems of this nature.

EXAMPLE 16.1D An insurance company offers to settle a claim either by making a payment of $50 000 immediately or by making payments of $8000 at the end of each year for ten years. What offer is preferable if interest is 12% compounded annually?

Solution Present value of $8000 at the end of each year for ten years is the present value of an ordinary annuity in which R = 8000, $n = 10$, and $i = 12\%$.

$$A_n = 8000\left(\frac{1 - 1.12^{-10}}{0.12}\right) = 8000(5.650223) = \$45\ 202$$

Programmed solution

0 FV 8000 PMT 10 N 12 %i CPT PV 45 201.784

Since the immediate payment is larger than the present value of the annual payments of $8000, the immediate payment of $50 000 is preferable.

DID YOU KNOW?

Investors often use various financial ratios when deciding to invest in the stock market. For example, did you know that the Price-Earnings (P/E) Ratio is one of the most widely used of all the financial ratios? The P/E ratio of a company is calculated by dividing the price of a company's stock by its earnings per share. Because the price of the company's stock is a part of the P/E ratio, the ratio reflects investors' assessment of the company's current performance. If the P/E ratio of a company is low compared to the P/E ratio of similar firms, the company's stock is more attractive. Assuming the company is sound, a low P/E ratio suggests that the stock price is not overvalued compared to that of similar firms.

However, many professional investors prefer the Price-to-Cash-Flow (P/CF) Ratio to the P/E ratio. This is because the effects of different accounting policies are removed from the earnings per share figure. The P/CF ratio of a company is calculated by dividing the price of a company's stock by its cash flow per share. (Cash flow per share is the sum of the company's net income, depreciation, and deferred taxes—all items from the company's financial statements.) A lower P/CF ratio suggests a higher future return on the stock. For both the P/E and P/CF ratios, you must compare a company's ratios to the ratios of similar companies in the same industry to make a valid assessment. The "typical" P/E and P/CF ratios can be very different from one industry to the next.

EXAMPLE 16.1E   Sheridan Credit Union needs to decide whether to buy a duplicating machine for $6000 and enter a service contract requiring the payment of $45 at the end of every three months for five years, or to enter a five-year lease requiring the payment of $435 at the beginning of every three months. If leased, the machine can be bought after five years for $600. At 9% compounded quarterly, should the credit union buy or lease?

Solution   To make a rational decision, the credit union should compare the present value of the cash outlays if buying the machine with the present value of the cash outlays if leasing the machine.

Present value of the decision to buy

Present value of cash payment for the machine	$=$	$6000
Present value of the service contract involves an ordinary annuity in which R = 45, $n = 20$, $i = 2.25\%$		

$$= 45\left(\frac{1 - 1.0225^{-20}}{0.0225}\right) = 45(15.963712) \qquad = \qquad \underline{718}$$

Present value of decision to buy $=$ $6718

Present value of the decision to lease

Present value of the quarterly lease payments involves an annuity due: R = 435, $n = 20$, $i = 2.25\%$

$$= 435(1.0225)\left(\frac{1 - 1.0225^{-20}}{0.0225}\right) = 435(1.0225)(15.963712) \qquad = \qquad \$7100$$

Present value of purchase price after five years
$$= 600(1.0225^{-20}) = 600(0.6408165) \qquad\qquad = \qquad \underline{384}$$

Present value of decision to lease $=$ $7484

Programmed solution

Present value of the decision to buy

Present value of cash payment for the machine	=	$6000

Present value of the service contract

0 [FV] 45 [PMT] 20 [N] 2.25 [%i] [CPT] [PV] [718.36705]

Present value of decision to buy is $6000 + 718 = $6718.

Present value of the decision to lease
Present value of the quarterly lease payments

0 [FV] 435 [PMT] 20 [N] 2.25 [%i] [DUE] [PV] [7100.4597]

Present value of purchase price after five years

0 [PMT] 600 [FV] 20 [N] 2.25 [%i] [CPT] [PV] [384.48988]

Present value of the decision to lease is $7100 + 384 = $7484.

In the case of costs, the selection criterion follows the the-smaller-the-better principle. Since the present value of the decision to buy is smaller than the present value of the decision to lease, the credit union should buy the duplicating machine.

EXAMPLE 16.1F Sheridan Service needs a brake machine. The machine can be purchased for $4600 and after five years will have a salvage value of $490, or the machine can be leased for five years by making monthly payments of $111 at the beginning of each month. If money is worth 10%, should Sheridan Service buy or lease?

Solution

Alternative 1: Buy machine

Present value of cash price	=	$4600
Less: Present value of salvage value		
$= 490(1.10^{-5}) = 490(0.6209213)$	=	304
Present value of decision to buy	=	$4296

Alternative 2: Lease machine
The monthly lease payments form a general annuity due in which

$$R = 111; \quad c = \frac{1}{12}; \quad n = 60; \quad i = 10\%;$$

$$f = 1.10^{\frac{1}{12}} - 1$$
$$= 1.0079741 - 1 = 0.79741\%$$

Present value of the monthly lease payments

$$= 111(1.0079741)\left(\frac{1 - 1.0079741^{-60}}{0.0079741}\right)$$

$$= 111(1.0079741)(47.538503)$$
$$= \$5319$$

The present value of the decision to lease is $5319.

Programmed solution

Alternative 1: Buy machine

Present value of cash price   = $4600

Less: Present value of salvage value

0 [PMT] 490 [FV] 5 [N] 10 [%i] [CPT] [PV] [304.25145]

Present value of decision to buy is $4600 − 304 = $4296.

Alternative 2: Lease machine

Present value of the monthly lease payments

0 [FV] 111 [PMT] 60 [N] 0.79741 [%i] [DUE] [PV] [5318.8569]

Since the present value of the decision to buy is smaller than the present value of the decision to lease, Sheridan Service should buy the machine.

Exercise 16.1

A. For each of the following situations, compute the present value of each alternative and determine the preferred alternative according to the discounted cash flow criterion.

1. The A company must make a choice between two investment alternatives. Alternative 1 will return the company $20 000 at the end of three years and $60 000 at the end of six years. Alternative 2 will return the company $13 000 at the end of each of the next six years. The A company normally expects to earn a rate of return of 12% on funds invested.

2. An obligation can be settled by making a payment of $10 000 now and a final payment of $20 000 in five years. Alternatively, the obligation can be settled by payments of $1500 at the end of every three months for five years. Interest is 10% compounded quarterly.

3. The B Company has a policy of requiring a rate of return on investment of 16%. Two investment alternatives are available but the company may choose only one. Alternative 1 offers a return of $50 000 after four years, $40 000 after seven years, and $30 000 after ten years. Alternative 2 will return the company $750 at the end of each month for ten years.

4. An unavoidable cost may be met by outlays of $10 000 now and $2000 at the end of every six months for seven years or by making monthly payments of $500 in advance for seven years. Interest is 17% compounded annually.

B. Answer each of the following questions.

1. A contract offers $25 000 immediately and $50 000 in five years or $10 000 at the end of each year for ten years. If money is worth 13%, which offer is preferable?

2. Bruce and Carol want to sell their business. They have received two offers. If they accept Offer A they will receive $15 000 immediately and $20 000 in three years. If they accept Offer B they will receive $3000 now and $3000 at the end of every six months for six years. If interest is 10%, which offer is preferable?

3. A warehouse can be purchased for $90 000. After twenty years the property will have a residual value of $30 000. Alternatively, the warehouse can be leased for twenty years at an annual rent of $12 000 payable in advance. If money is worth 15%, should the warehouse be purchased or leased?

4. A car costs $9500. Alternatively, the car can be leased for three years by making payments of $240 at the beginning of each month and can be bought at the end of the lease for $4750. If interest is 9% compounded semi-annually, which alternative is preferable?

16.2 NET PRESENT VALUE METHOD

A. Introductory examples

EXAMPLE 16.2A Net cash inflows from two ventures are as follows:

End of Year	1	2	3	4	5	Total
Venture A	12 000	14 400	17 280	20 736	24 883	89 299
Venture B	17 000	17 000	17 000	17 000	17 000	85 000

Which venture is preferable if the required yield is 20%?

Solution

Present value of Venture A

$$= 12\ 000(1.20^{-1}) + 14\ 400(1.20^{-2}) + 17\ 280(1.20^{-3})$$
$$+ 20\ 736(1.20^{-4}) + 24\ 883(1.20^{-5})$$
$$= 12\ 000(0.8333333) + 14\ 400(0.6944444) + 17\ 280(0.5787037)$$
$$+ 20\ 736(0.4822531) + 24\ 883(0.4018776)$$
$$= 10\ 000 + 10\ 000 + 10\ 000 + 10\ 000 + 10\ 000$$
$$= \$50\ 000$$

Present value of Venture B

$$= 17\ 000\left(\frac{1 - 1.20^{-5}}{0.20}\right) = 17\ 000(2.9906121) = \$50\ 840$$

Programmed solution

Present value of Venture A

0 PMT 12 000 FV 20 %i 1 N CPT PV 10 000.00

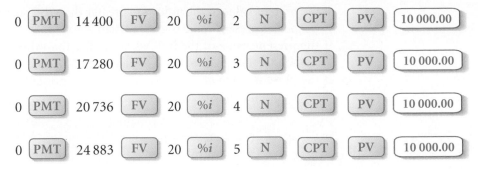

The present value of Venture A is $10 000 + 10 000 + 10 000 + 10 000 + 10 000 = $50 000.

Present value of Venture B

0 [FV] 17 000 [PMT] 20 [%i] 5 [N] [CPT] [PV] [50 840.406]

The present value of Venture B is $50 840.

Since at 20% the present value of Venture B is greater than the present value of Venture A, Venture B is preferable to Venture A.

EXAMPLE 16.2B   Assume for Example 16.2A that Venture A requires a non-recoverable outlay of $9000 while Venture B requires a non-recoverable outlay of $11 000. At 20%, which venture is preferable?

Solution

	Venture A	Venture B
Present value of cash inflows	$50 000	$50 840
Present value of immediate outlay	9000	11 000
Net present value	$41 000	$39 840

Since the net present value of Venture A is greater than the net present value of Venture B, Venture A is preferable.

B. The net present value concept

When only cash inflows were considered in Example 16.2A, Venture B was preferable. However, when outlays are different, as in Example 16.2B, the present value of the outlays as well as the present value of the cash inflows must be considered. The resulting difference is called the **net present value**

$$\begin{array}{c} \text{NET PRESENT VALUE} \\ \text{(NPV)} \end{array} = \begin{array}{c} \text{PRESENT VALUE} \\ \text{OF INFLOWS} \end{array} - \begin{array}{c} \text{PRESENT VALUE} \\ \text{OF OUTLAYS} \end{array}$$ ———— Formula 16.1

Since the net present value involves the difference between the present value of the inflows and the present value of the outlays, three outcomes are possible:

1. If the present value of the inflows is greater than the present value of the outlays, then the net present value is greater than zero.
2. If the present value of the inflows is smaller than the present value of the outlays, then the net present value is smaller than zero.
3. If the present value of the inflows equals the present value of the outlays, then the net present value is zero.

$$PV_{IN} > PV_{OUT} \longrightarrow NPV > 0 \text{ (positive)}$$
$$PV_{IN} = PV_{OUT} \longrightarrow NPV = 0$$
$$PV_{IN} < PV_{OUT} \longrightarrow NPV < 0 \text{ (negative)}$$

Criterion rule

At the organization's required rate of return, accept those capital investment projects that have a positive or zero net present value and reject those projects that have a negative net present value.

For a given rate of return:
ACCEPT if NPV > 0 or NPV = 0;
REJECT if NPV < 0.

To distinguish between a negative and a positive net present value, use

$$NPV = PV_{IN} - PV_{OUT}.$$

If a company is considering more than one project but can choose only one, the project with the greatest positive net present value is preferable.

Assumptions about the timing of inflows and outlays

The net present value method of evaluating capital investment projects is particularly useful when cash outlays are made and cash inflows received at various times. Since the *timing* of the cash flows is of prime importance, follow these assumptions regarding the timing of cash inflows and cash outlays.

Unless otherwise stated:

1. All cash inflows (benefits) are assumed to be received at the end of a period.
2. All cash outlays (costs) are assumed to be made at the beginning of a period.

C. Applications

EXAMPLE 16.2C   A company is offered a contract promising annual net returns of $36 000 for seven years. If it accepts the contract, the company must spend $150 000 immediately to expand its plant. After seven years, no further benefits are available from the contract and the plant expansion undertaken will have no residual value. Should the company accept the contract if the required rate of return is

(i) 12%?   (ii) 18%?   (iii) 15%?

Solution   The net inflows and outlays can be represented on a time graph.

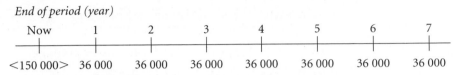

End of period (year)

Note: Cash outlays (costs) are identified in such diagrams by a minus sign or by using accounting brackets.

(i) For $i = 12\%$

Since we assume the annual net returns (benefits) are received at the end of a period unless otherwise stated, they form an ordinary annuity in which

$$R = 36\,000; \quad n = 7; \quad i = 12\%$$

$$PV_{IN} = 36\,000\left(\frac{1 - 1.12^{-7}}{0.12}\right) = 36\,000(4.5637565) \qquad = \$164\,295$$

$$PV_{OUT} = \text{Present value of 150 000 now} \qquad = \underline{150\,000}$$

The net present value (NPV)

$$= 164\,295 - 150\,000 \qquad\qquad = \underline{\underline{\$\ \ 14\,295}}$$

Since at 12% the net present value is greater than zero, the contract should be accepted. The fact that the net present value at 12% is positive means that the contract offers a return on investment of more than 12%.

(ii) For $i = 18\%$

$$PV_{IN} = 36\,000\left(\frac{1 - 1.18^{-7}}{0.18}\right) = 36\,000(3.8115276) \quad = \quad \$137\,215$$

$$PV_{OUT} \qquad\qquad\qquad\qquad\qquad\qquad = \underline{150\,000}$$

$$NPV = 137\,215 - 150\,000 \qquad\qquad = \underline{\underline{-\$\ \ 12\,785}}$$

Since at 18% the net present value is less than zero, the contract should not be accepted. The contract does not offer the required rate of return on investment of 18%.

(iii) For $i = 15\%$

$$PV_{IN} = 36\,000\left(\frac{1 - 1.15^{-7}}{0.15}\right) = 36\,000(4.1604197) \quad \doteq \$149\,775$$

$$PV_{OUT} \qquad\qquad\qquad\qquad\qquad\qquad = \underline{150\,000}$$

$$NPV = 149\,775 - 150\,000 \qquad\qquad = \underline{\underline{-\$225}}$$

The net present value is slightly negative, which means that the net present value method does not provide a clear signal as to whether to accept or reject the contract. The rate of return offered by the contract is almost 15%.

Programmed solution

(i) For $i = 12\%$

PV_{IN}: $\boxed{0}$ $\boxed{FV}$ $36\,000$ $\boxed{PMT}$ 7 $\boxed{N}$ 12 $\boxed{\%i}$ $\boxed{CPT}$ $\boxed{PV}$ $\boxed{164\,295.24}$

PV_{OUT} = Present value of 150 000 now = $150 000

The net present value (NPV) = $164 295 − 150 000 = $14 295.

(ii) For $i = 18\%$

PV_{IN}: $\boxed{0}$ $\boxed{FV}$ $36\,000$ $\boxed{PMT}$ 7 $\boxed{N}$ 18 $\boxed{\%i}$ $\boxed{CPT}$ $\boxed{PV}$ $\boxed{137\,214.99}$

PV_{OUT} = $150 000

NPV = $137 215 − 150 000 = −$12 785

(iii) For $i = 15\%$

PV_{IN}: $\boxed{0}$ $\boxed{FV}$ $36\,000$ $\boxed{PMT}$ 7 $\boxed{N}$ 15 $\boxed{\%i}$ $\boxed{CPT}$ $\boxed{PV}$ $\boxed{149\,775.11}$

PV_{OUT} = $150 000

NPV = $149 775 − 150 000 = −$225

EXAMPLE 16.2D A project requires an initial investment of $80 000 with a residual value of $15 000 after six years. It is estimated to yield annual net returns of $21 000 for six years. Should the project be undertaken at 16%?

Solution The cash flows are represented in the diagram below.

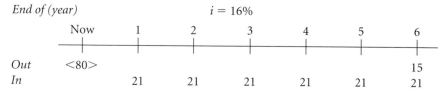

Note: The residual value of $15 000 is considered to be a reduction in outlays. Its present value should be subtracted from the present value of other outlays.

$$PV_{IN} = 21\,000\left(\frac{1 - 1.16^{-6}}{0.16}\right) = 21\,000(3.6847359) \qquad = \$77\,379$$

$$PV_{OUT} = 80\,000 - 15\,000(1.16^{-6})$$
$$= 80\,000 - 15\,000(0.4104423) = 80\,000 - 6157 \qquad = \underline{73\,843}$$
$$= \text{Net present value (NPV)} \qquad = \underline{\underline{\$\,3536}}$$

Programmed solution

PV_{IN}: $\boxed{0}$ $\boxed{FV}$ $21\,000$ $\boxed{PMT}$ 6 $\boxed{N}$ 16 $\boxed{\%i}$ $\boxed{CPT}$ $\boxed{PV}$ $\boxed{77\,379.454}$

PV_{OUT}: 0 [PMT] 15 000 [FV] 6 [N] 16 [%i] [CPT] [PV] [6156.6338]

$NPV = \$77\ 379 - (80\ 000 - 6157) = \$3536$

Since the net present value is positive (the present value of the benefits is greater than the present value of the costs), the rate of return on the investment is greater than 16%. The project should be undertaken.

EXAMPLE 16.2E The UBA Corporation is considering developing a new product. If undertaken, the project requires the outlay of $100 000 per year for three years. Net returns beginning in Year 4 are estimated at $65 000 per year for twelve years. The residual value of the outlays after fifteen years is $30 000. If the corporation requires a return on investment of 14%, should it develop the new product?

Solution

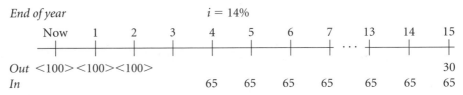

The net returns, due at the end of Year 4 to Year 15 respectively, form an ordinary annuity deferred for *three* years in which $R = 65\ 000, \quad n = 12, \quad d = 3, \quad i = 14\%$.

$$PV_{IN} = 65\ 000\left(\frac{1 - 1.14^{-12}}{0.14}\right)(1.14^{-3})$$

$$= 65\ 000(5.6602921)(0.6749715)$$
$$= \$248\ 335$$

The outlays, assumed to be made at the beginning of each year, form an annuity due in which $R = 100\ 000, \; n = 3, \; i = 14\%$.

$$PV_{OUT} = 100\ 000(1.14)\left(\frac{1 - 1.14^{-3}}{0.14}\right) - 30\ 000(1.14^{-15})$$

$$= 100\ 000(1.14)(2.3216320) - 30\ 000(0.1400965)$$
$$= 264\ 666 - 4203$$
$$= \$260\ 463$$
$$NPV = 248\ 335 - 260\ 463 = \ <\$12\ 128>$$

Programmed solution

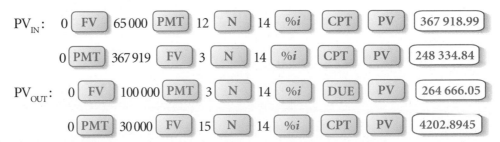

PV_{IN}: 0 [FV] 65 000 [PMT] 12 [N] 14 [%i] [CPT] [PV] [367 918.99]

0 [PMT] 367 919 [FV] 3 [N] 14 [%i] [CPT] [PV] [248 334.84]

PV_{OUT}: 0 [FV] 100 000 [PMT] 3 [N] 14 [%i] [DUE] [PV] [264 666.05]

0 [PMT] 30 000 [FV] 15 [N] 14 [%i] [CPT] [PV] [4202.8945]

$$\text{NPV} = \$248\,335 - (264\,666 - 4203) = -\$12\,128$$

Since the net present value is negative, the investment does not offer a 14% return. The corporation should not develop the product.

EXAMPLE 16.2F A feasibility study concerning a contemplated venture yielded the following estimates:

initial cost outlay: $1 300 000;
further outlays in Years 2 to 5: $225 000 per year;
residual value after 20 years: $625 000;
net returns: Year 5 to 10: $600 000 per year;
              Year 11 to 20: $500 000 per year.

Should the venture be undertaken if the required return on investment is 15%?

Solution

End of year $i = 15\%$

Now	1	2	3	4	5	6	9	10	11	12	19	20

Out <1300><225><225><225><225>
                                              625
In   600   600 ... 600   600   500   500 ... 500   500

$$\text{PV}_{\text{IN}} = 600\,000\left(\frac{1 - 1.15^{-6}}{0.15}\right)(1.15^{-4}) + 500\,000\left(\frac{1 - 1.15^{-10}}{0.15}\right)(1.15^{-10})$$

$$= 600\,000(3.7844827)(0.5717532) + 500\,000(5.0187686)(0.2471847)$$
$$= 1\,298\,274 + 620\,281$$
$$= \$1\,918\,555$$

$$\text{PV}_{\text{OUT}} = 1\,300\,000 + 225\,000\left(\frac{1 - 1.15^{-4}}{0.15}\right) - 625\,000(1.15^{-20})$$

$$= 1\,300\,000 + 225\,000(2.8549784) - 625\,000(0.0611003)$$
$$= 1\,300\,000 + 642\,370 - 38\,188$$
$$= \$1\,904\,182$$
$$\text{NPV} = 1\,918\,555 - 1\,904\,182 = \$14\,373$$

Programmed solution

PV_{IN}:   0 [FV] 600 000 [PMT] 15 [%i] 6 [N] [CPT] [PV] [2 270 689.60]

0 [PMT] 2 270 689 [FV] 15 [%i] 4 [N] [CPT] [PV] [1 298 274.10]

0 [FV] 500 000 [PMT] 15 [%i] 10 [N] [CPT] [PV] [2 509 384.30]

0 [PMT] 2 509 384 [FV] 15 [%i] 10 [N] [CPT] [PV] [620 281.42]

$\text{PV}_{\text{IN}} = \$1\,298\,274 + 620\,281 = \$1\,918\,555$

PV_{OUT}:

0 [FV] 225 000 [PMT] 15 [%i] 4 [N] [CPT] [PV] [642 370.13]

0 [PMT] 625 000 [FV] 15 [%i] 20 [N] [CPT] [PV] [38 187.674]

PV_{OUT} = \$1 300 000 + 642 370 − 38 188 = \$1 904 182
NPV = \$1 918 555 − 1 904 182 = \$14 373

Since the net present value is positive, the rate of return on investment is greater than 15%. The venture should be undertaken.

Exercise 16.2

A. For each of the following four investment choices, compute the net present value. Determine which investment should be accepted or rejected according to the net present value criterion.

1. A contract is estimated to yield net returns of \$3500 quarterly for seven years. To secure the contract, an immediate outlay of \$50 000 and a further outlay of \$30 000 three years from now are required. Interest is 12% compounded quarterly.

2. Replacing old equipment at an immediate cost of \$50 000 and an additional outlay of \$30 000 six years from now will result in savings of \$3000 per quarter for twelve years. The required rate of return is 10% compounded annually.

3. A business has two investment choices. Alternative 1 requires an immediate outlay of \$2000 and offers a return of \$7000 after seven years. Alternative 2 requires an immediate outlay of \$1800 in return for which \$250 will be received at the end of every six months for the next seven years. The required rate of return on investment is 17% compounded semi-annually.

4. Suppose you are offered two investment alternatives. If you choose Alternative 1, you will have to make an immediate outlay of \$9000. In return, you will receive \$500 at the end of every three months for the next ten years. If you choose Alternative 2, you will have to make an outlay of \$4000 now and \$5000 in two years. In return, you will receive \$30 000 ten years from now. Interest is 12% compounded semi-annually.

B. Answer each of the following questions.

1. Teck Engineering normally expects a rate of return of 12% on investments. Two projects are available but only one can be chosen. Project A requires an immediate investment of \$4000. In return, revenue payments of \$4000 will be received in four years and payments of \$9000 in nine years. Project B requires an investment of \$4000 now and another \$2000 in three years. In return, revenue payments will be received in the amount of \$1500 per year for nine years. Which project is preferable?

2. The owner of a business is presented with two alternative projects. The first project involves the investment of $5000 now. In return the business will receive a payment of $8000 in four years and a payment of $8000 in ten years. The second project involves an investment of $5000 now and another $5000 three years from now. The returns will be semi-annual payments of $950 for ten years. Which project is preferable if the required rate of return is 14% compounded annually?

3. Northern Teck is developing a special vehicle for Arctic exploration. The development requires investments of $60 000, $50 000, and $40 000 for the next three years respectively. Net returns beginning in Year 4 are expected to be $33 000 per year for twelve years. If the company requires a rate of return of 14%, compute the net present value of the project and determine whether the company should undertake the project.

4. The Kellog Company has to make a decision about expanding its production facilities. Research indicates that the desired expansion would require an immediate outlay of $60 000 and an outlay of a further $60 000 in five years. Net returns are estimated to be $15 000 per year for the first five years and $10 000 per year for the following ten years. Find the net present value of the project. Should the expansion project be undertaken if the required rate of return is 12%?

5. Agate Marketing Inc. intends to distribute a new product. It is expected to produce net returns of $15 000 per year for the first four years and $10 000 per year for the following three years. The facilities required to distribute the product will cost $36 000 with a disposal value of $9000 after seven years. The facilities will require a major facelift costing $10 000 each after three and after five years respectively. If Agate requires a return on investment of 20%, should the company distribute the new product?

6. A company is considering a project that will require a cost outlay of $15 000 per year for four years. At the end of the project the salvage value will be $10 000. The project will yield returns of $60 000 in Year 4 and $20 000 in Year 5. There are no returns after Year 5. Alternative investments are available that will yield a return of 16%. Should the company undertake the project?

7. Demand for a product manufactured by the Eagle Company is expected to be 15 000 units per year during the next ten years. The net return per unit is $2. The manufacturing process requires the purchase of a machine costing $140 000. The machine has an economic life of ten years and a salvage value of $20 000 after ten years. Major overhauls of the machine require outlays of $20 000 after four years and $40 000 after seven years. Should Eagle invest in the machine if it requires a return of 12% on its investments?

8. Magnum Electronics Company expects a demand of 20 000 units per year for a special purpose component during the next six years. Net return per unit is $4.00. To produce the component, Magnum must buy a machine costing $250 000 with a life of six years and a salvage value of $40 000 after

six years. The company estimates that repair costs will be $20 000 per year during Years 2 to 6. If Magnum requires a return on investment of 18%, should it market the component?

BUSINESS MATH NEWS BOX

Yamaha recently ran the following advertisement:

Lease a New

Virago 1100	Big Bear 4×4
for $175*	for $148*
per month for 36 months with $1500.00 down.	per month for 36 months with $1200.00 down.

*Plus applicable taxes, freight, and PDI. Does not include insurance, licence, or registration fees. Limited time offer. Consumer may be required to purchase leased goods at the end of the lease term for $3919.83 for Virago™ and $2417.01 for Big Bear™ plus applicable taxes. See your dealer for return of refinancing options.

QUESTIONS

To answer these questions, assume the combined PST and GST tax rate is 15%. Assume freight, PDI, insurance, licence, and registration costs are the same whether you lease or buy a vehicle.

1. Suppose the Virago 1100 has a Manufacturer's Suggested Retail Price (MSRP) of $7995.00 plus taxes.
   a) If you can earn 10% on your money, is it cheaper to lease or buy this motorcycle?
   b) If you can earn 20% on your money, is it cheaper to lease or buy this motorcycle?

2. Suppose the Big Bear 4×4 has an MSRP of $6395.00 plus taxes.

   a) If you can earn 20% on your money, is it cheaper to lease or buy this machine?
   b) If you can earn 23% on your money, is it cheaper to lease or buy this machine?
   c) Based on your calculators in parts (a) and (b), about how much interest would you have to earn on your money to make leasing a Big Bear 4×4 cost the same as buying it?

16.3 FINDING THE RATE OF RETURN ON INVESTMENT

A. Net present value, profitability index, rate of return

The **rate of return** on investment (R.O.I.) is widely used to measure the value of an investment. Since it takes interest into account, knowing the rate of return that results from a capital investment project provides useful information when evaluating a project.

The method of finding the rate of return that is explained and illustrated in this section uses the net present value concept introduced in Section 16.2. However, instead of being primarily concerned with a specific discount rate and with comparing the present value of the cash inflows and the present value of the cash outlays, this method is designed to determine the rate of return on the investment.

As explained in Section 16.2, three outcomes are possible when using Formula 16.1. These three outcomes indicate whether the rate of return is greater than, less than, or equal to the discount rate used in finding the net present value.

1. If the net present value is greater than zero (positive), then the rate of return is greater than the discount rate used to determine the net present value.
2. If the net present value is less than zero (negative), then the rate of return is less than the discount rate used.
3. If the net present value is equal to zero, then the rate of return is equal to the rate of discount used.

$$
\begin{aligned}
&\text{If NPV} > 0 \text{ (POSITIVE)} \longrightarrow \text{R.O.I.} > i \\
&\text{If NPV} < 0 \text{ (NEGATIVE)} \longrightarrow \text{R.O.I.} < i \\
&\text{If NPV} = 0 \longrightarrow \text{R.O.I.} = i
\end{aligned}
$$

It follows, then, that the rate of return on investment (R.O.I.) is that rate of discount for which the NPV = 0, that is, for which $PV_{IN} = PV_{OUT}$.

The above definition of the rate of return and the relationship between the net present value, the rate of discount used to compute the net present value, and the rate of return are useful in developing a method of finding the rate of return.

However, before computing the rate of return, it is useful to consider a ratio known as the **profitability index** or **discounted benefit-cost ratio**. It is defined as the ratio that results when comparing the present value of the cash inflows with the present value of the cash outlays.

$$
\text{PROFITABILITY INDEX (or DISCOUNTED BENEFIT-COST RATIO)} = \frac{PV_{IN}}{PV_{OUT}} \qquad \text{——— Formula 16.2}
$$

Since a division is involved, three outcomes are possible when computing this ratio.

1. If the numerator (PV_{IN}) is greater than the denominator (PV_{OUT}), then the profitability index is greater than one.

2. If the numerator (PV_{IN}) is less than the denominator (PV_{OUT}), then the profitability index is less than one.

3. If the numerator (PV_{IN}) is equal to the denominator (PV_{OUT}), then the profitability index is equal to one.

The three outcomes give an indication of the rate of return.

1. If the profitability index is greater than 1, then the rate of return is greater than the discount rate used.

2. If the profitability index is less than 1, then the rate of return is less than the discount rate used.

3. If the profitability index is equal to 1, then the rate of return equals the discount rate used.

The relationship between the present value of the inflows, the present value of the outlays, the net present value, the profitability index, and the rate of return at a given rate of discount i is summarized below.

PV_{IN} versus PV_{OUT}	Net Present Value (NPV)	Profitability Index	Rate of Return (R.O.I.)
$PV_{IN} > PV_{OUT}$	NPV > 0	> 1	> i
$PV_{IN} = PV_{OUT}$	NPV = 0	= 1	= i
$PV_{IN} < PV_{OUT}$	NPV < 0	< 1	< i

B. Procedure for finding the rate of return by trial and error

From the relationships noted above, the rate of return on investment can be defined as the rate of discount for which the present value of the inflows (benefits) equals the present value of the outlays (costs). This definition implies that the rate of return is the rate of discount for which the net present value equals zero or for which the profitability index (benefit-cost ratio) equals 1. This conclusion permits us to determine the rate of return by trial and error.

STEP 1   Arbitrarily select a discount rate and compute the net present value at that rate.

STEP 2   From the outcome of Step 1, draw one of the three conclusions.

(a) If NPV = 0, infer that the R.O.I. = i.

(b) If NPV > 0, infer that the R.O.I. > i.

(c) If NPV < 0, infer that the R.O.I. < i.

STEP 3   (a) If, in Step 1, NPV = 0, then R.O.I. = i and the problem is solved.

(b) If, in Step 1, NPV > 0 (positive), then we know that R.O.I. > i. A second attempt is needed. This second try requires choosing a discount rate greater than the rate used in Step 1 and computing the net present value using the higher rate.

If the resulting net present value is still positive, choose a still higher rate of discount and compute the net present value for that rate. Repeat this procedure until the selected rate of discount yields a negative net present value.

(c) If, in Step 1, NPV < 0 (negative), then we know that R.O.I. < i. The second try requires choosing a discount rate less than the rate used in Step 1 and computing the net present value using the lower rate.

    If the resulting net present value is still negative, choose a still lower rate of discount and compute the net present value for that rate. Repeat this procedure until the selected rate of discount yields a positive net present value.

STEP 4   The basic aim of Step 3 is to find one rate of discount for which the net present value is positive and a second rate for which the net present value is negative. Once this has been accomplished, the rate of return must be a rate between the two rates used to generate a positive and a negative net present value.

    You can now obtain a reasonably accurate value of the rate of return by using linear interpolation. To ensure sufficient accuracy in the answer, we recommend that the two rates of discount used when interpolating be no more than two percentage points apart. The worked examples in this section have been solved using successive even rates of discounts when interpolating.

STEP 5   (Optional) You can check the accuracy of the method of interpolation when using an electronic calculator by computing the net present value. Use as the discount rate the rate of return determined in Step 4. Expect the rate in Step 4 to be slightly too high. You can obtain a still more precise answer by further trials.

C. Selecting the rate of discount—using the profitability index

While the selection of a discount rate in Step 1 of the procedure is arbitrary, a sensible choice is one that is neither too high nor too low. Since the negative net present value immediately establishes a range between zero and the rate used, it is preferable to be on the high side. Choosing a rate of discount within the range 12% to 24% usually leads to quick solutions.

    While the initial choice of rate is a shot in the dark, the resulting knowledge about the size of the rate of return combined with the use of the profitability index should ensure the selection of a second rate that is fairly close to the actual rate of return.

    In making the second choice, use the profitability index.

1. Compute the index for the first rate chosen and convert the index into a percent.
2. Deduct 100% from the index and divide the difference by 4.
3. If the index is greater than 1, add the above result to obtain the rate that you should use for the second attempt. If, however, the index is smaller than 1, deduct the above result from the rate of discount initially used.

Assume that the rate of discount initially selected is 16%. The resulting $PV_{IN} = 150$ and the $PV_{OUT} = 120$.

1. The profitability index is $\dfrac{150}{120} = 1.25 = 125\%$.
2. The difference (125% − 100%) divided by 4 = 6.25%.
3. Since the index is greater than 1, add 6.25% to the initial rate of 16%; the recommended choice is 22%.

Assume that the rate of discount initially selected is 20%. The resulting $PV_{IN} = 200$ and the $PV_{OUT} = 250$.

1. The profitability index is $\dfrac{200}{250} = 0.80 = 80\%$.
2. The difference $(80\% - 100\%)$ divided by $4 = -5\%$.
3. Since the index is less than 1, subtract 5% from the initial rate of 20%; the recommended choice is 15%. (If, as in this text, you are using only even rates, try either 14% or 16%.)

D. Using linear interpolation

The method of linear interpolation used in Step 4 of the suggested procedure is illustrated in Example 16.3A below.

EXAMPLE 16.3A   Assume that the net present value of a project is $420 at 14% and −$280 at 16%. Use linear interpolation to compute the rate of return correct to the nearest tenth of a percent.

Solution   The data can be represented on a line diagram.

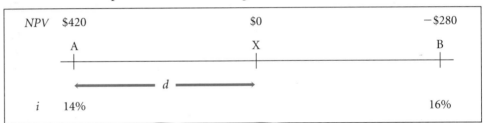

The line segment AB represents the distance between the two rates of discount that are associated with a positive and a negative net present value respectively.

At Point A, where $i = 14\%$, the NPV $= 420$;
at Point B, where $i = 16\%$, the NPV $= -280$;
at Point X, where i is unknown, the NPV $= 0$.

By definition, the rate of return is that rate of discount for which the net present value is zero. Since 0 is a number between 420 and −280, the NPV $= 0$ is located at a point on AB. This point is marked X.

We can obtain two useful ratios by considering the line segment from the two points of view shown in the diagram.

(i) In terms of the discount rate i,

$AB = 2\%$ ———————————— 16% − 14%
$AX = d\%$ ———————————— the unknown percent that must be added to 14% to obtain the rate of discount at which the NPV = 0

$$\frac{AX}{AB} = \frac{d\%}{2\%}$$

(ii) In terms of the net present value figures,

$$AB = 700 \qquad\qquad\qquad\qquad 420 + 280$$
$$AX = 420$$

$$\frac{AX}{AB} = \frac{420}{700}$$

Since the ratio AX:AB is written twice, we can derive a proportion statement.

$$\frac{d\%}{2\%} = \frac{420}{700}$$

$$d\% = \frac{420}{700} \times 2\%$$

$$d\% = 1.2\%$$

Therefore, the rate at which the net present value is equal to zero is 14% + 1.2% = 15.2%. The rate of return on investment is 15.2%.

E. Computing the rate of return

EXAMPLE 16.3B   A project requires an initial outlay of $25 000. The estimated returns are $7000 per year for seven years. Compute the rate of return (correct to the nearest tenth of a percent).

Solution   The cash flows (in thousands) are represented in the diagram below.
The inflows form an ordinary annuity since inflows are assumed to be received

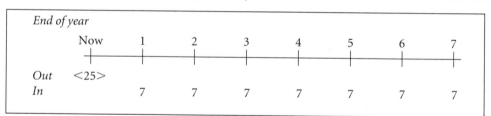

at the end of each year.

$$PV_{IN} = 7000\left[\frac{1 - (1 + i)^{-7}}{i}\right]$$

The outlays consist of an immediate payment.

$$PV_{OUT} = 25\,000$$

To determine the rate of return, we will choose a rate of discount, compute the net present value, and try further rates until we find two successive even rates. For one, the NPV > 0 (positive) and, for the other, NPV < 0 (negative).

STEP 1   Try $i = 12\%$.

$$PV_{IN} = 7000\left(\frac{1 - 1.12^{-7}}{0.12}\right) = 7000(4.5637565) \quad = \$31\,946$$

$$PV_{OUT} \qquad\qquad\qquad\qquad\qquad\qquad\qquad\qquad = \underline{25\,000}$$

$$NPV \text{ at } 12\% \qquad\qquad\qquad\qquad\qquad\qquad\quad = \underline{\underline{\$6\,946}}$$

Since the NPV > 0, R.O.I. > 12%.

STEP 2   Compute the profitability index to estimate what rate should be used next.

$$\text{INDEX} = \frac{PV_{IN}}{PV_{OUT}} = \frac{31\,946}{25\,000} = 1.278 = 127.8\%$$

Since at $i = 12\%$, the profitability index is 27.8% more than 100%, the rate of discount should be increased by $\frac{27.8\%}{4} = 7\%$ approximately. To obtain another even rate, the increase should be either 6% or 8%. In line with the suggestion that it is better to go too high, increase the previous rate by 8% and try $i = 20\%$.

STEP 3   Try $i = 20\%$.

$$PV_{IN} = 7000\left(\frac{1 - 1.20^{-7}}{0.20}\right) = 7000(3.6045918) \qquad = \$25\,232$$

$$PV_{OUT} \qquad\qquad\qquad\qquad\qquad\qquad\qquad\qquad = \underline{25\,000}$$
$$\text{NPV at 20\%} \qquad\qquad\qquad\qquad\qquad\qquad = \underline{\underline{\$\quad232}}$$

Since the NPV > 0, R.O.I. $> 20\%$.

STEP 4   Since the net present value is still positive, a rate higher than 20% is needed. The profitability index at 20% is $\frac{25\,232}{25\,000} = 1.009 = 100.9\%$. The index exceeds 100% by 0.9%; division by 4 suggests an increase of 0.2%. For interpolation, the recommended minimum increase or decrease is 2%. The next try should use $i = 22\%$.

STEP 5   Try $i = 22\%$.

$$PV_{IN} = 7000\left(\frac{1 - 1.22^{-7}}{0.22}\right) = 7000(3.4155064) \qquad = \quad\$23\,908$$

$$PV_{OUT} \qquad\qquad\qquad\qquad\qquad\qquad\qquad\qquad = \underline{25\,000}$$
$$\text{NPV at 22\%} \qquad\qquad\qquad\qquad\qquad\qquad = \underline{\underline{-\$\,1\,092}}$$

Since the NPV < 0, R.O.I. $< 22\%$.
Therefore, 20% $<$ NPV $<$ 22%.

STEP 6   Now that the rate of return has been located between two sufficiently close rates of discount, linear interpolation can be used as illustrated in Example 16.3A.

NPV $232		$0		<$1092>
	A		X	B
		←—— d ——→		
i 20%				22%

$$\frac{d}{2} = \frac{232}{232 + 1092}$$

$$d = \frac{232(2)}{1324} = 0.35$$

The rate of discount for which the NPV = 0 is approximately 20% + 0.35% = 20.35%. The rate of return is approximately 20.3%. (A more precisely computed value is 20.3382%.)

Note: Three attempts were needed to locate the R.O.I. between 20% and 22%. Three is the usual number of tries necessary. The minimum number is two attempts. Occasionally four attempts may be needed. To produce a more concise solution, organize the computation as shown below.

Since estimates are involved, it is sufficient to use present value factors with only three decimal positions. In the following examples, all factors are rounded to three decimals.

Present Value of Amounts in General Form	Attempts					
	i = 12%		*i* = 20%		*i* = 22%	
PV_{IN}	Factor	$	Factor	$	Factor	$
$7000\left[\dfrac{1-(1+i)^{-7}}{i}\right]$	4.5637565	31 946	3.6045918	25 232	3.4155064	23 908
PV_{OUT} 25 000 now		25 000		25 000		25 000
NPV		6 946		232		<1 092 >

Programmed solution

Present Value of Amounts in General Form	Attempts					
	i = 12%	*i* = 20%	*i* = 22%	*i* = 20.5%	*i* = 20.3%	*i* = 20.34%
PV_{IN} $7000\left[\dfrac{1-(1+i)^{-7}}{i}\right]$	0 FV 7000 PMT 7 N 12 %i CPT PV	0 FV 7000 PMT 7 N 20 %i CPT PV	0 FV 7000 PMT 7 N 22 %i CPT PV	0 FV 7000 PMT 7 N 20.5 %i CPT PV	0 FV 7000 PMT 7 N 20.3 %i CPT PV	0 FV 7000 PMT 7 N 20.34 %i CPT PV
PV_{IN}	31 946	25 232	23 908	24 890	25 026	24 999
PV_{OUT} 25 000 now	25 000	25 000	25 000	25 000	25 000	25 000
NPV	6 946	232	−1 092	−110	26	−1
R.O.I.	>12%	>20%	<22%	<20.5%	>20.3%	=20.34%

EXAMPLE 16.3C

A venture that requires an immediate outlay of $320 000 and an outlay of $96 000 after five years has a residual value of $70 000 after ten years. Net returns are estimated to be $64 000 per year for ten years. Compute the rate of return.

Solution

The cash flow is represented in the diagram below (in thousands).

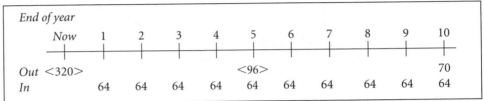

The computations are organized in a chart; explanations regarding the computations follow.

Present Value of Amounts in General Form	Attempts					
	$i = 20\%$		$i = 14\%$		$i = 12\%$	
PV of benefits	Factor	$	Factor	$	Factor	$
$64\,000\left[\dfrac{1-(1+i)^{-10}}{i}\right]$	4.192	268 288	5.216	333 824	5.650	361 600
PV of costs						
320 000 now		320 000		320 000		320 000
$96\,000(1+i)^{-5}$	0.402	38 592	0.519	49 824	0.567	54 432
$<70\,000(1+i)^{-10}>$	0.162	<11 340>	0.270	<18 900>	0.322	<22 540>
TOTAL		347 252		350 924		351 892
NPV		<78 964>		<17 100>		9 708

Explanations for computations

STEP 1

Try $i = 20\%$.
Since NPV < 0, R.O.I. $< 20\%$.

$$\text{Index at 20\%} = \frac{268\,288}{347\,252} = 0.773 = 77.3\%$$

$$\text{Reduction in rate} = \frac{22.7\%}{4} = 5.7\% \longrightarrow 6\%$$

STEP 2

Try $i = 14\%$.
NPV < 0; R.O.I. $< 14\%$

$$\text{Index} = \frac{333\,824}{350\,924} = 0.951 = 95.1\%$$

$$\text{Reduction in rate} = \frac{4.9\%}{4} = 1.2\% \longrightarrow 2\%$$

STEP 3

Try $i = 12\%$.
NPV > 0; R.O.I. $> 12\%$
$12\% <$ R.O.I. $< 14\%$

STEP 4 $\quad \dfrac{d}{2} = \dfrac{9708}{9708 + 17\,100} = \dfrac{9708}{26\,808} = 0.362131$

$d = 2(0.362131) = 0.724$

The rate of discount at which the net present value is zero is 12% + 0.72% = 12.72%. The rate of return is 12.7%.

Programmed solution

Present Value of Amounts in General Form	Attempts				
	$i = 20\%$	$i = 14\%$	$i = 12\%$	$i = 12.7\%$	$i = 12.68\%$
PV *of benefits* $64\,000\left[\dfrac{1-(1+i)^{-10}}{i}\right]$	0 FV / 64 000 PMT / 10 N / 20 %i / CPT / PV	0 FV / 64 000 PMT / 10 N / 14 %i / CPT / PV	0 FV / 64 000 PMT / 10 N / 12 %i / CPT / PV	0 FV / 64 000 PMT / 10 N / 12.7 %i / CPT / PV	0 FV / 64 000 PMT / 10 N / 12.68 %i / CPT / PV
PV_{IN}	268 318	333 831	361 614	351 484	351 767
PV *of costs* 320 000 now $96\,000(1+i)^{-5}$	320 000 / 0 PMT / 96 000 FV / 5 N / CPT / PV	320 000 / 0 PMT / 96 000 FV / 5 N / CPT / PV	320 000 / 0 PMT / 96 000 FV / 5 N / CPT / PV	320 000 / 0 PMT / 96 000 FV / 5 N / CPT / PV	320 000 / 0 PMT / 96 000 FV / 5 N / CPT / PV
	38 580	49 859	54 473	52 802	52 849
$<70\,000(1+i)^{-10}$	70 000 FV / 10 N / CPT / PV	70 000 FV / 10 N / CPT / PV	70 000 FV / 10 N / CPT / PV	70 000 FV / 10 N / CPT / PV	70 000 FV / 10 N / CPT / PV
	<11 303>	<18 882>	<22 538>	<21 177>	<21 214>
PV_{OUT}	347 275	350 977	351 935	351 625	351 635
NPV	<78 957>	<17 146>	9 679	<141>	132
R.O.I.	<20%	<14%	>12%	<12.7%	>12.68%

EXAMPLE 16.3D A project requires an immediate investment of $33 000 with a residual value of $7000 at the end of the project. It is expected to yield a net return of $7000 in Year 1, $8000 in Year 2, $11 000 per year for the following six years, and $9000 per year for the remaining four years. Find the rate of return.

Solution

The cash flows for the project (in thousands) are represented in the diagram below.

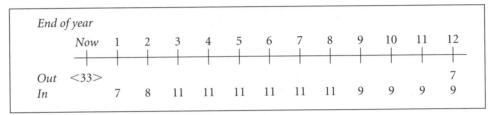

The computations are organized in the chart that follows.

Present Value of Amounts in General Form	Attempts					
	i = 20%		*i* = 28%		*i* = 26%	
PV of returns	**Factor**	**$**	**Factor**	**$**	**Factor**	**$**
$7000(1 + i)^{-1}$	0.833	5 831	0.781	5 467	0.794	5 558
$8000(1 + i)^{-2}$	0.694	5 552	0.610	4 880	0.630	5 040
$11\,000\left[\dfrac{1 - (1 + i)^{-6}}{i}\right]$	3.326		2.759		2.885	
	×	25 391	×	18 513	×	19 993
$\times (1 + i)^{-2}$	0.694		0.610		0.630	
$9000\left[\dfrac{1 - (1 + i)^{-4}}{i}\right]$	2.589		2.241		2.320	
	×	5 429	×	2 803	×	3 278
$\times (1 + i)^{-8}$	0.233		0.139		0.157	
TOTAL PV$_{IN}$		42 203		31 663		33 869
PV of costs						
33 000 now		33 000		33 000		33 000
$<7000(1 + i)^{-12}>$	0.112	<784>	0.052	<364>	0.062	<434>
TOTAL PV$_{OUT}$		32 216		32 636		32 566
NPV		9 987		<973>		1 303

Explanations for computations

STEP 1   The present value of the returns consists of $7000 discounted for one year, $8000 discounted for two years, the present value of an ordinary annuity of six payments of $11 000 deferred for two years, and the present value of an ordinary annuity of four payments of $9000 deferred for eight years. The present value of the costs consists of the lump sum of $33 000 less the salvage value of $7000 discounted for twelve years.

STEP 2 The rate of discount chosen for the first attempt is 20%.
For $i = 20\%$, NPV > 0; R.O.I. $> 20\%$

$$\text{Index} = \frac{42\ 203}{32\ 216} = 1.310 = 131.0\%$$

$$\text{Increase in rate} = \frac{31.0\%}{4} = 7.75\% \text{ or } 8\%$$

STEP 3 For $i = 28\%$, NPV < 0; R.O.I. $< 28\%$

$$\text{Index} = \frac{31\ 663}{32\ 636} = 0.970 = 97.0\%$$

$$\text{Decrease in rate} = \frac{3\%}{4} = 0.75\% \text{ or } 2\% \text{ (Rounded up)}$$

STEP 4 For $i = 26\%$, NPV > 0; R.O.I. $> 26\%$
$26\% < $ R.O.I. $< 28\%$

STEP 5 $$d = \frac{1303}{1303 + 973} \times 2 = \frac{2606}{2276} = 1.14499$$

The rate of discount for which the net present value is zero is approximately $26\% + 1.14\% = 27.14\%$. The rate of return, correct to the nearest tenth of a percent, is 27.1%.

Exercise 16.3

A. Use linear interpolation to determine the approximate value of the rate of return for each of the four projects below. State your answer correct to the nearest tenth of a percent.

	Positive NPV at i	**Negative NPV at i**
1.	$2350 at 24%	−$1270 at 26%
2.	$850 at 8%	−$370 at 10%
3.	$135 at 20%	−$240 at 22%
4.	$56 at 16%	−$70 at 18%

B. Find the rate of return for each of the six situations below (correct to the nearest tenth of a percent).

1. The proposed expansion of CIV Electronics' plant facilities requires the immediate outlay of $100 000. Expected net returns are

Year 1: Nil   Year 2: $30 000   Year 3: $40 000
Year 4: $60 000   Year 5: $50 000   Year 6: $20 000

2. The introduction of a new product requires an initial outlay of $60 000. The anticipated net returns from the marketing of the product are expected to be $12 000 per year for ten years.

3. Your firm is considering introducing a new product for which net returns are expected to be

Year 1 to Year 3 inclusive:	$2000 per year;
Year 4 to Year 8 inclusive:	$5000 per year;
Year 9 to Year 12 inclusive:	$3000 per year.

   The introduction of the product requires an immediate outlay of $15 000 for equipment estimated to have a salvage value of $2000 after twelve years.

4. A project requiring an immediate investment of $150 000 and a further outlay of $40 000 after four years has a residual value of $30 000 after nine years. The project yields a negative net return of $10 000 in Year 1, a zero net return in Year 2, $50 000 per year for the following four years, and $70 000 per year for the last three years.

5. You are thinking of starting a hot dog business that requires an initial investment of $16 000 and a major replacement of equipment after ten years amounting to $8000. From competitive experience, you expect to have a net loss of $2000 the first year, a net profit of $2000 the second year, and, for the remaining years of the first fifteen years of operations, net returns of $6000 per year. After fifteen years, the net returns will gradually decline and will be zero at the end of 25 years (assume returns of $3000 per year for that period). After 25 years, your lease will expire. The salvage value of equipment at that time is expected to be just sufficient to cover the cost of closing the business.

6. The Blue Sky Ski Resort plans to install a new chair lift to serve a new ski area. Construction of the lift is estimated to require an immediate outlay of $220 000. The life of the lift is estimated to be fifteen years with a salvage value of $80 000. Cost of clearing and grooming the new area is expected to be $30 000 for each of the first three years of operation. Net cash inflows from the lift are expected to be $40 000 for each of the first five years and $70 000 for each of the following ten years.

REVIEW EXERCISE

1. Wells Inc. has to choose between two investment alternatives. Alternative A will return the company $20 000 after three years, $60 000 after six years, and $40 000 after ten years. Alternative B will bring returns of $10 000 per year for ten years. If the company expects a return of 14% on investments, which alternative should it choose?

2. A piece of property may be acquired by making an immediate payment of $25 000 and payments of $37 500 and $50 000 three and five years from

now respectively. Alternatively, the property may be purchased by making quarterly payments of $5150 in advance for five years. Which alternative is preferable if money is worth 15% compounded semi-annually?

3. An investor has two investment alternatives. If he chooses Alternative 1, he will have to make an immediate outlay of $7000 and will receive $500 every three months for the next nine years. If he chooses Alternative 2, he will have to make an immediate outlay of $6500 and will receive $26 000 after eight years. If interest is 12% compounded quarterly, which alternative should the investor choose on the basis of the net present value criterion?

4. Replacing old equipment at an immediate cost of $65 000 and $40 000 five years from now will result in a savings of $8000 semi-annually for ten years. At 14% compounded annually, should the old equipment be replaced?

5. A real estate development project requires annual outlays of $75 000 for eight years. Net cash inflows beginning in Year 9 are expected to be $250 000 per year for fifteen years. If the developer requires a rate of return of 18%, compute the net present value of the project.

6. A company is considering a project that will require a cost outlay of $30 000 per year for four years. At the end of the project, the company expects to salvage the physical assets for $30 000. The project is estimated to yield net returns of $60 000 in Year 4, $40 000 in Year 5, and $20 000 for each of the following five years. Alternative investments are available yielding a rate of return of 14%. Compute the net present value of the project.

7. An investment requires an initial outlay of $45 000. Net returns are estimated to be $14 000 per year for eight years. Determine the rate of return.

8. A project requires an initial outlay of $10 000 and promises net returns of $2000 per year over a twelve-year period. If the project has a residual value of $4000 after twelve years, what is the rate of return?

9. Compute the rate of return for Question 5.

10. Compute the rate of return for Question 6.

11. The Superior Jig Company has developed a new jig for which it expects net returns as follows.

Year 1:	$8000
Year 2 to 6 inclusive:	$12 000 per year
Year 7 to 10 inclusive:	$6000 per year

The initial investment of $36 000 has a residual value of $9000 after ten years. Compute the rate of return.

12. The owner of a sporting goods store is considering remodelling the store in order to carry a larger inventory. The cost of remodelling and additional inventory is $60 000. The expected increase in net profit is $8000 per year for the next four years and $10 000 each year for the following six years. After ten years, the owner plans to retire and sell the business. She expects to recover the additional $40 000 invested in inventory but not the $20 000 invested in remodelling. Compute the rate of return.

13. Outway Ventures evaluates potential investment projects at 20%. Two alternative projects are available. Project A will return the company $5800 per year for eight years. Alternative B will return the company $13 600 after one year, $17 000 after five years, and $20 400 after eight years. Which alternative should the company choose according to the discounted cash flow criterion?

14. Project A requires an immediate investment of $8000 and another $6000 in three years. Net returns are $4000 after two years, $12 000 after four years, and $8000 after six years. Project B requires an immediate investment of $4000, another $6000 after two years, and $4000 after four years. Net returns are $3400 per year for seven years. Determine the net present value at 10%. Which project is preferable according to the net present value criterion?

15. Net returns from an investment are estimated to be $13 000 per year for twelve years. The investment involves an immediate outlay of $50 000 and a further outlay of $30 000 after six years. The investments are estimated to have a residual value of $10 000 after twelve years. Find the net present value at 20%.

16. The introduction of a new product requires an immediate outlay of $45 000. Anticipated net returns from the marketing of the product are expected to be $12 500 per year for ten years. What is the rate of return on the investment (correct to the nearest tenth of a percent)?

17. Games Inc. has developed a new electronic game and compiled the following product information.

	Production Cost	Promotion Cost	Sales Revenue
Year 1	$32 000	—	—
Year 2	32 000	$64 000	$ 64 000
Year 3	32 000	96 000	256 000
Year 4	32 000	32 000	128 000
Year 5	32 000		32 000

Should the product be marketed if the company requires a return of 16%?

18. Farmer Jones wants to convert his farm into a golf course. He asked you to determine his rate of return based on the following estimates.

Development cost for each of the first three years, $80 000.

Construction of a clubhouse in Year 4, $240 000.

Upon his retirement in fifteen years, improvements in the property will yield him $200 000.

Net returns from the operation of the golf course will be nil for the first three years and $100 000 per year afterwards until his retirement.

SELF-TEST

1. Opportunities Inc. requires a minimum rate of return of 15% on investment proposals. Two proposals are under consideration but only one may be chosen. Alternative A offers a net return of $2500 per year for twelve years. Alternative B offers a net return of $10 000 each year after four, eight, and twelve years respectively. Determine the preferred alternative according to the discounted cash flow criterion.

2. A natural resources development project requires an immediate outlay of $10 000 and $50 000 at the end of each year for four years. Net returns are nil for the first two years and $60 000 per year thereafter for fourteen years. What is the net present value of the project at 16%?

3. An investment of $100 000 yields annual net returns of $20 000 for ten years. If the residual value of the investment after ten years is $30 000, what is the rate of return on the investment (correct to the nearest tenth of a percent)?

4. A telephone system with a disposable value of $1200 after five years can be purchased for $6600. Alternatively, a leasing agreement is available that requires an immediate payment of $1500 plus payments of $100.00 at the beginning of each month for five years. If money is worth 12% compounded monthly, should the telephone system be leased or purchased?

5. A choice has to be made between two investment proposals. Proposal A requires an immediate outlay of $60 000 and a further outlay of $40 000 after three years. Net returns are $20 000 per year for ten years. The investment has no residual value after ten years. Proposal B requires outlays of $29 000 in each of the first four years. Net returns starting in Year 4 are $40 000 per year. The residual value of the investment after ten years is $50 000. Which proposal is preferable at 20%?

6. Introducing a new product requires an immediate investment in plant facilities of $180 000 with a disposal value of $45 000 after seven years. The facilities will require additional capital outlays of $50 000 each after three and five years respectively. Net returns on the investment are estimated to be $75 000 per year for each of the first four years and $50 000 per year for the remaining three years. Determine the rate of return on investment (correct to the nearest tenth of a percent).

CHALLENGE PROBLEMS

1. The owners of a vegetable processing plant can buy a new conveyor system for $85 000. The owners estimate they can save $17 000 per year on labour and maintenance costs. They can purchase the same conveyor system with an automatic loader for $114 000. They estimate they can save $22 000 per year with

this system. If the owners expect both systems to last ten years and they require at least 14% return per year, should the owners buy the system with the automatic loader?

2. CheeseWorks owns four dairies in your province and has planned upgrades for all locations. The owners are considering four projects, each of which is independent of the other three projects. The details of each project—A, B, C, and D—are shown below.

	Cost at Beginning	Revenues, and Cost Savings at End Of:				
Project	of Year 1	Year 1	Year 2	Year 3	Year 4	Year 5
A	300 000	150 000	120 000	120 000	0	0
B	360 000	0	40 000	200 000	200 000	200 000
C	210 000	10 000	10 000	100 000	120 000	120 000
D	125 000	30 000	40 000	40 000	40 000	40 000

The owners of CheeseWorks have $700 000 to invest in these projects. They expect at least 12% return on all of their projects. In which projects should the owners of CheeseWorks invest to maximize the return on their investment?

CASE STUDY 16.1 — TO LEASE OR NOT TO LEASE?

Rebecca is in the market for her first car. She has been studying the newspaper ads and has noticed that most car ads offer leasing information. Often, there is a paragraph of fine print that appears at the bottom of the ad. Rebecca has found an ad for a car that she would like to have. The advertisement states: "We make sure that leasing one of our cars is as simple as possible. The payments below are based on this year's Model A. They include transportation of $455, retailer preparation of the car, a full tank of fuel, and an acquisition fee of $350. Some things are extra, like taxes, licence, insurance, and a $300 non-taxable security deposit refundable at the end of the lease. This lease is based on 72 000 km over three years. At the end of three years, you have the option to purchase this car for $8886. Although retailers are free to set individual selling prices, the Manufacturer's Suggested Retail Price (MSRP) is $14 403."

Here's what you pay monthly	Amount of down payment or trade-in	Amount financed over the term of the lease
$223	$0	$5517
$208	$500	$5017
$193	$1000	$4517
$178	$1500	$4017
$163	$2000	$3517

Rebecca must decide whether to buy or lease this car. She lives in a province with a combined PST and GST tax rate of 15%. She will ignore the cost of licence and insurance in any calculations, but she realizes that both costs must be paid.

QUESTIONS

1. If Rebecca buys the car, what is the total purchase price, including taxes, transportation, and acquisition costs? Assume tax is charged on any additional costs.

2. Suppose Rebecca has no down payment and must finance the cost of the car if she pays cash for it. The dealer is offering a special finance rate of 4% per year.
   a) Is it cheaper to lease or buy the car at the special dealer rate of 4% per year?
   b) If Rebecca could obtain a loan at 5%, would it be cheaper to lease or buy the car at this rate?
   c) Using linear interpolation, find the rate of interest at which the cost of buying is the same as the cost of leasing. Calculate your answer to two decimal places.

3. Suppose Rebecca has a $2000 down payment for this car.
   a) What is the purchase price of the car if Rebecca pays cash for it? Assume the down payment is subtracted from the price of the car including tax.
   b) Is it cheaper to lease or buy the car if Rebecca can get the special dealer rate of 4%?
   c) Is there an advantage to having a $2000 down payment if you want to lease this car? Why or why not?

CASE STUDY 16.2 BUILDING A BUSINESS

MAS Manufacturing has demolished an old warehouse to make room for additional manufacturing capacity. The company has decided to construct a new building, but must decide how to proceed. It has two alternatives for the new building, both of which will create a building with an expected life of fifty years. The residual value is unknown but will be the same for either alternative.

Alternative A is to construct a new building that would have 180 000 square feet. Construction costs will total $2 100 000 at the end of Year 1. Maintenance costs are expected to be $15 000 per year. The building will need to be repainted every ten years (starting in ten years) at an estimated cost of $10 000.

Alternative B is to construct the building in two stages. The first stage is a building of 100 000 square feet now, and the second stage is an addition of 80 000 square feet in ten years. Construction costs for the first stage will be $1 600 000 at the end of Year 1. Construction costs for the second stage will be $900 000 when the addition is completed at the end of Year 10. Maintenance costs are expected to be $10 000 per year for the first ten years, then $17 000 per year after that. The building and the addition will have to be painted every ten years, beginning in Year 20, at an estimated cost of $10 000.

QUESTIONS

1. Suppose the company's required rate of return is 15%.
   a) What is the present value of Alternative A?
   b) What is the present value of Alternative B?
   c) Which alternative would you recommend on the basis of your discounted cash flow analysis?

2. Which alternative would you recommend if the company's required rate of return was 20%? Show all calculations.

3. Suppose the company could rent a portion of its building for $48 000 per year for the first ten years if it chose Alternative A.
   a) If the company's required rate of return is 15%, what is the net present value of Alternative A?
   b) On the basis of the new information, would you recommend Alternative A or Alternative B if the company's required rate of return is 15%?

SUMMARY OF FORMULAE

Formula 16.1

$$\underset{(\text{NPV})}{\text{NET PRESENT VALUE}} = \underset{\text{OF INFLOWS}}{\text{PRESENT VALUE}} - \underset{\text{OF OUTLAYS}}{\text{PRESENT VALUE}}$$

Formula 16.2

$$\text{PROFITABILITY INDEX} = \frac{\text{PRESENT VALUE OF INFLOWS}}{\text{PRESENT VALUE OF OUTLAYS}}$$

Formula 9.1B

$$P = \frac{S}{(1 + i)^n}$$

Formula 9.1C

$$P = S(1 + i)^{-n}$$

Formula 11.2

$$A_n = R\left[\frac{1 - (1 + i)^{-n}}{i}\right]$$

Formula 11.4

$$A_{nc} = R\left[\frac{1 - (1 + f)^{-n}}{f}\right]$$

where $f = (1 + i)^c - 1$

Formula 12.2

$$A_n(\text{due}) = R(1 + i)\left[\frac{1 - (1 + i)^{-n}}{i}\right]$$

Formula 12.4

$$A_{nc}(\text{due}) = R(1 + f)\left[\frac{1 - (1 + f)^{-n}}{f}\right]$$

where $f = (1 + i)^c - 1$

GLOSSARY

Discounted benefit-cost ratio   see *Profitability index*

Discounted cash flow   the present value of cash payments

Net present value   the difference between the present value of the inflows (benefits) and the present value of the outlays (costs) of a capital investment project

Profitability index   the ratio of the present value of the inflows (benefits) to the present value of the outlays (costs) of a capital investment project

Rate of return   the rate of discount for which the net present value of a capital investment project is equal to zero

APPENDIX I

Review of Basic Algebra

I.I   BASIC LAWS, RULES, AND DEFINITIONS

A. The fundamental operations

The fundamental operations of algebra are *addition, subtraction, multiplication,* and *division.* The symbols used to show these operations are the same as the symbols used in arithmetic.

For any two numbers 'a' and 'b', the fundamental operations are as follows.

1. *Addition* is denoted by '$a + b$' and referred to as the sum of 'a' and 'b'.
   If $a = 7$ and $b = 4$,
   then $a + b = 7 + 4 = 11$.
2. *Subtraction* is denoted by '$a - b$' and referred to as the difference between 'a' and 'b'.
   If $a = 7$ and $b = 4$,
   then $a - b = 7 - 4 = 3$.
3. *Multiplication* is denoted by '$a \times b$' '$(a)(b)$' or 'ab'. 'a' and 'b' are called **factors** and 'ab' is referred to as the product of 'a' and 'b'.
   If $a = 7$ and $b = 4$,
   then $ab = (7)(4) = 28$.
4. *Division* is denoted by '$a{:}b$' or '$\dfrac{a}{b}$' or 'a/b'. 'a' is the dividend, 'b' is the divisor, and '$\dfrac{a}{b}$' is the quotient.

   If $a = 7$ and $b = 4$,
   then $\dfrac{a}{b} = \dfrac{7}{4}$.

B. Basic laws

The basic laws governing algebraic operations are the same as those used for arithmetic operations.

1. The Commutative Laws for Addition and Multiplication

   (a) When adding two numbers, the two numbers (addends) may be interchanged.

   $$a + b = b + a$$ ———————— **Formula I.I**

If $a = 7$ and $b = 4$,
then $7 + 4 = 4 + 7 = 11$.

(b) When multiplying two numbers, the two factors may be interchanged.

$$\boxed{ab = ba}$$ ——————————— **Formula I.2**

If $a = 7$ and $b = 4$,
then $(7)(4) = (4)(7) = 28$.

2. **The Associative Laws for Addition and Multiplication**

(a) When adding three or more numbers, the numbers (addends) may be combined in any order.

$$\boxed{a + b + c = (a + b) + c = a + (b + c) = b + (a + c)}$$ ——— **Formula I.3**

If $a = 7$, $b = 4$, and $c = 2$,
then $7 + 4 + 2 = (7 + 4) + 2 = 7 + (4 + 2) = 4 + (7 + 2) = 13$.

(b) When multiplying three or more numbers, the numbers (factors) may be combined in any order.

$$\boxed{abc = (ab)c = a(bc) = b(ac)}$$ ——————— **Formula I.4**

If $a = 7$, $b = 4$, and $c = 2$,
then $7 \times 4 \times 2 = (7 \times 4) \times 2 = 7 \times (4 \times 2) = 4 \times (7 \times 2) = 56$.

3. **The Distributive Law of Multiplication over Addition**

The product of 'a' times the sum of 'b' and 'c' is equal to the sum of the products 'ab' and 'ac.'

$$\boxed{a(b + c) = ab + ac}$$ ——————————— **Formula I.5**

If $a = 7$, $b = 4$, and $c = 2$,
then $7(4 + 2) = 7 \times 4 + 7 \times 2 = 42$.

4. **Special Properties of '1'**

(a) $\boxed{a \times 1 = 1 \times a = a}$ When any number 'a' is multiplied by '1,' the product is the number 'a.'

If $a = 5$, then $5 \times 1 = 1 \times 5 = 5$.

(b) $\boxed{\dfrac{a}{1} = a}$ When any number 'a' is divided by '1,' the quotient is the number 'a.'

If $a = 5$, then $\dfrac{5}{1} = 5$.

(c) $\boxed{\dfrac{a}{a} = 1}$ When any number 'a' is divided by itself, the quotient is '1.'

If $a = 5$, then $\dfrac{5}{5} = 1$.

5. **Special Properties of '0'**

   (a) *Addition with '0'*

     $\boxed{a + 0 = 0 + a = a}$ When '0' is added to any number 'a,' the sum is the number 'a.'

     If $a = 5$, then $5 + 0 = 0 + 5 = 5$.

   (b) *Subtraction with '0'*

     (i) $\boxed{a - 0 = a}$ When '0' is subtracted from any number 'a,' the difference is the number 'a.'

       If $a = 5$, then $5 - 0 = 5$.

     (ii) $\boxed{0 - a = -a}$ When any number 'a' is subtracted from '0,' the difference is the inverse value of 'a,' that is, 'a' with the sign changed.

     If $a = 5$, then $0 - 5 = -5$.

   (c) *Multiplication with '0'*

     $\boxed{a \times 0 = 0 \times a = 0}$ When '0' is multiplied by any number 'a,' the product is '0.'

     If $a = 5$, then $5 \times 0 = 0 \times 5 = 0$.

   (d) *Division with '0'*

     (i) $\boxed{\dfrac{0}{a} = 0}$ When '0' is divided by any number 'a' other than '0,' the quotient is '0.'

     (ii) $\boxed{\dfrac{a}{0} = \text{undefined}}$ Division by '0' has no meaning.

       If $a = 5$, then $\dfrac{5}{0} = \text{undefined}$.

C. Definitions

1. An **algebraic expression** is a combination of numbers, variables representing numbers, and symbols indicating an algebraic operation.

$$7ab, \ 3a - 5b, \ x^2 - 3x + 4, \ \frac{3}{4}x - \frac{1}{5}y$$

2. A **term** is a part of an algebraic expression separated from other parts by a positive $(+)$ sign or by a negative $(-)$ sign. The preceding $(+)$ sign or $(-)$ sign is part of the term.

    The terms for the algebraic expressions listed in part (1) are

$$7ab; \quad 3a \text{ and } -5b; \quad x^2, -3x, \text{ and } +4; \quad \frac{3}{4}x \text{ and } -\frac{1}{5}y$$

3. A **monomial** is an algebraic expression consisting of *one* term, such as $7ab$.
   A **binomial** is an algebraic expression consisting of *two* terms, such as
   $3a - 5b$ or $\frac{3}{4}x - \frac{1}{5}y$.
   A **trinomial** is an algebraic expression consisting of *three* terms, such as
   $x^2 - 3x + 4$.
   A **polynomial** is an algebraic expression consisting of *more than one* term.

4. A **factor** is one of the numbers that when multiplied by another number or numbers yields a given product.

   The factors of the term $7ab$ are 7, a, and b.

5. A *factor of a term* is called the *coefficient* of the rest of the term.
   In the term $7ab$,   7 is the coefficient of ab,
                        $7a$ is the coefficient of b,
                        $7b$ is the coefficient of a.

6. The **numerical coefficient** is the part of a term formed by *numerals*.

   In the term $7ab$, the numerical coefficient is 7;
   in the term x^2, the numerical coefficient is *understood* to be 1 (1 is usually not written);
   in the term $-\frac{1}{5}y$, the numerical coefficient is $-\frac{1}{5}$ (the sign is considered to be part of the numerical coefficient).

7. The **literal coefficient** of a term is the part of the term formed with *letter* symbols.

   In the term $7ab$, ab is the literal coefficient;
   in the term $3x^2$, x^2 is the literal coefficient.

8. **Like terms** are terms having the *same* literal coefficients.

   $7a, -3a, a, -\frac{1}{3}a$ are like terms;
   $x^2, -2x^2, -\frac{1}{2}x^2, 5x^2$ are like terms.

9. **Combining like terms** or **collecting like terms** means *adding* like terms. Only like terms can be added.

10. **Signed numbers** are numbers preceded by a positive $(+)$ or a negative $(-)$ sign. Numbers preceded by a positive $(+)$ sign are called **positive numbers**, while numbers preceded by a negative $(-)$ sign are called **negative numbers**.

11. **Like signed numbers** are numbers that have the *same* sign while numbers with *different* signs are called **unlike signed numbers**.

    $+7$ and $+8$ are like signed numbers;
    -7 and -8 are like signed numbers;
    $+7$ and -8 are unlike signed numbers;
    -7 and 8 are unlike signed numbers.

Note: If no sign is written in front of a number, a plus $(+)$ sign is understood to precede the number.

'6' means '+6'.

12. The **absolute value** of a signed number is the value of the number *without* the sign and is denoted by the symbol $|\ |$.

The absolute value of $+5 = |+5| = 5$;
the absolute value of $-5 = |-5| = 5$.

Exercise I.1

A. Answer each of the following questions.

1. List the terms contained in each of the following expressions.
   a) $-3xy$
   b) $4a - 5c - 2d$
   c) $x^2 - \dfrac{1}{2}x - 2$
   d) $1.2x - 0.5xy + 0.9y - 0.3$

2. Name the numerical coefficient of each of the following terms.
   a) $-3b$ b) $7c$ c) $-a$ d) x
   e) $12a^2b$ f) $-3ax$ g) $-\dfrac{1}{2}x^2$ h) $\dfrac{x}{5}$

3. Name the literal coefficient of each of the following.
   a) $3x$ b) ab c) $-4y$ d) $-xy$
   e) $-15x^2y^2$ f) $3.5abx$ g) $\dfrac{4}{3}x^3$ h) $\dfrac{by}{6}$

I.2   FUNDAMENTAL OPERATIONS WITH SIGNED NUMBERS

A. Additions with signed numbers

1. *Addition of Like Signed Numbers*
   To add like signed numbers,

   (i) add their absolute values, and

   (ii) prefix the common sign.

EXAMPLE I.2A

Add each of the following.

   (i) -6 and -8

Solution

The absolute values are 6 and 8;
the sum of 6 and 8 is 14;
the common sign is $(-)$.
$(-6) + (-8) = -6 - 8 = -14$

(ii) $+6, +5,$ and $+12$

Solution   The absolute values are 6, 5, and 12;
the sum of 6, 5, and 12 is 23;
the common sign is $(+)$.
$(+6) + (+5) + (+12) = +6 + 5 + 12 = +23,$ or 23

(iii) $-9, -3, -1,$ and -15

Solution   The absolute values are 9, 3, 1, and 15;
the sum of the four numbers is 28;
the common sign is $(-)$.
$(-9) + (-3) + (-1) + (-15) = -9 - 3 - 1 - 15 = -28$

2. *Addition of Unlike Signed Numbers*
   To add unlike signed numbers,
   (i) subtract the smaller absolute value from the larger absolute value, and
   (ii) prefix the sign of the *larger* absolute value.

EXAMPLE I.2B   Add each of the following.

(i) 8 and -5

Solution   The absolute values are 8 and 5;
the difference between the absolute values is 3;
the sign of the larger absolute value is $(+)$.
$(+8) + (-5) = +8 - 5 = +3,$ or 3

(ii) 4 and -9

Solution   The absolute values are 4 and 9;
the difference between the absolute values is 5;
the sign of the larger absolute value is $(-)$.
$(+4) + (-9) = 4 - 9 = -5$

(iii) $-6, +8, +3, -4,$ and -5

Solution   When more than two numbers are involved and unlike signs appear, two approaches are available.

METHOD I   Add the first two numbers and then add the sum to the next number and so on.

$$(-6) + (+8) + (+3) + (-4) + (-5)$$
$$= -6 + 8 + 3 - 4 - 5$$
$$= +2 + 3 - 4 - 5 \quad\text{——— add } -6 \text{ and } +8, \text{ which equals } +2$$
$$= +5 - 4 - 5 \quad\text{——— add } +2 \text{ and } +3, \text{ which equals } +5$$
$$= +1 - 5 \quad\text{——— add } +5 \text{ and } -4, \text{ which equals } +1$$
$$= -4 \quad\text{——— add } +1 \text{ and } -5, \text{ which equals } -4$$

METHOD 2 First add the numbers having like signs and then add the two resulting unlike signed numbers.

$$(-6) + (+8) + (+3) + (-4) + (-5)$$
$$= -6 + 8 + 3 - 4 - 5$$
$$= (-6 - 4 - 5) + (+8 + 3)$$
$$= (-15) + (+11)$$
$$= -15 + 11$$
$$= -4$$

B. Subtraction with signed numbers

The subtraction of signed numbers is changed to addition by using the inverse of the *subtrahend*. Thus, to subtract with signed numbers, change the sign of the subtrahend and add.

EXAMPLE I.2C Perform each of the following subtractions.

(i) $(+6)$ from (4)

Solution
$$(+4) - (+6)$$
$$= (+4) + (-6) \quad \text{———— change the subtrahend } (+6) \text{ to } (-6) \text{ and change the}$$
$$= +4 - 6 \qquad\qquad\quad \text{subtraction to an addition}$$
$$= -2 \quad \text{———————— use the rules of addition to add } +4 \text{ and } -6$$

(ii) (-12) from $(+7)$

Solution
$$(+7) - (-12)$$
$$= (+7) + (+12) \quad \text{———— change the subtrahend } (-12) \text{ to } (+12)$$
$$= +7 + 12 \qquad\qquad\quad \text{and add}$$
$$= 19$$

(iii) $(+9)$ from (-6)

Solution
$$(-6) - (+9)$$
$$= (-6) + (-9)$$
$$= -6 - 9$$
$$= -15$$

C. Multiplication with signed numbers

The product of two signed numbers is positive or negative according to the following rules.

(a) If the signs of the two numbers are *like*, the product is *positive*.
$$(+)(+) = (+)$$
$$(-)(-) = (+)$$

(b) If the signs of the two numbers are *unlike*, the product is *negative*.
$$(+)(-) = (-)$$
$$(-)(+) = (-)$$

EXAMPLE I.2D

(i) $(+7)(+4)$ $= 28$ ——————— the signs are like (both positive); the product is positive

(ii) $(-9)(-3)$ $= 27$ ——————— the signs are like (both negative); the product is positive

(iii) $(-8)(3)$ $= -24$ ——————— the signs are unlike; the product is negative

(iv) $(7)(-1)$ $= -7$ ——————— the signs are unlike; the product is negative

(v) $(-8)(0)$ $= 0$ ——————— the product of any number and 0 is 0

(vi) $(-7)(3)(-4)$ $= (-21)(-4)$ ——————— (-7) times (3) is (-21)
$= 84$

(vii) $(-2)(-1)(-4)(3) = (2)(-4)(3) = (-8)(3) = -24$

Note: Brackets around one or both numbers indicate multiplication.

D. Division with signed numbers

The quotient of two signed numbers is positive or negative according to the following rules.

(a) If the signs are *like*, the quotient is *positive*.
$(+) \div (+) = (+)$
$(-) \div (-) = (+)$

(b) If the signs are *unlike*, the quotient is *negative*.
$(+) \div (-) = (-)$
$(-) \div (+) = (-)$

EXAMPLE I.2E

(i) $15 \div (+5)$ $= 3$ ——————— the signs are like; the quotient is positive

(ii) $(-24) \div (-4)$ $= 6$ ——————— the signs are like; the quotient is positive

(iii) $(-18) \div 2$ $= -9$ ——————— the signs are unlike; the quotient is negative

(iv) $(12) \div (-1)$ $= -12$ ——————— the signs are unlike; the quotient is negative

(v) $0 \div (-10)$ $= 0$ ——————— 0 divided by any number is 0

(vi) $(-16) \div 0$ $=$ undefined ——————— division by 0 has no meaning

E. Absolute value of signed numbers

The absolute value of signed numbers, denoted by $|\ |$, is the value of the numbers without the signs.

EXAMPLE I.2F

(i) $|-7| = 7$

(ii) $|-3 + 8| = |+5| = 5$

(iii) $|4 - 9| = |-5| = 5$

(iv) $|-9 - 4| = |-13| = 13$

(v) $|4(-7)| = |-28| = 28$

(vi) $|(-9)(-3)| = |27| = 27$

(vii) $|(-12) \div (4)| = |-3| = 3$

(viii) $|(-30) \div (-5)| = |+6| = 6$

Exercise I.2

A. Simplify.

1. $(+3) + (+7)$ 2. $(+12) + (+6)$ 3. $(-5) + (-9)$

4. $(-15) + (-12)$ 5. $4 + (+5)$ 6. $(+6) + 8$

7. $-8 + (-7)$ 8. $(-18) - 7$ 9. $+3 + 14$

10. $+12 + 1$ 11. $-6 - 9$ 12. $-14 - 3$

13. $-8 + 3$ 14. $-12 + 16$ 15. $8 - 12$

16. $0 - 9$ 17. $1 - 0.6$ 18. $1 - 0.02$

19. $(-4) + (6) + (-3) + (+2)$ 20. $12 + (-15) + (+8) + (-10)$

21. $-3 - 7 + 9 + 6 - 5$ 22. $10 - 8 - 12 + 3 - 7$

B. Simplify.

1. $(+9) - (+8)$ 2. $(+11) - (+14)$ 3. $(+6) - (-6)$

4. $(+11) - (-12)$ 5. $(-8) - (-7)$ 6. $(-9) - (-13)$

7. $(-4) - (+6)$ 8. $(-15) - (+3)$ 9. $0 - (-9)$

10. $1 - (-0.4)$ 11. $1 - (-0.03)$ 12. $0 - (+15)$

13. $6 - (-5) + (-8) - (+3) + (-2)$

14. $-12 - (-6) - (+9) + (-4) - 7$

C. Simplify.

1. $(+5)(+4)$ 2. $11(+3)$ 3. $(-4)(-6)$ 4. $-7(-3)$

5. $(+7)(-1)$ 6. $10(-5)$ 7. $-3(12)$ 8. $-9(1)$

9. $0(-6)$ 10. $-12(0)$ 11. $6(-4)(-3)(2)$ 12. $-3(5)(-2)(-1)$

D. Simplify.

1. $(+18) \div (+3)$ 2. $(32) \div (+4)$ 3. $(+45) \div (-9)$

4. $(63) \div (-3)$ 5. $(-28) \div (+7)$ 6. $(-36) \div (+12)$

7. $(-16) \div (-1)$ 8. $(-48) \div (-8)$ 9. $0 \div (-5)$

10. $0 \div 10$ 11. $(+4) \div 0$ 12. $(-12) \div 0$

E. Simplify.

1. $|-9|$ 2. $|+4|$ 3. $|6 - 10|$ 4. $|-5 + 12|$

5. $|-7 - 8|$ 6. $|0 - 3|$ 7. $|(-3) \times 3|$ 8. $|4 \times (-5)|$

9. $|20 \div (-5)|$ 10. $|(-35) \div (7)|$

I.3   COMMON FACTORING

A. Basic concept

In arithmetic, certain computations, such as multiplication and division involving common fractions, are helped by factoring. Similarly, algebraic manipulation can be made easier by the process of finding the factors that make up an algebraic expression.

Factoring an algebraic expression means writing the expression as a product in component form. Depending on the type of factors contained in the expression, the process of factoring takes a variety of forms. Only the simplest type of factoring applies to the subject matter dealt with in this text. Accordingly only this type, called *common factoring*, is explained in this section.

A **common factor** is one that is divisible without remainder into each term of an algebraic expression. The factor that is common to each term is usually found by inspection; the remaining factor is then obtained by dividing the expression by the common factor.

B. Examples

EXAMPLE I.3A

Factor $14a + 21b$.

Solution

By inspection, recognize that the two terms $14a$ and $21b$ are both divisible by 7.

The common factor is 7.
The second factor is now found by dividing the expression by 7.

$$\frac{14a + 21b}{7} = \frac{14a}{7} + \frac{21b}{7} = 2a + 3b$$

Thus the factors of $14a + 21b$ are 7 and $2a + 3b$.

$$14a + 21b = 7(2a + 3b)$$

EXAMPLE I.3B

Factor $18a - 45$.

Solution

By inspection, the highest common factor is 9;

the second factor is $\dfrac{18a - 45}{9} = 2a - 5$.

$$18a - 45 = 9(2a - 5)$$

Note: If 3 is used as the common factor, the second factor, $6a - 15$, contains a common factor 3 and can be factored into $3(2a - 5)$.

Thus, $18a - 45 = 3[6a - 15]$
$\qquad\qquad\quad = 3[3(2a - 5)]$
$\qquad\qquad\quad = 9(2a - 5)$

When factoring, the accepted procedure is to always take out the *highest* common factor.

EXAMPLE I.3C

Factor $mx - my$.

Solution

The common factor is m;

the second factor is $\dfrac{mx - my}{m} = x - y$.

$$mx - my = m(x - y)$$

EXAMPLE I.3D

Factor $15x^3 - 25x^2 - 20x$.

Solution

The common factor is $5x$.

The second factor is $\dfrac{15x^3 - 25x^2 - 20x}{5x} = 3x^2 - 5x - 4$.

$15x^3 - 25x^2 - 20x = 5x\,(3x^2 - 5x - 4)$

EXAMPLE I.3E

Factor $P + Prt$.

Solution

The common factor is P.

The second factor is $\dfrac{P + Prt}{P} = \dfrac{P}{P} + \dfrac{Prt}{P} = 1 + rt$.

$P + Prt = P(1 + rt)$

EXAMPLE I.3F

Factor $a(x + y) - b(x + y)$.

Solution

The common factor is $(x + y)$.

The second factor is $\dfrac{a(x + y) - b(x + y)}{x + y} = \dfrac{a(x + y)}{x + y} - \dfrac{b(x + y)}{x + y} = a - b$.

$a(x + y) - b(x + y) = (x + y)(a - b)$

EXAMPLE I.3G

Factor $(1 + i) + (1 + i)^2 + (1 + i)^3$.

Solution

The common factor is $(1 + i)$.

The second factor is $\dfrac{(1 + i) + (1 + i)^2 + (1 + i)^3}{(1 + i)}$

$= \dfrac{(1 + i)}{(1 + i)} + \dfrac{(1 + i)^2}{(1 + i)} + \dfrac{(1 + i)^3}{(1 + i)}$

$= 1 + (1 + i) + (1 + i)^2$

$(1 + i) + (1 + i)^2 + (1 + i)^3 = (1 + i)\left[1 + (1 + i) + (1 + i)^2\right]$

Exercise I.3

A. Factor each of the following.

　1. $8x - 12$ 　　　　　　　2. $27 - 36a$

　3. $4n^2 - 8n$ 　　　　　　4. $9x^2 - 21x$

　5. $5ax - 10ay - 20a$ 　　6. $4ma - 12mb + 24mab$

B. Factor each of the following.

　1. $mx + my$ 　　　　　　　2. $xa - xb$

　3. $m(a - b) + n(a - b)$ 　4. $k(x - 1) - 3(x - 1)$

　5. $P + Pi$ 　　　　　　　　6. $A - Adt$

　7. $r - r^2 - r^3$ 　　　　　　8. $(1 + i)^4 + (1 + i)^3 + (1 + i)^2$

SUMMARY OF FORMULAE (LAWS)

Formula I.1
$a + b = b + a$

The commutative law for addition that permits the addition of two numbers in any order

Formula I.2
$ab = ba$

The commutative law for multiplication that permits the multiplication of two numbers in any order

Formula I.3
$$a + b + c = (a + b) + c$$
$$= a + (b + c)$$
$$= b + (a + c)$$

The associative law for addition that permits the addition of three or more numbers in any order

Formula I.4
$$abc = (ab)c$$
$$= a(bc)$$
$$= b(ac)$$

The associative law for multiplication that permits the multiplication of three or more numbers in any order

Formula I.5
$$a(b + c) = ab + ac$$

The distributive law of multiplication over addition that provides the basis for the multiplication of algebraic expressions

GLOSSARY

Absolute value   the value of a number without its sign

Algebraic expression   a combination of numbers, variables representing numbers, and symbols indicating an algebraic operation

Binomial   an algebraic expression consisting of two terms

Collecting like terms   adding like terms

Combining like terms   see *Collecting like terms*

Common factor   a factor that is divisible without remainder into each term of an algebraic expression

Factor   one of the numbers that when multiplied with the other number or numbers yields a given product

Like signed numbers   numbers having the same sign

Like terms   terms having the same literal coefficient

Literal coefficient   the part of a term formed with letter symbols

Monomial   an algebraic expression consisting of one term

Negative numbers   signed numbers preceded by a minus ($-$) sign

Numerical coefficient   the part of a term formed with numerals

Polynomial   an algebraic expression consisting of more than one term

Positive numbers   signed numbers preceded by a plus ($+$) sign

Signed numbers   numbers preceded by a plus ($+$) or by a minus ($-$) sign

Term   a part of an algebraic expression separated from other parts by a plus ($+$) sign or by a minus ($-$) sign

Trinomial   an algebraic expression consisting of three terms

Unlike signed numbers   numbers having different signs

APPENDIX II

Linear Applications

II.1 COST-VOLUME-PROFIT ANALYSIS

A. Cost-volume-profit relationships

In our discussion of break-even analysis in Chapter 5, we used graphs to show the relationship between revenue and costs at different levels of output. We introduced the formulae that are used in cost-volume-profit analysis. We will begin this appendix by presenting the formulae from Chapter 5 in mathematical notation.

The following components are basic to cost-volume-profit relationships. The mathematical notations shown below will be used for these components throughout this appendix.

$$X = \text{Volume of output}$$
$$P = \text{Selling price (revenue) per unit of output}$$
$$TR = \text{Total revenue}$$
$$TC = \text{Total cost}$$
$$FC = \text{Fixed cost}$$
$$TVC = \text{Total variable cost}$$
$$VC = \text{Variable cost per unit of output}$$
$$NI = \text{Net income (profit)}$$

Recall that **fixed costs** are those costs that remain constant over the time period considered for all levels of output. **Variable costs** are those costs that are constant per unit of output regardless of volume. Variable costs fluctuate in total amount as volume fluctuates.

The accounting relationship (income statement equation) is basic to cost-volume-profit analysis.

> TOTAL REVENUE = TOTAL COST + NET INCOME

> TR = TC + NI ———————————————— **Formula II.1**

The following relationships are also useful.

> TOTAL REVENUE = VOLUME × UNIT REVENUE

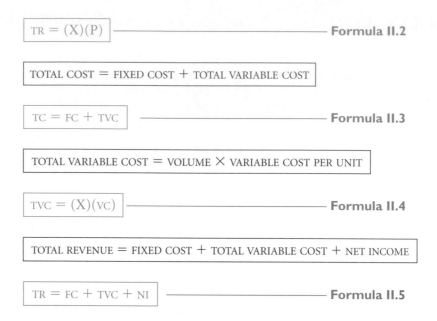

$$\boxed{TR = (X)(P)} \text{———————————— Formula II.2}$$

$$\boxed{TOTAL\ COST = FIXED\ COST + TOTAL\ VARIABLE\ COST}$$

$$\boxed{TC = FC + TVC} \text{———————————— Formula II.3}$$

$$\boxed{TOTAL\ VARIABLE\ COST = VOLUME \times VARIABLE\ COST\ PER\ UNIT}$$

$$\boxed{TVC = (X)(VC)} \text{———————————— Formula II.4}$$

$$\boxed{TOTAL\ REVENUE = FIXED\ COST + TOTAL\ VARIABLE\ COST + NET\ INCOME}$$

$$\boxed{TR = FC + TVC + NI} \text{———————————— Formula II.5}$$

B. Algebraic analysis of cost-volume-profit relationships

Recall from Chapter 5 that **break-even analysis** is a method of determining the level of output at which a business neither makes a profit nor sustains a loss. The **break-even point** is the level of output at which net income is zero. On a **break-even chart**, total revenues and total costs are shown for different levels of output. The point at which the total revenue line crosses the total costs line is the break-even point, since this is the level of output where no profit or loss is made. (See Chapter 5, page 217 for an example of a break-even chart.)

Break-even analysis focusses on one particular level of operations. However, the accounting relationship

$$TR = FC + TVC + NI \text{———————————— } \textbf{Formula II.5}$$

can be used to extend cost-volume-profit analysis to any desired level of operations. It is possible to determine the net income at any level of operations and to analyze what effect changes in selling price, fixed cost, or variable costs have on profitability at any level of operations.

EXAMPLE II.1A

Market research for a new product indicates that the product can be sold at $50.00 per unit. Cost analysis provides the following information.

Fixed cost per period = $8640.00
Variable cost per unit = $30.00
Production capacity per period = 900 units

Use this information to answer each of the following questions. (Note that this is the same scenario as Example 5.2A presented in Chapter 5.)

(i) What is the net income at a volume of

   (a) 385 units?   (b) 780 units?

Solution

TR = 50X

TC = 8640 + 30X

The basic accounting relationship (using Formula II.5) is

50X = 8640 + 30X + NI.

(a)   For X = 385,

   $$50(385) = 8640 + 30(385) + \text{NI}$$
   $$19\ 250 = 8640 + 11\ 550 + \text{NI}$$
   $$\text{NI} = -940 \ (\text{a loss})$$

The net income (loss) at a volume of 385 units is ($940).

(b)   For X = 780,

   $$50(780) = 8640 + 30(780) + \text{NI}$$
   $$39\ 000 = 8640 + 23\ 400 + \text{NI}$$
   $$\text{NI} = 6960$$

The net income at a volume of 780 units is $6960.

(ii) What is the net income at a sales volume of

   (a) $17 500?   (b) $40 000?

Solution

(a) At a sales volume of $17 500,

   $$50X = 17\ 500$$
   $$X = 350 \ (\text{units})$$
   $$50(350) = 8640 + 30(350) + \text{NI}$$
   $$17\ 500 = 8640 + 10\ 500 + \text{NI}$$
   $$\text{NI} = -1640$$

The net income (loss) at a volume of $17 500 is ($1640).

(b) At a sales volume of $40 000,

   $$50X = 40\ 000$$
   $$X = 800 \ (\text{units})$$
   $$50(800) = 8640 + 30(800) + \text{NI}$$
   $$40\ 000 = 8640 + 24\ 000 + \text{NI}$$
   $$\text{NI} = 7360$$

The net income at a sales volume of $40 000 is $7360.

(iii) What is the net income at a sales volume of

   (a) 36% of capacity?   (b) 95% of capacity?

Solution

(a) Sales volume is 36% of 900 = 324 units.

   $$50(324) = 8640 + 30(324) + \text{NI}$$
   $$16\ 200 = 8640 + 9720 + \text{NI}$$
   $$\text{NI} = -2160$$

The net income at 36% of capacity is ($2160).

(b) Sales volume is 95% of 900 = 855 units.

$$50(855) = 8640 + 30(855) + \text{NI}$$
$$42\ 750 = 8640 + 25\ 650 + \text{NI}$$
$$\text{NI} = 8460$$

The net income at 95% capacity is $8460.

(iv) What is the number of units that must be sold to generate a net income of
(a) ($1000)?   (b) $3000?

Solution

(a) $50X = 8640 + 30X - 1000$
$20X = 7640$
$X = 382$

To generate a net income of ($1000), the sales volume must be 382 units.

(b) $50X = 8640 + 30X + 3000$
$20X = 11\ 640$
$X = 582$

To generate a net income of $3000, the sales volume must be 582 units.

(v) What is the sales volume in dollars that generates a net income of
(a) ($1600)?   (b) $7200?

Solution

(a) $50X = 8640 + 30X - 1600$
$20X = 7040$
$X = 352$ (units)
The sales volume is $(352)(50) = \$17\ 600$.
(b) $50X = 8640 + 30X + 7200$
$20X = 15\ 840$
$X = 792$ (units)

The sales volume is $(792)(50) = \$39\ 600$.

(vi) What is the output required, as a percentage of capacity, to generate a net income of
(a) $360?   (b) $5760?

Solution

(a) $50X = 8640 + 30X + 360$
$20X = 9000$
$X = 450$ (units)

The required output is $\dfrac{450}{900} = 0.50 = 50\%$ of capacity.

(b) $50X = 8640 + 30X + 5760$
$20X = 14\ 400$
$X = 720$ (units)

The required output is $\dfrac{720}{900} = 0.80 = 80\%$ of capacity.

(vii) If fixed costs are increased to $10 400, what is the break-even point
(a) in units?　　(b) in dollars?　　(c) as a percent of capacity?

Solution
If fixed costs are increased to $10 400, the basic relationship (Formula II.5) becomes

$$50X = 10\,400 + 30X + \text{NI}.$$

To break even, NI $= 0$.

$$50X = 10\,400 + 30X$$
$$20X = 10\,400$$
$$X = 520 \text{ (units)}$$

(a) The break-even point in units is 520.
(b) The break-even point in dollars is $520(50) = \$26\,000$.
(c) The break-even point as a percent of capacity is

$$\frac{520}{900} = 0.57777778 = 57.8\%$$

(viii) What is the break-even point in dollars if fixed costs are reduced by $990 and variable cost per unit is increased by $2?

Solution
The new fixed cost is $8640 - 990 = \$7650$ and the new variable cost per unit is $30 + 2 = \$32$. The basic relationship (Formula II.5) becomes

$$50X = 7650 + 32X + \text{NI}.$$

To break even, NI $= 0$.

$$50X = 7650 + 32X$$
$$18X = 7650$$
$$X = 425 \text{ (units)}$$

The break-even point is $(425)(50) = \$21\,250$.

(ix) What is the break-even point as a percent of capacity if the selling price is reduced by 10%?

Solution
The new selling price $= 90\%$ of $50 = \$45$.
The basic relationship becomes

$$45X = 8640 + 30X + \text{NI}$$

To break even, NI $= 0$.

$$45X = 8640 + 30X$$
$$15X = 8640$$
$$X = 576 \text{ (units)}$$

The break-even point is $\dfrac{576}{900} = 0.64 = 64\%$ of capacity.

(x) To generate a profit of $4860, what dollar sales must be attained if the selling price per unit is
(a) reduced to $48?   (b) increased to $55?

Solution
(a) $48X = 8640 + 30X + 4860$
$\ 18X = 13\ 500$
$\ X = 750$ (units)

Sales volume must be $(750)(48) = \$36\ 000$.

(b) $55X = 8640 + 30X + 4860$
$\ 25X = 13\ 500$
$\ X = 540$ (units)

Sales volume must be $(540)(55) = \$29\ 700$.

(xi) What is the output as a percentage of capacity that must be achieved to generate a profit of $7830 if the production setup is modified so that fixed costs increase by 25% while variable costs are reduced by 10%?

Solution
The new fixed costs $= 1.25(8640) = \$10\ 800$; the new variable cost per unit $= (0.90)(30) = \$27$.

$50X = 10\ 800 + 27X + 7830$
$23X = 18\ 630$
$X = 810$ (units)

The required output is $\dfrac{810}{900} = 0.90 = 90\%$ of capacity.

EXAMPLE II.1B

The following information is available about the operations of the King Corp. for the current year.

Sales		$40 000
Fixed costs	$12 600	
Variable costs	16 000	
Total cost		28 600
Net income		$11 400

Capacity is a sales volume of $60 000.

Use this information to answer each of the following questions. (Note that this is the same scenario as Example 5.2B presented in Chapter 5.)

(i) What is the net income at a sales volume of $34 500?

Solution
Let X represent the sales volume.

$\text{TR} = X$
$\text{TC} = 12\ 600 + 40\%\ \text{of TR} = 12\ 600 + 0.40X$

The basic relationship (Formula II.5) is

$$X = 12\ 600 + 0.40X + \text{NI}.$$

At a sales volume of 34 500, $X = 34\ 500$.

$$34\ 500 = 12\ 600 + 0.40(34\ 500) + \text{NI}$$
$$34\ 500 = 12\ 600 + 13\ 800 + \text{NI}$$
$$\text{NI} = 8100$$

The net income at a volume of $34 500 is $8100.

(ii) What is the net income at a volume of 95% of capacity?

Solution

At 95% of capacity, $X = 0.95(60\ 000) = 57\ 000$.

$$57\ 000 = 12\ 600 + 0.40(57\ 000) + \text{NI}$$
$$57\ 000 = 12\ 600 + 22\ 800 + \text{NI}$$
$$\text{NI} = 21\ 600$$

The net income at 95% of capacity is $21 600.

(iii) What volume of output as a percentage of capacity is required to produce a net income of $13 320?

Solution

$$X = 12\ 600 + 0.40X + 13\ 320$$
$$0.60X = 25\ 920$$
$$X = 43\ 200$$

The volume of output required is $\dfrac{43\ 200}{60\ 000} = 72\%$ of capacity.

(iv) What sales volume is required to generate a net income of $3240?

Solution

$$X = 12\ 600 + 0.40X + 3240$$
$$0.60\ X = 15\ 840$$
$$X = 26\ 400$$

The sales volume required is $26 400.

(v) If fixed costs are increased by 25%, what is the break-even point
(a) in sales dollars?   (b) as a percentage of capacity?

Solution

New fixed cost is $12\ 600(1.25) = \$15\ 750$.

$$X = 15\ 750 + 0.40X + \text{NI}$$

To break even, $\text{NI} = 0$.

$$X = 15\ 750 + 0.40X$$
$$0.60X = 15\ 750$$
$$X = 26\ 250$$

(a) The break-even point is $26 250.

(b) The break-even point is $\dfrac{26\ 250}{60\ 000} = 43.75\%$ of capacity.

(vi) What is the break-even point in sales dollars if fixed costs are increased to $14 880 while variable costs are decreased to 38% of sales?

Solution
The basic relationship becomes

$$X = 14\ 880 + 38\% \text{ of } X + \text{NI}.$$
$$X = 14\ 880 + 0.38X + \text{NI}$$

To break even, NI = 0.

$$X = 14\ 880 + 0.38X$$
$$0.62X = 14\ 880$$
$$X = 24\ 000$$

The break-even point is $24 000.

(vii) To generate a profit of $5250, what output, as a percentage of capacity, must be attained if fixed costs are increased by 5% and variable costs by 10%?

Solution
$$\text{FV} = 12\ 600(1.05) = \$13\ 230$$
$$\text{TVC} = 1.10(40\% \text{ of TR})$$
$$= 1.10(0.40X)$$
$$= 0.44X$$

The basic relationship becomes

$$X = 13\ 230 + 0.44X + 5250.$$
$$0.56X = 18\ 480$$
$$X = 33\ 000$$

The required volume is $\dfrac{33\ 000}{60\ 000} = 55\%$ of capacity.

Exercise II.1

A. Answer each of the following questions. (Note that some of these are the same scenarios as the review and self-test questions presented in Chapter 5.)

1. Engineering estimates indicate the variable cost of manufacturing a new product will be $35 per unit. Based on market research, the selling price of the product is to be $120 per unit and variable selling expense is expected to be $15 per unit. The fixed costs applicable to the new product are estimated to be $2800 per period and capacity per period is 100 units. Determine

   a) the net income at a volume of 70 units;

b)   the net income at a volume of 30% of capacity;

c)   the net income at a sales volume of $10 200;

d)   the level of operations as a percentage of capacity to generate a net income of $2240;

e)   the number of units that must be sold to make a net income of $1050;

f)   the sales volume in dollars to suffer a loss of no more than $350;

g)   the break-even point in units if fixed costs are increased to $3150;

h)   the break-even point as a percentage of capacity if fixed costs are reduced by $160 and the variable cost of manufacturing is increased to $39 per unit;

i)   the break-even point in dollars if the selling price is reduced to $100 per unit.

2. The following data pertains to the operating budget of Matt Manufacturing.

Sales		$720 000
Fixed costs	$220 000	
Total variable costs	324 000	544 000
Net Income		$176 000

Capacity is a sales volume of $800 000 per period.
Determine

a)   the net income at 85% of capacity;

b)   the net income at 30% of capacity;

c)   the level of operations as a percentage of capacity to realize a net income of $66 000;

d)   the level of operations in dollars to sustain a loss of no more than $6600;

e)   the break-even point in dollars if fixed costs are increased by 15%;

f)   the break-even point as a percentage of capacity if fixed costs are decreased by $18 400 and variable costs are increased to 52% of sales.

3. The lighting division of Universal Electric Company plans to introduce a new streetlight based on the following accounting information.

Fixed costs per period are $3136; variable cost per unit is $157; selling price per unit is $185; and capacity per period is 320 units.

a)   Determine the net income at a sales volume of
(i) 25% of capacity;   (ii) $24 975.

b) Determine the level of operations as a percentage of capacity to generate a net income of

(i) $2240;   (ii) $6720.

4. The following information is available from the accounting records of Eva Corporation.

Fixed costs per period are $4800; sales volume for the last period was $19 360 and variable costs were $13 552. Capacity per period is a sales volume of $32 000.

a) Determine the net income at a sales volume of

(i) $24 000;   (ii) 30% of capacity.

b) Determine the level of operations as a percentage of capacity to generate a net income of $3264.

5. The operating budget of the Bea Company contains the following information.

Sales at 80% of capacity		$400 000
Fixed costs	$105 000	
Variable costs	260 000	365 000
Net Income		$ 35 000

a) Determine the net income at 40% of capacity.

b) Determine the sales volume as a percentage of capacity to generate a net income of $61 250.

6. A manufacturer of major appliances provides the following information about the operations of the refrigeration division.

Fixed costs per period are $26 880; variable costs per unit are $360; selling price per unit is $640; and capacity is 150 units.

a) Determine the net income at a sales volume of

(i) $78 080;   (ii) 48% of capacity.

b) Determine the volume of output as a percentage of capacity to generate a net income of $4200.

7. The Superior CD Company sells CDs for $10 each. Manufacturing cost is $2.60 per CD; marketing costs are $2.40 per CD; and royalty payments are 20% of selling price. The fixed cost of preparing the CDs is $18 000. Capacity is 15 000 CDs.

a) Determine the net income at a sales volume of 55% of capacity.

b) Determine the sales volume in dollars to generate a net income of $13 800.

8. The management of Lambda Corporation has received the following forecast for the next year.

Sales Revenue		$600 000
Fixed costs	$275 000	
Variable costs	270 000	545 000
Net Income		$ 55 000

Capacity is a sales volume of $800 000.

a) Determine the net income at 50% of capacity.

b) Determine the sales volume in dollars to generate a net income of $82 500.

9. The Peel Credit Union is organizing a charter flight to Bermuda for the March break. A package deal requires a fixed payment of $9900 plus $325 per person. The credit union intends to price the one-week package at $550 per person to cover the cost of flight, accommodation, meals, and tips. With a charge of $550 per person, the credit union estimates that the smallest number of participants would be 30 and the greatest number would be 70. If the price of the package is reduced to $475 per person, the minimum number of participants is expected to be 50 and the maximum number 120.

a) How many participants are needed to break even
   (i) at $550 per person?   (ii) at $475 per person?

b) What is the variation between the maximum and the minimum expected profit
   (i) at $550 per person?   (ii) at $475 per person?

10. The student senate of the college is planning the annual convocation dinner dance. Rental of facilities is $2000 and the local rock group can be hired for $660 plus 10% of gate receipts. Meal costs are $26 per couple. The senate expects to set a price of $40 per couple. At that price, estimated minimum ticket sales are 180 and maximum ticket sales are 400. The treasurer argues that the price should be set at $50 per couple at which price minimum sales are estimated at 100 tickets and maximum sales at 300.

a) What is the number of couples that must buy tickets to break even at
   (i) $40 per couple?   (ii) $50 per couple?

b) What is the variation between the maximum and the minimum expected profit
   (i) at $40 per couple?   (ii) at $50 per couple?

11. Eden Motels plan to build a motel complex that consists of 500 economy units, 300 deluxe units, and 200 luxury units. Rent is $40 per night for economy units, $60 per night for deluxe units, and $90 per night for luxury units. The complex will be open year-round and occupancy of the units is expected to be approximately proportional to the number of units of each type—that is, for every five economy units, three deluxe units and two luxury units will be rented. Annual fixed cost of the complex is estimated at $4 489 500 while variable cost per night is $15 per unit.

a) At what percent occupancy level will the motel complex break even?

b) How many units must be rented on average per night to generate an annual profit of $2 993 000?

12. One type of insecticide costs retailers $4.00 per package. The normal retail margin is 50% based on the retailer's cost. Total consumer spending on the product is expected to be $9 600 000. The insecticide is sold to retailers by wholesale distributors at a margin of 25% of the wholesale selling price.

Chemie Inc. has developed a competing product to be marketed under the brand name Bio-Kill. Market research indicates that Chemie Inc. will be able to sell the product to wholesalers at the same price charged by manufacturers of the first product to wholesalers. Chemie's variable costs are estimated to be $33\frac{1}{3}\%$ of Chemie's selling price and fixed costs for the first year of production are estimated to be $400 000. What market share must Bio-Kill attain for Chemie Inc. to break even on the product?

II.2 LINEAR PROGRAMMING—THE TWO-PRODUCT CASE

A. Basic concepts

Linear programming is a mathematical technique that helps managers make the best use of a firm's economic resources that are in limited supply, such as money, material, labour, machinery, space, etc. These limited resources have to be allocated among competing uses so as to maximize profits or minimize costs.

A typical problem of this type is the case of a manufacturer that produces four different products. Each requires a specified amount of time in each of five processes. In each of the five processes, only a limited number of hours are available per time period. Furthermore, the profit per unit of output is different for each of the five products.

The problem that must be solved requires optimizing output with the available resources. The optimal output in this context is the number of units of each product that should be produced to maximize the total profit.

Linear programming problems are of differing complexity. Simple linear programming problems involving two products only can be solved using two-dimensional graphs; multi-product problems require the use of more advanced algebraic techniques.

In this text, we are concerned only with introducing the concept of linear programming and solving the simplest cases. To deal with the two-product case graphically, we will take the following approach.

1. State the problem in algebraic terms.

   a) Represent the number of units of each product by X_1 and X_2 respectively, and organize the data in the form of a chart.

   b) State the **objective function** in equation form. The objective function is a mathematical presentation of the goal to be achieved—either a profit to be maximized or a cost to be minimized.

   c) List the **operational constraints** imposed on the objective function. The operational constraints state that the total amount of each type of economic resource used has to be consistent with the available amount of each resource.

   d) List the **non-negative constraints**. These constraints state that X_1 and X_2 cannot be *less* than zero; that is, the number of units produced cannot be negative.

2. Graphically represent the algebraic relationships.

   a) Represent the constraints graphically in a two-dimensional system of rectangular axes to obtain the **area of feasibility**. This area contains all points (X_1, X_2) that represent the *possible* combinations of X_1 and X_2 that can be produced consistent with the availability of the resources.

   b) Introduce graphs of the objective function to identify the **optimal point**. The optimal point is the point (X_1, X_2) for which the profit will be maximized or the cost will be minimized. If a single solution exists, the optimal point is *always* a corner point on the boundary of the area of feasibility.

3. Algebraically determine the coordinates of the optimal point to find the optimal solution and the value of the objective function at that point.

B. Graphic solution

EXAMPLE II.2A   A manufacturer markets two products. Each unit of Product A requires three hours in the molding department, four hours in the paint shop, and one hour in finishing. Each unit of Product B requires three hours in molding, two hours in painting, and two hours in finishing. Each week 210 hours are available in molding, 200 hours in painting, and 120 hours in finishing. Shipping can handle no more than 40 units of Product A per week. Each unit of Product A contributes $20.00 to profit while each unit of Product B contributes $30.00. Determine how many units of each product should be manufactured per week to maximize profit.

Solution

Algebraic Statement of Problem

(a) Let the number of units of Product A be represented by X_1; let the number of units of Product B be represented by X_2.

Constraints	Data Summary Resource Quantity per Unit For: Product A	Product B	Available Resource Quantity
1. Molding	3	3	210
2. Painting	4	2	200
3. Finishing	1	2	120
4. Shipping	1	N/A	40
Profit	$20	$30	Maximize

(b) **The objective function**

The goal is to maximize profit. The value of the total profit can be represented by P. For Product A the profit is $20.00 per unit or $20X_1$. For Product B the profit is $30.00 per unit or $30X_2$. The total profit is $20X_1 + 30X_2$. The objective function is $P = 20X_1 + 30X_2$ with X_1 and X_2 to be chosen so that P becomes as large as possible.

(c) **The operational constraints**

Production in the given situation depends on limited resources; the availability of time in the molding department, in the paint shop, and in finishing, as well as the ability of shipping to handle Product A.

Each constraint on the operations of the business can be expressed algebraically by relating the resource requirements per unit of product to the total resource available.

Each unit of Product A requires three hours in the molding department as does each unit of Product B. The total time used in the molding department to manufacture the two products must be less than or at most equal to 210 hours per week.

$$3X_1 + 3X_2 \leqq 210$$

Similarly, with respect to the paint shop,

$$4X_1 + 2X_2 \leqq 200$$

and with respect to finishing,

$$X_1 + 2X_1 \leqq 120$$

As far as shipping is concerned, the total number of units of Product A must be less than or equal to 40.

$$X_1 \leqq 40$$

(d) *The non-negative constraints*
The minimum number of units of each product that can be produced is zero. This fact is represented by the inequalities $X_1 \geqq 0$ and $X_2 \geqq 0$, called the non-negative constraints.

(e) *General form of a linear programming problem*
The problem is now stated in the general form of a linear programming problem consisting of three parts.

(i) The objective function $P = 20X_1 + 30X_2$
(ii) The operational constraints
    1. Molding $3X_1 + 3X_2 \leqq 210$
    2. Painting $4X_1 + 2X_2 \leqq 200$
    3. Finishing $X_1 + 2X_2 \leqq 120$
    4. Shipping $X_1 \leqq 40$
(iii) The non-negative constraints $X_1 \geqq 0$
                                                  $X_2 \geqq 0$

STEP 2   **Graphic Representation of the Algebraic Relationships**

(a) *Preliminary considerations*
    (i) *The non-negative constraints*
    Use a set of rectangular axes with the horizontal axis representing values of X_1 and the vertical axis representing values of X_2. The constraint $X_1 \geqq 0$ describes the region to the right of the vertical axis while the constraint $X_2 \geqq 0$ describes the region above the horizontal axis.

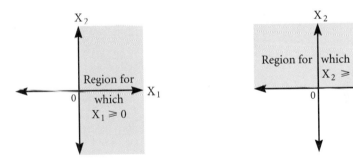

The region for which both conditions hold ($X_1 \geqq 0$ and $X_2 \geqq 0$) is the first quadrant. This is true for all linear programming problems.

    (ii) *Graphic representation of the objective function*
    The objective function may be represented graphically for various profit levels by assuming specific values for P.

Let $P_1 = 1500$.

    Then the specific objective function becomes

$20X_1 + 30X_2 = 1500$

For $X_1 = 0 \longrightarrow X_2 = 50 \longrightarrow$ Graph point A(0, 50)
For $X_2 = 0 \longrightarrow X_1 = 75 \longrightarrow$ Graph point B(75, 0)

The line AB (see Figure 1) joining the two points represents all combinations for which the profit is $1500.00.

$(0, 50)$ ⟶   0 units of Product A and 50 units of Product B
$(75, 0)$ ⟶ 75 units of Product A and 0 units of Product B
$(45, 20)$ ⟶ 45 units of Product A and 20 units of Product B
$(15, 40)$ ⟶ 15 units of Product A and 40 units of Product B

Let $P_2 = 3000$.

Then the specific objective function becomes

$$20X_1 + 30X_2 = 3000$$

For $X_1 = 0$ ⟶ $X_2 = 100$ Graph point C(0, 100)
For $X_2 = 0$ ⟶ $X_1 = 150$ Graph point D(150, 0)

The line CD joining the two points represents all combinations (X_1, X_2) for which the profit is $3000.00.

Similarly, additional lines may be drawn for any convenient profit figure such as $P_3 = 4500$ (see line EF in Figure 1) and $P_4 = 6000$ (see line GH).

FIGURE 1   Graphic Representation of the Objective Function

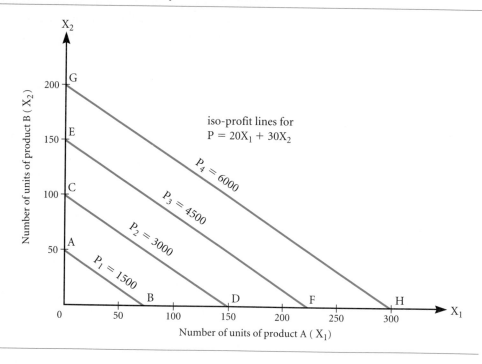

Note:

1. Each profit level results in a specific profit line. Since X_1 and X_2 cannot be negative, the lines are not extended across the two axes.

2. The various combinations of X_1 and X_2 that satisfy the equation of a particular profit will be points on the line and will produce the same amount of profit. Such lines are called **iso-profit lines**.

3. The various iso-profit lines have the same slope and run parallel to each other. All the possible iso-profit lines for a particular objective function represent a family of parallel lines.

4. The total profit represented by each iso-profit line increases with increasing distance of the line from the origin.

5. The parallel nature of the iso-profit lines and the increase in profit with the increase in distance from the origin is of crucial importance in locating the optimal point *graphically.*

(iii) *Graphing the operational constraints*

Each constraint involves an inequality that, when graphed, represents a region called the area of feasibility for the resource represented by the inequality. Each inequality can be graphed by first graphing the associated equality and testing for the region.

For the molding department, the inequality $3X_1 + 3X_2 \leqq 210$ is associated with the equation $3X_1 + 3X_2 = 210$.

For $X_1 = 0, X_2 = 70 \longrightarrow$ Graph the point $F(0, 70)$
For $X_2 = 0, X_1 = 70 \longrightarrow$ Graph the point $G(70, 0)$

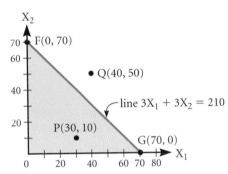

Test the point (0, 0)

$3X_1 + 3X_2 = 3(0) + 3(0) = 0 \leqq 210$

Since the coordinates $(0, 0)$ satisfy the inequality, the point $(0, 0)$ is a point in the region described by the inequality. Therefore, the region described by $3X_1 + 3X_2 \leqq 210$ is the area to the left of the line $3X_1 + 3X_2 = 210$. However, since X_1 and X_2 cannot be negative, the combinations (X_1, X_2) that are feasible are represented by the points inside the triangle OFG as shown in the diagram.

The point P(30, 10) lies inside the triangle OFG indicating that the combination $(30, 10)$ is possible. The coordinates $(30, 10)$ indicate a combination of 30 units of Product A and 10 units of Product B.

To produce 30 units of Product A requires $3(30) = 90$ hours in molding; to produce 10 units of Product B requires $3(10) = 30$ hours in molding. The combination requires a total of 120 hours in molding—less than the 210 hours available. The combination 30 units of Product A and 10 units of Product B is feasible.

The point Q (40, 50), representing a production of 40 units of Product A and 50 units of Product B, lies outside the area of feasibility. This combination is not possible.

To produce 40 units of Product A requires $3(40) = 120$ hours in molding; to produce 50 units of Product B requires $3(50) = 150$ hours in molding. The combination requires a total of 270 hours in molding; since only 210 hours are available, the combination 40 units of Product A and 50 units of Product B is not feasible.

For the paint shop, the inequality $4X_1 + 2X_2 \leqq 200$ is associated with the equation $4X_1 + 2X_2 = 200$.

For $X_1 = 0, X_2 = 100 \longrightarrow$ Graph point H(0, 100)
For $X_2 = 0, X_1 = 50 \longrightarrow$ Graph point J(50, 0)

The area of feasibility for the paint shop is the triangle OHJ as shown in the diagram below.

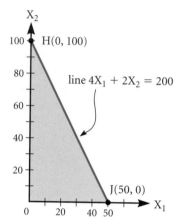

The area of feasibility for finishing, defined by the inequality $X_1 + 2X_2 \leqq 120$ and the non-negative constraints, is the triangle OAK as shown in the diagram below.

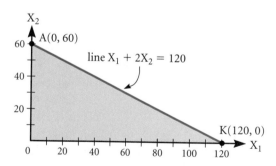

Finally, the area of feasibility for shipping, defined by the inequality $X_1 \leqq 40$ and the non-negative constraints, is the area between the X_2 axis and the line represented by $X_1 = 40$ as shown below.

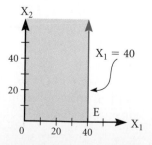

(b) *Graphing the area of feasibility*

The area of feasibility for the combined resources is the area containing the points that satisfy all operational constraints. This area is found by graphing the individual constraints on the same set of axes (see Figure 2). For molding and painting combined, the area of feasibility is the intersection of the two triangles OFG and OHJ, that is, the area OFCJ as shown below.

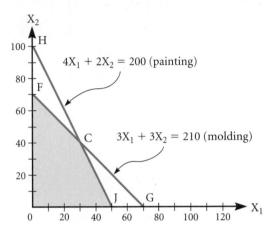

For molding, painting, and finishing combined, the area of feasibility is the area OABCJ as shown below.

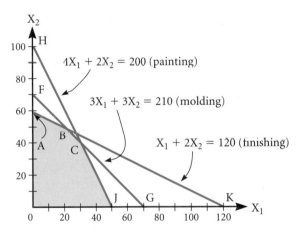

When shipping is also considered, the area of feasibility is reduced to the area OABCDE as shown in Figure 2.

FIGURE 2 **Area of Feasibility**

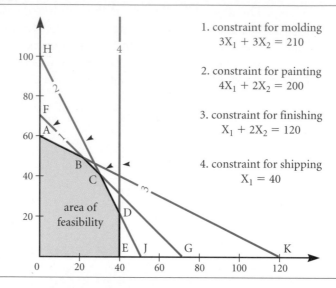

1. constraint for molding
$$3X_1 + 3X_2 = 210$$

2. constraint for painting
$$4X_1 + 2X_2 = 200$$

3. constraint for finishing
$$X_1 + 2X_2 = 120$$

4. constraint for shipping
$$X_1 = 40$$

(c) *Locating the optimal point*

Once we have determined the area of feasibility by graphing the operational constraints, we need to locate the optimal point—the point whose coordinates are the combination (X_1, X_2) which generates the maximum profit. One way to do this is by introducing graphs of the objective function $P = 20X_1 + 30X_2$ by the method previously explained.

In this case, a convenient value of $P = \$1500$.

For $X_1 = 0 \longrightarrow X_2 = 50 \longrightarrow$ Graph point $S(0, 50)$.
For $X_2 = 0 \longrightarrow X_1 = 75 \longrightarrow$ Graph point $T(75, 0)$.

Draw the profit line ST (see Figure 3).

Part of the iso-profit line ST passes through the area of feasibility. Any combination (X_1, X_2) that represents the coordinates of a point on this line provides a profit of $1500.

The line ST is one of the family of parallel lines defined by the equation $P = 20X_1 + 30X_2$. Some of the lines represent a profit lower than $1500.00, others a profit greater than $1500.00, depending on whether such lines are closer to the origin or farther away from the origin.

For example, a line parallel to ST through the point A(0, 60)—see Figure 3—yields a profit of

$$P = 20(0) + 30(60) = 0 + 1800 = \$1800.00.$$

This particular iso-profit line passes through the area of feasibility and any combination of (X_1, X_2) falling on this line generates a profit of $1800.00.

FIGURE 3   Locating the Optimal Point

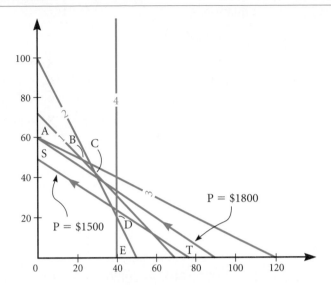

As long as a profit line passes through the area of feasibility OABCDE and is farther away from the origin, it will generate a profit higher than that which is obtainable from a profit line closer to the origin. However, for profit lines that do not pass through the area of feasibility, any combination (X_1, X_2) that represents a point on such a line does not satisfy all the constraints and is thus not attainable.

Therefore, the profit line that will generate the greatest possible profit is the line located farthest away from the origin such that at least one point on the line is still within the area of feasibility OABCDE.

When considering possible lines parallel to the two profit lines drawn in Figure 3, it becomes apparent that the profit line farthest from the origin that still passes through the area OABCDE is a line drawn through the point B. The point B must be the optimal point representing the combination (X_1, X_2) for which the profit is the maximum amount attainable with the given combination of resources.

Note: The optimal point is a point on the boundary of the area of feasibility. This location is generally true for any linear programming problem.

STEP 3   **Finding the Optimal Combination (X_1, X_2) and the Maximum Amount of Profit**
The coordinates of point B represent the number of units of Product A and Product B that should be produced to maximize the profit. This combination (X_1, X_2) provides for optimal utilization of the available resources; it can be found algebraically by solving the system of equations representing the two lines that form the point B.

From Figure 2, it is apparent that point B is formed by the intersection of line AK, represented by $X_1 + 2X_2 = 120$, and line FG, represented by $3X_1 + 3X_2 = 210$.

Equation ① ⟶ $X_1 + 2X_2 = 120$
Equation ② ⟶ $3X_1 + 3X_2 = 210$

To eliminate X_1,

multiply ① by 3 ⟶ $3X_1 + 6X_2 = 360$
subtract ② ⟶ $3X_1 + 3X_2 = 210$
$$3X_2 = 150$$
$$X_2 = 50$$

To find X_1, substitute $X_2 = 50$ in ①.

$$X_1 + 2(50) = 120$$
$$X_1 + 100 = 120$$
$$X_1 = 20$$

The solution to the system is $(X_1, X_2) = (20, 50)$.

For $(X_1, X_2) = (20, 50)$,
$P = 20X_1 + 30X_2 = 20(20) + 30(50) = 400 + 1500 = 1900$.

The optimal production is 20 units of Product A and 50 units of Product B for a maximum profit of $1900.00.

The Corner-Point Method of Finding the Optimal Combination (X_1, X_2)

As was mentioned earlier, the optimal point is a point on the boundary of the area of feasibility. In fact, if a single solution exists, the optimal point is *always* a corner point on the boundary of the area of feasibility. The **corner-point method** involves finding the coordinates of each corner point in the area of feasibility, then substituting into the objective function to identify the corner point that provides the greatest profit (or the least cost).

To check that point B is the optimal point, use the corner-point method and Figure 2.

The coordinates of point A, which can be read from Figure 2, are $A(X_1, X_2) = (0, 60)$.

The coordinates of point B, which were calculated above, are $B(X_1, X_2) = (20, 50)$.

From Figure 2, you can see that point C is formed by the intersection of line FG, represented by $3X_1 + 3X_2 = 210$, and line HJ, represented by $4X_1 + 2X_2 = 200$.

Equation ① ⟶ $3X_1 + 3X_2 = 210$
Equation ② ⟶ $4X_1 + 2X_2 = 200$

To eliminate X_2,

multiply ① by 2 ⟶ $6X_1 + 6X_2 = 420$
multiply ② by 3, and subtract ⟶ $12X_1 + 6X_2 = 600$
$$-6X_1 = -180$$
$$X_1 = 30$$

To find X_2, substitute $X_1 = 30$ in ①.

$$3(30) + 3X_2 = 210$$
$$90 + 3X_2 = 210$$
$$3X_2 = 120$$
$$X_2 = 40$$

The coordinates of point C are $C(X_1, X_2) = (30, 40)$.

From Figure 2, you can see that point D is formed by the intersection of line HJ, represented by $4X_1 + 2X_2 = 200$ and line DE, represented by $X_1 = 40$. Since $X_1 = 40$, substitute this into line HJ to find X_2.

$$4(40) + 2X_2 = 200$$
$$160 + 2X_2 = 200$$
$$2X_2 = 40$$
$$X_2 = 20$$

The coordinates of point D are $D(X_1, X_2) = (40, 20)$.

The coordinates of point E, which can be read from Figure 2, are $E(X_1, X_2) = (40, 0)$.

The optimum point is the corner point A, B, C, D, or E whose coordinates produce the greatest profit P when substituted into the objective function $P = 20X_1 + 30X_2$.

For $A(X_1, X_2) = (0, 60)$,
$P = 20(0) + 30(60) = 0 + 1800 = 1800$.

For $B(X_1, X_2) = (20, 50)$,
$P = 20(20) + 30(50) = 400 + 1500 = 1900$.

For $C(X_1, X_2) = (30, 40)$,
$P = 20(30) + 30(40) = 600 + 1200 = 1800$.

For $D(X_1, X_2) = (40, 20)$,
$P = 20(40) + 30(20) = 800 + 600 = 1400$.

For $E(X_1, X_2) = (40, 0)$,
$P = 20(40) + 30(0) = 800 + 0 = 800$.

Maximum profit is \$1900 by producing 20 units of Product A and 50 units of Product B.

Note: The available resources are used as follows.

Molding $3X_1 + 3X_2 = 3(20) + 3(50) = 60 + 150 = 210$
Since the maximum time in molding is 210 hours, molding capacity is totally used.

Painting $4X_1 + 2X_2 = 4(20) + 2(50) = 80 + 100 = 180$
Since the maximum available time is 200 hours, 20 hours are unused.

Finishing $X_1 + 2X_2 = 20 + 2(50) = 20 + 100 = 120$
Since the maximum available time is 120 hours, finishing capacity is totally used.

Shipping $X_1 = 20$. Since capacity is 40 units, 50% of shipping's capability to handle Product A is used.

EXAMPLE II.2B   A company makes two kinds of boots. X_1 is top quality; X_2 is ordinary quality. Producing top quality boots takes twice as long as ordinary quality. If only ordinary quality boots are made, 3000 pairs of boots can be made per week. Enough material is available to make 2400 pairs of boots. The top quality boots require a special zipper and enough zippers are available for 1100 pairs per week. Ordinary zippers are available to make 2200 ordinary pairs per week. Top quality boots give a profit of $32.00 per pair and ordinary quality boots give a profit of $24.00 per pair. Use the graphic method of linear programming to find the optimal production mix, the total contribution to profit of this mix, and the use of the available resources.

Solution

Constraints	Resource Quantity Required Per Pair of Boots		Available Resource Quantity
	Top Quality	Ordinary Quality	
1. Time units	2	1	3000
2. Material	1	1	2400
3. Special zipper	1	N/A	1100
4. Ordinary zipper	N/A	1	2200
PROFIT	$32	$24	MAXIMIZE

STEP 1   Statement of Problem in Algebraic Form

(a) Objective function $P = 32X_1 + 24X_2$

(b) Operational constraints   1. $2X_1 + X_2 \leq 3000$
                                2. $X_1 + X_2 \leq 2400$
                                3. $X_1 \leq 1100$
                                4. $X_2 \leq 2200$

(c) Non-negative constraints $X_1 \geq 0; X_2 \geq 0$

STEP 2   Graphic Solution
Area OABCDE is the area of feasibility. The optimal point is C.

FIGURE 4 **Graphic Solution**

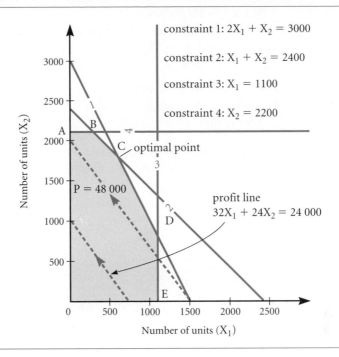

constraint 1: $2X_1 + X_2 = 3000$

constraint 2: $X_1 + X_2 = 2400$

constraint 3: $X_1 = 1100$

constraint 4: $X_2 = 2200$

C optimal point

$P = 48\ 000$

profit line
$32X_1 + 24X_2 = 24\ 000$

Number of units (X_2)

Number of units (X_1)

STEP 3   **Conclusion**

The optimal point C is formed by the intersection of

Constraint ① ⟶ $2X_1 + X_2 = 3000$ and
Constraint ② ⟶ $\underline{X_1 + X_2 = 2400}$
subtract ⟶ $X_1 = 600$
$X_2 = 1800$

The coordinates of the optimal point are (600, 1800).

Using the slope-point method, find the coordinates of the corner points of the area of feasibility, namely points A, B, C, D, and E. Then substitute the coordinates into the objective function to find the maximum profit P.

The coordinates of point A, which can be read from Figure 4, are $A(X_1, X_2) = (0, 2200)$.

From Figure 4, we see that point B is formed by the intersection of constraint 2, represented by $X_1 + X_2 = 2400$, and constraint 4, represented by $X_2 = 2200$. Since $X_2 = 2200$, substitute this into constraint 2 to find X_1.

$X_1 + 2200 = 2400$
$X_1 = 200$

Therefore, the coordinates of point B are $B(X_1, X_2) = (200, 2200)$.

The coordinates of point C, which were calculated above, are $C(X_1, X_2) = (600, 1800)$.

From Figure 4 we see that point D is formed by the intersection of constraint 1, represented by $2X_1 + X_2 = 3000$, and constraint 3, represented by $X_1 = 1100$. Since $X_1 = 1100$, substitute this into constraint 1 to find X_2.

$2(1100) + X_2 = 3000$

$2200 + X_2 = 3000$

$X_2 = 800$

Therefore, the coordinates of point D are $D(X_1, X_2) = (1100, 800)$.

The coordinates of point E, which can be read from Figure 4, are $E(X_1, X_2) = (1100, 0)$.

Substituting the coordinates of points A, B, C, D, and E into the objective function $P = 32X_1 + 24X_2$ gives the following results.

For $A(X_1, X_2) = (0, 2200)$,
$P = 32(0) + 24(2200) = 0 + 52\ 800 = 52\ 800$.

For $B(X_1, X_2) = (200, 2200)$,
$P = 32(200) + 24(2200) = 6400 + 52\ 800 = 59\ 200$.

For $C(X_1, X_2) = (600, 1800)$,
$P = 32(600) + 24(1800) = 19\ 200 + 43\ 200 = 62\ 400$.

For $D(X_1, X_2) = (1100, 800)$,
$P = 32(1100) + 24(800) = 35\ 200 + 19\ 200 = 54\ 400$.

For $E(X_1, X_2) = (1100, 0)$,
$P = 32(1100) + 24(0) = 35\ 200 + 0 = 35\ 200$.

Remember that $O(0,0)$ is a corner point of the area of feasibility, but no profit will be made if no products are produced.

The coordinates of the optimal point are (600, 1800), the coordinates for point C. Point C generates the greatest profit.

The optimal solution requires producing 600 pairs of top quality boots and 1800 pairs of ordinary quality boots.

The maximum profit that can be generated is

$P = 32(600) + 24(1800) = 19\ 200 + 43\ 200 = \$62\ 400$

Resource use for the optimal production is as follows:

1. Time used $2(600) + 1800 = 3000$; since 3000 time units are available, time capacity is totally used
2. Material $600 + 1800 = 2400$; since material for 2400 pairs is available, the supply of material is totally used.
3. Special zippers   600 pairs used; 1100 pairs available; 500 pairs unused.
4. Ordinary zippers 1800 pairs used; 2200 pairs available; 400 pairs unused.

Exercise II.2

A. Solve each of the following two linear programming problems. Show in your answer

   a) an algebraic statement of the problem;

   b) a graph of the area of feasibility showing the optimal point;

   c) an algebraic computation of the optimal solution including the amount of profit and utilization of the resources.

   1. A manufacturer produces two products. Product A contributes $7.00 per unit to profit and Product B contributes $5.00 per unit. The manufacturing process requires time on each of three machines. Product A requires eight hours on Machine I, two hours on Machine II, and four hours on Machine III. Product B requires five hours on each of Machines I and II, and six hours on Machine III. Machine I is available for 4200 hours, Machine II for 2000 hours, and Machine III for 2800 hours.

   2. Swim Quip has production facilities for assembling and distributing residential pool heaters and pool filters. The facilities consist of departments for subassembly, final assembly, finishing, and testing. Each filter requires twelve hours in subassembly, two hours in final assembly, and one hour in finishing. Each heater requires thirty-six hours in subassembly, 3.2 hours in final assembly, four hours in finishing, and two hours in testing. Capacity is 3600 hours in subassembly, 480 hours in final assembly, 324 hours in finishing, and 100 hours in testing. Each filter contributes $60.00 to profit and each heater contributes $180.00 to profit.

B. Solve each of the following problems.

   1. A manufacturer produces two types of product. Product A requires three units of material, one unit of time in fabricating, and one unit of time in finishing. Product B requires one unit of material, three units of time in fabricating, and one unit of time in finishing. Maximum daily resources are 24 units of material, 30 units of time in fabricating, and 12 units of time in finishing. Product A contributes $30.00 per unit to profit while Product B contributes $40.00 per unit.

   a) State the problem in algebraic form.

   b) Graphically solve the problem.

   c) Find the optimal solution algebraically and determine the maximum profit.

2. A manufacturer makes two types of brackets. Brackets of both types are formed in Department A from a piece of steel of which 750 are available for the time period. Each ordinary bracket requires four time units in Department A while each fancy bracket requires ten time units. The total number of time units available in Department A for the time period is 4800. The ordinary bracket is finished in Department B and requires four time units while the fancy bracket is finished in Department C and requires six time units. 2400 time units are available in each of the two finishing departments. The ordinary bracket contributes $4.00 to profit and the fancy bracket contributes $6.00.

   a) State the problem in algebraic form.

   b) Graphically solve the problem.

   c) Find the optimal solution algebraically and determine the maximum profit.

3. The Debris Company intends to market two types of containers. Each square container costs the company $20.00 and each round container costs $30.00. Each square container occupies 20 square units of floor space while each round container occupies 10 square units. There is $12 000.00 available per period to buy containers of either type and 8000 units of floor space available to store them. Each container weighs 100 kg and the floor of the storage room will not support more than 45 000 kg. Each square container contributes $30.00 to profit while each round container contributes $20.00. Demand is such that no more than 350 round containers can be sold. Using the graphic method of linear programming or the corner-point method, find the optimum product mix and the total contribution to profit of this mix.

SUMMARY OF FORMULAE

Formula II.1

$TR = TC + NI$

$$\text{TOTAL REVENUE} = \text{TOTAL COST} + \text{NET INCOME}$$

Formula II.2

$TR = (X)(P)$

$$\text{TOTAL REVENUE} = \text{VOLUME IN UNITS} \times \text{UNIT REVENUE}$$

Formula II.3

$TC = FC + TVC$

$$\text{TOTAL COST} = \text{FIXED COST} + \text{TOTAL VARIABLE COST}$$

Formula II.4

$TVC = (X)(VC)$

$$\text{TOTAL VARIABLE COST} = \text{VOLUME IN UNITS} \times \text{VARIABLE COST PER UNIT}$$

Formula II.5

$$\text{TR} = \text{FC} + \text{TVC} + \text{NI}$$

TOTAL REVENUE = FIXED COST + TOTAL VARIABLE COST + NET INCOME

GLOSSARY

Area of feasibility   in a linear programming graph, the area containing all the points (X_1, X_2) that represent the possible combinations in the product mix

Break-even analysis   a method of determining the level of output at which a business neither makes a profit nor sustains a loss

Break-even chart   a graphic representation of cost-volume-profit relationships used to identify the break-even point

Break-even point   the level of output at which net income is zero

Corner-point method   the method of substituting the coordinates of each corner point of the graphical area of feasibility into the objective function to determine the optimal point

Fixed costs   costs that remain constant for the time period for all levels of output considered

Iso-profit line   the line representing the various possible combinations in the product mix that yield the same amount of profit

Linear programming   a mathematical technique used to determine the optimal allocation of limited resources

Non-negative constraints   algebraic expressions stating that the variables used are limited to positive values

Objective function   an algebraic representation of the goal to be achieved in a linear programming problem

Operational constraints   an algebraic representation of the limitations imposed on operations because of the limited availability of various resources

Optimal point   the point whose coordinates represent the product mix at which the profit is maximized or the cost minimized

Variable costs   costs that are constant per unit of output regardless of volume; they fluctuate in total amount as volume fluctuates

Finding the Rate of Interest (i) Without Preprogramming

A. Finding the conversion rate i without preprogramming when the future value of a simple annuity is known

Finding the periodic rate of interest when S_n, R, and n are known is a rather awkward problem. Substituting the known values in Formula 11.1 or the general solution of the formula for i results in an exponential equation that is difficult to solve.

For example, if $S_n = 25\,000.00$, R = 500.00, and $n = 32$, the substitution in Formula 11.1 gives

$$25\,000.00 = 500.00\left(\frac{[(1 + i)^{32} - 1]}{i}\right)$$

$$50.00 = \frac{[(1 + i)^{32} - 1]}{i}$$

$$50.00i = (1 + i)^{32} - 1$$

$$(1 + i)^{32} - 50.00i - 1 = 0$$

However, instead of trying to solve the equation, the value of i can be found by using an approximation method based on trial and error. A value for i is arbitrarily selected and the compounding factor $\frac{(1 + i)^n - 1}{i}$ is computed. The numerical value of the factor indicates whether the rate to be found is more or less than the selected rate. The process of choosing a rate, computing the compounding factor, and comparing this factor with the actual compounding factor is repeated until an approximation sufficiently close to the actual rate is obtained.

To avoid writing the accumulation factor repeatedly, the factor $\frac{(1 + i)^n - 1}{i}$ is represented by the symbol $s_{\overline{n}|i}$ (read "s angle n at i").

$$\frac{(1 + i)^n - 1}{i} = s_{\overline{n}|i}$$

$$S_n = Rs_{\overline{n}|i}$$

EXAMPLE III.1A

Find the nominal rate of interest at which $200.00 deposited at the end of each quarter for fifteen years will amount to $20 000.00.

Solution

$S_n = 20\,000.00;\quad R = 200.00;\quad n = 15(4) = 60$

$$s_{\overline{n}|i} = \frac{(1+i)^{60}-1}{i} = \frac{20\,000}{200} = 100.0000$$

We want to find the quarterly rate i for which the accumulation factor $s_{\overline{60}|i} = 100.0000$. The first selection of i should allow for a reasonable range within which the nominal rate might be expected to fall. For most practical purposes, this range is 6% to 20%. Thus, we will try 12% as our initial selection.

Try $i = \dfrac{12\%}{4} = 3\% = 0.03.$

$$s_{\overline{60}|3\%} = \frac{(1.03)^{60}-1}{0.03} = 163.05344$$

Since $s_{\overline{60}|3\%} = 163.05344$ is greater than $s_{\overline{60}|i} = 100.0000$, the selected rate of 3% is greater than the actual rate i. The actual nominal rate must be less than 12%.

We must now choose a second selection for i. This selection should allow for the relationship between the value of the actual compounding factor and the factor computed for the first selected value of i. It should preferably result in a compounding factor smaller than 100.00. A considerable drop in rate is indicated since $s_{\overline{60}|3\%}$ is considerably greater than $s_{\overline{60}|i}$.

Try a nominal rate of 6% where $i = 1.5\% = 0.015.$
$s_{\overline{60}|1.5\%} = 96.214651$
This means $s_{\overline{60}|1.5\%} < s_{\overline{60}|i}$, that is, $i > 1.5\%$.

By now we know that $1.5\% < i < 3\%$. The nominal rate lies between 6% and 12%. Furthermore, because of the closeness of $s_{60|1.5\%}$ to $s_{\overline{60}|i}$, the actual nominal rate must be much closer to 6% than to 12%.

Try a nominal rate of 7% where $i = 1.75\% = 0.0175.$
$s_{\overline{60}|1.75\%} = 104.67522$
$1.5\% < i < 1.75\%$ and $6\% <$ nominal rate $< 7\%$.

For a closer approximation, further rates can be used. In doing so, pay attention to the size of the computed accumulation factors relative to the actual accumulation factor.

For $i = 1.6\%,\ s_{\overline{60}|1.6\%} = 99.495336 \quad i > 1.6\%$

For $i = 1.62\%,\ s_{\overline{60}|1.62\%} = 100.16772 \quad i < 1.62\%$

For $i = 1.61\%,\ s_{\overline{60}|1.61\%} = 99.830835 \quad i > 1.61\%$

$1.61\% < i < 1.62\%$

$i = 1.615\%$ approximately

$6.44\% <$ nominal rate of interest $< 6.48\%$

The nominal rate of interest is 6.46% approximately.

Programmed solution

0 [PV] 20 000 [FV] 200 [PMT] 60 [N] [CPT] [%i] [1.6150267]

(or −200) Please wait

The accuracy of the approximation becomes apparent when comparing the answer with the precise computed value of 1.6150267% or a nominal rate of 6.4601068%.

EXAMPLE III.1B

A debt of $4000.00 is due in two years. An agreement was made whereby the debt could be paid off by making monthly payments of $145.00 at the end of each month for the next two years. What is the nominal rate of interest allowed on the payments?

Solution

$S_n = 4000.00; \quad R = 145.00; \quad n = 24$

$$s_{\overline{24}|i} = \frac{4000.00}{145.00} = 27.586207$$

Try a nominal rate of 12%. $i = 1\% = 0.01$

$s_{\overline{24}|1\%} = 26.973465 \longrightarrow i > 1\%$

Try a nominal rate of 18%. $i = 1.5\% = 0.015$

$s_{\overline{24}|1.25\%} = 28.633520 \longrightarrow 1\% < i < 1.5\%$

Try a nominal rate of 15%. $i = 1.25\% = 0.0125$

$s_{\overline{24}|1.25\%} = 27.788083 \longrightarrow 1\% < i < 1.25\%$

For $i = 1.15\%$, $s_{\overline{24}|1.15\%} = 27.458606 \longrightarrow 1.15\% < i < 1.25\%$

For $i = 1.19\%$, $s_{\overline{24}|1.19\%} = 27.589811 \longrightarrow i = 1.19\%$ approximately

The nominal rate of interest is approximately 14.28%.

Programmed solution

0 [PV] 4000 [FV] 145 [PMT] 24 [N] [CPT] [%i] [1.1889046]

(or −145)

The computed value of $i = 1.1889046\%$ or a nominal rate of 14.266855%.

B. Finding the conversion rate i without preprogramming when the present value of a simple annuity is known

When A_n, R, and n are known, the periodic rate of interest can be found by a method similar to the one used for finding the rate of interest when S_n is known. The only difference is that the present value factor $\dfrac{1 - (1 + i)^{-n}}{i}$ is to be approximated.

To avoid writing the present value factor repeatedly, the factor $\frac{1 - (1 + i)^{-n}}{i}$ is represented by the symbol $a_{\overline{n}|i}$ (read "a angle n at i").

$$\frac{1 - (1 + i)^{-n}}{i} = a_{\overline{n}|i}$$

$$A_n = Ra_{\overline{n}|i}$$

However, take care to allow for the fact that the value of $a_{\overline{n}|i}$ is inversely related to i; that is, the greater i, the smaller will be $a_{\overline{n}|i}$.

EXAMPLE III.1C

What is the nominal rate of interest on a loan of $5000.00 repaid by payments of $425.00 made at the end of each quarter for four years?

Solution

$A_n = 5000.00; \quad R = 425.00; \quad n = 16$

$$a_{\overline{n}|i} = \frac{1 - (1 + i)^{-n}}{i} = \frac{A_n}{R}$$

$$a_{\overline{16}|i} = \frac{5000.00}{425.00} = 11.764706$$

For a nominal rate of 12%, $i = 3\%$ and $a_{\overline{16}|3\%} = 12.561102$.
Since $a_{\overline{16}|3\%} > a_{\overline{16}|i}$, $3\% < i$ due to the inverse relationship between $a_{\overline{n}|i}$ and i. Therefore, the next attempt should involve a rate *greater* than 3%.

For $i = 4\%$, $\quad a_{\overline{16}|4\%} \quad = 11.652296 \longrightarrow 3\% < i < 4\%$

For $i = 3.8\%$, $\quad a_{\overline{16}|3.8\%} \quad = 11.826111 \longrightarrow 3.8\% < i < 4\%$

For $i = 3.9\%$, $\quad a_{\overline{16}|3.9\%} \quad = 11.738726 \longrightarrow 3.8\% < i < 3.9\%$

For $i = 3.87\%$, $a_{\overline{16}|3.87\%} \quad = 11.764841$

Thus, $i = 3.87\%$ (approximately) and the nominal rate is 15.48%.

Programmed solution

0 [FV] 5000 [PV] 425 [PMT] 16 [N] [CPT] [%i] [3.870155]

The computed value of $i = 3.870155\%$ or a nominal rate of 15.48062%.

EXAMPLE III.1D

A car can be bought for $8240.00 plus GST of 7%. A financing plan is available requiring a down payment of $800.00 and monthly instalments of $226.00 for three and a half years. What is the nominal rate of interest?

Solution

$A_n = 8240.00 + 7\%$ of $8240.00 - 800.00 = 8016.80$

$R = 226.00; \quad n = (3.5)(12) = 42$

$$a_{\overline{42}|i} = \frac{8016.80}{226.00} = 35.472566$$

For $i = 1\%$, $a_{\overline{42}|1\%} = 34.158108 \longrightarrow i < 1\%$

For $i = 0.8\%$, $a_{\overline{42}|0.8\%} = 35.552612 \longrightarrow 0.8\% < i < 1\%$

For $i = 0.9\%$, $a_{\overline{42}|0.9\%} = 34.845543 \longrightarrow 0.8\% < i < 0.9\%$

For $i = 0.85\%$, $a_{\overline{42}|0.85\%} = 35.196583 \longrightarrow 0.8\% < i < 0.85\%$

For $i = 0.82\%$, $a_{\overline{42}|0.82\%} = 35.409596 \longrightarrow 0.8\% < i < 0.82\%$

For $i = 0.81\%$, $a_{\overline{42}|0.81\%} = 35.4810031 \longrightarrow 0.81\% < i < 0.82\%$

For $i = 0.811\%$, $a_{\overline{42}|0.811\%} = 35.473853$

The value of $i = 0.811\%$ approximately and the nominal rate is approximately 9.732%.

Programmed solution

0 [FV]   8016.80 [PV]   226 [PMT]   42 [N]   [CPT]   [%i]   [0.8111800]

The more precise computed value of $i = 0.81118\%$ and the nominal rate $= 9.73416\%$.

Exercise III.1 (same as portions of Exercise 13.3)

A. Compute the nominal rate of interest for each of the following four ordinary annuities.

	Future value S_n	Present value A_n	Periodic rent	Payment interval	Term	Compounding period
1.	$9000.00		$143.54	3 months	8 years	quarterly
2.	$4800.00		$ 49.00	1 month	5 years	monthly
3.		$7400.00	$119.06	1 month	7 years	monthly
4.		$5540.00	$800.00	6 months	5 years	semi-annually

B. Answer each of the following questions.

1. Compute the nominal rate of interest at which $350.00 paid at the end of every three months for six years accumulates to $12 239.76.

2. What is the nominal rate of interest if a four-year loan of $6000.00 is repaid by monthly payments of $178.58?

3. Réné contributed $250.00 every three months into an RRSP for ten years. What was the nominal rate of interest earned by the RRSP if the balance in Réné's account just after he made his last contribution was $19 955.40?

4. Rita converted a RRSP balance of $119 875.67 into an RRIF that will pay her $1800.00 at the end of every month for nine years. What is the nominal rate of interest?

5. A car valued at $11 400.00 can be bought for 10% down and monthly payments of $318.56 for three and a half years. What is the effective cost of financing?

6. A property worth $40 000.00 can be purchased for 20% down and quarterly mortgage payments of $1100.00 for 25 years. What effective rate of interest is charged?

III.2 FINDING THE CONVERSION RATE i FOR ANNUITIES DUE

A. Finding i when the future value S_n(due) is known

Since Formula 12.1 is awkward for finding i, we can develop the formula into a more suitable form.

$$S_n(\text{due}) = R(1 + i)\left[\frac{(1 + i)^n - 1}{i}\right] \quad\text{———— Formula 12.1}$$

$$= R\left[\frac{(1 + i)^{n+1} - (1 + i)}{i}\right] \quad\text{———— multiplying by } (1 + i)$$

$$= R\left[\frac{(1 + i)^{n+1} - 1 - i}{i}\right]$$

$$= R\left[\frac{(1 + i)^{n+1} - 1}{i} - \frac{i}{i}\right]$$

$$\boxed{S_n(\text{due}) - R\left[\frac{(1 + i)^{n+1} - 1}{i} - 1\right]}$$

Since the factor $\dfrac{(1 + i)^{n+1} - 1}{i}$ may be represented by the symbol $s_{\overline{n+1}|i}$,

$$\boxed{S_n(\text{due}) = R(s_{\overline{n+1}|i} - 1)} \quad\text{———— \textbf{Formula III.1}}$$

EXAMPLE III.2A   At what nominal rate of interest compounded semi-annually will $320.00 deposited at the beginning of every six months for twelve years accumulate to $15 000.00?

Solution $S_n(\text{due}) = 15\ 000.00; \quad R = 320.00; \quad n = 12(2) = 24$

$$15\ 000.00 = 320.00\left[\frac{(1 + i)^{24+1} - 1}{i} - 1\right] \quad\text{—— substituting in Formula III.1}$$

$$\frac{15\,000.00}{320.00} = \frac{(1 + i)^{25} - 1}{i} - 1$$

$$46.875 + 1 = \frac{(1 + i)^{25} - 1}{i} = s_{\overline{25}|i}$$

$$s_{\overline{25}|i} = 47.875$$

Choose a reasonable nominal rate, such as 12%; $i = 6\%$.

For $i = 6\%$, $s_{\overline{25}|6\%} = 54.864512 \longrightarrow i < 6\%$

For $i = 4\%$, $s_{\overline{25}|4\%} = 41.645908 \longrightarrow 4\% < i < 6\%$

For $i = 5\%$, $s_{\overline{25}|5\%} = 47.727098 \longrightarrow 5\% < i < 6\%$

Since 47.727098 is much closer to 47.875 than 54.864512, i is much closer to 5% than to 6%; try a value of i very close to 5%, such as 5.1%.

For $i = 5.1\%$, $s_{\overline{25}|5.1\%}$ $= 48.390405$ $5\% < i < 5.1\%$

For $i = 5.02\%$, $s_{\overline{25}|5.02\%}$ $= 47.858911$ $5.02\% < i < 5.1\%$

For $i = 5.023\%$, $s_{\overline{25}|5.023\%}$ $= 47.878720$ $i = 5.023\%$ approximately

Since the semi-annual rate of interest is approximately 5.023%, the nominal rate of interest = 2(5.023%) = 10.046%.

B. Finding i when the present value A_n(due) is known

Formula 12.2 too is awkward to use when finding i and can be developed into a more suitable form.

$$A_n(\text{due}) = R(1 + i)\left[\frac{1 - (1 + i)^{-n}}{i}\right] \text{———— Formula 12.2}$$

$$= R\left[\frac{(1 + i) - (1 + i)^{-n + 1}}{i}\right] \text{———— multiplying by } (1 + i)$$

$$= R\left[\frac{1 + i - (1 + i)^{-(n - 1)}}{i}\right]$$

$$= R\left[\frac{i}{i} + \frac{1 - (1 + i)^{-(n - 1)}}{i}\right]$$

$$\boxed{A_n(\text{due}) = R\left[\frac{1 - (1 + i)^{-(n - 1)}}{i} + 1\right]}$$

Since the factor $\dfrac{1 - (1 + i)^{-(n - 1)}}{i}$ can be represented by the symbol $a_{\overline{n - 1}|i}$

$$\boxed{A_n(\text{due}) = R(a_{\overline{n - 1}|i} + 1)} \text{———— Formula III.2}$$

EXAMPLE III.2B

A lease contract valued at $16 000.00 is to be fulfilled by making payments of $325.00 at the beginning of each month for ten years. What is the nominal rate of interest paid if interest is compounded monthly?

Solution

$A_n(\text{due}) = 16\,000.00; \quad R = 225.00; \quad n = 10(12) = 120$

$$16\,000.00 = 225.00\left[\frac{1 - (1 + i)^{-(120 - 1)}}{i} + 1\right] \text{ — substituting in Formula III.2}$$

$$\frac{16\,000.00}{225.00} = \frac{1 - (1 + i)^{-119}}{i} + 1$$

$$71.111111 - 1 = \frac{1 - (1 + i)^{-119}}{i} = a_{\overline{119}|i}$$

$$a_{\overline{119}|i} = 70.111111$$

For a nominal rate of 12%, $i = 1\%$.

For $i = 1\%$, $\quad a_{\overline{119}|i} = 69.397527$

$a_{\overline{119}|1\%} < a_{\overline{119}|i}$ and $i < 1\%$

For $i = 0.5\%$, $\quad a_{\overline{119}|0.5\%} = 89.523821 \quad 0.5\% < i < 1\%$

For $i = 0.9\%$, $\quad a_{\overline{119}|0.9\%} = 72.854305 \quad 0.9\% < i < 1\%$

For $i = 0.99\%$, $a_{\overline{119}|0.99\%} = 69.732134 \quad 0.9\% < i < 0.99\%$

For $i = 0.95\%$, $a_{\overline{119}|0.95\%} = 71.094814 \quad 0.94 < i < 0.95\%$

For $i = 0.94\%$, $a_{\overline{119}|0.94\%} = 71.441651 \quad 0.94 < i < 0.95\%$

For $i = 0.948$, $\quad a_{\overline{119}|0.948} = 71.163982 \quad 0.948 < i < 0.95\%$

$i = 0.949$ approximately

The nominal rate of interest $= 12(0.949) = 11.39\%$ (approximately).

Exercise III.2 (Same as portions of Exercise 13.3)

A. Find the unknown interest rate in each of the following four annuities due.

	Future Value	Present Value	Periodic Payment	Payment Period	Term	Interest Rate	Conversion Period
1.	$70 000.00		$ 367.00	1 year	25 years	?	annually
2.		$42 000.00	$ 528.00	1 month	10 years	?	monthly
3.		$28 700.00	$2015.00	6 months	15 years	?	semi-annually
4.	$36 000.00		$ 235.00	3 months	12 years	?	quarterly

B. Answer each of the following questions.

1. What nominal rate of interest was paid if contributions of $250.00 made into an RRSP at the beginning of every three months amounted to $14 559.00 after ten years?

2. A vacation property valued at $20 000.00 was bought for fifteen payments of $2750.00 due at the beginning of every six months. What nominal rate of interest was charged?

3. What is the effective rate of interest on a lease contract valued at $13 500.00 if payments of $1500.00 are made at the beginning of every six months for seven years?

4. An insurance policy provides a benefit of $250 000.00 twenty years from now. Alternatively, the policy pays $4220.00 at the beginning of each year for twenty years. What is the effective rate of interest paid?

III.3 FINDING THE RATE OF INTEREST FOR DEFERRED ANNUITIES WHEN THEIR PRESENT VALUE IS KNOWN

A. Finding the rate of interest of a deferred annuity without preprogramming

The rate of interest for a deferred annuity can be determined by trial and error using a method similar to the one previously explained. We obtain a suitable formula for determining i by solving the general problem of finding the present value of a deferred annuity represented in Figure 1.

FIGURE 1 **Graphic representation of the deferred ordinary annuity**

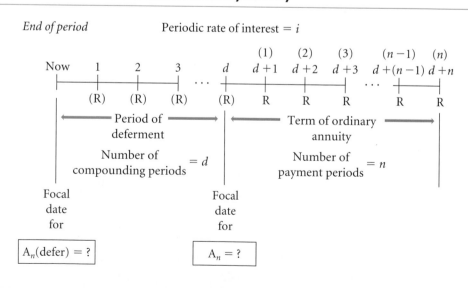

However, since this text uses only the original approach to finding the present value of a deferred annuity when finding R, n, or i, only the formula for this approach is developed.

STEP I   Find the present value of the ordinary annuity at the end of the period of deferment.

$$A_n = R\left[\frac{1 - (1 + i)^{-n}}{i}\right] = Ra_{\overline{n}|i}$$

STEP 2   Find the present value of A_n at the focal point 'now.'

$$P = A_n(1 + i)^{-d}$$

STEP 3   Since P represents the present value of the deferred annuity,

$$\boxed{A_n(\text{defer}) = R(1 + i)^{-d}(a_{\overline{n}|i})}\text{———— Formula III.3}$$

EXAMPLE III.3A   Payments of $900.00 are made at the end of every three months for fifteen years from a fund of $8000.00 earning interest compounded quarterly. If the payments were deferred for ten years, what was the nominal rate of interest?

Solution   The payments form a deferred ordinary annuity. $A_n(\text{defer}) = 8000.00$;

R = 900.00; $n = 15(4) = 60$; $d = 10(4) = 40$

$$8000.00 = 900.00(1 + i)^{-40}\left[\frac{1 - (1 + i)^{-60}}{i}\right]\text{———— using Formula III.3}$$

$$8.8888889 = (1 + i)^{-40}\left[\frac{1 - (1 + i)^{-60}}{i}\right]$$

$$a_{\overline{60}|i} \times (1 + i)^{-40} = 8.8888889$$

For a nominal rate of 12%, the quarterly rate $i = 3\%$.

For $i = 3\%$, $a_{\overline{60}|3\%} \times (1 + 0.03)^{-40}$
$$= (27.675564)(0.3065568) = 8.4841334$$

Since $a_{\overline{60}|3\%} \times (1 + 0.03)^{-40} < a_{\overline{60}|i} \times (1 + i)^{-40}$ ⟶ $3\% > i$,

For $i = 2.9\%$, $a_{\overline{60}|2.9\%} \times (1 + 0.029)^{-40}$
$$= (28.278648)(0.3187022) = 9.0124664 \qquad 2.9\% < i < 3\%$$

For $i = 2.93\%$, $a_{\overline{60}|2.93\%} \times (1 + 0.0293)^{-40}$
$$= (28.095572)(0.3150076) = 8.8503199 \qquad 2.9\% < i < 2.93\%$$

For $i = 2.92\%$, $a_{\overline{60}|2.92\%} \times (1 + 0.0292)^{-40}$
$$(28.156390)(0.3162342) = 8.9040149 \qquad 2.92\% < i < 2.93\%$$

For $i = 2.923\%$, $\qquad a_{\overline{60}|2.923\%} \times (1 + 0.02923)^{-40}$

$$= (28.138123)(0.3158658) = 8.8878694 \qquad i = 2.923\%$$

approximately

The nominal rate of interest $= 4(2.923\%) = 11.69\%$ approximately.

B. Finding the rate of interest of a deferred annuity with programming

While no direct solution is possible with the current generation of prepro-grammed pocket calculators, the preprogramming features can be used in the trial and error method.

Programmed solution for Example III.3A

First, substitute in Formula III.3 and determine the numerical value of the factor containing i.

$$8000.00 = 900.00(1 + i)^{-40}(a_{\overline{60}|i})$$
$$8.8888889 = a_{\overline{60}|i}(1 + i)^{-40}$$

Second, find approximations to the above factor using the following steps repeatedly.

STEP 1   Find $a_{\overline{60}|i}$.

	Press	*Display shows*	
1	PMT	1	
assumed i	%i	i	—— its assumed value
60	N	60	
	CPT PV RESULT A		

STEP 2   Find $(1 + i)^{-40}$.
Now use result A, the value of $a_{\overline{60}|i}$ for the assumed value of i, as the future value for finding $(1 + i)^{-40}$. Result A need not be keyed in; just press FV immediately after PV .

	Press	*Display shows*	
	FV RESULT A		
0	PMT	0	
assumed i	%i	i	—— its assumed value
40	N	40	—— $d = 40$
	CPT PV RESULT B		

Result B is the factor that is to be compared with 8.8888889.

Try $i = 3\%$.

	Press	Display shows	
1	PMT	1	—— start of Step 1
3	%i	3	—— assumed value of i
60	N	60	
CPT	PV	27.675564	—— result A
	FV	27.675564	—— start of Step 2
0	PMT	0	
3	%i	3	—— assumed value of i
40	N	40	—— $d = 40$
CPT	PV	8.4841334	—— result B

Since $a_{\overline{60}|3\%} \times (1 + 0.03)^{-40} < a_{\overline{60}|i} \times (1 + i)^{-40} \longrightarrow 3\% > i,$

Try $i = 2.9\%$,   Result A = 28.278648
Result B = 9.0124664
$2.9\% < i < 3\%$

Try $i = 2.93\%$,   Result B = 8.8503199
$2.9\% < i < 2.93\%$

Try $i = 2.92\%$,   Result B = 8.904149
$2.92\% < i < 2.93\%$

Try $i = 2.923\%$,   Result B = 8.8878694
$i = 2.923\%$ quarterly (approximately)

The nominal rate of interest = 4(2.923%) = 11.69%.

EXAMPLE III.3B

Payments of $400.00 are to be made at the beginning of each month for four years starting two years after a contract valued at $12 000 was signed. What nominal rate of interest compounded monthly has been charged?

Solution

Since the payments are at the beginning of each month, the problem involves a deferred annuity due.

$A_n(\text{defer}) = 12\ 000.00$; $R = 400.00$; $n = 48$; $d = 24$

$12\ 000.00 = 400.00(1 + i)^{-24}(a_{\overline{48}|i})(1 + i)$

$$30 = (1 + i)^{-23}(a_{\overline{48}|i})$$

$$30 = a_{\overline{48}|i}(1 + i)^{-23}$$

For $i = 1.5\%$ Result B = 24.171475   → $i < 1.5\%$

For $i = 1.0\%$,   Result B = 30.206075   → $1.0 < i < 1.5$

For $i = 1.1\%$,   Result B = 28.876037   → $1.0 < i < 1.1$

For $i = 1.01\%$,   Result B = 30.070047   → $1.01 < i < 1.1$

For $i = 1.015\%$, Result B = 30.00229   → $i = 1.015\%$

The nominal rate of interest is 12.18% approximately.

Exercise III.3

A. For each of the following deferred annuities, find i.

	Present Value	Periodic Payment	Made at	Payment Interval	Period of Deferment	Term	Compounding Period
1.	$45 000.00	$7250.00	end	6 months	7 years	16 years	semi-annually
2.	$ 7 500.00	$920.00	beginning	3 months	9 years	7 years	quarterly

B. Answer each of the following questions.

1. Andreas invested $3500.00 in an annuity deferred for twenty-five years that paid him $3000.00 at the end of every six months for twenty years. What rate of interest compounded semi-annually did Andreas receive on his investment?

2. A ten-year $15 000.00 promissory note is redeemed by making semi-annual payments of $4200.00 for fifteen years. If the first payment is due at the date of maturity of the promissory note, what is the effective rate if interest is compounded semi-annually?

3. Judith Ball invested $10 000.00 on her 35th birthday in an annuity that will pay her $5000.00 every six months for twenty years. If the first payment is due six months after her 60th birthday, what is the nominal annual rate of interest compounded semi-annually?

4. A lease can be bought for $64 000.00. If the lease requires payments of $2700.00 every three months for ten years and the first payment is due two years after the lease is purchased, what is the effective annual rate of interest based on quarterly compounding?

III.4 FINDING THE CONVERSION RATE i FOR GENERAL ANNUITIES AND DEFERRED GENERAL ANNUITIES WITHOUT PREPROGRAMMED CALCULATORS

A. Finding i for general annuities without a preprogrammed calculator

Finding the equivalent effective rate per payment period can be done by trial and error using the same method found in Section III.1. When the amount S_{nc} is known, use Formula 11.3, if the present value A_{nc} is given, Formula 11.4 applies.

EXAMPLE III.4A An ordinary annuity of $500.00 per quarter accumulates to $12 500.00 in five years. What rate of interest compounded monthly do the deposits earn?

Solution $S_{nc} = 12\,500.00; \quad R = 500.00; \quad n = 5(4) = 20; \quad c = \dfrac{12}{4} = 3$

The equivalent effective quarterly rate of interest

$f = (1 + i)^3 - 1$

$12\,500.00 = 500.00\, s_{\overline{20}|f}$ ———————————— substituting in Formula 11.3

$\qquad 25.0 = s_{\overline{20}|f}$

For $f = 3\%$,	$s_{\overline{20}|3\%}$	$= 26.870374$	$\longrightarrow f < 3\%$
For $f = 2\%$,	$s_{\overline{20}|2\%}$	$= 24.297369$	$\longrightarrow 2\% < f < 3\%$
For $f = 2.3\%$,	$s_{\overline{20}|2.3\%}$	$= 25.036609$	$\longrightarrow 2\% < f < 2.3\%$
For $f = 2.28\%$,	$s_{\overline{20}|2.28\%}$	$= 24.986482$	$\longrightarrow 2.28\% < f < 2.3\%$
For $f = 2.29\%$,	$s_{\overline{20}|2.29\%}$	$= 24.011530$	$\longrightarrow 2.28\% < f < 2.29\%$
For $f = 2.285\%$,	$s_{\overline{20}|2.285\%}$	$= 24.999002$	$\longrightarrow 2.285\% < f < 2.29\%$
For $f = 2.2854\%$,	$s_{\overline{20}|2.2854\%}$	$= 25.000004$	$\longrightarrow f = 2.2854\%$ approx.

$$(1 + i)^3 = 1.022854$$
$$1 + i = 1.022854^{\frac{1}{3}}$$
$$i = 1.0075607 - 1$$
$$i = 0.0075607 = 0.75607\%$$

The nominal rate of interest is $12(0.75607\%) = 9.07284\%$ compounded monthly.

EXAMPLE III.4B A twenty-year residential mortgage of $45 000.00 is repaid by making payments of $546.83 at the end of each month. What is the rate of interest compounded semi-annually on the mortgage?

Solution $A_{nc} = 45\,000.00; \quad R = 546.83; \quad n = 20(12) = 240; \quad c = \dfrac{2}{12} = \dfrac{1}{6}$

The equivalent effective monthly interest

$f = (1 + i)^{\frac{1}{6}} - 1$

$45\,000.00 = 546.83 a_{\overline{240}|f}$ ———————————— substituting in Formula 11.4

$a_{\overline{240}|f} = 82.292486$

For $f = 1\%$, $a_{\overline{240}|f} = 90.819416$ ⟶ $1\% < f$

For $f = 1.2\%$, $a_{\overline{240}|f} = 78.574552$ ⟶ $1\% < f < 1.2\%$

For $f = 1.14\%$, $a_{\overline{240}|f} = 81.943828$ ⟶ $1\% < f < 1.14\%$

For $f = 1.13\%$, $a_{\overline{240}|f} = 82.529073$ ⟶ $1.13\% < f < 1.14\%$

For $f = 1.134\%$, $a_{\overline{240}|f} = 82.294136$ ⟶ $f = 1.134\%$ approximately

$$(1 + i)^{\frac{1}{6}} = 1.01134$$

$$1 + i = 1.01134^6$$

$$i = 1.0699983 - 1$$

$$i = 0.069983 = 7\% \text{ approximately}$$

The interest rate on the mortgage is 14% compounded semi-annually.

B. Finding the conversion rate *i* for general annuities due

When finding the rate of interest for a general annuity due, first determine the equivalent effective interest per payment period f. Do this calculation using Formula 12.3 when the future value S_{nc}(due) is known or Formula 12.4 when the present value A_{nc}(due) is known.

The computation, however, is made easier by using the two alternate formulae

$$S_{nc}(\text{due}) = R\left[\frac{(1 + f)^{n + 1} - 1}{f} - 1\right] \text{ or } S_{nc}(\text{due}) = R(a_{\overline{n+1}|f} - 1)$$ —— Formula III.4

$$A_{nc}(\text{due}) = R\left[\frac{(1 - f)^{-(n - 1)} + 1}{f} + 1\right] \text{ or } A_{nc}(\text{due}) = R(s_{\overline{n-1}|f} + 1)$$ —— Formula III.5

EXAMPLE III.4C   Deposits of $300.75 made at the beginning of every three months accumulate to $10\,000.00 at the end of six years. What rate of interest compounded monthly has been earned by the deposits?

Solution $S_{nc}(\text{due}) = 10\ 000.00; \quad R = 300.75; \quad n = 6(4) = 24; \quad c = \dfrac{12}{4} = 3;$

$10\ 000.00 = 300.75(s_{\overline{24+1}|f} - 1)$ ——————— substituting in Formula III.4

$33.250208 = s_{\overline{25}|f} - 1$

$\quad\quad s_{\overline{25}|f} = 34.250208$

For $f = 3\%$, $\quad\quad s_{\overline{25}|3\%} \quad = 36.459264 \longrightarrow f < 3\%$

For $f = 2\%$, $\quad\quad s_{\overline{25}|2\%} \quad = 32.030299 \longrightarrow 2\% < f < 3\%$

For $f = 2.5\%$, $\quad\quad s_{\overline{25}|2.5\%} \quad = 34.157763 \longrightarrow 2.5\% < f < 3\%$

For $f = 2.52\%$, $\quad\quad s_{\overline{25}|2.52\%} \quad = 34.246386 \longrightarrow 2.52\% < f < 3\%$

For $f = 2.521\%$, $\quad s_{\overline{25}|2.521\%} \quad = 34.250824 \longrightarrow 2.52\% < f < 2.521\%$

For $f = 2.5208\%$, $\quad s_{\overline{25}|2.5208\%} = 34.249937 \longrightarrow 2.5208\% < f < 2.521\%$

For $f = 2.5209\%$, $\quad s_{\overline{25}|2.5209\%} = 34.250381 \longrightarrow 2.5208\% < f < 2.5209\%$

For $f = 2.52086\%$, $\; s_{\overline{25}|2.52086\%} = 34.250203 \longrightarrow f = 2.52086\%$

$$(1 + i)^3 = 1.0252086$$

$$1 + i = 1.0252086^{\frac{1}{3}} = 1.0083332$$

$$i = 0.0083332 = 0.83332\%$$

The rate of interest is $12(0.83332\%) = 9.99988\%$ or 10% compounded monthly.

EXAMPLE III.4D A property valued at $74 250.00 can be bought by making payments of $913.32 at the beginning of each month for fifteen years. What rate of interest compounded semi-annually is being charged?

Solution $A_{nc}(\text{due}) = 74\ 250.00; \quad R = 913.32; \quad n = 15(12) = 180;$

$c = \dfrac{2}{12} = \dfrac{1}{6} \; ; \; f = (1 + i)^{\frac{1}{6}} - 1$

$74\ 250.00 = 913.32(a_{\overline{180-1}|f} + 1)$ ——————— substituting in Formula III.5

$81.296807 = a_{\overline{179}|f} + 1$

$\quad\quad a_{\overline{179}|f} = 80.296807$

For $f = 1\%$, $\quad\quad a_{\overline{179}|1\%} \quad = 83.154881 \longrightarrow 1\% < f$

For $f = 1.1\%$, $\quad\quad a_{\overline{179}|1.1\%} \quad = 78.081342 \longrightarrow 1\% < f < 1.1\%$

For $f = 1.05\%$, $\quad a_{\overline{179}|1.05\%} \quad = 80.555264 \longrightarrow 1.05\% < f < 1.1\%$

For $f = 1.06\%$, $\quad a_{\overline{179}|1.06\%} \quad = 80.050665 \longrightarrow 1.05\% < f < 1.06\%$

For $f = 1.055\%$, $\quad a_{\overline{179}|1.055\%} = 80.302340 \longrightarrow 1.055\% < f < 1.06\%$

For $f = 1.0551\%$, $\; a_{\overline{179}|1.0551\%} = 80.297295 \longrightarrow 1.0551\% < f < 1.06\%$

For $f = 1.05511\%$, $a_{\overline{179}|1.05511\%} = 80.296790 \longrightarrow f = 1.05511\%$

$$(1 + i)^{\frac{1}{6}} = 1.0105511$$

$$1 + i = 1.0105511^6 = 1.0650002$$

$$i = 0.0650002 = 6.5\%$$

The rate of interest is $2(6.5\%) = 13\%$ compounded semi-annually.

C. Finding the rate for deferred general annuities

You can determine the rate of interest for a deferred general annuity by trial and error as previously explained. For deferred ordinary general annuities, use the formula

$$A_{nc}(\text{defer}) = R(1 + f)^{-d}\left[\frac{1 - (1 + f)^{-n}}{f}\right] = R(1 + f)^{-d}\,a_{\overline{n}|f}$$

where $f = (1 + i)^{c-1}$ and d is the number of deferred payment intervals

——— Formula III.6

For deferred general annuities due, multiply Formula III.6 by $(1 + f)$.

EXAMPLE III.4E

A retirement annuity of $12 000.00 payable at the end of each year for fifteen years is bought for $7560.73. If the payments are deferred for twenty-five years, what is the rate of interest compounded quarterly on the annuity?

Solution

$A_{nc}(\text{defer}) = 7560.73$; $R = 12\ 000.00$; $n = 15$; $d = 25$;

$c = 4$; $f = (1 + i)^4 - 1$

For a deferred ordinary general annuity, use Formula III.6.

$$7560.73 = 12\ 000.00(1 + f)^{-25}\left[\frac{1 - (1 + f)^{-15}}{f}\right]$$

$$(1 + f)^{-25}\left[\frac{1 - (1 + f)^{-15}}{f}\right] = 0.6300608$$

We need to find the annual rate of interest f for which

$$a_{\overline{15}|f} \times (1 + f)^{-25} = 0.6300608$$

For $f = 12\%$, $a_{\overline{15}|12\%} \times (1 + 0.12)^{-25}$
              $= (6.8108645)(0.0588233) = 0.4006376 \longrightarrow f < 12\%$

For $f = 10\%$, $a_{\overline{15}|10\%} \times (1 + 0.10)^{-25}$
              $= (7.6060795)(0.0922960) = 0.7020107 \longrightarrow 10\% < f < 12\%$

For $f = 10.4\%$, $a_{\overline{15}|10.4\%} \times (1 + 0.104)^{-25}$
$= (7.4355148)(0.0842894) = 0.6267354 \longrightarrow$ 10%
$< f < 10.4\%$

For $f = 10.38\%$, $a_{\overline{15}|10.38\%} \times (1 + 0.1038)^{-25}$
$= (7.4438978)(0.0846721) = 0.6302904 \longrightarrow$ 10.38%
$< f < 10.4\%$

For $f = 10.381\%$, $a_{\overline{15}|0.381\%} \times (1 + 0.10381)^{-25}$
$= (7.4434783)(0.0846529) = 0.6301121 \longrightarrow$ 10.381%
$< f < 10.4\%$

For $f = 10.3813\%$, $a_{\overline{15}|10.3813\%} \times (1 + 0.103813)^{-25}$
$= (7.4433525)(0.0846472) = 0.6300586 \longrightarrow f = 10.3813\%$

Since $(1 + i)^4 = (1 + f) = 1.103813$
$\qquad 1 + i = 1.103813^{\frac{1}{4}}$
$\qquad 1 + i = 1.025$
$\qquad\quad i = 0.025 = 2.5\%$

The rate of interest is $4(2.5\%) = 10\%$ compounded quarterly.

EXAMPLE III.4F

Payments of \$500.00 are to be made at the beginning of each month for four years starting two years after a contract valued at \$12 000.00 was signed. What nominal rate of interest compounded quarterly has been charged?

Solution

Since the payments are at the beginning of each month, the problem involves a deferred general annuity.

$A_{nc}(\text{defer}) = 12\ 000.00; \quad R = 500.00; \quad n = 48; \quad d = 24;$

$c = \dfrac{4}{12} = \dfrac{1}{3}$

To find the equivalent monthly rate of interest f, substitute the given values in Formula III.6, multiply by $(1 + f)$, and determine the factor for which f is to be computed.

$12\ 000.00 = 400.00(1 + f)^{-24}(a_{\overline{48}|f})(1 + f)$

$\qquad 24 = (1 + f)^{-23}(a_{\overline{48}|f})$

$\qquad 24 = a_{\overline{48}|f} \times (1 + f)^{-23}$

We need to find the monthly rate f for which

$a_{\overline{48}|f} \times (1 + f)^{-23} = 24$

$f = 1.516\%$

$(1 + i)^{\frac{1}{3}} = 1.01516$

$1 + i = 1.01516^3$

$1 + i = 1.046173$

$i = 0.046173$

$i = 4.6173\%$

The nominal rate of interest compounded quarterly is about 18.469%.

Exercise III.4 *(in part same as portions of Exercise 13.3)*

A. For each of the following four ordinary general annuities, determine the nominal rate of interest represented by the question mark.

	Future Value S_{nc}	Present Value A_{nc}	Periodic Payment R	Payment Interval	Term	Nominal Rate of Interest	Conversion Period
1.	$39 200.00		$1100.00	1 year	12 years	?	monthly
2.		$9 600.00	$1220.00	6 months	5 years	?	monthly
3.		$62 400.00	$5200.00	6 months	25 years	?	annually
4.	$55 500.00		$75.00	1 month	20 years	?	semi-annually

B. For each of the following four general annuities due, determine the nominal rate of interest.

	Future Value S_{nc} (due)	Present Value A_{nc} (due)	Periodic Payment R	Payment Interval	Term	Nominal Rate of Interest	Conversion Period
1.	$ 6 400.00		$200.00	6 months	9 years	?	monthly
2.	$25 000.00		$790.00	1 year	15 years	?	quarterly
3.		$ 7 500.00	$420.00	3 months	5 years	?	monthly
4.		$60 000.00	$725.00	1 month	25 years	?	semi-annually

C. 1. Compute the rate of interest compounded monthly at which $400.00 paid at the end of every three months for eight years accumulates to $20 000.00.

2. What is the rate of interest compounded quarterly if a loan of $21 500.00 is repaid in seven years by payments of $2500.00 made at the end of every six months?

3. A mortgage of $27 500.00 is repaid by making payments of $280.00 at the end of each month for fifteen years. What is the rate of interest compounded semi-annually?

4. A property worth $35 000.00 is purchased for 10 percent down and semi-annual payments of $2750.00 for twelve years. What is the effective rate of interest if interest is compounded quarterly?

5. What is the rate of interest compounded annually on a lease valued at $21 600.00 if payments of $730.00 are made at the beginning of each month for three years?

6. An insurance policy provides for a lump sum benefit of $50 000.00 fifteen years from now. Alternatively, payments of $1700.00 may be received at the beginning of each of the next fifteen years. What is the effective rate of interest if interest is compounded quarterly?

7. A business venture requiring an initial investment of $5000.00 yields no returns for the first three years and net returns of $650.00 at the end of every three months for the following seven years. What rate of interest compounded semi-annually does the venture yield?

8. A $40 000.00 lease requires semi-annual payments of $6750.00 for five years due in advance. If the payments are deferred for two years, what is the nominal annual rate of interest charged?

9. An annuity bought for $52 000.00 provides ordinary annuity payments of $5200.00 every three months for fifteen years. If the payments are deferred for ten years, what rate of interest compounded semi-annually is paid on the investment?

10. A leasing agreement with a cash value of $24 500.00 requires semi-annual payments of $3500.00 for five years. If the first payment is due three years from the date of the agreement, what is the effective rate of interest on the lease if interest is compounded monthly?

III.5 FINDING THE ACCURATE YIELD RATE FOR BONDS BY TRIAL AND ERROR

A method of trial and error similar to the one used to find the nominal rate of interest can be used to obtain as precise an approximation to the yield rate as desired. When using this method, use the rate obtained by the method of averages for the first attempt by substituting in Formula 15.1

$$PP = S(1 + i)^{-n} + R\left[\frac{1 - (1 + i)^{-n}}{i}\right] = S(1 + i)^{-n} + Ra_{\overline{n}|i}$$

EXAMPLE III.5A Compute the yield rate for Example 15.4B (see page 672).

Solution The approximate value of i by the method of averages is 5.48%; the quoted price is $25 875.00.

Our aim is to find the value of i for which Formula 15.1 gives a purchase price equal to the quoted price of $25 875.00.

$$S = 25\,000.00; \quad R = 1437.50; \quad n = 20$$

$$PP = 25\,000.00(1 + i)^{-20} + 1437.50a_{\overline{20}|i}$$

For $i = 5.48\%$, $PP = 25\,000.00(1.0548^{-20}) + 1437.50a_{\overline{20}|5.48\%}$

$$= 8600.77 + 17\,207.22$$

$$= \$25\,807.99$$

Programmed solution

The purchase price is $8600.77 + 17\,207.22 = \$25\,807.99$.

Since the computed purchase price of \$25 807.99 is less than the quoted price of \$25 875.00, $i < 5.48\%$.

For $i = 5.46\%$, $\quad PP = 8633.46 + 17\,235.83 = 25\,869.29 \longrightarrow i < 5.46\%$
For $i = 5.456\%$, $PP = 8640.01 + 17\,241.56 = 25\,881.57 \longrightarrow 5.456\% < i < 5.46\%$
For $i = 5.458\%$ $\;PP = 8636.73 + 17\,238.70 = 25\,875.43 \longrightarrow i = 5.458\%$

Note: Because the computed purchase price is almost exactly equal to the quoted price, $i = 5.458\%$ is a precise value.

The yield rate is $2(5.458\%) = 10.916\%$.

EXAMPLE III.5B   Compute the yield rate for Example 15.4D (see page 673).

Solution   The approximate value of i by the method of averages $= 4.75\%$; the quoted price on December 2, 2000, is \$5187.50.

We want to find the value of i for which Formula 15.1 gives a purchase price equal to the quoted price of \$5187.50.

When the date of purchase is between interest dates, we can approximate the precise value of i by using the theoretically correct number of interest conversion intervals in fractional form.

The number of days from the date of purchase (December 2, 2000) to the next interest payment date (January 15, 2001) is 44;
the number of conversion periods from December 2, 2000, to July 15, 2012, is

$$23 + \frac{44}{184} = 23.23913.$$

$$S = 5000.00; \quad R = 250.00$$

Substituting in Formula 15.1,

$$PP = 5000.00(1 + i)^{-23.23913} + 250.00a_{\overline{23.23913}|i}$$

For $i = 4.75\%$, PP $= 5000.00(1.0475^{-23.23913}) + 250.00a_{\overline{23.23913}|4.75\%}$
$$= 1700.62 + 3473.03$$
$$= \$5173.65$$

Programmed solution

$$0 \boxed{\text{PMT}} \ 5\,000 \boxed{\text{FV}} \ 23.23913 \boxed{\text{N}} \ 4.75 \boxed{\%i} \ \boxed{\text{CPT}} \ \boxed{\text{PV}} \ \boxed{1\,700.62222}$$

$$0 \boxed{\text{FV}} \ 250 \boxed{\text{PMT}} \ \boxed{\text{CPT}} \ \boxed{\text{PV}} \ \boxed{3473.0293}$$

The purchase price is $1700.62 + 3473.03 = \$5173.65$.

Since the purchase price of $5173.65 is less than the quoted price of $5187.50, $i < 4.75\%$.

For $i = 4.73\%$,   PP $= 1708.19 + 3479.72 = 5187.91 \longrightarrow 4.73 < i < 4.75\%$

For $i = 4.731\%$,   PP $= 1707.81 + 3479.38 = 5187.19 \longrightarrow 4.73\% < i < 4.731\%$

For $i = 4.7305\%$, PP $= 1708.00 + 3479.55 = 5187.55 \longrightarrow i = 4.7305\%$

The yield rate is $2(4.7305\%) = 9.461\%$.

EXAMPLE III.5C

A $10 000.00, 11.5% bond with quarterly coupons redeemable at 106 on September 1, 2001, was purchased on April 10, 1992, at 94½. What is the yield rate?

Solution

The quoted price is $10\,000.00(0.945) = \$9450.00$;

the redemption value is $10\,000.00(1.06) = \$10\,600.00$;

the average book value is $\dfrac{(9450.00 + 10\,600.00)}{2} = \$10\,025.00$.

The interest payment dates are December 1, March 1, June 1, and September 1; the interest date closest to April 10 is March 1.

Assuming that the price was quoted on March 1, 1992, the time to maturity is 9 years and 6 months; the number of interest payments to maturity is $4(9.5) = 38$;

the quarterly interest payment is $10\,000.00\left(\dfrac{0.115}{4}\right) = \$287.50$;

the total interest payments are $38(287.50) = \$10\,925.00$;

the discount is $10\,600.00 - 9450.00 = \$1150.00$.

The average income per interest payment interval $= \dfrac{(10\,925.00 + 1150.00)}{38}$

$$= \$317.76$$

The approximate value of $i = \dfrac{317.76}{10\,025.00} = 0.0316968 = 3.17\%$

The number of days from April 10 to June 1 is 52;
the number of days in the interest payment interval March 1 to June 1 is 92;
the exact number of interest payment intervals from April 10, 1992 to

September 1, 2001 is $37 + \frac{52}{92} = 37.565217$.

$S = 10\,600.00$; $R = 287.50$; $n = 37.565217$

Substituting in Formula 15.1,

$PP = 10\,600.00(1 + i)^{-37.565217} + 287.50a_{\overline{37.565217}|i}$

For $i = 3.17\%$, $PP = 10\,600.00(0.3096438) + 287.50(21.777797)$
$$= 3282.22 + 6261.12$$
$$= \$9543.34$$

Programmed solution

0 [PMT] $10\,000$ [FV] 37.565217 [N] 3.17 [%i] [CPT] [PV]

[3 282.2247]

0 [FV] 287.50 [PMT] [CPT] [PV] [6261.1166]

The purchase price is $\$3282.22 + 6261.12 = \$9543.34$.

Since $9543.34 > 9450.00$ $i > 3.17\%$

For $i = 3.20\%$, $PP = 3246.57 + 6232.64 = 9479.21 \longrightarrow i > 3.20\%$
For $i = 3.22\%$, $PP = 3223.03 + 6213.76 = 9436.79 \longrightarrow 3.20\% < i < 3.22\%$
For $i = 3.214\%$, $PP = 3230.07 + 6219.41 = 9449.48 \longrightarrow i = 3.214\%$

The yield rate is $4(3.214) = 12.856\%$.

EXAMPLE III.5D   Ram Snead purchased a $5000.00, 10% bond with semi-annual coupons redeemable at par at $93\frac{3}{4}$ twenty years before maturity. He sold the bond nine years later at $100\frac{1}{2}$. What yield rate did Ram realize?

Solution   Ram's purchase price is $5000.00(0.9375) = \$4687.50$ ——— original book value
Ram's selling price is $5000.00(1.005) = \$5025.00$ ——— final book value

The average book value is $\frac{1}{2}(4687.50 + 5025.00) = \$4856.25$.

The semi-annual coupon is $5000.00\left(\frac{0.10}{2}\right) = \$250.00$;

the number of interest payments received by Ram is $9(2) = 18$;

the total interest payments are $18(250.00) = \$4500.00$;

the gain on the sale is $5025.00 - 4687.50 = \$337.50$ ——— discount

The average income per interest interval is $\dfrac{(4500.00 + 337.50)}{18} = \$268.75$

The approximate value of i is $\dfrac{268.75}{4856.25} = 0.0553411 = 5.53\%$.

Our aim is to find the value of i for which Formula 15.1 gives a purchase price of $\$4687.50$ given that

$S = 5025.00; \quad R = 250.00; \quad n = 18$

$PP = 5025.00(1 + i)^{-18} + 250.00a_{\overline{18}|i}$

For $i = 5.53\%$, $PP = 5025.00(1.0553^{-18}) + 250.00a_{\overline{18}|5.53\%}$

$\qquad\qquad\qquad = 5025.00(0.3795186) + 250.00(11.220278)$

$\qquad\qquad\qquad = \$4712.15$

Programmed solution

0 [PMT] 5025 [FV] 18 [N] 45.53 [%i] [CPT] [PV] [1 907.0812]

0 [FV] 250 [PMT] [CPT] [PV] [2 805.0694]

The purchase price is $\$1907.08 + 2805.07 = \$4712.15$.

Since $4712.15 > 4687.50, \quad i > 5.53\%$.

For $i = 5.55\%$, $PP = 1900.59 + 2800.78 = 4701.37 \longrightarrow i > 5.55\%$
For $i = 5.57\%$, $PP = 1894.12 + 2796.51 = 4690.63 \longrightarrow i > 5.57\%$
For $i = 5.577\%$, $PP = 1891.86 + 2795.01 - 4686.87 \longrightarrow 5.57\% < i < 5.577\%$
For $i = 5.576\%$, $PP = 1892.18 + 2795.22 = 4687.40 \longrightarrow i = 5.576\%$

The yield rate is $2(5.576\%) = 11.152\%$.

Exercise III.5

A. Use trial and error to find the yield rate for each of the following bonds.

1. A $\$1000.00$, 11.5% bond with semi-annual coupons redeemable at par on November 15, 2004, is bought on April 5, 1991, at $96\tfrac{3}{4}$.

2. A $\$5000.00$, 16% bond with interest payable quarterly redeemable at 110 on July 1, 2003, is bought on October 26, 1990, at $101\tfrac{7}{8}$.

3. A $\$10\ 000.00$, 7% bond with semi-annual coupons was bought seventeen years before maturity at $102\tfrac{1}{4}$ and sold at $99\tfrac{1}{2}$ five years later.

4. Four $\$1000.00$, 10.5% bonds with interest payable semi-annually redeemable at 101 on August 15, 2011, were bought on October 14, 1994, at $87\tfrac{3}{4}$ and sold on May 25, 1998, at $91\tfrac{1}{2}$.
   a) What would have been the yield rate if held to maturity?
   b) What was the yield rate realized by selling the bond on May 25, 1998?

5. A $25 000.00, 9.5% bond with semi-annual coupons redeemable at par is bought sixteen years before maturity at 78¼.

6. A $10 000.00, 12% bond with quarterly coupons redeemable at 102 on October 15, 2007, is bought on May 5, 1995, at 98¾.

SUPPLEMENTARY FORMULAE

Formula III.1

$S_n(\text{due}) = R(s_{\overline{n+1}|i} - 1)$

Alternate form of the formula for finding the future value of an annuity due

Formula III.2

$A_n(\text{due}) = R(a_{\overline{n-1}|i} + 1)$

Alternate form of the formula for finding the present value of an annuity due

Formula III.3

$A_n(\text{defer}) = R(1 + i)^{-d} a_{\overline{n}|i}$

Finding the present value of a deferred ordinary annuity using the symbol $a_{\overline{n}|i}$ for the discount factor

Formula III.4

$S_{nc}(\text{due}) = R(s_{\overline{n+1}|f} - 1)$

Alternate form of the formula for finding the future value of a general annuity due

Formula III.5

$A_{nc}(\text{due}) = R(a_{\overline{n-1}|f} - 1)$

Alternate form for finding the present value of a general annuity due

Formula III.6

$A_{nc}(\text{defer}) = R(1 + f)^{-d} a_{\overline{n}|f}$

Alternate form for finding the present value of a deferred ordinary general annuity

where $f = (1 + i)^c - 1$ and d is the number of deferred payment intervals

Answers to Odd-Numbered Problems, Review Exercises, and Self-Tests

Chapter 1

Exercise 1.1

A. 1. 14
3. 53
5. 23
7. 24
9. 1.3333333

Exercise 1.2

A. 1. $\frac{2}{3}$
3. $\frac{7}{12}$
5. $\frac{8}{5}$
7. $\frac{2}{5}$
9. $\frac{5}{73}$
11. 5

B. 1. 1.375
3. 1.6666667
5. 1.8333333
7. 1.0833333

C. 1. 3.375
3. 8.3333333
5. 33.333333
7. 7.7777778

D. 1. 5.63
3. 18.00
5. 57.70
7. 13.00

E. 1. 720
3. 630.85
5. 1911
7. 220 000

9. 4000

Exercise 1.3

A. 1. 0.64
3. 0.025
5. 0.005
7. 2.5
9. 4.5
11. 0.009
13. 0.0625
15. 0.99
17. 0.0005
19. 0.005
21. 0.09375
23. 1.625
25. 0.0025
27. 0.0175
29. 1.375
31. 0.00875
33. 0.3333333
35. 0.1666667
37. 1.8333333
39. 1.3333333

B. 1. $\frac{1}{4}$
3. $\frac{7}{4}$
5. $\frac{3}{8}$
7. $\frac{1}{25}$
9. $\frac{2}{25}$
11. $\frac{2}{5}$
13. $\frac{5}{2}$

15. $\frac{1}{8}$
17. $\frac{9}{400}$
19. $\frac{1}{800}$
21. $\frac{3}{400}$
23. $\frac{1}{16}$
25. $\frac{1}{6}$
27. $\frac{3}{400}$
29. $\frac{1}{1000}$
31. $\frac{5}{6}$
33. $\frac{4}{3}$
35. $\frac{5}{3}$

C. 1. 350%
3. 0.5%
5. 2.5%
7. 12.5%
9. 22.5%
11. 145%
13. 0.25%
15. 9%
17. 75%
19. $166\frac{2}{3}$%
21. 4.5%
23. 0.75%
25. 1.125%
27. 37.5%

29. $133\frac{1}{3}$%
31. 65%

Exercise 1.4

A. 1. $409 062.50
3. $1147.50
5. $176.00

B. 1. $0.41
3. 2.9

Exercise 1.5

A. 1. a) $955.50
  b) $12.25
  c) $1157.63
3. a) $7.26
  b) $1185.50
5. a) $16.47
  b) $875.94
7. $1568.06
9. a) $225.00
  b) $332.25
11. 9.25%
13. $19 680
15. $425.21
17. $7.26

Exercise 1.6

A. 1. $38 819.90
3. $1.05
5. $1.31
7. $2843.88
9. $38.88

Review Exercise

1. a) 29
  b) −8
  c) 11

d) 8

e) 1000

f) 0.15

g) 340

h) 950

i) 625

j) 1250

2. a) 1.85

b) 0.075

c) 0.004

d) 0.00025

e) 0.0125

f) 0.0075

g) 1.625

h) 0.1175

i) 0.0833333

j) 0.8333333

k) 2.6666667

l) 0.10375

3. a) $\dfrac{1}{2}$

b) $\dfrac{3}{8}$

c) $\dfrac{1}{6}$

d) $\dfrac{5}{3}$

e) $\dfrac{1}{200}$

f) $\dfrac{3}{40}$

g) $\dfrac{3}{400}$

h) $\dfrac{1}{160}$

4. a) 225%

b) 2%

c) 0.9%

d) 12.75%

e) 125%

f) 137.5%

g) 2.5%

h) 28%

5. a) 20.2083333 kg

b) $24.25

c) 5.05 kg

d) $6.06

6. $35, $150, $147, $252; Total $584

7. a) $11.19

b) $9.60

8. $13 875

9. $13 680

10. a) $9.24

b) $918.61

11. a) $1456.00

b) $9.60

c) 16.5 hours

12. a) $845.52

b) $10.84

c) $1048.77

13. a) $367.50

b) $8.55

14. a) $387.45

b) $26.65

15. $1924.25

16. a) $398.65

b) $11.39

17. 4.25%

18. $21 750

19. $8.44

20. a) $8.40

b) 13 hours

21. $5945.00

22. $10.56

23. 41.5 hours

24. $4272.80

25. $5344.50

26. $26.25

27. 15.56%

28. Ripley pays $20.91 more

29. a) 46.3538

b) $1635.70

c) 2.05128

d) $71.49

Self-Test

1. a) 4417.2

b) 94.5

c) 2606.4

d) 4560

e) 4800

2. a) 1.75

b) 0.00375

3. a) $\dfrac{1}{40}$

b) $\dfrac{7}{6}$

4. a) 112.5%

b) 2.25%

5. $7080

6. $203

7. $7.35

8. $299 250

9. $650

10. 15.5%

11. $2382.41

12. $788.50

13. $8.90

14. $687.00

15. $9.00

16. $7318.80

17. $45 500

18. Alberta, $18.08
B.C., Man. Sask.,
$19.26
Ont. Que., $19.43
P.E.I., $19.77
N.B., N.S., Nfld.,
$19.27

Chapter 2

Exercise 2.1

A. 1. $19a$

3. $-a - 10$

5. $0.8x$

7. $1.4x$

9. $-x^2 - x - 8$

11. $x - 7y$

13. $-2a^2 - 6ab + 5b^2$

15. $14 - 9x + y$

B. 1. $-12x$

3. $-10ax$

5. $-2x^2$

7. $60xy$

9. $-2x + 4y$

11. $2ax^2 - 3ax - a$

13. $35x - 30$

15. $-20ax + 5a$

17. $3x^2 + 5x - 2$

19. $x^3 + y^3$

21. $7x^2 + 3x + 39$

C. 1. $4ab$

3. $4x$

5. $10m - 4$

7. $-2x^2 + 3x + 6$

D. 1. -5

3. 378

5. 3000

7. 902

9. 1400

Exercise 2.2

A. 1. 81

3. 16

5. $\dfrac{16}{81}$

7. 0.25

9. 1

11. $\dfrac{1}{9}$

13. 125

15. $\dfrac{1}{1.01}$

B. 1. 2^8

3. 4^3

5. 2^{15}

7. a^{14}

9. 3^{11}

11. 6

13. $\dfrac{3^{11}}{5^{11}}$

15. $\dfrac{(-3)^{11}}{2^{11}}$

17. 1.025^{150}

19. 1.04^{80}

21. $(1 + i)^{200}$

23. $(1 + i)^{160}$

25. $a^5 b^5$

27. $m^{24} n^8$

29. 16

31. $\dfrac{b^8}{a^8}$

Exercise 2.3

A. 1. 72

3. 3

5. 1.0758857

7. 1.0132999

B. 1. 55
3. 12.25
5. 1.0711221
7. 0.6299605
9. 163.05343

Exercise 2.4

A. 1. $9 = \log_2 512$
3. $-3 = \log_5 \frac{1}{125}$
5. $\ln 18 = 2j$
B. 1. $2^5 = 32$
3. $10^1 = 10$
C. 1. 0.6931472
3. -2.2537949
5. 6.8253032

Exercise 2.5

A. 1. 3
3. 80
5. 18
7. -35
9. -4
11. -8
13. 5
15. 20
17. 200
B. 1. $x = 4$;
L.S. $= 17 =$ R.S.
3. $x = 0$;
L.S. $= -7 =$ R.S.

Exercise 2.6

A. 1. $x = -10$;
L.S. $= 320 =$ R.S.
3. $x = -3$;
L.S. $= -15 =$ R.S.
B. 1. 20
3. -1
5. $\frac{1}{2}$
C. 1. -1
3. $\frac{5}{6}$
D. 1. $h = \frac{2A}{b}$

3. $C = \frac{5}{9}(F - 32)$
5. $r = \frac{A - P}{Pt}$

Exercise 2.7

A. 1. $28.28
3. 192
5. $670.00
7. $23 500.00
9. 18
11. 20 dimes;
56 nickels;
16 quarters

Review Exercise

1. a) $-2x - 7y$
b) $1.97x$
c) $6a - 7$
d) $x + 3y$
e) $9a^2 - 4b - 4c$
f) $-x^2 + 3x + 1$
2. a) $-15a$
b) $28mx$
c) -7
d) $-3ab$
e) $36xy$
f) $24abc$
g) $-12x + 20y + 4$
h) $x - 2x^2 - x^3$
i) $-6x + 4$
j) $7a - 4$
k) $26a - 29$
l) $14ax - 2a^2 + 10a$
m) $2m^2 - 7m + 5$
n) $3a^3 - 8a^2 - 5a + 6$
o) $-14x^2 + 34x + 36$
p) $-26am^2 + 26am + 37a$
3. a) -47
b) $6\frac{1}{3}$
c) 0.16
d) 200

e) 644.40
f) 2500
4. a) -243
b) $\frac{16}{81}$
c) 1
d) $\frac{-1}{3}$
e) $\frac{625}{16}$
f) 1
g) $-19\,683$
h) 1024
i) 59 049
j) m^{12}
k) $\frac{16}{81}$
l) $\frac{25}{16}$
m) 1.03^{150}
n) $(1 + i)^{80}$
o) 1.05^{150}
p) $16x^4y^4$
q) $\frac{81}{a^8b^4}$
r) $\frac{1}{(1 + i)^n}$
5. a) 0.96
b) 1.0121264
c) 1.07
d) 0.9684416
e) 1.0986123
f) -2.9957323
g) 7.0875403
h) 9.8716396
6. a) -7
b) 880
c) -21
d) -18
e) 3
f) -11
g) 250
h) 40
i) -5
j) 7
k) 39
l) 56

7. a) $x = -7$;
L.S. $= -203 =$ R.S.
b) $x = 5$;
L.S. $= -32 =$ R.S.
c) $x = -3$;
L.S. $= \frac{-23}{14} =$ R.S.
d) $x = -\frac{7}{12}$;
L.S. $= \frac{11}{9}$ R.S.
e) $x = 7$;
L.S. $= 25 =$ R.S.
f) $x = -\frac{1}{3}$;
L.S. $= -1 =$ R.S.
g) $x = -\frac{1}{2}$;
L.S. $= -\frac{31}{6} =$ R.S.
8. a) $r = \frac{i}{Pt}$
b) $t = \frac{S - P}{Pr}$
c) $F = \frac{1}{D} - E$
d) $T_2 = \frac{S\,T\,W_2}{W\,S_2}$
e) $h = \frac{v^2}{2g}$
9. a) 138
b) $63 350
c) $117
d) $44 500
e) heat $814;
power $1056;
water $341
f) $37 500
g) Machine A, 17;
Machine B, 25;
Machine C, 35
h) superlight, 27;
ordinary, 45
i) 164

j) $1400; $1680;
   $3200

Self-Test

1. a) $-2 - 8x$
   b) $-2x - 9$
   c) $-16a - 7$
   d) $-6x^2 + 6x + 12$
2. a) -7
   b) $18\frac{2}{3}$
   c) 0.192
   d) 0.40
   e) 1474.00
   f) 1450.00
3. a) -8
   b) $\frac{4}{9}$
   c) 1
   d) 2187
   e) $\frac{9}{16}$
   f) $-x^{15}$
4. a) 1.0253241
   b) 23.114772
   c) 0.024926
   d) 0.8986123
   e) 5.7559717
   f) 7.2707892
5. a) $n = 6$
   b) $n = 5$
6. a) -36
   b) 9.00
   c) 20
   d) -3
   e) 3
   f) 35
   g) 25
   h) 2
7. a) $P = \dfrac{I}{rt}$
   b) $d = \dfrac{S - P}{St}$
8. a) $240
   b) 4600
   c) 55
   d) $4500

Chapter 3

Exercise 3.1

A. 1. a) $3 : 8$
     b) $3 : 2$
   c) $5 : 8 : 13$
   d) $3 : 6 : 13$
3. a) $5 : 16$
   b) $2 : 7$
   c) $2 : 7 : 11$
   d) $23 : 14 : 5$
   e) $5 : 4$
   f) $25 : 21$
   g) $9 : 16 : 18$
   h) $28 : 40 : 25$
   i) $8 : 15$
   j) $9 : 10$
B. 1. $8 : 7$
   3. $2 : 3 : 12$
C. 1. $2295; $510; $255
   3. $5250; $2800; $1400

Exercise 3.2

A. 1. 4
   3. 56
   5. 7.4
   7. 2.4
   9. $\dfrac{7}{10}$
   11. 1
B. 1. 21 months
   3. 600 km
   5. a) $3600
      b) $9000
   7. $100 800

Exercise 3.3

A. 1. 36
   3. 300
   5. 18
   7. 6
   9. 0.50
   11. 2
   13. 7.50
   15. 17.50
B. 1. $16
   3. $1950
   5. $9
   7. $200
   9. $600
   11. $49

13. $135
15. $60
C. 1. $15.60
   3. $1.62
   5. $48.40
   7. $22.42
D. 1. 20
   3. 440
   5. 36
   7. 30
E. 1. 60%
   3. 115%
   5. 5%
   7. 600%
   9. $166\frac{2}{3}\%$
F. 1. $200
   3. $3.60
   5. $3.06
   7. $200
   9. $1.10
   11. $240
   13. 500%
   15. $300
G. 1. $28
   3. $1500
   5. $45 000
   7. $45 000$

Exercise 3.4

A. 1. 168
   3. $1140
   5. $88
B. 1. 50%
   3. 200%
   5. 2%
C. 1. 32
   3. $130
   5. $4.40
**Exercise 3.5*

A. 1. 27
   3. 12.5%
   5. $4320
   7. a) $180 000
      b) $225 000
B. 1. $14.52

3. $150
5. $85.10
7. $5000
9. $83\frac{1}{3}\%$
11. 325%
13. $96.69
15. $680
17. $44 800
19. $900

Exercise 3.6

A. 1. $558.90 US
   3. $204.11 Cdn
B. 1. $479.17 Cdn
   3. 258.95 francs
   5. 742.47 marks

Exercise 3.7

A. 1. $10 193.60
   3. $7897.80

Exercise 3.8

A. 1. 156.52, 110.59, 69.05
B. 1. a) $0.78, $0.73
      b) $0.94

Review Exercise

1. a) $5 : 6$
   b) $6 : 1$
   c) $9 : 40$
   d) $6 : 1$
   e) $240 : 20 : 1$
   f) $15 : 4 : 3$
2. a) 3
   b) 18
   c) 1.61
   d) 2.70
   e) $\dfrac{9}{5}$
   f) 2
3. a) 210
   b) 7.20
   c) 195
   d) 3.60

4. a) $112
  b) $930
  c) $1155
  d) $1320
5. a) $6.66
  b) $8.30
  c) $90.00
  d) $27.72
6. a) 62.5%
  b) 175%
  c) $0.48
  d) $22.50
  e) $280
  f) $440
  g) 2%
  h) 500%
  i) $132
  j) $405
7. a) $18
  b) $1955
  c) $16\frac{2}{3}$%
  d) 550%
  e) $56
  f) $340

g) $140
8. $1200; $1800; $1500
9. $2400; $4200; $4800
10. $63 000; $47 250; $70 875; $7875
11. $75 000; $50 000; $60 000
12. 16 minutes
13. $182 000
14. a) $14 700
  b) $36 750
15. 540
16. a) 59 250
  b) 19 750
17. $56 250; $84 375; $9375
18. a) $42 600
  b) $8520
19. a) $400 000
  b) $280 000
20. a) 50.00%; 22.22%; 27.78%

b) 125%
21. a) 7.5%
  b) $16\frac{2}{3}$%
22. a) 8%
  b) 92%
23. a) $166\frac{2}{3}$%
  b) $266\frac{2}{3}$%
24. $350 000
25. $165
26. $84 000
27. $15 000
28. a) $300 000
  b) $23 400
  c) $17 550
  d) 37.5%
29. a) $80 000
  b) $250 000
  c) 312.5%
30. a) $1 C = $0.73 US
  b) $529.25 US
31. $158.82 US
32. $19 762.30
33. a) $50.68
  b) $42 500

1. a) $350.00
  b) $76.05
  c) $145.00
  d) $13.20
2. a) 20
  b) 3
3. 45%
4. $4800
5. $10 000
6. $72
7. $16 875; $11 250; $6750; $5625
8. 14%
9. $17.50
10. 5%
11. 180
12. $72 000
13. a) 1.247 mark
  b) 623.44 mark
14. $1049.18 Cdn
15. $10 011.60
16. $0.69

Chapter 4

Exercise 4.1

A. **1.** A$(-4, -3)$ B$(0, -4)$ C$(3, -4)$ D$(2, 0)$ E$(4, 3)$
  F$(0, 3)$ G$(-4, 4)$ H$(-5, 0)$

3. a)

x	-5	-4	-3	-2	-1	0	1	2	3
y	-3	-2	-1	0	1	2	3	4	5

b)

x	3	2	1	0	-1	-2
y	5	3	1	-1	-3	-5

c)

x	3	2	1	0	-1	-2	-3
y	6	4	2	0	-2	-4	-6

d)

x	-5	-4	-3	-2	-1	0	1	2	3	4	5
y	5	4	3	2	1	0	-1	2	-3	-4	-5

B. 1.

x	0	3	2
y	-3	0	-1

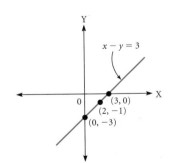

3.

x	0	-2	2
y	0	2	-2

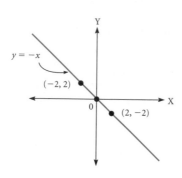

5.

x	0	4	-4
y	-3	0	-6

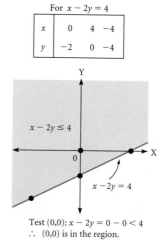

7.

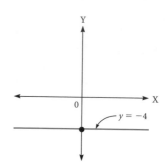

9.

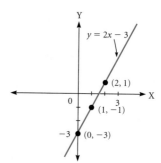

Exercise 4.2

A. 1.

For $x + y = 4$

x	0	4	2
y	4	0	2

3.

For $x - 2y = 4$

x	0	4	-4
y	-2	0	-4

Test $(0,0)$: $x - 2y = 0 - 0 < 4$
∴ $(0,0)$ is in the region.

5.

Graph $2x = -3y$

x	0	-3	3
y	0	2	-2

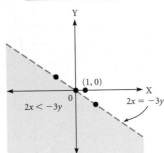

7.

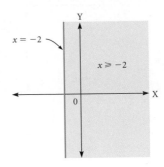

Exercise 4.3

A. 1.

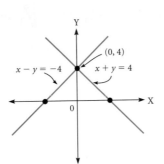

5.

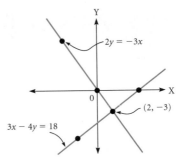

3.

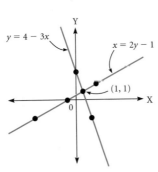

7.

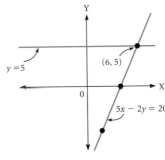

B. 1.

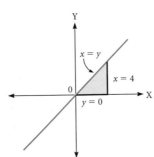

3.

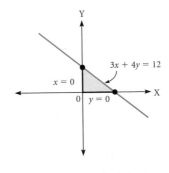

C. **1.**

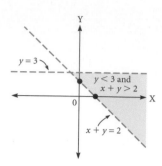

3.

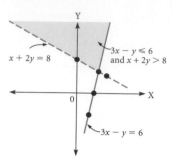

5.

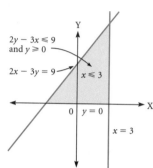

7.

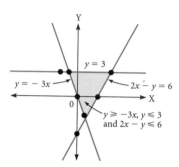

Exercise 4.4

A. **1.** $x = -8, y = -1$
   3. $x = 10, y = 12$
   5. $x = -3, y = 3$
B. **1.** $x = -4, y = 3$
   3. $x = -1, y = 3$
   5. $x = 4, y = 3$

C. **1.** $x = 12, y = 8$
   3. $x = 1.5, y = 2.5$
   5. $x = 6, y = 10$
   7. $x = \frac{1}{2}, y = \frac{3}{4}$

Exercise 4.5

A. **1.** $x = -5, y = 4,$
     $z = 3$
   3. $a = 10, b = 12,$
     $c = 15$
   5. $m = 0.8, n = 0.6,$
     $k = 1.2$

Exercise 4.6

A. **1.**

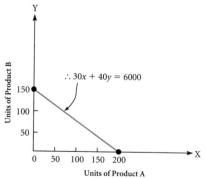

3.

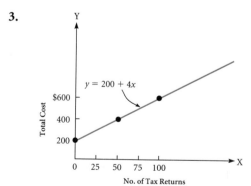

B. **1.** 15; 9
   3. Brand X, 90;
     No-name, 50
   5. Kaya, \$31 500;
     Fred, \$23 500

7. Type A, 42;
     Type B, 18
9. 20 dimes;
     56 nickels;
     16 quarters

Review Exercise

1. a) $m = -\frac{7}{3}$
  $b = 2$

b) $m = \frac{1}{2}$
  $b = 0$

c) $m = \frac{3}{2}$
  $b = 4$

d) $m = -6$
  $b = 10$

e) m is undefined
  b does not exist

f) $m = \frac{1}{3}$
  $b = -3$

g) $m = \frac{1}{4}$
  $b = -1$

h) $m = 0$
  $b = 5$

2. a)

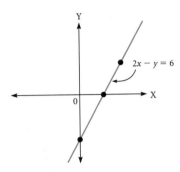

$2x - y = 6$

b)

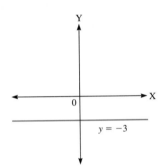

$3x + 4y = 0$

c)

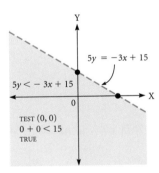

$5x + 2y = 10$

d)

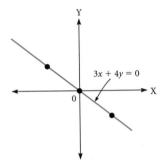

$y = -3$

e)

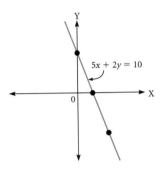

$5y = -3x + 15$

$5y < -3x + 15$

TEST $(0, 0)$
$0 + 0 < 15$
TRUE

f)

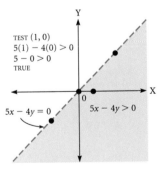

TEST $(1, 0)$
$5(1) - 4(0) > 0$
$5 - 0 > 0$
TRUE

$5x - 4y = 0$ $5x - 4y > 0$

g)

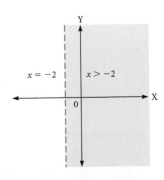

$x = -2$ $x > -2$

h)

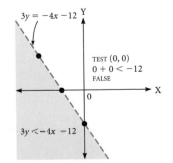

$3y = -4x - 12$

TEST $(0, 0)$
$0 + 0 < -12$
FALSE

$3y < -4x - 12$

3. a)

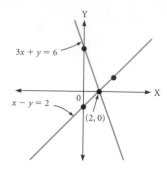

b)

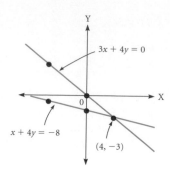

c)

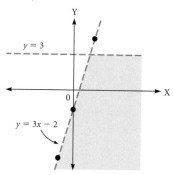

d)

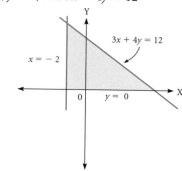

4. a) $y < 3x - 2$ and $y < 3$

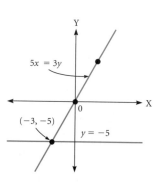

c) $x \geq -2, y \geq 0,$ and $3x + 4y \geq 12$

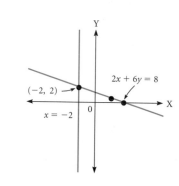

b) $y > -2x$ and $x < 4$

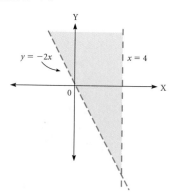

d) $x \geq 0, y \geq -2$ and $5x + 3y \leq 15$

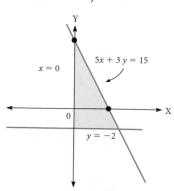

5. a) $x = -1, y = 1$
  b) $x = 5, y = -1$
  c) $x = -1, y = 10$
  d) $x = -3, y = 4$
  e) $x = 2, y = -3$
  f) $x = -4, y = 1$
  g) $a = 4, b = -2, c = 2$
  h) $a = 10, b = 6, c = -20$
  i) $a = 1, b = -3, c = +2$
  j) $a = -2, b = 1, c = 3$
  k) $m = 6, n = 8, k = 10$
  l) $m = \frac{2}{3}, n = \frac{2}{5}, k = \frac{3}{4}$

6. a)

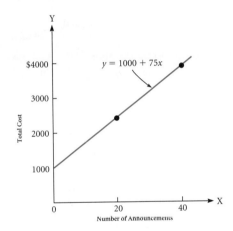

b)

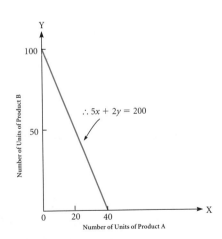

7. a) first number 8; second number 9
  b) 275 at \$2.50; 175 at \$3.50
  c) \$105
  d) white \$36; red \$66
  e) 17, 25, 35
  f) heat \$814; power \$1056; water \$341

g) direct selling \$37 500; TV advertising \$37 750; newspaper advertising \$12 250
h) 164 quarters; 16 50¢ coins; 25 \$1 coins

Self-Test

1. a) $m = 4; \ b = 11$
  b) $m = -6; \ b = -9$
  c) $m = -\frac{1}{3}; \ b = 0$
  d) $m = 0; \ b = -3$
  e) m is undefined; b does not exist
  f) $m = -\frac{a}{b}; \ b = \frac{c}{b}$

2. a)

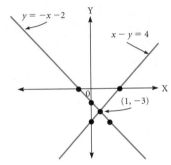

b)

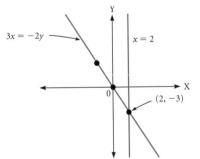

3. a)

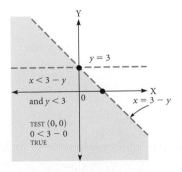

b)

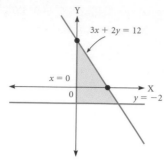

4. a) $x = 4, y = -3$
  b) $x = 0, y = 3$
  c) $a = 3, b = 2, c = -2$
  d) $a = 2, b = -2, c = 5$
5. $8000; $4000
6. $7500
7. $1400; $1680; $3200

Chapter 5
Exercise 5.1

A. 1. a) annual depreciation $3500
  b) depreciation year 1 to 4, $3705.75; year 5 to 7, $3477.00; year 8 to 10, $3248.25
  c) depreciation per unit $0.35; year 1 to 4, $3762.50; year 5 to 7, $3430.00; year 8 to 10, $3220.00
  d) constant part 636.3636; year 1, $6363.64; year 10, $636.35
  e) rate 20%; year 1, $8000.00; year 10, $368.71
  f) rate 18.77476%; year 1, $7509.90; year 10, $1155.72
  g) rate 20%; year 1, $8000; year 10, $1073.74
B. 1. a) $375 500; $12 300
  b) $263 000; $15 000
  c) $259 443.09; $12 972.15
  d) $253 985.20; $13 041.02

Exercise 5.2

A. 1. a) i) Revenue = $120x$
    ii) Cost = $2800 + 50x$
  b)

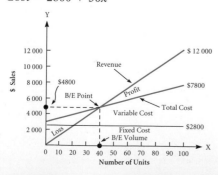

c) i) 40
  ii) 40%
  iii) $4800
3. a) i) Revenue = x
    ii) Cost = $220\,000 + 0.45x$
  b)

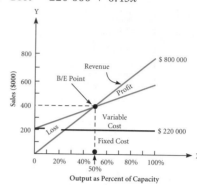

c) i) not applicable
  ii) 50%
  iii) $400\,000

Review Exercise

1. a) constant value $265; depreciation year 1, $2120; year 8, $265
  b) rate 25%; depreciation year 1, $3000; year 8, nil
  c) rate 17.97066%; depreciation year 1, $2156.48; year 8, $538.93
2. a) $6784.00; $1260.80
  b) $1934.77; $484.92
  c) $6038.19; $483.06
  d) $1111.79; $171.92
3. constant part is 330; depreciation year 1, $1980; year 6, $330
4. $22 903.79
5. $1974.82
6. a)

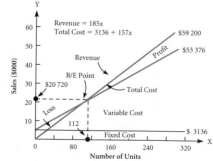

b) i) 112
  ii) 35%
  iii) $20 720
c) i) 30%
  ii) 38.75%
  iii) 70%

7. a) Revenue $= x$; cost $= 4800 + 0.70x$

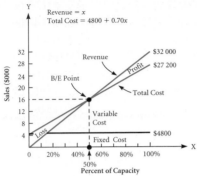

b) i) $16 000
ii) 50%
c) i) 43.75% or $14 000
ii) 39.375% or $12 600

8. a)

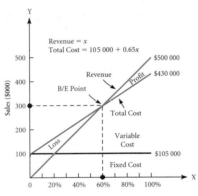

b) i) 60%
ii) $300 000
c) $335 000
9. a) i) 96
ii) 64%
iii) $61 440
b) $73 600
c) 62%

Self-Test

1. $35 000
2. $6100
3. $800.65
4. a)

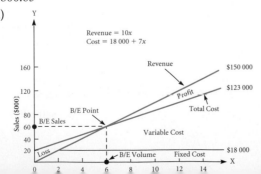

b) i) 6000
ii) 60 000
iii) 40%
c) 5600
d) 5500
5. a) i) $500 000
ii) 62.5%
b) $525 000

Chapter 6

Exercise 6.1

A. 1. $13.53
3. $134.96

5. $33\frac{1}{3}$%

7. $30.24; 32.5%
9. $137.89; 48.55%;
11. $1583.33; 61%
B. 1. a) $127.68
b) $112.32
c) 46.8%
3. 15.9%
5. a) 38.75%
b) 48.267%
7. $74.10
9. 15%
11. $426.00
13. $180.00

Exercise 6.2

A. 1. $640.00
3. $776.11
5. $1136.80
7. $4581.50
B. 1. $582.00; $850.00
3. $564.50; $536.28
5. $810.00; $810.00
C. 1. a) Sept. 10
b) $5276.85
c) $103.20
3. $2507.19
5. $2184.00
7. a) $1164.00
b) $733.54
c) $600.00
9. a) $1925.00
b) $3400.00

Exercise 6.4

A. 1. a) $6.00
   b) $3.84
   c) $2.16
   d) 25%
   e) 20%
3. a) $35.00
   b) $31.50
   c) $3.50
   d) $66\frac{2}{3}$%
   e) 40%
5. a) $10.50
   b) $12.75
   c) −$2.25
   d) $38\frac{8}{9}$%
   e) 28%

B. 1. $6.25; 25%; 20%
3. $102.40; 60%; 37.5%
5. $75.95; $21.70; 28.6%
7. $44.24; $22.12; $33\frac{1}{3}$%
9. $78.10; $46.86; 150%
11. $111.30; $133.56; 20%

C. 1. $5.12
3. a) $75.00
   b) $63.00
   c) $8160
   d) 147.14%
5. a) 120%
   b) 54.55%
7. a) $22.80
   b) $26.22
   c) 13.04%
9. a) $53.25
   b) 28.57%
11. a) $32.00
    b) 150%

Exercise 6.5

A. 1. $68.00; $85.00; $62.90
3. 200%; $120.00; 37.5%
5. $45.50; 24.36%; $96.25

B. 1. $51.00; $59.00; −$8.00
3. $96.40; $30.65; $7.91
5. $160.00; 12%; $124.20

C. 1. a) $228.69
   b) 54%
3. $70.00
5. a) 40%
   b) −$8.00
   c) 10.294%
   d) $9\frac{1}{3}$%
7. −$6.50
9. a) $19.00
   b) $4.00
   c) 21.05%
11. −$97.50
13. −$82.50

Review Exercise

1. a) $31.92
   b) $24.08
   c) 43%
2. 37.5%
3. 45.66%
4. $2.16
5. 15%
6. $465.00
7. $30.00
8. a) June 10
   b) $2584.00
9. $2520.67
10. a) $1940.00
    b) $2813.00
11. a) $2000.00
    b) $9310.00
12. a) $1645.00
    b) $1500.00
13. a) $7.92
    b) $3.12
    c) 39.4%
    d) 65%
    e) $6.96
    f) −$0.96
14. a) $90.00
    b) $58.50
    c) 53.85%
    d) $74.88
    e) −$6.48
15. a) $6.60
    b) 25.9%
16. a) $77.50
    b) 42.86%
17. a) $1217.70
    b) 32%
18. $240.00
19. a) 25%
    b) −$3.06
    c) 25%
20. a) −$0.60
    b) 21.25%
21. a) $253.00
    b) $189.75
    c) 25%
22. a) −$13.20
    b) 25%
23. 12.5%
24. a) $189.00
    b) 21.25%
    c) $133\frac{1}{3}$%
25. a) $154.00
    b) 27.27%
    c) $138.95
    d) 21%
26. a) $2152.40
    b) 69.43%
    c) 40.98%

Self-Test

1. $295.77
2. 37.5%
3. 50.5%
4. 6.5%
5. $1635.04
6. $1940.00
7. $1450.00
8. $1587.50
9. $240.00
10. $1010.00
11. $348.36
12. $1360.00
13. 180%
14. $110.00
15. 23.4%
16. $1130.00
17. −$660.45
18. −$94.77

Chapter 7

Exercise 7.1

A. 1. 0.125; 1.25
3. 0.1025; $\frac{165}{365}$

Exercise 7.2

A. 1. 112 days
3. 166 days
B. 1. 244 days
3. 341 days

Exercise 7.3

A. 1. $945.00
3. $215.80
5. $75.34
B. 1. $10.87
3. $31.71

Exercise 7.4

A. 1. $1224.00
3. $10.75%
5. 14 months
7. 144 days
B. 1. $3296.00
3. 9.5%
5. 11 months
7. $876.00
9. $400 000

Exercise 7.5

A. 1. $516.16
   3. $892.26

Exercise 7.6

A. 1. $266.00; $39.90
   3. $517.50; $547.17
   5. $2025.00; 292 days
B. 1. $1222.00
   3. $1704.60

Exercise 7.7

A. 1. $829.33
   3. $617.50
   5. $1108.24
   7. $885.05
   9. $622.41
   11. $1113.78
B. 1. $1156.80
   3. $519.17
   5. $1438.68
   7. $929.75

Review Exercise

1. a) 172 days
   b) 186 days
2. a) $63.98
   b) $41.81
3. a) $1160.00
   b) $601.77
4. a) 7.5%
   b) 265 days
   c) 11%
   d) 10 months
5. a) $640.00
   b) $5709.97
6. $1225.03
7. $3000.17
8. 9.25%
9. 8.25%
10. 7 months
11. 196 days
12. $4642.75
13. $1601.89

14. $1440.00
15. $3200.00
16. $3467.89
17. $1736.47
18. $3158.35
19. $2668.00
20. $1022.07
21. $3415.20
22. $2351.17
23. $1592.18
24. $3544.91
25. $961.50
26. $1056.12
27. $1653.61
28. $1850.98

Self-Test

1. $64.20
2. 9 months
3. 6.5%
4. $9797.92
5. $5901.04
6. $4781.68
7. $4769.78
8. 7.5%
9. 359 days
10. $1369.96
11. $7293.39
12. $51.47
13. $1163.85
14. $2910.69
15. $1799.33
16. $1335.77

Chapter 8

Exercise 8.1

A. 1. December 30,
      1998
   3. $530.00
   5. 154 days
   7. $549.01
B. 1. a) March 3, 2000
      b) 155 days
      c) $42.81
      d) $882.81

3. a) April 3, 2000
   b) 63 days
   c) $22.65
   d) $1272.65

Exercise 8.2

A. 1. $644.61
   3. $837.19

Exercise 8.3

A. 1. $455.00
B. 1. $1166.60
   3. $1618.41

Exercise 8.4

A. 1. $989.23; $10.77
   3. $857.48; $12.43

Exercise 8.5

A. 1. $98 448.77
   3. 7.065%
   5. a) $23 841.62
      b) 5.255%
      c) $24 448.96
      d) 4.929%

Exercise 8.6

A. 1. $33.75
   3. $278.14
B. 1. $1825.63
   3. $178.66

Exercise 8.7

A. 1. a) $0.45
      b) $5.88
      c) $1.66
      d) $10.00
      e) $−958.30

Exercise 8.8

A. 1. Totals are
      $1233.69; $33.69;
      $1200.00

Review Exercise

1. a) November 2
   b) $35.62
   c) $1635.62
2. $1274.22
3. $750.00
4. $3132.02
5. $5251.51
6. $940.00
7. $814.17
8. $1897.52; $19.98
9. $1259.04
10. $704.47; $11.98
11. 6.1493%
12. a) 15.8956%
    b) 5.477%
    c) 8.948%
13. $450.96
14. $79.46
15. a) $68.20; $79.15;
       $91.48; $90.97;
       $93.16
    b) $10 717.96
16. Totals are
    $3081.35; $81.35;
    $3000.00

Self-Test

1. $19.79
2. $1169.77
3. $1160.00
4. $1766.13
5. $1670.61
6. $24 797.22
7. a) $98 116.43
   b) 3.68%
8. $216.13
9. $340.26
10. a) $54.69; $73.23;
       $70.08
    b) −$10 230.63
11. Totals are
    $4070.41; $70.41;
    $4000.00

Chapter 9

Exercise 9.1

A. 1. 1; 0.12; 5
   3. 4; 0.03375; 36
   5. 2; 0.0775; 27
   7. 12; 0.0125; 150
   9. 2; 0.06125; 9
B. 1. 1.7783812
   3. 1.6349754
   5. 4.5244954
   7. 2.7092894
   9. 1.7074946
C. 1. a) 48
      b) 2.5%
      c) 1.025^{48}
      d) 3.2714896

Exercise 9.2

A. 1. $713.39
   3. $2233.21
   5. $5468.38
   7. $6639.54
   9. $662.02
B. 1. $9167.68;
      $4167.68
   3. $2075.07
   5. a) $199.26
      b) $202.24
      c) $203.81
      d) $204.89
   7. a) $148.59; $48.59
      b) $220.80;
         $120.80
      c) $487.54;
         $387.54
   9. 161
   11. a) Bank $6982.27
          (preferred);
          Credit union
          $6914.10
       b) $68.17
C. 1. $3010.85
   3. $1452.79
   5. $3942.41
   7. $1102.13
   9. $1444.24

Exercise 9.3

A. 1. $574.37
   3. $371.86
   5. $409.16
   7. $500.24
B. 1. $1095.53; $590.47
   3. $762.84
   5. $3129.97

Exercise 9.4

A. 1. $1494.52; $505.48
   3. $2418.10; $916.08
   5. $1638.87; $361.19
B. 1. $3681.95
   3. $1345.06
   5. $3800.24
   7. $1532.09

Exercise 9.5

A. 1. $7153.84
   3. $2537.13
   5. $1673.49
   7. $641.36
   9. $1560.25
B. 1. $3426.73
   3. $1536.03
   5. $974.21
C. 1. a) $2269.71
      b) $2847.12
      c) $4000.00
      d) $7049.37
   3. $6805.32
   5. $693.04
   7. $2423.97
   9. a) $3113.90
      b) $1847.95
   11. a) $646.41
       b) $946.41

Review Exercise

1. a) $1198.28
   b) $1221.61
   c) $1227.05
2. a) $15 191.84
   b) $24 317.66
c) $80 919.18
3. a) $2890.09
   b) $890.09
4. a) $6519.80
   b) $6530.25
5. a) 6144.45;
      $4344.45
   b) $3305.25;
      $2055.25
6. a) $1770.06;
      $1829.94
   b) $6424.27;
      $2575.73
7. $9791.31
8. $5537.42
9. $850.05
10. $3190.62
11. $7182.20
12. $15 636.83
13. $2824.29
14. $2082.25;
    $1912.75
15. $2838.60
16. 50 710.59
17. $3277.40
18. $17 082.87
19. $71 551.24
20. a) $2742.41
    b) $2911.55
    c) $3281.79
21. 3841.72
22. $4796.96
23. $2954.39
24. $1820.32
25. $3032.54
26. $3574.57

Self-Test

1. $898.83
2. $2194.01
3. 2.7118780
4. $6919.05
5. $9449.31
6. $14 711.80
7. $1955.28
8. $4504.29
9. $774.01
10. $16 001.64
11. $2425.52
12. $2661.85

Chapter 10

Exercise 10.1

A. 1. a) $4152.58
      c) $3820.34
   2. a) $429.44
      c) $1120.13
B. 1. $3712.50
   3. $1006.76
   5. $17 116.96

Exercise 10.2

A. 1. a) $311.27
      c) $4344.21
   2. a) $3050.92
      c) $250.75
B. 1. $1398.85
   3. $8452.52
   5. $2346.36

Exercise 10.3

A. 1. $3204.82
   3. $2642.50
   5. $893.45
   7. $2116.39
B. 1. $3230.60
   3. $1798.33
   5. $1972.80
   7. $1830.97

Exercise 10.4

A. 1. a) 9.726%
      c) 5.116%
      e) 12.114%
   2. a) 12.5%
      c) 9.6%
      e) 9.778%
   3. a) 13.4 years
      c) 117.8 months
      e) 37.313 quarters

B. **1.** 9.237%
   3. a) 10.402%
     b) 7.585%
   5. 6.991%
   7. 8.945%
   9. 9.329 years
  11. 17.501 years
  13. 2.818 years
  15. November 1, 2001
  17. 21 months

Exercise 10.5

A. **1. a)** $n = 10$ quarters
     (2.5 years)
    c) $n = 2.2506112$
     (69 days)
  2. a) 12.891%
    c) 7.397%
  3. a) $608.78
    c) $2316.07
  4. a) $1487.00
    c) $3869.15
  5. a) 12.187%
B. **1.** $n = 33.791662$
    months (2 years,
    298 days)
  3. $n = 7.2571412$
    half-years (3 years,
    230 days)
  5. 7.385%
  7. $5.88
  9. $2757.71
  11. 5.031%
  13. a) 11.552453 years
     (11 years, 202
     days)
    b) 6.08 years
  15. 6.94%

Review Exercise

  1. $2854.72
  2. $11 102.50
  3. $10 681.77
  4. $6913.53
  5. $55 276.80
  6. $26 048.42

  7. $996.10
  8. $4194.33
  9. $1256.08
 10. 14.072%
 11. 6.03%
 12. 19.596642 months
    (1 year, 231 days)
 13. $1269.12
 14. $690.09
 15. 22.571 half-years
    (11 years, 95 days)
 16. 6.983%
 17. a) $5326.87
    b) $11 263.47
 18. a) $6703.20
    b) $5515.58
 19. a) 13.08%
    b) 14.35%
    c) 8.833%
    d) 8.24%
    e) 8.33%
 20. a) 11.02%
    b) 13.32%
    c) 9.417%
 21. a) 8.44%
    b) 11.495%
 22. a) $n = 16$ half-
    years (8 years)
    b) $n = 49.374482$
    quarters (12
    years, 118 days)
    c) $n = 36.001416$
    months (3
    years)
    d) $n = 7.7016353$
    years (7 years,
    256 days)
 23. $n = 18.813466$
    months (1 year,
    208 days)
 24. $n = 3.4514466$
    half-years (1 year,
    265 days)
 25. $n = 27.315156$
    quarters (6 years,
    303 days —
    September 30,

    2004)
 26. $2035.07
 27. $5122.89
 28. 36.2 months
 29. 10.663 years (10
    years, 242 days)
 30. 6.880%

Self-Test

  1. 63 months
  2. $2177.36
  3. 16.07545%
  4. 12.7932%
  5. 19 months
  6. 13.456508%
  7. 9.7134 years
  8. 10.0%
  9. $24 253.31
 10. $12 984.30
 11. $756.81
 12. $4341.18

Chapter 11

Exercise 11.1

A. **1. a)** annuity certain
    b) annuity due
    c) general annuity
  3. a) perpetuity
    b) deferred
     annuity
    c) general annuity
  5. a) annuity certain
    b) deferred
     annuity due
    c) simple annuity

Exercise 11.2

A. **1.** 54 193.60
  3. 59 185.19
  5. 17 915.08
B. **1.** $13 045.68
  3. $32 434.02
  5. a) $41 220.21
    b) $4500.00
    c) $36 720.21

  7. $62 177.25

Exercise 11.3

A. **1.** $9515.19
  3. $24 213.90
  5. $10 544.91
B. **1.** $6897.00
  3. a) $9906.20
    b) $2093.80
  5. a) $2123.82
    b) $372.06
  7. $12 710.96
  9. a) $11 999.88
    b) $1443.26
    c) $12 738.11
    d) $738.23
    e) $35.66

Exercise 11.4

A. **1.** $45 855.46
  3. $16 317.75
  5. $64 166.42
  7. $32 876.06
B. **1.** $23 268.48
  3. $2326.66
  5. a) $13 265.50
    b) $3265.50
  7. $31 293.63

Exercise 11.5

A. **1.** $47 853.23
  3. $42 505.50
  5. $5095.74
  7. $34 627.57
B. **1.** $6281.74
  3. $31 736.56
  5. a) $25 786.03
    b) $9213.97
  7. $80 000.00
  9. $15 592.21

Review Exercise

  1. a) $26 734.60
    b) $17 280.00
    c) $9454.60

2. **a)** $64 576.40
   b) $85 500.00
   c) 20 923.60
3. $722.62
4. $5232.46
5. $19 792.33
6. $28 435.42
7. $64 125.83
8. $35 830.48
9. $101 517.64
10. $3620.11
11. $75 962.59
12. $88 440.69
13. $24 418.00
14. $34 031.63
15. **a)** $16 978.26
    b) $3102.78
    c) $18 558.65
    d) $102.78

Self-Test

1. $18 277.44
2. $7882.30
3. $108 276.76
4. $5020.59
5. $4468.10
6. $12 308.20
7. $40 385.38
8. $5231.73

Chapter 12

Exercise 12.1

A. 1. $135 334.71;
      $71 813.10
   3. $69 033.69;
      $35 581.76
   5. $43 738.24;
      $7278.61
B. 1. $39 593.70
   3. $33 338.44
   5. **a)** $1238.56
      b) $1575.00
      c) $336.44
   7. **a)** $29 513.14
      b) $10 313.14

9. $2150.38

Exercise 12.2

A. 1. $62 800.18
   3. $11 304.61
B. 1. $59 113.10
   3. $24 111.11

Exercise 12.3

A. 1. $5048.76
   3. $1325.85
   5. $3058.17
   7. $10 272. 72
   9. $3135.48
B. 1. $126 738.20
   3. $40 000.51
   5. **a)** $6265.33
      b) $19 200.00
      c) $12 934.67
   7. $8822.89

Exercise 12.4

A. 1. $73 529.41
   3. $12 029.76
   5. $91 027.09
   7. $88 446.04
B. 1. $27 951.82
   3. $214.60
   5. $189 473.41
   7. $138.46
   9. $1393.91

Review Exercise

1. **a)** $11 223.89;
      $5799.35
   b) $11 728.44;
      $6060.33
2. **a)** $6172.13;
      $3823.78
   b) $6141.42;
      $3804.76
3. **a)** $19 792.33
   b) $20 392.06
4. **a)** $28 435.42
   b) $28 552.68

5. $33 291.15
6. $19 153.93
7. **a)** $60 229.26
   b) $62 662.52
   c) $20 620.76
   d) $36 229.72
   e) $86 633.66
   f) $90 133.66
8. **a)** $22 492.54
   b) $20 000.05
   c) $6407.77
   d) $4668.08
   e) $23 632.98
   f) $23 872.98
9. $17 367.81
10. $42 092.97
11. $124 638.48
12. $20 964.79
13. $12 885.42
14. $34 543.54
15. $318 181.82
16. $92 210.53
17. $105.30
18. $28 089.24
19. **a)** $2638.84
    b) $3444.00
    c) $805.16
20. **a)** $8164.11
    b) $7200.00
    c) $964.11

Self-Test

1. $84 209.75
2. $153 600.00
3. $66 043.50
4. $69 783.50
5. $21.97
6. $43 246.07
7. $9207.27
8. $30 380.89
9. $32 695.51
10. $46 807.18

Chapter 13

Exercise 13.1

A. 1. $821.39
   3. $1117.37
   5. $272.73
   7. $702.87
   9. $271.68
B. 1. $204.80
   3. $636.55
   5. $716.80
   7. $903.61
C. 1. $576.10
   3. $147.55
D. 1. $207.87
   3. $591.66
   5. $330.63
   7. $117.26
   9. $300.36
   11. $459.47
   13. $10 203.89
   15. $1655.40
   17. $229.33
   19. $3141.41
   21. $114.89
   23. $2568.82
   25. $2752.22

Exercise 13.2

A. 1. $n = 14.6023569$
      years
   3. $n = 247.77343$
      months
   5. $n = 15.577578$
      half-years
   7. $n = 15.425835$
      half-years
   9. $n = 58.307344$
      months
B. 1. $n = 112.589158$
      months
   3. $n = 7.7784905$
      years
   5. $n = 34.333804$
      half-years
   7. $n = 17.348624$
      quarters
C. 1. $n = 15.850822$
      quarters

3. $n = 117.01114$
months

D. 1. $n = 74.4983386$
months

3. $n = 105.21875$
months

5. $n = 20.924449$
quarters

7. $n = 52.541832$
quarters

9. $n = 17.531631$
quarters

11. $n = 109.48123$
months

13. $n = 39.878728$
months

15. $n = 34.152966$
months

17. $n = 96.882620$
months

19. $n = 6.8625067$
years

Exercise 13.3

A. 1. $i = 3.999896$;
nominal rate =
16%

3. $i = 0.75\%$;
nominal rate = 9%

5. $i = 13.4942582\%$;
nominal rate =
13.494%

7. $i = 6.2492018$;
nominal rate =
12.5%

B. 1. $f = 18.32\%$;
$i = 1.41173\%$;
nominal rate =
16.94%

3. $f = 8.1696\%$;
$i = 17.0\%$;
nominal rate =
17%

5. $f = 5.77432\%$;
$i = 0.94\%$;
nominal rate =

11.28%

7. $f = 1.22638\%$;
$i = 0.40713\%$;
nominal rate =
4.89%

C. 1. $i = 3.1249761\%$;
nominal rate =
12.5%

3. $i = 3.25\%$;
nominal rate =
13%

5. $i = 1.3\%$; effective
rate = 16.765%

7. $i = 1.75\%$;
nominal rate = 7%

9. $i = 7.78\%$;
effective rate =
16.165%

11. $f = 2.7189\%$;
$i = 0.98920\%$;
nominal rate =
10.778%

13. $f = 0.7555\%$;
$i = 4.61948\%$;
nominal rate =
9.24%

15. $f = 1.1690263\%$;
$i = 14.97\%$;
nominal rate =
14.97%

Review Exercise

1. a) $411.57
b) $403.50
2. a) $201.34
b) $202.85
3. a) $61.81
b) $1261.46
4. a) $796.00
b) $2563.40
c) $1198.61
d) $18 231.17
e) $222.27
f) $2455.83
5. $n = 9.8850381$
years

6. $n = 99.053253$
months

7. $n = 108.31780$
months

8. $n = 9.8407692$
half-years

9. a) $n = 34.2738$
quarters
b) $n = 27.9824$
half-years

10. 10.43%
11. 16.94%
12. 12.33%
13. 25.10%
14. $361.31
15. $n = 8.5838838$
half-years

16. a) $n = 6.777030$
half-years
b) $n = 7.5111015$
years
c) $n = 10.111897$
quarters
d) $n = 8.86133$
half-years

17. 6.21%
18. 8.57%
19. $n = 25.389533$
years
20. $n = 106.15677$
months
21. 5.881%
22. $26 945.42
23. $n = 24.971014$
quarters
24. a) $15 749.42
b) $3149.42
c) $432.91
25. a) $85 882.89
b) $118 117.11
c) $196.16
d) $168 691.20
26. $1320.05
27. $4079.07
28. $742.45
29. $8908.36
30. $910.15

31. $4964.12
32. $n = 27.206912$
months
33. $n = 53.470007$
quarters
34. $1.24
35. $3329.46
36. $n = 90.10018$
months
37. $n = 28.4623$ years
38. $n = 420.01797$
months
39. $n = 12.21035$
half-years
40. a) $16 102.46
b) $3120.21
c) $14 740.76
d) $120.21
41. $709.95
42. $n = 28.811254$
months
43. $n = 97.758303$
months
44. $n = 83.065997$
quarters
45. $n - 48.295933$
months
46. $n = 59.909808$
quarters
47. $n = 28.605079$
quarters

Self-Test

1. $540.36
2. 10.90%
3. $n = 38.37$ quarters
4. $755.60
5. $143.98
6. 15.6%
7. $n = 29.713747$
quarters =
90 months
8. $6056.04
9. $994.55
10. $1258.38
11. 11.426%

12. 12%
13. $n = 31.9965$ quarters
14. $3268.62
15. $168.36
16. $1170.69
17. $357.34

Chapter 14

Exercise 14.1

A. 1. a) $588.56
  b) $5858.52
  c) $175.76
  d) $412.80
 3. a) $1103.73
  b) $4913.61
  c) $196.54
  d) $907.19
 5. a) $136.87
  b) $4094.16
  c) $20.71
  d) $106.16
B. 1. a) $n = 19.47532$
  b) $2493.97
 3. a) $n = 14.530933$
  b) $23 234.20
C. 1. a) $1282.84
  b) $15 052.64
  c) $59 234.20
  d) $23 234.20
 3. Payment
  $2054.05; total
  paid $14 378.41;
  interest paid
  $4378.41
 5. Total paid
  $14 943.16; interest paid $5743.16
 7. $651.11
 9. $1160.09
 11. a) $3621.90
  b) $1035.27
  c) $2799.85
  d) Totals
   $115 900.80;
   $30 900.80;

$85 000.00
13. a) $n = 14.022508$
  b) $957.79
  c) $1910.53
  d) Totals
   $35 065.45;
   $11 065.45;
   $24 000.00

Exercise 14.2

A. 1. a) $1829.69
  b) $20 286.42
  c) $819.57
  d) $1010.12
 3. a) $164.04
  b) $4563.55
  c) $20.54
  d) $141.50
 5. a) $2790.38
  b) $33 701.74
  c) $1545.30
  d) $1245.08
B. 1. a) $n = 17.13251$
  b) $2685.85
 3. a) $n = 14.894792$
  b) $1585.00
C. 1. a) $252.15
  b) $34 200.11
  c) $7277.51
  d) $292.24
 3. a) $n = 15.413529$
  b) $2911.17
  c) $4311.17
 5. Payments
  $3212.01; total
  paid $22 484.09;
  interest paid
  $6484.08
 7. $752.68
 9. a) $318.15
  b) $3323.12
  c) $259.36
  d) $364.44
  e) Balances
   $37 056.14;
   $36 913.71

Exercise 14.3

A. (Using Method 1)
 1. $725.07
 3. $73.74
 5. $700.62
 7. $146.80
B. 1. a) $n = 29.434057$
  b) $157.46
 3. $511.30
 5. $301.45
 7. $1152.87
 9. a) $n = 61.523813$
  b) $724.48
  c) $84 599.48
  d) $68 599.48

Exercise 14.4

A. 1. a) $715.83
  b) $83 375.45
  c) $641.41
 3. a) $503.15
   rounded to
   $550.00;
   $n = 104.522813$
  b) $288. 05
  c) $2889.95
 5. $i = 4.75$; nominal
  rate = 9.50%
 7. a) $86 514.51
  b) $n = 165.56125$
  c) $54 269.19
 9. Payments $378.81
  rounded to
  $380.00; Balance
  Dec. 1 $38 794.01
 11. Balance Dec. 1
  $38 795.58

Review Exercise

1. a) $1491.37
  b) $12 723.84
  c) $15 771.75
  d) $338.49
  e) $1247.91
  f) Totals

$47 723.84;
$12 723.84;
$35 000.00
2. a) $166.07
  b) $1964.20
  c) $5964.19
  d) $28.30
  e) $150.70
  f) Totals
   $9964.20;
   $1964.20;
   $8000.00
3. a) $n = 24.830989$
  b) $28 940.29
  c) $426.66
  d) $1807.58
  e) Totals
   $49 664.41;
   $9664.41;
   $40 000.00
4. a) $370.43
  b) $4232.15
  c) $1277.53
  d) $338.60
  e) Totals
   $42 541.80;
   $38 906.83;
   $3634.97
5. a) $735.80
  b) $280.57
  c) $23 981.91
  d) $1000.89
  e) Totals
   $24 843.84;
   $11 088.04;
   $13 755.80
6. a) $n = 16.294188$
  b) $7464.05
  c) $707.75
  e) Totals
   $46 478.84;
   $28 978.84;
   $17 500.00
7. a) $n = 9.3198366$
  b) $1139.87
8. a) $n = 160.53831$
  b) $485.59

9. a) $n = 11.7444464$
   b) $3211.27
10. a) $n = 19.700707$
    b) $14 240.01
11. a) $1091.28
    b) $125 324.69
    c) $1023.15
12. a) $1326.31
    b) $168 986.32
    c) $1455.70
13. a) $n = 117.33209$
    b) $748.93
    c) $2119.07
14. a) $n = 216.41765$
    b) $627.84
    c) $21 569.76
15. a) $161.75
    b) $1264.00
    c) $5086.52
    d) $21.41
    e) Totals
       $7764.00;
       $1264.00;
       $6500.00
16. a) $n = 9.266195$
    b) $3394.38
    c) Totals
       $41 721.42;
       $9721.47;
       $32 000.00
17. $i = 4.125\%$;
    nominal rate =
    8.25%
18. $i = 9.40\%$;
    nominal rate =
    9.40%
19. a) $601.20
    b) $1651.04
    c) $25 598.05
    d) $638.94
20. a) $n = 19.225855$
    b) $227.49

Self-Test

1. $6027.52
2. $71.90

3. $12 866.98
4. $689.88
5. a) $1406.95
   b) $174 506.12
   c) $1479.65
6. a) $n = 179.20906$
   b) $282.98
   c) $518.02
7. $i = 5.00\%$;
   nominal rate
   = 10. 00%
8. Balances
   $11 867.56;
   $9754.86; totals
   $23 232.00;
   $11 232.00;
   $12 000.00

Chapter 15

Exercise 15.1

A. 1. $107 592.94
   3. $27 477.23
   5. $53 909.88
   7. $9706.28
   9. $11 939.29
   11. $9294.84
B. 1. $403.02
   3. $937.89
   5. $4 278 802
   7. $39 020.77
   9. a) $19 656.14
      b) $792.35
      c) $18 863.79
   11. $5449.01

Exercise 15.2

A. 1. a) $3822.93
      (discount)
      b) $21 177.07
   3. a) $1773.12
      (discount)
      b) $8628.88
   5. a) $9837.48
      (discount)
      b) $54 962.51

7. a) $194.24
   (discount)
   b) $880.01
B. 1. a) $30 384.99
      (discount);
      $69 615.01
      b) $18 481.46
      (discount);
      $81 518.44
   3. a) $269.95
      (premium);
      $5469.95
      b) $199.89
      (premium);
      $5399.89
   5. a) $3098.85
      (discount)
      b) $9362.53
      c) $9007.10
   7. $4 630 385

Exercise 15.3

A. 1. a) $967.90
      (discount);
      $4032.10; totals
      $1575.00;
      $2542.90;
      $967.90
   3. $49.18
      (premium);
      $1079.18; totals
      $420.00; $370.82;
      $49.18
B. 1. $976.84 (gain)
   3. $64.02 (loss)
   5. $313.43 (gain)

Exercise 15.4

A. 1. 11.83%
   3. 12.12%
   5. 13.28%

Exercise 15.5

A. 1. a) $558.24
      b) $6399.60

3. a) $22.03
   b) $3104.14
5. a) $495.27
   b) $9598.44
B. 1. a) $700.00
      b) $265.25
      c) $965.25
      d) $10 868.38
   3. a) $62.50
      b) $143.33
      c) $205.83
      d) $2246.16
   5. a) $4275.00
      b) $1123.59
      c) $5398.59
      d) $36 997.28
C. 1. a) $2699.00
      b) $64 776.00
      c) $10 024.00
   3. Deposits
      $2419.29;
      totals
      $16 935.03;
      $3064.99;
      $20 000.02
   5. $2840.83
   7. a) $302.01
      b) $21 903.91
      c) $257.62
      d) $764.19
      e) Balances
         $911.71;
         $97 252.61;
         totals
         $54 361.80;
         $45 637.43;
         $99 999.23
   9. a) $24 750
      b) $8604
      c) $33 354
      d) $13 931
      e) $107 196
      f) totals
         $172 073;
         $127 927;
         $300 000

Review Exercise

1. a) $5336.73
   b) $4550.35
2. a) $9443.35
   b) $8927.93
3. $24 894.85
4. $746.05
5. a) $929.50
   (premium);
   $20 929.50
   b) $148.72
   (premium);
   $21 548.72
6. a) $2243.20
   (premium);
   $11 243.20
   b) Nil; $9000.00
   c) $883.64
   (discount);
   $8116.36
7. a) $9962.95
   (discount)
   b) $93 969.33
   c) $90 115.74
8. a) $225.87
   (premium)
   b) $43 556.85
   c) $42 624.98
9. $4527.64
10. $1071.17
11. a) −$3469.30
    (discount)
    b) $24 625.42
    c) $23 330.78
12. 12.56%
13. −$72.73
    (discount);
    $927.27; totals
    $870.00; $942.73;
    $72.73
14. $272.16
    (discount);

$4727.84; totals
$4287.50;
$4559.66; $272.16
15. $381.32
    (premium);
    $21 381.32; totals
    $9300.00;
    $8918.68; $381.32
16. $6124.75 (loss)
17. $993.69 (gain)
18. 12.18%
19. 15.20%
20. 14.40%
21. a) 46 025.91
    b) $48 240.30
    c) $1572.20 (gain)
22. $92 388.48
23. 15.24%
24. $977.39 (loss)
25. a) $92 388.48
    b) $28 862.02
    c) $1873.21
    d) Totals
       $92 687.50;
       $17 312.53;
       $110 000.03
26. a) $1201.97
    b) $17 570.15
    c) $2443.36
    d) Totals
       $38 463.04;
       $26 536.90;
       $64 999.94
27. a) $13 750.00
    b) $8279.90
    c) $22 029.90
    d) $72 194.23
    e) $5989.29
    f) Totals
       $66 239.23;
       $33 760.07;
       $100 000.00

28. a) $13 875.00
    b) $5349.00
    c) $38 448.00
    d) $235 779.00
    e) $11 270.00
    f) Totals
       $160 472.00;
       $139 528.00;
       $300 000.00
29. a) $2469.40
    b) $10 612.00
    c) $21 194.78
    d) $788.92
30. a) $1058.60
    b) Totals
       $7410.20;
       $2589.75;
       $9999.95
31. a) $n = 38.468063$
    b) $8318.12
32. a) $13 920.00
    b) $5211.80
    c) $19 131.80
    d) $70 723.83
    e) Totals
       $52 117.95;
       $43 882.05;
       $96 000.00

Self-Test

1. $9269.44
2. $1110.97
3. $304.02
   (premium)
4. $21 459.38
5. $4613.34
6. −$327.27
   (discount); totals
   $2300.00;
   $2627.27; $327.27
7. 12.46%
8. $2062.19

9. 12.92%
10. $58 197.77
11. $371.86
12. $1297.87
13. $622 192.28
14. Payments
    $2798.01
    totals $16 788.06;
    $8211.95;
    $25 000.01

Chapter 16

Exercise 16.1

A. 1. Alternative 2; pre-
      sent values are
      $44 634; $53 448
   3. Alternative 1; pre-
      sent values are
      $48 569; $46 604
B. 1. Offer 2; present
      values are $52 138;
      $54 262
   3. Lease; present val-
      ues are $88 167;
      $86 379

Exercise 16.2

A. 1. Reject; NPV is
      −$5367
   3. Alternative 1;
      NPVs are $234;
      $203
B. 1. Project B; NPVs
      are $1787; $2568
   3. No; NPV is
      −$8561
   5. Yes; NPV is
      $5696
   7. Yes; NPV is $5142

Exercise 16.3

A. **1.** 25.3%

   3. 20.7%

B. **1.** at 18%, NPV = $6101; at 20%, NPV = −$292; R.O.I. = 19.9%

   3. at 18%, NPV = $1286; at 20%, NPV = −$104; R.O.I. = 19.9%

   5. at 22%, NPV = $148; at 24%, NPV = −$1538; R.O.I. = 22.2%

Review Exercise

1. Alternative B; present values are $51 624; $52 161

2. Alternative 1; present values are $73 559; $74 653

3. Alternative 1; NPVs are $3916; $3597

4. Yes; NPV = $508

5. −$22 227

6. $404

7. at 26%, NPV = $370; at 28%, NPV = −$1939; R.O.I. = 26.3%

8. at 18%, NPV = $135; at 20%, NPV = −$673; R.O.I. = 18.3%

9. at 16%, NPV = $47 272; at 18%, NPV = −$22 227; R.O.I. = 17.4%

10. at 14%, NPV = $404; at 16%, NPV = −$4383; R.O.I. = 14.2%

11. at 24%, NPV = $2035; at 26%, NPV = −$184; R.O.I. = 25.8%

12. at 12%, NPV = $3307; at 14%, NPV = −$2876; R.O.I. = 13.1%

13. Project B; present values are $22 256; $22 909

14. Project B; NPVs are $3510; $4862

15. −$1215

16. at 24%, NPV = $1023; at 26%, NPV = −$1690; R.O.I. = 24.8%

17. Yes; NPV = $28 940

18. at 14%, NPV = $36 347; at 16%, NPV = −$7635; R.O.I. = 15.7%

Self-Test

1. Alternative A; present values are $13 552; $10 856

2. $3887

3. at 16%, NPV = $3466; at 18%, NPV = −$4368; R.O.I. = 16.9%

4. Present values are $5939; $6040; purchase

5. Proposal B, net present values are $701; $1427

6. at 26%, NPV = $356; at 28%, NPV = −$7526; R.O.I. = 26.1%

Index

$$M = E + P$$

Formula 6.11 $\dfrac{\text{RATE OF MARKUP}}{\text{BASED ON COST}} = \dfrac{\text{MARKUP}}{\text{COST}} = \dfrac{M}{C}$

Finding the rate of markup as a percent of cost

Formula 6.12 $\dfrac{\text{RATE OF MARKUP BASED ON SELLING PRICE}}{} = \dfrac{\text{MARKUP}}{\text{SELLING PRICE}} = \dfrac{M}{S}$

Finding the rate of markup as a percent of selling price

Formula 7.1A $I = Prt$

Finding the amount of interest when the principal, the rate, and the time are known

Formula 7.2 $S = P + I$

Finding the future value (maturity value) when the principal and the amount of interest are known

Formula 7.3A $S = P(1 + rt)$

Finding the future value (maturity value) at simple interest directly when the principal, rate of interest, and time are known

Formula 9.1A $S = P(1 + i)^n$

Finding the future value of the compound amount (or maturity value) when the original principal, the rate of interest, and the time period are known

Formula 9.2 $i = \dfrac{j}{m}$

Finding the periodic rate of interest

Formula 10.1 $f = (1 + i)^m - 1$

Finding the effective rate of interest f for a nominal annual rate compounded m times per year

Formula 10.2A $S = Pe^{nj}$

Finding the compound amount when using continuous compounding

Formula 10.3 $f = e^j - 1$

Finding the effective rate of interest for a nominal rate compounded continuously

Formula 11.1 $S_n = R\left[\dfrac{(1 + i)^n - 1}{i}\right]$

Finding the future value (accumulated value) of an ordinary simple annuity

Formula 11.2 $A_n = R\left[\dfrac{1 - (1 + i)^{-n}}{i}\right]$

Finding the present value (discounted value) of an ordinary simple annuity

Formula 11.3 $S_{nc} = R\left[\dfrac{(1 + f)^n - 1}{f}\right]$

where $f = (1 + i)^c - 1$

Formula for finding the future value of an ordinary general annuity using the equivalent effective rate of interest per payment period

Formula 11.4 $A_{nc} = R\left[\dfrac{1 - (1 + f)^{-n}}{f}\right]$

where $f = (1 + i)^c - 1$

Formula for finding the present value of an ordinary general annuity using the equivalent effective rate of interest per payment period

Formula 12.1 $S_n(\text{due}) = R(1 + i)\left[\dfrac{(1 + i)^n - 1}{i}\right]$

Finding the future value of an annuity due